POSTCARDS FROM

Frommer's

London 2003

P9-CCH-848

Spanning the Thames River since 1894, the Tower Bridge is one of London's most photographed sights. You can ascend the towers for a panoramic view of the area. See chapter 7. © Wolfgang Kaehler Photography.

Enjoy the atmosphere, food, and drink at many historic watering holes on the World's Greatest Pub Crawl listed in chapter 10. Pubs and their fare are also described in chapter 6.
© Dave Bartruff Photography.

Buckingham Palace, home of the Queen and site of the Changing of the Guard. See chapter 7. © Chris Warren/International Stock.

Big Ben, the world's most famous timepiece, is housed in the clock tower of the Houses of Parliament. The name "Big Ben" refers to the largest bell in the chime, which weighs almost 14 tons. See chapter 7. © *Andrea Pistolesi Photography.*

Hyde Park, with adjoining Kensington Gardens, is one of London's "green lungs," covering 615 acres, with velvety lawns, a lake for boating, and the famous Speakers Corner. See chapter 7. © Robert Holmes Photography.

A full English breakfast is a complete meal, with eggs, bread, meat, cereal, and plenty of coffee, tea, and juice to wash it all down. In chapter 5, we've noted which hotels include a full English or continental breakfast in their room rate. © Dave Bartruff Photography.

Theatergoers can watch plays performed as they were in Shakespeare's day at the Globe Theatre, a modern reconstruction of the original. See chapter 9. © Kelly/Mooney Photography.

The Yeoman Warders, "Beefeaters," keep watch at the Tower of London, where famous prisoners such as Anne Boleyn, Lady Jane Grey, and Sir Thomas More lost their lives. See chapter 7. © Catherine Karnow Photography.

When Londoners speak of "The City," they mean the original square mile that's become the British version of Wall Street. © Lisl Dennis/The Image Bank.

Portobello Market was once known only for its produce (above), but now is a magnet for collectors of virtually anything, especially antiques (see facing page). See chapter 9.
© Jan Butchofsky-Houser/Houserstock, Inc. Photography; facing page © Kelly/Mooney Photography.

Westminster Abbey, where English rulers have been crowned for a thousand years. See chapter 7. © Kelly/Mooney Photography.

A New Star-Rating System & Other Exciting News from Frommer's!

In our continuing effort to publish the savviest, most up-to-date, and most appealing travel guides available, we've added some great new features.

Frommer's guides now include a new **star-rating system.** Every hotel, restaurant, and attraction is rated from 0 to 3 stars to help you set priorities and organize your time.

We've also added **seven brand-new features** that point you to the great deals, in-the-know advice, and unique experiences that separate travelers from tourists. Throughout the guide, look for:

Finds	Special finds—those places only insiders know about
Fun Fact	Fun facts—details that make travelers more informed and their trips more fun
Kids	Best bets for kids—advice for the whole family
Moments	Special moments—those experiences that memories are made of
Overrated	Places or experiences not worth your time or money
Tips	Insider tips—some great ways to save time and money
Value	Great values—where to get the best deals

We've also added a **"What's New"** section in every guide—a timely crash course in what's hot and what's not in every destination we cover.

Here's what the critics say about Frommer's:

"Amazingly easy to use. Very portable, very complete."
—*Booklist*

"Detailed, accurate, and easy-to-read information for all price ranges."
—*Glamour Magazine*

"Hotel information is close to encyclopedic."
—*Des Moines Sunday Register*

"Frommer's Guides have a way of giving you a real feel for a place."
—*Knight Ridder Newspapers*

Other Great Guides for Your Trip:

Frommer's Memorable Walks in London,
Frommer's England
Frommer's Great Britain
London For Dummies
Frommer's Portable London
Frommer's London from $85 a Day
Unofficial Guide to London
Irreverent Guide to London

Frommer's®

London

2003

by Darwin Porter & Danforth Prince

Wiley Publishing, Inc.

About the Authors

Authors **Darwin Porter** and **Danforth Prince** share their love of their favorite European city in this guide. Porter, a bureau chief for *The Miami Herald* at 21, who later worked in television advertising, wrote the first-ever book on London for Frommer's. Prince, formerly of the Paris bureau of the *New York Times,* joins him. Together, they're the authors of several best-selling Frommer's guides, notably England, France, the Caribbean, Italy, and Germany.

Published by:

Wiley Publishing, Inc.

909 Third Ave.
New York, NY 10022

ISBN 0-7645-6624-5
ISSN 1096-6439

Editor: Liz Albertson
Production Editor: M. Faunette Johnston
Cartographer: Nicholas Trotter
Photo Editor: Richard Fox
Production by Wiley Indianapolis Composition Services
Chapter 2 illustrations by Rashell Smith and Karl Brandt

Front cover photo: A Yeoman Warder (Beefeater) snaps a photo of another.
Back cover photo: Thames River, the Tower Bridge at night.

For information on our other products and services or to obtain technical support, please contact our Customer Care Department within the U.S. at 800-762-2974, outside the U.S. at 317-572-3993 or fax 317-572-4002.

Wiley also publishes its books in a variety of electronic formats. Some content that appears in print may not be available in electronic formats.

Manufactured in the United States of America

5 4 3 2 1

Contents

List of Maps

An Invitation to the Reader

In researching this book, we discovered many wonderful places—hotels, restaurants, shops, and more. We're sure you'll find others. Please tell us about them, so we can share the information with your fellow travelers in upcoming editions. If you were disappointed with a recommendation, we'd love to know that, too. Please write to:

Frommer's London 2003
Wiley Publishing, Inc. • 909 Third Ave. • New York, NY 10022

An Additional Note

Please be advised that travel information is subject to change at any time—and this is especially true of prices. We therefore suggest that you write or call ahead for confirmation when making your travel plans. The authors, editors, and publisher cannot be held responsible for the experiences of readers while traveling. Your safety is important to us, however, so we encourage you to stay alert and be aware of your surroundings. Keep a close eye on cameras, purses, and wallets, all favorite targets of thieves and pickpockets.

New! Frommer's Star Ratings & Icons

Every hotel, restaurant, and attraction listing in this guide has been ranked for quality, value, service, amenities, and special features using a star-rating scale. In country, state, and regional guides, we also rate towns and regions to help you narrow down your choices and budget your time accordingly. Hotels and restaurants in the Very Expensive and Expensive categories are rated on a scale of one (highly recommended) to three stars (exceptional). Those in the Moderate and Inexpensive categories rate from zero (recommended) to two stars (very highly recommended). Attractions, towns, and regions are rated according to the following scale: zero stars (recommended), one star (highly recommended), two stars (very highly recommended), and three stars (must-see).

In addition to the rating system, we also use seven icons to highlight insider information, useful tips, special bargains, hidden gems, memorable experiences, kid-friendly venues, places to avoid, and other useful information:

| *Finds* | *Fun Fact* | *Kids* | *Moments* | *Overrated* | *Tips* | *Value* |

The following abbreviations are used for credit cards:

| AE | American Express | DISC | Discover | V | Visa |
| DC | Diners Club | MC | MasterCard | | |

FROMMERS.COM

Now that you have the guidebook to a great trip, visit our website at **www.frommers.com** for travel information on nearly 2,500 destinations. With features updated regularly, we give you instant access to the most current trip-planning information available. At Frommers.com, you'll also find the best prices on airfares, accommodations, and car rentals—and you can even book travel online through our travel booking partners. At Frommers.com, you'll also find the following:

- Online updates to our most popular guidebooks
- Vacation sweepstakes and contest giveaways
- Newsletter highlighting the hottest travel trends
- Online travel message boards with featured travel discussions

What's New in London

London is the most volatile and ever-changing city in Europe. "The scene" is constantly shifting. Here are some of the latest developments:

ACCOMMODATIONS Prices go higher and higher and still people arrive by the thousands to check in.

Unlike most of the capitals of Europe, London continues to open new and exciting hotels in the heart of the city. Even the staid financial district, "the City," now has a new luxury hotel—**Threadneedles,** 5 Threadneedles St., EC2 (*℃* **020/7289-4878**). You can't find a more central London address than Hilton's first boutique hotel in London: **The Trafalgar,** 2 Spring Gardens (*℃* **020/7870-2900**), right on Trafalgar Square. The hotel chain converted the 19th century shipping headquarters of the Cunard line into this hotel.

Those who want to dwell directly across the street from the queen at Buckingham Palace can check into **The Rubens at The Palace,** 39 Buckingham Palace Rd. SW1 (*℃* **020/ 7834-6600**), the best of the increasingly popular deluxe "Red Carnation" properties.

For those who'd like to lodge right at the entrance to Hyde Park, there is the **Mandarin Oriental Hyde Park,** 66 Knightsbridge, SW1 (*℃* **020/ 7235-2000**), one of the best business hotels in London, with one of the finest spas.

Today, anything associated with the Notting Hill district is called "Notting Hill chic," and there's no finer (or "chicer") address in Notting Hill than

The Westbourne Hotel, 163–165 Westbourne Grove, W11 (*℃* **020/ 243-6008**), which some critics consider London's finest urban inn. Boasting a Japanese garden, the hotel is a gem.

Those with leaner purses will delight in knowing that the modestly priced **Aster House,** 3 Sumner Place, SW7 (*℃* **020/7581-5888**), is still as good as it was when it was voted London's best B&B. If anything, standards have improved since then. Also opening in the more moderately priced category, **Ten Manchester Street,** 10 Manchester St., W1 (*℃* **020/7486-6669**) was converted from a former residence hall for nurses into a smart town house hotel of red brick, located in the central Marylebone district.

DINING The explosion of top-notch restaurants in London continues with the opening of the aptly named **The Bridge,** 1 Paul's Walk, EC4 (*℃* **020/7236-000**), with its panoramic view of the Thames. Even without the stunning view, the international and modern British cuisine is reason enough to pay a visit. Another new dining star in the east of London is the (also aptly named) **Vertigo 42,** Tower 42, Old Broad St., EC2 (*℃* **020/7877-7842**), which offers the chance to dine with a panoramic view on the 42nd floor of a building in the heart of "the City," London's financial district. A high-speed elevator swoops you up to a first-class dining room with superb Continental and seafood cuisine.

Restaurants are popping up like spring crocuses out in the West End, notably **Hakkasan,** 8 Hanway Pl. (℗ **020/7907-1888**), created by Wagamama noodle shop's mastermind, Alan Yau. Asian mystique and delicate Chinese cuisine are served up at this posh dining venue. Theatergoers along Shaftesbury Avenue now have a destination for first-class Indian cuisine at **Mela,** 152–156 Shaftesbury Ave., WC2 (℗ **020/7836-8635**). Mela is one of the top four or five Indian restaurants in London, a city where the competition between good Indian restaurants is fierce.

No restaurant has created more excitement than the opening of **Gordon Ramsay at Claridge's,** Brook St., W1 (℗ **020/7499-0099**). With the fading of some old culinary legends, Ramsay is now the hottest chef in the country. His modern European cuisine is sublime. A very different spot, **Nahm,** in the Halkin Hotel, Halkin St., SW1 (℗ **020/7333-1234**) has become the Thai restaurant to watch. David Thompson is the London expert on Thai cookery, re-creating dishes lost for centuries in old Siam.

In Marylebone, the French cuisine of **John Burton–Race at the Landmark,** 222 Marylebone Rd., NW1 (℗ **022/7723-7800**) is making him a media darling. You dine here in real 1890s Belle Epoque style.

Some of London's finest Italian cuisine is served at **Assaggi,** 39 Chepstow Place, W2 (℗ **020/7792-5501**), above a pub near Notting Hill Gate.

EXPLORING One of London's most famous galleries, **The Saatchi Gallery,** is currently without a permanent residence. Since this collection of art is one of the greatest ever in private hands, it's worth checking with the London Tourist Board to see if it has a permanent or even temporary home at the time of your visit. It's well worth seeking out.

The British Museum, Great Russell St., WC1 (℗ **020/7323-8299**) is luring more and more visitors with its newly opened Sainsbury African Galleries, one of the finest collections of African art and artifacts in the world.

Those visitors who plan to call on the queen in 2003 at **Buckingham Palace,** at the end of the Mall (℗ **020/7839-1377**), will find her hiding away in Scotland in August. But she's granted permission for visitors to stroll through the royal family garden, with its lush foliage, rare birds, and panoramic views, while she's away in August.

London's first museum devoted to a composer has opened: **Handel Museum,** 25 Brook St., W1 (℗ **020/7495-1685**) is located in the home that George Frideric Handel lived in until his death in 1759. He composed "Messiah" here.

SHOPPING More and more decorators, both professional and of the do-it-yourself variety, are flocking to **LASSCO,** Mark St., off St. Paul St., EC2 (℗ **020/77749-9944**), the best place in London for architectural salvage, much of it from 19th-century buildings (you may even spot pieces from St. Paul's Cathedral).

AFTER DARK London continues to fulfill its reputation as one of the most cutting edge after-dark scenes among all the European capitals. What's amazing is that many of the old reliables are still around and still as popular as ever. But there is some new competition, notably from **The End,** 16A West Central St., WC1 (℗ **020/7419-9199**), which has recently enlarged itself and vastly improved its ambience with 3 large dance floors and 4 bars. Since it made its debut, **Fabric,** 77A Charterhouse St., EC1 (℗ **020/7336-8898**) has exploded into one of London's major nighttime diversions. Its chief asset? It has a license for 24-hour dancing and music

Thursday through Sunday nights, including live music on Friday nights. It is not open Monday through Wednesday.

For the hippest nighttime venue, head for the **Notting Hill Art Club,** 21 Notting Hill Gate, W11 (© 020/ 7460-4459), where you might run into Madonna, or at least Liam Gallagher and Courtney Love.

SIDE TRIPS Visitors flocking to take in Shakespeare's plays at Stratford-upon-Avon in 2003 will find the famous Box restaurant in the Royal Shakespeare Theatre at Waterside closed. The good news is that it's been replaced by **Quarto's** (© 01789/ 403415), at the same location and offering the same excellent Continental menu.

The Best of London

The British capital is more eclectic and electric than it's been in years. *Newsweek* hailed London as a "hip compromise between the nonstop newness of Los Angeles and the aspic-preserved beauty of Paris—sharpened to New York's edge." *Wine Spectator* proclaims more modestly: "The sun is shining brighter in London these days."

The sounds of Brit-pop and techno pour out of Victorian pubs; experimental theater is popping up on stages built for Shakespeare's plays; upstart chefs are reinventing the bland dishes British mums have made for generations; and Brits are even running the couture houses of Dior and Givenchy. In food, fashion, film, music, the visual arts, and just about everything else, London, as it moves deeper into the 21st century, stands at the cutting edge again, just as it did in the 1960s.

If this sea of change worries you more than it appeals to you, rest assured that traditional London survives, basically intact under the veneer of hip. This ancient city has withstood a thousand years of invasion, from the Normans to the Blitz, so a few hipsters aren't going to change anything fundamental. From high tea at Brown's to the changing of the guard at Buckingham Palace, the city still abounds with the culture and charm of days gone by.

Discovering London and making it your own can be a bit of a challenge, especially if you have limited time. Even in the 18th century, Daniel Defoe found London "stretched out in buildings, straggling, confused, out of all shape, uncompact and unequal; neither long nor broad, round nor square." The actual City of London proper is 1 square mile of very expensive real estate around the Bank of England. All of the gargantuan rest of the city is made up of separate villages, boroughs, and corporations—each with its own mayor and administration. Together, however, they add up to a mammoth metropolis.

Luckily, whether you're looking for Dickens's house or the Dr. Marten's Superstore, only the heart of London's huge territory need concern you. The heart of this behemoth is one of the most fascinating places on earth. With every step you take, you'll feel the tremendous influence this city has exerted.

London is a mass of contradictions. On the one hand, it's a decidedly royal city, studded with palaces, court gardens, coats of arms, and other regal paraphernalia; yet it's also the home of the world's second-oldest parliamentary democracy. (Iceland was the first.)

Today, London has grown less English and more international. The gent with the bowler hat has long gone out of fashion; today's Londoner might have a turban, a Mohawk, or even a baseball cap. It's becoming easier to find a *café au lait* and a croissant than a scone and a cup of tea. The city is home to thousands of immigrants and refugees, both rich and poor, from all reaches of the world.

What's amazing is that this city—ancient and modern, sprawling and compact, stolidly English and increasingly multicultural—works as well as it does.

1 Frommer's Favorite London Experiences

- **Watching the Sunset at Waterloo Bridge:** This is the ideal place for watching the sun set over Westminster. You can see the last rays of light bounce off the dome of St. Paul's and the city spires in the East End. See chapter 4.

- **Enjoying a Traditional Afternoon Tea:** Try the Goring Hotel, dating from 1910. From the lounge, you'll look out on a small garden as you enjoy finger sandwiches (often watercress or cucumber), the hotel's special Ceylon-blend tea, scones and clotted cream, and the chef's famous light fruitcake. See p. 109.

- **Cruising London's Waterways:** In addition to the Thames, London has an antique canal system, with towpath walks, bridges, and wharves. Replaced by the railroad as the prime means of transportation, the canal system remained forgotten until it was recently rediscovered by a new generation. Now in a process of urban renewal, the old system has been restored, with bridges painted and repaired, and paths cleaned up, for you to enjoy. See "River Cruises Along the Thames," in chapter 7.

- **Spending Sunday Morning at Speakers' Corner:** At the northeastern corner of Hyde Park, a British tradition carries on. Speakers sound off on any subject, and "in your face" hecklers are part of the fun. You might hear anything from denunciations of the monarchy to anti-gay rhetoric. Anyone can get up and speak. The only rules: You can't blaspheme, be obscene, or incite a riot. The tradition began in 1855—before the legal right to assembly was guaranteed in 1872—when a mob of 150,000 gathered to attack a proposed Sunday Trading Bill. See p. 264.

- **Studying the Turners at the Tate:** When he died in 1851, J. M. W. Turner bequeathed his personal collection of 19,000 watercolors and some 300 paintings to the people of Britain. He wanted his finished works, about 100 paintings, displayed under one roof. Today at the Tate, you see not only the paintings, but also glimpses of Turner's beloved Thames through the museum's windows. The artist lived and died on the river's banks and painted its many changing moods. See p. 231.

- **Strolling Through Covent Garden:** George Bernard Shaw got his inspiration for *Pygmalion* here, where the Cockney lass who inspired the character of Eliza Doolittle sold violets to wealthy opera-goers. The old market (p. 71), with its cauliflower peddlers and butchers in blood-soaked aprons, is long gone. What's left is London's best example of urban renewal and one of its hippest shopping districts. In the footsteps of Chippendale and Dickens, you can discover colorful street stalls, boutiques, and shops selling one-of-a-kind items, and enjoy some of the city's best sidewalk entertainment. There's an antiques market on Monday and a crafts market Tuesday through Saturday. When you're parched, there are plenty of pubs to quench your thirst, like the Nag's Head (p. 327), an Edwardian pub that'll serve you a draft Guinness and a plate of pork cooked in cider.

- **Rowing on the Serpentine:** When the weather's right, we head to Hyde Park's 17-hectare

Central London

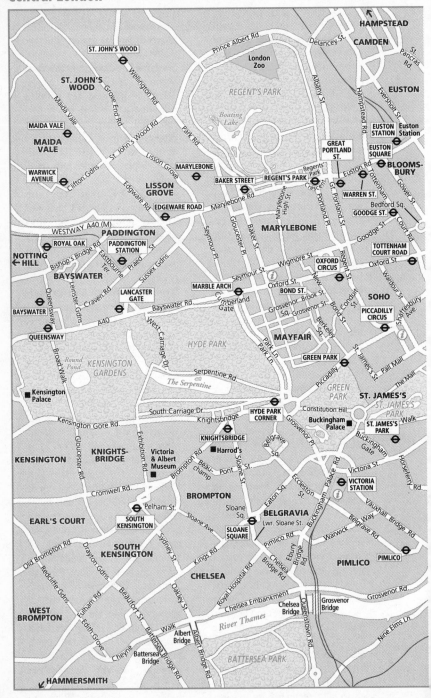

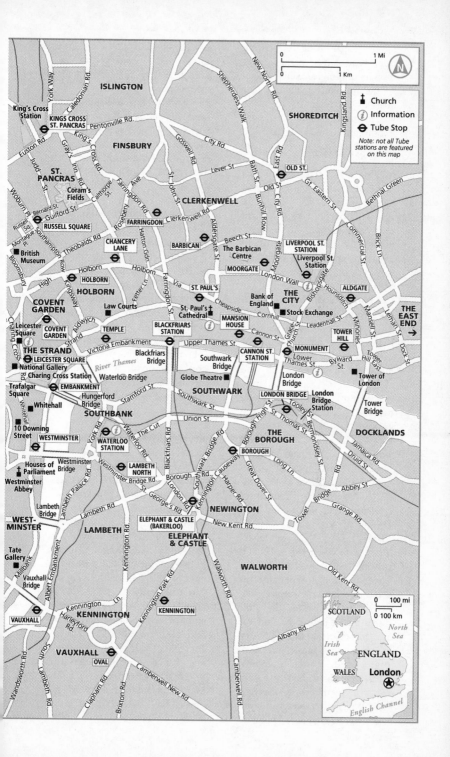

(41-acre) man-made lake dating from 1730, whose name derives from its winding, snakelike shape. At the Boathouse, you can rent boats by the hour. It's an idyllic way to spend a sunny afternoon. Renoir must have agreed; he depicted the custom on canvas. See p. 264.

- **Making a Brass Rubbing:** Take home some costumed ladies and knights in armor from England's age of chivalry. Make your very own brass rubbing in the crypt of St. Martin-in-the-Fields in Trafalgar Square; the staff there will be happy to show you how. See p. 242.

- **Getting to Know North London on a Sunday:** Begin by looking for some smart fashion at Camden Market, a Sunday event in the Camden High Street where stall-holders hawk designer jewelry and clothing. Next, walk up to Hampstead Heath off Well Walk and take the right fork, which leads to an open field with a panoramic view of London. Cap your jaunt with a visit to the **Freud Museum** (p. 270), open on Sunday until 5pm. See "Attractions on the Outskirts," in chapter 7 for more information on North London.

- **Dining at Rules:** Rules, at 35 Maiden Lane, WC2, was established as an oyster bar in 1798; it may be the oldest restaurant in London. Long a venue for the theatrical elite and literary *beau monde*, it still serves the same dishes that delighted Edward VII and his mistress, Lillie Langtry, who began their meals with champagne and oysters upstairs. Charles Dickens had a regular table. Over the years, everyone from William Thackeray to Clark Gable has enjoyed Rules' pheasant and grouse. And where else can you get a good purée of parsnips these days? If you're looking for an old-fashioned British dessert, finish off with the treacle sponge or apple suet pudding. See p. 163.

- **Spending a Night at a West End Theater:** London is the theatrical capital of the world. The live stage offers a unique combination of variety, accessibility, and economy— and maybe a look at next season's Broadway hit. See "The Play's the Thing: London's Theater Scene," in chapter 9.

- **Crawling the London Pubs:** Americans barhop; Londoners pub-crawl. With some 5,000 pubs within the city limits, you would certainly be crawling if you tried to have a drink in each of them! We have suggested the traditional pubs that we think will make a worthwhile crawl. While making the rounds, you can partake of that quintessentially British fare known as "pub grub," which might include everything from a ploughman's lunch (a hunk of bread, cheese, and a pickle) to shepherd's pie. In the right places, some of that pub grub today tastes better than the fare served in many restaurants. Our favorite crawl gives you a chance to see several London districts. Begin at **Ye Olde Cheshire Cheese** (p. 152), Wine Office Court, 145 Fleet St., EC4, before heading to **Cittie of Yorke** (p. 323), 22–23 High Holborn, WC1. Have a pint in the heart of the West End at the **Red Lion** (p. 327), 2 Duke of York St., SW1. If you're still standing, rush to **Shepherd's Tavern** (p. 328), 50 Hertford St., W1, in Mayfair, before the publican rings the bell for "final call."

2 Best Hotel Bets

London is home to some of the finest hotels in the world (and some of the priciest). Happily, there are good, affordable options as well.

- **Best Newcomer:** The first luxury hotel to be built in London's financial district, the City, is the charmingly named **Threadneedles,** 5 Threadneedles St., EC2 (✆ **020/7432-8450**). The hotel was installed in an 1856 former bank building, and is located near the Bank of England. See p. 91.

- **Best Historic Hotel:** Founded by the former manservant to Lord Byron, stylish **Brown's Hotel,** Albemarle St., W1 (✆ **020/7493-6020**), dates back to Victorian times. It's one of London's most genteel hotels, from its legendary afternoon tea to its centenary *Times* clock (which displays everything from the days of the week and the tides to the zodiac) in the reception area. See p. 105.

- **Best for Business Travelers:** Wheelers and dealers head to **The Langham Hilton,** 1C Portland Place, W1 (✆ **020/7636-1000**), Hilton's flagship hotel in Europe, which boasts sleek styling and grand public rooms. At times, it seems that all the world's business is conducted from this nerve center. See p. 126.

- **Best for a Romantic Getaway:** **The Gore,** 189 Queen's Gate, SW7 (✆ **020/7584-6601**), has been sheltering lovers both on and off the record since 1892. The place is eccentric and lots of fun, and the staff doesn't bother you, but is always available if you need something. For nostalgia-accented romance, request the Venus Room—Judy Garland once owned its bed. See p. 123.

- **Best Trendy Hotel: St. Martins Lane,** 45 St. Martins Lane (✆ **020/7300-5500**), is almost without challenge in this category. Ian Schrager has brought New York cutting-edge style to a 1960s office building in Covent Garden. It's his first hotel outside the United States, and it's eccentric, irreverent, and whimsical. Would Madonna go anywhere else? See p. 102.

- **Best Lobby for Pretending You're Rich: The Dorchester,** 53 Park Lane, W1 (✆ **020/7629-8888**), has a long promenade with London's largest floral display and rows of faux-marble columns with ornate gilt capitals. Even if you can't afford to stay at this citadel of luxury, come by for the traditional afternoon tea. See p. 106.

- **Best Quirky Hotel: The Rookery,** 12 Peter's Lane, Cowcross St., EC1 (✆ **020/7336-0931**), is eccentric but fun, loaded with atmosphere, luring some of London's most discerning visitors. Its individually decorated rooms offer charm and comfort; the bathrooms even retain their Victorian cast-iron fittings. The owners combed London's antiques stores and flea markets to create the decor. See p. 91.

- **Best Grande Dame:** The **Sheraton Park Lane Hotel,** Piccadilly, W1 (✆ **020/7499-6321**), is English to the core, evoking the grand old days of debutante balls. Suites still have their 1920s styling and Art Deco bathrooms. Parts of *Brideshead Revisited* were filmed here. See p. 107.

- **Best Quintessentially English Hotel: Durrants Hotel,** George Street, W1 (✆ **020/7935-8131**), established in 1789, is often called "the poor man's Brown's" (see the review of Brown's, p. 105.) A soothing retreat, it's been run by the Miller family for a century. They have joined several houses into a unified Georgian hotel. Stay here for charm and comfort, not grand style. See p. 127.

- **Best for Showing Off:** Anouska Hempel's luxurious **Blake's Hotel,** 33 Roland Gardens, SW7 (© 020/7370-6701), is personalized, elegant, and fun, with beautiful bathrooms in marble, opulent accessories, and a restaurant packed with London glitterati. Wait until after your stay to worry about how much you spent. See p. 122.

- **Best for Thoroughly British Ambience:** In a gas-lit courtyard in back of St. James's Palace, **Dukes Hotel,** 35 St. James's Place, SW1 (© 020/7491-4840), has an unsurpassed dignity. From the bread-and-butter pudding served in the clubby dining room to the impeccable service, at Dukes there will always be an England. See p. 107.

- **Best Modern Design: The Hempel,** 31–35 Craven Hill Garden Sq., W2 (© 020/7298-9000), may be housed in a trio of 1800s row houses, but the renovations by designer Anouska Hempel are pure modern. A grand Italian sense of proportion is balanced with Asian simplicity, and soothing monochromatic tones prevail. On site is one of London's best Thai restaurants, I-Thai. See p. 133.

- **Best Re-creation of an English Country House:** Tim and Kit Kemp are hoteliers of charm, taste, and sophistication. They combined two Georgian town houses into the **Dorset Square Hotel,** 39–40 Dorset Sq., NW1 (© 020/7723-7874), creating an English country house in the heart of the city. Gilt-framed paintings, antiques, tapestry cushions, and

mahogany bathrooms make you feel warm, cozy, and refined. See p. 127.

- **Best Service: 22 Jermyn Street,** 22 Jermyn St., SW1 (© 020/7734-2353), does more for its guests than any other hotel in London. The owner has fitted a room on the 6th floor with a superbly equipped computer center, which guests are free to use. He also informs you of the hottest and newest restaurants, along with old favorites, the best shopping, and even what's hot in theater. The staff won't deny any reasonable request—they even grant some unreasonable ones. See p. 109.

- **Best Location:** Creaky, quirky **Fielding Hotel,** 4 Broad Court, Bow Street, WC2 (© 020/7836-8305), is hardly London's finest hotel, but oh, the location! It's in an alleyway in the center of Covent Garden, in the heart of the excitement of London, almost opposite the Royal Opera House, with pubs, shops, markets, restaurants, even street entertainment, right outside your door. Stay here, and London is at your fingertips. See p. 102.

- **Best Health Club & Pool: The Savoy,** The Strand, WC2 (© 020/7836-4343), has a health club and large swimming pool atop the historic Savoy Theatre, overlooking the heart of London. It's the best gym in central London; the views make it extra special. There's a massage room, plus state-of-the-art health and beauty treatments. See p. 102.

- **Best Boutique Hotel: The Beaufort,** 33 Beaufort Gardens, SW3 (© 020/7584-5252), is a gem that's sure to charm. Personal service and tranquillity combine for a winning choice, a private but not snobbish place 200 yards from the famed Harrods Department Store. Even longtime patrons of Claridge's and the Dorchester have deserted those bastions of luxury to check into The Beaufort. See p. 118.

- **Best Small Hotel:** Housed in three historic homes on Soho Square, **Hazlitt's 1718,** 6 Frith St., W1 (© 020/7434-1771), was a fashionable address 2 centuries ago—and is again today. One of London's best small hotels, it's a favorite with artists, actors, media people, and models. Many bedrooms boast four-poster beds. See p. 104.

- **Best Moderately Priced Hotel:** In the heart of Bloomsbury, you can find cozy charm at the attractively priced **Morgan Hotel,** 24 Bloomsbury St., WC1 (© 020/7636-3735), which occupies a row of 1790s Georgian houses. Warmth and hospitality await you in accommodations overlooking the British Museum. See p. 99.

- **Best Inexpensive Hotel:** In this price category, it's hard to be chic, but **The Pavilion,** 34–36 Sussex Gardens, W2 (© 020/7262-0905) fits the bill. Known for its bedrooms' wacky themes, this theatrical and slightly outrageous hotel attracts models and music industry folks. Rooms range in

decor from "Oriental Bordello" to "Honky-Tonk Afro." See p. 135.

- **Best for Families Who Don't Want to Break the Bank: Colonnade Town House,** 2 Warrington Crescent, W9 (© 020/7286-1052), stands in the canal-laced Little Venice section. This family-friendly hotel lets children under 12 stay free in their parents' room. The staff can also arrange baby-sitting. This residential area of London is safe at night, with tree-lined avenues leading down to a canal. It's got a real neighborhood feel to it. See p. 139.

- **Best B&B: Vicarage Private Hotel,** 10 Vicarage Gate, W8 (© 020/7229-4030), provides old-fashioned English charm and hospitality—at affordable prices. Close to Kensington High Street, the family-run B&B charges a modest price for a cozy nest—if you can do without a private bath. See p. 124.

- **Best Value:** Savvy hotel shoppers seek out **Aston's Apartments,** 39 Rosary Gardens, SW7 (© 020/7590-6000). The accommodations range widely in price, varying from basic rooms to designer suites, each with a kitchenette if you want to avoid London's high-priced restaurants for some meals. See p. 124.

3 Best Dining Bets

London's restaurant scene is booming. What follows is a sampling of its best restaurants, in enough categories for us to name our favorites:

- **Best Newcomer of the Year:** London's hottest chef is now installed at its most prestigious hotel: **Gordon Ramsay at Claridge's,** Brook St., W1 (© 020/7499-0099). His modern European menu delights the senses. See p. 178.

- **Best Place for a Business Lunch:** Impress your clients by taking

them to **Poons in the City,** 2 Minster Pavement, Minster Court, Mincing Lane, EC3 (© 020/7626-0126). This famous Chinese restaurant is outfitted with furniture and accessories from China, and the menu is wide-ranging. After a taste of the finely chopped wind-dried meats or the crispy aromatic duck, it'll be a snap to seal the deal. See p. 152.

- **Best Spot for a Celebration:** There's no spot in all of London that's more fun than **Quaglino's,** 16 Bury St., SW1 (© 020/7930-6767), which serves up Continental cuisine. On some nights, as many as 800 diners show up at Sir Terence Conran's gargantuan Mayfair eatery. It's the best place in London to celebrate almost any occasion—and the food's good, too. There's live jazz on Friday and Saturday nights. See p. 185.

- **Best Wine List:** The renowned wine list at the **Tate Gallery Restaurant,** in the Tate Gallery, Millbank, SW1 (© 020/7887-8877), reads like a "who's who" of famous French châteaux. Plus, the Tate offers the city's best bargains on fine wines; management keeps the markups between 40% and 65%, instead of the 100% to 200% that most restaurants add per bottle. See p. 232.

- **Best Value:** At cheap and cheerful **Simply Nico,** 48A Rochester Row, SW1 (© 020/7630-8061), grand chef Nico Ladenis offers some of the best value fixed-price meals in London. This isn't the fabled haute cuisine Nico serves on Park Lane, but quality ingredients are beautifully distilled into some of the best French food in London. Breast of guinea fowl with lentils and other specialties will keep you coming back. See p. 186.

- **Best Modern British Cuisine:** In a former smokehouse just north of Smithfield Market, **St. John,** 26 St. John St., EC1 (© 020/7251-0848), serves a modern interpretation of British cuisine like none other in town. The chefs here believe in offal (those parts of the animal that are usually discarded)—after all, why use just parts of the animal when you can use it all? Although some diners

are a bit squeamish at first, they're usually hooked once they get past the first bite. Book ahead of time. See p. 155.

- **Best Traditional British Cuisine:** There is no restaurant in London quite as British as **Simpson's-in-the-Strand,** 100 The Strand, WC2 (© 020/7836-9112), which has been serving the finest English roast beef since 1828. Henry VIII, were he to return, would surely pause for a feast here. This place is such a British institution, you'll think they invented roast saddle of mutton. See p. 163.

- **Best for Kids: YO! Sushi,** 52 Poland St., W1 (© 020/7287-0443), is a kind of sushi Disneyland. It's filled with gimmicks and high-tech gadgets, but the food is good. Robots serve the drinks, and color- coded sushi dishes cruise by on the world's longest conveyor belt (you can just pick whatever looks good from the conveyor belt). There's nothing else like this in London. See p. 176.

- **Best Continental Cuisine: Le Gavroche,** 43 Upper Brook St., W1 (© 020/7408-0881), was the forerunner of the modern French approach to cuisine in London, and it's lost none of its appeal. If you want to know why, order *pigeonneau de Bresse en vessie aux deux celeris:* The whole bird is presented at your table, enclosed in a pig's bladder; the pigeon is removed, and then carved and served on a bed of braised fennel and celery. Trust us—it's fabulous. See p. 179.

- **Best Indian Cuisine:** London's finest Indian food is served at **Cafe Spice Namaste,** in a landmark Victorian hall near Tower Bridge, 16 Prescot St., E1 (© 020/7488-9242). You'll be tantalized with an array of spicy southern and northern Indian dishes. We like the cuisine's strong Portuguese influence; the chef, Cyrus Todiwala, is from Goa (a Portuguese territory absorbed by India long ago), where he learned many of his culinary secrets. See p. 152.

- **Best Italian Cuisine:** At **Zafferano,** 15 Lowndes St., SW1 (© 020/7235-5800), master chefs prepare delectable cuisine with ingredients that conjure up the Mediterranean shores. The most refined palates of Knightsbridge come to this chic/rustic trattoria for refined dishes like pheasant and black truffle ravioli with rosemary. See p. 189.

- **Best Innovative Cuisine:** The strikingly modern **Vong,** in the Berkeley Hotel, Wilton Place, SW1 (© 020/7235-1010), just steps from Harrods Department Store, is the London showcase of Jean-Georges Vongerichten, whose French and Thai cuisine is innovative, subtle, and inspired. Vong tempts you with melt-in-your-mouth dishes such as *foie gras* with fresh ginger and mango. See p. 192.

- **Best View:** From the terrace of **The Bridge,** 1 Paul's Walk, EC4 (© 020/7236-0000), next to the Millennium Bridge, the panoramic view encompasses a vista of the Thames that stretches from Shakespeare's Globe Theatre to the Tate Modern. The modern British cooking is good, too. See p. 151.

- **Best for Spotting Celebrities:** **Archipelago,** 110 Whitfield St., W1 (© 020/7383-3346), is small and intimate, a cozy retreat for the likes of Madonna and other celebs in London. Media headliner Michael Von Hruschka runs this Thai and French restaurant with a sort of whimsy and with many precious touches, such as a drink list inserted in an ostrich eggshell. But the cuisine doesn't depend on gimmicks. It's first-rate both in ingredients and preparation. See p. 159.

- **Best Seafood: Back to Basics,** 21A Foley St., W1 (© 020/7436-2181), is no fish and chips joint. Stefan Plaumer's Fitzrovia bistro serves some of the freshest seafood in town. You name it: broiled, grilled, baked, or poached; anything except fried—and the chefs will cook the fish to your specifications. An array of delicacies from the sea awaits you here, from plump tasty mussels to sea bass given an extra zing with chili oil. See p. 162.

- **Best Wine Bar Food: Cork & Bottle Wine Bar,** 44–46 Cranbourn St., WC2 (© 020/7734-7807), serves the best wine bar food in London. Don Hewitson's raised ham-and-cheese pie alone is worth the trek across town. It's hardly your typical quiche. Taste the Mediterranean prawns with garlic and asparagus or the lamb in ale. The wine selection is superb, with a strong emphasis on selections from Australia. See p. 168.

- **Best Cantonese Cuisine: Fung Shing,** 15 Lisle St., WC2 (© 020/7437-1539), is a culinary landmark, serving the finest Cantonese cuisine in London, both traditional and innovative. The seasonal specials are the way to go. Stewed duck with yam, tender ostrich in a yellow bean sauce, and a delectable whole sea bass are just some of the delicious treats. See p. 166.

- **Best Late Night Dining: Atlantic Bar & Grill,** 20 Glasshouse St., W1 (© 020/7734-4888), is a titanic restaurant installed in a former Art Deco ballroom off Piccadilly Circus. Modern British cuisine is served in a cosmopolitan atmosphere until 3am Monday through Saturday with an emphasis on organic and homegrown products. See p. 171.

- **Best Japanese Cuisine:** Robert De Niro and his gang have generated much excitement about **Nobu,** in the Metropolitan Hotel, 19 Old Park Lane, W1 (© 020/7447-4747). The staff here is as brilliant and innovative as their New York counterparts. The sushi chefs create gastronomic pyrotechnics with their raw dishes, and do wonders with cooked dishes as well. See p. 179.
- **Best Trendy Restaurants:** Following chic and trendy London as it moves east to Shoreditch, **Les Trois Garçons,** 1 Club Row, E1 (© 020/7613-1924), attracts fashionable young London after dark. In an amusing kitschy setting, it is known for its first-rate French cuisine. See p. 156.
- **Best People-Watching:** In Karl Marx's former apartment house, **Quo Vadis,** 26–29 Dean St., W1 (© 020/7437-9585), is the joint venture of London's *enfant terrible* chef, Marco Pierre White, and Damien Hirst, the artist who wowed the London art world with his cow carcasses in formaldehyde. This is the hottest see-and-be-seen venue in town. The food's not bad, either. See p. 174.
- **Best Afternoon Tea:** While everyone else is donning fancy hats and heading for the Ritz, you should retreat to the **Palm Court at the Waldorf Meridien,** Aldwych, WC2 (© 020/7836-2400), in the grand 1908 Waldorf Hotel. Its Sunday ballroom tea dances are legendary: Originating with the "Tango Teas" of the 1920s and 1930s, they've been going strong ever since, interrupted only by war and a few other inconveniences. See p. 208.
- **Best Pre-Theater Menu:** Opposite the Ambassador Theatre, **The Ivy,** 1–5 West St., WC2 (© 020/7836-4751), is popular for both pre- and après-theater dining. The brasserie-style food reflects English and modern Continental influences. Try favorites such as potted shrimp or tripe and onions, or imaginative dishes like butternut pumpkin salad or wild mushroom risotto. See p. 168.
- **The Best Pizza:** We think **Pizzeria Condotti,** 4 Mill St., W1 (© 020/7499-1308), consistently serves up some of London's most savory pies—with an array of hot, bubbling, and delectable toppings. In attractive, rather expensive-looking surroundings, the restaurant serves pizzas on thin, crisp crusts. All are prepared to order and fresh from the oven. Each is a meal unto itself. See p. 183.
- **Best Picnic Fare:** For a picnic fit for a queen, go to **Fortnum & Mason,** 181 Piccadilly, W1 (© 020/7734-8040), the world's most famous grocery store. You'll find a wide array of foodstuffs to take away to your favorite park. See p. 210.

4 The Best Pubs

- **Fox and Anchor,** 115 Charterhouse St., EC1 (© 020/7253-5075), is a favorite among early-morning pub crawlers and club trawlers who fancy a pint and a bite to start (or end) the day. The array of breakfast goodies is "gut-busting"—everything from black pudding to fried bread and baked beans. After the "full house" breakfast here (including at least eight breakfast items, such as sausage or black pudding), you won't be ready to eat again until the following morning. See p. 154.

- **Grenadier,** 18 Wilton Row, SW1 (© **020/7235-3074**), was the favorite of the Duke of Wellington's officers who downed many a pint here on leave from fighting Napoleon's troops. It's a traditional pub with the aura of 19th-century England pervading, thanks to the portrait of the Duke of Wellington hanging over the fireplace, the wooden stools and benches, and the pewter-topped bar counter. See p. 326.

- **The Cow,** 89 Westbourne Park Rd., W2 (© **020/7221-0021**), attracts patrons who haven't been in an English pub for years. Leading the revolution in upgrading pub cuisine, The Cow manages to secure the biggest and juiciest oysters in town. Ox tongue poached in milk? Don't knock it 'til you've tried it. Proof that the London pub scene has changed radically: The hip young staff serves finger bowls (for before-dinner

cleansing) to its even hipper clientele. See p. 206.

- **Red Lion,** 2 Duke of York St., SW1 (© **020/7321-0782**), is where you'd take Oscar Wilde on a date if he should miraculously reappear. The writer would feel that nothing had changed in London since his departure. As you gaze upon the Belle Epoque decorations, you'll think Victoria is still on the throne. See p. 327.

- **Salisbury,** 90 St. Martin's Lane, WC2 (© **020/7836-5863**), decked out in Art Deco, is the ideal spot for a pint in the theater district. Regrettably, Lord Olivier isn't around anymore, but you might just spot a young actor who will be the Olivier of 2010. See p. 327.

- **Nag's Head,** 53 Kinnerton St., SW1 (© **020/7235-1135**), is where you go to escape tourists and hang with the locals. This quaint discovery is one of the most unspoiled pubs in London. Only minutes from Harrods, it's intimate and traditional, like something you'd encounter in a country village in Devon. See p. 327.

5 Best for Kids

Complete details on these sights and activities can be found in chapter 7, "Exploring London."

- **Sightseeing:** London is filled with attractions that appeal to young and old—take **Madame Tussaud's** wax museum (p. 259), that all-time favorite. There's more: everything from the **London Transport Museum** (p. 259) to the **National Army Museum** (p. 260), and, of course, the **Natural History Museum** (p. 261). A cruise along the Thames (see "River Cruises Along the Thames," in chapter 7) is a great way to spend an afternoon,

as is a trip to the **London Zoo** (p. 264).

- **Trips Out of London:** Board a riverboat for a **cruise to Greenwich** (p. 266), with its **National Maritime Museum** and other amusements. Part of the fun is getting there. In Greenwich you'll find many attractions, including the **Old Royal Observatory.** See "Greenwich," under "Attractions on the Outskirts," in chapter 7.

- **Royal London:** No kid would want to leave London without a visit to the **Tower of London**

(p. 233). And of course, children will want to see the **Changing of the Guard** (p. 224). For castles that evoke Disney, take them on a trip to **Windsor Castle** (p. 334) or **Hampton Court Palace** (p. 273).

- **Playgrounds:** London brims with a system of parks, nicknamed "green lungs," including **Regent's Park** with its two boating lakes, one just for children. An afternoon in sprawling **Hampstead Heath** (see "Hampstead," under "Attractions on the Outskirts," in chapter 7) can fill more enjoyable hours, as can a stroll through **Kensington Gardens** with its playgrounds. **Battersea Park** has a small children's zoo and adventure playground. For more information on **Regent's Park, Kensington Gardens** and **Battersea Park**, see "Parks and Gardens," under "More Central London Attractions," in chapter 7.

- **Entertainment:** London has a number of theaters designed for children, notably **Little Angel Theatre,** which hosts regular visiting puppeteers. The minimum age is 3. See p. 275.

A Traveler's Guide to London's Art & Architecture

By Reid Bramblett

There's no one artist, period, or museum that defines London's art and architecture; rather the city builds upon the work of artists and craftsman from its earliest days to a thriving, sometimes shocking art scene today, which could shape the look and view of the city in the future. You can see the art of London in medieval illuminated manuscripts, Thomas Gainsborough portraits, and Damien Hirst's pickled cows and sharks, its architecture from Roman walls and Norman castles to baroque St. Paul's Cathedral and towering postmodern skyscrapers. Let us illuminate some of the art and architecture that surrounds you in this graceful, exciting city.

1 Art 101

CELTIC & MEDIEVAL (CA. 800 BC–16TH CENTURY)

The Celts, mixed with Scandinavian and Dutch tribes, ruled England until the Romans established rule in A.D. 43. Celtic art survived the Roman conquest and Dark Ages Christianity mainly as carved swirls and decorations on the "Celtic Crosses" in medieval cemeteries. During the Dark and Middle Ages, colorful Celtic images and illustrations decorated "illuminated manuscripts" copied by monks. Plenty of these have ended up in London's libraries and museums.

Important examples and artists of this period include:

- **Wilton Diptych,** National Gallery. The first truly British painting was crafted in the late 1390s for Richard II by an unknown artist who mixed Italian and Northern European influences.
- **Lindisfarne Gospels,** British Library. One of Europe's greatest illuminated manuscripts from the 7th century.
- **Matthew Paris** (died 1259). A Benedictine monk who illuminated his own writings, Paris was the St. Albans Abbey chronicler. Examples are now in the British Library and Cambridge's Corpus Christi College.

THE RENAISSANCE & BAROQUE (16TH–18TH CENTURIES)

While the Renaissance was more of a Southern European movement, London's museums contain many important old masters from Italy and Germany. Renaissance means "rebirth," in this case, the renewed use of classical styles and forms. Artists strove for greater naturalism, using newly developed techniques such as linear perspective to achieve new heights of realism. A few foreign Renaissance artists did come to English courts, and had an influence on some local artists, but significant Brits didn't emerge until the baroque.

The baroque mixes a kind of super-realism based on using peasants as models and an exaggerated use of light and dark, called *chiaroscuro*, with compositional complexity and explosions of dynamic fury, movement, color, and figures.

Significant artists of this period include:

- **Pietro Torrigiano** (1472–1528). An Italian sculptor, Pietro fled Florence after breaking the nose of his classmate, Michelangelo. In London, he crafted tombs for the Tudors in Westminster Abbey, including Henry VII and Elizabeth of York. The Victoria and Albert Museum preserves Pietro's terra-cotta bust of Henry VII.

- **Hans Holbein the Younger** (1497–1543). A German Renaissance master of penetrating portraits, Holbein the Younger cataloged many significant figures in 16th-century Europe. You'll find examples in the National Gallery, National Portrait Gallery, and Windsor Castle.

- **Anton Van Dyck** (1599–1641). This Belgian painted royal portraits in the baroque style for Charles I and other Stuarts, setting the tone for British portraiture for the next few centuries and gaining a knighthood. You'll find his works in the National Portrait Gallery, National Gallery, Wallace Collection, and Wilton House, with more in Oxford's Ashmolean Museum.

- **William Hogarth** (1697–1764). Influenced by Flemish masters, Hogarth painted and engraved scenes of everyday life. His serial work such as *Rake's Progress* (in the John Soane Museum) were popular morality tales presented as a sort of early version of a comic strip. Seek out his other works in the National Gallery and Tate Britain, and Cambridge's Fitzwilliam Museum.

- **Joshua Reynolds** (1723–92). A staunch traditionalist and fussy baroque painter, Reynolds was the first president of London's Royal Academy of Arts. Reynolds spent much of his career casting his noble patrons as ancient gods in portrait compositions cribbed from old masters. Many of his works are in the National Gallery, Tate Britain, Wallace Collection, and Dulwich Picture Gallery, and in Oxford's Cathedral Hall.

- **Thomas Gainsborough** (1727–88). Although Gainsborough was a classical/baroque portraitist like Reynolds, he could be more original. When not immortalizing noble patrons such as Jonathan Buttell (better known as "Blue Boy") he painted quite a collection of landscapes for himself. His works grace the National Gallery and National Portrait Gallery, Cambridge's Fitzwilliam Museum, Oxford's Cathedral Hall and Ashmolean Museum, and Gainsborough's House, a museum and gallery in his birthplace in Suffolk.

THE ROMANTICS (LATE 18TH–19TH CENTURIES)

The Romantics idealized the Romantic tales of chivalry, had a deep respect for nature, human rights, and the nobility of peasantry, and a suspicion of progress. Their paintings tended to be heroic, historic, dramatic, and beautiful. They were inspired by critic and art theorist **John Ruskin** (1819–1900), who was among the first to praise pre-Renaissance painting and Gothic architecture.

Significant artists of this period include:

- **William Blake** (1757–1827). Romantic archetype, Blake snubbed the Royal Academy of Arts to do his own engraving, prints, illustrations, poetry, and painting. He believed in divine inspiration, but it was the vengeful Old Testament God he channeled; his works were filled with melodrama, muscular figures, and sweeping lines. See his work at the Tate Britain.

- **John Constable** (1776–1837). A little obsessed with clouds, Constable was a great British landscapist, whose scenes (especially those of happy, agrarian peasants) got more idealized with each passing year—while his compositions and brushwork became freer. You'll find his best stuff in the National Gallery and the Victoria and Albert Museum.

- **J. M. W. Turner** (1775–1851). Turner, called by some "The First Impressionist," was a prolific artist whose mood-laden, freely brushed watercolor landscapes influenced Monet. London, and the River Thames, were frequent subjects. He bequeathed his collection of some 19,000 watercolors and 300 paintings to the people of Britain. The Tate Britain's Clores Gallery displays the largest number of Turner's works, and others grace the National Gallery and Cambridge's Fitzwilliam Museum.

- **Pre-Raphaelites** (1848–70). This "Brotherhood" declared art had gone all wrong with Raphael (1483–1520) and set about to emulate the 15th-century Italian painters that preceded him—though their symbolically imbued, sweetly idealized, hyper-realistic work actually looks nothing like it. They loved depicting scenes from Romantic poetry and Shakespeare as well as the Bible. There were seven founders and many followers, the most important were Dante Rossetti, William Hunt, and John Millais; you can see work by all three at the Tate Britain and Oxford's Ashmolean Museum.

THE 20TH CENTURY

The only artistic movement or era the Brits can claim a major stake in is contemporary art, with many young British artists bursting onto the international gallery scene just before and after World War II. The 20th century, if anything, has shown the greatest artists searching for a unique, individual expression rather than adherence to a particular school.

Important artists of this period include:

- **Henry Moore** (1898–1986). A sculptor, Moore saw himself as a sort of reincarnation of Michelangelo. He mined his marble from the same quarries as the Renaissance master and let the stone itself dictate the flowing, abstract, surrealistic figures carved from it. Moore did several public commissions (*Knife Edge* [1967] at Abingdon St. Gardens underground garage; *The Arch* [1979] on the east bank of the Longwater in Kensington Gardens), and started working in bronze after the 1950s. His sculptures also grace the Tate Modern and Cambridge's Fitzwilliam Museum and Clare College.

- **Ben Nicholson** (1894–1982). The most famous of Britain's abstract artists, Nicholson is known for his low-relief abstract paintings using layered cardboard and minimalist colors (his most famous are just white). His work is in the Tate Modern and Cambridge's Fitzwilliam Museum.

- **Francis Bacon** (1909–92). A dark, brooding expressionist, Bacon used formats such as the triptych, which were usually reserved for religious subjects, to show man's foibles. Examples of his work are in the Tate Modern, including *Triptych August 1972* (1972).

- **Lucien Freud** (born 1922). Freud's portraits and nudes live in a depressing world of thick paint, fluid lines, and harsh light. The grandson of psychiatrist Sigmund Freud, this artist has pieces at the Tate Modern, including *Girl With a White Dog* (1950–51) and *Standing in Rags* (1988–89).

- **David Hockney** (born 1937). Hockney employs a less Pop Arty style than American Andy Warhol—though Hockney does reference modern technologies and culture—and is much more playful with artistic traditions. The Tate Modern is the place to see his creations, including *Mr. and Mrs. Clark and Percy* (1970–71).

- **Damien Hirst** (born 1965). The guy who pickles cows, Hirst is a celebrity/artist whose work sets out to shock. He's a winner of Britain's Turner Prize, and his work is prominent in the collection of Charles Saatchi (whose Saatchi Gallery in London displays his holdings) and was featured in "Sensation," the exhibition that prompted protest, vandalism, and the formation of a decency commission in New York City.

2 Architecture 101

While each architectural era in London has its own distinctive features, there are some elements, floor plans, and terms common to many.

From the Romanesque period on, most **churches** consist either of a single-wide **aisle** or a wide central **nave** flanked by two narrow, less-tall aisles. The aisles are separated from the nave by a row of **columns,** or square stacks of masonry called **piers,** connected by **arches.** Sometimes—especially in the medieval Norman and Gothic eras—there is a second level to the nave, above these arches (and hence above the low roof over the aisles) punctuated by windows called a **clerestory.** Often, between the arches and clerestory windows there is a small passageway inside the wall called the **triforium,** open on the nave side via a series of small arches.

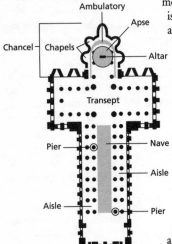

Church Floor Plan

This main nave/aisle assemblage is usually crossed by a perpendicular corridor called a **transept** near the far, east end of the church so that the floor plan looks like a **Latin Cross.** The shorter, east arm of the nave is called the **chancel;** it often houses the stalls of the **choir** and the **altar.** Some churches use a **rood screen** (so called because it supports a *rood,* the Saxon word for *crucifixion*) to separate the nave from the chancel. If the far end of the chancel is rounded off, we call it an **apse.** An **ambulatory** is a corridor outside the altar and choir area, separating it from the ring of smaller chapels radiating off the chancel and apse.

Some churches, especially after the Renaissance when mathematical proportion became important, were built on a **Greek Cross** plan, each axis the same length, like a giant +.

It's worth pointing out that very few buildings (especially churches) were built in only one style. They often took centuries to complete, during which time tastes would change and plans would be altered.

NORMAN (1066–1200)

Aside from a smattering of ancient sights—**pre-classical** stone circles at Stonehenge and Avebury, **Roman** ruins such as the Bath spa and Hadrian's Wall—the oldest surviving architectural style in England dates to when the 1066 Norman Conquest brought the Romanesque era to Britain, where it flourished as the **Norman style.**

Churches were large, with a wide nave and aisles to fit the masses that came to hear Mass and worship at the altars of various saints. But to support the weight of all that masonry, the walls had to be thick and solid (pierced only by few and small windows) resting on huge piers, giving Norman churches a dark, somber, mysterious feeling.

Some of the features of this style include

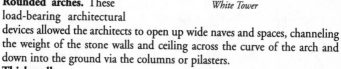

White Tower

- **Rounded arches.** These load-bearing architectural devices allowed the architects to open up wide naves and spaces, channeling the weight of the stone walls and ceiling across the curve of the arch and down into the ground via the columns or pilasters.
- **Thick walls.**
- **Infrequent and small windows.**
- **Huge piers.** These are square stacks of masonry.
- **Chevrons.** These zigzagging decorations often surround a doorway or wrap around a column.

White Tower, London (Gundulf, 1078), William the Conqueror's first building in Britain, is the central keep of the Tower of London. The tower's fortress-thick walls and rounded archways provide a textbook example of a Norman-era castle. **St. John's Chapel,** located in the White Tower, is one of the few remaining Norman churches in England.

GOTHIC (1150–1550)

The French Gothic style invaded England in the late 12th century, trading rounded arches for pointy ones—an engineering discovery that freed architects from the thick walls of Norman structures and allowed ceilings to soar, walls to thin, and windows to proliferate.

Instead of dark, somber, relatively unadorned Norman interiors that forced the eyes of the faithful toward the altar, the Gothic interior enticed the churchgoers' gaze upward to high ceilings filled with light. While the priests conducted Mass in Latin, the peasants could "read" the Bible stories in the stained glass windows.

The squat exteriors of the Norman churches were replaced by graceful buttresses and soaring spires, which rose from town centers.

The Gothic style made comebacks in the 17th century as **Laudian Gothic** in some Oxford and Cambridge buildings, in the 18th century as **rococo** or **Strawberry Hill Gotick,** and the 19th century as **Victorian Gothic Revival,** discussed below.

The Gothic proper in Britain can be divided into three periods or styles: **Early English** (1150–1300), **Decorated** (1250–1370), and **Perpendicular** (1350–1550). Although each has identifiable features, they all include:

- **Pointed arches.** The most significant development of the Gothic era was the discovery that pointed arches could carry far more weight than rounded ones.
- **Ribbed vaulting.** In Gothic buildings, the square patch of ceiling between four columns arches up to a point in the center, creating four sail shapes. This is called a cross-vault. The "X" separating these four sails is often reinforced with ridges called ribbing. As the Gothic progressed, the spaces between the structural ribbing became more decorative, often filled with **tracery** (delicate and lace-like carved stone). In the Perpendicular style, **fan vaulting** (cone-shaped concave vaults springing from the same point) was often used.

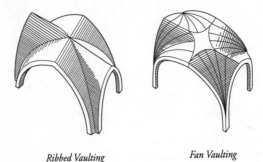

Ribbed Vaulting   *Fan Vaulting*

- **Flying buttresses.** These freestanding exterior pillars connected by graceful, thin arms of stone help channel the weight of the building and its roof out and down into the ground.
- **Plate tracery.** The tip of a window, or the tips of two side-by-side windows, is often filled with a flat plate of stone pierced by a **light** (tiny window), which is either round or in a **trefoil** (3 round petals, like a clover) or **quatrefoil** (4 petals) shape.
- **Stained glass.** The multitude and size of Gothic windows allowed them to be filled with Bible stories and symbolism writ in the colorful patterns of stained glass. The use of stained glass was more common in the later Gothic periods.
- **Rose windows.** These huge circular windows, often the centerpieces of facades, are filled with elegant tracery and "petals" of stained glass.
- **Spires.** These pinnacles seem to defy gravity and reach toward Heaven itself.
- **Gargoyles.** These are drain spouts disguised as wide-mouthed creatures or human heads.
- **Choir screen.** Serving as the inner wall of the ambulatory and outer wall of the choir section, the choir screen is often decorated with carvings or tombs.

Among England's towering Gothic achievements, **Salisbury Cathedral** (1220–65) is almost unique for the speed with which it was built and the uniformity of its architecture. **King's College Chapel** (1446–1515) at Cambridge has England's most magnificent fan vaulting along with some fine stained glass. At Windsor are two great examples, the **College Chapel** at Eton College (the stained glass is modern, and the fan vaulting painstakingly redone in 1957, but the 15th century murals are original), and the **St. George's Chapel** in Windsor

Castle (a gorgeous nave vault with fan vaulting in the aisles, and carved choir stalls).

RENAISSANCE (1550–1650)

While Italy and even France were experimenting with the Renaissance ideals of proportion, classical inspiration, and mathematical precision to create unified, balanced structures, England was trundling along with the late **Tudor Gothic** Perpendicular style (the Tudor use of red brick became a major feature of later Gothic revivals) in places such as Hampton Court Palace.

It wasn't until the Elizabethan era that the Brits turned to the **Renaissance** style sweeping the Continent. Architect **Inigo Jones** (1573–1652), England's greatest Renaissance architect, brought back from his travel in Italy a fevered imagination full of the exactingly classical theories of **Palladianism,** as developed by **Andrea Palladio** (1508–80). Although Jones applied what he'd learned to several English structures, most English architects at this time tempered the Renaissance style with a heavy dose of Gothic-like elements.

Little specifically identifies Renaissance buildings, except

Salisbury Cathedral

- **A sense of proportion.**
- **A reliance on symmetry.**
- **The use of classical orders.** This idea specifies three different column types: Corinthian, Ionic, or Doric.

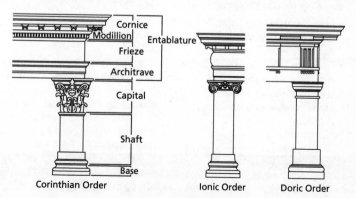

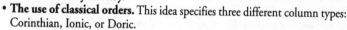

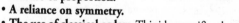

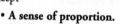

Cornice
Modillion
Frieze
Architrave
Entablature
Capital
Shaft
Base

Corinthian Order

Ionic Order

Doric Order

Classical Orders

Noteworthy structures in this style by Inigo Jones include **Queen's House,** Greenwich (1616–18 and 1629–35); the **Queen's Chapel,** St. James Palace (1623–25) and the **Banqueting House,** Whitehall (1619–22), both in London; and the state rooms of Wiltshire's **Wilton House** (1603), where Shakespeare performed and D-Day was planned. Recently, **Shakespeare's Globe Theatre** dusted off one of Jones's never-realized plans and used it to construct their new indoor theater.

BAROQUE (1650–1750)

England's greatest architect was **Christopher Wren** (1632–1723), a scientist and member of Parliament who got the job of rebuilding London after the Great Fire of 1666. He designed 53 replacement churches alone, plus the new St. Paul's Cathedral and numerous other projects.

The identifiable features of the baroque as practiced by Wren and others include

- **Classical architecture rewritten with curves.** The baroque is similar to the Renaissance, but many of the right angles and ruler-straight lines are exchanged for curves of complex geometry and an interplay of concave and convex surfaces. The overall effect is to lighten the appearance of structures and to add some movement of line.
- **Complex decoration.** Unlike the sometimes severe and austere designs of Renaissance and other classically inspired styles, the baroque was often playful and apt to festoon structures with decorations to liven things up.

St. Paul's Cathedral, London (1676–1710), is the crowning achievement both of the English baroque and of Christopher Wren himself. The city's other main Wren attraction is **Royal Naval College,** Greenwich (1696).

A student of Wren's, **Nicholas Hawksmoor** practiced a baroque more fanciful than that of his teacher. Hawksmoor left London several churches, including **St. Mary Woolnoth** (1716–24), **St. George's,** Bloomsbury (1716–30), **Christ Church,** Spitalfields (1714–29), and **St. Anne's,** Limehouse (1714–30).

NEOCLASSICAL AND GREEK REVIVAL (1714–1837)

Many 18th-century architects cared little for the baroque, and during the Georgian era (1714–1830) a restrained, simple neoclassicism reigned, balanced between a resurgence of the precepts of Palladianism (see "Renaissance," above) and an even more distilled vision of classical theory called Greek Revival.

Buildings in these styles may be distinguished by

- **Mathematical proportion, symmetry, and classical orders.** These classical ideals first rediscovered during the Renaissance are the hallmark of every classically styled era.
- **Crescents and circuses.** The Georgians were famous for these seamless curving rows of identical stone town houses with tall windows, each one simple yet elegant inside.
- **Open double-arm staircases.** This feature was a favorite of the neo-Palladians.

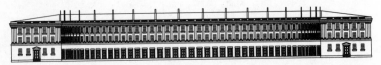

Crescent

The chapel in Greenwich Hospital (1779–88) is a fine example of the style, courtesy of the most textbook of Greek Revivalists, James "Athenian" Stuart. The greatest sight by Greek Revivalist John Soane is his own idiosyncratic house at No. 13 Lincoln's Inn Fields (1812–13), now the John Soane Museum (other Soane buildings include the Dulwich Picture Gallery and the facade of the Bank of England in Bartholomew Lane). Another example of this style is the British Museum (Robert & Sidney Smirke, 1823).

VICTORIAN GOTHIC REVIVAL (1750–1900)

While neoclassicists were reinterpreting the classical age, the Romantic movement swept up many others with rosy visions of the past. Their imaginary and fairytale version of the Middle Ages led to such creative developments as the Pre-Raphaelite painters (see "The Romantics," earlier in this chapter) and Gothic revival architects, who really got a head of steam under their movement during the eclectic Victorian era.

Buildings in the Victorian Gothic Revival style can be distinguished by their:

- **Mishmash of Gothic features.** Look at the Gothic features described earlier, and then imagine going on a shopping spree through them at random. How to tell the copycats from the original? Victorian buildings are much younger so tend to be in better shape. They're often much larger.
- **Eclecticism.** Few Victorians bothered with getting all the formal details of a particular Gothic era right (London's Houses of Parliament comes closest). They just wanted to make sure the overall effect was pointy with pinnacled turrets, busy with decorations, and medieval.
- **Grand scale.** These buildings tend to be very large. This was usually accomplished by using Gothic only on the surface, with industrial age engineering underneath.

Palace of Westminster

Charles Barry designed the British seat of government, **Palace of Westminster** (Houses of Parliament) (1835–52), in a Gothic idiom that, sticks pretty faithfully to the old Perpendicular period's style. His clock tower, usually called "Big Ben" after its biggest bell, has become an icon of London.

The massive pinnacled and redbrick Victorian mansion, **St. Pancras Station** (George Gilbert Scott, 1867), makes for a quirky entrance to the Industrial Age phenomenon of rail travel. (And, while purely industrial and not Gothic, the station's steel-and-glass train shed was an engineering marvel, widest in the world at its time.) **Albert Memorial** (George Gilbert Scott, 1863–72), a massive Gothic canopy by the same architect, was commissioned by Queen Victoria in memory of her husband. Like St. Pancras, the **Natural History Museum**

(Alfred Waterhouse, 1873–81), is another delightful marriage of imposing neo-Gothic clothing hiding an industrial age steel-and-iron framework.

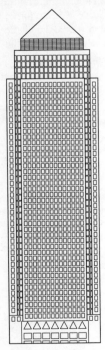

Canary Wharf Tower

THE 20TH CENTURY

For the first half of the 20th century, London was too busy expanding into suburbs (in an architecturally uninteresting way) and fighting World Wars to pay much attention to architecture. After the Blitz, much of central London had to be rebuilt, but most of the new buildings that went up in the City held to a functional school of architecture aptly named **Brutalism.** It wasn't until the late 1970s and 1980s that **postmodern** architecture gave British architects a bold, new direction.

Identifiable features of postmodern architecture in London include

- **The skyscraper motif.** Glass and steel as high as you can stack it.
- **A reliance on historic details.** Like the Victorians, postmodernists also recycled elements from architectural history, from classical to exotic.

Lloyd's Building (1978–86) is *the* British postmodern masterpiece by architect Richard Rogers, who had a hand in the design of Paris's funky Centre Pompidou. Britain's tallest building, **Canary Wharf Tower** (César Pelli, 1986), is the centerpiece of the early 1990s Canary Wharf office complex and commercial development. **Charing Cross** (Terry Farrell, 1991) capped the famous old train station with an enormous postmodern office-and-shopping complex in glass and pale stone.

3

Planning Your Trip to London

This chapter tackles the hows of your trip to London—those issues required to get your trip together and get on the road, whether you're a frequent traveler or a first-timer.

1 Visitor Information

The British Tourist Authority maintains a website at **www.visitbritain. com**. You can also get information from **British Tourist Authority** offices. There's one in the **United States,** at 551 Fifth Ave., Suite 701, New York, NY 10176-0799 (© **800/ 462-2748** or 212/986-2200; fax 212/986-1188). In **Canada,** it's at 5915 Airport Rd., Mississagua, ON L4V 1T1 (© **888/VISITUK;** fax 905/405-1835). In **Australia,** the office is at Level 16, Gateway, 1 Macquarie Place, Sydney, NSW 2000 (© **02/9377-4400;** fax 02/9377-4499). In **New Zealand,** go to the Fay Richwhite Building, 17th Floor, 151 Queen St., Auckland 1 (© **09/ 303-1446;** fax 09/377-6965). For a full information pack on London, write to the **London Tourist Board,** Glen House, Stag Place, Victoria, SWIE 5LT (© **020/7932-2000**). You can also call the recorded-message service, **Visitorcall** (© **0839/ 123456**), 24 hours a day. This number cannot be dialed outside Britain. Various topics are listed; calls cost 60p ($1) per minute.

Time Out, the most up-to-date magazine for what's happening in London, is online at **www.timeout. co.uk**. You can pick up a print copy at any international newsstand.

London Guide (www.cs.ucl.ac.uk) is run by London's University College and has information on cheap dining and accommodations in the Bloomsbury area. There are also travelogues and tips for theatergoers.

To book accommodations with a credit card (MasterCard or Visa), call the **London Tourist Board Booking Office** at © **020/7604-2890,** or fax them at 020/7372-2068. They're available Monday through Friday from 9am to 6pm (London time). There is a £5 ($7.50) fee for booking.

WHAT'S ON THE WEB? The most useful site was created by a very knowledgeable source, the British Tourist Authority itself, and U.S. visitors are its target audience. A wealth of information is available at **www.usa gateway.visitbritain.com**, which lets you order brochures online, provides trip planning hints, and even grants prompt answers to e-mail questions. This site covers all of Great Britain. Go to **www.heathrow.co.uk** for a guide and terminal maps for Heathrow, Gatwick, Stansted, and other lesser airports, including flight arrival times, duty-free shops, airport restaurants, and info on getting from the airports to downtown London. Getting around London can be confusing, so you might want to visit

Destination: London—Red Alert Checklist

- Citizens of EU countries can cross into Britain for as long as they wish with an identity card. Citizens of other countries must have a passport.
- If you purchased traveler's checks, have you recorded the check numbers and stored that document separately from the checks?
- Did you pack your camera and an extra set of camera batteries, and purchase enough film? If you packed film in your checked baggage, did you invest in protective pouches to shield film from airport x-rays?
- Do you have a safe, accessible place to store money?
- Did you bring ID cards that may entitle you to discounts, such as AAA and AARP cards, student IDs, and so forth?
- Did you bring emergency drug prescriptions and extra glasses and/or contact lenses?
- Do you have your credit card pin numbers?
- If you have an E-ticket, do you have documentation (a printout with the confirmation number)?
- Did you leave a copy of your itinerary with someone at home?
- Did you check to see if any travel advisories have been issued by the **U.S. State Department** (http://travel.state.gov/travel_warnings.html) regarding your destination?
- Do you have the address and phone number of your country's embassy with you?

www.londontransport.co.uk for up-to-the-minute info. For the latest details on London's theater scene, consult **www.officiallondontheatre.co.uk**. At **www.multimap.com**, you can access detailed street maps of the whole United Kingdom—just key in the location or even just the postal code and a map of the area with the location circled will appear. For directions to specific places in London, consult **www.streetmap.co.uk**.

2 Entry Requirements & Customs Regulations

Citizens of the United States, Canada, Australia, New Zealand, and South Africa require a passport to enter the United Kingdom, but no visa. Irish citizens and citizens of European Union countries need only an identity card. The maximum stay for non-European Union visitors is 6 months. Some Customs officials request proof that you have the means to leave the country (usually a round-trip ticket) and means of support while you're in Britain (someone in the UK will have to vouch that they are supporting you,

or you may be asked to show documents that indicate that you have an income). If you're planning to fly on from the United Kingdom to a country that requires a visa, it's wise to secure the visa before you leave home.

Your valid driver's license and at least 1 year's experience is required to drive personal or rented cars. You must be 25 or over to rent a car.

PASSPORT INFORMATION
Safeguard your passport—if you lose it, visit your nearest consulate right

away for a replacement. Passport applications can be downloaded from Internet sites listed below under the individual country.

FOR RESIDENTS OF THE UNITED STATES

For general information, call the **National Passport Agency** (© **202/647-0518**; www.travel.state.gov). If you're applying for a first-time passport, you must do it in person at one of 13 passport offices throughout the United States; a federal, state, or probate court; or a major post office (not all post offices accept applications; call the number below to find the ones that do). To find your regional office, call or access the **National Passport Information Center** on the Web (© **900/225-5674**; www.travel.state. gov). The call costs 35¢ per minute; $1.05 per minute for operator-assisted calls), or call © 888/362-8668 with a Visa, MasterCard, or American Express card for a flat $4.95 charge.

See the website or passport form for acceptable forms of identification needed to acquire a passport. You'll need to present a birth certificate as proof of citizenship, and submit proof of identity, so bring along a driver's license, state or military ID, and social security card. You can renew your passport by mail. Pick up a form at any post office, or download it from the website listed above. Allow 3 to 6 weeks (especially during spring and summer) to receive your new passport, though for an extra $35, you can get "expedited service" with a turnaround time of 2 weeks or less. You'll need

two identical passport-size photos (2 in. by 2 in.), which you can usually get taken at a drugstore.

FOR RESIDENTS OF CANADA

Passport applications, which must be accompanied by two identical passport-size photographs and proof of Canadian citizenship, are available at travel agencies throughout Canada, at any of 28 regional passport offices, or from the central **Passport Office, Department of Foreign Affairs and International Trade,** Ottawa, ON K1A 0G3 (© **800/567-6868;** in U.S. 819/994-3500; www.dfait-maeci.gc. ca). Children under 16 may be included on a parent's passport, but they need their own to travel unaccompanied by the parent.

FOR RESIDENTS OF IRELAND

Passport applications are available at all Garda stations, at post offices with Passport Express Service, and from the **Passport Offices** at Setanta Centre, Molesworth Street, Dublin 2 (© **353-1/671-1633**), or at 1A South Mall, Cork (© **353-021/272-525;** www.irl-gov.ie). For additional information, visit the Department of Foreign Affairs' website at www.irlgov.ie/ iveagh and click on "Traveling Abroad."

FOR RESIDENTS OF AUSTRALIA

Apply at your local post office or passport office, or search the government website at www.passports.gov.au. Passports for adults are A$136 and for

---

⌒Tips   Surfing for Passports

U.S. citizens can save the 35¢ to $4.95 per minute it costs to call the National Passport Information Center by pointing browsers at travel.state.gov/passport_services.html, where you can locate the nearest place to apply for a passport, check the lists of frequently asked questions, and print application and renewal forms.

those under 18, A$68. For information, call ℂ **02/13-12-32.**

FOR RESIDENTS OF NEW ZEALAND

Pick up a passport application at any travel agency or Link Centre, or on the Web at www.passports.govt.nz. For more info, contact the **Passport Office,** P.O. Box 805, Wellington (ℂ**0800/225-050;**www.passport. govt.nz). Passports for adults are NZ$80 and for those under 16, NZ$40.

CUSTOMS REGULATIONS
WHAT YOU CAN BRING INTO LONDON

For Non-EU Nationals You can bring in, duty-free, 200 cigarettes, 20 cigarillos, 50 cigars, or 250 grams of smoking tobacco. This amount for these goods is doubled if you live outside Europe.

You can also bring in 2 liters of wine and either 1 liter of alcohol over 22 proof or 2 liters of wine under 22 proof. In addition, you can bring in 50 grams (1.75 oz.) of perfume, a quarter liter (250ml) of eau de toilette, 500 grams (1 lb.) of coffee, and 200 grams (½ lb.) of tea. Visitors 15 and over may also bring in other goods totaling 182.40€ ($162.90); the allowance for those 14 and under is 91.20€ ($81.45). (Customs officials tend to be lenient about general merchandise, realizing the limits are unrealistically low.)

You can't bring your pet straight to England. Six months' quarantine is required before it is allowed in. An illegally imported animal may be destroyed.

For EU Citizens Visitors from fellow European Union countries can bring into Britain any amount of goods as long as the goods are intended for their personal use—not for resale.

The current policy for bringing pets into the UK from the EU is under review. Right now, animals or pets of any kind are forbidden from entering without a long quarantine period.

WHAT YOU CAN BRING HOME

For U.S. Citizens If you've been out of the country for 48 hours or more, you can bring $400 worth of goods (per person) back into the States without paying a duty. On the first $1,000 worth of goods over $400 you pay a flat 10%. Beyond that, it works on an item-by-item basis. There are a few restrictions on amounts: 1 liter of alcohol (you must be over 21), 200 cigarettes, and 100 cigars. Antiques over 100 years old and works of art are exempt from the $400 limit, as is anything you mail home. Once per day, you can mail yourself $200 worth of goods duty-free; mark the package "For Personal Use." You can also mail $100 worth of goods per person per day to other people; label each package "Unsolicited Gift." Any package must state a description of the contents and their values on the exterior. You can't mail alcohol, perfume (it contains alcohol), or tobacco products.

For more details on regulations, check out the **U.S. Customs Service** website at www.customs.ustreas.gov or contact the Customs office at P.O. Box 7407, Washington, DC 20044 (ℂ **202/354-1000**) to request the free "Know Before You Go" pamphlet.

To prevent the spread of diseases, you can't bring in any plants, fruits, vegetables, meats, or other foodstuffs. This includes cured meats like salami. You may bring in the following: bakery goods, all but the softest cheeses (the rule is vague, but if the cheese is at all spreadable, don't risk confiscation), candies, roasted coffee beans and dried tea, fish (packaged salmon is okay), seeds for veggies and flowers (but not for trees), and mushrooms. Check out the USDA's website at www.aphis.usda.gov/oa/travel.html for more details.

For Canadian Citizens For a clear summary of Canadian rules, write for the booklet "I Declare," issued by **Canadian Customs Revenue Agency,** 333 Dunsmuir St., Vancouver, BC V6B 5R4 CANADA (© **800/461-9999**), or check out the website at www.ccra-adrc.gc.ca. Canada allows its citizens a C$750 tax exemption if you're gone for 7 days or longer (only C$200 if you're gone between 48 hr. and 7 days), and you're allowed to bring back, duty-free, 200 cigarettes, 50 cigars, and 1.5 liters of wine *or* 1.14 liters of liquor *or* 8.5 liters of beer or ale. In addition, you're allowed to mail gifts to Canada at the rate of C$60 a day, provided they're unsolicited and aren't alcohol or tobacco (write "Unsolicited Gift, Under $60 Value" on the package).

For Australian Citizens The duty-free allowance in Australia is A$400 or, for those under 18, A$200. Upon returning to Australia, citizens can bring in 250 cigarettes or 250 grams of loose tobacco and 1.125 liters of alcohol. A helpful brochure, available from Australian consulates or Customs offices, is "Know Before You Go." For more information, contact **Australian Customs Services,** GPO Box 8, Sydney NSW 2001 (© **02/921-32-000** within Australia; 02/6275-6666; www.customs.gov.au from overseas).

For New Zealand Citizens The duty-free allowance for New Zealand is NZ$700. Citizens over 17 can bring back 200 cigarettes or 50 cigars or 250 grams of tobacco (or a mix of all 3 if their combined weight does not exceed 250g); plus 4.5 liters of wine or beer, plus 1.125 liters of liquor. Most questions are answered in the free "Advice to Travellers" pamphlet available at New Zealand consulates and Customs offices. For more information, contact **New Zealand Customs,** 50 Anzac Ave., P.O. Box 29, Auckland (© **09/359-6655**).

3 Money

POUNDS & PENCE

Britain's decimal monetary system is based on the pound (£), which is made up of 100 pence (written as "p"). Pounds are also called "quid" by Britons. There are £1 and £2 coins, as well as coins of 50p, 20p, 10p, 5p, 2p, and 1p. Banknotes come in denominations of £5, £10, £20, and £50.

As a general guideline, the price conversions in this book have been computed at the rate of £1 = $1.50 (U.S.). Bear in mind, however, that exchange rates fluctuate daily.

ATMS

ATMs are easily found throughout London. ATMs are also connected to

---

Tips Make Sure Your PIN Works

Make sure that the PINs on your bankcards and credit cards will work in Britain. You'll need a four-digit code (six digits won't work), so if you have a six-digit code you'll have to get a new PIN from your bank before your trip. If you're unsure about this, contact Cirrus or PLUS (above). Be sure to check the daily withdrawal limit at the same time.

The U.S. Dollar & the British Pound

Rates are subject to change, although they have been around this level for the past few years. Point your browser to www.x-rates.com/calculator.html for exchange rates, updated daily, between any two major currencies.

U.S.$	U.K.£	U.S.$	U.K.£
0.25	0.17	15	9.99
0.50	0.33	20	13.32
0.75	0.50	25	16.65
1.00	0.67	50	33.30
2.00	1.33	75	49.95
3.00	2.00	100	66.60
4.00	2.66	150	99.90
5.00	3.33	200	166.50
7.00	4.66	300	199.80
10.00	6.66	500	333.00

the major networks at airports such as Heathrow and Gatwick. You'll usually get a better exchange rate by withdrawing money at an ATM (currency exchange booths take a huge commission or give an unfavorable rate, or both), but your bank may charge a fee for using a foreign ATM. You may also need a different PIN to use overseas ATMs. Call your bank to check and get a new PIN if needed before you go.

The most popular ATM networks are **Cirrus** (© 800/424-7787; www.mastercard.com) and **PLUS** (© 800/843-7587; www.visa.com); check the back of your ATM card to see which network your bank belongs to. You can use the 800 numbers in the U.S. (also on your card) to locate ATMs in your destination or ask your bank for a list of overseas ATMs. You can find the locations of ATMs on www.visa.com and www.mastercard.com.

These days, traveler's checks seem less necessary because most English cities and towns, especially London, have 24-hour ATMs, allowing you to withdraw small amounts of cash as needed. But if you prefer the security of the tried and true, you might want to stick with traveler's checks—provided that you don't mind showing an ID every time you want to cash a check.

Exchange rates are more favorable at your destination. Nevertheless, it's often helpful to exchange at least some money before going abroad (standing in line at the *cambio* [exchange bureau] in the London airport could make you miss the next bus leaving for downtown after a long flight). Check with any of your local American Express or Thomas Cook offices or major banks. Or, order pounds in advance from the following: **American Express** (© 800/221-7282; www.americanexpress.com), **Thomas Cook** (© 800/223-7373; www.thomascook.com), or **Capital for Foreign Exchange** (© 888/842-0880).

It's best to exchange currency or traveler's checks at a bank, not a *cambio,* hotel, or shop. Currency and traveler's checks (which garner a better exchange rate than cash) can be changed at all principal airports and at some travel agencies, such as American Express and Thomas Cook. Note the rates and ask about commission

What Things Cost in London	U.K.£	U.S.$
Taxi from Heathrow Airport to central London	£35	$52.50
Underground from Heathrow Airport to central London	£3.50	$ 5.25
Local telephone call	20p	30¢
Double room at The Dorchester (Very expensive)	£320	$480
Double room at Hallam Hotel (Moderate)	£105	$157.50
Double room at Glynne Court (Inexpensive)	£75	$112.50
Lunch for one at The Ivy (Expensive)	£24	$36
Lunch for one at Ye Olde Cheshire Cheese (Moderate)	£18	$27
Dinner for one, without wine, at Bibendum The Oyster Bar (Expensive)	£35	$52.50
Dinner for one, without wine, at Porter's English Restaurant (Moderate)	£18	$27
Dinner for one, without wine at Stockpot (Inexpensive)	£6.50	$9.75
Pint of beer	£1.75	$2.65
Coca-Cola	£1.60	$2.40
Cup of coffee	£1.50	$2.25
Roll of ASA 100 color film, 36 exposures	£6	$9.00
Admission to the British Museum	Free	
Movie ticket	£6.50	$9.75
Theater ticket	£18–£60	$27–$90

fees; it can sometimes pay to shop around and ask.

Keep a record of your traveler's checks' serial numbers—separate from the checks, of course—so you're ensured a refund in an emergency.

CREDIT CARDS

Credit cards are a safe way to carry money and provide a convenient record of all your expenses. You can also withdraw cash advances from your credit cards at any bank (although you'll pay interest on the advance the moment you receive the cash, and you won't get frequent-flyer miles on an airline credit card). At most banks you can get a cash advance at the ATM with your PIN. If you don't have a PIN, call your credit card company and ask for one. It usually takes 5 to 7 business days, but some banks provide the number over the phone if you pass a security clearance.

CURRENCY EXCHANGE

When exchanging money, you'll have to pay a service charge at banks and when using ATMs (because you are withdrawing the currency of the country that you're in, this is considered a currency exchange). London banks are usually open Monday through Friday from 9:30am to 3:30pm. Many of the major branches are open until 5pm; a handful of central London branches are open until noon on Saturday, including **Barclays,** 208 Kensington High St., W8 (© **0845/755-5555;** www.Ibank.barklays.co.uk). Money exchange is also available at competitive rates at major London **post offices,** with a 1% service charge. Money can be exchanged during off-hours at change bureaus throughout the city; these bureaus are found at small shops and in hotels, railway stations (including the international terminal at Waterloo Station), travel agencies, and airports, but their rates are poor and they charge high service fees. Examine and compare prices and rates before handing over your dollars, as there's no consumer organization to regulate the activities of privately run change bureaus.

In a recent *Time Out* survey of exchange facilities, **American Express** came out on top, with the lowest commission charged on dollar transactions. They're at 30–31 Haymarket, SW1 (© **800/221-7282** or 020/7484-9600; www.americanexpress.com) and other locations throughout the city. They charge no commission when cashing traveler's checks. However, a flat rate of £2 ($3) is charged when exchanging the dollar to the pound. Most other agencies tend to charge a percentage rate commission

(usually 2%) with a £2 to £3 ($3–$4.50) minimum charge. Other reputable firms are **Thomas Cook,** 35 Great Russell St., WI (© **800/ 223-7373** or 0800/622-101), which has branches at Victoria Station, Marble Arch, and other city locations; and, for 24-hour foreign exchange, **Chequepoint,** at 548 Oxford St., W1N 9HJ (© **020/7723-1005**) and other locations throughout London (hours vary). Try not to change money at your hotel; the rates tend to be horrendous.

WHAT TO DO IF YOUR CREDIT CARDS ARE STOLEN

Almost every credit card company has an emergency 800 number that you can call if your wallet or purse is stolen. Write these numbers down and carry them separately from your cards if they are not listed below. Card companies may be able to wire you an advance off your credit card immediately and, in many places, can deliver an emergency credit card in a day or two. Call © **800/555-1212** for your card issuer's phone number. **Visa's** U.S. emergency number is © **800/ 336-8472** in the U.S., or © **410/ 581-3836** outside the U.S. **American Express** cardholders should call © **800/233-5432** to report a lost card, and traveler's check holders should call © **800/221-7282.**

Tips **Emergency Cash—The Fastest Way**

If you need emergency cash over the weekend when all the banks and American Express offices are closed, you can have money wired to you from **Western Union** (© **800/325-6000;** www.westernunion.com). You must present valid ID to pick up the cash at the Western Union office. However, in most countries, you can pick up a money transfer even if you don't have valid identification, as long as you can answer an identifying test question provided by the sender. Be sure to let the sender know in advance that you don't have ID. If you need to use a test question instead of ID, the sender must take cash to his or her local Western Union office, rather than transferring the money over the phone or online.

MasterCard holders should call 𝄢 **800/307-7309** in the U.S., or call 𝄢 **0800/964-767** toll-free.

Odds are that if your wallet is gone, the police won't recover it. However, it is still worth informing them; your credit-card company or insurer might require a police report number.

4 When to Go

CLIMATE

Charles Dudley Warner once said that the trouble with the weather is that everybody talks about it but nobody does anything about it. Well, Londoners talk about weather more than anyone, but they have also done something about it: air pollution control has resulted in the virtual disappearance of the pea soup fogs that once blanketed the city.

A typical London-area weather forecast for a summer day predicts "scattered clouds with sunny periods and showers, possibly heavy at times."

Summer temperatures seldom rise above 78°F, nor do they drop below 35°F in winter. London, being in one of the mildest parts of the country, can be very pleasant in the spring and fall. Yes, it rains, but you'll rarely get a true downpour. Rains are heaviest in November, when the city averages 2½ inches.

The British consider chilliness wholesome and usually try to keep room temperatures about 10°F below the American comfort level, so bring sweaters year-round if you tend to get cold.

London's Average Daytime Temperature & Rainfall

	Jan	Feb	Mar	Apr	May	June	July	Aug	Sept	Oct	Nov	Dec
Temp. (°F)	40	40	44	49	55	61	64	64	59	52	46	42
Temp. (°C)	4.4	4.4	6.7	9.4	12.8	16.1	17.8	17.8	15.0	11.1	7.8	5.6
Rainfall (inches)	2.1	1.6	1.5	1.5	1.8	1.8	2.2	2.3	1.9	2.2	2.5	1.9

CURRENT WEATHER CONDITIONS

In the United States, you can dial 𝄢 **1/900-WEATHER,** and then press the first four letters of the desired foreign city—in this case, LOND for London—for the time of day in that city, plus current temperatures, weather conditions, and forecasts. The cost is 95¢ per minute. Another good way to check conditions is at the Weather Channel's website: **www.weather.com.** In London, you can listen to BBC One–TV for the weather.

HOLIDAYS

In England, public holidays include New Year's Day, Good Friday, Easter Monday, May Day (first Mon in May), spring and summer bank holidays (last Mon in May and Aug, respectively), Christmas Day, and Boxing Day (Dec 26).

LONDON CALENDAR OF EVENTS

January

January Sales. Most shops offer good reductions. Many sales start as early as late December to beat the post-Christmas slump. The truly voracious shoppers camp overnight outside Harrods to get in first.

London Parade, from Parliament Square to Berkeley Square in Mayfair. Bands, floats, and carriages. January 1. Procession starts around 12pm.

Tips   Best Weather in London

If balmy weather is your dream, the month of July is as warm as it gets in London. Temperatures range from the 50s (Fahrenheit) in the morning, rising to the low 70s (Fahrenheit) in the afternoon. But it still rains 1 day in 5. For some "real weather," with wind, storms, freezing and all the works, visit during the other months.

London International Boat Show, Earl's Court Exhibition Centre, Warwick Road. The largest boat show in Europe. Call ℂ **020/8385-1200** for details. Early January.

Charles I Commemoration. Anniversary of the execution of King Charles I "in the name of freedom and democracy." Hundreds of cavaliers march through central London in 17th-century dress, and prayers are said at the Banqueting House in Whitehall. Free. Last Sunday in January.

February

Chinese New Year. The famous Lion Dancers in Soho. Free. Either in late January or early February (based on the lunar calendar).

Great Spitalfields Pancake Race. Teams of four run in relays, tossing pancakes. At Old Spitalfields Market, Brushfield Street, E1. To join in, call ℂ **020/7375-0441.** At noon on Shrove Tuesday (last day before Lent).

March

St. David's Day. A member of the Royal Family presents the Welsh Guards with the principality's national emblem, a leek; call ℂ **020/7414-3291** for information. March 1 (or nearest Sun). This takes place at the Chelsea Barracks.

Chelsea Antiques Fair, a twice-yearly gathering of England's best dealers, held at Old Town Hall, King's Road, SW3 (ℂ **0144/ 448-2514**). Mid-March (and again in mid-Sept).

Oranges and Lemons Service, at St. Clement Danes, Strand, WC2. As a reminder of the nursery rhyme "Bells of St. Clements," children are presented with the fruits during the church service, and the church bells ring out the rhyme (part of which is "Oranges and Lemons, Say the bells of St. Clements") at 9am, noon, 3pm, and 6pm; call ℂ **020/7242-8282** for information. Third week of March.

Westminster Abbey on Holy Week Tuesday; call ℂ **020/7222-7110** for information. Free. Late March or early April.

April

Easter Parade, around Battersea Park. Floats and marching bands; a full day of Easter Sunday activities. Free. Easter Sunday.

Harness Horse Parade, a morning parade of heavy-working horses in superb gleaming brass harnesses and plumes, at Battersea Park. Call ℂ **020/8871-7531.** Easter Monday.

Boat Race, Putney to Mortlake. Oxford and Cambridge University eights battle upstream with awesome power. Park yourself at one of the Thames-side pubs along the route to see the action. Early April; check *Time Out* for exact dates and times.

Glyndebourne Festival Opera Season, Sussex. Exclusive performances in a beautiful setting, with champagne picnics before or after the shows. Since the completion of the Glyndebourne opera house, one of the world's best, tickets are a bit easier to come by (© 1273/812-321). The season runs from mid-April to late August.

London Marathon. Thirty thousand competitors run from Greenwich Park to Buckingham Palace; call © 020/7902-0189 (www.london-marathon.co.uk) for information. Mid- to late April.

The Queen's Birthday is celebrated with 21-gun salutes in Hyde Park, and on Tower Hill at noon by troops in parade dress. April 21.

National Gardens Scheme. More than 100 private gardens in London are open to the public on set days, and tea is sometimes served. Pick up the NGS guidebook for £5 ($7.50) from most bookstores, or contact the National Gardens Scheme Charitable Trust, Hatchlands Park, East Clandon, Guildford, Surrey GU4 7RT (© 01483/211-535). Late April to early May.

May

May Fayre and Puppet Festival, Covent Garden. Procession at 10am, service at St. Paul's at 11:30am, then Punch and Judy shows until 6pm at the site where British diarist Pepys watched it in 1662; call © 020/7375-0441. Second Sunday in May.

The Royal Windsor Horse Show is held at Home Park, Windsor Castle (© 01753/860-633); you might even spot a royal. Mid-May.

Chelsea Flower Show, Chelsea Royal Hospital. The best of British gardening, with displays of plants and flowers of all seasons. The show runs from 8am to 8pm; tickets are £28 ($42). On the last day, the show runs from 8am to 5:30pm, and tickets are £26 ($39). Tickets are available through Ticketmaster

(© 020/7344-4444). Tickets must be purchased in advance. Call © 020/7649-1885 for information. Three days in mid-May.

June

Trooping the Colour, Horse Guards Parade, Whitehall. The official birthday of the queen (as opposed to her actual birthday, which is April 21) is held on a designated date in June. Seated in a carriage, the monarch inspects her regiments and takes their salute as they parade their colors. It's a quintessentially British event, with exquisite pageantry and pomp. Tickets for the parade and for two reviews, held on preceding Saturdays, are allocated by ballot. Those interested in attending must apply for tickets between January 1 and the end of February, enclosing a stamped, self-addressed envelope, or International Reply Coupon—exact dates and ticket prices are supplied later. The drawing is held in mid-March, and successful applicants *only* are informed in April. For details, and to apply for tickets, write to **HQ Household Division,** Horse Guards, Whitehall, London SW1X 6AA, enclosing a self-addressed envelope and International Reply Coupon (available at any post office).

Vodafone Derby Stakes, the famous horseracing event is held at Epsom Racecourse, Epsom, Surrey. It's the best-known event on the British horseracing calendar and a chance for men to wear top hats and women, including the queen, to put on silly millinery creations. Grandstand tickets range from £19 to £27 ($28.50–$40.50). Call © 1372/470-047 for more information. The "darby" (as it's pronounced) is run the first or second Saturday in June.

Royal Academy's Summer Exhibition. This institution, founded in 1768 with Sir Joshua Reynolds as president and Thomas Gainsborough as a member, has sponsored summer exhibitions of living painter's work for some 2 centuries. Visitors can browse and purchase art. Exhibitions are presented at Burlington House in Piccadilly Circus, W1. Call ℭ **020/7439-7438** for details. Early June to mid-August.

Grosvenor House Art and Antique Fair, Le Méridien Grosvenor House, Park Lane, W1. A very prestigious antiques fair featuring the world's leading antiques dealers and more than 400 million pounds worth of fine art and antiques. Call ℭ **020/7399-8100** for more information. June 11–17 in 2003.

Royal Ascot Week. Ascot Racecourse is open year-round for guided tours, events, exhibitions, and conferences. There are 25 race days throughout the year with the feature race meetings being the Royal Meeting in June, Diamond Day in late July, and the Festival at Ascot in late September. For Royal Ascot week, which runs from June 17 through June 20, in 2003, everyone (including the queen) shows up in their finery to watch 24 races over 4 days. For further information, contact **Ascot Racecourse,** Ascot, Berkshire, SL5 7JN (ℭ **1344/622-211**).

Lawn Tennis Championships, Wimbledon, Southwest London. Ever since players in flannels and bonnets took to the grass courts at Wimbledon in 1877, this tournament has drawn a socially prominent crowd. You'll still find an excited hush at Centre Court (where the most hotly contested championship matches are held)

and a thrill in being there. Savoring strawberries and cream is part of the experience. Tickets for Centre and Number One courts are handed out through a lottery; write to **All England Lawn Tennis Club,** P.O. Box 98, Church Road, Wimbledon, London SW19 5AE (ℭ **020/8946-2244**) between August and December. Include a self-addressed and stamped envelope with your letter. A number of tickets are set aside for visitors from abroad, so you may be able to purchase some in spring for this year's games; call to inquire. Outside court tickets are available daily, but *be prepared to wait in line.* Late June to early July.

City of London Festival is an annual arts celebration held throughout the city. Call ℭ **020/7377-0540** for information about programs and venues. June and July.

Shakespeare Under the Stars. If you want to see *Macbeth, Hamlet,* or *Romeo and Juliet* (or any other Shakespeare play), our advice is to bring a blanket and a bottle of wine to watch the Bard's works performed at the Open Air Theatre, Inner Circle, Regent's Park, NW1. Take the Tube to Regent's Park or Baker Street. Performances are Monday through Saturday at 8pm; Wednesday, Thursday, and Saturday also at 2:30pm. Call ℭ **020/7935-5756** for more information. Previews begin in late June and performances last throughout the summer.

July

Kenwood Lakeside Concerts. These annual concerts are staged on the north side of Hampstead Heath (ℭ **020/8348-1286**). Fireworks and laser shows enliven the excellent performances. Classical music drifts to the fans across the lake every Saturday and Sunday in summer from early July to early September.

Hampton Court Palace Flower Show, East Molesey, Surrey. This 5-day international show is eclipsing its sister show in Chelsea; here, you can purchase the exhibits on the last day. Call ✆ **020/7834-4333** for exact dates and details. Early July.

The Proms. "The Proms"—the annual Henry Wood Promenade Concerts at Royal Albert Hall—attract music aficionados from around the world. Staged almost daily (except for a few Sun), the concerts were launched in 1895 and are the principal summer venue for the BBC Symphony Orchestra. Cheering, clapping, banners, balloons, and Union Jacks on parade contribute to the festive summer atmosphere. Call ✆ **020/7589-3203** for more information. Mid-July to mid-September.

August

Notting Hill Carnival, Notting Hill. One of the largest street festivals in Europe, attracting more than a half-million people annually. Live reggae and soul music combine with great Caribbean food. Free. Call ✆ **020/8964-0544** for information. Two days in late August (usually the last Sun and Mon).

September

Chelsea Antiques Fair, Chelsea Old Town Hall, King's Road, SW3 (see "March," above, for details). Mid-September.

Open House, a 2-day event during which members of the public have access to buildings of architectural significance that are normally closed. Call ✆ **020/7267-7697** for schedule and further information. Mid-September.

Horse of the Year Show. At Wembley Arena, outside London, this is the premier equestrian event on the English calendar. Riders fly in from all over to join in this festive display of jumping, parading, and pony showing (much appreciated by the queen herself). For more information, call ✆ **020/8902-8833.** End of September to early October.

Raising of the Thames Barrier, Unity Way, SE18. Once a year, in September, a full test is done on this miracle of modern engineering, as all 10 of the massive steel gates are raised against the high tide. Call ✆ **020/8854-1373** for exact date and time.

October

Opening of Parliament, House of Lords, Westminster. Since the 17th century, when Charles I was beheaded, the British monarch hasn't had the right to enter the House of Commons. Instead, the monarch opens Parliament in the House of Lords, reading an official speech written by the Prime Minister's office. The monarch rides from Buckingham Palace to Westminster in a royal coach accompanied by the Yeoman of the Guard and the Household Cavalry. The Strangers' Gallery is open to spectators on a first-come, first-served basis. Call ✆ **020/7219-4272.** First Monday in October.

Judges Service, Westminster Abbey. The judiciary attends a service in Westminster Abbey to mark the opening of the law term. Afterward, in full regalia—wigs and all—they form a procession and walk to the House of Lords for their "Annual Breakfast." You'll have a great view of the procession from behind the Abbey. First Monday in October, at 10am.

Quit Rents Ceremony, Royal Courts of Justice, WC2. The City Solicitor pays one of the queen's officials a token rent for properties leased from the kingdom long, long ago. The ceremony includes splitting sticks and counting horse-shoes. Call ℂ **020/7947-6000** for free tickets. Late October.

November

Guy Fawkes Night. Anniversary of the Gunpowder Plot, an attempt to blow up King James I and his Parliament. Huge bonfires are lit throughout the city, and Guy Fawkes, the most famous conspirator, is burned in effigy. Free. Check *Time Out* for locations. Early November.

Lord Mayor's Procession and Show, from the Guildhall to the Royal Courts of Justice, in the City of London. This annual event marks the inauguration of the new lord mayor of the City of London.

The queen must ask permission to enter the City—a right jealously guarded by London merchants during the 17th century. You can watch the procession from the street; the banquet is by invitation only. Second week in November.

December

Caroling Under the Norwegian Christmas Tree. There's caroling most evenings beneath the tree in Trafalgar Square. Early December.

Harrods After-Christmas Sale, Knightsbridge. Call ℂ **020/7730-1234** for dates. Late December.

Watch Night, St. Paul's Cathedral, where a lovely New Year's Eve service takes place at 11:30pm; call ℂ **020/7236-4128** for information. December 31.

5 Health & Insurance

TRAVEL INSURANCE AT A GLANCE

Since you'll be away from home, and there is always the possibility of things going awry—lost luggage, trip cancellation, a medical emergency—you may want to consider the following types of trip insurance.

Check your existing insurance policies before you buy travel insurance to cover trip cancellation, lost luggage, medical expenses, or car rental insurance. You're likely to have partial or complete coverage. If your standard insurance doesn't cover travel and you decide that you'd like to purchase additional insurance, first ask your travel agent about a comprehensive package, which may be less expensive. The cost of travel insurance varies widely, depending on the cost and length of your trip, your age and overall health, and the type of trip you're taking.

For information in the U.S., contact one of the following popular insurers:

- **Access America** (ℂ 800/284-8300; www.accessamerica.com)
- **Travel Assistance International** (ℂ 800/821-2828; www.travelassistance.com)
- **Travel Guard International** (ℂ 800/826-1300; www.travelguard.com)
- **Travel Insured International** (ℂ 800/243-3174; www.travelinsured.com)
- **Travelex Insurance Services** (ℂ 800/228-9792; www.travelexinsurance.com)

For information in Great Britain, contact the following agency:

- **Columbus Direct,** 17 Devonshire Sq., London, EC2 M4S (ℂ 020/7375-0011; www.columbusdirect.com)

For information in Canada contact:

- **Travel Guard International** (see contact information above)

TRIP-CANCELLATION INSURANCE (TCI)

There are three major types of trip-cancellation insurance—one works in the event that you pre-pay a tour that gets canceled, and you can't get your money back; a second helps if you or someone in your family gets sick or dies, and you can't travel (but beware that you may not be covered for a pre-existing condition); and a third aids if bad weather makes travel impossible. Some insurers provide coverage for events like jury duty; natural disasters close to home, like floods or fire; even the loss of a job. A few have added provisions for cancellations because of terrorist activities. Always check the fine print before signing on, and don't buy trip-cancellation insurance from the tour operator that may be responsible for the cancellation; buy it only from a reputable travel insurance agency. Don't overbuy. You won't be reimbursed for more than the cost of your trip.

MEDICAL INSURANCE

Most health insurance policies cover you if you get sick away from home—but check, particularly if you're insured by an HMO. With the exception of certain HMOs and Medicare/Medicaid, your medical insurance should cover emergency medical treatment—even hospital care—overseas. However, most out-of-country hospitals make you pay your bills up front, and send you a refund after you've returned home and filed the necessary paperwork. Members of **Blue Cross/ Blue Shield** can now use their insurance cards at select hospitals in most major cities worldwide. Call *©* **800/810-BLUE** or go to www. bluecares. com for a list of hospitals.

Some credit cards (American Express and certain gold and platinum Visa and MasterCard, for example) offer automatic flight insurance against death or dismemberment in case of an airplane crash if you charged the cost of your ticket.

If you require additional medical insurance, try one of the following companies:

- **MEDEX International,** 9515 Deereco Rd., Timonium, MD 21093-5375 (*©* **888/MEDEX-00** or 410/453-6300; fax 410/453-6301; www.medexassist.com)
- **Travel Assistance International** (*©* **800/821-2828;** www.travel assistance.com), 9200 Keystone Crossing, Suite 300, Indianapolis, IN 46240 (for general information on services, call the company's Worldwide Assistance Services, Inc., at *©* 800/777-8710)

The cost of travel medical insurance varies widely. Check your existing policies before you buy additional coverage. Also, check to see if your medical insurance covers you for emergency medical evacuation. If you have to buy a one-way same-day ticket home and forfeit your nonrefundable round-trip ticket, you may be out big bucks.

LOST-LUGGAGE INSURANCE

On international flights (including U.S. portions of international trips), lost baggage is reimbursed to approximately $9.07 per pound, with a limit of about $635 per checked bag. If you plan to check items more valuable than the standard liability, you may purchase "excess valuation" coverage from the airline, which provides up to $5,000 in reimbursement. Be sure to take any valuables or irreplaceable items with you in your carry-on luggage. If you file a lost luggage claim, be prepared to answer detailed questions about the contents of your baggage, and be sure to file a claim immediately, as most airlines enforce a 21-day deadline. Before you leave home, compile an inventory of all packed items and a rough estimate of the total value to ensure that you're properly compensated if your luggage is lost. You will only be reimbursed for what you lost, no more. Once you've filed a complaint, persist in securing your reimbursement; there are no laws governing the length of time it takes for a carrier to reimburse you. If you arrive at a destination without your bags, ask the airline to forward them to your hotel or to your next destination; they will usually comply. If your bag is delayed or lost, the airline may reimburse you for reasonable expenses, such as a toothbrush or a set of clothes, but the airline is under no legal obligation to do so.

Lost luggage may also be covered by your homeowner's or renter's policy. Many platinum and gold credit cards cover you as well. If you choose to purchase additional lost-luggage insurance, be sure not to buy more than you need. Buy in advance from the insurer or a trusted agent (prices will be much higher at the airport).

CAR RENTAL INSURANCE (LOSS/DAMAGE WAIVER OR COLLISION DAMAGE WAIVER)

If you hold a private auto insurance policy, you probably are covered in the U.S., but not abroad, for loss or damage to the car, and liability in case a passenger is injured. The credit card you used to rent the car also may provide some coverage.

Car rental insurance probably does not cover liability if you caused the accident. Check your own auto insurance policy, the rental company's policy, and your credit card's policy to figure out the extent of coverage. Is your destination covered? Are other drivers covered? How much liability is covered if a passenger is injured? (If you rely on your credit card for coverage, you may want to bring a second credit card with you, as damages may be charged to your card and you may find yourself stranded with no money.)

Car rental insurance costs about $20 a day.

WHAT TO DO IF YOU GET SICK AWAY FROM HOME

If you need an ambulance, call © 999. If you need a doctor, your hotel can recommend one, or you can contact your embassy or consulate. Outside London, dial © 100 and ask the operator for the local police, who will give you the name, address, and telephone number of a doctor in your area. Also see "Fast Facts: London," in chapter 4. *Note:* U.S. visitors who become ill while they're in England are eligible only for free *emergency* care. For other treatment, including follow-up care, you'll be asked to pay.

If you worry about getting sick away from home, consider purchasing **medical travel insurance** and carry your ID card in your purse or wallet. In most cases, your existing health plan will provide the coverage you need. See "Medical Insurance," above in this section for more information.

If you suffer from a chronic illness, consult your doctor before your departure. For conditions like epilepsy, diabetes, or heart problems,

---

Tips **Quick Baggage I.D.**

Tie a colorful ribbon or piece of yarn around your luggage handle, or slap a distinctive sticker on the side of your bag. This makes it less likely that someone will mistakenly appropriate it. And if your luggage gets lost, it will be easier to find.

wear a **Medic Alert Identification Tag** (© **800/825-3785;** www.medic alert.org), which will immediately alert doctors to your condition and give them access to your records through Medic Alert's 24-hour hot line.

Carry prescription medications in their original containers and pack them in your carry-on luggage. Also bring along copies of your prescriptions in case you lose your pills or run out. Carry the generic name of prescription medicines, in case a local pharmacist is unfamiliar with the brand name.

And don't forget to bring along an extra pair of contact lenses or prescription glasses.

Contact the **International Association for Medical Assistance to Travelers (IAMAT)** (© **716/754-4883** or 519/836-3412; www.sentex.net/ ~iamat) for tips on travel and health concerns in London or England. In Canada, call © 519/836-0102. The United States **Centers for Disease Control and Prevention** (© **800/ 311-3435;** www.cdc.gov) provides up-to-date information on necessary vaccines and health hazards by region or country (their booklet, *Health Information for International Travel,* is $25 by mail; on the Internet, it's free).

THE HEALTHY TRAVELER

You'll encounter few health risks while traveling in England. The tap water is safe to drink, the milk is pasteurized, and health services are good. The mad cow disease crisis appears to be over, as does the epidemic of foot-and-mouth disease, which began in the spring of 2001 (and which affected only animals). Traveling to London doesn't pose any health risk.

THE SAFE TRAVELER

Like all big cities, London has its share of crime, but in general it is one of the safer destinations in Europe. Pickpockets are the most major concern. Violent crime is relatively rare, especially in the heart of London, which hasn't seen a Jack the Ripper in a long time. Even so, it is not wise to go walking in parks at night. King's Cross at night can also be a dangerous area, frequented by prostitutes and their clients. In London, take all the precautions a prudent traveler would in going to any city, be it in Los Angeles, Paris, or New York. Conceal your wallet or hold onto your purse, and don't flaunt your wealth by displaying jewelry or cash. In other words, do as your mother told you. In these uncertain times, it is always prudent to check the U.S. State Department's travel advisories at http://travel.state. gov/travel_warnings.html.

6 Tips for Travelers with Special Needs

TRAVELERS WITH DISABILITIES

Many London hotels, museums, restaurants, and sightseeing attractions have wheelchair ramps. Persons with disabilities are often granted special discounts at attractions and, in some cases, nightclubs. These discounts are called "concessions" in Britain. It always pays to ask. Free information and advice is available from **Holiday Care Service,** Imperial Building, 2nd floor, Victoria Road, Horley, Surrey

RH6 7PZ (© **01293/774-535;** fax 01293/784-647; www.holidaycare. org.uk.)

Bookstores in London often carry *Access in London* (£10 or $15), a publication listing hotels, restaurants, sights and shops for persons with disabilities, among other things.

The transport system, cinemas, and theaters are still extremely hard for the disabled to negotiate, but **Transport for London** does publish a leaflet called *Access to the Underground,* which gives details of elevators and ramps at individual Underground stations; call ✆ **020/7918-3312.** And the **London black cab** is perfectly suited for those in wheelchairs; the roomy interiors have plenty of room for maneuvering.

London's most visible organization for information about access to theaters, cinemas, galleries, museums, and restaurants is **Artsline,** 54 Chalton St., London NW1 1HS (✆ **020/7388-2227;** fax 020/7383-2653; www.artsline.org.uk). It offers free information about wheelchair access, theaters with hearing aids, easily wheelchair-accessible tourist attractions and cinemas, and sign language–interpreted tours and theater productions. Artsline will mail information to North America, but it's more helpful to contact them once you arrive in London; the line is staffed Monday through Friday from 9:30am to 5:30pm.

An organization that cooperates closely with Artsline is **Tripscope,** The Courtyard, 4 Evelyn Rd., London W4 5JL (✆ **020/8580-7021;** www.justmobility.co.uk), which offers advice on travel in Britain and elsewhere for persons with disabilities.

AGENCIES/OPERATORS

- **Flying Wheels Travel** (✆ **800/535-6790;** www.flyingwheelstravel.com) offers escorted private tours in minivans with lifts.
- **Access Adventures** (✆ **716/889-9096**), a Rochester, New York–based agency, offers customized itineraries for a variety of travelers with disabilities.
- **Accessible Journeys** (✆ **800/TINGLES** or 610/521-0339; www.disabilitytravel.com) caters specifically to slow walkers and wheelchair travelers and their families and friends, with escorted trips.

ORGANIZATIONS

- **The Moss Rehab Hospital** (✆ **215/456-5995;** www.mossresourcenet.org) provides helpful phone assistance through its **Travel Information Service.**
- **The Society for Accessible Travel and Hospitality** (✆ **212/447-7285;** fax 212/725-8253; www.sath.org) offers a wealth of travel resources about all types of disabilities and informed recommendations on destinations, access guides, travel agents, tour operators, vehicle rentals, and companion services. Annual membership costs $45 for adults; $30 for seniors and students.
- **The American Foundation for the Blind** (✆ **800/232-5463;** www.afb.org) provides information on traveling with Seeing Eye dogs.

PUBLICATIONS

- **Mobility International USA** (✆ **541/343-1284;** www.miusa.org) publishes a 658-page book of resources, *A World of Options,* and a biannual newsletter, *Over the Rainbow.* Annual membership is $35.
- **Twin Peaks Press** (✆ **360/694-2462**) publishes travel books for those with special needs.
- *Open World for Disability and Mature Travel* magazine, published by the Society for Accessible Travel and Hospitality (see above), is full of good resources and information. A year's subscription is $13 ($21 outside the U.S.).

GAYS & LESBIANS

London has one of the most active gay and lesbian scenes in the world; we've recommended a number of the city's best gay clubs in chapter 9, "London After Dark."

AGENCIES/OPERATORS

- **Above and Beyond Tours** (© **800/ 397-2681** or 760/325-0702; fax 760/325-1702) caters to gay couples, mainly men, with travel planning and escorted tours.

ORGANIZATIONS

- **The International Gay & Lesbian Travel Association (IGLTA)** (© **800/448-8550** or 954/776-2626; fax 954/776-3303; www. iglta.org) links travelers with appropriate gay-friendly service organizations or tour specialists. With around 1,200 members, it offers quarterly newsletters, mailings, and a membership directory. Membership is geared to gay or lesbian businesses, but it is open to individuals for an annual $300 membership fee, $200 for renewals. Members are informed of gay and gay-friendly hoteliers, tour operators, and airline and cruise-line representatives. Contact the IGLTA for a list of its member agencies, who will also be listed in IGLTA's information resources.

- **Lesbian and Gay Switchboard** (© **020/7837-7324**) is open 24 hours a day, providing information about gay-related activities in London, plus general advice. The **Bisexual Helpline** (© **020/8569-7500**) offers useful information, but only on Tuesdays and Wednesdays from 7:30 to 9:30pm, and Saturdays between 9:30am and noon.

PUBLICATIONS

- *Out and About,* 995 Market St., San Francisco, CA 94103 (© **800/ 929-2268** or 415/644-8044; fax 415/644-7985; www.outand about.com), has been hailed for its "straight" reporting about gay travel. *Out and About*'s guidebooks are available at most major bookstores.

- The **Ferrari Guides** (© **800/962-2912;** www.ferrariguides.com) are another good series of gay and lesbian guidebooks.

- For up-to-the-minute information, we recommend the monthly *Gay Times* (London).

- You can pick up the latest edition of *Frommer's Gay & Lesbian Europe,* which covers the scene in a number of European capitals.

- London's best gay-oriented bookstore is **Gay's the Word,** 66 Marchmont St., WC1 (© **020/ 7278-7654;** www.gaystheword. co.uk; Tube: Russell Square), the largest such store in Britain. The staff is friendly and helpful and will offer advice about the ever-changing gay scene in London. It's open Monday through Saturday from 10am to 6:30pm and Sunday from 2 to 6pm. At Gay's the Word, as well as at other gay-friendly venues, you can find a number of gay publications, many free, including the popular *Boyz* and *Pink Paper* (this one has a good lesbian section). Also check out *9X,* filled with data about all the new clubs and whatever else is hot on the scene.

SENIOR TRAVEL

Many discounts are available to seniors. Be advised that in England you often have to be a member of an association to get discounts. Public-transportation reductions, for example, are available only to holders of British Pension books. However, many attractions do offer discounts for seniors (women 60 or over, and men 65 or over). Even if discounts aren't posted, ask if they're available.

If you're over 60, you're eligible for special 10% discounts on **British Airways** through its Privileged Traveler program. You also qualify for reduced restrictions on Advanced Purchases airline ticket cancellations. Discounts are also granted for British Airways' tours and for intra-Britain air tickets booked in North America. **British Rail** offers seniors discounted rates on first-class rail passes around Britain. See "By Train," under "Getting There," below.

Don't be shy about asking for discounts, but carry some kind of identification that shows your date of birth. Also, mention that you're a senior when you make your hotel reservations. Many hotels offer seniors discounts. In most cities, people over the age of 60 qualify for reduced admission to theaters, museums, and other attractions, and discounted fares on public transportation.

Members of **AARP** (formerly known as the American Association of Retired Persons), 601 E St. NW, Washington, DC 10049 (© 800/424-3410 or 202/434-2277; www.aarp.org) get discounts on hotels, airfares, and car rentals. AARP offers members a wide range of benefits. Anyone over 50 can join.

AGENCIES/OPERATORS
- **Grand Circle Travel** (© 800/221-2610 or 617/350-7500; www.gct.com) offers package deals for the 50-plus market, mostly of the tour-bus variety, with free trips thrown in for individuals who organize groups of 10 or more.
- **Elderhostel** (© 877/426-8056; www.elderhostel.org) arranges extremely affordable study programs for those aged 55 and over (and a spouse or companion of any age) in the U.S. and in more than 80 countries around the world, including Britain. Most

courses last 5 to 7 days in the U.S. or 2 to 4 weeks abroad, and many include airfare, accommodations in university dormitories or modest inns, meals, and tuition.
- **Interhostel** (© 800/733-9753; www.learn.unh.edu/interhostel), organized by the University of New Hampshire, also offers educational travel for senior citizens. On these escorted tours, the days are packed with seminars, lectures, and field trips, with sightseeing led by academic experts. **Interhostel** takes travelers 50 and over (with companions over 40), and offers 1- and 2-week trips, mostly international.

PUBLICATIONS
- **The Alliance for Retired Americans,** 8403 Colesville Rd., Suite 1200, Silver Spring, MD 20910 (© 301/578-8422; www.retiredamericans.org), puts out a newsletter six times a year including discounts on hotel and auto rentals. Annual dues are $13 per person or couple. *Note:* Members of the former National Council of Senior Citizens receive automatic membership in the Alliance.

STUDENT TRAVEL
AGENCIES/OPERATORS
- The best resource for students is the **Council on International Educational Exchange,** or CIEE (© 212/822-2700; www.ciie.org). Their travel agency branch, **Council Travel Service** (© 800/2COUNCIL; www.counciltravel.com), is the biggest student travel agency in the world. It can get you discounts on plane tickets, rail passes, and the like. Ask for a list of CTS offices in major cities so that you can keep the discounts flowing (and aid lines open) as you travel.

You can purchase the student traveler's best friend from CIIE, the $22 **International Student Identity Card (ISIC).** It's the only officially accepted form of student identification, good for cut rates on rail passes, plane tickets, and other discounts. It also offers basic health and life insurance and a 24-hour help line. If you're no longer a student but are still under 26, you can get a **GO 25** card from the CIEE, which gets you the insurance and some of the discounts (but not student admission prices in museums).

- In Canada, **Travel CUTS,** 200 Ronson Dr., Suite 320, Toronto, Ontario M9W 5Z9 (© **800/667-2887** or 416/614-2887; fax 416/614-9670; www.travelcuts. com), offers services similar to those of the Council on International Educational Exchange (see above).
- **USIT Campus,** 52 Grosvenor Gardens, London SW1W 0AG (© **020/7730-3402** or 0870/240-1010; www.usitworld.com), opposite Victoria Station, is Britain's leading specialist in student and youth travel.
- **STA Travel,** 86 Old Brompton Rd., London SW7 3LQ (© **800/781-4040;** www.statravel.com; Tube: South Kensington), is the only worldwide company specializing in student- and youth-discounted airfares. STA also specializes in low-cost package tours. It's open Monday through Friday from 8:30am to 7pm, Saturday from 10am to 5pm, and Sunday from 10am to 2pm.

ORGANIZATIONS
- **The International Student House,** 229 Great Portland St.,

W1 (© **020/7631-8300;** www. ish.org.uk), lies at the foot of Regent's Park across from the Tube stop for Great Portland Street. It's a beehive of activity, offering discos and film showings. It rents blandly furnished, institutional rooms for £31 ($46.50) single, £25 ($37.50) per person double, £20 ($30) per person triple, and £11.99 ($18) per person in a dorm. Laundry facilities are available, and a £10 ($15) key deposit is charged. Reserve way in advance.
- **University of London Student Union,** 1 Malet St., WC1E 7HY (© **020/7664-2000;** www.ulu. lon.ac.uk; Tube: Goodge Street or Russell Square), is the best place to go to learn about student activities in the Greater London area. The Union has a swimming pool, a fitness center, a gymnasium, a general store, a sports shop, a ticket agency, banks, bars, inexpensive restaurants, venues for live events, an office of STA Travel (see above), and many other facilities. It's open Monday through Thursday from 8:30am to 11pm, Friday from 8:30am to 1pm, Saturday from 9am to 2pm, and Sunday from 9:30am to 10:30pm. Bulletin boards at the Union provide a rundown on events, some of which you will be able to attend; although others might be "closed door."

PUBLICATIONS
The Hanging Out Guides (www. frommers.com/hangingout/) published by Frommer's, are the top student travel series for today's students, covering everything from adrenaline sports to the hottest club and music scenes.

SINGLE TRAVELERS

Unfortunately for the 85 million or so single Americans, the travel industry is geared toward couples, and so singles often wind up paying the penalties of traveling alone, if they don't know how to avoid them.

AGENCIES/OPERATORS

- **Experience Plus** (© **800/685-4565;** fax 970/493-0377; www.experienceplus.com) has a varied selection of single-only trips, both escorted and custom-tailored.
- **Travel Buddies** (© **800/998-9099;** www.travelbuddiesworldwide.com) runs single-friendly tours with no singles supplement.
- It pays to travel with someone. One company that resolves this problem is **Travel Companion Exchange,** which matches single travelers with like-minded companions. It's headed by Jens Jurgen, who charges $159 for an annual listing in his well-publicized records. People seeking travel companions fill out forms stating their preferences and needs and receive a listing of potential travel partners. Companions of the same or opposite sex can be requested. For $48 you can get a bimonthly newsletter, averaging 70 large pages, that gives numerous money-saving travel tips of special interest to solo travelers. A sample copy is available for $6. For an application and more information, contact Jens Jurgen at **Travel Companion Exchange,** P.O. Box 833, Amityville, NY 11701 (© **800/392-1256** or 631/454-0880; fax 631/454-0170; www.whytravelalone.com).

FAMILY TRAVEL

For the best places to stay and eat, see "Family-Friendly Hotels," in chapter 5 and "Family-Friendly Restaurants," in chapter 6. For details on sightseeing, check out the section called "Especially for Kids" in chapter 7. On airlines, you must request a special menu for children at least 24 hours in advance. Bring your own baby food; you can ask a flight attendant to warm it.

Arrange ahead of time for such necessities as a crib, bottle warmer, and car seat (in England, small children aren't allowed to ride in the front seat). If you're staying with friends, you can rent baby equipment from **Chelsea Baby Hire,** 108 Dorset Rd., SW19 3HD (© **020/8540-8830;** www.chelseababyhire.co.uk). The **London black cab** is a lifesaver for families; the roomy interior allows a stroller to be lifted right into the cab without unstrapping baby.

A recommended babysitting service is **Childminders** (© **020/7487-5040;** www.babysitter.co.uk). Babysitters can also be found for you at most hotels. Just ask at the front desk.

To find out what's on for kids while you're in London, pick up the leaflet *Where to Take Children,* published by the London Tourist Board. If you have specific questions, ring **Kidsline** (© **0845/458-3536;** www.kidsline.co.uk) Monday through Friday from 4 to 6pm and summer holidays from 9am to 4pm, or the **London Tourist Board's** special children's information line (© **0839/123-425**) for listings of special events and places to visit for children. The number is accessible in London at 50p (75¢) per minute.

AGENCIES/OPERATORS

- **Familyhostel** (© **800/733-9753;** www.learn.unh.edu/familyhostel) takes the whole family on moderately priced domestic and international learning vacations. The program staff handles all trip details, and a team of academics guides lectures, field trips, and sightseeing. This program is geared towards kids ages 8 to 15 accompanied by their parents and/or grandparents.

PUBLICATIONS

- *How to Take Great Trips with Your Kids* (The Harvard Common Press) is full of good general family travel advice.
- *Family Travel Times,* which is published 10 times a year by Travel With Your Children (TWYCH), includes a weekly call-in service for subscribers, which provides last minute updates to the publication. Subscriptions cost $40 a year and can be ordered by contacting TWYCH, 40 5th Ave., New York, NY 10011 (© **212/477-5524;** www.familytraveltimes.com).

7 Getting There

BY PLANE

Don't worry about which airport, Heathrow versus Gatwick, to fly into unless you are extremely pressed for time. Heathrow is closer to central London than Gatwick, but there is fast train service from both of the airports to the West End (see "By Plane," under "Orientation," in chapter 4). **High season** on most airlines' routes to London is usually from June to the beginning of September. This is the most expensive and most crowded time to travel. **Shoulder season** is from April to May, early September to October, and December 15 to 24. **Low season** is from November 1 to December 14 and December 25 to March 31.

FROM THE UNITED STATES
American Airlines (© **800/433-7300;** www.im.aa.com) offers daily nonstop flights to London's Heathrow Airport from five U.S. gateways: New York's JFK (6 times daily), Chicago's O'Hare (3 times daily), Boston's Logan (twice daily), and Miami International and Los Angeles International (once daily).

British Airways (© **800/247-9297;** www.british-airways.com) offers mostly nonstop flights from 21 U.S. cities to Heathrow and Gatwick. With more add-on options than any other airline, British Airways can make a visit to Britain cheaper than you might expect. Of particular interest are the "Value Plus," "London on the Town," and "Europe Escorted" packages that include airfare and discounted accommodations throughout Britain.

Continental Airlines (© **800/525-0280;** www.continental.com) flies daily to Gatwick Airport from Newark, Houston, and Cleveland.

Depending on the day and season, **Delta Air Lines** (© **800/221-1212;** www.delta.com) runs either one or two daily nonstop flights between Atlanta and Gatwick. Delta also offers nonstop daily service from Cincinnati.

Although **Air India** (© **800/223-7776** or 212/751-6200) doesn't immediately come to mind when you think of flying from the U.S. to London, it's a viable option and is competitively priced. Air India (www.airindia.com) offers daily flights from New York's JFK and three flights a week—Tuesday, Friday, and Sunday—from Chicago to London's Heathrow Airport.

Northwest Airlines (© **800/225-2525;** www.nwa.com) flies nonstop from Minneapolis and Detroit to Gatwick, with connections from cities such as Boston and New York.

United Airlines (© **800/241-6522;** www.ual.com) flies nonstop from New York's JFK and Chicago's O'Hare to Heathrow two or three times a day, depending on the season. United also offers nonstop service three times a day from Dulles Airport, near Washington, D.C., to London's

---

Tips   Airport Taxes

You pay a departure tax of £10 ($15) for flights within Britain and the European Union; and £20 ($30) for flights to the U.S. and other countries. Your airline ticket may or may not include this tax. Ask in advance to avoid a surprise at the gate.

Gatwick plus once-a-day service to Heathrow from Newark, Los Angeles, San Francisco, and Boston.

Virgin Atlantic Airways (© 800/862-8621; www.fly.virgin.com) flies daily to either Gatwick or Heathrow from Boston, Newark, New York's JFK, Los Angeles, San Francisco, Washington, D.C.'s Dulles, Miami, Orlando, and Chicago.

FROM CANADA For travelers departing from Canada, **Air Canada** (© 888/247-2262 in U.S. or 800/268-7240 in Canada; www.aircanada.ca) flies daily to London Heathrow nonstop from Vancouver, Montreal, and Toronto. There are also frequent direct flights from Calgary and Ottawa.

FROM AUSTRALIA Qantas (© 131313; www.qantas.com) flies from both Sydney and Melbourne daily. **British Airways** (© 800/227-4500; www.british-airways.com) has five to seven flights weekly from Sydney and Melbourne. Both airlines have a stop in Singapore

FROM SOUTH AFRICA South African Airways (© 0861/FLYSAA; www.flysaa.com) schedules two daily flights from Johannesburg and two daily flights from Cape Town. From Johannesburg, both **British Airways** (© 0845/773-3377; www.british-airways.com) and **Virgin Atlantic Airways** (© 011/340-3400; www.fly.virgin.com) have daily flights to Heathrow. British Airways flies five times weekly from Cape Town.

NEW AIR TRAVEL SECURITY MEASURES

In the wake of the terrorist attacks on September 11, 2001, the airline industry is implementing sweeping security measures in airports. Expect a lengthy check-in process and extensive delays. Although regulations vary from airline to airline, you can expedite the process by taking the following steps:

- **Arrive early.** Arrive at the airport at least 2 hours before your scheduled flight.

- **Try not to drive your car to the airport.** Parking and curbside access to the terminal may be limited. Call ahead and check.

- **Don't count on curbside check-in.** Some airlines and airports have stopped curbside check-in altogether, whereas others offer it on a limited basis. For up-to-date information on specific regulations and implementations, check with the individual airline.

- **Be sure to carry plenty of documentation.** A government-issued photo ID (federal, state, or local), such as a passport or driver's license, is now required. You may need to show this at various checkpoints. With an E-ticket, you may be required to have a printed confirmation of purchase with you, and perhaps even the credit card with which you bought your ticket (see "All about E-Ticketing," below). This varies from airline to airline, so call ahead to make sure you have the proper documentation. And be sure that your ID is **up-to-date;** an expired driver's license, for example, may keep you from boarding the plane altogether.

- **Know what you can carry on—and what you can't.** Travelers in the United States are now limited to one carry-on bag, plus one personal bag (such as a purse or a briefcase). The Transportation Security Administration (TSA) has also issued a list of newly restricted carry-on items; see the box "What You Can Carry On—and What You Can't," below.
- **Prepare to be searched.** Expect spot-checks. Electronic items, such as a laptop or cellular phone, should be readied for additional screening. Limit the metal items you wear on your person.
- **It's no joke.** When a check-in agent asks if someone other than you packed your bag, don't decide that this is the time to be funny. The agents will not hesitate to call an alarm.

- **No ticket, no gate access.** Only ticketed passengers will be allowed beyond the screener checkpoints, except for those people with specific medical or parental needs.

FLYING FOR LESS: TIPS FOR GETTING THE BEST AIRFARE

Passengers within the same airplane cabin are rarely paying the same fare. Business travelers who need to purchase tickets at the last minute, change their itinerary at a moment's notice, or get home for the weekend pay the premium rate. Passengers who can book their ticket long in advance, who can stay over Saturday night, or who are willing to travel on a Tuesday, Wednesday, or Thursday after 7pm, will pay a fraction of the full fare. Here are a few other easy ways to save:

- **Take advantage of APEX fares.** Advance-purchase booking, or APEX, fares are often the key to getting the lowest fare. You generally must be willing to make your plans and buy your tickets as far

---

Tips   What You Can Carry On—And What You Can't

The Transportation Security Administration (TSA), the governement agency that now handles all aspects of airport security, has devised new restrictions for carry-on baggage, not only to expedite the screening process, but also to prevent potential weapons from passing through airport security. Passengers are now limited to bringing just one carry-on bag and one personal item onto the aircraft (previous regulations allowed two carry-on bags and one personal item, like a briefcase or a purse). For more information, go to the TSA's website www.tsa.gov. The agency has released an updated list of items that passengers are not allowed to carry onto an aircraft.

Not permitted: knives and box cutters, corkscrews, straight razors, metal scissors, golf clubs, baseball bats, pool cues, hockey sticks, ski poles, ice picks.

Permitted: nail clippers, nail files, tweezers, eyelash curlers, safety razors (including disposable razors), syringes (with documented proof of medical need), walking canes and umbrellas (must be inspected first).

The airline you fly may have additional restrictions on items you can and cannot carry on board. Call ahead to avoid problems.

Tips All About E-Ticketing

Only yesterday **electronic tickets (E-tickets)** were the fast and easy doc-ument-free alternative to paper tickets. E-tickets allowed passengers to avoid long lines at airport check-in, all the while saving the airlines money on postage and labor. With the increased security measures in airports, however, an E-ticket no longer guarantees an accelerated check-in. You often can't go straight to the boarding gate, even if you have no bags to check. You'll probably need to show your printed E-ticket receipt or confirmation of purchase, as well as a photo I.D., and sometimes even the credit card with which you purchased your E-ticket. That said, buying an E-ticket is still a fast, convenient way to book a flight; instead of having to wait for a paper ticket to come through the mail, you can book your fare by phone or on the com-puter, and the airline will immediately confirm by fax or e-mail. In addition, airlines often offer frequent flier miles as an incentive for electronic bookings.

ahead as possible: The **14-day APEX** is almost as popular as the **21-day APEX,** with a stay in Eng-land of 7 to 30 days for both. Because the number of seats allo-cated to APEX fares is sometimes less than 25% of the plane's capac-ity, the early bird gets the low-cost seat. There's often a surcharge for flying on a weekend, and cancella-tion and refund policies can be strict.

• **Watch for sales.** You'll almost never see sales during July and August or the Thanksgiving or Christmas seasons, but at other times you can get great deals. In the last couple of years, there have been amazing prices on winter flights. If you already hold a ticket when a sale breaks, it might pay to exchange it, even if you incur a $50 to $75 penalty charge. Note, however, that the lowest-priced fares are often nonrefundable, and require advance purchase of 1 to 3 weeks and a certain length of stay. Sale tickets may also carry penal-ties for changing dates of travel. Make sure you know exactly what

the restrictions are before you commit.

• If your schedule is flexible, ask if you can secure a cheaper fare by **staying an extra day** or by **flying midweek.** (Many airlines won't volunteer this information.)

• **Consolidators,** also known as "bucket shops," are a good place to find low fares. Consolidators buy seats in bulk from the airlines, and then sell them to the public at prices below even the airlines' dis-counted rates. Their ads usually run in the Sunday travel section of newspapers at the bottom of the page. Before you pay a consolida-tor, however, ask for a record loca-tor number and confirm your seat with the airline itself. Be prepared to book your ticket with a differ-ent consolidator—there are many to choose from—if the airline can't confirm your reservation. Also be aware that bucket shop tickets are usually nonrefundable or have stiff cancellation fees, often as high as 50% to 75% of the ticket price.

- We've gotten great deals on many occasions from **Cheap Tickets** ✦ (✆ **800/377-1000;** www.cheap tickets.com). **Council Travel** (✆ **800/2COUNCIL;** www. counciltravel.com) and **STA Travel** (✆ **800/781-4040;** www. sta.travel.com) cater especially to young travelers, but their bargain-basement prices are available to people of all ages. Other reliable consolidators include **Lowestfare. com** (✆ **888/278-8830;** www. lowestfare.com); **Cheap Seats** (✆ **800/451-7200;** www.cheap seatstravel.com); and **1-800/FLY-CHEAP** (www.flycheap.com).
- Join a travel club such as **Moment's Notice** (✆ **718/234-6295;** www.moments-notice.com) or **Sears Discount Travel Club** (✆ **800/433-9383,** or 800/255-1487 to join; www.travelers advantage.com), which supply unsold tickets at discounted prices. You pay an annual membership fee to get the club's hot line number. Of course, you're limited to what's available, so you have to be flexible.
- Join **frequent-flier clubs.** It's best to accrue miles on one program, so you can rack up free flights and achieve elite status faster. But it makes sense to open as many accounts as possible, no matter how seldom you fly a particular airline. It's free, and you'll get the best choice of seats, faster response to phone inquiries, and prompter service if your luggage is lost or stolen, your flight is canceled or delayed, or if you want to change your seat.
- Search the **Internet** for cheap fares—though it's still best to compare your findings with the research of a dedicated travel agent, if you're lucky enough to have one, especially when you're booking more than just a flight. Among the better-respected virtual travel agents are **Travelocity** (www.travelocity.com), **Expedia** (www.expedia.com), and **Yahoo! Travel** (http://travel.yahoo.com).

BY CAR

If you plan to take a rented car across or under the Channel, check with the rental company about license and insurance requirements before you leave.

FERRIES FROM THE CONTINENT

There are many "drive-on, drive-off" car-ferry services across the Channel. The most popular ports in France for Channel crossings are Boulogne and Calais, where you can board Stena ferries or hovercraft taking you to the English ports of Dover and Folkestone. For details, see "Ferries & Hovercraft," under "By Boat," below.

LE SHUTTLE

The Chunnel accommodates not only trains, but also passenger cars, charter buses, taxis, and motorcycles. Le Shuttle, a half-mile long train carrying motor vehicles under the English Channel (✆ **08705/353-535;** www. eurotunnel.com), connects Calais, France, with Folkestone, England, and vice versa. It operates 24 hours a day, 365 days a year, running every 15 minutes during peak travel times and at least once an hour at night.

Tips Canceled Plans

If your flight is canceled, don't book a new fare at the ticket counter. Find the nearest phone and call the airline directly to reschedule. You'll be relaxing while other passengers are still standing in line.

> ⌐ **Tips** **Getting from One London Airport to the Other**
>
> Some visitors will need to transfer from one airport to the other. Two bus companies offer these transfers. **Speedlink/Jetlink** (© **08705/747-777**; www.speedlink.co.uk) buses leave from all four terminals at Heathrow. Trip time is about an hour, a one-way fare costing £17 ($25.50). **AirLinks** (© **01223/423-900**) also runs between the two airports in the same time frame, a one-way ticket costing only £8 ($12). The difference between the two is that Speedlink/Jetlink offers service every 15 minutes and AirLink's Cambridge Coach provides service every hour. Both services run at all hours.

With Le Shuttle, gone are weather-related delays, seasickness, and a need for reservations. Before boarding Le Shuttle, you stop at a tollbooth to pay, and then pass through Immigration for both countries at one time. During the ride, you travel in bright, air-conditioned carriages, remaining inside your car or stepping outside to stretch your legs. An hour later, when you reach England, you drive off toward London. The cost of Le Shuttle varies according to the season and the day of the week. Count on at least £178 ($267) per car for a round-trip ticket.

Stores selling duty-free goods, restaurants, and service stations are available to travelers on both sides of the Channel. A bilingual staff is on hand to assist travelers at both the British and French terminals.

Hertz offers **Le Swap,** a service for passengers taking Le Shuttle. At Calais, you can switch cars for one with the steering wheel on the opposite side depending upon which country you're heading for.

BY TRAIN
VIA THE CHUNNEL FROM THE CONTINENT
Since 1994, when the Channel Tunnel opened, the *Eurostar Express* train has been operating twice-daily passenger service between London and both Paris and Brussels. The $15-billion tunnel, one of the great engineering feats of all time, is the first link between Britain and the Continent since the Ice Age.

Rail Europe (© **800/361-RAIL;** www.raileurope.com) sells tickets on the *Eurostar* for direct train service between Paris or Brussels and London. A round-trip fare between Paris and London, for example, costs $369 for first class, or $279 in second class. You can reduce that rate further, to $79, with a second-class, 14-day advance purchase (nonrefundable) round-trip fare. In London, make reservations for *Eurostar* at © **0870/530-0003,** or 800/EUROSTAR in the U.S. (www.eurostar.com). *Eurostar* trains arrive and depart from London's Waterloo Station, Paris's Gare du Nord, and Brussels's Central Station.

VIA BRITRAIL FROM OTHER PARTS OF EUROPE
If you're traveling to London from elsewhere in the United Kingdom, consider buying a **BritRail Classic Pass,** which allows unlimited rail travel during a set time period (8 days, 15 days, 22 days, or 1 month). *Remeber:* Eurailpasses aren't accepted in Britain, although they are in Ireland. For 8 days, a pass costs $400 in first class and $265 in standard class; for 15 days, it's $600 and $400, respectively; for 22 days, it's $760 and $499; and for 1 month, it's $900 and $600. If a child age 5 to 15 is traveling with a full-fare adult, the child's fare is half the adult fare. Children under age

5 travel free if they are not occupying a seat. Senior citizens (60 and over) qualify for discounts on first-class travel: It's $340 for an 8-day pass, $510 for a 15-day pass, $639 for a 22-day pass, and $759 for a 1-month pass. Travelers between 16 and 25 can purchase a **BritRail Classic Youth Pass,** which allows unlimited second-class travel: $215 for 8 days, $280 for 15 days, $355 for 22 days, or $420 for 1 month.

Britain on Track (www.britainon-track.com) is the most comprehensive British Rail website out there, providing fares, schedules, maps, and in-depth information on how to travel Britain by rail. You can order your BritRail pass online by downloading a faxable order form or using the BritRail pass "shopping cart" feature. You can also check out BritRail's point-to-point fares-at-a-glance chart and compare your British rail pass cost with point-to-point fares.

Travelers who arrive from France by boat (see "By Boat," below) and pick up a British Rail train at Dover, arrive at **Victoria Station,** in the center of London. Those journeying south by rail from Edinburgh arrive at **King's Cross Station.**

BY BUS

If you're traveling to London from elsewhere in the United Kingdom, consider purchasing a **Britexpress Card,** which entitles you to a 30% discount on National Express (England and Wales) and Caledonian Express (Scotland) buses. Contact a travel agent for details.

Bus connections to Britain from the Continent, using the Euro-tunnel (Chunnel) or ferry services, are generally not very comfortable, although some lines are more convenient than others. One line with a relatively good reputation is **Eurolines,** 52 Grosvenor Gardens, London SW1W OAU (© **0870/514-3219;** www.eurolines.

co.uk). They book passage on buses traveling two times a day between London and Paris (9 hr.); three times a day from Amsterdam (12 hr.); three times a week from Munich (24 hr.); and three times a week from Stockholm (44 hr.). On longer routes, which use alternating drivers, the bus proceeds almost without interruption, taking only occasional breaks for meals.

BY BOAT
CROSSING THE ATLANTIC

The **Cunard Line,** 6100 Blue Lagoon Dr., Suite 400, Miami, FL 33126 (© **800/528-6273;** www.cunardline.com) boasts that its flagship, *Queen Elizabeth 2,* is the only five-star-plus luxury ocean liner providing regular transatlantic service—some 18 voyages a year between April and December. Many passengers appreciate the cruise's graceful introduction to British mores, as well as the absolute lack of jet lag.

Fares vary, based on the season and the cabin grade. The average 6-day crossing begins at $1,625 per person and can go up to as high as $23,374 per person for one of the standard outside suites. All prices are double occupancy; passengers also pay $275 port and handling charges. Many packages are offered, which include inexpensive airfare from your home city to the point of departure plus a return flight to your home city from London on British Airways.

FERRIES & HOVERCRAFT

For centuries, sailing ships and ferryboats have traversed the English Channel bearing supplies, merchandise, and passengers. Today, the major carriers are **P&O Stena Lines** (© **0870/600-0611;** www.posl.com) and **HoverSpeed** (© **800/677-8585;** www.hoverspeed.com). Once you arrive in Dover, you can pick up a BritRail train to London (see "By Train," above).

CAR & PASSENGER FERRIES

P&O Stena Lines (© 0870/600-0611; www.posl.com) operates car and passenger ferries between Dover (England) and Calais (France) only. Trip time is 75 minutes at a cost of £59.50 ($89.25) one-way for a car and driver, or £28 ($42) for a foot passenger. P&O European Ferry (© 087/0242-4999; www.poferries.com) operates from Portsmouth (England) to Cherbourg (France). Depending on the vessel, this trip can take from 2 hours and 45 minutes up to 5 hours. One-way car passage costs £118 ($177) for up to two adults and two children. One-way foot passengers pay £20 ($30).

HOVERCRAFT & SEACATS

Traveling by Hovercraft or Seacat offers a speedy journey from the Continent to Britain, and vice versa. HoverSpeed operates at least six daily 35-minute hovercraft crossings, as well as slightly longer crossings via Seacat (a catamaran propelled by jet engines; these go 4 times daily and take about 50 min.), between Boulogne and Folkestone. A Hovercraft trip is definitely fun, as the vessel is technically "flying" over the water. Seacats also travel from the mainland of Britain to the Isle of Wight, Belfast, and the Isle of Man. For reservations and information, call HoverSpeed at © 0870/524-0241 (www.hoverspeed.com). For foot passengers, a typical adult fare, round-trip with a 5-day return policy, is £24 ($36). Children pay half fare.

8 Escorted Tours & Package Deals

Before you start your search for the lowest airfare, you may want to consider booking your flight as part of a travel package such as an escorted tour or a package tour. What you lose in adventure, you'll gain in time and money saved when you book accommodations, and maybe even food and entertainment, along with your flight.

ESCORTED TOURS

The two largest tour operators conducting escorted tours of Europe are Globus/Cosmos (©800/221-0090; www.globusandcosmos.com) and Trafalgar (www.trafalgartours.com). Both companies have first-class tours that run about $100 a day and budget tours for about $75 a day. The differences are mainly in hotel location and the number of activities. There's little difference in the companies' services, so choose your tour based on the itinerary and preferred date of departure. Brochures are available at travel agencies, and all tours must be booked through travel agents.

PACKAGE TOURS FOR INDEPENDENT TRAVELERS

Package tours are not the same thing as escorted tours. With a package tour, you travel independently but pay a group rate. Packages usually include airfare, a choice of hotels, and car rentals, and packagers often offer several options at different prices. In many cases, a package including airfare, hotel, and transportation to and from the airport will cost you less than just the hotel alone would have, had you booked it yourself. That's because packages are sold in bulk to tour operators—who resell them to the public at a cost that drastically undercuts standard rates.

FINDING A GENERAL PACKAGE

The best place to start your search is the travel section of your local Sunday newspaper. Also check the ads in the back of national travel magazines such as *Travel & Leisure, National*

Geographic Traveler, and *Condé Nast Traveler.*

Liberty Travel (© **888/271-1584** to be connected with the agent closest to you; www.libertytravel.com), one of the biggest packagers in the Northeast, often runs a full-page ad in the Sunday papers.

American Express Travel (© **800/ 941-2639;** www.americanexpress.com) is another option. Check out its **Last Minute Travel Bargains** (www.lastminute.com) site, offered in conjunction with **Continental Airlines,** with deeply discounted vacation packages and reduced airline fares that differ from the "E-savers" bargains that

Continental e-mails weekly to subscribers. **Northwest Airlines** (www.nwa.com) offers a similar service. Posted on Northwest's website every Wednesday, **Cyber Saver Bargain Alerts** offer special hotel rates, package deals, and discounted airline fares.

Another good resource is the airlines themselves, which often package their flights together with accommodations. Among the airline packagers, your best bets are **American Airlines Vacations** (© **800/321-2121;** www.aavacations.com) and **US Airways Vacations** (© **800/455-0123;** www.usairwaysvacations.com).

9 Planning Your Trip Online

Researching and booking your trip online can save time and money. Then again, it may not. It is simply not true that you always get the best deal online. Most booking engines do not include schedules and prices for budget airlines, and from time to time you'll get a better last-minute price by calling the airline directly, so when you find an Internet fare that looks good, its always best to call the airline to see if you can get an even better bargain before booking online.

On the plus side, Internet users today can tap into the same travel-planning databases that were once accessible only to travel agents—and do it at the same speed. Sites such as **Frommers.com, Travelocity.com, Expedia.com,** and **Orbitz.com** allow consumers to comparison shop for airfares, access special bargains, book flights, and reserve hotel rooms and rental cars.

But don't fire your travel agent just yet. Although online booking sites offer tips and hard data to help you bargain shop, they cannot endow you with the hard-earned experience that makes a seasoned, reliable travel agent an invaluable resource, even in the Internet age. And for consumers with

---

Frommers.com: The Complete Travel Resource

For an excellent travel planning resource, we highly recommend **Arthur Frommer's Budget Travel Online** (www.frommers.com). We're a little biased, of course, but we think you'll find the travel tips, reviews, monthly vacation giveaways, and online-booking capabilities indispensable. Among the special features are **Arthur Frommer's Daily Newsletter,** for the latest travel bargains and insider travel secrets; the electronic version of Frommer's travel guides, including expert travel tips, hotel and dining recommendations, and recommended sights in more than 2000 destinations worldwide; and guidebook updates. Once your research is done, the **Online Reservation System** (www.frommers.com/booktravelnow) takes you to Frommer's favorite sites for booking your vacation at affordable prices.

a complex itinerary, a trusty travel agent is still the best way to arrange the most direct flights to and from the best airports.

Some sites such as Expedia.com will send you **e-mail notification** when cheap fares become available to your selected destinations. Some sites will also tell you when fares to a particular destination are lowest.

TRAVEL PLANNING & BOOKING SITES

Keep in mind that because several airlines are no longer willing to pay commissions on tickets sold by online travel agencies, these agencies may either add a $10 surcharge to your bill if you book on that carrier—or neglect to offer those carriers' schedules.

The list of sites below is selective, not comprehensive. Some sites will have evolved or disappeared by the time you read this.

- **Travelocity** (www.travelocity.com or www.frommers.travelocity.com) and **Expedia** (www.expedia.com) are among the most popular sites, each offering an excellent range of options. Travelers search by destination, dates and cost.
- **Qixo** (www.qixo.com) is another powerful search engine that allows you to search for flights and accommodations from some 20 airline and travel-planning sites (such as Travelocity) at once. Qixo sorts results by price.

SMART E-SHOPPING

The savvy traveler is one armed with good information. Here are a few tips to help you navigate the Internet successfully and safely.

- **Know when sales start.** Last-minute deals may vanish in minutes. If you have a favorite booking site or airline, find out when last-minute deals are released to the public. (For example, Southwest's

specials are posted every Tuesday at 12:01am central time.)
- **Shop around.** Compare results from different sites and airlines—and against a travel agent's best fare, if you can. If possible, try a range of times and alternate airports before you make a purchase.
- **Follow the rules of the trade.** Book in advance, and choose an off-peak time and date if possible. Some sites will tell you when fares to a particular destination tend to be cheapest.
- **Stay secure.** Book only through secure sites (some airline sites are not secure). Look for a key icon (Netscape) or a padlock (Internet Explorer) at the bottom of your web browser before you enter credit card information or other personal data.
- **Avoid online auctions.** Sites that auction airline tickets and frequent-flier miles are the number-one perpetrators of Internet fraud, according to the National Consumers League.
- **Maintain a paper trail.** If you book an E-ticket, print out a confirmation, and write down your confirmation number, keep it safe and accessible and take the printout with you to the airport—or your trip could be a virtual one!

ONLINE TRAVELER'S TOOLBOX

Following is a selection of online tools to bookmark and use:

- **Visa ATM Locator** (www.visa.com) or **MasterCard ATM Locator** (www.mastercard.com). Find ATMs in hundreds of cities in the U.S. and around the world. The Visa locator also located PLUS network ATMs, and the MasterCard locator also find Cirrus ATMs.

- **Foreign Languages for Travelers** (www.travlang.com). Learn basic terms in more than 70 languages and click on any underlined phrase to hear what it sounds like. *Note:* Free audio software and speakers are required.
- **Intellicast** (www.intellicast.com). Weather forecasts for all 50 states and cities around the world. *Note:* Temperatures are in Celsius for many international destinations.
- **Mapquest** (www.mapquest.com). The best of the mapping sites, Mapquest lets you choose a specific address or destination, and in seconds, it returns a map and detailed directions.

- **Cybercafes.com** (www.cybercafes. com) or **Net Café Guide** (www. netcafeguide.com). Locate Internet cafes at hundreds of locations around the globe. Catch up on your e-mail and log onto the Web for a few dollars per hour.
- **Universal Currency Converter** (www.xe.com). See what your dollar or pound is worth in more than 100 other countries.
- **U.S. State Department Travel Warnings** (www.travel.state.gov). Reports on places where health concerns or unrest might threaten U.S. travelers. It also lists the locations of U.S. embassies around the world.

10 Recommended Books

GENERAL HISTORY

Anthony Sampson's *The Changing Anatomy of Britain* (Random House) still gives great insight into the idiosyncrasies of English society. *London Perceived* (Hogarth), by novelist and literary critic V. S. Pritchett, is a witty portrait of the city—its history, art, literature, and life. Virginia Woolf's *The London Scene: Five Essays* (Random House), a literary gem, brilliantly depicts 1930s London. *In Search of London* (Methusen Publishers), by H. V. Morton, is filled with anecdotal history and is well worth reading even though it was written in the 1950s.

In *London: The Biography of a City* (Penguin), popular historian Christopher Hibbert paints a lively portrait of the city. For 17th-century history, you can't beat the *Diary of Samuel Pepys* (1660–69), and for the flavor of the 18th century, try Daniel Defoe's *Tour Thro' London About the Year 1725*. Winston Churchill's *History of the English-Speaking Peoples* (Dodd Mead) is a four-volume tour de force, while his *The Gathering Storm* (Houghton-Mifflin) captures London and Europe on the brink of World War II.

Americans in London (William Morrow), by Brian N. Morton, is a street-by-street guide to the clubs, homes, and favorite pubs of more than 250 illustrious Americans (Mark Twain, Joseph Kennedy, Dwight Eisenhower, and Sylvia Plath among them) who made London their temporary home.

Children of the Sun (Basic Books), by Martin Green, depicts the decadent post-World War I period in Britain and the lives of such people as Randolph Churchill, Rupert Brooke, Edward VIII (the then Prince of Wales), and Christopher Isherwood.

George Williams's *Guide to Literary London* (Batsford) charts a series of literary tours through London, from Chelsea to Bloomsbury. Peter Gibson's *The Capital Companion* (Webb & Bower), containing more than 1,200 alphabetical entries, is filled with facts and anecdotes about the streets of London and their inhabitants.

Bloomsbury at Home, by Pamela Todd (Phaidon Press, Inc.), brings alive famous literati crowd, the Bloomsbury group, who embodied the Arts and Letters society in London at the turn of the 20th century. Star members include Virginia and Leonard Woolf, Vanessa Bell, Dora Carrington, Lytton Strachley, and others who were passionately (some say obsessively) devoted to the arts, liberal ideas, and literature, and who were, individually and collectively, notorious for their "loose sexuality."

Sarah Valente Kettler and Carole Trimble have written the *Amateur Historian's Guide to Medieval and Tudor London* (Capital Books, Inc.), which is one of the best compendiums of these two important areas. Rather exhaustive, it focuses on the sometimes offbeat aspects of London's charm.

A unique walking tour for London, *Our Sisters' London: Feminist Walking Tours*, by Katherine Sturtevant (Chicago Review Press), hits the trail of some of the most illustrious (or notorious) women who called London home.

ARCHITECTURE

The Architect's Guide to London (Reed International), by Renzo Salvadori, documents 100 landmark buildings with history, descriptions, photographs, and maps. *Nairn's London* (Penguin) is Ian Nairn's stimulating, opinionated discourse on London's buildings. Donald Olsen's *The City as a Work of Art: London, Paris, and Vienna* (Yale University Press) is a well-illustrated text tracing the evolution of these great cities. *London One: The Cities of London and Westminster* (Penguin) and *London Two: South* (Penguin) are labors of love by well-known architectural writers Bridget Cherry and Nikolaus Pevsner.

In one of the best overviews of its kind, Ann Saunders tackles *The Art and Architecture of London: An Illustrated Guide* (Phaidon Press, Inc.). The book is particularly articulate about the City of London, its medieval core and modern-day financial district, but it covers all neighborhoods well.

The fascinating story of the recreation of London's most famous theater is told in *Shakespeare's Globe Rebuilt*, edited by J.R. Mulryne (Cambridge University Press). Theater buffs especially will appreciate this keen insight into the Elizabethan stage.

FICTION & BIOGRAPHY

A good feel for English life, both urban and rural, has been created by some of the country's leading exponents of mystery and suspense fiction. Agatha Christie, P. D. James, Dorothy Sayers, and Ruth Rendell are just a few of the familiar authors. Of course, the great London mystery character is Sir Arthur Conan Doyle's Sherlock Holmes. Any of these writers will give pleasure and insight into London.

England's literary heritage is so vast that it's hard to select particular titles, but here are a few favorites. Master storyteller Charles Dickens re-creates Victorian London in such books as *Oliver Twist, David Copperfield, Great Expectations,* and his earlier, satirical *Sketches by Boz.*

Edwardian London and the 1920s and 1930s are wonderfully captured in any of Evelyn Waugh's social satires and comedies. Any work from the Bloomsbury Group will also prove enlightening—Virginia Woolf's *Mrs. Dalloway,* for example, which peers behind the surface of the London scene. For a portrait of wartime London, there's Elizabeth Bowen's *Heat of the Day.*

For an American slant on London and on England, Henry James's *The Awkward Age* dissects the social order of the English upper class when a young woman finds herself impossibly spoiled for the marriage market by her contact with her mother's "fast set."

Colin MacInnes's novels *City of Spades* and *Absolute Beginners* focus on more recent social problems. Among contemporary writers, Margaret Drabble and Iris Murdoch are both challenging.

No "man about town" in London became more famous than Shakespeare, and the Bard's life and the English Renaissance are illuminated in Dennis Kay's *Shakespeare: His Life, Work, and Era* (Morrow). Another interesting portrait emerges in *Shakespeare, the Latter Years,* by Russell Fraser (Columbia University Press).

An equally famous man about London was Sir Winston Churchill (1874–1965). Although no one told the story of his life more eloquently than did the Nobel Prize-winning prime minister himself, the latest engaging study emerges in *Churchill: A Life* by Martin Gilbert (Holt).

Richard Ellmann's *Oscar Wilde* (Knopf) is a masterpiece, bringing the Victorian era and such personalities as Lillie Langtry, Gilbert and Sullivan, and Henry James to light. More recently, *The Lives of John Lennon* by Albert Goldman (William Morrow) traces the life of the most famous of all 1960s musicians.

Just for fun on a foggy night in Londontown, read *The Ultimate Jack the Ripper Companion,* edited by Steward P. Evans and Keith Skinner (Carrol & Graf). This 650-page tome doesn't even attempt to answer the question of who Jack the Ripper really was (other books have unsuccessfully tried that already), but it lays out the evidence and leaves the conclusion up to you, the keen-eyed detective.

The British Tourist Authority has produced *A Movie Map of Britain*, available at local visitor centers, pinpointing London locales used in various films.

4

Getting to Know London

England's largest city is like a great wheel, with Piccadilly Circus at its hub and dozens of communities branching out from it. Since London is such a large conglomeration of neighborhoods and areas, each with its own personality, first-time visitors are sometimes intimidated until they get the hang of it. Many visitors spend all their time in the West End, where most of the attractions are, with a visit to The City (London's financial district) to see the Tower of London.

This chapter provides a brief orientation to the city's neighborhoods and tells you how to get around London by public transport or on foot. In addition, the "Fast Facts" section helps you find everything from babysitters to camera repair shops.

1 Orientation

ARRIVING

BY PLANE

LONDON HEATHROW AIRPORT Located west of London in Hounslow (© **0870/000-0123** for flight information), Heathrow is one of the world's busiest airports. It has four terminals, each relatively self-contained. Terminal 4 handles the long haul and transatlantic operations of British Airways. Most transatlantic flights on U.S.-based airlines arrive at Terminal 3. Terminals 1 and 2 receive the intra-European flights of several European airlines.

It takes 50 minutes by **Underground** and costs £3.50 ($5.25) to make the 24km (15-mile) trip from Heathrow to the center of the city.

The British Airport Authority now operates **Heathrow Express** (© **0845/ 600-1515** or 877/677-1066; www.heathrowexpress.com), a 100-mph train service running every 15 minutes daily from 5:10am until 11:40pm between Heathrow and Paddington Station in the center of London. Trips cost £12 ($18) each way in economy class, rising to £20 ($30) in first class. Children under 15 go for free (when accompanied by an adult). You can save £1 ($1.50) on the fare by booking online or by phone. The trip takes 15 minutes each way between Paddington and Terminals 1, 2, and 3, or 23 minutes from Terminal 4. The trains have special areas for wheelchairs. You can buy tickets in advance, at the Heathrow Express stations in, or on board with a surcharge of £2). From Paddington, passengers can connect to other trains or hail a taxi. You can buy tickets on the train or at self-service machines at Heathrow Airport (also available from travel agents). At Paddington, a bus link, Hotel Express, takes passengers to a number of hotels in central London. The cost is £2 ($3) for adults, £1 ($1.50) for children 5 to 15, and free for children under 5. This service has already revolutionized travel to and from the airport, much to the regret of London cabbies. Hotel Express buses are clearly designated outside the station, and there are frequent departures throughout the day.

GATWICK AIRPORT   While Heathrow still dominates, more and more scheduled flights land at Gatwick (© **0129/353-5353** for flight information), located some 40km (25 miles) south of London in West Sussex, but only a 30-minute train ride away from central London (Victoria Station). From Gatwick, the fastest way to get to London is via the **Gatwick Express** trains (**08705/301-530;** www.gatwickexpress.co.uk), which leave for Victoria Station in London every 15 minutes during the day and every hour at night. The one-way charge is £10.50 ($15.75) "Express Class" for adults, £17 ($25.50) for First Class, half price for children 5 to 15, free for children under 5. There are also Airbus **buses** from Gatwick to Victoria coach station (which is adjacent to Victoria Rail Station) operated by **National Express** (© **0870/580-8080;** www. gobycoach.com), approximately every hour from 4:15am to 9:15pm; the round-trip fare is £12.50 ($18.75) per person, and the trip takes approximately 1½ hours. A **taxi** from Gatwick to central London usually costs £55 to £70 ($82.50–$105). However, you must negotiate a fare with the driver before you enter the cab; the meter doesn't apply because Gatwick lies outside the Metropolitan Police District. For further transportation information, call © **020/ 7222-1234.**

LONDON STANSTED AIRPORT   Located some 81km (50 miles) northeast of London's West End, Stansted, in Essex (© **08700/0000-303**), mostly handles flights to and from the European continent. From Stansted, your best bet for getting to central London is the **Stansted Express train** (© **01332/ 387-601;** www.stanstedexpress.com) to Liverpool Street Station which runs every 15 minutes from 8am to 5pm, and every 30 minutes in the early mornings, evening weekdays, and weekends, and costs £13 ($19.50) for a standard ticket, and £18 ($27) for business class and takes 42 minutes. By bus, you can take the A6 Airbus (www.gobycoach.com), which runs regular departures 24 hours a day from the airport to both Victoria rail and coach stations, and costs £7 ($10.50). Trip time is 1 hour, 15 minutes to 1 hour, 35 minutes.

LONDON CITY AIRPORT   London City Airport (© **020/7646-0000**) receives mainly short-haul flights from Britain and northern Europe, making it popular with business travelers.

It's easy to reach the center of London from London City Airport. You can ride the **blue-and-white bus** for £6 ($9) each way to and from the Liverpool Street Station, where you can connect to rail and Underground transport to almost anywhere in England. The bus runs daily every 10 minutes, during the airport's open hours—roughly from 6:50am to 9:20pm (airport closes at 1pm Sat). Then, there's a **shuttle bus from the airport to Canary Wharf,** where trains from the Docklands Light Railway make frequent 10-minute runs to the heart of London's financial district, the City. Here, passengers can catch an Underground from the Bank Tube stop. The **London Transport bus no. 473** goes from the City Airport to East London, where passengers can pick up the Underground at the Plaistow Tube stop.

BY TRAIN

Each of London's train stations is connected to the city's vast bus and Underground network, and each has phones, restaurants, pubs, luggage storage areas, and London Regional Transport Information Centres.

If you're coming from France, the fastest way to get to London is by the **HoverSpeed** connection between Calais and Dover (see "Hovercraft & Seacats,"

London's Neighborhoods

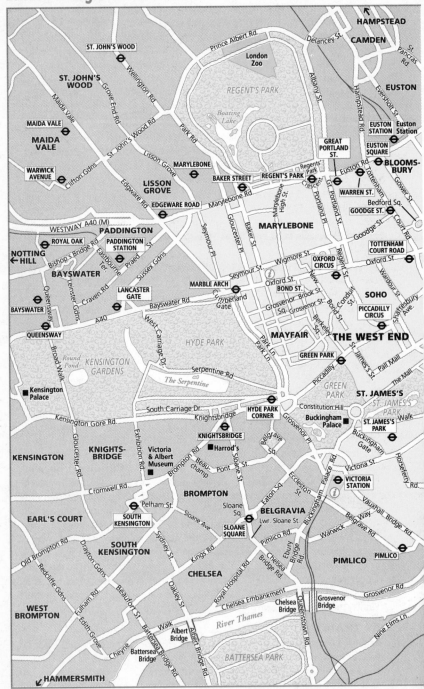

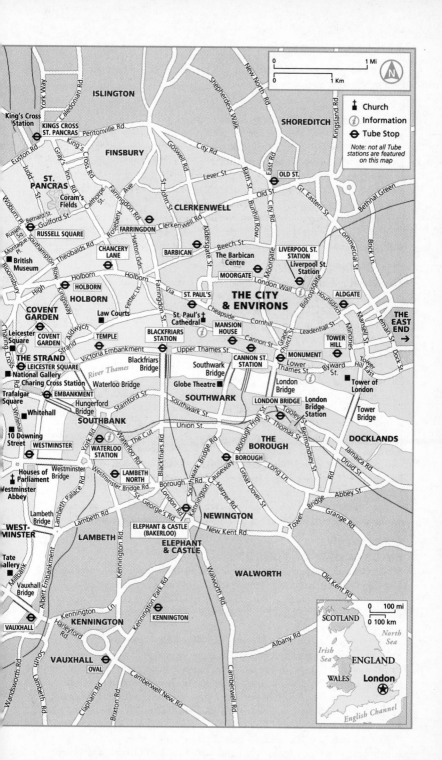

under "Getting There by Boat," in chapter 3), where you can get a BritRail train into London. For one-stop travel, you can take the Chunnel train direct from Paris to Waterloo Station in London.

BY CAR

Once you arrive on the English side of the channel, the M20 takes you directly into London. *Remember to drive on the left.* Two roadways encircle London: the A406 and A205 form the inner beltway; the M25 rings the city farther out. Determine which part of the city you want to enter and follow signposts.

We suggest you confine driving in London to the bare minimum, which means arriving and parking. Because of parking problems and heavy traffic, getting around London by car is not a viable option. Once there, leave your car in a garage and rely on public transportation or taxis. Before arrival in London, call your hotel and inquire if it has a garage (and what the charges are), or ask the staff to give you the name and address of a garage nearby.

VISITOR INFORMATION

The **British Travel Centre,** Rex House, 4–12 Lower Regent St., London SW1 4PQ (Tube: Piccadilly Circus), caters to walk-in visitors with information about all parts of Britain. There's no telephone service; you must go in person and there is often a wait in a lengthy line. On the premises you'll find a British Rail ticket office, travel and theater ticket agencies, a hotel-booking service, a book-shop, and a souvenir shop. It's open Monday through Friday from 9am to 6:30pm, Saturday and Sunday from 10am to 4pm, with extended hours on Saturday from June to September.

London Tourist Board's **Tourist Information Centre,** Victoria Station Forecourt, SW1 (walk-ins only; no phone; Tube: Victoria Station), can help you with almost anything. The center deals chiefly with accommodations in all price categories and can handle most travelers' questions. It also arranges ticket sales for tours, and theater reservations, and offers a wide selection of books and souvenirs. From Easter to October, the center is open daily from 8am to 7pm; from November to Easter, it's open Monday through Saturday from 8am to 6pm and Sunday from 9am to 4pm.

The Tourist Board also has offices at **Heathrow Terminals 1, 2, and 3,** and on the Underground concourse at **Liverpool Street Railway Station.**

CITY LAYOUT
AN OVERVIEW OF LONDON

While **Central London** doesn't formally define itself, most Londoners today would probably accept the Underground's Circle Line as a fair boundary.

"The City" (the financial district) is where London began; it's the original square mile that the Romans called *Londinium,* and it still exists as its own self-governing entity. Rich in historical, architectural, and social interest, the City is one of the world's great financial areas. **The West End,** where most of London's main attractions are found, is unofficially bounded by the Thames to the south, Farringdon Road/Street to the east, Marylebone Road/Euston Road to the north, and Hyde Park and Victoria Station to the West. Most visitors will spend their time in the West End, whether at Buckingham Palace, the British Museum, or the shops and theaters in Soho. You'll also find the greatest concentration of hotels and restaurants in the West End.

Farther west are the upscale neighborhoods of Belgravia, Kensington, Knightsbridge, Chelsea, Paddington and Bayswater, Earl's Court, and Notting

Hill. This is also prime hotel and restaurant territory. To the east of the City is the **East End,** which forms the eastern boundary of **Inner London** (Notting Hill and Earl's Court roughly form the western boundary). Inner London is surrounded, like a donut, by the sprawling hinterland of **Outer London.** Even though the City is jeweled with historic sights, it empties out in the evenings and on weekends, and there are lots of better places to stay if you are looking for a hopping nightlife scene. Despite attempts to extend central London's nocturnal life to the south side of the Thames (notably the ambitious South Bank Arts Centre—London's energy fades when it crosses the river. Still, the new urban development of Docklands, the tourist attraction of the new Globe Theatre, and some up-and-coming residential neighborhoods are infusing energy into the area across the river.

FINDING YOUR WAY AROUND

It's not easy to find an address in London, as the city's streets—both names and house numbers—follow no pattern whatsoever. London is checkered with innumerable squares, mews, closes, and terraces that jut into, cross, overlap, or otherwise interrupt whatever street you're trying to follow. And house numbers run in odds and evens, clockwise and counterclockwise—when they exist at all. Many establishments, such as the Four Seasons Hotel and Langan's Brasserie, don't have numbers, even though the building right next door is numbered. Just ask if you're having trouble finding something. Throughout this book, street addresses are followed by designations like SW1 and EC1, which are postal areas. The original post office was at St. Martin-le-Grand in the City, so the postal districts are related to where they lie geographically from there. Victoria is SW1 since it's the first area southwest of St. Martin-le-Grand; Covent Garden is west (west central), so its postal area is WC1 or WC2; Liverpool Street is east central of there, so its postal area is EC1.

If you plan to explore London in any depth, you'll need a detailed street map with an index. No Londoner is ever without a *London A to Z,* the ultimate street-by-street reference guide, available at bookstores and newsstands. There's even a *Mini A to Z,* which all but the most myopic will find easier to carry around. If you can't find the map you're looking for, **Foyle's Ltd.,** 113–119 Charing Cross Rd., WC2 (② **020/7440-3225;** Tube: Leicester Square), carries a wide range. Also, we have included a foldout street map at the back of this book.

LONDON'S NEIGHBORHOODS IN BRIEF

The City & Environs

The City   When Londoners speak of "the City" (EC2, EC3) they mean the original square mile that's now the British version of Wall Street. The buildings of this district are known all over the world: the Bank of England, the London Stock Exchange, and famed insurance company Lloyd's of London. The City was the original site of *Londinium,* the first settlement of the Roman conquerors. Despite its age, the City doesn't easily reveal its past. Although it retains some of its medieval character, much of the City has been swept away by the Great Fire of 1666, the bombs of 1940, the IRA bombs of the 1990s, and the zeal of modern developers. Landmarks include Sir Christopher Wren's masterpiece, **St. Paul's Cathedral,** which stood virtually alone in the rubble after the Blitz. Some 2,000 years of history unfold at the City's **Museum of London**

and at the **Barbican Centre,** opened by Queen Elizabeth in 1982.

Following the Strand eastward from Trafalgar Square you'll come to Fleet Street. In the 19th century, this corner of London became the most concentrated newspaper district in the world. William Caxton printed the first book in English here, and the *Daily Consort,* the first daily newspaper printed in England, was launched at Ludgate Circus in 1702. In recent times, however, most London tabloids have abandoned Fleet Street for the Docklands across the river. Where the Strand becomes Fleet Street stands Temple Bar, where the actual City of London begins. The Tower of London looms at the eastern fringe of the City, shrouded in legend, blood, and history, and permanently besieged by battalions of visitors.

The average visitor will venture into the City during the day to sample its attractions or to lunch at pubs such as Ye Olde Cheshire Cheese, then return to the West End for evening amusement. As a hotel district, the City wasn't even on the map until recent times. The opening of the Great Eastern Hotel has brought a lot of business clients who prefer to stay here to avoid the traffic jams involved in getting into and out of the City. Stay in the City if you would prefer a hotel in New York's Wall Street instead of a midtown address. If you can't afford the Great Eastern, then consider the cheaper Rookery in newly fashionable Smithfield. The City lures hotel guests who prefer its quirky, quiet, offbeat flavor at night, when it's part ghost town, part movie set. There is some nightlife here, including pubs and restaurants. It's fun to wander the area when all the crowds are gone, pondering the thought that you're walking the same streets Samuel Johnson trod so long ago.

The City of London still prefers to function on its own, separate from the rest of London. It maintains its own **Information Centre** at St. Paul's Churchyard, EC4 (*©* **020/ 7332-1456**). It is open Monday through Friday from 9am to 5pm and Saturday from 9am to noon.

The East End Traditionally, this was one of London's poorest districts, nearly bombed out of existence during World War II. In the words of one commentator at the time, Hitler created "instant urban renewal" here. The East End extends east from the City Walls, encompassing Stepney, Bow, Poplar, West Ham, Canning Town, and other districts. The East End is the home of the Cockney. To be a true Cockney, it's said that you be born within the sound of the Bow Bells of St. Mary-le-Bow church, an old church rebuilt by Sir Christopher Wren in 1670. Many immigrants to London have found a home here.

London is pushing eastward, and the East End might even become fashionable, somewhat like the Lower East Side of New York. But that day isn't quite here, and except for the Docklands area (see below) much of the East End doesn't concern the average visitor. Attractions that you may want to visit if you are in the area include St. Clements Danes church, the Temple of Mithras, and Sir Christopher Wren's Monument to the Great Fire of 1666.

Docklands In 1981, the London Docklands Development Corporation (LDDC) was formed to redevelop Wapping, the Isle of Dogs, the Royal Docks, and Surrey Docks in the most ambitious scheme of its kind in Europe. The area is bordered roughly by Tower Bridge to the west and London City Airport and the Royal Docks to the east. Many businesses have moved here; Thames-side warehouses have been converted to Manhattan-style lofts; and museums, entertainment complexes, shops, and an ever-growing list of restaurants have popped up at this 21st-century river city in the making.

Canary Wharf, on the Isle of Dogs, is the heart of Docklands. This 71-acre site is dominated by an 800-foot-high tower, which is the tallest building in the United Kingdom, and was designed by Cesar Pelli. The Piazza is lined with shops and restaurants. On the south side of the river at Surrey Docks, Sir Terence Conran has converted the Victorian warehouses of Butler's Wharf into offices, workshops, houses, shops, and restaurants. Butler's Wharf is also home to the **Design Museum.** Chances are you'll venture here for sights and restaurants, not for lodging, unless you've got business in the area. But it's fun during the day, and you'll find some of London's finest restaurants here, offering good food and a change of pace from the West End—this is post-millennium London, whereas the West End is the essence of traditional. See our recommendations in chapter 6, "Where to Dine." To get to Docklands, take the Underground to Tower Hill and pick up the **Docklands Light Railway** (© **0877/677-1066**), which operates Monday through Friday from 5:30am to 12:30am, with selected routes offering weekend service from 6am to 12:30am Saturday and from 7:30am to 11:30pm Sunday.

South Bank Although not officially a district, you'll find the **South Bank Arts Centre,** the largest art center in Western Europe and still growing. Reached by Waterloo Bridge (or on foot by Hungerford Bridge), it lies across the Thames from the Victoria Embankment. Culture buffs flock to its galleries and halls, which encompass the **National Theatre, Queen Elizabeth Hall, Royal Festival Hall,** and the **Hayward Gallery.** The center also houses the National Film Theatre and the Museum of the Moving Image (MOMI).

Although its day as a top hotel district in London may come in a decade or so (since there's no room left in the West End), that hasn't happened yet. The South Bank is a destination for daytime adventures, or for evening cultural attractions. You may want to dine here during a day's and evening's exploration of the area. See our recommendations in chapter 6, "Where to Dine."

Nearby are such neighborhoods as Elephant and Castle, and Southwark, home to **Southwark Cathedral.** To get here, take the Tube to Waterloo Station.

Clerkenwell This neighborhood, north and a bit west of the City, was the site of London's first hospital and is the home of several early churches. **St. Bartholomew-the-Great,** built in 1123, still stands as London's oldest church and the best example of large-scale Norman building in the city. In the 18th century, Clerkenwell declined into a muck-filled cattle yard, home to cheap gin distilleries. During a 19th-century revival, John Stuart Mill's London Patriotic Club moved here in 1872 and William Morris's socialist press called Clerkenwell home in the 1890s; Lenin worked here editing *Iskra.* The neighborhood fell into disrepair, but has recently been reinvented by the moneyed and groovy. A handful of hot restaurants and clubs have sprung up, and art galleries line St. John's Square and the border of Clerkenwell Green. Lest you think that the whole area has become trendy, know that trucks still rumble into **Smithfield Market** throughout the night, unloading thousands of beef carcasses. Farringdon is Clerkenwell's central Tube stop.

No one ever accused Clerkenwell of being a hotel district. But it is increasingly known for containing some of London's better restaurants, which have been pushed out of the West End because of high rents. See our recommendations in chapter 6, "Where to Dine."

West End Neighborhoods

Bloomsbury This district, a world within itself, is bounded roughly by Euston Road to the north, Gower Street to the west, and Clerkenwell to the east. It is, among other things, the academic heart of London; you'll find the **University of London,** several other colleges, and many **bookstores.** Writers like Virginia Woolf, who lived within its bounds (it figured in her novel *Jacob's Room*), have fanned the neighborhood's reputation as a place devoted to liberal thinking, arts, and "sexual frankness." The novelist and her husband, Leonard, were unofficial leaders of a group of artists and writers known as "the Bloomsbury Group." Despite its student population, it is a fairly staid neighborhood. The heart of Bloomsbury is **Russell Square,** whose outlying streets are lined with moderately priced to expensive hotels and B&Bs. It's a noisy but central place to stay. Most visitors come to visit the **British Museum,** one of the world's greatest repositories of treasures from around the globe. The **British Telecom Tower** (1964) on Cleveland Street is a familiar landmark.

Of all the areas described so far, this is the only one that could be called a hotel district. Hotel prices have risen dramatically in the past decade, but are nowhere near the levels of those in Mayfair and St. James's. In price, Bloomsbury's hotels are comparable to Marylebone's to the west. But Bloomsbury is more convenient. At its southern doorstep lie the restaurants and nightclubs of Soho, the theater district, and the markets of Covent Garden. If you stay here, it's a 10-minute Tube ride to the heart of the action of the West End.

The western edge of Bloomsbury is **Fitzrovia,** bounded by Great Portland, Oxford, and Gower streets, and reached by the Goodge Street Tube. Goodge Street, with its many shops and pubs, forms the heart of the village. Fitzrovia was once the stamping ground for writers and artists like Ezra Pound, Wyndham Lewis, and George Orwell, among others. The bottom end of Fitzrovia is a virtual extension of Soho, with a cluster of Greek restaurants.

Holborn The old borough of Holborn (*Ho*-burn), which abuts the City southeast of Bloomsbury, encompasses the heart of legal London—this is where you'll find the city's barristers, solicitors, and law clerks. Still Dickensian in spirit, the area preserves the Victorian author's literary footsteps in the two Inns of Court (where law students perform their apprenticeships and where barristers chambers are located) and the Bleeding Heart Yard of *Little Dorrit* fame. **The Old Bailey** courthouse, where judges and lawyers still wear old-fashioned wigs, has stood for English justice through the years; Fagin went to the gallows from this site in *Oliver Twist.* Everything in Holborn is steeped in history. For example, as you're downing a half-pint of bitter at the **Viaduct Tavern,** 126 Newgate St. (Tube: St. Paul's), you can reflect on the fact that the pub was built over the notorious Newgate Prison. You might come here for some sightseeing, perhaps quenching your thirst in a historic pub.

Covent Garden & The Strand
The flower, fruit, and "veg" market is long gone (since 1970), but memories of Professor Higgins and his "squashed cabbage leaf," Eliza Doolittle, linger on. **Covent Garden** contains the city's liveliest group of restaurants, pubs, and cafes outside Soho, as well as some of the city's hippest shops—including the world's only Dr. Martens Super Store. The restored marketplace, with its glass and iron roofs, has been called a magnificent example of urban recycling. London's **theater district** begins in Covent Garden and spills over into Leicester Square and Soho. Inigo Jones's **St. Paul's Covent Garden** is known as the actors' church; over the years, it has attracted everybody from Ellen Terry to Vivien Leigh. The **Theatre Royal Drury Lane** was where Charles II's mistress Nell Gwynne made her debut in 1665 and the Irish actress Dorothea Jordan caught the eye of the Duke of Clarence, later William IV. The **Strand** forms the southern border of Covent Garden. It's packed with theaters, shops, first-class hotels, and restaurants. **Ye Olde Cheshire Cheese** pub, **Dr. Johnson's House,** tearooms fragrant with brewing Twinings English tea—all these evoke memories of the rich heyday of this district. The Strand runs parallel to the River Thames, and to walk it is to follow in the footsteps of Charles Lamb, Mark Twain, Henry Fielding, James Boswell,

William Thackeray, and Sir Walter Raleigh, among others. The Strand's **Savoy Theatre** helped make Gilbert and Sullivan household names.

You'll probably come here for theater or dining rather than for a hotel room. Covent Garden has few hotels (although the ones that do exist are very nice). We recommend the best ones (beginning on p. 101). Expect to spend a lot for the privilege of staying in such a central zone. The Strand, of course, has always been known for its swank Savoy Hotel.

Piccadilly Circus & Leicester Square Piccadilly Circus, with its statue of Eros, is the heart and soul of London. The circus isn't Times Square yet, but its traffic, neon, and jostling crowds might indeed make "circus" an apt word to describe this place. Piccadilly, which was the western road out of town, was named for the "picadil," a ruffled collar created by Robert Baker, a 17th-century tailor. If you want more grandeur, retreat to the Regency promenade of exclusive shops, the **Burlington Arcade,** designed in 1819. The English gentry—tired of being mud-splashed by horses and carriages along Piccadilly—came here to do their shopping. Some 35 shops, housing a treasure trove of expensive goodies, await you. A bit more tawdry is **Leicester Square,** a hub of theaters, restaurants, movie palaces, and nightlife. Leicester Square is London's equivalent of New York's Times Square. The square changed forever in the Victorian era, when four towering entertainment halls were opened. In time, the old palaces changed from stage to screen; three of them still show films. The old Café de Paris is no longer a chic cabaret—now it's a disco.

There are a few hotels here, although they're invariably expensive, and this is certainly not the best place to stay for most people. Stay here if you'd want a hotel in Times Square in New York. It's convenient for those who want to be at the center of the action. The downside is noise, congestion, and pollution.

Soho   A nightclubber's paradise, Soho is a confusing grid of streets crammed with restaurants. It's a great place to visit, but you probably won't want to stay there (there aren't many hotels, anyway). These densely packed streets in the heart of the West End are famous for their cosmopolitan mix of people and trades. A decade ago, much was heard about the decline of Soho with the influx of sex shops; even the pub where Dylan Thomas used to drink himself into oblivion became a sex cinema. Since then, non–sex-oriented businesses have returned, and fashionable restaurants and shops prosper. Soho is now the heart of London's expanding gay scene.

Soho starts at Piccadilly Circus and spreads out, more or less bordered by Regent Street to the west, Oxford Street to the north, Charing Cross Road to the east, and the **theaters along Shaftesbury Avenue** to the South. Carnaby Street, a block from Regent Street, was the center of the universe in the Swinging '60s, but is now just a schlocky tourist trap. Across Shaftesbury Avenue is London's **Chinatown,** centered on Gerrard Street. It's small, authentic, and packed with good restaurants. But **Soho's heart**—featuring great delicatessens, butchers, fish stores, and wine merchants—is farther north,

on Brewer, Old Compton, and Berwick streets; Berwick is also a wonderful open-air fresh food market. To the north of Old Compton Street, Dean, Frith, and Greek streets have fine restaurants, pubs, and clubs. The British movie industry is centered in Wardour Street. The average visitor comes to Soho to dine. Its many restaurants are convenient to the theater district. Most travelers don't stay in Soho, but a certain action-oriented visitor prefers the *joie de vivre* of the neighborhood as compared to staid Bloomsbury or swank Mayfair. Does this sound like you? Check out Soho's accommodations starting on p. 103.

Marylebone   West of Bloomsbury and Fitzrovia, Marylebone extends from the eastern edge of Hyde Park. Most first-time visitors head here to explore **Madame Tussaud's** waxworks or walk along **Baker Street** in the footsteps of Sherlock Holmes. The streets form a near-perfect grid, with the major ones running north-south between Regent's Park and Oxford Street. Architect Robert Adam laid out **Portland Place,** one of the most characteristic squares, from 1776 to 1780. At **Cavendish Square** Mrs. Horatio Nelson waited for the return of Admiral Nelson. Marylebone Lane and High Street retain some small town atmosphere, but this is otherwise a rather anonymous area. Dickens wrote nearly a dozen books while he resided here. At **Regent's Park,** you can visit Queen Mary's Gardens or, in summer, see Shakespeare performed in an open-air theater. **Marylebone** has emerged as a major "bedroom" district for London, competing with Bloomsbury to its east. It's not as convenient as Bloomsbury, but the hub of West End's action is virtually at your doorstep if you lodge here, northwest of Piccadilly Circus and facing Mayfair to the south. The area extends north of Marble Arch at Hyde Park. Once known only for its town houses turned into B&Bs, the district now offers accommodations in all price ranges, catering to lodgers from rock stars to frugal family travelers.

Mayfair Bounded by Piccadilly, Hyde Park, and Oxford and Regent streets, this is the most elegant, fashionable section of London, filled with luxury hotels, Georgian town houses, and swank shops. **Grosvenor Square** (pronounced *Grov*-nor) is nicknamed "Little America" because it's home to the American Embassy and a statue of Franklin D. Roosevelt; **Berkeley Square** (*Bark*-ley) was made famous by the song "A Nightingale Sang in Berkeley Square." You'll want to dip into this exclusive section at least once. One of the curiosities of Mayfair is **Shepherd Market,** a village of pubs, two-story inns, restaurants, and book and food stalls, nestled within Mayfair's grandness. If you're seeking sophisticated, albeit expensive, accommodations, close to the **Bond Street** shopping, boutiques, and art galleries, then Mayfair is for you.

The hotels of Mayfair, especially those along Park Lane, are the most expensive and grand in London. If "address" is important to you, and you're willing to pay for a good one, Mayfair has a bed waiting for you. The area is sandwiched between Piccadilly Circus and Hyde Park. It's convenient to London's best shopping and close to the West End theaters, yet (a bit snobbily) removed from the peddlers and commerce of Covent Garden and Soho.

St. James's Often called "Royal London," St. James's basks in its associations with everybody from the "merrie monarch" Charles II to Elizabeth II, who lives at its most famous address, **Buckingham Palace.** The neighborhood begins at **Piccadilly Circus** and moves southwest, incorporating **Pall Mall, The Mall, St. James's Park,** and **Green Park.** It's "frightfully convenient," as the English say; within its confines are American Express and many of London's leading department stores. This is where the English gentleman seeks haven at that male-only bastion of English tradition, the gentlemen's club, where poker is played, drinks are consumed, and pipes are smoked (St. James's Club is one of the most prestigious clubs). Be sure to stop in at **Fortnum & Mason,** 181 Piccadilly, the world's most luxurious grocery store. Launched in 1788, the store sent hams to the Duke of Wellington's army and baskets of tinned goodies to Florence Nightingale in the Crimea. Hotels in this neighborhood tend to be expensive, but if the Queen should summon you to Buckingham Palace, you're right there.

Westminster Westminster has been the seat of the British government since the days of Edward the Confessor (1042–66). Dominated by the **Houses of Parliament** and **Westminster Abbey,** the area runs along the Thames to the east of St. James's Park. **Trafalgar Square,** at the area's northern end and one of the city's major landmarks, remains a testament to England's victory over Napoleon in 1805. The square is home to the landmark National Gallery, which is filled with glorious paintings. Whitehall is the main thoroughfare, linking Trafalgar Square with **Parliament**

Square. You can visit Churchill's Cabinet War Rooms and walk down **Downing Street** to see **Number 10,** home to Britain's prime minister. No visit is complete without a call at **Westminster Abbey,** one of the great Gothic churches in the world. It has witnessed a parade of English history, beginning when William the Conqueror was crowned here on Christmas Day, 1066.

Westminster also encompasses **Victoria,** an area that takes its name from bustling Victoria Station, "the gateway to the Continent." Many B&Bs and hotels have sprouted up here because of the neighborhood's proximity to the rail station. Victoria is cheap and convenient, if you don't mind the noise and crowds.

Welfare recipients occupy many hotels along Belgrave Road. If you've arrived without a hotel reservation, you'll find the pickings better on the streets off Belgrave Road. Your best bet is to walk along Ebury Street, east of Victoria Station and Buckingham Palace Road. Here you'll find some of the best moderately priced lodgings in central London. Since you're near Victoria Station, the area is convenient for day trips to Oxford, Windsor, or Canterbury.

Beyond the West End

Knightsbridge   One of London's most fashionable neighborhoods, Knightsbridge is a top residential, hotel, and shopping district, just south of Hyde Park. **Harrods** on Brompton Road is its chief attraction. Founded in 1901, Harrods has been called "the Notre Dame of department stores." Right nearby, **Beauchamp Place** (*Bee*-cham) is one of London's most fashionable shopping streets, a Regency-era boutique-lined street with a scattering of restaurants. Most hotels here are deluxe or first class.

Knightsbridge is one of the most convenient areas of London; ideally located if you want to head east to the theater district or the Mayfair shops, or west to Chelsea or Kensington's restaurants and attractions. Knightsbridge is also a swank address, with many fine hotels, although none are at the level of the palaces of Mayfair.

Belgravia   South of Knightsbridge, this area has long been the aristocratic quarter of London, rivaling Mayfair in grandeur. Although it reached its pinnacle of prestige during the reign of Queen Victoria, the duke and duchess of Westminster still live at **Eaton Square,** and Belgravia remains a hot area for chic hotels. The neighborhood's centerpiece is **Belgrave Square.** When town houses were built in 1825 to 1835, aristocrats followed—the duke of Connaught, the earl of Essex, even Queen Victoria's mother.

Belgravia is a tranquil district. If you lodge here, no one will ever accuse you of staying on the "wrong side of the tracks." Belgravia is convenient to the little restaurants and pubs of Chelsea, to Belgravia's immediate west. Victoria Station is located to its immediate east, so Belgravia is convenient if you're planning to take day trips from London.

Chelsea   This stylish Thames-side district lies south and to the west of Belgravia. It begins at **Sloane Square,** with **Gilbert Ledward's Venus fountain** playing watery music. The area has always been a favorite of writers and artists, including Oscar Wilde (who was arrested here), George Eliot, James Whistler, J.M.W. Turner, Henry James, and Thomas Carlyle (whose former home can be visited). Mick Jagger and Margaret Thatcher (not together) have been more recent residents, and the late Princess Diana and her "Sloane Rangers" (a term used to described posh women, derived from Chelsea's Sloane Square) of the 1980s gave it even more recognition. There are some swank hotels here and a scattering of modestly priced ones. The main drawback to Chelsea is inaccessibility. Except for Sloane Square, there's a dearth of Tube stops, and unless you like to take a lot of buses or expensive taxis, you may find getting around a chore.

Chelsea's major boulevard is **King's Road,** where Mary Quant launched the miniskirt in the 1960s and where the English punk look began. King's Road runs the length of Chelsea; it's at its liveliest on Saturday. The outrageous fashions of the King's Road boutiques aren't typical of otherwise upmarket Chelsea, an elegant village filled with town houses and little mews dwellings which only successful stockbrokers and solicitors can afford to occupy. On the Chelsea/Fulham border is **Chelsea Harbour,** a luxury development of apartments and restaurants with a marina. You can spot its tall tower from far away; the golden ball on top moves up and down to indicate the tide level.

Kensington This Royal Borough (W8) lies west of Kensington Gardens and Hyde Park and is traversed by two of London's major shopping streets, **Kensington High Street** and **Kensington Church Street.** Since 1689, when asthmatic William III fled Whitehall Palace for Nottingham House (where the air was fresher), the district has enjoyed royal associations. In time, Nottingham House became Kensington Palace, and the royals grabbed a chunk of Hyde Park to plant their roses. Queen Victoria

was born here. Kensington Palace, or "KP," as the royals say, was home to the late Princess Margaret (who had 20 rooms with a view), and is still home to Prince and Princess Michael of Kent, and the duke and duchess of Gloucester. Kensington Gardens is now open to the public, ever since George II decreed that "respectably dressed" people would be permitted in on Saturday—providing that no servants, soldiers, or sailors came (as you might imagine, that rule is long gone). During the reign of William III, Kensington Square developed, attracting artists and writers. Thackeray wrote *Vanity Fair* while living here. With all those royal associations, Kensington is a fashionable neighborhood. If you're a frugal traveler, head for South Kensington (see below) for moderately priced hotels and B&Bs. Southeast of Kensington Gardens and Earl's Court, primarily residential **South Kensington** is often called "museumland" because it's dominated by a complex of museums and colleges, including the **Natural History Museum,** the **Victoria and Albert Museum,** and the **Science Museum;** nearby is **Royal Albert Hall.** South Kensington boasts some fashionable restaurants and town house hotels. One of the neighborhood's curiosities is the **Albert Memorial,** completed in 1872 by Sir George Gilbert Scott; for sheer excess, this Victorian monument is unequaled in the world.

A hotel room in Kensington is a prestigious address. But as Princess Margaret may have told you, you're at the far stretch of the West End, lying some 20 minutes by Tube from the heart of the theater district. As for South Kensington, it was once considered the "boondocks," although with the boundaries of the West End expanding, South Kensington is much closer to the action than it has ever been before.

Earl's Court   Earl's Court lies below Kensington, bordering the western half of Chelsea. For decades a staid residential district, drawing genteel ladies wearing pince-nez glasses, Earl's Court now attracts a new younger crowd (often gay), particularly at night, to its pubs, wine bars, and coffeehouses. It's a popular base for budget travelers thanks to its wealth of B&Bs and budget hotels and its convenient access to central London: A 15-minute Tube ride takes you into the heart of Piccadilly.

Once regarded as a hinterland, nearby **West Brompton** is seen today as an extension of central London. It lies directly south of Earl's Court (take the Tube to West Brompton) and southeast of West Kensington. Its focal point is the sprawling **Brompton Cemetery,** a flower-filled "green lung" (park) and burial place of such famous names as Frederick Leyland, the Pre-Raphaelite patron who died in 1892. It has many good restaurants, pubs, and taverns, as well as some budget hotels.

Paddington & Bayswater   The **Paddington** section radiates out from Paddington Station, north of Hyde Park and Kensington Gardens. It's one of the major B&B centers in London, attracting budget travelers who fill the lodgings in Sussex Gardens and Norfolk Square. After the first railway was introduced in London in 1836, a circle of sprawling railway terminals, including Paddington Station, which was built in 1838 and spurred the growth of this middle-class area followed it. Just south of Paddington, north of Hyde Park, and abutting more fashionable

Notting Hill to the west is **Bayswater,** also filled with a large number of B&Bs attracting budget travelers. Inspired by Marylebone and elegant Mayfair, a relatively prosperous set of Victorian merchants built terrace houses around spacious squares.

Paddington and Bayswater are a sort of "in between" area of London. If you've come to London to see the attractions in the east, including the British Museum, the Tower of London, and the theater, you'll find yourself commuting a lot. Stay here for the moderately priced lodgings (there are expensive hotels, too) and for convenience to transportation. Rapidly being gentrified, this area ranges from seedy to swank.

On the other (north) side of Westway/Marylebone Road are **Maida Vale** and **St. John's Wood,** two villages that have been absorbed by central London. Maida Vale lies west of **Regent's Park,** north of Paddington, and next to the more prestigious St. John's Wood (home to the Beatles' Abbey Road Studios). The area is very sports oriented; if you take the Tube to Maida Vale, you'll find Paddington Recreation Ground, plus a smaller "green lung": Paddington Bowling and Sports Club. The area is also home to some of the BBC studios.

Notting Hill   Increasingly fashionable Notting Hill is bounded on the east by Bayswater and on the south by Kensington. Hemmed in on the north by Westway and on the west by the Shepherd's Bush ramp leading to the M40, it has many turn-of-the-century mansions and small houses sitting on quiet, leafy streets, plus a growing number of hot restaurants and clubs. Gentrified in recent years, it's becoming an extension of central London. Hotels are few, but increasingly chic.

Even more remote than Paddington and Bayswater, Notting Hill lies at least another 10 minutes west of those districts. In spite of that, many young professional visitors to London wouldn't stay anywhere else.

In the northern half of Notting Hill is the hip neighborhood known as **Notting Hill Gate.** Portobello Road is home to one of London's most famous street markets. The area Tube stops are Notting Hill Gate, Holland Park, and Ladbroke Grove.

Nearby **Holland Park,** an expensive residential neighborhood, promotes itself as "10 minutes by Tube from practically anywhere," a bit of an exaggeration.

Shepherd's Bush To the immediate west of Notting Hill Gate, this increasingly fashionable area is attracting a slew of artists and photographers and in their wake a number of trendy new hangouts. Old milk-bottling factories are being turned into chic dives, and on and on. The area is close to more upscale districts such as Holland Park and Notting Hill Gate. All of these places are less than 1.6km (1 mile) from each other. The main BBC national office is in Shepherd's Bush, and, yes, that is Kate Moss rushing along Goldhawk Road.

Farther Afield

Greenwich To the southeast of London, this suburb, which contains the prime meridian—"zero" for the reckoning of terrestrial longitudes—enjoyed its heyday under the Tudors. Henry VIII and both of his daughters, Mary I and Elizabeth I, were born here. Greenwich Palace, Henry's favorite, is long gone, though; today's visitors come to this lovely port village for nautical sights along the Thames, including visits to the 1869 tea

clipper, *Cutty Sark,* and the tiny *Gipsy Moth IV,* a 54-foot ketch in which Sir Francis Chichester sailed solo around the world from 1966 to 1967. Other attractions include the **National Maritime Museum.**

Hampstead This residential suburb of north London, beloved by Keats and Hogarth, is a favorite excursion destination for Londoners. Everybody from Sigmund Freud and D. H. Lawrence to Anna Pavlova and John Le Carré has lived here, and it's still one of the most desirable districts in the Greater London area. It has very few hotels, and, of course, is quite far from central London. Nonetheless, it's an attractive residential area and many visitors appreciate its bucolic charms. Staying there is rather like going to a hotel in Westchester when you visit New York City. Hampstead's centerpiece is Hampstead Heath, nearly 320 hectares (800 acres) of rolling meadows and woodland; it maintains its rural atmosphere even though it's surrounded by cityscapes on all sides. The hilltop village of Hampstead is filled with cafes, tearooms, and restaurants, and there are pubs galore, some with historic pedigrees. Take the Northern Line to Hampstead Heath station.

Highgate Along with Hampstead, Highgate in north London is another choice residential area, particularly on or near **Pond Square** and along Hampstead High Street. Once celebrated for its "sweet salutarie airs," Highgate has long been a desirable place for Londoners to live; locals still flock to its taverns and pubs for "exercise and harmless merriment" as they did in the old days. Today, most visitors come to see moody **Highgate Cemetery,** London's most famous burial ground. It's the final resting place of

The Outskirts of London

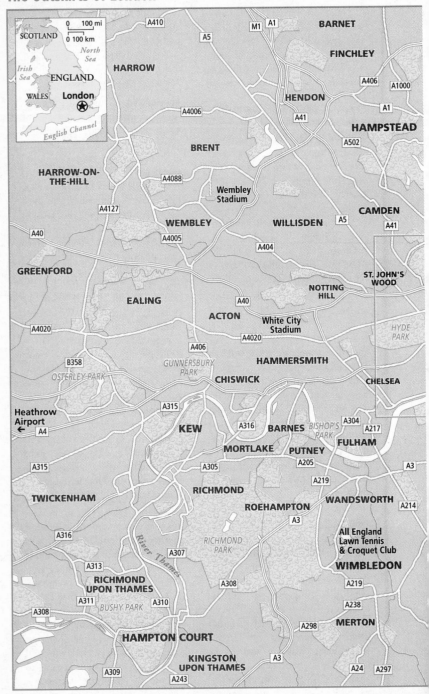

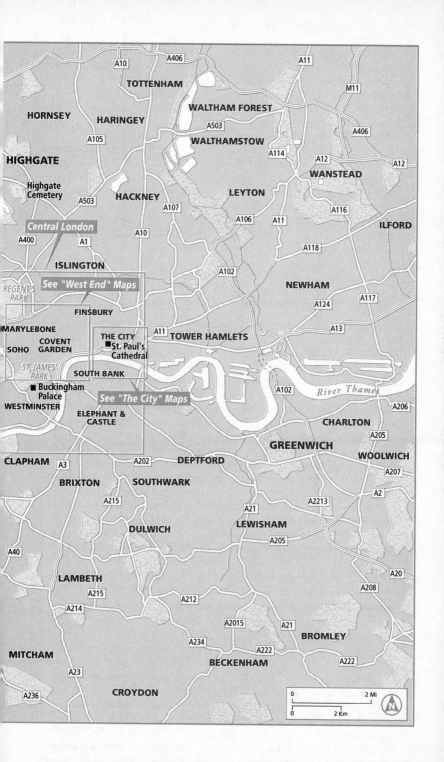

such famous figures as Karl Marx and George Eliot.

Hammersmith Sitting on the north bank of the Thames, just to the west of Kensington, Hammersmith will fool you at first into thinking it's an industrial park, thanks to the stretch of factories between Putney and Hammersmith bridges. Actually, the area is predominantly residential. Its most attractive feature is its waterfront, filled with boathouses, small businesses, some very good restaurants, and artists' studios. Beyond Hammersmith Bridge, the neighborhood blossoms with balconied 18th-century homes behind lime and catalpa trees, more boathouses, and old pubs that spill out onto the riverbank as soon as warm weather hits. Some of London's best chefs have fled the heart of the West End and ridiculous rents to open quality dining rooms here. For our recommendations, see p. 108.

Nearby is the delightful old village of **Barnes,** with its ironwork-decorated Barnes Terrace. **Hammersmith Terrace,** a favorite stamping ground of artists, adds color to the neighborhood. Another stretch of gracious homes lies along **Chiswick Mall,** curling into Church Street. This area deftly imitates an English village before thrusting you back into teeming London along Great West Road.

2 Getting Around

BY PUBLIC TRANSPORTATION

The London Underground and the city's buses operate on the same system of six fare zones. The fare zones radiate out in rings from the central zone 1, which is where most visitors spend the majority of their time. Zone 1 covers the area from Liverpool Street in the east to Notting Hill in the west, and from Waterloo in the south to Baker Street, Euston, and King's Cross in the north. To travel beyond zone 1, you need a two-zone ticket. Note that all one-way, round-trip, and 1-day pass tickets are valid only on the day of purchase. Tube and bus maps should be available at any Underground station. You can also download them before you travel from the excellent **London Transport (LT)** website: www.londontransport.co.uk. (You can also send away for a map by writing to **London Transport,** Travel Information Service, 55 Broadway, London SW1H 0BD.) There are also **LT Information Centres** at several major Tube stations: Euston, King's Cross, Oxford Circus, St. James's Park, Liverpool Street Station, and Piccadilly Circus, as well as in the British Rail stations at Euston and Victoria and in each of the terminals at Heathrow Airport. Most of them are open daily (some close Sun) from at least 9am to 5pm. **A 24-hour public transportation information service** is also available at © 020/7222-1234.

TRAVEL DISCOUNTS   If you plan to use public transportation a lot, investigate the range of fare discounts available. **Travelcards** offer unlimited use of buses, Underground, and British Rail services in Greater London for any period ranging from a day to a year. Travelcards are available from Underground ticket offices, Travel Information Centres, main post offices in the London area, and some newsstands. You need to bring a passport-size photo to purchase a Travelcard; you can take a photo at any of the instant photo booths in London's train stations. Children under age 5 generally travel free on the Tube and buses.

The **One-Day Travelcard** allows you to go anywhere throughout Greater London. For travel anywhere within zones 1 and 2, the cost is £5.30 ($7.95) for adults or £2.60 ($3.90) for children 5 to 15. The **Off-Peak One-Day Travelcard,** which isn't valid until after 9:30am on weekdays (or on night buses), is even cheaper. For two zones, the cost is £4.10 ($6.15) for adults and £2 ($3) for children 5 to 15.

Weekend Travelcards are valid for 1 weekend, plus the Monday if it's a national holiday. They're not valid on night buses. Travel anywhere within zones 1 and 2 for the whole weekend costs £6.10 ($9.15) for adults or £3 ($4.50) for children 5 to 15.

One-Week Travelcards cost adults £21 ($31.50) and children £8.50 ($12.75) for travel in zones 1 and 2.

The 1-day **Family Travelcard** allows as many journeys as you want on the Tube, buses (excluding night buses) displaying the London Transport bus sign, and even the Docklands Light Railway or any rail service within the travel zones designated on your ticket. The family card is valid Monday through Friday after 9:30am and all day on weekends and public holidays. It's available for families as small as two (1 adult and 1 child) to as large as six (2 adults and 4 children). The cost is £3 ($4.50) per adult, 80p ($1.20) per child.

You can also buy **Carnet** tickets, a booklet of 10 single Underground tickets valid for 12 months from the issue date. Carnet tickets are valid for travel only in zone 1 (Central London), and cost £11.50 ($17.25) for adults and £5 ($7.50) for children (up to 15). A book of Carnet tickets gives you a savings of £2 ($3) over the cost of 10 separate single tickets.

THE UNDERGROUND

The Underground, or Tube, is the fastest and easiest way to get around. All Tube stations are clearly marked with a red circle and blue crossbar. Routes are conveniently color-coded.

With British coins, you can get your ticket at a vending machine. Otherwise, buy it at the ticket office. You can transfer as many times as you like, as long as you stay in the Underground. The flat fare for one trip within the central zone is £1.60 ($2.40). Trips from the central zone to destinations in the suburbs range from £1.90 to £3.60 ($2.85–$5.40) in most cases. You can also purchase weekly passes for £16.20 ($24.30) for adults and £6.20 ($9.30) for children in the central zone, or £28.10 ($42.15) for adults and £13 ($19.50) for children for travel in four zones. See "Travel Discounts," above, for information on various types of Underground cards and fare bargains.

Value **Don't Leave Home Without It!**

If you will use public transportation a lot while in London, buy a **London Visitor Travelcard** before you leave home. This card, which allows unlimited transport within all six zones of Greater London's Underground (as far as Heathrow) and bus network, as well as some discounts on London attractions, isn't available in the U.K. A pass for 3 consecutive days of travel is $34 for adults, $15 for children 5 to 15; for 4 consecutive days of travel, it's $43 for adults, $17 for children; and for 7 consecutive days of travel, it's $64 for adults, $27 for children. Contact **BritRail Travel International**, 500 Mamaroneck Ave., Suite 314, Harrison, NY 10528 (© **800/677-8585;** 800/555-2748 in Canada; www.raileurope.com). It will take up to 21 days for the card to reach you at home.

Feed your ticket into the slot at the gate, pick it up as it comes through on the other side and *hold on to it while you ride the Underground*—it must be presented when you exit the station at your destination. If you're caught without a valid ticket, you'll be fined £10 ($15) on the spot. If you owe extra money, you'll be asked to pay the difference by the attendant at the exit. The Tube runs roughly from 5am to 11:30pm. After that you must take a taxi or night bus to your destination. For more information on the London Tube system, call the **London Underground** at ℂ **020/7222-1234,** but expect to stay on hold for a good while before a live person comes on the line. Information is also available on the comprehensive London Transport website, **www.londontransport.co.uk**.

The long-running saga known as the Jubilee Line Extension is beginning to reach completion. This line, which once ended at Charing Cross, has been extended eastward to serve the growing suburbs of the southeast and the Docklands area. This east-west axis helps ease traffic on some of London's most hard-pressed Underground lines. The line also makes it much easier to reach Greenwich.

BY BUS

The first thing you learn about London buses is that nobody just boards them. You "queue up"—that is, form a single-file line at the bus stop.

The comparably priced bus system is almost as good as the Underground and gives you better views of the city. To find out about current routes, pick up a free bus map at one of London Transport's Travel Information Centres, listed above. The map is available in person only, not by mail. You can also obtain a map at **www.londontransport.co.uk/buses/**.

London still has some old-style Routemaster buses, with both driver and conductor. After you board this type of bus, a conductor comes to your seat; you pay a fare based on your destination and receive a ticket in return. This type of bus is being replaced with buses that have only a driver; you pay the driver as you enter and you exit via a rear door. As with the Underground, fares vary according to distance traveled. Generally, bus fares are 70p to £1 ($1.05–$1.50), slightly less than Tube fares. If you travel for two or three stops, the cost is £1.50 ($2.25). If you want your stop called out, simply ask the conductor or driver.

Buses generally run between about 5am and 11:30pm. There are night buses on special routes, running once an hour or so; most pass through Trafalgar Square. Keep in mind that night buses are sometimes so crowded (especially on weekends) that they are unable to pick up passengers after a few stops. You might find yourself waiting a long time, so consider taking a taxi if the bus is too packed. There are various bargains for bus riders including an all-zone 1-day pass for £2 ($3) and an all-zone 7-day pass for £8.50 ($12.75). Call the 24-hour **hot line** (ℂ **020/7222-1234**) for bus schedules and fare information.

BY TAXI

London cabs are among the most comfortable and best designed in the world. You can pick one up either by heading for a cab stand or by hailing one in the street (the taxi is available if the yellow taxi sign on the roof is lit); once they have stopped for you, taxis are obliged to take you anywhere you want to go within 9.5km (6 miles) of the pick-up point, provided it's within the metropolitan area. To **call a cab,** phone ℂ **020/7272-0272** or 020/7253-5000. The minimum taxi fare is £3.80 ($5.70). The meter starts at £3.60 ($5.40), with increments of 20p (35¢) thereafter, based on distance or time. Each additional passenger is charged 40p (70¢). Passengers pay 10p (15¢) for each piece of luggage in the driver's compartment and any other item more than .6m (2 ft.) long. Surcharges are imposed after 8pm and on weekends and public holidays. All these tariffs include VAT. Fares usually increase annually. It's recommended that you tip 10% to 15% of the fare.

If you call for a cab, the meter starts running when the taxi receives instructions from the dispatcher, so you could find that the meter already reads a few pounds more than the initial £3.60 when you step inside.

Minicabs, small cars, are also available, and they're often useful when the regular taxis become scarce or when the Tube stops running. These cabs are meterless, so the fare must be negotiated in advance. Unlike regular cabs, minicabs are forbidden by law to cruise for fares. They operate from sidewalk kiosks, such as those around Leicester Square. If you need to call one, try **Brunswick Chauffeurs/Abbey Cars** (© 020/8969-2555) in west London; **London Cabs, Ltd.** (© 020/8778-3000) in east London; or **Newname Minicars** (© 020/8472-1400) in south London. Minicab kiosks can be found near many Tube or BritRail stops, especially in outlying areas. You can also hail a minicab if you spot one on the street. If you have a complaint about taxi service, or if you leave something in a cab, contact the **Public Carriage Office,** 15 Penton St., N1 9PU (Tube: Angel Station). If it's a complaint, you must have the cab number, which is displayed in the passenger compartment. Call © 020/7230-1631 with complaints.

Cab sharing is permitted in London, with cabbies permitted to carry two to five persons going to different destinations. Taxis accepting such riders display a notice on yellow plastic, with the words "Shared Taxi." Each of two riders sharing is charged 65% of the fare a lone passenger would be charged. Three persons pay 55%, four pay 45%, and five (the seating capacity of all new London cabs) pay 40% of the single-passenger fare.

BY CAR

Don't drive in congested London. It is easy to get around without a car, traffic and parking are nightmares, and depending on where you're from, you mayhave to drive from what you normally consider the passenger seat, on the wrong side of the road. It all adds up to a big headache.

BY BICYCLE

One of the most popular bike rental shops is **On Your Bike,** 52–54 Tooley St., London Bridge, SE1 (© 020/7378-6669; Tube: London Bridge), open Monday through Friday from 9am to 6pm, Saturday from 9:30am to 5:30pm, and Sunday from 11am to 4pm. The first-class mountain bikes, with high seats and low-slung handlebars, cost £15 ($22.50) per day, £30 ($45) per weekend, or £70 ($105) per week, and require a £200 ($300) deposit on a credit card. Heavy traffic makes biking in London's streets difficult, but biking in the parks is a pleasure.

 FAST FACTS: London

American Express The main Amex office is at 30–31 Haymarket, SW1 (© 020/7484-9600; Tube: Piccadilly Circus). Full services are available Monday through Saturday from 9am to 6pm. On Sundays from 10am to 5pm, only the foreign-exchange bureau is open.

Babysitters Babysitting organizations provide registered nurses and carefully screened mothers, as well as trained nannies, as sitters. One such company is **Childminders** (℃ 020/7935-2049; www.babysitter.co.uk; Tube: Baker Street). You pay £6.80 ($10.20) per hour in the daytime and £5.20 to £6.40 ($7.80–$9.60) per hour at night. There's a 4-hour minimum, and hotel guests pay a £10 ($15) booking fee each time they use a sitter. You must also pay reasonable transportation costs.

Business Hours Banks are usually open Monday through Friday from 9:30am to 3:30pm. Business offices are open Monday through Friday from 9am to 5pm; the lunch break lasts an hour, but most places stay open during that time. Pubs and bars stay open from 11am to 11pm Monday through Saturday and from noon to 10:30pm on Sunday. Stores generally open at 9am and close at 5:30pm, staying open until 7pm on Wednesday or Thursday. Most central shops close on Saturday around 1pm. In a recent change, some stores are now open for 6 hours on Sunday, usually from 11am to 5 pm.

Camera Repair **Sendean,** Shop 2, 9–12 St. Anne's Court, W1V (℃ 020/7439-8418), gives free estimates and does quick work. It's open weekdays from 10am to 5:30pm (Fri until 6pm) and accepts MasterCard and Visa.

Climate See "When to Go," in chapter 3.

Currency Exchange See "Money," in chapter 3.

Dentists For dental emergencies, call **Eastman Dental Hospital** (℃ **020/7915-1000;** Tube: King's Cross or Chancery Lane).

Doctors Call ℃ **999** in a medical emergency. Some hotels have physicians on call for emergencies. For non-emergencies try **Medical Express,** 117A Harley St., W1 (℃ **020/7499-1991;** Tube: Regent's Park), a private British clinic; it's not part of the free British medical establishment. For filling the British equivalent of a U.S. prescription, there's sometimes a surcharge of £20 ($30) on top of the cost of the medications. The clinic is open Monday through Friday from 9:30am to 6pm and Saturday from 9:30am to 2:30pm.

Documents See "Entry Requirements & Customs Regulations," in chapter 3.

Drugstores In Britain they're called chemists. Every police station has a list of emergency chemists (dial 0 and ask the operator for the local police). One of the most centrally located, keeping long hours, is **Bliss the Chemist,** 5 Marble Arch, W1 (℃ 020/7723-6116; Tube: Marble Arch), open daily from 9am to midnight. Every London neighborhood has a branch of **Boots the Chemist,** Britain's leading pharmacy, which is also open until midnight.

Electricity British current is 240 volts, AC, so you'll need a converter or transformer for U.S.-made electrical appliances, as well as an adapter that allows the plug to match British outlets. Some (but not all) hotels supply them for guests. If you've forgotten one, you can buy a transformer/adapter at most branches of **Boots the Chemist.**

Embassies & High Commissions If you lose your passport or experience some other emergency, here's a list of addresses and phone numbers: **Australia** The high commission is at Australia House, Strand, WC2 (℃ 020/7379-4334; Tube: Charing Cross or Aldwych); it's open Monday through

Friday from 10am to 4pm. **Canada** The high commission is located at Mac-Donald House, 38 Grosvenor Sq., W1 (© **020/7258-6600;** Tube: Bond Street); it's open Monday through Friday from 8am to 4pm. **Ireland** The embassy is at 17 Grosvenor Place, SW1 (© **020/7235-2171;** Tube: Hyde Park Corner); it's open Monday through Friday from 9:30am to 1pm and 2:15 to 5pm. **New Zealand** The high commission is at New Zealand House, 80 Haymarket at Pall Mall, SW1 (© **020/7930-8422;** Tube: Charing Cross or Piccadilly Circus); it's open Monday through Friday from 9am to 5pm, but hours vary by department. **The United States** The embassy is at 24 Grosvenor Sq., W1 (© **020/7499-9000;** Tube: Bond Street). For passport and visa information, go to the U.S. Passport & Citizenship Unit, 55–56 Upper Brook St., W1 (© **020/7499-9000,** ext. 2563 or 2564; Tube: Marble Arch or Bond Street). Embassy hours are Monday through Friday from 8:30am to 5:30pm. Passport and Citizenship unit hours are Monday through Friday from 8:30am to 11:30am and Monday, Wednesday, and Friday from 2 to 4pm.

Emergencies For police, fire, or an ambulance, dial © **999.**

Eyeglass Repair **David Clulow** has 10 offices in Central London; the one in Soho, 70 Old Compton St., W1 (© **020/7287-1128**), can handle most repairs.

Holidays See "When to Go," in chapter 3.

Hospitals The following offer emergency care in London 24 hours a day, with the first treatment free under the National Health Service: **Royal Free Hospital,** Pond Street, NW3 (© **020/7794-0500;** Tube: Belsize Park), and **University College Hospital,** Grafton Way, WC1 (© **020/7387-9300;** Tube: Warren Street or Euston Square). Many other London hospitals also have accident and emergency departments.

Hot Lines For police or medical emergencies, dial © **999** (no coins required). If you're in some sort of **legal emergency,** call **Release** at © **020/7729-9904,** 24 hours a day. **The Rape Crisis Line** is © **020/7837-1600** or 020/8572-0100, accepting calls after 6pm. **Samaritans,** 46 Marshall St., W1 (© **020/7734-2800;** Tube: Oxford Circus or Piccadilly Circus), maintains a crisis hot line that helps with all kinds of trouble, even threatened suicides. Doors are open from 9am to 9pm daily, and phones are open 24 hours. **Alcoholics Anonymous** (© **020/7833-0022**) answers its hot line daily from 10am to 10pm. The **AIDS** 24-hour hot line is © **0800/567-123.**

Liquor Laws No alcohol is served to anyone under 18. Children under 16 aren't allowed in pubs, except in certain rooms, and then only when accompanied by a parent or guardian. Pubs are open Monday through Saturday from 11am to 11pm and Sunday from noon to 10:30pm. Restaurants are allowed to serve liquor during the same hours as pubs; however, only people eating a meal on the premises can be served. You can buy beer, wine, and liquor in supermarkets, liquor stores (called off-licenses), and many local grocery stores during any hour that pubs are open. In hotels, liquor may be served from 11am to 11pm to both residents and nonresidents; after 11pm, only residents may be served. Any nightclub that charges admission is allowed to serve alcohol until 3am or so. Don't drink and drive; penalties are stiff.

Mail An airmail letter to North America costs 45p (68¢)) for 10 grams; postcards require a 40p (60¢) stamp; letters generally take 7 to 10 days to arrive from the United States. See "Post Offices," below, for locations.

Maps See "Finding Your Way Around," under "Orientation," earlier in this chapter.

Money See "Money," in chapter 3.

Newspapers/Magazines The *Times, Daily Telegraph, Daily Mail,* and *Guardian* are dailies carrying the latest news. The *International Herald Tribune*, published in Paris, and an international edition of *USA Today*, beamed via satellite, are available daily (*USA Today* will be printed as a newsletter). Copies of *Time* and *Newsweek* are sold at most newsstands. Magazines such as *Time Out, City Limits,* and *Where* contain useful information about the latest happenings in London.

Police In an emergency, dial © **999** (no coins required). You can also go to a local police station in central London, including New Scotland Yard, Broadway, SW1 (© **020/7230-1212;** Tube: St. James's Park).

Post Offices The **main post office** is at 24–28 William IV St. (© **020/ 7484-9307;** Tube: Charing Cross). It operates as three separate businesses: inland and international postal service and banking (Mon–Fri 8am–8pm and Sat 9am–8pm); philatelic postage stamp sales (Mon–Sat 8am–8pm) for collectors; and the post shop, selling greeting cards and stationery (Mon–Sat 8am–8pm). Other post offices and post office branches are open Monday through Friday from 9am to 5:30pm and Saturday from 9am to 12:30pm. Many post office branches and some main post offices close for an hour at lunchtime.

Radio There are 24-hour radio channels operating throughout the United Kingdom, including London. They offer mostly pop music and chat shows at night. Some "pirate" stations add more spice. So-called legal FM stations are **BBC1** (104.8); **BBC2** (89.1); **BBC3** (between 90 and 92); and the classical station, **BBC4** (95). There is also the **BBC Greater London Radio** (94.9) station, with lots of rock, plus **LBC Crown** (97.3), with news and reports of "what's on" in London. Pop/rock U.S. style is heard on **Capital FM** (95.8); if you like jazz, reggae, or salsa, tune in to **Choice FM** (96.9). **Jazz FM** (102.2) offers jazz, blues, and big-band music.

Restrooms They're marked by PUBLIC TOILETS signs in streets, parks, and Tube stations; many are automatically sterilized after each use. The English often call toilets "loos." You'll also find well-maintained lavatories in all larger public buildings, such as museums and art galleries, large department stores, and railway stations. It's not really acceptable to use the lavatories in hotels, restaurants, and pubs if you're not a customer, but we can't say that we always stick to this rule. Public lavatories are usually free, but you may need a small coin to get in or to use a proper washroom.

Smoking Most U.S. cigarette brands are available in London. Smoking is forbidden in the Underground (on the cars and the platforms) and on buses, and it's increasingly frowned upon in many other places. But London still isn't a particularly friendly place for the nonsmoker. Most restaurants have nonsmoking tables, but they're usually separated from the smoking section by only a little bit of space. Nonsmoking rooms are available in the bigger hotels. Some of the smaller hotels claim to have nonsmoking rooms, but we've often found that this means the room is smoke-free only during our visit; if you're bothered by the odor, ask to be shown another room.

Taxes   There is a 17.5% national **value-added tax (VAT)** added to all hotel and restaurant bills and included in the price of many items you purchase. It can be refunded if you shop at stores that participate in the Retail Export Scheme (signs are posted in the window). See the "How to Get Your VAT Refund" box in chapter 8.

You also pay a departure tax of £10 ($15) for flights within Britain and the European Union; it's £20 ($30) for flights to the U.S. and other countries. Your airline ticket may or may not include this tax. Ask in advance to avoid a surprise at the gate.

To encourage energy conservation, the British government levies a 25% tax on gasoline (petrol). If you've read our warnings about driving in London, this will be of no importance to you whatsoever.

Taxis   See "Getting Around," earlier in this chapter.

Telephone   For directory assistance in London, dial © 142; for the rest of Britain, © 192.

To call London from the United States, dial **011** (international code), **44** (Britain's country code), **20** (the area code for anywhere in London), and the eight-digit local phone number. Always omit the zero from the area code when calling London from outside of England (London's official area code is 020, but you will dial 20).To make an international call from London, dial the international access code (00), then the country code, then the area code, and finally the local number. Or call through one of the following long-distance access codes: **AT&T USA Direct** (© **0800/ 890011**), **Canada Direct** (© **0800/890016**), **Australia** (© **0800/890061**), and **New Zealand** (© **0800/890064**). Common country codes are **U.S. and Canada**, 1; **Australia**, 61; **New Zealand**, 64; **South Africa**, 27.

To make calls within London, just dial the local seven- or eight-digit number. Phone numbers outside the major cities consist of an exchange name plus telephone number. To dial the number, you need to dial the exchange code first. Information sheets on call-box walls give the codes in most instances. If your code isn't there, call the operator by dialing 100.

There are three types of public pay phones: those taking only coins, those accepting only phonecards (called Cardphones), and those taking both phonecards and credit cards. At coin-operated phones, insert your coins before dialing. The minimum charge is 10p (15¢).

Phonecards are available in four values—£2 ($3), £5 ($7.50), £10 ($15), and £20 ($30)—and are reusable until the total value has expired. Cards can be purchased from newsstands and post offices. You can also use credit cards—Access (MasterCard), Visa, American Express, and Diners Club—at credit-call pay phones, commonly found at airports and large railway stations.

Time   England follows Greenwich Mean Time (5 hr. ahead of Eastern Standard Time). Most of the year Britain is 5 hours ahead of the time observed on the East Coast of the United States. When it's noon in New York, it's

5pm in London. Because the U.S. and Britain observe Daylight Saving Time at slightly different times of year, there's a brief period (about a week) in the spring when London is 6 hours ahead of New York.

Tipping In restaurants, service charges in the 15% to 20% range are usually added to the bill. Sometimes this is clearly marked; at other times, it isn't. When in doubt, ask. If service isn't included, it's customary to add 15% to the bill. Sommeliers get about £1 ($1.50) per bottle of wine served. You can leave small change if the service is good. There's no tipping in pubs. In cocktail bars, the server usually gets about 75p ($1.15) per round of drinks.

Hotels, like restaurants, often add a service charge of 10% to 15% to most bills. In smaller B&Bs, the tip isn't likely to be included. Therefore, tip people who performed special services, such as for the person who served you breakfast. If several persons have served you in a B&B, many guests ask that 10% or 15% be added to the bill and divided among the staff. Tip chambermaids $1 per day for cleaning up (more if you've made their job extra difficult).

It's standard to tip taxi drivers 10% to 15% of the fare, although a tip for a taxi driver should never be less than 30p (45¢), even for a short run. Barbers and hairdressers expect 10% to 15%. Tour guides expect £2 ($3), although it's not mandatory. Theater ushers don't expect tips.

Transit Information See "Getting Around," earlier in this chapter. For more information on travel on London's Tube and bus system, call ℭ **020/7222-1234**, 24 hours a day.

Water London's water is safe to drink. Tap water is free in restaurants, so be sure to ask for it if you don't want to pay for bottled water.

Weather Call ℭ **020/7922-8844** for current weather information, but chances are the line will be busy. You can also tune into 1152 AM (The Voice of London) for weather reports.

5

Where to Stay

More than 10,000 hotel rooms have opened to the public between 2000 and 2002. That's good news given the overcrowding that was plaguing London's accommodations. The downside is that most of these hotels are in districts far from the city center and are of the no-frills budget chain variety.

Some hoteliers have decided to adapt former public or institutional buildings rather than start from scratch. The imposing County Hall building in the S1 district now boasts two chains: a luxurious Marriott and a leaner, meaner Travel Inn. Another trend is a shift away from the West End to such respectable sections as Greenwich (now a virtual suburb of London), Docklands, and even the City (London's financial district).

With all the vast improvements and upgrades made at the turn of the 21st century, chances are you'll like your room. What you won't like is the price. Even if a hotel remains scruffy, London hoteliers have little embarrassment about jacking up prices. Hotels in all categories remain overpriced.

London boasts some of the most famous hotels in the world—temples of luxury like Claridge's and the Dorchester and more recent rivals like the Four Seasons. The problem is that there are too many of these and not enough moderately priced options.

Even at the luxury level, you might be surprised at what you don't get. Many of the stately Victorian and Edwardian gems are so steeped in tradition that they lack many modern conveniences that are standard in other luxury hotels around the world. Some have modernized with a vengeance, but others retain amenities from the Boer War era. London does have some cutting-edge, chintz-free hotels that seem to have been flown in straight from Los Angeles—complete with high-end sound systems and gadget-filled marble bathrooms. However, these cutting edge hotels are not necessarily superior; though they're streamlined and convenient, they frequently lack the personal service and spaciousness that characterize the grand old hotels.

In the late 1990s, the opening of a number of new boutique hotels generated lots of excitement. With their charm, intimacy, and attention to detail, they're an attractive alternative to the larger, stuffier establishments. The "boutiquing" of the hotel scene continues; the city offers more personally run and privately operated hotels than ever. We've surveyed the best of them, concentrating on the reasonably priced choices.

If you're looking for budget options, don't despair. London does have some good-value places in the lower price ranges, and we've included the best of these. An affordable option is a **bed-and-breakfast.** At their best, B&Bs are clean, comfortable, and friendly. Good B&Bs are in short supply; don't reserve a room at one without a recommendation you can trust. The following services will arrange a B&B room for you: **Bed & Breakfast** (© **800/367-4668** in the U.S. or

Tips   **Upstairs, Downstairs**

Elevators are called "lifts." Some of them are just as Victorian as the edifices in which they operate. They are, however, regularly inspected and completely safe. Many hotels (and especially B&Bs) lack even these rudimentary elevators, making them inaccessible for individuals with disabilities. If you have mobility issues, call ahead and make sure there isn't a steep, narrow staircase between the lobby and your guest room.

423/690-8484), and **London Bed & Breakfast Association** (© **800/852-2632** in the U. S., fax 020/8749-7084; fax from U.S. 619/531-1686). **The London Bed and Breakfast Agency Limited** (© **020/7586-2768;** fax 020/7586-6567) is another reputable agency that can provide inexpensive accommodations in selected private homes. Prices range from £23 to £42 ($34.50–$63) per person per night, based on double occupancy, although some will cost a lot more. **US/European B&B** (© **800/872-2632** in the U.S. or 619/531-1179; fax 619/531-1686; www.londonbandb.com) offers B&B accommodations in private family residences or unhosted apartments. Homes are inspected for quality and comfort, amenities, and convenience.

You can almost always get a room at a deluxe hotel if you're willing to pay the price. But during certain peak periods, including the high season (roughly Apr–Oct) and during certain trade shows, seasonal events, and royal occasions, rooms in all kinds of hotels might be snatched up early. Book ahead. If you arrive without a reservation, begin your search for a room as early in the day as possible. If you arrive late at night, you might have to take what you can get, often at a much higher price than you'd like.

A NOTE ABOUT PRICES   Unless otherwise noted, prices are published rack rates for rooms with a private bathroom. Many include breakfast (usually continental) and a 10% to 15% service charge. The British government also imposes a VAT (value-added tax) that adds 17.5% to your bill. This is not included in the prices quoted in the guide. Always ask for a better rate, particularly at the first-class and deluxe hotels (B&Bs generally charge a fixed rate). Parking rates are per night.

RATE REGULATIONS   All hotels, motels, inns, and guesthouses in Britain with four bedrooms or more (including self-catering accommodations) must display notices showing minimum and maximum overnight charges in a prominent place in the reception area or at the entrance, and prices must include any service charge and may include VAT, and it must be made clear whether these items are included; if VAT isn't included, then it must be shown separately. If meals are provided, this must be stated. If prices aren't standard for all rooms, then only the lowest and highest prices need be given.

1 In & Around the City

There are precious few hotels within the confines of the City (the financial district). If you plan to do a lot of business or sightseeing in the City, and you're not very interested in shopping, theater, and nightlife, then the location might be perfect for you. (For a map showing the location of the following hotels as well as restaurants in the City, see "Where to Dine & Stay In and Around 'The City,'" in chapter 6.)

VERY EXPENSIVE

Great Eastern Hotel ★★   Terrence Conran's monolithic hotel is one of only three hotels in London's financial district. One London writer claimed that the City was "nosebleed territory" for visitors to London. "Just try meeting someone for a drink who lives in fashionable Chelsea." In terms of the theater, Great Eastern would be Broadway, The Rookery (see below) a play in New York's West Greenwich Village. Great Eastern lies at the doorstep of two increasingly trendy London "villages," Shoreditch and Hoxton with their explosive arts scenes. Back in 1884, the Great Eastern sprouted up next to the Liverpool Street Station. The building was the creation of Charles Barry, better known for his Houses of Parliament. The hotel was a tired and dreary relic when it closed in 1997. Today, it is abloom outside in all its Victorian glory, with a stained-glass dome and roof towers, but inside it is sleek and modern. Jacob Jacobsen's chrome-plated architect's lamps (those goose-necked ones you find in offices) light up the night. In the bedrooms, the upholstery comes in traditional fabrics such as houndstooth and herringbone. Full bathrooms are state of the art, and the beds offer grand comfort.

Liverpool St., London EC2M 7QN. ⓒ **020/7618-5000.** Fax 020/7618-5001. www.great-eastern-hotel.co.uk. 267 units. £299–£515 ($448.50–$772.50) double. AE, DC, MC, V. Tube: Liverpool Street Station. **Amenities:** 4 restaurants, 3 bars; fitness center; concierge; tour desk; business center; 24-hr. room service; laundry. *In room:* A/C, TV, minibar.

Threadneedles ★★ *(Finds)*   This is the first luxury hotel to be built in the City, home to many of London's major financial institutions. In 1856, the building housing the hotel was constructed as a bank, with solid oak doors and marble columns. The conversion to its new role is successful. Contemporary comforts are found in the midsize to spacious bedrooms and suites. The limestone bathrooms contain tub and shower combination, and there are such elegant touches as Egyptian cotton and duck down duvets on the beds. The luxury boutique hotel lies near the Bank of England, called "The Old Lady of Threadneedle Street"—hence, the name of the hotel.

5 Threadneedles St., London EC2R. ⓒ **020/7432-8450.** Fax 020/7289-4878. www.smallandeleganthotels. com. 69 units. £265–£310 ($397.50–$465) double; from £790 ($1,185) suite. AE, DC, MC, V. Tube: Bank. **Amenities:** Restaurant, bar; health club; concierge; tour desk; 24-hr. room service; babysitting; laundry/ dry cleaning. In room: A/C, TV, minibar, hair dryer, safe.

EXPENSIVE

The Rookery ★ *(Finds)*   Newly fashionable Smithfield, just east of Farringdon Road, now has a quirky hotel. The only remaining Georgian houses in Peter's Lane now form a delightful small hotel a short walk from the Square Mile. The brainchild of Peter McKay and Douglas Blain, who gave the world trendy Hazlitt's in Soho, the Rookery has been restored with its period features relatively intact—even the coal-fired bread ovens still survive in the basement, a former bakery. The decorators spent thousands of hours combing auction rooms, antiques shops, and flea markets for funky, yet elegant pictures, furniture, beds, and carpets to create maximum atmosphere. Regardless of where the bed is from, each is fitted with a superb mattress and fine bed linen. Each room is different and full of character. The Rook's Nest, for example, is on two levels with a 40-foot ceiling, boasting a panoramic view across London's rooftops from

Guide to London Hotel Maps

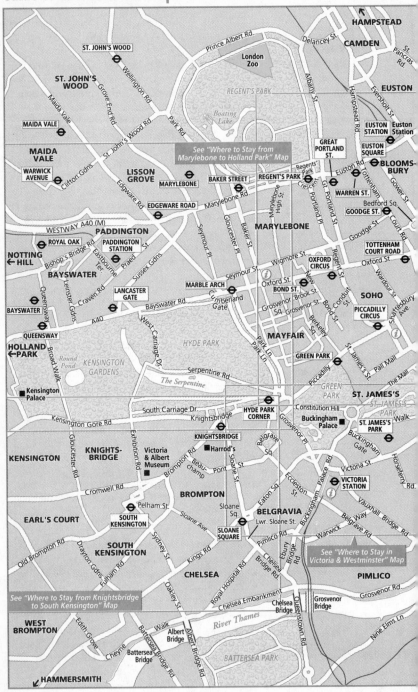

HAMPSTEAD

CAMDEN

St. Pancras Rd.

Delancey St.

Prince Albert Rd.

ST. JOHN'S WOOD

London Zoo

Albany St.

Hampstead Rd.

Eversholt St.

EUSTON

REGENT'S PARK

Euston Rd.

EUSTON STATION · Euston Station

ST. JOHN'S WOOD

Boating Lake

EUSTON SQUARE

BLOOMS-BURY

Wellington Rd.

Grove End Rd.

Park Rd.

MAIDA VALE

Maida Vale

See "Where to Stay from Marylebone to Holland Park" Map

GREAT PORTLAND ST.

Tottenham Court Rd.

Gower St.

MAIDA VALE

Clifton Gdns.

St. John's Wood Rd.

LISSON GROVE

MARYLEBONE

BAKER STREET

REGENT'S PARK

Regents Park Crescent

Euston Rd.

Gt. Portland St.

WARREN ST.

Bedford Sq.

GOODGE ST.

WARWICK AVENUE

Edgware Rd.

Marylebone Rd.

Portland Pl.

Court Rd.

EDGEWARE ROAD

Marylebone High St.

MARYLEBONE

Goodge St.

WESTWAY A40 (M)

Gloucester Pl.

Baker St.

Regent St.

TOTTENHAM COURT ROAD

PADDINGTON

Seymour Pl.

Wigmore St.

OXFORD CIRCUS

Oxford St.

Warburg St.

ROYAL OAK

PADDINGTON STATION

Bishop's Bridge Rd.

Eastbourne Ter.

Praed St.

Sussex Gdns.

Seymour St.

Oxford St.

New Bond St.

SOHO

NOTTING HILL

BAYSWATER

Leinster Gdns.

Craven Rd.

A40

MARBLE ARCH

Cumberland Gate

BOND ST.

Grosvenor Sq.

Brook St.

Grosvenor St.

Bond St.

Berkeley St.

PICCADILLY CIRCUS

Shaftesbury Ave.

LANCASTER GATE

Bayswater Rd.

BAYSWATER

Queensway

MAYFAIR

QUEENSWAY

HYDE PARK

Park Ln.

Park Ln.

GREEN PARK

Piccadilly

St. James's St.

Pall Mall

HOLLAND PARK

Broad Walk

Round Pond

KENSINGTON GARDENS

West Carriage Dr.

Serpentine Rd.

The Serpentine

GREEN PARK

The Mall

ST. JAMES'S

Kensington Palace

South Carriage Dr.

Knightsbridge

HYDE PARK CORNER

Constitution Hill

Buckingham Palace

ST. JAMES'S PARK

Walk

Kensington Gore Rd.

KNIGHTSBRIDGE

Grosvenor Pl.

ST. JAMES'S PARK

Buckingham Gate

KENSINGTON

KNIGHTS-BRIDGE

Victoria & Albert Museum

Harrod's

Brompton Rd.

Beauchamp Pl.

Pont St.

Sloane St.

Belgrave Sq.

Victoria St.

Horseferry Rd.

VICTORIA STATION

Cromwell Rd.

Pelham St.

BROMPTON

Eaton Sq.

Eccleston St.

Buckingham Palace Rd.

EARL'S COURT

SOUTH KENSINGTON

Sloane Ave.

Sloane Sq.

BELGRAVIA

Belgrave Rd.

Old Brompton Rd.

Drayton Gdns.

Sydney Rd.

Fulham Rd.

SOUTH KENSINGTON

SLOANE SQUARE

Lwr. Sloane St.

Pimlico Rd.

Ebury Bridge Rd.

Warwick Way

Belgrave Rd.

Vauxhall Bridge Rd.

Kings Rd.

CHELSEA

Royal Hospital Rd.

Chelsea Bridge Rd.

PIMLICO

Grosvenor Rd.

See "Where to Stay in Victoria & Westminster" Map

WEST BROMPTON

Edith Grove

Cheyne Walk

Battersea Bridge Rd.

Albert Bridge

Albert Bridge Rd.

Chelsea Embankment

River Thames

Chelsea Bridge

Queenstown Rd.

Grosvenor Bridge

Nine Elms Ln.

See "Where to Stay from Knightsbridge to South Kensington" Map

Oakley St.

Battersea Bridge

BATTERSEA PARK

HAMMERSMITH

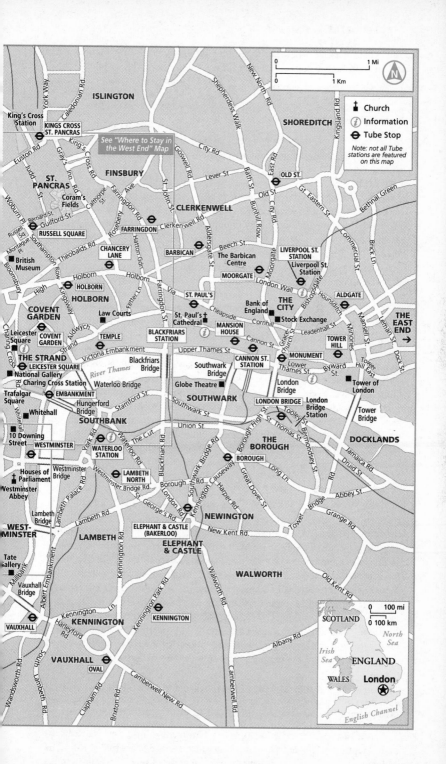

ISLINGTON

King's Cross Station
KINGS CROSS ST. PANCRAS

SHOREDITCH

See "Where to Stay in the West End" Map

ST. PANCRAS

FINSBURY

OLD ST.

Coram's Fields

CLERKENWELL

RUSSELL SQUARE

FARRINGDON

LIVERPOOL ST. STATION

CHANCERY LANE

BARBICAN

The Barbican Centre

Liverpool St. Station

British Museum

MOORGATE

HOLBORN

ST. PAUL'S

London Wall

Bank of England

THE CITY

ALDGATE

HOLBORN

COVENT GARDEN

Law Courts

Cheapside

St. Paul's Cathedral

THE EAST END →

Leicester Square

COVENT GARDEN

TEMPLE

Cornhill

Stock Exchange

TOWER HILL

BLACKFRIARS STATION

MANSION HOUSE

Cannon St.

THE STRAND

LEICESTER SQUARE

Victoria Embankment

Upper Thames St.

CANNON ST. STATION

MONUMENT

National Gallery

Blackfriars Bridge

Lower Thames St.

Charing Cross Station

Waterloo Bridge

Southwark Bridge

London Bridge

Tower of London

EMBANKMENT

Hungerford Bridge

Globe Theatre

SOUTHWARK

LONDON BRIDGE

Tower Bridge

Trafalgar Square

Whitehall

London Bridge Station

SOUTHBANK

Southwark St.

DOCKLANDS

10 Downing Street

WESTMINSTER

Union St.

THE BOROUGH

Houses of Parliament

WATERLOO STATION

BOROUGH

Westminster Abbey

Westminster Bridge

LAMBETH NORTH

WEST-MINSTER

Lambeth Bridge

NEWINGTON

Tate Gallery

LAMBETH

ELEPHANT & CASTLE (BAKERLOO)

New Kent Rd.

Vauxhall Bridge

ELEPHANT & CASTLE

WALWORTH

VAUXHALL

KENNINGTON

KENNINGTON

VAUXHALL

OVAL

St. Paul's to the Old Bailey. The bathrooms with shower-tub combinations are a special treat, with Victorian cast-iron fittings and polished-copper pipe work.

12 Peter's Lane, Cowcross St., London EC1M 6DS. ⓒ **020/7336-0931.** Fax 020/7336-0932. www.rookery hotel.com. 33 units. £225 ($337.50) double; £275 ($412.50) suite. AE, DC, MC, V. Tube: Farringdon. **Amenities:** 24-hr. room service; babysitting; laundry/dry cleaning; a garden (unusual for a City location). *In room:* TV, minibar, fridge, hair dryer, iron/ironing board, safe.

2 The West End

BLOOMSBURY
EXPENSIVE

Academy Hotel ✪ The Academy is in the heart of London's publishing district. Looking out your window, and you'll see where Virginia Woolf and other members of the literary Bloomsbury Group used to pass by. Many original architectural details were preserved when these three 1776 Georgian row houses were joined. The hotel was substantially upgraded in the 1990s, with a bathroom added to every bedroom (whether there was space or not). Fourteen have a tub-shower combination; the rest have showers only. The beds, so they say, were built to "American specifications." True or not, they assure you of a restful night's sleep. Grace notes include the glass panels, colonnades, and intricate plasterwork on the facade. With their overstuffed armchairs and half-canopied beds, rooms here evoke English country-house living, but that of the poorer relations. *Warning:* If you have a problem with stairs, this may not be the place for you—there are no elevators rising to the four floors. Return guests always request rooms opening on the garden in back and not those in front with ducted fresh air, although the front units have double-glazing to cut down on the noise. The theater district and Covent Garden are within walking distance. The in-house, award-winning restaurant, Alchemy, has been recently refurbished to a much more modern design and offers a reasonably priced menu of modern European food.

17–21 Gower St., London WC1E 6HG. ⓒ **800/678-3096** in the U.S., or 020/7631-4115. Fax 020/7636-3442. www.etontownhouse.com. 48 units. £152–£185 ($228–$277.50) double; £205 ($307.50) suite. AE, DC, MC, V. Tube: Tottenham Court Rd., Goodge St., or Russell Sq. **Amenities:** Restaurant, bar; room service; laundry/dry cleaning; library; patio garden. *In room:* A/C, TV, hair dryer, safe.

Blooms Town House Hotel ✪ This restored town house has a pedigree: It stands in what were formerly the grounds of Montague House (now the British Museum). It has had a distinguished, if eccentric, list of former occupants: everybody from Richard Penn (the Whig member of Parliament from Liverpool) to Dr. John Cumming, who firmly believed he'd witness the end of the world (on long winter nights, his ghostly presence has supposedly been spotted). Even though it's in the heart of London, the house has a country-home atmosphere, complete with fireplace, period art, and copies of *Country Life* in the magazine rack. Guests take morning coffee in a walled garden overlooking the British Museum. In summer, light meals are served. The small- to medium-size bedrooms are individually designed with traditional elegance, in beautifully muted tones, each with a firm mattress. The shower-only bathrooms here are well maintained.

7 Montague St., London WC1B 5BP. ⓒ **020/7323-1717.** Fax 020/7636-6498. www.bloomshotel.com. 27 units. £205–£210 ($307.50–$315) double. Extra person £45 ($67.50). AE, DC, MC, V. Tube: Russell Sq. **Amenities:** 24-hr. room service; babysitting; laundry/dry cleaning. *In room:* TV, minibar, coffeemaker, hair dryer.

The Montague on the Gardens ✪✪ This member of the deluxe Red Carnation Hotel Group—others include The Rubens at the Palace (p. 110) and The Milestone (p. 120)—offers a winning combination of plush accommodations and exceptional service. The location is right across the street from the British Museum, and a short walk from the West End and the shopping on Oxford and Bond streets. One staff member aptly describes the Montague as a "country house hotel in the heart of London." The public rooms are meticulously (if not minimally) decorated in various woods, light fabrics, and antiques, conjuring the atmosphere of an expensive manor home. Indulge in afternoon tea on an outdoor patio that overlooks a secluded garden, work out in the small gym, or have a nightcap while listening to live jazz music in the Scottish-themed bar. The cordial and professional staff is extremely helpful.

Guest rooms are individually sized and decorated; most aren't huge, but all are cozy, spotless, and loaded with amenities ranging from bathrobes and slippers to complimentary bottled waters and jellybeans. The beds are most comfortable; some are four-posters and most sport half-canopies. Offering good value for the money are the bi-level deluxe king rooms, which feature pullout couches and would be classified as suites in many other hotels. Rooms overlooking the garden offer the nicest views and are especially quiet, although guaranteeing one for your stay will cost you a bit more. And though some families do stay here, the hotel doesn't offer interconnecting rooms and caters mostly to couples and single travelers. *Note:* Always ask about discount rates when you book; the hotel usually offers a number of promotions throughout the year.

15 Montague St., London WC1B 5BJ. ℂ 877/955-1515 (U.S./Canada), or 020/7627-1001. Fax 020/7637-2516. www.redcarnationhotels.com. 104 units. £135–£230 ($202.50–$345) double; £225–£440 ($337.50–$660) double. AE, DC, MC, V. Tube: Russell Square. **Amenities:** Restaurant, 4 lounges, bar; gym; steam room; sauna; concierge; business center; 24-hr. room service; laundry/dry cleaning/pressing; nonsmoking rooms. *In room:* A/C, TV, fax (in some rooms), tea/coffeemaker, hair dryer, iron, safe.

Myhotel ★ *Finds* Creating shock waves among staid Bloomsbury hoteliers, Myhotel is a London row house on the outside decorated Asian *moderne*-style on its interior. It is designed according to *feng shui* principles—the ancient Chinese art of placement that analyzes the flow of energy in a space. Tipping is discouraged, and each guest is assigned a personal assistant responsible for that guest's happiness. Aimed at today's young, hip traveler, Myhotel lies within a short walk of Covent Garden and the British Museum. The rooms have mirrors but they're positioned so you don't see yourself when you first wake up—*feng shui* rule no. 1 (probably a good rule, *feng shui* or no *feng shui*). Rooms are havens of comfort, taste, and tranquillity. Excellent sleep-inducing beds are found in all rooms, plus a small bathroom with shower stall.

11–13 Bayley St., Bedford Sq., London WC1B 3HD. ℂ 020/7667-6000. Fax 020/7667-6044. www.holidaycity.com/myhotel-london/. 76 units. £195–£225 ($292.50–$337.50) double; from £315 ($472.50) family room. AE, DC, MC, V. Tube: Tottenham Court Rd. **Amenities:** Breakfast cafe, restaurant, bar; 24-hr. room service; babysitting. *In room:* A/C, TV, minibar, hair dryer, safe.

MODERATE

Harlingford Hotel *Value* This hotel is comprised of three town houses built in the 1820s, and joined together around 1900 with a bewildering array of staircases and meandering hallways. Set in the heart of Bloomsbury, it's run by a management that seems genuinely concerned about the welfare of their guests, unlike many of their neighboring rivals. (They even distribute little mincemeat pies to their guests during the Christmas holidays.) Double-glazed windows cut down on the street noise, and all the bedrooms are comfortable and inviting. Shower-only bathrooms are small, however, since the house wasn't originally designed for them. The most comfortable rooms are on the second and third levels, but expect to climb some steep English stairs (there's no elevator). Say no to

Where to Stay in the West End

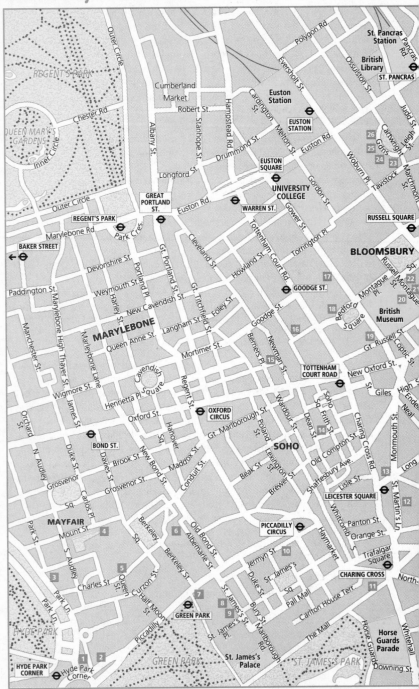

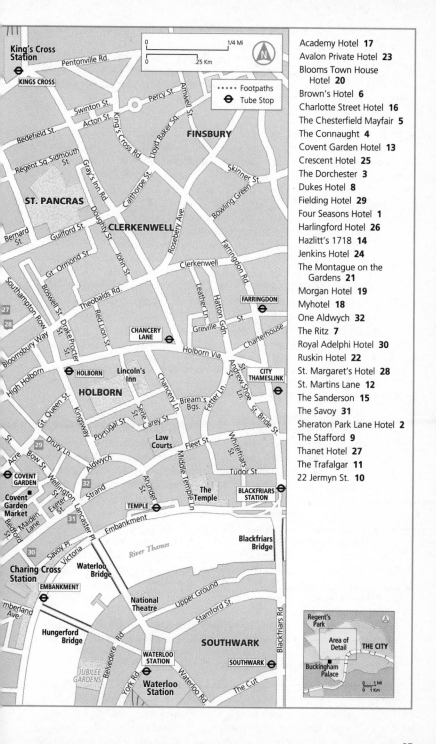

Academy Hotel **17**
Avalon Private Hotel **23**
Blooms Town House Hotel **20**
Brown's Hotel **6**
Charlotte Street Hotel **16**
The Chesterfield Mayfair **5**
The Connaught **4**
Covent Garden Hotel **13**
Crescent Hotel **25**
The Dorchester **3**
Dukes Hotel **8**
Fielding Hotel **29**
Four Seasons Hotel **1**
Harlingford Hotel **26**
Hazlitt's 1718 **14**
Jenkins Hotel **24**
The Montague on the Gardens **21**
Morgan Hotel **19**
Myhotel **18**
One Aldwych **32**
The Ritz **7**
Royal Adelphi Hotel **30**
Ruskin Hotel **22**
St. Margaret's Hotel **28**
St. Martins Lane **12**
The Sanderson **15**
The Savoy **31**
Sheraton Park Lane Hotel **2**
The Stafford **9**
Thanet Hotel **27**
The Trafalgar **11**
22 Jermyn St. **10**

the rooms on ground level, as they are darker and have less security. You'll have use of the tennis courts in Cartwright Gardens.

61–63 Cartwright Gardens, London WC1H 9EL. ℭ 020/7387-1551. Fax 020/7387-4616. www.holidaycity. com. 44 units. £90 ($135) double; £100 ($150) triple; £108 ($162) quad. Rates include English breakfast. AE, DC, MC, V. Tube: Russell Sq., King's Cross, or Euston. **Amenities:** Use of tennis courts in Cartwright Gardens. *In room:* TV, coffeemaker, hair dryer.

INEXPENSIVE

Avalon Private Hotel   A bit of a comedown after the Harlingford (see above), this hotel is easier on the purse. One guidebook from Victoria's day claimed Bloomsbury attracted "medical and other students of both sexes and several nationalities, American folk passing through London, literary persons 'up' for a week or two's reading in the British Museum, and Bohemians pure and simple." The same might be said for today's patrons of this hotel, which was built in 1807 as two Georgian houses in residential Cartwright Gardens. Guests have use of a semiprivate garden across the street with tennis courts. Top-floor rooms, often filled with students, are reached via steep stairs, but bedrooms on the lower levels have easier access. The place obviously didn't hire a decorator—everything is mismatched in the bedrooms and the lounge—but the price is right. The bedrooms were recently renewed with new linens and fresh curtains. Private bathrooms with showers are extremely small. Most guests in rooms without bathrooms have to use the corridor bathrooms (4 bedrooms to a bathroom), which are generally adequate and well maintained.

46–47 Cartwright Gardens, London WC1H 9EL. ℭ 020/7387-2366. Fax 020/7387-5810. www.avalonhotel. co.uk. 28 units (5 with shower). £49 ($73.50) double without shower; £69 ($103.50) double with shower; £59 ($88.50) triple without shower; £79 ($118.50) triple with shower; £69 ($103.50) quad without shower, £89 ($133.50) quad with shower. Rates include English breakfast. AE, DC, MC, V. Tube: Russell Sq., King's Cross, or Euston. **Amenities:** Use of tennis courts; tour desk; laundry. *In room:* TV, coffeemaker, safe.

Crescent Hotel   Although Ruskin and Shelley no longer pass by, the Crescent still stands in the heart of academic London. The private square is owned by the City Guild of Skinners (who are furriers, as you might have guessed) and guarded by the University of London, whose student residential halls are across the street. You have access to the gardens and private tennis courts belonging to the Skinners. Mrs. Bessolo and Mrs. Cockle, the managers, are the kindest hosts along the street; they view Crescent as an extension of their home and welcome you to its comfortably elegant Georgian surroundings, which date from 1810. Some guests have been returning for 4 decades. Bedrooms range from small singles with shared bathrooms to more spacious twin and double rooms with private showers. All have extras such as alarm clocks. Twins and doubles have private plumbing, with tiny bathrooms. Many rooms are singles, however, ranging in price from £45 to £70 ($67.50–$105), depending on the plumbing. The good ladies will even let you do your ironing, so that you'll look sharp when you go out on the town.

49–50 Cartwright Gardens, London WC1H 9EL. ℭ 020/7387-1515. Fax 020/7383-2054. www.crescent hoteloflondon.com. 27 units, 18 with bathroom (some with shower only, some with tub and shower). £87 ($130.50) double with bathroom. Rates include English breakfast. MC, V. Tube: Russell Sq., King's Cross, or Euston. **Amenities:** Use of tennis courts in Cartwright Gardens. *In room:* TV, coffeemaker, hair dryer.

Jenkins Hotel ⚑ *Value*   Followers of the Agatha Christie TV series "Poirot" will recognize this Cartwright Gardens residence—it was featured in the series. The antiques are gone and the rooms are small, but some of the original charm of the Georgian house remains—enough so that the London *Mail on Sunday* proclaimed it one of the "ten best hotel values" in the city. All the rooms have been redecorated and many have been completely refurbished. Only a few rooms have private shower-only bathrooms, and they're quite small, but the corridor bathrooms are adequate and well maintained. The location is great, near the British Museum, London University, theaters, and antiquarian bookshops. There are some drawbacks: no lift and no reception or sitting room. But this is a place where you can settle in and feel at home.

45 Cartwright Gardens, London WC1H 9EH. ☎ 020/7387-2067. Fax 020/7383-3139. www.jenkinshotel. demon.co.uk. 13 units. £85 ($127.50) double; £105 ($157.50) triple. Rates include English breakfast. MC, V. Tube: Russell Sq., King's Cross, or Euston. *In room:* TV, minibar, fridge, coffeemaker, hair dryer, iron/ironing board, safe.

Morgan Hotel   In a row of Georgian houses, each built in the 1790s, this much-restored hotel is easily recognizable by its gold-tipped iron fence railings. The flower boxes outside preview the warmth and hospitality inside. The family management does all the work themselves, and have such a devoted following that it's hard to get a reservation in summer. Several rooms, each individually designed, overlook the British Museum. Even if things are a bit cramped and the stairs are rather steep, the rooms are pleasant and the atmosphere congenial. The carpeted bedrooms in this completely refurbished hotel have big beds (by British standards), dressing tables with mirrors, ample wardrobe space, and batik bedspreads; about 11 of the rooms have air-conditioning. The suites are worth the extra money if you can afford it. They're furnished tastefully with polished dark English pieces, framed English prints, and decorator fabrics, all with spacious bathrooms equipped with showers. Suites also have irons and kitchenettes.

24 Bloomsbury St., London WC1B 3QJ. ☎ 020/7636-3735. Fax 020/7636-3045. 21 units. £90 ($135) double; £135 ($202.50) triple; £125 ($187.50) suite. Rates include English breakfast. MC, V. Tube: Russell Sq. or Tottenham Court Rd. *In room:* TV, kitchenette in suites, hair dryer, iron in suites, safe.

Ruskin Hotel   Although the hotel is named for author John Ruskin, the ghosts of other literary legends who lived nearby haunt you: Mary Shelley plotting her novel, *Frankenstein;* James Barrie fantasizing about *Peter Pan;* and even the provocative Olive Schreiner (1855–1920), who advocated that women should be independent in sexual matters. For 2 decades, this hotel has been managed by a hard-working family that enjoys a repeat clientele. They keep the place spick-and-span, although you shouldn't expect a decorator's flair. The mattresses are good, but the furnishings, although well polished, are worn. Double-glazed windows in the front blot out street noise, but we prefer the old-fashioned chambers in the rear, as they open onto a park. Sorry, no elevator. The greenery in the cellar-level breakfast room provides a nice touch, and the breakfast is big enough to fortify you for a full day at the British Museum next door. *Insider tip:* Although the private bathrooms are small, the shared bathrooms in the hall are generous and well maintained; all have shower units.

23–24 Montague St., London WC1B 5BH. ☎ 020/7636-7388. Fax 020/7323-1662. 32 units, 6 with bathroom. £67 ($100.50) double without bathroom, £84 ($126) double with bathroom; £82 ($123) triple without bathroom, £92 ($138) triple with bathroom. Rates include English breakfast. AE, DC, MC, V. Tube: Russell Sq. or Tottenham Court Rd. *In room:* Coffeemaker, hair dryer, iron/ironing board.

St. Margaret's Hotel   As you trudge along Bedford Place in the footsteps of Hogarth, Yeats, and Dickens, you'll come across this hotel, composed of four interconnected Georgian town houses. Furnishings are a mismatched medley, a bit tattered here and there, but endurable and fine nevertheless. All is forgiven on a spring day when you look out back onto the Duke of Bedford's private gardens in full bloom. Rooms are fairly large, except for a cramped single here or there. Many still retain their original fireplaces, which is how the rooms were once heated. Families should ask for no. 53, with a glassed-in garden along the back. A single guest who doesn't mind sharing a shower-only bathroom will find ample space in no. 24. Guests have use of two lounges, one with a TV. The staff here is so loyal that they often work here, and only here, until they retire.

26 Bedford Place, London WC1B 5JH. ℂ **020/7636-4277.** Fax 020/7323-3066. 64 units, 16 with bathroom (5 with shower). £60.50 ($90.75) double without shower; £75 ($112.50) double with shower; £90 ($135) double with shower and bathroom. Rates include English breakfast. MC, V. Tube: Holborn or Russell Sq. *In room:* TV.

Thanet Hotel   Most of the myriad hotels around Russell Square become almost indistinguishable at some point, but the Thanet stands out. It no longer charges the same rates it did when it appeared in *England on $5 a Day*, but it's still a winning choice, and an affordable option close to the British Museum, the theater district, and Covent Garden. It's a landmark-status building on a quiet Georgian terrace between Russell and Bloomsbury squares. Although it has been restored many times, many original features remain. Third-generation hoteliers,

---

 Family-Friendly Hotels

Although the bulk of their clients are business travelers, the major hotel chains try to create the impression that they are fully geared for family fun. Look for special summer packages at most hotel chains between June and August. Some of the most generous offers come from the **Travelodge** (ℂ **800/435-4542** in the U.S.) and **Hilton International** (ℂ **800/445-8667** in the U.S.) chains. For best results, call the 800 number and ask about family packages. Here are some other family-friendly spots:

Hart House Hotel *(Marylebone; p. 130)*   This small, family-run B&B is right in the center of the West End, near Hyde Park. Many of its rooms are triples; if you need even more room, special family suites, with connecting rooms, can be arranged.

The Colonnade Townhouse *(p. 139)*   In the canal-laced Little Venice section of London, this hotel lets children under 12 stay free in their parents' room. The staff can also arrange babysitting. This residential area is safe, with tree-lined avenues leading down to a canal. With its shops, cafes, and restaurants, Little Venice has a real neighborhood feel to it.

Columbia Hotel *(p. 135)*   A big hotel comprised of five Victorian town houses lies conveniently north of Hyde Park. The hotel has several connecting bedrooms and also offers rooms with four beds at inexpensive rates—great for families on a budget. There are even five-bedroom units if you count a rollaway bed. Nearby bus stops and Underground stations give families immediate access to all parts of London.

James House/Cartref House *(Near Victoria Station; p. 114)*   This is one of London's finest B&Bs. Some of the large accommodations have bunk beds that make them ideal for families.

the Orchard family offers small, adequately furnished rooms. However, scattered throughout the hotel are some unacceptable bedrooms. One guest reported that the foot of her lumpy bed was higher than the head. Try to see the room before accepting it. This place is always full, so it must be doing something right, and indeed many of the bedrooms are fine. It depends largely on which rooms were most recently renovated—ask for those. All rooms are equipped with shower-only bathrooms that are very small but neatly maintained. Washbasins in the bathrooms were designed for Tiny Tim.

8 Bedford Place, London WC1B 5JA. ℂ 020/7636-2869. Fax 020/7323-6676. www.scoot.co.uk/thanet. hotel. 16 units. £92 ($138) double; £99 ($148.50) triple; £108 ($162) quad. Rates include English breakfast. AE, MC, V. Tube: Holborn or Russell Sq. *In room:* TV, coffeemaker, hair dryer.

COVENT GARDEN & THE STRAND
VERY EXPENSIVE

Covent Garden Hotel ★★★   This former hospital building lay neglected for years until it was reconfigured in 1996 by hot hoteliers Tim and Kit Kemp—their flair for interior design is legendary—into one of London's most charming boutique hotels in one of the West End's hippest shopping neighborhoods. *Travel and Leisure* called this hotel one of the 25 hottest places to stay in the *world.* It remains so. Across from Neal's Yard, a charming alleyway, and behind a bottle-green facade reminiscent of a 19th-century storefront, the hotel has a welcoming lobby outfitted with elaborate inlaid furniture and elegant draperies, plus two charming restaurants. Upstairs, above a dramatic stone staircase, soundproof bedrooms are furnished in English style with Asian fabrics, many adorned with hand-embroidered designs. The hotel has a decorative trademark—each room has a clothier's mannequin, a lithe female form draped in the fabric that decorates that particular room. Each room comes with luxurious amenities—two phone lines with voicemail, full marble bathrooms with double vanities, and deep soaking tubs. Some guests prefer the attic rooms with sloping ceilings and small arched windows. The staff works hard to please—the friendly concierge walked blocks in a downpour to hail us a cab.

10 Monmouth St., London WC2H 9HB. ℂ 800/553-6674 in the U.S., or 020/7806-1000. Fax 020/7806-1100. www.firmdale.com. 58 units. £220–£280 ($330–$420) double; £325–£595 ($487.50–$892.50) suite. AE, MC, V. Tube: Covent Garden or Leicester Sq. **Amenities:** Brasserie, bar; small gym; concierge; tour desk; business services; 24-hr. room service; massage; babysitting; laundry; video library. *In room:* A/C, TV, VCR, CD player, minibar, hair dryer, safe.

One Aldwych ★★   Just east of Covent Garden, this five-star hotel occupies the classic-looking 1907 building that served as headquarters for the now defunct *Morning Post.* Before its conversion in 1998, all but a fraction of its interior was gutted and replaced with an artful simplicity. Although a first-rate hostelry in every way, it lacks the cutting-edge chic of the Covent Garden Hotel (see above). Bedrooms are outfitted with simple lines and rich colors and accessorized with raw silk curtains and electrical outlets that can handle both North American and European electrical currents. The bedrooms are sumptuous, with deluxe furnishings; and bathrooms boasting full tubs and showers and luxurious toiletries.

1 Aldwych, London WC2B 4RH. ℂ 800/223-6800 in the U.S., or 020/7300-1000. Fax 020/7300-1001. www.onealdwych.co.uk. 105 units. £310–£325 ($465–$487.50) double; from £475 ($712.50) suite. AE, DC, MC, V. Parking £30 ($45). Tube: Temple. **Amenities:** Restaurant, cafe/bistro; pool; state-of-the-art health club; sauna; concierge; tour desk; 24-hr. room service; massage; babysitting; laundry/dry cleaning. *In room:* A/C, TV, modem, minibar, hair dryer, safe.

The Savoy ✦✦✦   Although not as swank as the Dorchester, this London landmark is the premier hotel in the Strand/Covent Garden area. Richard D'Oyly Carte built it in 1889 as an annex to his nearby Savoy Theatre, where many Gilbert and Sullivan operettas were staged. Each room is individually decorated with color-coordinated accessories, solid and comfortable furniture, large closets, and an eclectic blend of antiques, such as gilt mirrors, Queen Anne chairs, and Victorian sofas. 48 units have their own sitting rooms. The handmade beds, real luxury models, have top-of-the-line crisp linen clothing and lavish appointments. Some bathrooms have shower stalls, but most have a combination shower and tub. Bathrooms are spacious, with deluxe toiletries. The riverview suites are the most sought after, and for good reason—the vistas are the best in London. *Tip:* You can ask for one of the newer rooms in what was formerly a riverview storage space. They are among the best in the hotel, with views of the Thames and Parliament.

The Strand, London WC2R 0EU. ℂ **800/63-SAVOY** in the U.S. or 020/7836-4343. Fax 020/7240-6040. www. savoy-group.co.uk. 263 units. £345–£370 ($517.50–$555) double; from £495 ($742.50) suite. AE, DC, MC, V. Parking £36 ($54). Tube: Charing Cross or Covent Garden. **Amenities:** Celebrated Savoy Grill, River Restaurant overlooking Thames, bistro; city's best health club; valet; concierge; tour desk; business center; 24-hr. room service; laundry/dry cleaning. *In room:* A/C, TV, minibar, fridge, hair dryer, safe.

St. Martins Lane ✦✦✦   "Eccentric and irreverent, with a sense of humor," is how Ian Schrager describes his cutting-edge Covent Garden hotel, which he transformed from a 1960s office building into a chic enclave. This was the first hotel that Schrager designed outside the United States, after a string of successes from New York to West Hollywood. The hip mix of design and a sense of cool have been imported across the pond. Whimsical touches abound. For example, a string of daisies replaces DO NOT DISTURB signs. Rooms are all white, but you can use the full-spectrum lighting to make them any color. Floor-to-ceiling glass windows in every room offer a panoramic view of London, and down comforters and soft pillows ensure a good night's sleep. Some rooms are nonsmoking. Bathrooms are spacious and state-of-the-art, with deluxe toiletries, shower-tub combinations, and full plumbing.

45 St. Martins Lane, London WC2N 4HX. ℂ **020/7300-5500.** Fax 020/7300-5565. www.ianschrager hotels.com. 204 units. £285–£520 ($427.50–$780) double; from £700 ($1,050) suite. AE, DC, MC, V. Tube: Covent Garden or Leicester Sq. **Amenities:** Asia de Cuba restaurant, outdoor garden restaurant, 24-hr. brasserie, bar; gym; concierge; tour desk; business center; 24-hr. room service; laundry/dry cleaning; nonsmoking rooms. *In room:* A/C, TV, minibar, hair dryer, safe.

MODERATE

Fielding Hotel ✦ *Finds*   One of London's more eccentric hotels, the Fielding is cramped, quirky, and quaint, and also an enduring favorite. Luring media types, the hotel is named after novelist Henry Fielding of *Tom Jones* fame, who lived in Broad Court. It lies on a pedestrian street still lined with 19th-century gas lamps; the Royal Opera House is across the street; and the pubs, shops, and restaurants of lively Covent Garden are just beyond the front door. Rooms are small, but charmingly old-fashioned and traditional. Some units are redecorated or at least "touched up" every year. Floors dip and sway, and the furnishings and fabrics have known better times. The bathrooms, some with antiquated plumbing, are equipped with shower-tub combinations. But with a location like this, in the heart of London, the Fielding keeps guests coming back; in fact, many love the hotel's rickety charm. There's no room service or restaurant, but breakfast is served.

4 Broad Ct., Bow St., London WC2B 5QZ. $\textcircled{C}$ **020/7836-8305.** Fax 020/7497-0064. www.the-fielding-hotel. co.uk. 24 units. £100–£130 ($150–$195) double; £140 ($210) triple; £185 ($277.50) suite. AE, DC, MC, V. Tube: Covent Garden. **Amenities:** Bar. *In room:* TV, coffeemaker.

INEXPENSIVE

Royal Adelphi Hotel   If you care most about being in a central location, consider the Royal Adelphi. Close to Covent Garden, the theater district, and Trafalgar Square, it's an unorthodox choice but it's away from the typical B&B stamping grounds. Villiers Street, on which the hotel sits, was named for George Villiers, Duke of Buckingham and 17th-century courtier. The hotel is above an Italian restaurant. Although the bedrooms call to mind London's swinging 1960s heyday, accommodations are decently maintained and comfortable, with good beds. Plumbing, however, is a bit creaky. The lack of air-conditioning can make London feel like summer in the Australian outback during the city's few hot days. London has far better B&Bs, but not in this part of town.

21 Villiers St., London WC2N 6ND. $\textcircled{C}$ **020/7930-8764.** Fax 020/7930-8735. www.royaladelphi.co.uk. 47 units, 34 with bathroom. £68 ($102) double without bathroom; £90 ($135) double with bathroom; £120 ($180) triple with bathroom. Extra bed £15 ($22.50). AE, DC, MC, V. Tube: Charing Cross or Embankment. *In room:* TV, coffeemaker, hair dryer.

TRAFALGAR SQUARE
EXPENSIVE

The Trafalgar ★★   In the heart of landmark Trafalgar Square, this is Hilton's first boutique hotel in London. The chain calls it its first lifestyle hotel, whatever that means. The facade of this 19th-century structure was retained, while the guest rooms inside were rebuilt to modern standards. Because of the original architecture, many of the rooms are uniquely shaped and sometimes offer split-level layouts. Large windows open onto panoramic views of Trafalgar square. The decor in the rooms is minimalist, and comfort is combined with simple luxury, including the deluxe tiled bathrooms with tub and shower combinations. The greatest view of London's cityscape is from the Hilton's rooftop garden.

Unusual for London, the bar, Rockwell, specializes in bourbon, with more than 100 brands. Jago is the hotel's organic produce restaurant serving "comfort food."

2 Spring Gardens, Trafalgar Square, London SW1A 2TS. $\textcircled{C}$ **800/774-1500** in the U.S., or 020/870-2900. Fax 020/870-2911. www.hilton.com. 129 units. £270–£320 ($405–$480) double; from £380 ($570) suite. AE, DC, MC, V. Tube: Charing Cross. **Amenities:** Restaurant; bar; concierge; tour desk; business services; room service; babysitting; laundry/dry cleaning. *In room:* A/C, TV, minibar, hair dryer, safe.

SOHO
VERY EXPENSIVE

The Sanderson ★★★   New York's golden boy hotel designer, Ian Schrager, strikes again. For his latest London hotel, Schrager secured the help of talented partners, Philippe Starck and Andra Andrei, to create an "ethereal, transparent urban spa," in which boring old opaque walls are replaced by glass and layers of curtains. The location is near Oxford Street, north of Soho. The king of New York hip has come to London. The hotel has a lush bamboo-filled roof garden, a large courtyard, and a spa. Alain Ducasse, one of the world's great chefs, directs its restaurant. The accommodations are cutting edge. How does Schrager explain this hotel? Enigmatically he says, "the envelope is minimalist, but the contents are baroque, which gives rise to a certain tension." A former corporate headquarters, the transformation into a hotel has been remarkable, although the dreary aluminum and glass grid facade remains (the minimalist envelope?) Your bed is likely to be an Italian silver-leaf sleigh attended by spidery polished steel night tables and draped with a fringed pashmina shawl the color of dried lemon verbena (a brownish-lavender, in case you were wondering).

50 Berners St., London W1P 3AD. ⓒ 020/7300-1400. Fax 020/7300-1401. www.hotels-london.co.uk/fivestar-sandersons/. 150 units. £235–£650 ($352.50–$975) double. Ask about weekend specials. AE, DC, MC, V. Tube: Oxford Circus. **Amenities:** 2 restaurants, 3 bars, health bar; yoga and fitness studio; concierge; tour desk; children's area; 24-hr. room service; laundry/dry cleaning. *In room:* A/C, TV, minibar, hair dryer, safe.

EXPENSIVE

Charlotte Street Hotel ★★ *(Finds)* Located in North Soho, a short walk from the action of Soho Square, this town house has been converted into a high-end hotel that is London chic at its finest, featuring everything from a Los Angeles–style juice bar to a private screening room. The latter has made it a hit with the movie, fashion, and media crowd, many of whom had never ventured to North Soho before. Since both Charlotte Street and Hazlitt's (see below) attract media folk, what's the difference? One local told us, "Hazlitt's is when you want to land in old-fashioned London, and Charlotte Street is for those who'd like to imagine themselves in California." The hotel achieves a happy blend of old English mixed with hip, modern flair. Midsize to spacious bedrooms have modern English interiors with every amenity from two-line phones with voicemail, to modem points and fax machines. Bathrooms are state of the art, designed in solid granite and oak with twin basins, walk-in showers, even color TVs. Guests relax in the elegant drawing room and library in front of a log-burning fireplace. The library decor evokes memories of the Bloomsbury set of Virginia Woolf.

15 Charlotte St., London W1P 1R3. ⓒ 800/553-6674 in the U.S., or 020/7806-2000. Fax 020/7806-2002. www.firmdale.com. 52 units. £195–£280 ($292.50–$420) double; from £330 ($495) suite. AE, DC, MC, V. Tube: Tottenham Court. **Amenities:** Large brasserie and long pewter bar; gym; concierge; tour desk; 24-hr. room service. *In room:* A/C, TV, VCR, DVD player, minibar, hairdryer, safe.

Hazlitt's 1718 ★★ *(Finds)* This gem, housed in three historic homes on Soho Square, is one of London's best small hotels. Built in 1718, the hotel is named for William Hazlitt, who brought the Unitarian church to Boston, and wrote four volumes on the life of his hero, Napoleon.

Hazlitt's is a favorite with artists, actors, media people, and models. It's eclectic, filled with odds and ends picked up around the country at estate auctions. Some find the Georgian decor a bit spartan, but the 2,000 original prints hanging on the walls brighten it considerably. Many bedrooms have four-poster beds, and some bathrooms have their original claw-foot tubs (only one unit has just a shower). If you can afford it, opt for the elegant Baron Willoughby suite, with its giant four-poster bed and wood-burning fireplace. Some of the floors dip and sway and there's no elevator, but it's all part of the charm. It has just as much character as the quirky Fielding Hotel (see above) but is a lot more comfortable. Some rooms are a bit small, but most are spacious, and all contain state-of-the-art appointments. For example, most of the bathrooms have 19th-century styling with oversize tubs and old brass fittings, but they also have up-to-date plumbing. The showers, however, are mostly hand-held. Accommodations in the back are quieter but perhaps too dark, and only those on the top floor have air-conditioning. Swinging Soho is at your doorstep, and the young, hip staff will be happy to direct you to the local hot spots.

6 Frith St., London W1V 5TZ. © **020/7434-1771.** Fax 020/7439-1524. www.hazlittshotel.com. 23 units. £200 ($300) double; £300 ($450) suite. AE, DC, MC, V. Tube: Leicester Sq. or Tottenham Court Rd. **Amenities:** 24-hr. room service; babysitting; laundry/dry cleaning; video rentals. *In room:* TV, minibar, hair dryer, safe.

MAYFAIR
VERY EXPENSIVE

Brown's Hotel ★★★ Almost every year a new hotel sprouts up trying to evoke an English country house ambience with Chippendale furniture and chintz, but this quintessential town house hotel always comes out on top. James Brown, a former manservant to Lord Byron, who was intimate with the tastes of well-bred gentlemen and wanted to create a dignified, club-like place for them, founded Brown's. Brown's opened its doors in 1837, the same year Queen Victoria took the throne. The hotel is near Green Park, Piccadilly Circus, Soho, and some of the West End's major theaters.

Brown's, which occupies 14 historic houses off Berkeley Square, is still true to its founder's vision. The guest rooms vary in decor, but all show stately, restrained taste; even the washbasins are tasteful antiques. Accommodations, which range from small to extra spacious, have such extras as voicemail, dual phone lines, and dataports. Bathrooms come in a variety of sizes, are equipped with robes, cosmetics, tubs, and showers. In keeping with the atmosphere of the rest of the hotel, the lounges pay homage to the past: They include the Roosevelt Room (TR honeymooned here in 1886), the Rudyard Kipling Room (the author was a frequent visitor), and the paneled St. George's Bar.

Albemarle St., London W1X 4BP. © **020/7493-6020.** Fax 020/7493-9381. www.brownshotel.com. 118 units. £290–£420 ($435–$630) double; from £455 ($682.50) suite. AE, DC, MC, V. Off-site parking £40 ($68). Tube: Green Park. **Amenities:** Restaurant, bar; health club; concierge; tour desk; business center; 24-hr. room service; library. *In room:* A/C, TV, minibar, hair dryer, safe.

The Connaught ★★★ This elegant hotel, in the heart of Mayfair, is one of Europe's most prestigious. It is not the most glamorous, nor even the most fashionable in London, but it nonetheless coddles you in comfort and luxury, with a hospitality that's legendary. It has the atmosphere of a English country house, and guarantees privacy even if you're a film star sex symbol. Barbara Bush would prefer the Connaught. Visiting Saudi princes stay here. Near Grosvenor Square, this brick house is like a club, with many repeat guests demanding their favorite room. You enter a world of fresh flowers, crystal chandeliers, Wedgwood, and antiques. There is something of an aura of aristocratic decay here, just as the country gentry like it. The Dorchester (see below) has more flash.

Rooms range from medium to large, and are a world of antiques, chintz, and tasteful details such as gilt-trimmed white paneling. Sumptuous beds are dressed in the finest Irish linen bed clothing. Marble fireplaces, ornate plasterwork, and oak paneling add to its stately allure. The large, old-fashioned bathrooms are still intact and are outfitted with robes and deep tubs.

The on-site **Grill Connaught Restaurant,** decked out in mahogany paneling, and the smaller Georgian-style **Grill Room,** are among the premier dining venues of London. Yes, they still serve Irish stew on Tuesday, but they also dazzle with the finest haute cuisine of the Escoffier tradition. One loyal patron who comes here twice a week to dine told us, "I picked up the habit from my great-grandfather."

Carlos Place, London W1Y 6AL. © **800/63-SAVOY** in the U.S., or 020/7499-7070. Fax 020/7495-3262. www. savoy-group.co.uk. 92 units. £390–£405 ($585–$607.50) double; from £495 ($742.50) suite. AE, DC, DISC, MC, V. Parking £37 ($55.50). Tube: Green Park. **Amenities:** Restaurant, grill, bar; access to nearby health club;

concierge; tour desk; 24-hr. room service; babysitting; laundry/dry cleaning. *In room:* A/C, TV, minibar, hair dryer, iron/ironing board, safe, trouser press.

The Dorchester ★★★   This is one of London's best hotels. It has all the elegance of the Connaught without the upper-crust attitude that can verge on snobbery. Few hotels have the time-honored experience of "The Dorch," which has maintained a tradition of fine comfort and cuisine since 1931.

Breaking from the neoclassical tradition, the most ambitious architects of the era designed a building of reinforced concrete clothed in terrazzo (polished marble pieces set in cement) slabs. Within, you'll find a 1930s take on Regency motifs: monumental arrangements of flowers and the elegance of the gilded-cage promenade, appropriate for a diplomatic reception, yet with a comfort that puts guests from all over the world at ease. The Dorchester boasts guest rooms outfitted with Irish linen on deluxe mattresses, plus all the gadgetry you'd expect (a button to call waiters, individually controlled heating, and the like), and double- and triple-glazed windows, along with plump armchairs, cherry wood furnishings, and, in many cases, four-poster beds piled high with pillows. The large bathrooms are equally stylish, with Carrara marble and Lalique-style sconces, plus makeup mirrors and toiletries, and deep tubs. The best rooms open onto views of Hyde Park.

The hotel's restaurant, **The Grill Room,** is among the finest establishments in London, and the **Dorchester Bar** is a legendary meeting place. The promenade, with its gloriously lush sofas, is the ideal setting to enjoy afternoon tea and watch the world go by. The hotel also offers Cantonese cuisine at **The Oriental,** London's most exclusive—and expensive—Chinese restaurant.

53 Park Lane, London W1A 2HJ. (✆) **800/727-9820** in the U.S. or 020/7629-8888. Fax 020/7409-0114. www. dorchesterhotel.com. 248 units. £350 ($525) double; from £475 ($712.50) suite. AE, DC, MC, V. Parking £32 ($48). Tube: Hyde Park Corner or Marble Arch. **Amenities:** 3 restaurants, bar; health club; spa; concierge; car rental desk; tour desk; business services; salons; 24-hr. room service; babysitting; laundry/dry cleaning. *In room:* A/C, TV, minibar, hair dryer, iron/ironing board, safe.

Four Seasons Hotel ★★   This deluxe hostelry has captured the imagination of glamour-mongers the world over ever since it was inaugurated by Princess Alexandra in 1970. Its clientele include heads of state, superstars, and top business execs. Sitting tastefully behind a modern facade in one of the most exclusive neighborhoods in the world, it's opposite its major competitors, the London Hilton and the Inter-Continental, but has better food, better rooms, and more style and refinement than either of its rivals. Even so, it falls just a little bit short of the platinum credentials of the longer established Dorchester and Connaught (see above). Inside, acres of superbly crafted paneling and opulent but conservative decor create the impression that the hotel is far older than it is.

The guest rooms are large and beautifully outfitted with well-chosen chintz, reproductions, plush upholstery, and dozens of well-concealed electronic extras. Most rooms are medium size, although some are quite large, and all are maintained in state-of-the-art condition, with plenty of desk space, TV/VCRs, and in many instances tall windows opening to stand-up balconies. Mattresses are of the finest quality, as are the bed linens. Bathrooms are good-size with thought-out extras such as deep tubs, robes, and deluxe toiletries.

Lanes Restaurant is modern and trendy, offering fine hotel dining from an international menu. Tables are arranged for grand views of Park Lane.

Hamilton Place, Park Lane, London W1A 1AZ. (✆) **800/332-3442** in the U.S. or 020/7499-0888. Fax 020/7493-1895. www.fourseasons.com. 220 units. £325–£350 ($487.50–$525) double; £470 ($705) conservatory

---

(*Tips* **The Most Important Meal of the Day**

A **continental breakfast** consists of coffee or tea and some sort of roll or pastry. An **English breakfast** is a fairly lavish, traditionally hearty meal of tea or coffee, cereal, eggs, bacon, ham or sausage, toast, and jam.

---

double; from £590 ($885) suite. AE, DC, MC, V. Parking £26 ($39). Tube: Hyde Park Corner. **Amenities:** Restaurant, bar; fitness club; business services; concierge; tour desk; 24-hr. room service; massage; babysitting; laundry/dry cleaning; garden. *In room:* A/C, TV/VCR, minibar, hair dryer, safe.

Sheraton Park Lane Hotel ★★ Since 1924, this has been the most traditional of the Park Lane mansions, even more so than The Dorchester. The hotel was sold in 1996 to the Sheraton Corporation, which upgraded it but maintained its quintessential Britishness. Today, its Silver Entrance remains an Art Deco marvel that has been used as a backdrop in many films, including the classic BBC miniseries *Brideshead Revisited.*

Overlooking Green Park, the hotel offers luxurious accommodations that are a surprisingly good deal—well, for pricey Park Lane, where anything under $500 a night is a bargain. Many suites have marble fireplaces and original marble bathrooms. The rooms have all benefited from impressive refurbishment. Bathrooms are generally spacious and well equipped with tub-and-shower combos; many also have robes. All have double-glazed windows to block out noise. The most tranquil rooms open onto the rear, but those opening onto the court are dark. In the more deluxe rooms, you get trouser presses and better views.

Piccadilly, London W1Y7BX. © 800/325-3535 in the U.S. or 020/7499-6321. Fax 020/7499-1965. www. sheraton.com. 305 units. £199 ($298.50) double; from £298 ($447) suite. AE, DC, MC, V. Parking £35 ($52.50). Tube: Hyde Park Corner or Green Park. **Amenities:** Restaurant, fabled 1920s palm court; fitness center; concierge; tour desk; business center; 24-hr. room service, laundry/dry cleaning. *In room:* A/C (in most rooms), TV, minibar, hair dryer.

EXPENSIVE

The Chesterfield Mayfair ★ An air of Victorian respectability and easy access to Berkeley Square contribute to the allure of this Mayfair hotel, once partly the home of the Earl of Chesterfield (he resided in the main building). The owners take great pride and care in their decorating techniques: Each room contains rich-looking accessories, an antique or two, or some artifact that suggests a venerable English home. Each bedroom is equipped with an immaculately kept tiled bathroom with tub-and-shower combo.

35 Charles St., London W1J 5EB. © 020/7491-2622. Fax 020/7491-4793. www.redcarnationhotels.com. 110 units. £195–£250 ($292.50–$375) double; £395 ($592.50) suite. AE, DC, MC, V. Tube: Green Park. **Amenities:** Restaurant, supper club and bar; 24-hr. room service; babysitting; laundry/dry cleaning; conservatory. *In room:* A/C, TV, coffeemaker, hair dryer, iron/ironing board, safe.

ST. JAMES'S
VERY EXPENSIVE

Dukes Hotel ★★★ Dukes provides elegance without ostentation in what was presumably someone's "Upstairs, Downstairs" town house. Along with its competitors, the Stafford and 22 Jermyn Street, it caters to those looking for charm, style, and tradition in a hotel. It stands in a quiet courtyard off St. James's Street with turn-of-the-century gas lamps that create the appropriate mood as you walk through the front door. Each well-furnished guest room is decorated in the style of a particular English period, ranging from Regency to Edwardian.

All rooms feature marble bathrooms, equipped with shower-tub combinations. Buckingham Palace, St. James's Palace, and the Houses of Parliament are just a short walk away. Shoppers will appreciate that they're near Bond Street and Piccadilly. Even though it's claustrophobically small—it was once described as England's smallest castle—Dukes offers full hotel services.

35 St. James's Place, London SW1A 1NY. ℂ 800/381-4702 in the U.S. or 020/7491-4840. Fax 020/7493-1264. www.dukeshotel.co.uk. 89 units. £225–£260 ($337.50–$390) double; from £295 ($442.50) suite. AE, DC, MC, V. Parking £32 ($48). Tube: Green Park. **Amenities:** Restaurant bar; small health spa; concierge; tour desk; business services; 24-hr. room service; babysitting; laundry/dry cleaning. *In room:* A/C, TV, minibar, hair dryer, safe.

The Ritz 🏅🏅🏅   Built in the French-Renaissance style and opened by César Ritz in 1906, this hotel, overlooking Green Park, is synonymous with luxury: Gold-leafed molding, marble columns, and potted palms abound, and a gold-leafed statue, *La Source*, adorns the fountain of the Palm Court. After a major restoration, the hotel is better than ever: New carpeting and air-conditioning have been installed, and an overall polishing has recaptured much of the Ritz's original splendor. The Belle Epoque guest rooms, each with its own character, are spacious and comfortable. Many have marble fireplaces, elaborate gilded plasterwork, and a decor of soft pastel hues. A few rooms have their original brass beds and marble fireplaces. The bathrooms are elegantly appointed in either tile or marble and filled with deep tubs with showers, robes, phones, and deluxe toiletries. Corner rooms are grander and more spacious.

The Ritz's **Ritz Palm Court** is still the most fashionable place in London for tea (p. 210). The **Ritz Restaurant,** one of the loveliest dining rooms in the world, has been restored to its original splendor.

150 Piccadilly, London W1J 9BR. ℂ 877/748-9536 or 020/7493-8181. Fax 020/7493-2687. www.theritz london.co.uk. 133 units. £315–£425 ($472.50–$637.50) double; from £495 ($742.50) suite. Children under 12 stay free in parents' room. AE, DC, MC, V. Parking £50 ($75). Tube: Green Park. **Amenities:** Restaurant, Palm Court; fitness center; concierge; tour desk; business services; 24-hr. room service; massage; babysitting; laundry/dry cleaning. *In room:* A/C, TV, minibar, hair dryer, safe.

The Stafford 🏅🏅🏅   Famous for its American Bar, its clubby St. James's address, and the warmth of its Edwardian decor, the Stafford is in a cul-de-sac off one of London's most centrally located and busiest neighborhoods. You can reach it via St. James's Place or through a cobble-covered courtyard known today as the Blue Ball Yard. The recently refurbished late-19th-century hotel has retained a country-house atmosphere, with antique charm and modern amenities. The Stafford competes well with Dukes and 22 Jermyn Street for a tasteful, discerning clientele and seems to maintain a slight edge in attracting an upmarket clientele.

Tips **How to Avoid Getting Knocked Up**

If you don't want a rude awakening, remember to hang the DO NOT DISTURB sign on your doorknob (or bolt the door, if that's an option). English hotel service personnel—most of whom aren't English—have a disconcerting habit of bursting in simultaneously with their knock. (As you might have deduced, "knocking someone up" doesn't have the same meaning in England as it does in the United States.)

All the guest rooms are individually decorated, reflecting the hotel's origins as a private home. Many singles contain queen-size beds. Some of the deluxe units also offer four-posters that make you feel like Henry VIII. Nearly all the bathrooms are clad in marble with tubs and stall showers, toiletries, and chrome fixtures. A few of the hotel's newest accommodations, located in the restored stable mews, require a walk across the yard. These rooms are superior in some ways to those in the main building, and much has been done to preserve their original style, including saving the original A-beams on the upper floors. But you can bet that no 18th-century horse ever slept with the electronic safes, stereo systems, and quality furnishings, mostly antique reproductions, that these rooms feature. Rooms on the top floor are small.

16–18 St. James's Place, London SW1A 1NJ. © **800/525-4800** in the U.S. or 020/7493-0111. Fax 020/7493-7121. www.thestaffordhotel.co.uk. 81 units. £240–£310 ($360–$465) double; from £360 ($540) suite. AE, DC, MC, V. Tube: Green Park. **Amenities:** Restaurant, famous American bar; health club privileges nearby; concierge; tour desk; secretarial services; 24-hr. room service; babysitting; laundry/dry cleaning. *In room:* A/C, TV, hair dryer, safe.

22 Jermyn Street ★★★   This is London's premier town house hotel, a bastion of elegance and discretion. Set behind a facade of gray stone with neoclassical details, this structure, only 50 yards from Piccadilly Circus, was built in 1870 for English gentlemen doing business in London. Since 1915, the Togna family has been in charge. After a radical renovation in 1990, 22 Jermyn revels in its new role as a chic, upscale boutique hotel. It offers an interior filled with greenery, and the kind of art you might find in an elegant private home. On the 6th floor it features one of the best-equipped computer centers in London, which guests may use for free. This hotel doesn't have the bar or restaurant facilities of Stafford or Dukes, but its rooms are more richly appointed, done in traditional English style with fresh flowers and chintz. Beds are luxurious and bathrooms are clad in granite and contain deep tubs and showers, luxurious toiletries, and phones. If you like space, ask for one of the studios in the rear.

22 Jermyn St., London SW1Y 6HL. © **800/682-7808** in the U.S. or 020/7734-2353. Fax 020/7734-0750. www.22jermyn.com. 18 units. £210 ($315) double; from £346 ($519) suite. AE, DC, MC, V. Valet parking £35 ($52.50). Tube: Piccadilly Circus. **Amenities:** Nearby health club; concierge; tour desk; business services; 24-hr. room service; babysitting; laundry/dry cleaning; video library; Internet access. *In room:* TV, minibar, hair dryer, safe.

3 Westminster & Victoria

VERY EXPENSIVE

Goring Hotel ★★★   For tradition and location, the Goring is our first choice in Westminster. Just behind Buckingham Palace, it lies within easy reach of the royal parks, Victoria Station, Westminster Abbey, and the Houses of Parliament. It also offers the finest personal service of all its nearby competitors.

Built in 1910 by O. R. Goring, this was the first hotel in the world to have central heating and a private bathroom in every room. Today's guest rooms still offer all the comforts, including refurbished bathrooms, which are luxurious, with extra-long tubs, red marble walls, dual pedestal basins, bidets, deluxe toiletries, and power showerheads. There is an ongoing refurbishment of all the bedrooms, including frequent replacement of linens. The beds, in fact, are among the most comfortable in London. The rooms overlooking the garden are best. Queen Anne and Chippendale are usually the decor style. The maintenance level is of the highest order. The charm of a traditional English country hotel is conjured in the paneled drawing room, where fires crackle in the ornate fireplaces on nippy evenings. The adjoining bar overlooks the rear gardens.

15 Beeston Place, Grosvenor Gardens, London SW1W OJW. ℭ 020/7396-9000. Fax 020/7834-4393. www. goringhotel.co.uk. 74 units. £240–£295 ($360–$442.50) double; from £320 ($480) suite. AE, DC, MC, V. Parking £25 ($37.50). Tube: Victoria. **Amenities:** Grand afternoon tea in the drawing room (a London highlight), classic restaurant, bar; free use of nearby health club; concierge; tour desk; 24-hr. room service; babysitting; dry cleaning. In room: A/C, TV, hair dryer, safe.

EXPENSIVE

The Rubens at the Palace ★★ *Value*   The very British Rubens is popular with Americans and Europeans seeking traditional English hospitality combined with the latest in creature comforts. And its location is one of the best in town—directly across the street from Buckingham Palace, only a 2-minute walk from Victoria Station. As at all deluxe Red Carnation properties, the public rooms are lavishly decorated with antiques, fabric wall-coverings, and fresh flowers. A pianist plays in the military-style Cavalry Bar, the ideal place for a nightcap, on most evenings. People-watchers should take tea in the Palace Lounge, which offers a view of the comings and goings at the Royal Mews,—you might see Harrods make a delivery to the queen in an old-fashioned horse and buggy. The staff is one of the friendliest we've ever encountered in a London hotel.

The size and decor of the comfortable guest rooms varies, but all have been renovated in the last 2 years and feature a host of amenities, including bathrobes and slippers, complimentary mineral water, and a selection of magazines. Bathrooms vary in size, but almost all have deep tubs. If you want to immerse yourself in the English experience, stay in one of the hotel's new "Royal Rooms." Housed in a private wing, each of the eight rooms is named for an English monarch, and is decorated in the style of that ruler's period, but also features such modern luxuries as DVD players and marble bathrooms with heated floors. Some Royal Rooms aren't particularly big. If it's available and your budget allows, we suggest the Henry the Eighth room, a relatively large Tudor fantasy done up in red and gold, with a half-canopy bed fit for a king, and a spacious marble bathroom. *Note*: Always ask about discount rates and check the hotel's website for specials; the hotel often runs promotions that can make it an exceptionally attractive value option.

39 Buckingham Palace, R.D. London SW1W OPS. ℭ 877/955-1515 (U.S./Canada), or 020/7834-6600. Fax 020/7838-5401. www.redcarnationhotels.com. 174 units. £150–£240 ($225–$360) double; £220–£280 ($330–$420) Royal Room; £245–£490 ($367.50–$735) suite. AE, DC, MC, V. Tube: Victoria: **Amenities:** 2 restaurants, lounge, bar; access to nearby health club; concierge; tour desk; business center; 24-hr. room service; laundry/dry cleaning; nonsmoking rooms. In room: A/C, TV, fax (in some rooms), minibar (in some rooms), tea/coffeemaker, hair dryer, iron, safe.

Tophams Belgravia ✦   Tophams came into being in 1937, when five small row houses were interconnected. With its flower-filled window boxes, the place has a bucolic flavor. It was completely renovated in 1997. The petite informal reception rooms are done in flowery chintzes and antiques. All rooms are tastefully furnished. The best are appointed with four-poster beds and private bathrooms equipped with shower-tub combinations. Not all have private bathrooms—ask for one when making reservations. The restaurant offers traditional and modern English cooking for lunch and dinner. And the location is great, especially if you're planning to cover a lot of ground by Tube or train: it's only a 3-minute walk to Victoria Station.

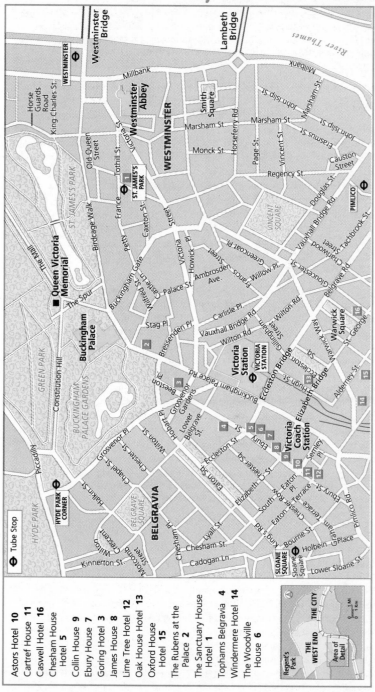

Astors Hotel **10**

Cartref House **11**

Caswell Hotel **16**

Chesham House
Hotel **5**

Collin House **9**

Ebury House **7**

Goring Hotel **3**

James House **8**

Lime Tree Hotel **12**

Oak House Hotel **13**

Oxford House
Hotel **15**

The Rubens at the
Palace **2**

The Sanctuary House
Hotel **1**

Tophams Belgravia **4**

Windermere Hotel **14**

The Woodville
House **6**

28 Ebury St., London SW1W 0LU. © **020/7730-8147.** Fax 020/7823-5966. www.tophams.co.uk. 40 units, 34 with bathroom. £130 ($195) double without bathroom; £140–£150 ($210–$225) double with bathroom; £170 ($255) triple with bathroom. AE, DC, MC, V. Tube: Victoria. **Amenities:** Restaurant, bar; access to nearby health club; room service; babysitting; laundry. *In room:* TV, hair dryer.

MODERATE

Lime Tree Hotel   The Wales-born Davies family, longtime veterans of London's B&B business, have transformed a rundown guesthouse into a cost-conscious, cozy hotel for budget travelers. The simply furnished bedrooms are scattered over four floors of a brick town house; each has been recently refitted with new curtains and cupboards. The front rooms have small balconies overlooking Ebury Street; units in the back don't have balconies, but are quieter and feature views over the hotel's small rose garden. The Lime Tree's rooms tend to be larger than other hotel rooms offered at similar prices, and breakfasts are generous. Six rooms come with a tub-and-shower combo, the rest with shower only. Buckingham Palace, Westminster Abbey, and the Houses of Parliament are within easy reach, as is Harrods. Nearby is the popular Ebury Wine Bar.

135–137 Ebury St., London SW1W 9RA. © **020/7730-8191.** Fax 020/7730-7865. www.limetreehotel.co.uk. 26 units. £115–£120 ($172.50–$180) double. Rates include English breakfast. AE, DC, MC, V. Tube: Victoria. *In room:* Hair dryer, safe.

The Sanctuary House Hotel ★   Only in the new London, where hotels are bursting into bloom like daffodils, would you find a hotel so close to Westminster Abbey. And a pub hotel, no less, with rooms on the upper floors above the tavern. Rooms have a rustic feel, but they have first-rate beds and mattresses, along with newly restored bathrooms with shower-tub combinations and state-of-the-art plumbing. The building was converted by Fuller Smith and Turner, a traditional brewery in Britain. Downstairs, a pub/restaurant, part of The Sanctuary, offers old-style British meals that have ignored changing culinary fashions. "We like tradition," one of the perky staff members told us. "Why must everything be trendy? Some people come to England nostalgic for the old. Let others be trendy." Actually, the food is excellent if you appreciate the roast beef, Welsh lamb, and Dover sole that pleased the palates of Churchill and his contemporaries. Naturally, there's always plenty of brew on tap.

33 Tothill St., London SW1H 9LA. © **020/7799-4044.** Fax 020/7799-3657. www.fullers.co.uk. 34 units. £104–£113 ($156–$169.50) double. AE, DC, MC, V. Parking £24 ($36). Tube: St. James's Park. **Amenities:** Restaurant, pub; room service. *In room:* A/C, TV, coffeemaker, hair dryer.

Windermere Hotel ★ *Value*   This award-winning small hotel is an excellent choice near Victoria Station. The Windermere was built in 1857 as a pair of private dwellings on the site of the old Abbot's Lane. The lane linked Westminster Abbey to its abbot's residence—so all the kings of medieval England trod here. A fine example of early Victorian classical design, the hotel has lots of English character. Most rooms have a small bathroom equipped with a shower; public bathrooms are adequate and well maintained. Rooms come in a wide range of sizes, some accommodating three or four lodgers, but the cheaper ones are somewhat cramped. The ground-floor rooms facing the street tend to be noisy at night.

142–144 Warwick Way, London SW1V 4JE. © **020/7834-5163.** Fax 020/7630-8831. www.windermere-hotel.co.uk. 23 units, 20 with bathroom. £89 ($133.50) double without bathroom; £109 ($163.50) double with bathroom; £139 ($208.50) triple with bathroom; £149 ($223.50) quad with bathroom. AE, MC, V. Tube: Victoria. **Amenities:** Restaurant, bar; limited room service; laundry/dry cleaning. *In room:* TV, coffeemaker, hair dryer, safe.

INEXPENSIVE

Astors Hotel This well-located choice is a stone's throw from Buckingham Palace and a 5-minute walk from Victoria Station. It was once home to Margaret Oliphant (1828–1897), a Victorian novelist; Noel Coward was a neighbor for 20 years, and H. G. Wells, Yeats, Bennett, and Shaw hung out down the street at no. 153 when poet, novelist, and racy autobiographer George Moore (1852–1933) was in residence. The guests today are travelers looking for a decent, affordable address in pricey London. Although more functional than glamorous, the rooms are satisfactory in every way. Much of the hotel, including the shower-only bathrooms, was renovated in 1998. Since space and furnishings vary greatly, ask to take a peek before committing to a room.

110–112 Ebury St., London SW1W 9QD. ℂ 020/7730-3811. Fax 020/7823-6728. www.astors.uk.com. 35 units, 12 with bathroom. £65 ($97.50) double without bathroom, £75 ($112.50) double with bathroom; from £125 ($187.50) family unit with bathroom. Rates include English breakfast. MC, V. Parking £30 ($45) nearby. Tube: Victoria. *In room:* TV, coffeemaker, no phone.

Caswell Hotel Run with consideration and thoughtfulness by Mr. and Mrs. Hare, Caswell is on a cul-de-sac, a calm oasis in a busy area. Mozart lived nearby while he completed his first symphony, as did that "notorious couple" of the literati, Harold Nicholson and Victoria Sackville-West. Beyond the chintz-filled lobby, the decor is understated. There are four floors of well-furnished but not spectacular bedrooms. Private bathrooms are small units with a shower stall; however, corridor bathrooms are adequate and well maintained. How does the Caswell explain their success? One staff member said, "This year's guest is next year's business."

25 Gloucester St., London SW1V 2DB. ℂ 020/7834-6345. www.hotellondon.co.uk. 18 units, 7 with bathroom. £55 ($82.50) double without bathroom, £70 ($105) double with bathroom. Rates include English breakfast. MC, V. Tube: Victoria. *In room:* TV, coffeemaker, hair dryer, safe.

Chesham House Hotel Just 5 minutes from Victoria Station, this hotel is often cited as one of the best B&Bs in London. Although Ebury Street is not as grand as before, it's still prime London real estate. Thomas Wolfe stayed at no. 75 in 1930 while working on *Of Time and the River*. The Chesham House consists of two brick Georgian buildings. Outside is a pair of old-fashioned carriage lamps and window boxes, a facade that has won various prizes in local competitions. The buildings are connected on the top floor and in the basement breakfast area. Livinia Sillars, the leaseholder, has decorated the bedrooms so as to create a warm, cozy ambience. Rooms without private bathrooms have hot and cold running water, with well-maintained and generous shared hallway bathrooms with showers.

64–66 Ebury St., London SW1W 9QD. ℂ 020/7730-8513. Fax 020/7730-1845. www.chesham-house-hotel.com. 23 units, 3 with bathroom. £50 ($75) double without bathroom, £70 ($105) double with bathroom. Rates include English breakfast. AE, MC, V. Tube: Victoria. *In room:* TV, no phone.

Collin House This B&B emerges as a winner on a street lined with the finest Victoria Station–area B&Bs. Queen Victoria was halfway through her long reign when this house was constructed. Private, shower-only bathrooms have been discreetly installed, and everything still works efficiently. For rooms without bathroom, there are adequate hallway facilities, some of which are shared by no more than two rooms. Traffic in this area of London is heavy outside, and the front windows are not soundproof, so be warned if you're a light sleeper. Year after year, owners make improvements in the furnishings and carpets. All bedrooms, which vary in size, are comfortably furnished and well maintained. Two rooms are large enough for families. A generous breakfast awaits you each morning in the basement of this nonsmoking facility.

104 Ebury St., London SW1W 9QD. ℂ and fax **020/7730-8031**. www.collinhouse.co.uk. 12 units, 8 with bathroom (shower only). £68 ($102) double without bathroom, £82 ($123) double with bathroom; £95 ($142.50) triple without bathroom. Rates include English breakfast. No credit cards. Tube: Victoria. **Amenities:** Breakfast room. *In room:* Safe, no phone.

Ebury House   In 1920, Ruth Draper wrote: "I was very lucky in finding a sunny top floor room . . . a lovely big double room in front and I am so comfortably fixed . . . for one guinea a week." Update the price and her statement is true today. On this highly competitive street, this comfortable guesthouse stands out, thanks to the welcome you get from its owner-manager, Peter Evans. The bedrooms, while no pacesetters, are well maintained. The B&B has also recently upgraded its plumbing and installed new shower-only bathrooms, although they're tiny. Guests in rooms without a private bathroom will find a bathroom on each floor, plus a pay phone in one of the stairwells. "We get just as many Canadians and Aussies as Yanks," one of the staff confided. Reserve well in advance in summer. A pine-paneled breakfast room is the morning rendezvous point.

102 Ebury St., London SW1W 9QD. ℂ **020/7730-1350**. Fax 020/7259-0400. www.ebury-house-hotel.com. 13 units, 6 with bathroom. £60 ($90) double without bathroom, £75 ($112.50) double with bathroom; £90 ($135) triple with bathroom; £105 ($157.50) family room for 4 with bathroom. Rates include English breakfast. MC, V. Tube: Victoria. *In room:* TV, hair dryer, no phone.

James House/Cartref House (Kids)   Hailed by many publications, including the *Los Angeles Times,* as one of the top 10 B&B choices in London, James House and Cartref House (across the street from each other) deserve their accolades. Each room is individually designed; some of the large ones have bunk beds that make them suitable for families. Clients in rooms with a private shower-only bathroom will find somewhat cramped quarters, but each room is tidily arranged. Corridor bathrooms are adequate and frequently refurbished. The English breakfast is so generous that you might end up skipping lunch. There's no elevator, but the guests don't seem to mind. Both houses are nonsmoking. You're just a stone's throw from Buckingham Palace should the queen invite you over for tea. *Warning:* Whether or not you like this hotel will depend on your room assignment. Some accommodations are fine but several rooms (often when the other units are full) are hardly large enough to move around in. This is especially true of some third-floor units. Some "bathrooms" reminded us of those found on small ocean-going freighters. Ask before booking.

108 and 129 Ebury St., London SW1W 9QD. James House ℂ **020/7730-7338**; Cartref House ℂ **020/7730-6176**. Fax 020/7730-7338. www.jamesandcartref.co.uk. 21 units, 11 with bathroom. £70 ($105) double without bathroom, £85 ($127.50) double with bathroom; £136 ($204) quad with bathroom. Rates include English breakfast. AE, MC, V. Tube: Victoria. *In room:* TV, hair dryer, no phone.

Oak House Hotel (Finds)   This little jewel of a hotel, perhaps the smallest in the area, is a real find for London, with lots of homespun charm. The Symingtons bring their Scottish hospitality to their home in the Victoria Station area. When Mr. Symington isn't putting on his kilt to do the Scottish war dance, he's out driving a London taxi. Mrs. Symington is here to welcome you to her tidily maintained bedrooms, small yet handsomely furnished and appointed. Half of the rooms have double beds; the others have twins. The closets are small, so you'll have to hang your garments on hooks and store other items on shelves.

Tips **Hot & Cold**

London hotel rooms aren't kept as warm as in other parts of the world. Bring a sweater if you find yourself chilly at a lower-than-usual room temperature. In summer, rooms without air-conditioning can get quite hot. Don't assume that your hotel, even at the luxury level, has central air; many have only partial air-conditioning or none at all. Call ahead and ask if this is a concern for you.

Shower-only bathrooms are adequate and spotlessly maintained. Rooms may be reserved only for 5 or more consecutive days.

29 Hugh St., London SW1V 1QJ. *©* **020/7834-7151.** 6 units. £46 ($69) single or double. No credit cards. Tube: Victoria. *In room:* TV, coffeemaker, hair dryer, no phone.

Oxford House Hotel *(Value)* Just a 10-minute walk from Victoria Station, Oxford House is known for value. Since many of its rooms sleep three to four guests, it's a family favorite as well. Yunus and Terry Kader operate this small hotel like the private family home that it is, and the atmosphere is informal. They even have pets. The biggest drawback is the lack of a private bathroom. Usually occupants of two bedrooms share one shower-only bathroom, so waiting time is minimal. Guests from all over the world converge in the TV lounge. Rooms are midsize and furnished with comfortable, well-chosen pieces, as Mr. Kader is an interior designer. Although in a heavily congested area of London, Cambridge Street is not a major thoroughfare, and rooms, although without double-glazed windows, tend to be tranquil.

92–94 Cambridge St., London SW1V 4QG. *©* **020/7834-6467.** Fax 020/7834-0225. 17 units, none with bathroom. £55 ($82.50) double; £65 ($97.50) triple; £88 ($132) quad. Rates include English breakfast. If you pay by credit card, a 5% surcharge is added. MC, V. Tube: Victoria. *In room:* No phone.

The Woodville House *(Finds)* It's virtually impossible to find a hotel charging a reasonable price in Belgravia. Yet, this small attractive hotel—a converted Georgian town house—amazingly exists, standing right in the center of that very pricey district. The owners are friendly and helpful, providing such thoughtful extras as buckets of ice and a warming cup of tea or coffee. Rooms are individually designed, with tasteful touches like canopied beds, and William Morris Arts and Crafts wallpaper. Rare for London, most of the accommodations are air-conditioned. Standard features include shaver outlets. A hearty English breakfast is served in the attractive dining room, and in the late afternoon guests meet each other and enjoy a drink on the patio. Occupants of 12 bedrooms share 3 bathrooms, so things get a little tight in the mornings.

107 Ebury St., SW1W 9QU. *©* **020/7730-1048.** Fax 020/7730-2547. www.woodvillehouse.co.uk. 12 units, none with bathroom. £62 ($93) double; £90 ($135) family room for 4; £115 ($172.50) family room for 5. Rates include English breakfast. MC, V. Tube: Victoria. *In room:* TV, hair dryer. Phone only for receiving calls.

4 Knightsbridge to South Kensington

KNIGHTSBRIDGE
VERY EXPENSIVE

Basil Street Hotel 🌟 An Edwardian charmer, the Basil is a favorite with travelers whose trips to London wouldn't be complete with a pilgrimage (or 2, or 3) to Harrods—"just 191 steps away." The Chelsea Flower Show is right near as

Where to Stay from Knightsbridge to South Kensington

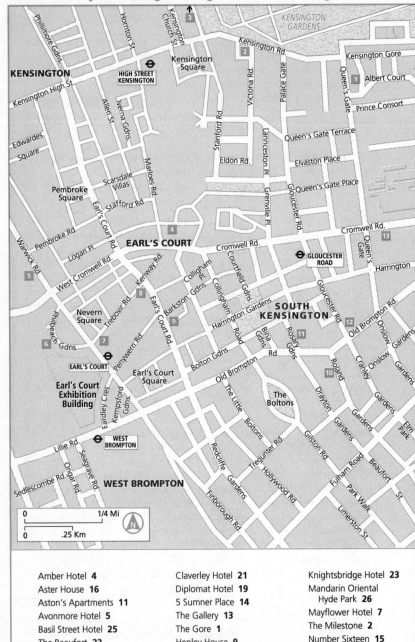

Amber Hotel **4**
Aster House **16**
Aston's Apartments **11**
Avonmore Hotel **5**
Basil Street Hotel **25**
The Beaufort **22**
Blake's Hotel **10**

Claverley Hotel **21**
Diplomat Hotel **19**
5 Sumner Place **14**
The Gallery **13**
The Gore **1**
Henley House **9**
Knightsbridge Green
   Hotel **24**

Knightsbridge Hotel **23**
Mandarin Oriental
   Hyde Park **26**
Mayflower Hotel **7**
The Milestone **2**
Number Sixteen **15**
Philbeach Hotel **6**

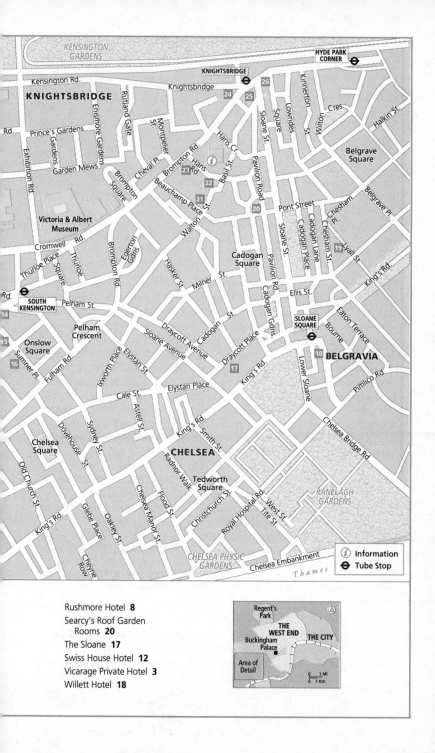

Rushmore Hotel **8**

Searcy's Roof Garden Rooms **20**

The Sloane **17**

Swiss House Hotel **12**

Vicarage Private Hotel **3**

Willett Hotel **18**

well. Several spacious, comfortable lounges are furnished in an English country house style befitting the lord of a manor, and are accented with 18th- and 19th-century accessories. There are smaller sitting rooms off the hotel's many corridors. Rooms come in varying shapes and dimensions, suggesting the era when hotels housed everyone from grand dukes in large suites, to their valets in small rooms on the upper floors. Nearly all units are traditional in decor. Persons with disabilities should check in elsewhere because the stairs make this hotel an Olympic feat to traverse. Even so, some older clients particularly like this hotel, which calls itself a "Hotel for Those Who Hate Hotels." We love its old-fashioned Edwardian gentility, particularly the antiquated bathrooms with deep tubs that still function perfectly. The best rooms are those overlooking the court-yard, because they are the most quiet. Front rooms are subject to the sound of heavy traffic.

8 Basil St., London SW3 1AH. (℡) 020/7581-3311. Fax 020/7581-3693. www.absite.com/basil. £198 ($297) double; £275 ($412.50) family room. AE, DC, MC, V. Parking £26 ($39) at 24-hr. lot nearby. Tube: Knightsbridge. **Amenities:** Restaurant, bar; 24-hr. room service; babysitting; laundry/dry cleaning. In room: TV, coffeemaker, hair dryer.

The Beaufort ★★ If you'd like to stay at one of London's finest boutique hotels, offering personal service in an elegant, tranquil town house atmosphere, head here. The Beaufort, only 200 yards from Harrods, sits on a cul-de-sac behind two Victorian porticoes and an iron fence. Owner Diana Wallis, a television producer, combined a pair of adjacent houses from the 1870s, ripped out the old decor, and created a graceful and stylish hotel that has the feeling of a private house. You register at a small desk extending off a bay-windowed parlor, and then climb the stairway used by the queen of Sweden during her stay. Each guest room is bright and individually decorated in a modern color scheme and adorned with well-chosen paintings by London artists; they come with earphone radios, flowers, and a selection of books. Bedrooms are exceedingly small, but tasteful and efficiently organized. The most deluxe and spacious rooms are in the front. Those in the back are smaller and darker. Included in the rates are a 24-hour free bar, continental breakfast, and light meals from room service, plus English cream tea each afternoon, and brandy, chocolates, and shortbread in each room. The junior suites offer a personal fax/answering machine, modem, and use of a mobile phone. Bathrooms are adequate, with tidy maintenance, and shower-tub combination. The all-female staff is exceedingly helpful.

33 Beaufort Gardens, London SW3 1PP. (℡) 888/668-8141 in the U.S. or Canada, or 020/7584-5252. Fax 020/7589-2834. www.thebeaufort.co.uk. 28 units. £180–£260 ($270–$390) double; £295 ($442.50) junior suite. Rates include continental breakfast, bar, light meals, and afternoon tea. AE, DC, MC, V. Tube: Knightsbridge. **Amenities:** Bar; access to nearby health club; 24-hr. room service; babysitting; laundry/dry cleaning; junior suites include complimentary limo to or from the airport or aromatherapy massage. In room: A/C, TV, VCR, CD player, hair dryer, trouser press.

Mandarin Oriental Hyde Park ★★★ Right on Hyde Park itself, with the Royal household's cavalry trotting by en route to Buckingham Palace, the old Hyde Park Hotel lives again under a new name. This *grande dame,* known for decades as one of the best-located and most glamorous hotels, has garnered praise from all over. In the heart of Knightsbridge, the hotel is consistently voted among the top 100 hotels in the world by numerous rating institutions. It was recently hailed by Condé Nast as the best business hotel in the UK. The hotel's new spa is also one of the finest hotel spas in England. That's not all, as it's Mandarin Bar was voted one of the top 10 bars in London by *The Evening Standard,* and its fine dining restaurant, Foliage, was voted hotel restaurant of the year by *Square Meal* magazine. All of the bedrooms, which are generous in size and maintained beautifully, benefited from a £45 million renovation. Furnishings are deluxe, and comfort is first class all the way. Butlers are assigned to each floor to assist guests.

66 Knightsbridge, SW1X 7LA. © 020/7235-2000. Fax 020/7235-4552. www.mandarinoriental.com. 200 units. £295–£475 ($442.50–$712.50) double; from £495 ($742.50) suite. AE, DC, MC, V. Tube: Knightsbridge. **Amenities:** 2 restaurants; bar; gym; spa; concierge; tour desk; business center; 24-hr. room service; babysitting; laundry/dry cleaning. *In room:* A/C, TV, minibar, hair dryer, safe.

EXPENSIVE

Aster House ★★ *Value* This is the winner of the London Tourism Award for best B&B in London for 2001. It's just as good now as it was then. Within an easy walk of Kensington Palace, the late Princess Diana's home, and the museums of South Kensington, it is a friendly, inviting, and well-decorated lodging on a tree-lined street. The area surrounding the hotel, Sumner Place, looks like a Hollywood set depicting Victorian London. Aster House guests eat breakfast in a sunlit conservatory and can feed the ducks in the pond outside. Since the B&B is a Victorian building spread across five floors, no unit is similar in size or shape to the other. Rooms range from spacious with a four-poster bed to a Tiny Tim special with a single bed. Some beds are draped with fabric tents for extra drama, and each room is individually decorated in the style of an English manor house. The small bathrooms are beautifully kept with shower ("the best in Europe," wrote one guest) or tub and shower.

3 Sumner Place, London SW7 3EE. © 020/7581-5888. Fax 020/7584-4925. http://welcome2london.com/asterhouse/. £135–£180 ($202.50–$270) double. MC, V. Tube: South Kensington. **Amenities:** Lounge, breakfast conservatory. *In room:* A/C, TV, coffeemaker, hair dryer, safe.

Claverley Hotel ★ On a quiet cul-de-sac, this tasteful hotel, one of the neighborhood's very best (and winner of the Spencer Trophy for the Best Bed & Breakfast Hotel in Central London), is just a few blocks from Harrods Department Store. It's a small, cozy place accented with Georgian-era accessories. The lounge has the atmosphere of a country house, and complimentary tea, coffee, and biscuits are served all day in the Reading Room. Most rooms have wall-to-wall carpeting and comfortably upholstered armchairs, and each has a tidy bathroom with a shower stall. Recently refurbished rooms have a marble bathroom and "power shower." Rooms are individually decorated, some with four-poster beds.

13–14 Beaufort Gardens, London SW3 1PS. © 800/747-0398 in the U.S., or 020/7589-8541. Fax 020/7584-3410. www.claverleyhotel.co.uk. 29 units. £120–£190 ($180–$285) double; £160–£215 ($240–$322.50) junior suite. Rates include English breakfast. AE, DC, MC, V. Free parking on weekends. £35 ($52.50) during the week. Tube: Knightsbridge. **Amenities:** Breakfast room; dry cleaning/same-day valet service. *In room:* TV, hair dryer, safe.

Knightsbridge Green Hotel ★ Repeat guests from around the world view this dignified 1890s structure as their home away from home. In 1966, when it was converted into a hotel, the developers kept its wide baseboards, cove moldings, high ceilings, and spacious proportions. Even without kitchens, the well-furnished suites come close to apartment-style living. The well-appointed marble bathrooms come with tubs and power showers. Most rooms are spacious, with custom-made decorator colors and adequate storage space. Bedrooms are often individualized—one has a romantic sleigh bed. This is a solid choice for lodging, just around the corner from Harrods.

159 Knightsbridge, London SW1X 7PD. ℭ **020/7584-6274**. Fax 020/7225-1635. www.theKGHotel.co.uk. 28 units. £145 ($217.50) double; £170 ($255) suite. AE, DC, MC, V. Tube: Knightsbridge. **Amenities:** Limited room service; babysitting; laundry/dry cleaning. *In room:* A/C, TV, hair dryer, coffeemaker, safe.

Knightsbridge Hotel ✪   The Knightsbridge Hotel attracts visitors from all over the world seeking a small, comfortable hotel in a high-rent district, and is popular with families. It's fabulously located, sandwiched between fashionable Beauchamp Place and Harrods, with many of the city's top theaters and museums close at hand. Built in the early 1800s as a private town house, this family-run place sits on a tranquil, tree-lined square, free from traffic. Small and unpretentious, with a subdued Victorian ambience, it's recently been renovated to a high standard. All the well-furnished rooms have shower-only private bathrooms. Most bedrooms are spacious and furnished with traditional English fabrics. The best are numbers 311 and 312 at the rear, each with a pitched ceiling and a small sitting area. Bathrooms are clad in marble or tile.

10 Beaufort Gardens, London SW3 1PT. ℭ **020/7589-9271**. Fax 020/7823-9692. www.firmdalehotels.com. 40 units. £150–£200 ($225–$300) double; from £170 ($255) suite. Rates include English or continental breakfast. AE, MC, V. Tube: Knightsbridge. **Amenities:** Bar; small fitness center; 24-hr. room service; laundry/dry cleaning. *In room:* TV, minibar, hair dryer.

Searcy's Roof Garden Rooms ✪ *(Finds)*   Searcy's, one of London's best catering firms, operates the surprise of the year: an old pumping station that has been turned into a hotel that's only a hop, skip, and a jump from Harrods and the boutiques of Sloane Street. At this Knightsbridge oasis, you press a buzzer and are admitted to a freight elevator that carries you to the third floor. Upstairs you encounter handsomely furnished rooms with occasional antiques, tasteful fabrics, comfortable beds (some with canopies), and often a sitting alcove. Coming as a surprise, some of the bathtubs are placed right in the room instead of in a separate unit. Opt, if possible, for rooms 7, 14, and 15. For an extra charge, the staff will bring you a continental breakfast.

30 Pavilion Rd., London SW1X 0HJ. ℭ **020/7584-4921**. Fax 020/7823-8694. www.searcys.co.uk/roofgardens.html. 10 units. £130 ($195) double; £160–£190 ($240–$285) apt. AE, DC, MC, V. Tube: Knightsbridge. **Amenities:** Communal kitchen; rooftop garden. *In room:* TV, hair dryer, safe.

KENSINGTON
VERY EXPENSIVE

The Milestone ✪✪✪ *(Kids)*   This outstanding boutique hotel, conveniently located in a Victorian town house across the street from Kensington Palace, offers modern luxury in an intimate, traditional setting. The Milestone's beautiful public rooms are awash with fresh flowers, dark woods, antique furnishings, and fabric wall coverings, creating the cozy atmosphere of a private manor home. But it's the service that really sets this property apart. The staff is gracious, and guests aren't just pampered—they're spoiled rotten. Highlights include a welcome basket of tea and fruit upon arrival, bathrobes and slippers, complimentary umbrellas, CD players equipped with music pre-selected by guests, and deluxe toiletries and scented candles in the bathrooms. There's a small but well-equipped health club—a real rarity in London hotels of this size. And this is one of the few luxury hotels we've seen where the staff dotes on children just as much as they do on adults.

Guest rooms and suites are spread over six floors and vary in size and shape (a few rooms are a bit small). They feature a full range of amenities, luxurious beds, and marble bathrooms, some of which have Jacuzzis. All accommodations are individually and creatively decorated, though some are more theme-intensive

Book your air, hotel, and transportation all in one place.

Hotel or hostel? Cruise or canoe? Car? Plane? Camel? Wherever you're going, visit Yahoo! Travel and get total control over your arrangements. Even choose your seat assignment. So. One hump or two? travel.yahoo.com

YAHOO!
Travel

than others. The masculine Savile Row Room is "papered" in pinstriped material and sports a tailor's dummy and books on men's fashion; the serene Royal Studio has a small balcony and a magnificent sleigh bed; and the bi-level Club Suite offers an English library-style lounge, complete with an antique billiards table. You can request rooms overlooking the palace and Kensington Gardens, but be advised that these have original leaded windows, which look wonderful but can't be double-glazed, so traffic noise does leak through. *Note:* This hotel often offers special deals on its website, so it's possible to stay here for a princely rather than kingly sum.

1 Kensington Court, London W8 5DL. ℂ **877/955-1515** (U.S./Canada), or 020/7917-1000. Fax 020/7917-1010. www.redcarnationhotels.com. 57 units. £250–£325 ($375–$487.50) double; £380–£800 ($570–$1,200) suite. AE, DC, MC, V. Tube: Kensington High Street. **Amenities:** Restaurant, 2 lounges, bar; health club; Jacuzzi; concierge; business center; 24-hr. room service; babysitting; laundry/dry cleaning/pressing; non-smoking rooms. *In room:* A/C, TV/DVD w/pay movies, fax, dataport (with U.S. modem lines), minibar, tea/coffeemaker, hair dryer, iron, safe, 24-hr. butler service (suites only).

BELGRAVIA
EXPENSIVE

Diplomat Hotel ⭐ Part of the Diplomat's charm is that it is small and reasonably priced in an otherwise prohibitively expensive neighborhood. Only minutes from Harrods Department Store, it was built in 1882 as a private residence by the noted architect Thomas Cubbitt. It's very well appointed: The registration desk is framed by the sweep of a partially gilded circular staircase; above it, cherubs gaze down from a Regency-era chandelier. The staff is helpful, well mannered, and discreet. The high-ceilinged guest rooms are tastefully done in Victorian style, and many were renovated in 1996. You get good—not grand—comfort here. Rooms are a bit small and usually furnished with twin beds. Bathrooms are also small but well maintained; they have shower stalls.

2 Chesham St., London SW1X 8DT. ℂ **020/7235-1544.** Fax 020/7259-6153. www.btinternet.com/~diplomat. hotel. 27 units. £120–£175 ($180–$262.50) double. Rates include English buffet breakfast. AE, DC, MC, V. Tube: Sloane Sq. or Knightsbridge. **Amenities:** Snack bar; nearby health club; business services; back-and-neck shiatsu massage to arriving guests; dry cleaning. *In room:* TV, coffeemaker, hair dryer.

CHELSEA
EXPENSIVE

The Sloane ⭐⭐ This "toff" (dandy, in case you were wondering) address, a redbrick Victorian-era town house that has been tastefully renovated during recent years, is located in Chelsea near Sloane Square. It combines valuable 19th-century antiques with modern comforts—if you happen to admire a piece of furniture, the staff at the front desk will probably quote you a price that could be attractive enough for you to actually buy it. Our favorite spot here is the rooftop terrace; with views opening onto Chelsea, it's ideal for a relaxing breakfast or drink. Bedrooms come in varying sizes, ranging from small to spacious, but all are opulently furnished with flouncy draperies, tasteful fabrics, and sumptuous beds. Many rooms have draped four-poster or canopied beds and, of course, antiques. The deluxe bathrooms have combination tub and shower, with chrome power showers, and wall-width mirrors (in most rooms) and luxurious toiletries.

29 Draycott Place, London SW3 2SH. ℂ **800/324-9960** in the U.S., or 020/7581-5757. Fax 020/7584-1348. www.sloanehotel.com. 22 units. £150–£240 ($225–$360) double; £225 ($337.50) suite. AE, DC, MC, V. Tube: Sloane Sq. **Amenities:** Light meals 24-hr. a day; 24-hr. room service; massage; laundry/dry cleaning. *In room:* A/C, TV.

MODERATE

Willett Hotel ★ *Value*   On a tree-lined street leading off Sloane Square, this dignified Victorian town house lies in the heart of Chelsea. Named for the famous London architect, William Willett, its stained glass and chandeliers reflect the opulence of the days when Prince Edward was on the throne. Under a mansard roof, with bay windows projecting, the hotel is a 5-minute walk from the shopping mecca of King's Road and close to such stores as Peter Jones, Harrods, and Harvey Nichols. Individually decorated bedrooms come in a wide range of sizes. All rooms have well-kept bathrooms, equipped with shower-tub combinations. Some are first class with swagged draperies, matching armchairs, and canopied beds. But a few of the twins are best left for Lilliputians.

32 Sloane Gardens, London SW1 8DJ. ℂ 020/7824-8415. Fax 020/7730-4830. www.eeh.co.uk. 19 units. £110–£175 ($165–$262.50) double. Rates include English or continental breakfast. AE, DC, MC, V. Tube: Sloane Sq. *In room:* TV, fridge, coffeemaker, hair dryer, trouser press.

SOUTH KENSINGTON
VERY EXPENSIVE

Blake's Hotel ★★★   Actress Anouska Hempel's opulent and highly individual creation is one of London's best small hotels. No expense was spared in converting this former row of Victorian town houses into one of the city's most original hotels. It offers an Arabian Nights atmosphere down in old Kensington: The richly appointed lobby boasts British Raj–era furniture from India; and individually decorated, elaborately appointed rooms contain such treasures and touches as Venetian glassware, cloth-covered walls, swagged draperies, even Empress Josephine's daybed. Live out your fantasy: Choose an ancient Egyptian funeral barge or a 16th-century Venetian boudoir. Rooms in the older section have the least space and aren't air-conditioned, but are chic nevertheless. Beds are deluxe, and the marble bathrooms are richly appointed with combo tub and shower and robes. Rooms also have dataports. Go for a deluxe room if you can manage it; the standard singles and doubles are tiny.

33 Roland Gardens, London SW7 3PF. ℂ **800/926-3173** in the U.S. or 020/7370-6701. Fax 020/7373-0442. www.blakeshotels.com. 51 units. £255–£335 ($382.50–$502.50) double; from £545 ($817.50) suite. AE, DC, MC, V. Parking £32 ($48). Tube: Old Brompton Rd. **Amenities:** Restaurant; access to nearby health club; concierge; tour desk; secretarial services; 24-hr. room service; massage; babysitting; laundry/dry cleaning. *In room:* TV, minibar, hair dryer, safe.

EXPENSIVE

5 Sumner Place ★   This little charmer is frequently cited as one of the best B&Bs in the greater Kensington area, and we agree. Completely restored in an elegant, classically English style that captures the flavor of the bygone Victorian era, this terrace (ca. 1848) house enjoys landmark status. You'll feel the warm ambience as soon as you enter the reception hall and are welcomed by the staff. After you register, you're given your own front-door key, and London is yours. An elevator takes you up to the guest floors, where the well-maintained rooms are tastefully done in period furnishings, and all have refrigerators. Bedrooms are medium size, with extremely comfortable, soft beds. Bathrooms are small but tidily kept and supplied with a shower. The breakfast room is a Victorian-style conservatory with greenery, which leads out onto a patio where you can relax in warm weather.

5 Sumner Place, London SW7 3EE. ℂ **020/7584-7586.** Fax 020/7823-9962. www.sumnerplace.com. 14 units. £130–£140 ($195–$210) double. Rates include English breakfast. AE, MC, V. Parking £20 ($30). Tube: South Kensington. **Amenities:** Room service; laundry/dry cleaning. *In room:* TV, refrigerator, hair dryer, iron.

The Gore ★★ Once owned by the Marquess of Queensberry's family, the Gore has been a hotel since 1892, and it's always been one of our favorites. Victorians would still feel at home here among the walnut and mahogany woods, Oriental carpets, and walls covered in antique photos and some 4,000 English prints. The Gore has always been known for eccentricity. Each room is different, so try to find one that suits your personality. The Venus Room has a bed once owned by Judy Garland. The dark-paneled Tudor Room is the most fascinating, with its gallery and fireplace. Rooms no longer go for the 1892 price of 50p, but they're still a good value (yes, even at $300 a night). Although most are a bit small, there is room enough for a sitting area. Well-maintained bathrooms have custom brass taps. Some units have a shower stall but no tub, although most have a tub-and-shower combination. Some of the plumbing would be familiar to Queen Victoria, but everything works smoothly. Many rooms feature four-poster beds.

189 Queen's Gate, London SW7 5EX. ℂ 800/637-7200 in the U.S. or 020/7584-6601. Fax 020/7589-8127. www.gorehotel.com. 53 units. £194 ($291) double; £285–£338 ($427.50–$507) suite. AE, DC, MC, V. Tube: Gloucester Rd. **Amenities:** Restaurant; bar; access to health club next door; secretarial services; room service; babysitting; laundry/dry cleaning. *In room:* TV, minibar, hair dryer.

Number Sixteen ★ This luxurious pension is composed of four early-Victorian town houses linked together. The hotel was named the best B&B in London in 1992, and the high standards remain. The scrupulously maintained front and rear gardens make this one of the most idyllic spots on the street. The rooms are done in an eclectic mix of English antiques and modern paintings, although some look a little faded. The rooms range from small to spacious and have themes such as tartan or maritime. The beds are comfortable, and bathrooms are tiled and outfitted with vanity mirrors, heated towel racks, and hand-held showers over small tubs. There's an honor-system bar in the library. On chilly days, a fire roars in the fireplace of the flowery drawing room, although some prefer the more masculine library. Breakfast is served in your bedroom. You can also take breakfast in the conservatory or, if the weather's good, in the garden, with its bubbling fountain and fishpond.

16 Sumner Place, London SW7 3EG. ℂ 800/592-5387 in the U.S. or 020/7589-5232. Fax 020/7584-8615. www.numbersixteenhotel.co.uk. 39 units, 35 with bathroom. £145 ($217.50) double without bathroom; £170–£195 ($255–$292.50) double with bathroom; £210 ($315) suite. Rates include continental breakfast. AE, DC, MC, V. Parking £25 ($37.50). Tube: South Kensington. **Amenities:** Access to nearby health club; babysitting; laundry/dry cleaning; conservatory. *In room:* TV, minibar, hair dryer, safe.

MODERATE

Avonmore Hotel ★ *Finds* The recently refurbished Avonmore is easily accessible to West End theaters and shops, yet it's located in a quiet neighborhood, only 2 minutes from the West Kensington stop on the District Line. This privately owned place—a former National Award winner as the best private hotel in London—boasts wall-to-wall carpeting and radio alarms in each tastefully decorated room. All rooms have small shower-only bathrooms. The owner, Margaret McKenzie, provides lots of personal service. An English breakfast is served in a cheerful breakfast room, and a wide range of drinks is available in the cozy bar.

66 Avonmore Rd., London W14 8RS. ℂ 020/7603-4296. Fax 020/7603-4035. www.avonmorehotel.co.uk. 9 units. £100 ($150) double; £120 ($180) triple. Rates include English breakfast. AE, MC, V. Tube: West Kensington. **Amenities:** Bar; room service; babysitting; laundry/dry cleaning. *In room:* TV, minibar, coffeemaker, hair dryer.

The Gallery ⭐ *Finds*   This is the place to go if you want to stay in an exclusive little town house hotel, but don't want to pay £300 a night for the privilege. Two splendid Georgian residences have been restored and converted into this remarkable hotel (which remains relatively unknown). The location is ideal, near the Victoria and Albert Museum, Royal Albert Hall, Harrods, Knightsbridge, and King's Road. Bedrooms are individually designed and elegantly decorated in Laura Ashley style, with half-canopied beds and luxurious marble-tiled bathrooms with brass fittings and tub-and-shower combos. The junior suites have private roof terraces, minibars, Jacuzzis, and air-conditioning. A team of butlers takes care of everything. The lounge, with its mahogany paneling and moldings and deep colors, has the ambience of a private club. The drawing room beckons you to relax and read in a quiet corner. The Gallery Room displays works for sale by known and unknown artists.

8–10 Queensberry Place, London SW7 2EA. 📞 020/7915-0000. Fax 020/7915-4400. www.eeh.co.uk. 36 units. £130–£145 ($195–$217.50) double; from £220 ($330) junior suite. Extra bed £35 ($52.50). Rates include buffet English breakfast. AE, DC, MC, V. Tube: South Kensington. **Amenities:** Bar; access to nearby health club; babysitting; laundry/dry cleaning; 24-hr. butler service. *In room:* TV, coffeemaker, hair dryer, safe.

INEXPENSIVE

Aston's Apartments ⭐ *Value*   This carefully restored row of Victorian town houses offers comfortably furnished studios and suites that are among London's best values. Heavy oak doors and 18th-century hunting pictures give the foyer a rich traditional atmosphere. Accommodations range in size and style from budget to designer; every one has a compact but complete kitchenette concealed behind doors. The air-conditioned designer studios and two-room designer suites are decorated with rich fabrics and furnishings, and each has its own marble bathroom with a shower.

39 Rosary Gardens, London SW7 4NQ. 📞 800/525-2810 in the U.S., or 020/7590-6000. Fax 020/7590-6060. www.astons-apartments.com. 76 units. Standard studios £90 ($135) double; £125 ($187.50) triple; £165 ($247.50) quad. Designer studios £125 ($187.50) double. AE, MC, V. Tube: South Kensington. **Amenities:** Secretarial services; laundry. *In room:* A/C, TV, kitchenette, coffeemaker, hair dryer, iron/ironing board.

Swiss House Hotel ⭐   This appealing B&B, in a Victorian row house, has a portico festooned with flowers and vines. It's conveniently located in the heart of South Kensington, near the museums, Kensington Gardens, and the main exhibition centers of Earl's Court and Olympia. Some of the individually designed country-style guest rooms have fireplaces, and there's enough chintz to please even the most avid Anglophile. Try to avoid the rooms along the street—traffic is heavy, and even with double-glazing, rooms get noisy. Instead, book one of the rear bedrooms, which overlook a communal garden and have a view of the London skyline. Most of the rooms are small, but beds are quite comfortable. Sometimes there's a private safe in the room. Bathrooms are also small and contain shower stalls. And there's a luxury that you won't get in most B&Bs: Room service—nothing elaborate, just soup and sandwiches—is available from noon to 9pm.

171 Old Brompton Rd., London SW5 0AN. 📞 and fax 020/7373-2769. www.swiss-hh.demon.co.uk. 16 units. £110 ($165) double; £140 ($210) triple with bathroom; £140 ($210) quad with bathroom. Rates include continental breakfast. AE, DC, MC, V. Tube: Gloucester Rd. **Amenities:** Room service; massage; babysitting; laundry. *In room:* TV, hair dryer, safe (in most rooms).

Vicarage Private Hotel ⭐ *Finds*   Owners Eileen and Martin Diviney enjoy a host of admirers on all continents. Their hotel is tops for old-fashioned English charm, affordable prices, and hospitality. Situated on a residential garden square close to Kensington High Street, not far from Portobello Road Market, this Victorian town house retains many original features. Individually furnished in a country-house style, the bedrooms can accommodate up to four, making it a great place for families. If you want a little nest to hide away in, opt for the very private top-floor aerie (no. 19). Guests find the corridor shower-only bathrooms adequate, and well maintained. Guests meet in a cozy sitting room for conversation and to watch the telly. As a thoughtful extra, hot drinks are available 24 hours a day. In the morning, a hearty English breakfast awaits.

10 Vicarage Gate, London W8 4AG. ℂ 020/7229-4030. Fax 020/7792-5989. www.londonvicaragehotel. com. 18 units, 5 with bathroom. £100 ($150) double with bathroom; £76 ($114) double without bathroom; £93 ($139.50) triple without bathroom; £100 ($150) family room for 4 without bathroom. Rates include English breakfast. No credit cards. Tube: High St. Kensington or Notting Hill Gate. *In room:* Coffeemaker, hair dryer (upon request), no phone.

EARL'S COURT
MODERATE

Amber Hotel 🛋   This charming, graceful hotel is an inviting oasis in a sea of bad B&Bs. The welcoming staff makes you feel at home at this 1860 house, located on a terraced street close to Kensington Gardens, the South Kensington museums, and Holland Park. The majority of the rooms are singles, but there are also twins and double-bedded rooms, along with two very attractive executive rooms. The conservatively decorated rooms have such extras as a refreshment tray, but rooms are all on the small side. The private bathrooms are cramped but well maintained, each with a shower. The private garden out back is almost reason enough to stay here. Breakfast is served buffet style in the lounge.

101 Lexham Gardens, London W8 6JN. ℂ **020/7373-8666.** Fax 020/7835-1194. www.amberhotel.co.uk. 38 units. £110–£120 ($165–$180) double; £55 ($82.30) single. Rates include buffet breakfast. AE, DC, MC, V. Tube: Earl's Court. *In room:* TV, coffeemaker, hair dryer, trouser press.

Henley House *Value*   This newly refurbished B&B stands out from the pack around Earl's Court—and it's a better value. The redbrick Victorian row house is on a communal fenced-in garden that you can enter by borrowing a key from the reception desk. The staff takes a keen interest in the welfare of its guests and is happy to take bewildered newcomers under their wing, so this is a great place for London first-timers. A ground-floor sitting room overlooks a rear courtyard. The decor is bright and contemporary; a typical room has warmly patterned Anna French wallpaper, chintz fabrics, and solid-brass lighting fixtures. Each is fitted with a well-maintained private shower-only bathroom. Breakfast is a cheerful event, served in a room decorated with terra-cotta accents and pots of dried flowers. For those who prefer to stay in rather than hitting the area's hot spots (mostly gay bars), there's a shelf of books you're welcome to borrow.

30 Barkston Gardens, London SW5 0EN. ℂ **020/7370-4111.** Fax 020/7370-0026. www.henlyhousehotel. com. 20 units. £89 ($133.50) double. Rates include continental breakfast. AE, DC, MC, V. Tube: Earl's Court. *In room:* TV, coffeemaker, hair dryer, safe.

Mayflower Hotel   Originally a private Victorian town house, this family-run hotel extends a warm welcome. This hotel stands out among the many B&B disasters along this street by offering clean, comfortable, and inviting (if unremarkable) accommodations. The queen of England doesn't send overflow guests here, but frugal travelers delight in the prices. The area is young and vibrant, and is just beginning to experience gentrification. Don't expect frills, but you get comfort instead. Each room has good linens on comfortable beds, and neat, shower-only bathrooms. An elevator carries guests to every floor, and there are also luggage storage facilities if you want to venture into the countryside with a lighter load than you brought to London (or acquired in London).

26–28 Trebovir Rd., London SW5 9NJ. ℂ 020/7370-0991. Fax 020/7370-0994. www.mayflower-group. co.uk. 48 units. £80 ($120) double. Rates include continental breakfast. AE, MC, V. Parking £17 ($25.50). Tube: Earl's Court. **Amenities:** Laundry. *In room:* TV, coffeemaker, hair dryer (on request), iron/ironing board (on request).

INEXPENSIVE

Philbeach Hotel One of Europe's largest gay hotels, the Philbeach is a Victorian row house on a wide crescent behind the Earl's Court Exhibition Centre, open to both men and women. It offers standard budget-hotel rooms; the showers are tiny, but the shared baths are clean. Room no. 8A, a double with bathroom, has a balcony overlooking the small back garden.

30–31 Philbeach Gardens, London SW5. ℂ 020/7373-1244. Fax 020/7244-0149. www.philbeachhotel. freeserve.co.uk. 40 units, 16 with bathroom. £55 ($82.50) single without bathroom; £65 ($97.50) single with bathroom; £70 ($105) double without bathroom; £90 ($135) double with bathroom. Rates include continental breakfast. AE, DC, MC, V. Tube: Earl's Court. **Amenities:** Gay bar and restaurant in basement ("Wilde About Oscar"). *In room:* TV.

Rushmore Hotel Although it became quite run-down in the early 1970s, this Victorian row house (behind a brick-faced Italianate facade) received a complete overhaul in 1987; today, it's one of the most pleasing hotels in a low-budget neighborhood. The hotel stands on the former site of the Manor House of Earl's Court Farm, where manorial courts were held until the mid-1850s. As long as you don't require atriums and minibars, the Rushmore proves that it's still possible to get good service and a fine room in London at an affordable price. The multilingual staff works hard to make your visit rewarding. The rooms are individually decorated in a variety of period schemes, but each has a comfortable feel. Those with shower bathrooms have nice touches like marble tiling and brass fittings. The breakfast room is beautifully outfitted with French limestone floors, unique Murano glass wall- and floor-lighting created by Missoni, wrought-iron furniture from Tuscany, and antique terra-cotta urns holding exotic cacti.

11 Trebovir Rd., London SW5 9LS. ℂ 020/7370-3839. Fax 020/7370-0274. www.rushmorehotel.co.uk. 22 units. £79–£85 ($118.50–$127.50) double; £89–£95 ($133.50–$142.50) triple; £99–£110 ($148.50–$165) family room for 4 or 5. Rates include continental breakfast. AE, DC, MC, V. Tube: Earl's Court. **Amenities:** Breakfast room; laundry; security boxes at reception. *In room:* TV, coffeemaker.

5 Marylebone to Holland Park

MARYLEBONE
VERY EXPENSIVE

The Langham Hilton ★★★ After it was bombed in World War II, this extremely well-located hotel languished as dusty office space for the BBC until the early 1990s, when Hilton International took it over. Its restoration was painstaking; and today, it's Hilton's European flagship. The Langham's public rooms reflect the power and majesty of the British Empire at its apex. Guest rooms are somewhat less opulent, but still attractively furnished and comfortable, featuring French provincial furniture and red oak trim. Major refurbishment was carried out in 1999. All bathrooms are well kept and contain full tub-and-shower units. Ask for one of the rooms in the "52" series as they are much grander and more spacious. And the location is terrific: within easy reach of Mayfair and Soho restaurants and theaters and Oxford and Regent Street shopping; Regent's Park is just blocks away.

1C Portland Place, London W1B 1JA. ℭ **800/774-1500** in the U.S., or 020/7636-1000. Fax 020/7323-2340. www.langham.hilton.com. 429 units. £250 ($375) double; £320 ($480) executive room; from £720 ($1,080) suite. Rates include breakfast for executive rooms and suites. AE, DC, MC, V. Tube: Oxford Circus. **Amenities:** 2 restaurants (one Russian), bar, Edwardian-style palm court; indoor pool; health club; concierge; tour desk; business center; salon; 24-hr. room service; massage; babysitting; laundry/dry cleaning. *In room:* A/C, TV, mini-bar, hair dryer, trouser press, safe.

EXPENSIVE

Dorset Square Hotel ✦✦✦   Situated just steps away from Regent's Park, this is one of London's best and most stylish "house hotels," overlooking Thomas Lord's (the man who set up London's first private cricket club) first cricket pitch. Hot hoteliers Tim and Kit Kemp have furnished the interior of these two Georgian town houses in a comfy mix of antiques, reproductions, and chintz that makes you feel as though you're in an elegant private home. The impressive rooms come with full marble bathrooms. About half are air-conditioned. All are decorated in a personal, beautiful style—the owners are interior decorators known for their bold and daring taste. Eight rooms offer crown-canopied beds, but all appointments are of a very high standard. The bathrooms are exquisite, with robes, deluxe toiletries, and shower-tub combinations.

39–40 Dorset Sq., London NW1 6QN. ℭ **020/7723-7874.** Fax 020/7724-3328. www.firmdale.com. 37 units. £140–£195 ($210–$292.50) double; from £240 ($360) suite. AE, MC, V. Parking £25 ($37.50). Tube: Baker St. or Marylebone. **Amenities:** Restaurant, bar; business center; 24-hr. room service; massage; babysitting; laundry/dry cleaning; rides in owner's chauffeured vintage Bentley. *In room:* TV, minibar, hair dryer, safe.

Durrants Hotel ✦   This historic hotel off Manchester Square (established in 1789) with its Georgian-detailed facade, is snug, cozy, and traditional. We find it one of the most quintessentially English of all London hotels. Hazlitt's (p. 104) and Fielding (p. 102) compete with Durrants for similar crowds, folks who enjoy vintage English charm. The difference is that you could invite the queen of England to Durrants for tea, whereas the other two competitors would be the place to take Meg Ryan out on the town. Over the 100 years that they have owned the hotel, the Miller family has incorporated several neighboring houses into the original structure. A walk through the pine-and-mahogany paneled public rooms is like stepping back in time: You'll even find an 18th-century letter-writing room. The rooms are rather bland except for elaborate cove moldings and very comfortable furnishings, including good beds. Some are air-conditioned, and some are, alas, small. Bathrooms are also tiny, with shower-tub combinations, but little room to maneuver.

The in-house restaurant serves full afternoon tea and satisfying French or traditional English cuisine in one of the most beautiful Georgian rooms in the neighborhood. The less formal breakfast room is ringed with 19th-century political cartoons by a noted Victorian artist. The pub, a neighborhood favorite, has Windsor chairs, a fireplace, and decor that hasn't changed much in 2 centuries.

George St., London W1H 6BJ. ℭ **020/7935-8131.** Fax 020/7487-3510. 90 units. £90–£145 ($135–$217.50) double; £180 ($270) family room for 3; from £285 ($427.50) suite. AE, MC, V. Tube: Bond St. or Baker St. **Amenities:** Restaurant, pub; 24-hr. room service; babysitting; laundry. *In room:* A/C in some rooms, TV, hair dryer.

MODERATE

Hallam Hotel   This heavily ornamented stone-and-brick Victorian—one of the few on the street to escape the Blitz—is just a 10-minute stroll from Oxford

Where to Stay from Marylebone to Holland Park

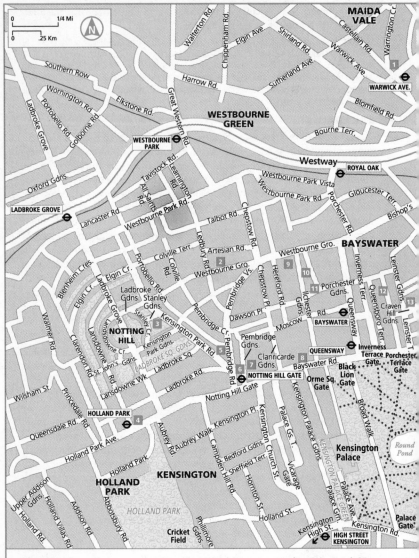

The Abbey Court **7**	Europa House Hotel **21**	Ivanhoe Suite Hotel **37**
Boston Court Hotel **26**	Fairways Hotel **17**	Kensington Guest House **4**
The Byron Hotel **12**	Garden Court **10**	Kenwood House Hotel **30**
Colonnade Town House **1**	The Gate Hotel **5**	The Langham Hilton **35**
Columbia Hotel **14**	Georgian House Hotel **28**	London Elizabeth Hotel **16**
Darlington Hyde Park **23**	Glynne Court **24**	Manor Court Hotel **8**
Dorset Square Hotel **31**	Hallam Hotel **34**	Miller's **9**
Durrants Hotel **36**	Hart House Hotel **29**	Mornington Hotel **15**
Edward Lear Hotel **25**	The Hempel **13**	Norfolk Court & St. David's Hotel **20**

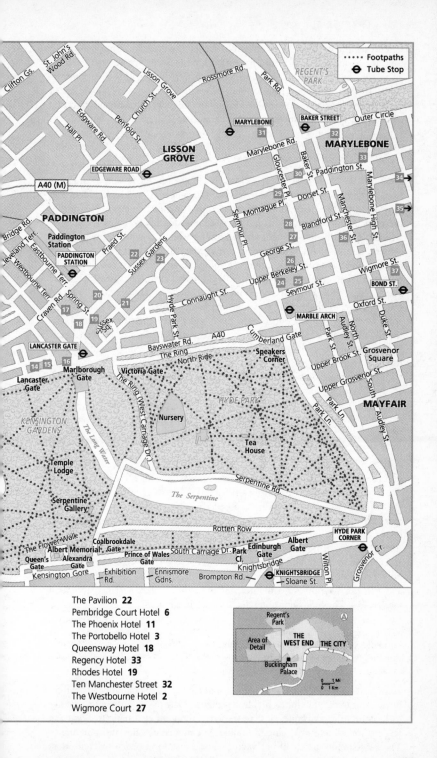

Circus. It's the property of brothers Grant and David Baker, who maintain it well. It's warm and friendly, and the very central location that you get for these prices can't be beat. The guest rooms, which were redone in 1991, are comfortably furnished with good beds. Some of the singles are so small they're called "cabinettes." Several of the twin-bedded rooms are quite spacious and have adequate closet space. Bathrooms, which have shower stalls, are a bit cramped.

12 Hallam St., Portland Place, London W1N 5LJ. © 020/7580-1166. Fax 020/7323-4527. 25 units. £89.50 ($134.25) single; £95 ($142.50) double. Rates include English breakfast. AE, DC, MC, V. Tube: Oxford Circus. *In room:* TV, minibar, coffeemaker, hair dryer, iron/ironing board.

Hart House Hotel ⭐ *Kids*   Hart House is a long-enduring favorite with Frommer's readers. In the heart of Marylebone, this well-preserved historic building (one of a group of Georgian mansions occupied by exiled French nobles during the French Revolution) lies within easy walking distance of many theaters, as well as some of the most sought-after shopping areas in London. Cozy and convenient, it's run by Andrew Bowden, one of Marylebone's best B&B hosts. The rooms—done in a combination of furnishings ranging from Portobello antique to modern—are spic-and-span, each with a different character. Favorites include no. 7, a triple with a big bathroom and shower, and no. 11, a brightly lit nest on the top floor. Housekeeping gets high marks here. Bedrooms are comfortably appointed with chairs, an armoire, a desk, and a large chest of drawers. Bathrooms, although small, are efficiently organized, and feature showers. Hart House has long been known as a good, safe place for traveling families. Many rooms are triples. Larger families can avail themselves of family accommodations with connecting rooms. Literary buffs, take note: Poet Elizabeth Barrett resided at no. 99 with her family for many years.

51 Gloucester Place, Portman Sq., London W1U 8JF. © 020/7935-2288. Fax 020/7935-8516. www. harthouse.co.uk. 16 units. £105 ($157.50) double; £130 ($195) triple; £150 ($225) quad. Rates include English breakfast. AE, MC, V. Tube: Marble Arch or Baker St. **Amenities:** Babysitting; laundry/dry cleaning. *In room:* TV, coffeemaker, hair dryer, iron/ironing board, safe.

Ivanhoe Suite Hotel *Value*   Born-to-shop buffs flock to this discovery located in a part of town off Oxford Street that's not usually known for its hotels. "It's like having my own little flatlet every time I come to London," one satisfied guest told us. Above a restaurant, on a pedestrian street of boutiques and restaurants, close to the shop-filled New and Old Bond streets, this town house hotel boasts attractively furnished small and medium singles and doubles, each with a sitting area. Each room has its own entry and security video. Bedrooms were redecorated in 1998. The newly tiled bathrooms are small—half have showers only. Breakfast is served in a very small area at the top of the first flight of stairs, and you can stop off for a nightcap at the corner pub, a real neighborhood locale. *Note:* The four-floor hotel doesn't have an elevator.

1 St. Christopher's Place, Barrett St. Piazza, London W1M 5HB. © 020/7935-1047. Fax 020/7224-0563. www.smoothhound.co.uk/hotels/ivanhoe.html. 8 units. £88–£98 ($132–$147) double; £120 ($180) triple. Rates include continental breakfast. AE, DC, MC, V. Tube: Bond St. **Amenities:** Secretarial service; 24-hr. room service; babysitting; laundry. *In room:* TV, kitchenette, minibar, fridge, coffeemaker, hair dryer, iron/ironing board.

Ten Manchester Street ⭐ *Value*   Constructed in 1919 as a residence hall for nurses, this terraced redbrick building is now a smart town house hotel. We like its location in Marylebone, close to those top shopping destinations, Bond and Regent Streets, and near chic boutiques and numerous cafes and restaurants. The guest rooms are small but well designed, and furnished with comfort in mind. Each room has a well-organized bathroom with tub and shower. There is the aura of a private home here, upheld by an inviting atmosphere and a helpful staff.

10 Manchester St., London W1M 5PG. © **020/7486-6669.** Fax 020/7224-0348. 46 units. www.10manchester street.com. £120–£150 ($180–$225) double; £150–£195 ($225–$292.50) suite. Rates include continental breakfast. AE, DC, MC, V. Tube: Marble Arch. **Amenities:** Public lounge, breakfast room. *In room:* TV, small refrigerator, coffeemaker, hair dryer, trouser press.

INEXPENSIVE

Boston Court Hotel Upper Berkeley is a classic street of B&Bs. In days of yore, it was home to Elizabeth Montagu (1720–1800), "queen of the blue-stockings" (a pejorative term for the women's literary clubs that sprang up in the 18th century) who defended Shakespeare against attacks by Voltaire, who was fond of saying such things as: "Shakespeare is a savage with sparks of genius which shine in a horrible night." Today, it's a good, safe retreat at an affordable price. This simply decorated hotel offers accommodations in a centrally located Victorian-era building within walking distance of Oxford Street shopping and Hyde Park. The small, basic rooms have been refurbished and redecorated with a no-nonsense decor. Rooms contain well-kept bathrooms with private showers.

26 Upper Berkeley St., Marble Arch, London W1H 7PF. © **020/7723-1445.** Fax 020/7262-8823. www.boston courthotel.co.uk. 15 units (7 with shower only). £65 ($97.50) double with shower only; £79 ($118.50) double with bathroom; £85–£89 ($127.50–$133.50) triple with bathroom. Rates include continental breakfast. MC, V. Tube: Marble Arch. **Amenities:** Video rentals; laundry. *In room:* TV, fridge, coffeemaker, hair dryer.

Edward Lear Hotel This popular hotel, situated 1 block from Marble Arch, is made all the more desirable by the bouquets of fresh flowers in the public rooms. It occupies a pair of brick town houses dating from 1780. The western house was the London home of 19th-century artist and poet Edward Lear, famous for his nonsense verse, and his illustrated limericks adorn the walls of one of the sitting rooms. Steep stairs lead up to cozy rooms which range from spacious to broom-closet size. Things are a bit tattered here and there, but with this location and price level, few can complain, as this is an area of £400- ($600) a-night mammoths. If you're looking for classiness, know that the bacon on your plate came from the same butcher used by the queen. One major drawback to the hotel: This is a very noisy part of town. Rear rooms are quieter. Bathrooms are tidy and well maintained, each with a shower unit.

28–30 Seymour St., London W1H 5WD. © **020/7402-5401.** Fax 020/7706-3766. www.edlear.com. 31 units, 12 with bathroom. £66 ($99) double without bathroom; £82–£93 ($123–$139.50) double with bathroom; from £110 ($165) suite. Rates include English breakfast. MC, V. Tube: Marble Arch. **Amenities:** Breakfast room. *In room:* TV.

Georgian House Hotel Central London, filled with luxury hotels, suffers an acute lack of small, personally run places, but Georgian House fills this gap. It lies near Sherlock Holmes's Baker Street and is within walking distance of Oxford Street and Regent's Park. Run by the same family since 1973, the Georgian House has a dedicated staff and management intent on improving the hotel. We especially like the top-quality English breakfast served here, and the way that original architectural features were retained even as modern comforts were added. Rooms have private bathrooms, and there's an elevator to all floors. Bedrooms are neutral in style and the ground-floor rooms are the least preferred. Don't expect views from some of the back rooms, which open onto a wall.

87 Gloucester Place (Baker St.), London W1H 3PG. ✆ **020/7935-2211.** Fax 020/7486-7535. www.london centralhotel.com. 20 units. £100 ($150) double; £110 ($165) triple; £130 ($195) family room. Rates include English breakfast. AE, MC, V. Tube: Baker St. *In room:* TV, coffeemaker.

Glynne Court In the Marble Arch area of Marylebone, this clean, comfortable B&B is a desirable place to stay due to its proximity to Hyde Park and Oxford Street. The guesthouse is run by a bright and helpful staff. Carriage lamps on either side of the front door welcome you home. The rooms are mostly en suite or have a private shower-tub combination. Each room has its own character and all are comfortably, but relatively simply, furnished. Fax service is available upon request. The staff is attentive. Continental breakfast is served in your room in the morning.

41 Great Cumberland Place, London W1H 7LG. ✆ **020/7262-4344.** Fax 020/7724-2071. 15 units, 10 with bathroom. £60 ($90) double without bathroom, £75 ($112.50) double with bathroom. Rates include continental breakfast. AE, DC, MC, V. Tube: Marble Arch. *In room:* TV, tea/coffeemakers, hair dryer.

Kenwood House Hotel This 1812 Adam-style town house is a historical landmark (the front balcony is said to be original). It has been converted into a small hotel, run by English-born Arline Woutersz and her Dutch husband, Bryan. Guests gather in the mirrored lounge with its antimacassars (those small coverings on the backs and arms of chairs) in place, just as they were in Victoria's day. Most of the basically furnished bedrooms were upgraded and restored in 1993. Some rooms have private bathrooms with shower-units. Spick-and-span modern public bathrooms with showers are on every floor.

114 Gloucester Place, London W1H 3DB. ✆ **020/7935-3473.** Fax 020/7224-0582. www.kenwoodhouse hotel.com. 19 units, 12 with bathroom. £58 ($87) double without bathroom, £68 ($102) double with bathroom; £78 ($117) triple with bathroom; £88 ($132) family room for 4 with bathroom. Rates include English breakfast. AE, DC, MC, V. Parking £10 ($15). Tube: Baker St. **Amenities:** Babysitting. *In room:* TV, hair dryer, iron/ironing board.

Regency Hotel The building is from the 1800s, and there has been a hotel of some kind here since the Blitz. In 1991 it was gutted and renovated into its present form. One of the better hotels on the street, it offers simple, conservatively decorated modern bedrooms scattered over four floors and a breakfast room set in what used to be the cellar. Bathrooms, although small, are well kept and come mostly with shower-tub combinations. The neighborhood is protected as a historic district, and Marble Arch, Regent's Park, and Baker Street all lie within a 15-minute walk.

19 Nottingham Place, London W1U 5LQ. ✆ **020/7486-5347.** Fax 020/7224-6057. www.regencyhotel westend.co.uk. 20 units. £89 ($133.50) double; £125 ($187.50) family room. Rates include English breakfast. AE, DC, MC, V. Parking £18 ($27) nearby. Tube: Baker St. or Regent's Park. **Amenities:** Room service; laundry. *In room:* TV, minibar, coffeemaker, hair dryer, iron/ironing board, trouser press.

Wigmore Court *(Value)* A convenient family hotel, this inn lies near the street made famous as the fictional address of Sherlock Holmes—Baker Street. It is close to Marble Arch, Oxford Street, and Madame Tussaud's. A somber Victorian structure, it has been converted into a fine B&B suitable only for serious stair climbers as there is no elevator. There's traffic noise outside, so request a room in the rear. Bedrooms, many quite spacious, are comfortably furnished. Most units contain double or twin beds, plus a small bathroom. About half of the bathrooms have shower-tub combinations.

23 Gloucester Place, London W1H 3PB. ✆ **020/7935-0928.** Fax 020/7487-4254. www.wigmore-court-hotel.com. 18 units. £80–£92 ($120–$138) double; £120 ($180) triple. MC, V. Tube: Marble Arch. **Amenities:** Guest kitchen; laundry. *In room:* TV, coffeemaker.

HOLLAND PARK
INEXPENSIVE

Kensington Guest House *Kids*   A family-run B&B, two doors from the Holland Park tube station, this is worth the commute from central London. On a section of tree-lined avenue, it is a neat and well-kept guesthouse. The Kensington offers twin bedrooms, and two are large enough to be made into family units. Another three have their own private toilet and shower. A full English breakfast is part of the package. And, all of the rooms have full kitchen facilities, including fridge, stove, sink, and crockery.

72 Holland Park Ave., London W11 3QZ. © 020/7460-7080. Fax 020/7221-1077. www.hotelondon.co.uk. 6 units, 3 with private bathroom. £55 ($82.50) double without bathroom, £65 ($97.50) double with bathroom; £65 ($97.50) triple without bathroom, £75 ($112.50) triple with bathroom. Rates include English breakfast. AE, MC, V. Tube: Holland Park. *In room:* TV, kitchen, no phone.

PADDINGTON & BAYSWATER
VERY EXPENSIVE

The Hempel ★★★   Set in a trio of nearly identical 19th-century row houses, this hotel is the newest statement of flamboyant interior designer Anouska Hempel. Don't expect the swags, tassels, and the elegance of her better-established hotel, Blake's (p. 122)—the feeling here is radically different. The Hempel manages to combine a grand Italian sense of proportion with Asian Zen-like simplicity. Soothing monochromatic tones prevail. The deliberately sparse lobby is flanked by symmetrical fireplaces; throughout the hotel are carefully positioned mementos from Asia, including Thai bullock carts that double as coffee tables.

Bedrooms continue the minimalist theme, except for their carefully concealed battery of electronic accessories, which includes a VCR, satellite TV control, CD player, twin phone lines, and a modem hookup. Bathrooms have cut-stone walls, countertops and bathtubs. The hotel mostly caters to business travelers from around the world, most of whom appreciate its tactful service and undeniably snobbish overtones.

31–35 Craven Hill Garden Sq., London W2 3EA. © **020/7298-9000.** Fax 020/7402-4666. www.the-hempel. co.uk. 47 units. £255–£295 ($382.50–$442.50) double; from £440 ($660) suite. AE, DC, DISC, MC, V. Tube: Lancaster Gate, Queensway, or Paddington. **Amenities:** Restaurant, bar; access to health club; concierge; tour desk; business services; 24-hr. room service; massage; babysitting; laundry/dry cleaning. *In room:* A/C, TV, VCR, minibar, coffeemaker, hair dryer, safe.

EXPENSIVE

Darlington Hyde Park ★   Although it's not flashy and lacks the full range of services, the Darlington Hyde Park is a winning choice for central London. Newly renovated rooms are decorated in an updated Victorian style: tasteful and neat, albeit a bit short of flair. They range from small to medium, and each is fitted with a good mattress and a tiny but adequate bathroom with a shower-tub combination. The maintenance is good, and a happy blend of business people and vacationers check in here. The in-room amenities are superior to other hotels along this street. Five bedrooms are nonsmoking. There is no bar, but guests are invited to BYOB and drink in the lounge. A number of neighboring restaurants cater room service for the hotel; they are listed in a restaurant book found in each room.

111–117 Sussex Gardens, London W2 2RU. © **020/7460-8800.** Fax 020/7460-8828. www.hydeparkhotels-uk.com. 40 units. £130–£140 ($195–$210) double; £145 ($217.50) family room; £150 ($225) suite. Rates include continental breakfast. AE, DC, MC, V. Tube: Paddington or Lancaster Gate. **Amenities:** Dining room; nearby health club; laundry/dry cleaning; nonsmoking rooms. *In room:* TV, hair dryer, safe.

London Elizabeth Hotel ✯   This elegant Victorian town house is ideally situated, overlooking Hyde Park. Amid the buzz and excitement of central London, the hotel's gentle, graceful atmosphere is an oasis of charm and refinement. Even before the hotel's recent £3 million restoration, it oozed character. Individually decorated rooms range from executive to deluxe and remind us of staying in an English country-house. Deluxe rooms are fully air-conditioned; some contain four-poster beds. Executive units usually contain one double bed. Some rooms have special features like Victorian antique fireplaces, and all contain first-rate bathrooms with showers. Suites are pictures of grand comfort and luxury—the Conservatory Suite boasts its own veranda, part of the house's original 1850 conservatory.

Lancaster Terrace, Hyde Park, London W2 3PF. ✆ **020/7402-6641.** Fax 020/7224-8900. www.london elizabethhotel.co.uk. 49 units. £115–£140 ($172.50–$210) double; £180–£250 ($270–$375) suite. AE, DC, MC, V. Parking £10 ($15). Tube: Lancaster Gate or Paddington. **Amenities:** Restaurant, bar; limited business services; 24-hr. room service; laundry/dry cleaning. *In room:* A/C, TV, hair dryer, iron/ironing board.

Miller's ✯ *(Finds)*   A stay here is like a night spent in the Old Curiosity Shop of Charles Dickens. Others say that the little hotel looks like a set of *La Traviata*. Miller's calls itself an 18th-century rooming house, and there's nothing quite like it in London. A roaring log fire blazes in the large book-lined drawing room in winter. The individually designed rooms are named after romantic poets. They vary in shape and size, but all are luxuriously furnished with antiques, prints, and tasteful curios. Each room contains a small bathroom with a shower stall. Miller's also offers sumptuous apartments with multiple bedrooms, a drawing room and a kitchen, for guests who are staying longer than a week.

111A Westbourne Grove, London W2 4UW. ✆ **020/7243-1024.** Fax 020/7243-1064. www.millersuk.com. 8 units. £165 ($247.50) double; £185 ($277.50) suite; from £1800/week ($2700/week) apt. Rates include continental breakfast. AE, DISC, MC, V. Tube: Bayswater or Notting Hill Gate. **Amenities:** Breakfast room; babysitting; laundry. *In room:* TV.

MODERATE

The Byron Hotel *(Value)*   A mostly American clientele appreciates this family-run hotel, just north of Kensington Gardens, for its country-house atmosphere, its helpful staff (who spend extra time with guests to make sure their stay in London is special), and the good value it offers. This is one of the best examples of a Victorian house conversion that we've seen; it was modernized without ruining its traditional appeal. The interior was recently redesigned and refurbished, and the rooms are better than ever, with ample closets, and tile bathrooms with good showers. An elevator services all floors, and breakfast is served in a bright and cheery room.

36–38 Queensborough Terrace, London W2 3SH. ✆ **020/7243-0987.** Fax 020/7792-1957. www.capricorn hotels.co.uk. 45 units. £110–£125 ($165–$187.50) double; £140–£150 ($210–$225) suite. Rates include English/continental breakfast. AE, DC, MC, V. Tube: Bayswater or Queensway. **Amenities:** 24-hr. room service; laundry/dry cleaning. *In room:* A/C, TV, coffeemaker, hair dryer, iron/ironing board, safe, trouser press.

Mornington Hotel ✯   Affiliated with Best Western, the Mornington brings a touch of northern European hospitality to the center of London. Just north of Hyde Park and Kensington Gardens, the hotel has a Victorian exterior and a Scandinavian-inspired decor. The area isn't London's most fashionable, but the location is close to Hyde Park and convenient to Marble Arch, Oxford Street shopping, and the ethnic restaurants of Queensway. The recently renovated guest rooms are tasteful and comfortable; all have pay movies, and Internet access; and you may discover a Mornington teddy bear on your bed after a long day of sightseeing. Bathrooms are small but tidy, with showers. Every year we get a Christmas card from "the gang"—the hotel staff, and what a helpful crew they are.

12 Lancaster Gate, London W2 3LG. ✆ **800/528-1234** in the U.S. or 020/7262-7361. Fax 020/7706-1028. www.mornington.com. 66 units. £135 ($202.50) double; £150 ($225) triple. Rates include Scandinavian and English cooked breakfast. AE, DC, MC, V. Tube: Lancaster Gate. **Amenities:** Bar; 24-hr. room service; laundry/dry cleaning; library. *In room:* TV, coffeemaker.

The Pavilion *(Finds)*   Until the early 1990s, this was a rather ordinary looking B&B. Then, a team of entrepreneurs with ties to the fashion industry took over and redecorated the rooms with sometimes wacky themes, turning it into an idiosyncratic little hotel. The result is a theatrical and often outrageous decor that's appreciated by the many fashion models and music-industry folks that regularly make this their temporary home in London. Rooms are, regrettably, rather small, but each has a distinctive style. Examples include a "kitsch 1970s" room ("Honky-Tonk Afro"), an Oriental bordello theme ("Enter the Dragon"), and even some with 19th-century ancestral themes. One Edwardian-style room, a gem of emerald brocade and velvet, is called "Green with Envy." Each contains tea-making facilities and small, but efficiently organized, bathrooms with excellent showers.

34–36 Sussex Gardens, London W2 1UL. ✆ **020/7262-0905.** Fax 020/7262-1324. www.msi.com.mt/pavilion. 28 units. £100 ($150) double. Rates include continental breakfast. AE, DC, MC, V. Parking £5 ($7.50). Tube: Edgware Rd. **Amenities:** Lounge. *In room:* TV, coffeemaker.

The Phoenix Hotel   This hotel, a member of the Best Western chain, occupies the entire south side of one of the most famous garden squares in Europe. Well situated in an ethnically mixed neighborhood, the Phoenix was created from a series of 1854 town houses. The atmosphere is welcoming. Well-furnished bedrooms keep to a smart international standard, with a palette of muted tones, and beds with firm mattresses. Everything is designed for comfort and ease, including the luggage racks. Bathrooms, most of which contain shower-tub combinations, are a bit small but well kept. The bar is a good place to unwind; moderately priced meals are served in the downstairs cafe. Our biggest complaint? The public areas are too small for a hotel of this size.

1–8 Kensington Garden Sq., London W2 4BH. ✆ **800/528-1234** in the U.S. or 020/7229-2494. Fax 020/7727-1419. www.phoenixhotel.co.uk/. 130 units. £125 ($187.50) double; £150 ($225) suite; £165 ($247.50) family room. Rates include buffet breakfast. AE, DC, MC, V. Tube: Bayswater Station. **Amenities:** Cafe, bar; limited business service; 24-hr. room service; laundry/dry cleaning. *In room:* TV, hair dryer.

INEXPENSIVE

Columbia Hotel *(Kids)*   On the north side of Hyde Park, less than a mile from Marble Arch, five Victorian houses were linked together to form this hotel. And a good one it is. Its character has shifted over the years. It was an American Red Cross Hospital in World War I, and after World War II became the American Officers Club in London. Since 1975, it's been the Columbia Hotel. The hotel just keeps improving, while still managing to retain elements of its Victorian allure. An elegant lounge, bar, and spacious breakfast room are part of the facilities. Extras include free overnight luggage storage. The public rooms here are so large it's like wandering the Victoria & Albert Museum; bedrooms are spacious, with high ceilings and often three to four beds (or even five, if you count a rollaway). The hotel offers several connecting rooms, which make it suitable for families. All units come with well-kept bathrooms containing shower-tub combinations. Some rooms are suited for persons with disabilities, and many of the bedrooms open onto Hyde Park.

95–99 Lancaster Gate, London W2 3NS. ✆ **020/7402-0021.** Fax 020/7706-4691. www.columbiahotel.co.uk.
103 units. £86 ($129) double; £112 ($168) triple; £130 ($195) quad. Rates include English breakfast. AE, MC, V.
Tube: Lancaster Gate. **Amenities:** Restaurant, bar; laundry. *In room:* TV, coffeemaker, hair dryer.

Europa House Hotel Another budget find along Sussex Gardens, this
family-run hotel attracts those who want a room with a private bathroom, but
at shared-bathroom prices. Like most hotels along Sussex Gardens, the bedrooms are a bit cramped, but they're well maintained; each has color-coordinated decor, and most of the rooms have been recently refurbished. Some units
are custom built for groups, with three, four, or five beds per unit. Some of the
multiple rooms have rather thin mattresses, but most are firm and comfortable.
A hearty English breakfast awaits you in the bright dining room every morning.

151 Sussex Gardens, London W2 2RY. ✆ **020/7723-7343.** Fax 020/7224-9331. www.europahousehotel.
com.net. 20 units. £56–£65 ($84–$97.50) double; from £20 ($30) per person family room. Rates include
English breakfast. AE, DC, MC, V. Free parking. Tube: Paddington. *In room:* TV, coffeemaker, hair dryer.

Fairways Hotel Jenny and Steve Adams welcome you into one of the finest
B&Bs along Sussex Gardens. Even though it doesn't enjoy the pedigree it used
to, this little place near Hyde Park is still a favorite of bargain hunters. The
black-and-white town house is easily recognizable: Just look for its colonnaded
front entrance with a wrought-iron balustrade stretching across the second floor.
Scorning the modern, the Adams opt for traditional charm and character. They
call their breakfast room "homely" (Americans might say homey); it's decorated
with photographs of the family and a collection of china. Bedrooms are attractive and comfortably furnished, with hot and cold running water and intercom.
Bathrooms are small but tidy and some have shower units. Those who share the
corridor bathrooms will find them clean and well maintained. The home-
cooked breakfast is plenty of fortification for a full day of sightseeing.

186 Sussex Gardens, London W2 1TU. ✆ and fax **020/7723-4871.** www.fairways-hotel.co.uk. 17 units,
10 with bathroom. £70 ($105) double without bathroom, £76 ($114) double with bathroom. Rates include
English breakfast. MC, V. Tube: Paddington or Lancaster Gate. *In room:* TV, coffeemaker, hair dryer (on
request), safe.

Garden Court This hotel was constructed in 1870 on a tranquil Victorian
garden square in the heart of the city. Two private houses were combined to form
one efficiently run hotel, located near such attractions as Kensington Palace,
Hyde Park, and the Portobello Antiques Market. Each year, rooms are redecorated and refurbished, although there would seem to be a lack of an overall renovation plan. Most accommodations are spacious, with good lighting, generous
shelf and closet space, and comfortable furnishings. If you're in a room without
a bathroom, you'll generally have to share with the occupants of only one other
room. There are many homey touches throughout the hotel, including ancestral
portraits and silky flowers. Each room is individually decorated, and "comfy";
it's like visiting your great-aunt. Rooms open onto the square in front or the gardens in the rear. Shower-only bathrooms are installed in areas never intended for
plumbing, thus tend to be very cramped. There is no elevator.

30–31 Kensington Gardens Sq., London W2 4BG. ✆ **020/7229-2553.** Fax 020/7727-2749. www.garden
courthotel.co.uk. 32 units, 16 with bathroom. £60 ($90) double without bathroom, £90 ($135) double with
bathroom; £75 ($112.50) triple without bathroom, £95 ($142.50) triple with bathroom. Rates include English
breakfast. MC, V. Tube: Bayswater or Queensway. *In room:* TV, hair dryer.

Norfolk Court & St. David's Hotel George and Foula Neokledos, two of
the most welcoming hosts in this highly-concentrated B&B area, run these two
properties with a certain friendly, personalized style. Only a 2-minute walk from

Paddington Station, these small, friendly hotels were built when Norfolk Square knew a grander age, attracting such Victorian luminaries as John Addington Symonds (1840–93), the scholar and author of the seven-volume *The Renaissance in Italy*. The bluebloods are long gone, but the area is still safe and recommendable. An interior designer might turn up his nose at the mismatched decor, but each room is well maintained and furnished comfortably, and you can't beat the price. In the rooms that do have showers, a cubicle shower does the job, though it's not the best spot for lingering. We are big fans of the large breakfast.

16–20 Norfolk Sq., London W2 1RS. ℂ 020/7723-4963. Fax 020/7402-9061. 78 units (45 with shower). £59 ($88.50) double without bathroom; £69 ($103.50) double with bathroom or shower; £65 ($97.50) triple without bathroom; £80 ($120) triple with shower; £80 ($120) quad without bathroom; £90 ($135) quad with shower. Rates include English breakfast. MC, V. Tube: Paddington. *In room:* TV.

Queensway Hotel   On a tree-lined road close to Hyde Park and Marble Arch, this hotel, composed of two Victorian houses, is ideal for shopping along Oxford Street, Bond Street, and Knightsbridge. Personal service and hospitality have long characterized this place, which received much refurbishment during the mid-1990s. The hotel is one of the most immaculate along Sussex Gardens. Bedrooms are moderately spacious and comfortably furnished, with sleek shower-only bathrooms. A reception room has its original mantelpiece and deep-cove moldings, evoking the hotel's former life as a private residence for a "family of character." The dining room is elegantly decorated with pink tablecloths and wall art, and it serves a generous breakfast.

147–149 Sussex Gardens, London W2 2RY. ℂ 020/7723-7749. Fax 020/7262-5707. www.londonreservations. co.uk. 43 units. £78 ($117) double. Rates include continental breakfast. AE, MC, V. Tube: Paddington. *In room:* TV, coffeemaker, hair dryer, trouser press.

Rhodes Hotel   This elegant late-Georgian house, just a short stroll from Hyde Park, is decorated with a certain theatrical flair. The owners, Chris and Maria Crias, have poured many pounds into their hotel to give it a cozy charm, with a Victorian curtained lounge, Greek murals, lacquered walls, and *trompe l'oeil* bambinis on puffy clouds. Creature comforts weren't ignored either. You'll find air-conditioning—a bit of a rarity in the neighborhood, especially at these prices—plus new rugs and clean bathrooms with shower units in all the bedrooms. The best place for a rendezvous is the little roof terrace, where you can sit out and enjoy a drink if you BYOB. There's an excellent bunkroom for families. Good coffee and lively conversation makes breakfast here an event.

195 Sussex Gardens, London W2 2RJ. ℂ 020/7262-0537. Fax 020/7723-4054. www.rhodeshotel.co.uk. 36 units. £72–£87 ($108–$130.50) double; £110–£123 ($165–$184.50) triple. Rates include continental buffet breakfast. MC, V. Tube: Paddington or Lancaster Gate. *In room:* A/C, TV, fridge, tea/coffeemaker, hair dryer.

NOTTING HILL GATE
EXPENSIVE

The Abbey Court ✦   This first-rate hotel is a small white-fronted mid-Victorian town house with a flower-filled patio in front and a conservatory in back. Its recently renovated lobby has a sunny bay window, floral draperies, and a comfortable sofa and chairs. You'll always find fresh flowers in the reception area and the hallways. Each room, although small, has carefully coordinated fabrics and fine furnishings (mostly 18th- and 19th-century country antiques). Done in Italian marble, bathrooms are equipped with a Jacuzzi bath, shower, and heated towel racks. Light snacks and drinks are available from room service 24 hours a day and breakfast is served in the newly renovated conservatory. Kensington Gardens is a short walk away, as are the antiques stores along Portobello

Road and Kensington Church Street. *Note:* There is more than one Abbey Court Hotel in London, but this is the one we like best.

20 Pembridge Gardens, London W2 4DU. © 020/7221-7518. Fax 020/7792-0858. www.abbeycourthotel. co.uk. 22 units. £155–£175 ($232.50–$262.50) double; £210 ($315) suite with four-poster bed. AE, DC, MC, V. Tube: Notting Hill Gate. **Amenities:** Access to nearby health club; Jacuzzi; tour desk; business services; 24-hr. room service; babysitting; laundry/dry cleaning. *In room:* TV, fax, dataport, hair dryer, safe, trouser press.

Pembridge Court Hotel ✫   This hotel, featuring an elegant cream-colored neoclassical facade, is located in the increasingly fashionable Notting Hill Gate residential neighborhood. Avid antiques hunters will like its proximity to Portobello Road. Most guest rooms contain at least one antique, as well as 19th-century engravings and plenty of warm-toned floral fabrics. Some of the largest and most stylish rooms are on the top floor. Bathrooms are tiled in Italian marble and feature shower-tub combinations. Three air-conditioned deluxe rooms, all with VCRs, overlook Portobello Road: The Spencer and Churchill Rooms are decorated in blues and yellows, and the Windsor Room has a contrasting array of tartans.

34 Pembridge Gardens, London W2 4DX. © 020/7229-9977. Fax 020/7727-4982. www.pemct.co.uk. 20 units. £190–£195 ($285–$292.50) double. Rates include English breakfast. AE, DC, MC, V. Tube: Notting Hill Gate. **Amenities:** Bar; access to nearby health club; secretarial services; 24-hr. room service; babysitting; laundry/dry cleaning. *In room:* A/C, TV, hair dryer, iron/ironing board, safe.

The Portobello Hotel ✫   On an elegant Victorian terrace near the Portobello antiques market, these two 1850-era town houses have been combined to form a quirky property that has its devotees. We remember these rooms when they looked better, but they still have plenty of character. Who knows what will show up in what nook? Perhaps a Chippendale, a claw-foot tub, or a round bed tucked under a gauze canopy. Try for no. 16, with a full-tester bed facing the garden. Some of the cheaper rooms are so tiny they're cabinlike garrets, but others have been combined into large doubles. Comfortable beds are a standard; most of the small bathrooms have showers but no tubs. An elevator goes to the third floor; after that, it's the stairs. Since windows are not double-glazed, request a room in the rear, which is quiet. Some rooms are air-conditioned. Don't expect top-notch service; it's erratic at best, but this is still a good choice.

22 Stanley Gardens, London W11 2NG. © 020/7727-2777. Fax 020/7792-9641. www.portabello-hotel. co.uk. 24 units. £185–£280 ($277.50–$420) double; £320 ($480) suite. Rates include continental breakfast. AE, MC, V. Tube: Notting Hill Gate or Holland Park. **Amenities:** 24-hr. bar and restaurant in basement; health club nearby; room service. *In room:* TV, hair dryer, minibar.

The Westbourne Hotel ✫✫ *(Finds)*   Call it "Notting Hill chic" or "London's best urban inn," this hotel is a gem, from its Japanese garden to its bespoke furniture. The design was inspired by such fabled architects as Frank Lloyd Wright and Mies Van der Rohe. Visitors checking in during its first year found the Westbourne a "new hotel experience," the creation of a series of entrepreneurs known heretofore mainly for their wildly successful night clubs. One of the backers, Orlando Campbell, has a strong interest in modern art. He asked four well-known British artists to design a room each, and also displays of art in the other 16 units. This is the first of a series of hotels projected in fashionable residential areas of London. Bedrooms are midsize with modern designs and queen-size beds and tiled bathrooms with tub-and-shower combination. You get 20 accommodations of serenity with all sorts of flat screen multi-media technology.

163–165 Westbourne Grove, London W11 2RS ℂ **020/243-6008.** Fax 020/229-7201. www.hotel-london. co.uk/site/features.php?hotel_id=80. 20 units. £189–£269 ($283.50–$403.50) double. Rates include continental breakfast. AE, MC, V. Tube: Notting Hill Gate. **Amenities:** Restaurant and bar (for guests and their friends); room service; laundry/dry cleaning. *In room:* A/C, TV, hair dryer, safe, trouser press.

INEXPENSIVE

The Gate Hotel *Finds* This antiques-hunters' favorite is the only hotel along the length of Portobello Road—and because of rigid zoning restrictions, it will probably remain the only one for years to come. It was built in the 1820s as housing for farmhands at the now-defunct Portobello Farms and has functioned as a hotel since 1932. It has two cramped but cozy bedrooms on each of its three floors, plus a renovated breakfast room in the cellar. Be prepared for some *very* steep English stairs. Rooms are color-coordinated, with a bit of style, and have such extras as full-length mirrors and built-in wardrobes. Bathrooms are small but adequate, with tiled shower stalls; housekeeping is excellent. Especially intriguing are the wall paintings that show what the Portobello Market was: Every character looks like they are straight from a Dickens novel. The onsite manager can direct you to the antiques markets and the attractions of Notting Hill Gate and nearby Kensington Gardens, both within a 5-minute walk.

6 Portobello Rd., London W11 3DG. ℂ **020/7221-0707.** Fax 020/7221-9128. www.gatehotel.com. 6 units. £100 ($150) double. Rates include continental breakfast. AE, MC, V. Tube: Notting Hill Gate. *In room:* TV, coffeemaker, fridge.

Manor Court Hotel This B&B lies on a cul-de-sac at the edge of Kensington Gardens. Still slightly run-down, the neighborhood is improving, and real estate prices are soaring as young professionals seek town houses here. A Victorian home, Manor Court lies only a 15-minute stroll to Portobello Road of antiques fame. A family favorite, it offers a simple decor with basic, not stylish, furnishings, comfortable beds and generous space. If you look carefully, you'll see elements that need restoration, but the comfort is high and the cleanliness immaculate. Bedrooms come in a variety of shapes and sizes, with the smaller units on the top floors. Those units that have a private bathroom come with shower stalls.

7 Clanricarde Gardens, London W2 4JJ. ℂ **020/7792-3361.** Fax 020/7229-2875. 20 units, 16 with bathroom. £55–£65 ($82.50–$97.50) double with bathroom; £75 ($112.50) triple with bathroom; £85 ($127.50) family room with bathroom. There is a 10% discount for any stay over 4 nights. Rates include continental breakfast. AE, MC, V. Tube: Notting Hill Gate. **Amenities:** Roof terrace. *In room:* TV, hair dryer.

IN NEARBY MAIDA VALE
MODERATE

Colonnade Town House *Kids* Tired of large chain hotels? Head for this boutique charmer in the canal-riddled "Little Venice" area of London, an appellation bestowed by Lord Byron. A handsome Victorian edifice, the hotel was built in 1886 as two different structures, one of which was a hospital. An unusually shaped elevator remains from when it was used to transport stretchers. Before he purchased his own home in Homestead, Sigmund Freud stayed here in 1938. Each midsize bedroom is individually decorated, many with four-posters and small terraces. Tasteful fabrics and antiques evoke town house living. The least desirable units are two small basement bedrooms. They are impeccably furnished, but subject to rumblings from the Underground at night. Families opt for the spacious two-level JFK suite. All units have well maintained bathrooms with shower-tub combinations. Half the rooms are for nonsmokers. Thoughtful extras abound, including Penhaligon toilet articles, Frette Egyptian cotton bed linens, complimentary fresh fruit, and dual-line phones with voicemail.

2 Warrington Crescent, London W9 1ER. © **020/7286-1052.** Fax 020/7286-1057. www.etontownhouse. com. 43 units. £126–£179 ($189–$268.50) double; £230–£245 ($345–$367.50) suite. AE, DC, MC, V. Tube: Warwick Ave. **Amenities:** 24-hr. room service. *In room:* A/C, TV, minibar, coffeemaker, hair dryer, iron/ironing board, safe, trouser press.

6 A Bit Farther Afield

HAMPSTEAD
See the "Hampstead" map on p. 269 for the locations of the following hotels.

MODERATE
Swiss Cottage Hotel ✦   On the border of Hampstead,, this hotel lies only a 15-minute Tube ride to central London. A charming Victorian building, Swiss Cottage has been a hotel for 3 decades. The interior is modernized, but each unit is individually furnished with an eye to comfort, as reflected by the well-kept bathrooms with shower-tub combinations and old-fashioned ambience, enhanced by the use of antiques. The hotel also welcomes children and offers a breakfast room (the only meal served). For more substantial meals, many restaurants are within walking distance.

4 Adamson Rd., London NW3 3HP. © **020/7722-2281.** Fax 020/7483-4588. 53 units. £115–£135 ($172.50–$202.50) double; £160 ($240) suite. Rates include English breakfast. AE, DC, MC, V. Tube: Swiss Cottage. **Amenities:** Bar. *In room:* A/C, TV, minibar, coffeemaker, hair dryer (on request).

INEXPENSIVE
La Gaffe ✦ *Finds*   A 15-minute Tube ride from central London, this little gem is nestled in Hampstead Heath. It dates from 1734 and was a shepherd's cottage before being turned into a residential inn. Although relatively small, it offers many of the luxuries its large competitors do. The well-furnished rooms are small but cozy, with firm beds, plus small bathrooms with shower stalls. Special rooms include a honeymoon room with a four-poster and a Jacuzzi, plus a triple room with a queen-size four-poster.

107–111 Heath St., Hampstead, London NW3 6SS. © **020/7435-8965.** Fax 020/7794-7592. www.lagaffe. co.uk. 18 units. £90 ($135) double; £125 ($187.50) honeymoon room or triple. Rates include continental breakfast. AE, DISC, MC, V. Tube: Hampstead Heath. **Amenities:** Italian restaurant, bar. *In room:* TV, hair dryer.

ISLINGTON
INEXPENSIVE
Kandara Guesthouse   If you don't mind the trek up to Islington, this family-run B&B, a tradition for nearly 50 years, is along a leafy residential road. The house stands in one of Islington's designated conservation areas. A nonsmoking guesthouse, Kandara has recently redecorated its bedrooms. The public shower-only bathrooms are neatly kept, and improvements in the plumbing have made them more accessible. The location is only 20 minutes from London's West End.

68 Ockendon Rd., London N1 3NW. © **020/7226-5721.** Fax 020/7226-3379. www.kandara.co.uk. 11 units, none with bathroom. £51–£59 ($76.50–$88.50) double. Rates include English breakfast. MC, V. *In room:* TV, coffeemaker, hair dryer. No phone.

7 Near the Airports

NEAR HEATHROW
The reason for staying at one of the hotels below is obvious: You either want to catch an early plane or are arriving too late to search for a hotel in central London.

Unless you like plane-spotting, there isn't much reason to hang out. Incidentally, the hotels below provide transportation to and from the airport.

VERY EXPENSIVE

Radisson Edwardian Heathrow ✿   The poshest digs at Heathrow, this deluxe hotel lies just south of the M4 about 5 minutes east of the long tunnel that leads to Terminals 1, 2, and 3. Since 1991 it has housed tired air travelers from all over the world. Its grand spa has a swimming pool and two whirlpools. You enter a courtyard with potted trees and a koi pond. Persian rugs, brass-railed staircase, and chandeliers live up to the "Edwardian" in the hotel's name. Rooms are medium in size but adorned with hand-painted hardwood furnishings. The bathrooms are in tile and marble, with robes, a shower, and a tub. All in-room televisions have a channel reserved to broadcast flight information.

140 Bath Rd., Hayes UB3 5AW. © 800/333-3333 in the U.S., or 020/8759-6311. Fax 020/8759-4559. www. radisson.com. 459 units. £219–£253 ($328.50–$379.50) double; from £363 ($544.50) suite. AE, DC, MC, V. Parking £8 ($12). Heathrow Hoppa bus service. **Amenities:** Restaurant, brasserie, bar; plunge pool; health club; steam room; spa; sauna; 24-hr. room service; laundry/dry cleaning. *In room:* A/C, TV, minibar, hair dryer, safe.

EXPENSIVE

Hilton London Heathrow ✿   This first-class hotel with its five-story atrium evoking the feel of a hangar is linked to Heathrow's Terminal 4 by a covered walkway. A glass wall faces the runways, so you can see planes land and take off. You can take buses to Terminals 1, 2, or 3. Medium-size bedrooms are standard, but comfortably decorated with built-in wood furniture, and comfortable sofas. Bathrooms are tiled and trimmed in marble, containing a phone, tub, and shower. The best accommodations are on the fifth floor; they have better extras (bathrobes, and so forth) as well as a private lounge with airport vistas.

Terminal 4, Hounslow TW6 3AF. © 020/8759-7755. Fax 020/8759-7579. www.hilton.com. 395 units. £120–£270 ($180–$405) double; £430 ($645) suite. AE, DC, MC, V. Parking from £6.50 ($9.75). Tube: Piccadilly. **Amenities:** 3 restaurants, 2 bars; business services; 24-hr. room service; babysitting; laundry/dry cleaning; TV with flight information. *In room:* A/C, TV, coffeemaker, hair dryer.

Renaissance London Heathrow Hotel ✿   This bustling hotel factory lies just inside the perimeter of the airport and is spotted just before you reach the long airport entrance tunnel. Three cantilevered concrete floors attract a bevy of international travelers. Rooms have recently been renovated and are fairly standard, although they are a bit small. They feature bedside controls, inlaid wood and laminate furnishings, along with tiled combination baths (tub-and-shower) plus marble sinks. We prefer the units facing the airport itself—double-glazing keeps out the noise of planes taking off and landing.

Bath Rd., Hounslow TW6 2AQ. © 020/889-6363. Fax 020/8897-1113. www.renaissancehotels.com. 650 units. Mon–Thurs £119–£169 ($178.50–$253.50) double; Fri–Sun £70–£90 ($105–$135) double; all week from £315 ($472.50) suite. AE, DC, MC, V. Parking £5 ($7.50). Heathrow Hoppa bus service to most terminals. **Amenities:** Brasserie, bar; health club; sauna; 24-hr. room service; laundry/dry cleaning; solarium. *In room:* A/C, TV, minibar, coffeemaker, hair dryer.

MODERATE

Holiday Inn London-Heathrow   Once you get past the regrettable 1960s architecture—critics have compared it to a roll of toilet paper—this is your best bet in the moderate range at London's major airport. The decor is bland, but not unpleasant. Or, you can pay a lot more and live more elegantly at one of the big chains. The Holiday Inn has been massively upgraded—ask for one of the new millennium rooms. Rooms are midsize with immaculate bathrooms containing shower stalls; some are nonsmoking.

118 Bath Rd., Hayes, Middlesex UB3 5AJ. ℂ **800/225-5843** in the U.S., or 8704/009-040. Fax 020/8564-9265. www.london-heathrow.holiday-inn.com. 186 units. Mon–Thurs £119–£129 ($178.50–$193.50) double; Fri–Sun £59–£79 ($88.50–$118.50) double. AE, DC, MC, V. Parking £30 ($45). Hotel Hoppa bus H2 from Terminals 1 and 3, H12 from Terminal 4. **Amenities:** Bar/restaurant, rotisserie; room service; laundry/dry cleaning. *In room:* A/C, TV, minibar, coffeemaker, hair dryer, trouser press.

Stanwell Hall This sunny Victorian house was purchased in 1951 by the Parke family, who converted it into a comfortable hotel. The cheery house with its side garden is located in a small village minutes from Heathrow; it's perfect for businesspeople tired of staying in standard airport hotels. About half the rooms have been fully renovated; they are comfortably furnished, papered in warm shades, with chintz curtains covering the windows—a dramatic improvement over the washed-out, prerenovation rooms. All rooms have bathrooms equipped with shower-tub combinations. Bathrooms are efficiently organized and tidy.

St. Anne's Restaurant, located on the ground floor, is small but inviting and serves modern British cuisine.

Town Lane, Stanwell, Staines, Middlesex TW19 7PW. ℂ **01784/252292.** Fax 01784/245250. www.stanwell-hall.co.uk. 19 units, 18 with bathroom. £70–£100 ($105–$150) double; £150 ($225) suite. Rates include continental breakfast. AE, DC, MC, V. Free parking. No bus or Tube service. **Amenities:** Restaurant, bar; limited room service; laundry/dry cleaning. *In room:* TV, coffeemaker, hair dryer.

INEXPENSIVE

The Swan Dating from the days of Samuel Pepys, the Swan is on the south bank of the Thames, beside Staines Bridge and within a 15-minute drive of Heathrow. Bedrooms were newly refurbished in 1999. The shower-only bathrooms are small, but the corridor bathroom is adequate. The attractive inn also has a reputation for good food ranging from bar snacks to traditional English fare. The food is served in a gazebo-style dining room. Staines was an important Roman settlement, and many buildings in the area date from the 17th century.

The Hythe, Staines, Middlesex TW18 3JB. ℂ **0178/445-2494.** Fax 0178/446-1593. 11 units, 10 with bathroom. £65–£80 ($97.50–$120) double without bathroom; £85–£100 ($127.50–$150) double with bathroom; £105–£130 ($157.50–$195) suite. Rates include English breakfast. AE, DC, MC, V. Tube: Heathrow (you must take a taxi from there). **Amenities:** Restaurant; laundry/dry cleaning. *In room:* TV, hair dryer.

NEAR GATWICK
EXPENSIVE

Hilton London Gatwick Airport ✦ This deluxe five-floor hotel—Gatwick's most convenient—is linked to the airport terminal with a covered walkway; an electric buggy service transports people between hotel and airport. The most impressive part of the hotel is the first floor lobby. Its glass-covered portico rises four floors and contains a scale replica of the de Havilland Gypsy Moth airplane *Jason,* used by Amy Johnson on her solo flight from England to Australia in 1930. The reception area has a lobby bar and lots of greenery. The well-furnished, soundproof rooms have triple-glazed windows and tidily kept bathrooms equipped with a tub and shower. Recently, most of the rooms were refurbished, in addition to the executive floor and all their junior suites. Now 300 of the rooms have minibars.

South Terminal, Gatwick Airport, West Sussex RH6 0LL. ℂ **800/HILTONS** in the U.S., or 01293/518080. Fax 01293/528980. www.hilton.com. 565 units. £160–£240 ($240–$360) double; from £260 ($390) suite. AE, MC, V. Parking £11.50 ($17.25). **Amenities:** 3 restaurants, 2 bars; health club; business center; 24-hr. room service; babysitting; laundry/dry cleaning; bank. *In room:* A/C, TV, hair dryer.

INEXPENSIVE

The Manor House   Owners Steve and Jo Jeffries include transportation from Gatwick as part of the price of their lodgings. Their home is a sprawling neo-Tudor affair on 2 acres of land, amid fields, which surround it on all sides. It was built in 1894 as a supplemental home for the Lord of Ifield, who occupied a larger house nearby and never actually moved in. Two of the rooms share a bathroom, the others have bathrooms with shower. Regardless of its plumbing, each accommodation has flowered wallpaper, and simple, traditional accessories. Breakfast is the only meal served.

Bonnetts Lane, Ifield, Crawley, Sussex RH11 0NY. *C* **01293/510000**. Fax 01293/518046. www.manorhouse-gatwick.co.uk. 6 units, 4 (doubles) with private bathroom. £45 ($67.50) double; £70 ($105) family unit. Rates include English breakfast. MC, V. Free parking. *In room:* TV, tea/coffeemaker. No phone.

6

Where to Dine

George Mikes, Britain's famous Hungarian-born humorist, wrote about the cuisine of his adopted country: "The Continentals have good food. The English have good table manners."

Quite a lot has happened since.

London has emerged as one of the great food capitals of the world. Both its veteran and upstart chefs have fanned out around the globe for culinary inspiration and returned with innovative dishes, flavors, and ideas that London diners have never seen before. These chefs are pioneering a style called "Modern British," which is forever changing and innovative, yet familiar in many ways.

Traditional British cooking has made a comeback, too. The dishes that British mums have been forever feeding their families are fashionable again. Yes, we're talking British soul food: bangers and mash, Norfolk dumplings, nursery puddings, cottage pie. This may be a rebellion against the minimalism of the nouvelle cuisine of the 1980s, but maybe it's just plain nostalgia. Pig's nose with parsley-and-onion sauce may not be your idea of cutting-edge cuisine, but Simpson's-in-the-Strand is serving it for breakfast.

These days, many famous chefs spend more time writing cookbooks and on TV than in their own kitchens. That chef you've read about in *Condè Nast Traveler* or *Travel & Leisure* may not be in the kitchen when you get here. But don't worry: the cuisine isn't suffering. An up-and-coming new chef, perhaps even better than the one you heard about, has probably taken over the kitchen.

If you want a lavish meal, London is the place: Gourmet havens such as Le Gavroche, and a half-dozen others are reviewed in the following pages. We've also included many affordable restaurants where you can dine well and still pay off your mortgage. You'll find that London's food revolution has infiltrated every level of the dining scene—even the lowly pub has entered the culinary sweepstakes. Believe the unthinkable: At certain pubs, you can now dine better than in many restaurants. In some, standard pub grub has given way to Modern British and Mediterranean-style fare; in others, oyster bars have taken hold.

SOME DINING NOTES

HOURS Restaurants in London keep varied hours, but in general, lunch is offered from noon to 2pm and dinner from 7:30 to 9:30pm, although more restaurants are staying open later. Sunday is the usual closing day for restaurants, but there are exceptions. (Many also close for a few days around Christmas, so call ahead during the holidays.) We've listed serving hours in the descriptions below.

RESERVATIONS Nearly all places, except pubs, cafeterias, and fast-food joints, prefer or require reservations. Almost invariably, you get a better table if you book in advance. For a few of the famous places, you might need to reserve weeks in advance, even before leaving home. (Reservations should always be confirmed when you land in London.) However, if you haven't made reservations, even at a "reservations required" restaurant, it's worth trying to walk in to the restaurant if you are in the area. If they do have room, you won't be turned down.

TAXES & TIPPING   All restaurants and cafes are required to display the prices of their food and drink in a place visible from outside. Charges for service, as well as any minimums or cover charges, must also be made clear. The prices shown must include 17.5% VAT. Most restaurants add a 10% to 15% service charge to your bill, but check to make sure. If nothing has been added, leave a 10% to 15% tip. It is not considered rude to tip, so feel free to leave something extra if service was good.

A NOTE ABOUT PRICES   When restaurants are classified as Moderate or Inexpensive, most main courses are at the lower end of the price scale. That doesn't mean that the chefs don't prepare some expensive dishes. Often they do, especially if they offer shellfish. But if you avoid the highest-priced dishes, you can dine moderately or inexpensively in our selections.

1 Restaurants by Cuisine

AFTERNOON TEA

The Blue Room, Soho (p. 211, $)

Brown's Hotel, Mayfair ✭ (p. 208, $$$)

Claridge's, Mayfair ✭ (p. 208, $$$)

The Garden Café, Notting Hill (p. 212, $)

The Georgian Restaurant, Knightsbridge (p. 210, $$$)

The Lanesborough, Knightsbridge (p. 210, $$$)

MJ Bradley's, Covent Garden & the Strand (p. 211, $)

The Orangery, Kensington ✭ (p. 211, $)

The Palm Court, Mayfair (p. 209, $$$)

Palm Court at the Waldorf Meridien, Covent Garden & the Strand (p. 208, $$$)

Richoux, Knightsbridge (p. 210, $$)

Ritz Palm Court, St. James's ✭✭✭ (p. 210, $$$)

St. James Restaurant & The Fountain Restaurant, St. James's (p. 210, $$$)

The Tearoom at the Chelsea Physic Garden, Chelsea (p. 211, $)

AMERICAN

Ed's Easy Diner, Soho (p. 176, $)

Hard Rock Cafe, Mayfair (p. 181, $$)

Pizzeria Condotti, Mayfair (p. 183, $)

Spoon+, Soho ✭ (p. 169, $$$$)

ASIAN

(See also Cantonese, Chinese, Japanese, Pekinese, Szechuan, and Thai)

Mezzo, Soho (p. 173, $$)

BELGIAN

Belgo Centraal, Piccadilly Circus & Leicester Square (p. 166, $$)

BRITISH—MODERN

Admiral Codrington, Kensington & South Kensington ✭ (p. 198, $)

Alastair Little, Soho ✭ (p. 169, $$$)

Atlantic Bar & Grill, Soho (p. 171, $$)

Balans, Soho (p. 176, $)

The Bridge, the City (p. 151, $$)

Circus, St. James's (p. 184, $$)

Clarke's, Kensington & South Kensington ✭ (p. 195, $$$)

Key to Abbreviations: $$$$ = Very Expensive $$$ = Expensive $$ = Moderate $ = Inexpensive

Guide to London Restaurant Maps

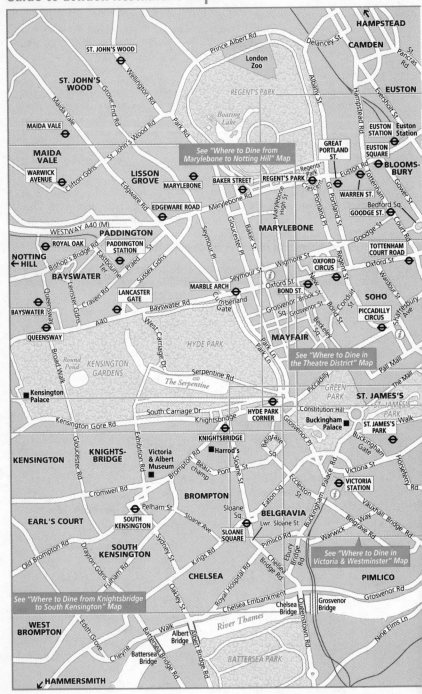

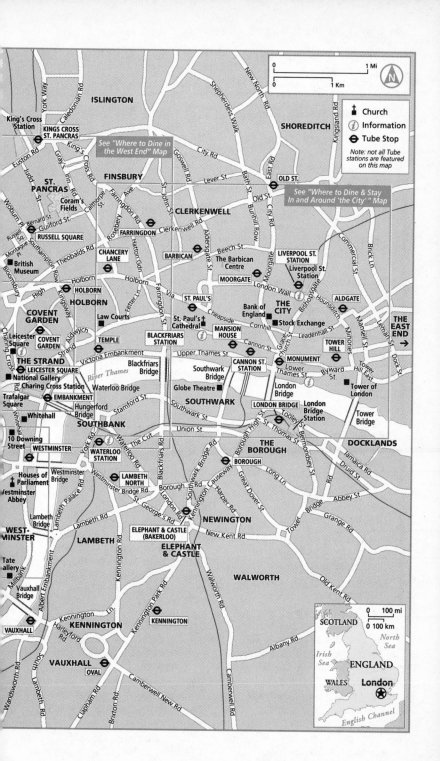

The Collection, Knightsbridge ✶
(p. 189, $$$)

The Cow, Notting Hill Gate ✶
(p. 206, $$)

The Criterion Brasserie, Soho ✶
(p. 170, $$$)

Greenhouse, Mayfair (p. 181, $$)

The Ivy, Piccadilly Circus &
Leicester Square ✶ (p. 168, $$)

Joe's, Kensington & South Kens-
ington ✶ (p. 196, $$)

Launceston Place, Kensington
& South Kensington ✶
(p. 195, $$$)

Mirabelle, Mayfair ✶
(p. 180, $$$)

Oxo Tower Restaurant, South
Bank ✶ (p. 157, $$$)

The Portrait Restaurant, Trafalgar
Square ✶ (p. 178, $$)

Prism, the City ✶✶ (p. 151, $$$)

Quo Vadis, Soho ✶ (p. 174, $$)

Rhodes in the Square, Westminster
& Victoria ✶✶✶ (p. 186, $$$)

Simpson's-in-the-Strand, Covent
Garden & the Strand ✶
(p. 163, $$$)

St. John, Clerkenwell (p. 155, $$)

Tate Gallery Restaurant,
Westminster & Victoria ✶
(p. 188, $$)

Teatro Club & Restaurant, Soho
✶ (p. 171, $$$)

The Titanic, Soho (p. 175, $$)

BRITISH—TRADITIONAL

British Museum Restaurant,
Bloomsbury (p. 162, $)

Bush Bar & Grill, Marylebone ✶
(p. 202, $$)

Butler's Wharf Chop House,
Docklands ✶ (p. 156, $$$)

The Enterprise, Kensington &
South Kensington (p. 196, $$)

Fox and Anchor, the City ✶
(p. 154, $)

The George, Covent Garden &
the Strand (p. 164, $)

The George & Vulture, the City
(p. 154, $)

The Granary, Mayfair (p. 183, $)

Langan's Bistro, Marylebone
(p. 202, $$)

Langan's Brasserie, Mayfair
(p. 181, $$)

Porter's English Restaurant,
Covent Garden & the Strand ✶
(p. 164, $$)

Rules, Covent Garden & the
Strand ✶ (p. 163, $$$)

Shepherd's, Westminster &
Victoria (p. 186, $$$)

Simpson's-in-the-Strand, Covent
Garden & the Strand ✶
(p. 163, $$$)

The Stockpot, Piccadilly Circus
& Leicester Square (p. 169, $)

Veronica's, Paddington &
Bayswater ✶ (p. 205, $$)

Ye Olde Cheshire Cheese, the City
(p. 152, $$)

CANTONESE

China City, Piccadilly Circus &
Leicester Square (p. 167, $$)

Fung Shing, Piccadilly Circus
& Leicester Square ✶
(p. 166, $$$)

Jenny Lo's Teahouse, Westminster
& Victoria (p. 188, $)

Ming, Soho (p. 173, $$)

Royal China, Paddington &
Bayswater ✶ (p. 204, $$$)

CHINESE

Chuen Cheng Ku, Soho
(p. 172, $$)

Dumpling Inn, Piccadilly Circus
& Leicester Square (p. 167, $$)

Hakkasan, Soho ✶ (p. 172, $$)

Poons in the City, the City ✶
(p. 152, $$)

CONTINENTAL

Admiral Codrington, Kensington
& South Kensington ✶
(p. 198, $)

Alastair Little, Soho ✶
(p. 169, $$$)

Blue Bird, Chelsea ✶ (p. 193, $$$)

Hilaire, Kensington & South
Kensington ✶ (p. 195, $$$)

L'Oranger, St. James's ✶
(p. 183, $$$)

Maison Novelli, Clerkenwell ✵✵
(p. 154, $$$)
Mash, Marylebone ✵ (p. 203, $$)
Noble Rot, Mayfair ✵
(p. 181, $$$)
Prism, the City ✵✵ (p. 151, $$$)
Quaglino's, St. James's ✵
(p. 185, $$)
Shampers, Soho (p. 175, $$)
The Stockpot, Piccadilly Circus &
Leicester Square (p. 169, $)
The Square, Mayfair ✵✵✵
(p. 180, $$$$)
Union Cafe, Marylebone
(p. 203, $$)
Vertigo 42, the City ✵ (p. 154, $)
Villandry, Marylebone ✵
(p. 203, $$)

CYPRIOT

Halepi, Paddington & Bayswater
✵ (p. 204, $$)
Sarastro, Covent Garden & the
Strand ✵ (p. 164, $)

ECLECTIC

Incognico, Piccadilly Circus &
Leicester Square ✵✵
(p. 167, $$)

EUROPEAN

The Engineer, Camden Town ✵
(p. 207, $$)
The Enterprise, Kensington &
South Kensington (p. 196, $$)
Front Page, Chelsea (p. 194, $)
Gordon Ramsay at Claridge's,
Mayfair ✵✵✵ (p. 178, $$$$)
Kensington Place, Kensington &
South Kensington (p. 197, $$)
Mezzo, Soho (p. 173, $$)
Oxo Tower Restaurant, South
Bank ✵ (p. 157, $$$)
Pharmacy Restaurant and Bar,
Notting Hill Gate ✵
(p. 205, $$$)

FRENCH

Archipelago, Bloomsbury ✵
(p. 159, $$$)
Aubergine, Chelsea ✵✵
(p. 192, $$$$)

Bam-Bou, Soho ✵ (p. 171, $$)
Bibendum/The Oyster Bar,
Kensington & South
Kensington ✵ (p. 194, $$$)
Bush Bar & Grill, Marylebone ✵
(p. 202, $$)
Crivelli's Garden, Trafalgar Square
✵ (p. 177, $$)
Gordon Ramsay, Chelsea ✵✵✵
(p. 193, $$$$)
Incognico, Piccadilly Circus
& Leicester Square ✵✵
(p. 167, $$)
John Burton—Race at the
Landmark, Marylebone ✵✵
(p. 198, $$$$)
La Tante Claire, Knightsbridge
✵✵✵ (p. 188, $$$$)
Langan's Bistro, Marylebone
(p. 202, $$)
Langan's Brasserie, Mayfair
(p. 181, $$)
Le Gavroche, Mayfair ✵✵✵
(p. 179, $$$$)
Les Trois Garçons, Shoreditch ✵
(p. 156, $$$)
L'Odéon, Soho ✵ (p. 170, $$$)
Maison Novelli, Clerkenwell ✵✵
(p. 154, $$$)
Mirabelle, Mayfair ✵
(p. 180, $$$)
Orrey, Marylebone ✵✵
(p. 199, $$$)
Petrus, Mayfair ✵✵ (p. 179, $$$$)
Pied-á-Terre, Bloomsbury ✵
(p. 159, $$$$)
Simply Nico, Westminster &
Victoria ✵ (p. 186, $$$)
Townhouse Brasserie, Bloomsbury
✵ (p. 162, $$)
Vong, Belgravia ✵ (p. 192, $$$)

GREEK

Halepi, Paddington & Bayswater
✵ (p. 204, $$)

HUNGARIAN

The Gay Hussar, Soho ✵
(p. 172, $$)

INDIAN

The Bengal Clipper, Docklands ✦
(p. 157, $$)
Cafe Spice Namaste, the City ✦
(p. 152, $$)
Mela, Soho ✦ (p. 173, $$)
Rasa Samundra, Soho ✦
(p. 174, $$)
Soho Spice, Soho (p. 175, $$)
Tamarind, Mayfair (p. 182, $$)
Veeraswamy, Soho (p. 177, $)

INTERNATIONAL

The Bridge, the City (p. 151, $$)
Chelsea Kitchen, Chelsea
(p. 194, $)
Circus, St. James's (p. 184, $$)
The Collection, Knightsbridge ✦
(p. 189, $$$)
Cork & Bottle Wine Bar,
Piccadilly Circus & Leicester
Square ✦ (p. 168, $)
The Ivy, Piccadilly Circus &
Leicester Square ✦ (p. 168, $$)
Le Metro, Knightsbridge
(p. 192, $)
Le Pont de la Tour, Docklands ✦
(p. 156, $$$)
Odin's, Marylebone ✦
(p. 199, $$$)
Orrey, Marylebone ✦✦
(p. 199, $$$)
Prince Bonaparte, Notting Hill
Gate (p. 206, $)
Townhouse Brasserie, Bloomsbury
✦ (p. 162, $$)
Villandry, Marylebone ✦
(p. 203, $$)

ITALIAN

Assaggi, Marylebone ✦✦
(p. 199, $$$)
Caldesi, Marylebone (p. 202, $$)
Crivelli's Garden, Trafalgar Square
✦ (p. 177, $$)
Floriana, Knightsbridge ✦
(p. 189, $$$)
I-Thai, Paddington & Bayswater
✦ (p. 204, $$$$)
Neal Street Restaurant, Covent
Garden & the Strand ✦
(p. 163, $$$)

Pizzeria Condotti, Mayfair
(p. 183, $)
The River Café, Hammersmith
✦✦ (p. 207, $$$$)
Zafferano, Knightsbridge ✦
(p. 189, $$$$)

JAPANESE

I-Thai, Paddington & Bayswater ✦
(p. 204, $$$$)
Nobu, Mayfair ✦ (p. 179, $$$$)
Satsuma, Soho (p. 174, $$)
Wagamama, Bloomsbury
(p. 162, $$)
YO! Sushi, Soho (p. 176, $$)

LEBANESE

Phoenicia, Kensington & South
Kensington (p. 197, $$)

MEDITERRANEAN

Bibendum/The Oyster Bar,
Kensington & South
Kensington ✦ (p. 194, $$$)
Bistro 190, Kensington & South
Kensington (p. 196, $$)
Cantina Vinopolis, South Bank ✦
(p. 158, $$)

MOROCCAN

Momo, Mayfair (p. 182, $$)
Pasha, Kensington & South
Kensington (p. 197, $$)

NORTH AFRICAN

Momo, Mayfair (p. 182, $$)
Moro, Clerkenwell ✦ (p. 155, $$)

PACIFIC RIM

Bali Sugar, Notting Hill Gate ✦
(p. 205, $$$)
The Sugar Club, Soho ✦
(p. 170, $$$)
Suze, Mayfair (p. 183, $)

PEKINESE

Ming, Soho (p. 173, $$)

RUSSIAN

Firebird Restaurant, Mayfair ✦
(p. 180, $$$)

SEAFOOD

Back to Basics, Bloomsbury ✦
(p. 162, $$)

Greens Restaurant & Oyster Bar, St. James's (p. 184, $$)

J. Sheekey, Piccadilly Circus & Leicester Square ⭐ (p. 166, $$$)

Livebait's Café Fish, Piccadilly Circus & Leicester Square ⭐ (p. 168, $$)

Lou Pescadou, South Kensington (p. 198, $)

North Sea Fish Restaurant, Bloomsbury ⭐ (p. 162, $$)

Vertigo 42, the City ⭐ (p. 154, $)

SPANISH
Moro, Clerkenwell ⭐ (p. 155, $$)

SUDANESE
Mondola, Notting Hill Gate (p. 206, $)

SZECHUAN
Jenny Lo's Teahouse, Westminster & Victoria (p. 188, $)

Royal China, Paddington & Bayswater ⭐ (p. 204, $$$)

Zen Central, Mayfair (p. 182, $$)

THAI
Archipelago, Bloomsbury ⭐ (p. 159, $$$)

Blue Elephant, Kensington & South Kensington ⭐ (p. 196, $$)

Chiang Mai, Soho (p. 176, $)

The Engineer, Camden Town ⭐ (p. 207, $$)

I-Thai, Paddington & Baywater ⭐ (p. 204, $$$$)

Nahm, Mayfair ⭐⭐ (p. 185, $$$$)

Vong, Belgravia ⭐ (p. 192, $$$)

TURKISH
Sarastro, Covent Garden & the Strand ⭐ (p. 164, $)

VEGETARIAN
Mildreds, Soho ⭐ (p. 176, $)

VIETNAMESE
Bam-Bou, Soho ⭐ (p. 171, $$)

2 In & Around the City

THE CITY
EXPENSIVE

Prism ⭐⭐ MODERN BRITISH/CONTINENTAL   Located in the financial district, this restaurant attracts London's movers and shakers, especially those with demanding palates. Harvey Nichols—known for his chic department store in Knightsbridge—took this 1920s neo-Grecian hall (the former Bank of New York) and installed Mies van der Rohe chairs in chrome and lipstick red leather. In such a setting, traditional English dishes are given a light touch—try the tempura of Whitby cod or the cream of Jerusalem artichoke soup with roasted scallops and truffle oil. For a first course, you might opt for a small seared calves' liver with mushroom risotto, or a Savoy cabbage salad with Parma ham, seasoned with flecks of Parmesan cheese. The menu reveals the chef's penchant for foreign travel—note the Moroccan-spiced chicken livers, the lemon and parsley couscous, and the zesty chili sauce. Unusual for a restaurant, the staff will compose a set menu for each individual table. You can discuss what you'd like and what's available that day and the chef will prepare the tailored dishes for your table.

147 Leadenhall St., EC3. ☎ 020/7256-3888. Reservations required. Main courses £14–£23 ($21–$34.50). Set menus £21 ($31.50). AE, DC, DISC, MC, V. Mon–Fri noon–3pm and 6–10pm. Tube: Bank.

MODERATE

The Bridge INTERNATIONAL/MODERN BRITISH   As far as restaurants go, the most panoramic view of the new riverside architecture is from the terrace of this glass-walled restaurant next to the Millennium Bridge. It looks out across the Thames to Shakespeare's Globe Theatre and the Tate Modern. Peter Gladwin, the executive chef, roams the world for inspiration—perhaps a velvety smooth gazpacho from Spain, duck confit from France, or a chicken satay from Malaysia. For appetizers, try such delights as the baby squid salad, the sautéed seaweed, or the delectable iced lobster bisque. For something really English, opt for the thinly sliced and quick-seared calves' liver, served with smoky bacon and mashed potatoes laced with sage. If you want to drop in for a drink and a look at that view, you can order dim sum at the bar. The house wine, Nutbourne Sussex Reserve, comes from Gladwin's own Sussex vineyard, and has won several awards. Desserts feature the chef's own homemade ice cream and such delights as an elderflower and lemon tart with crème fraîche and fresh raspberry sauce.

1 Paul's Walk, EC4. ℂ **020/7236-0000.** Reservations required. Main courses £11.50–£14 ($17.25–$21). AE, MC, V. Mon–Fri 11am–10pm. Tube: St. Paul's.

Cafe Spice Namaste ✿ INDIAN   Along with Tamarind (see later in this chapter), this is our favorite Indian restaurant in London. It's housed in a landmark Victorian hall near Tower Bridge, just east of the Tower of London. The chef, Cyrus Todiwala, is Parsi and is a former resident of Goa (a Portuguese territory absorbed by India long ago), where he learned many of his culinary secrets. He concentrates on southern and northern Indian dishes with a strong Portuguese influence. Chicken and lamb are prepared a number of ways, from mild to spicy-hot. Todiwala occasionally offers a menu of emu dishes; when marinated, the meat is rich and spicy and evocative of lamb. Emu is not the only dining oddity here. Ever have ostrich gizzard kebab, alligator tikka, or minced moose, bison, and blue boar? Many patrons journey here for the complex chicken curry known as *xacutti*. Lambs' livers and kidneys are also cooked in the tandoor. A weekly specialty menu complements the long list of regional dishes. The homemade chutneys alone are worth the trip; our favorite is made with kiwi. All dishes come with fresh vegetables and Indian bread. With the exotic ingredients, the often time-consuming preparation, the impeccable service, the warm hospitality, and the spicy but subtle flavors, this is a real winner.

16 Prescot St., E1. ℂ **020/7488-9242.** Reservations required. Main courses £10.50–£15 ($15.75–$22.50). AE, DC, MC, V. Mon–Fri noon–3pm and 6:15–10:30pm; Sat 6:30–10:15pm. Tube: Tower Hill.

Poons in the City ✿ CHINESE   Since 1992, Poons has operated this branch in the City, less than a 5-minute walk from the Tower of London. The restaurant is modeled on the Luk Yew Tree House in Hong Kong. Main courses feature crispy, aromatic duck, prawns with cashew nuts, and barbecued pork. Poons's famous *lap yuk soom* (like Cantonese tacos) includes finely chopped wind-dried bacon. Special dishes can be ordered on 24-hour notice. At the end of the L-shaped restaurant is an 80-seat fast-food area and take-out counter that's accessible from Mark Lane. The menu changes every 2 weeks.

2 Minster Pavement, Minster Court, Mincing Lane, EC3. ℂ **020/7626-0126.** Reservations recommended for lunch. Fixed-price lunch and dinner £15–£30.80 ($22.50–$46.20); a la carte main courses £6–£9 ($9–$13.50). AE, DC, MC, V. Mon–Fri noon–10:30pm. Tube: Tower Hill or Monument.

Ye Olde Cheshire Cheese *Kids* TRADITIONAL BRITISH   The foundation of this building was laid in the 13th century, and it holds the most famous of the old City chophouses and pubs. Established in 1667, it claims to be the spot where Dr. Samuel Johnson entertained admirers with his acerbic wit. Charles Dickens and other literary lions also patronized the place. Later, many of the ink-stained journalists of 19th- and early-20th-century Fleet Street made it their watering hole. You'll find six bars and two dining rooms here. The house

Where to Dine & Stay In & Around "The City"

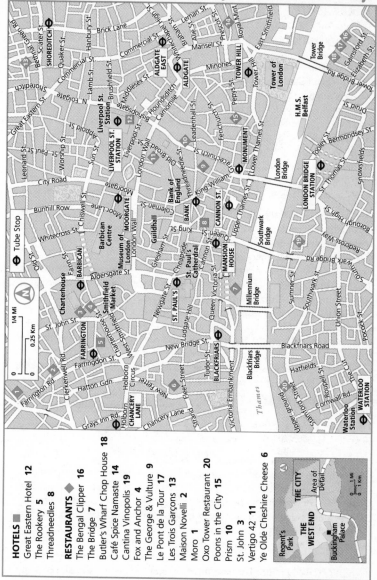

HOTELS
Great Eastern Hotel **12**
The Rookery **5**
Threadneedles **8**

RESTAURANTS
The Bengal Clipper **16**
The Bridge **7**
Butler's Wharf Chop House **18**
Café Spice Namaste **14**
Cantina Vinopolis **19**
Fox and Anchor **4**
The George & Vulture **9**
Le Pont de la Tour **17**
Les Trois Garçons **13**
Maison Novelli **2**
Moro **1**
Oxo Tower Restaurant **20**
Poons in the City **15**
Prism **10**
St. John **3**
Vertigo 42 **11**
Ye Olde Cheshire Cheese **6**

specialties include "Ye Famous Pudding" (steak, kidney, mushrooms, and game) and Scottish roast beef with Yorkshire pudding and horseradish sauce. Sandwiches, salads, and classic pub favorites such as steak-and-kidney pie are also available. When your kid says, "What's an English pub?" the Cheshire is the best and safest venue to take him or her to see an example of this British institution.

Wine Office Court, 145 Fleet St., EC4. (**020/7353-6170**. Main courses £7.25–£10 ($10.90–$15). AE, DC, MC, V. Meals Mon–Fri noon–10pm; Sat noon–2:30pm and 6–10pm; Sun noon–2:30pm. Drinks and bar snacks daily 11:30am–11pm. Tube: St. Paul's or Blackfriars.

INEXPENSIVE

Fox and Anchor ★ *Finds* TRADITIONAL BRITISH   For British breakfast at its best, try this place, which has been serving traders from the nearby Smithfield meat market since 1898. Breakfasts are gargantuan, especially if you order the "Full House"—a plate with at least eight items, including sausage, bacon, kidneys, eggs, beans, black pudding, and fried bread, along with unlimited tea or coffee, toast, and jam. Add a Black Velvet (champagne with Guinness), or the more fashionable Bucks Fizz (orange juice and champagne, known in the U.S. as a Mimosa). The Fox and Anchor is noted for its fine English ales, which are all available at breakfast. Butchers from the market, spotted with blood, still appear, as do nurses getting off their shifts, and clerks and City tycoons who've been making millions all night.

115 Charterhouse St., EC1. ② 020/7253-5075. Reservations recommended. "Full house" breakfast £7 ($10.50). AE, MC, V. Mon–Fri from 7am. Closing time varies from 8–10pm. Tube: Barbican or Farringdon.

The George & Vulture TRADITIONAL BRITISH   Dickens enthusiasts still seek out this Pickwickian place. Founded in 1660, it claims that it's "probably" the world's oldest tavern and refers to an inn that operated on this spot in 1175. While they no longer put up overnight guests here, The George & Vulture does serve English lunches (but no dinners) in a warren of small dining rooms scattered over the tavern's three floors. Besides the daily specials, the menu includes a mixed grill, a loin chop, a lamb-based hot pot, and fried Dover sole filets with tartar sauce. Potatoes and buttered cabbage are the standard vegetables, and the apple tart is always reliable. The system is to arrive and give your name, then retire any of the three different pubs on the same narrow street for a drink (Simpson's Bar, the Cross Key's Pub or the Jamaican pub across the way); you're "fetched" when your table is ready. After, be sure to explore the mazes of pubs, shops, wine houses, and other old buildings near the tavern. The Pickwick Club, a private literary group, meets here four times a year for reunion dinners. Cedric Dickens, the octogenarian great-great-grandson of Charles Dickens, heads the literary club.

3 Castle Court, Cornhill, EC3. ② 020/7626-9710. Reservations accepted before 12:45pm. Main courses £8–£15 ($12–$22.50). AE, DC, MC, V. Mon–Fri noon–2:45pm. Tube: Bank.

Vertigo 42 ★ *Finds* SEAFOOD/CONTINENTAL   This is a relatively unknown little spot that offers one of London's most spectacular views from the 42nd floor of Tower 42, located in the heart of the city. After securing a special security pass downstairs, you're taken to Vertigo in a high-speed elevator. Dining here is like being on top of the world, as you take in the view of London that eagles enjoy, from the Canada Tower to the Law Courts. We prefer to come here as the sun sets on London and the city lights begin to twinkle on. Blue binoculars are provided if you want a more intimate view of the cityscape. Seven champagnes are served by the glass, and there's an array of well-presented, very tasty food, ranging from lobster to Iranian fresh caviar to excellent sushi. The organic smoked salmon in salsa verde is a delight, and the fresh Cornish crab arrives from the West Country of England.

Tower 42, Old Broad St., EC2. ② 020/7877-7842. Reservations required. Main courses £3.50–£5.25 ($5.25–$7.90). AE, DC, MC, V. Mon–Fri 11:45am–3pm and 5–11pm. Closed weekends. Tube: Liverpool St.

CLERKENWELL
EXPENSIVE

Maison Novelli ★★ CONTINENTAL/MODERN FRENCH   Those who leave the heart of London can experience some of the city's finest and most imaginative cookery. High rents have driven stellar chefs, such as Jean-Christophe Novelli, to up-and-coming areas. Novelli is a devotee of bold flavors, the freshest ingredients, and imaginative culinary twists.

The ground floor is a brasserie, with outdoor tables in fair weather. More formal service is upstairs. The brasserie and restaurant share a blue-violet decor, lined with modern art. The brasserie serves such hearty fare as mackerel-and-lemon-grass kebabs, and braised onions filled with cubed lamb. But it is in the restaurant that Novelli truly shines. His signature dish is a perfumed halibut that we could dine on every day. You can opt for the baby squid and scallop *nage,* followed by the sublime grilled John Dory (St-Pierre to the French) or the ever-popular corn-fed chicken, which comes with a sliver of *foie gras* and a green pea-pod emulsion. Stuffed pigs' trotters are rich and appear with mashed almonds for an exquisite flavor.

29–31A Clerkenwell Green, EC1. ℭ 020/7251-6606. Reservations recommended. Main courses in restaurant and brasserie £14.50–£23 ($21.75–$34.50). AE, DC, MC, V. Mon–Fri noon–3pm; Mon–Sat 6–11pm. Closed 2 weeks July–Aug. Tube: Farringdon.

MODERATE

Moro ⋆ SPANISH/NORTH AFRICAN   If you've been hearing about all the trendy restaurants in Clerkenwell and want to try one, make it Moro. With its streamlined interior, and kitchen in open view, it attracts the chic and fashionable. The aromas of delicious meats on the charcoal grill will attract carnivores, but vegetarian meals are also available. At the long zinc bar, you can fill up on some of the city's best tapas, or a Maghreb-inspired dinner of impeccable quality. The restaurant's recipes were inspired by the epoch when Arab culture met European in southern Spain (8th–15th centuries). From the charcoal grill emerges a delectable veal chop with spicy chorizo and cabbage, and the leg of lamb is tantalizingly prepared with okra and coriander. The quail on flatbread makes the angels weep. Begin with the lusty white-bean soup and the night is yours. Extra-fresh products go into the creation of the dishes, and no seasoning or flavor overpowers.

34–36 Exmouth Market, EC1. ℭ 020/7833-8336. Reservations recommended. Main courses £10.50–£17.50 ($15.75–$26.25). AE, DC, MC, V. Mon–Fri 12:30–2:30pm; Mon–Sat 7–10:30pm. Tube: Farringdon.

St. John MODERN BRITISH   Located in a former smokehouse, just north of Smithfield Market, this air-conditioned, canteen-like dining room is the restaurant of choice for carnivores. It is a showcase for the talents of owner/chef Fergus Henderson, a leader in the offal movement, which advocated the use of all animal parts in cuisine. In true British tradition, he doesn't use just part of the animal, he uses it all—we're talking neck, trotters, tail, liver, heart, the works. It's called nose-to-tail cookery.

Don't think you'll be served warmed-over haggis: The food is excellent and flavor-packed. There's an earthiness and simplicity to this cuisine that's unequaled in London. The grilled lamb chops, garnished with sliced pig's tongue, bacon, salsify, and dandelion, are matchless. Roast bone marrow appears with a parsley salad, and pork chops are called pig chops. It's hard these days to find an eel, bacon, and clam stew, but you'll discover one here. French wines wash it all down. Desserts run to puddings such as vanilla-rice or dates and walnuts with butterscotch. Dessert oddity? Where else can you get a good goat curd, marc (the product of grapes, seeds and fruits after pressing), and rhubarb concoction these days? The breads served here can be purchased in an on-site bakery.

26 St. John St., EC1. ☎ 020/7251-0848. Reservations required. Main courses £10.20–£16.50 ($15.30–$24.75). AE, DC, DISC, MC, V. Mon–Fri noon–11pm; Sat 6–11pm. Tube: Farringdon.

SHOREDITCH
EXPENSIVE

Les Trois Garçons ★ *Finds* FRENCH   As trendy London moves east, and once seedy districts like Shoreditch (north of the City) became cutting edge, eye-popping restaurants like Les Trois Garçons are bound to follow. The three "garçons" of the restaurants name are Hassan Abdullah, Michel Lassere, and Stefan Karlson. They took this pub, which opened early in Victoria's reign, and turned it into one of the hottest reservations for London's young, fashionable set. This fun, campy restaurant lies among a row of garages and second-hand shops. You won't miss the flaming torches guarding the entrance. Inside, stuffed animals, including a British bulldog, are adorned with glittering tiaras. That's Quentin the crocodile balanced on top of the baby grand. In such a setting, the cuisine could be second to the entertainment. But, happily, the restaurant serves an excellent and modern French menu, beautifully prepared and making full use of first-rate ingredients. The fish soup with rouille (a creamy garlic and red pepper sauce) is an excellent starter, as are the seared scallops and tiger prawns in a lemon grass sauce. For main courses, we've enjoyed roast rump of lamb in a sweet garlic cream sauce, served with a bean and tomato cassoulet or wild strip loin of boar with roasted chestnuts and cracked black pepper sauce. For dessert, try one of the freshly made tarts of the day.

1 Club Row, E1. ☎ 020/7613-1924. Reservations essential. Main courses £17.50–£23 ($26.25–$34.50). AE, MC, V. Mon–Sat 7–10:30pm. Tube: Liverpool St.

DOCKLANDS
EXPENSIVE

Butler's Wharf Chop House ★ TRADITIONAL BRITISH   Of the four restaurants housed in Butler's Wharf (other Butler's Wharf restaurants are listed in this chapter), this one is the closest to Tower Bridge. It maintains its commitment to moderate prices. The Chop House was modeled after a large boat-house, with banquettes, lots of exposed wood, flowers, candles, and windows overlooking Tower Bridge and the Thames. Lunchtime crowds include workers from the city's financial district; evening crowds are made up of friends dining together leisurely.

Dishes are largely adaptations of British recipes: fish and chips with mushy peas; steak-and-kidney-pudding with oysters; stewed rabbit leg with bitter leaves and mustard; roast rump of lamb, garlic mash, and rosemary; and grilled pork filet with apples, chestnuts, and cider sauce. After, there might be a dark-chocolate tart with whiskey cream or toffee pudding. The bar offers such choices as Theakston's best bitter, several English wines, and a half-dozen French clarets by the jug.

36E Shad Thames, SE1. ☎ 020/7403-3403. Reservations recommended. Fixed-price 2-course lunch £19.75 ($29.65); fixed-price 3-course lunch £23.75 ($35.65); dinner main courses £12.50–£25 ($18.75–$37.50). AE, DC, MC, V. Sun–Fri noon–3pm (last order); Mon–Sat 6–11pm. Tube: Tower Hill.

Le Pont de la Tour ★ INTERNATIONAL   At the edge of the Thames, near Tower Bridge, the Butler's Wharf complex holds condos, rental apartments, offices, and an assortment of food and wine shops collectively known as the Gastrodome. Built in the mid–19th century as a warehouse, it's now another Terence Conran–designed playland. From its windows, diners and shoppers enjoy sweeping views of some of the densest river traffic in Europe.

The **Bar and Grill**'s live piano music (on evenings and weekends), plus a wide choice of wines and cocktails, creates a convivial atmosphere. Although such dishes as ham and *foie gras* terrine; a half-lobster with roast peppers, olives, and fennel; and langoustines mayonnaise are featured, the culinary star is a huge platter of fresh shellfish—perfect for sharing with a friend, accompanied by a bottle of wine.

In bold contrast to the Bar and Grill is the more formal room known simply as **The Restaurant.** Filled with burr oak furniture and decorated with framed lithographs of early-20th-century Parisian cafe society, it offers excellent food and a polite English reserve. The menu might list such temptations as roast rabbit wrapped in herbs, with pancetta and a mustard vinaigrette, or whole roast-buttered lobster with herbs. One winning selection is the best end of lamb, with a black olive and herb crust, in a red-pepper sauce. All the fish is excellent, but none is better than the Dover sole, which can be ordered grilled or meunière (breaded and sprinkled with lemon juice and parsley).

36D Shad Thames, Butler's Wharf, SE1. ℂ 020/7403-8403. Reservations not accepted in the Bar and Grill; recommended in the restaurant. Bar and Grill main courses £12.95–£20 ($19.40–$30); Restaurant main courses £15.50–£34 ($23.25–$51); fixed-price 3-course lunch £28.50 ($42.75). AE, DC, MC, V. Restaurant Mon–Fri noon–2:30pm; Mon–Sat 6–10:30pm; Sun 12:30–2:30pm and 6–10:30pm. Bar and Grill daily 11:30am–10:30pm. Tube: Tower Hill or London Bridge.

MODERATE

The Bengal Clipper ✧ INDIAN   This former spice warehouse by the Thames serves what it calls "India's most remarkable dishes." The likable and often animated restaurant is outfitted with cream-colored walls, tall columns, and modern artwork inspired by the Moghul Dynasty's depictions of royal figures, soaring trees, and well-trained elephants. Seven windows afford sweeping views over the industrialized Thames-side neighborhood, and live piano music plays in the background. The cuisine includes many vegetarian choices derived from the formerly Portuguese colony of Goa and the once-English colony of Bengal. There is a zestiness and spice to the cuisine, but never overpowering. The chefs keep the menu fairly short so that all ingredients can be purchased fresh every day.

A tasty specialty is stuffed *murgh masala,* a tender breast of chicken with potatoes, onions, apricots, and almonds, cooked with yogurt and served with a delectable curry sauce. The perfectly cooked duckling (off the bone) comes in a tangy sauce with a citrus bite. One of the finest dishes we tasted in North India is served here, and has lost nothing in the transfer: marinated lamb simmered in cream with cashew nuts and seasoned with fresh ginger. One of the best offerings from the Goan repertoire is the karkra chop, a spicy patty of minced crab blended with mashed potatoes and peppered with Goan spices.

Shad Thames, Butler's Wharf, SE1. ℂ 020/7357-9001. Reservations recommended. Main courses £10–£25 ($15–$37.50); set menu from £14 ($21); Sunday buffet £9 ($13.50). AE, DC, MC, V. Daily noon–2:30pm and 6–11:30pm. Tube: Tower Hill.

SOUTH BANK
EXPENSIVE

Oxo Tower Restaurant ✧ MODERN BRITISH/EUROPEAN   In the South Bank complex, on the eighth floor of the Art Deco Oxo Tower Wharf, is this dining sensation. It's called "the other tower" and is operated by the department store Harvey Nichols. Down the street from the newly rebuilt Globe Theater, this 140-seat restaurant could be visited for its view alone, but the cuisine

Family-Friendly Restaurants

Pizzeria Condotti *(Mayfair; p. 183)* If your young one insists on pizza, here's where to get it. Pies with succulent toppings emerge bubbling hot from the oven. The "American Hot" comes with mozzarella, pepperoni, sausages, and hot peppers—and the menu isn't just confined to pizzas.

Ye Olde Cheshire Cheese *(The City; p. 152)* Fleet Street's famous chophouse, established in 1667, is an eternal favorite. If "ye famous pudding" turns your kids off, sandwiches and roasts will tempt them.

Hard Rock Cafe *(Mayfair; p. 181)* This is a great place for kids old enough to busy themselves with rock-and-roll memorabilia as they wait for their familiar burgers, fries, and salads with Thousand Island dressing.

Porter's English Restaurant *(Covent Garden & the Strand; p. 164)* This restaurant serves traditional English meals that most kids love—especially the pies, stews, and steamed "spuds." They'll get a kick out of ordering the wonderfully named bubble-and-squeak and mushy peas.

Simpson's-in-the-Strand *(Covent Garden & the Strand; p. 163)* If your offspring is an aspiring Henry VIII, take him here for the best roasts in London, including tender roast sirloin of beef. For dessert, he might be introduced to such English favorites as a treacle roll.

Royal China *(Paddington & Bayswater; p. 204)* If there's a dim sum lover in your family, head for this eatery. We saw a young brother and sister devouring a dish of seafood golden cups—stir-fried scallops, prawns, water chestnuts, and mushrooms in crispy puff pastry.

is also stellar. You'll enjoy a sweeping view of St. Paul's Cathedral and the City, all the way to the House of Parliament. The decor is chic 1930s style.

The cuisine, under Chef Simon Arkless, is rich and prepared with finesse. Menu items change based on the season and the market. Count on a modern interpretation of British cookery, as well as the English classics. The fish is incredibly fresh here. The whole sea bass for two is delectable, as is the cannon of lamb with creamed garlic. The grilled escalopes of salmon with smoked chili and mango salsa are exotic and tasty, and the pan-fried filet of John Dory with scallops is served with a delicately flavored *fines herbes* risotto and a champagne sauce.

Barge House St., South Bank, SE1. ✆ 020/7803-3888. Main courses £17–£30 ($25.50–$45); fixed-price lunch £20.50 ($30.75). AE, DC, MC, V. Mon–Fri noon–3pm; Mon–Sat 6–11:30pm; Sun 6–10:30pm. Tube: Blackfriars or Waterloo.

MODERATE

Cantina Vinopolis ★ *Finds* MEDITERRANEAN Not far from the re-created Globe Theatre, this place is a "Walk-Through Wine Atlas." This brick-walled, high-vaulted brasserie was converted from abandoned Victorian railway arches, and is located in the revitalized Bankside neighborhood (which was once the entertainment center of London). Inside, you'll find both the Vinopolis

Wine Gallery and the Cantina Restaurant. Although many come here just to drink wine, the food is prepared with quality ingredients (very fresh), and the menu is sensibly priced. Start with a bit of heaven like a pumpkin and Parmesan soup with a lime-flavored crème fraîche or chargrilled asparagus with artichoke hearts and rocket. Dishes are flavorful and never overcooked. Squid fried in a crispy batter won us over, along with its side dish, wasabi slaw. The rump of lamb was tender and perfectly flavored, served with a polenta cake. Seared blue tuna arrived with sliced warm new potatoes, plus a tomato confit and a chorizo salad. Many of the other dishes have the hearty rustic taste that defines the trattorias of southern Italy. Naturally, the wine list is the biggest in the UK.

1 Bank End, London Bridge, SE1. ℂ 020/7940-8333. Reservations required. Main courses £12.50–£15 ($18.75–$22.50). MC, V. Daily noon–3pm; Mon–Sat 6–10:30pm. Tube: London Bridge.

3 The West End

BLOOMSBURY
VERY EXPENSIVE

Pied-à-Terre ✿ MODERN FRENCH   This foodie heaven understates its decor in favor of an intense focus on its subtle, sophisticated cuisine. You'll dine in a strictly minimalist room, where gray and pale pink walls compliment metal furniture and focused lighting that reveals a collection of modern art. France is the inspiration for the impressive wine list and some of the cuisine. The menu changes with the seasons but might include braised snails with celeriac, garlic, and a morel-flavored cream sauce; roasted scallops with apple and puréed ginger; halibut filets with queen scallops and caramelized endive; roasted partridge with pear; and the house specialty, a ballotine (stuffed and rolled into a bundle) of duck confit. If you're not dining with a vegetarian, braised pigs' head is another specialty. Our favorite item on the menu? Sea bass with vichyssoise (a thick soup of potatoes, leeks and cream) and caviar sauce. The food is beautifully presented on hand-painted plates with lush patterns.

34 Charlotte St., W1T. ℂ 020/7636-1178. Reservations recommended. Fixed-price 3-course lunch £23–£35 ($34.50–$52.50); fixed-price 3-course dinner £45–£60 ($67.50–$90); 8-course tasting menu £65 ($97.50). AE, DC, MC, V. Mon–Fri noon–2:30pm (last order); Mon–Sat 7–11pm. Closed last week of Dec and first 3 weeks of Jan. Tube: Goodge St.

EXPENSIVE

Archipelago ✿ THAI/FRENCH   This cozy restaurant is a celebrity favorite, attracting the likes of Madonna and Hugh Hefner when they are in town. Archipelago is definitely on the see-and-be-seen circuit. Media darling Michael Von Hruschka has decorated this restaurant in a whimsical style, with everything from birdcages to a Buddha serving as props. There are precious touches, such as the drink list written on delicate paper and inserted in an ostrich eggshell. Everything is presented in exquisite boxes, and even the bill comes in a book. Amazingly, with all the attention paid to the environment, the cuisine does not suffer in ingredients or preparation. Launch your repast with a coconut-and-lemon-grass soup or the most delectable small carrot spring rolls. Vegetable couscous and fish-and-banana risotto are delectable, and tiramisu is given an original touch with the addition of ginger wine.

110 Whitfield St., W1. ℂ 020/7383-3346. Reservations required as far in advance as possible. Set lunch £15.50–£20.50 ($23.25–$30.75); set dinner £32.50–£38.50 ($48.75–$57.75). MC, V. Mon–Fri noon–3pm; Mon–Sat 6–10:30pm. Tube: Goodge St.

Where to Dine in the West End

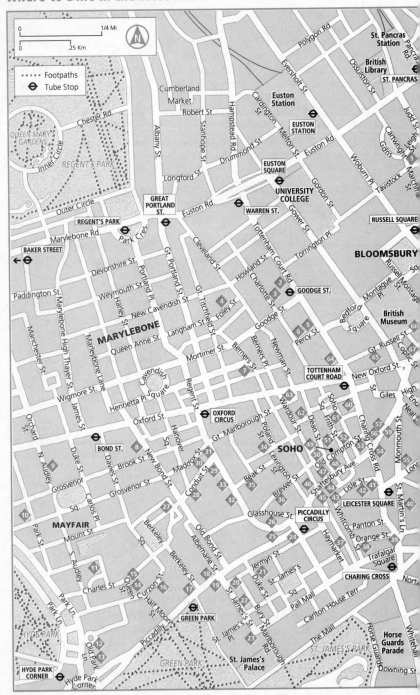

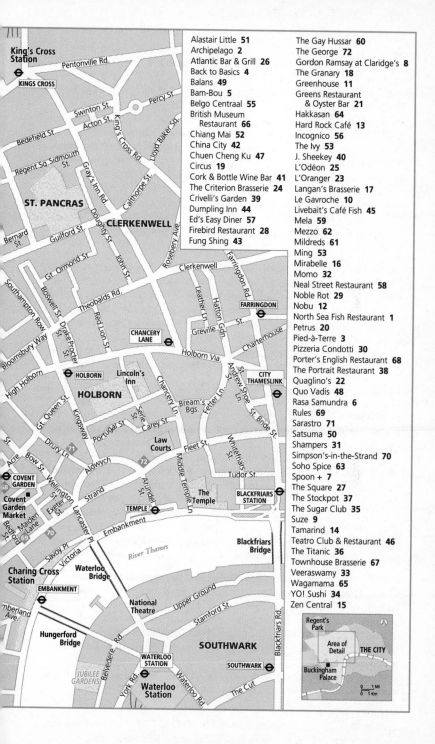

MODERATE

Back to Basics ✦ SEAFOOD   Stefan Plaumer's Fitzrovia bistro draws discerning palates seeking some of the freshest seafood in London. When the weather's fair, you can dine outside. Otherwise, retreat inside to a vaguely Parisian setting with a blackboard menu and checked tablecloths. The fish is served in large portions, and you can safely forgo an appetizer unless you're ravenous. More than a dozen seafood dishes are offered; the fish can be broiled, grilled, baked, or poached, but frying is not permitted. In other words, this is no fish and chippie. Start with a bowl of tasty, plump mussels or sea bass flavored with fresh basil and chili oil. Brill appears with green peppercorn butter, and plaice is jazzed up with fresh ginger and soy sauce. For the meat eater, there is Scotch rib eye or perhaps lamb steak. Freshly made salads accompany most meals, and an excellent fish soup is offered daily. For dessert, try the bread pudding or freshly made apple pie.

21A Foley St., W1. ✆ 020/7436-2181. Reservations recommended. Main courses £10.50–£15 ($15.75–$22.50). AE, DC, MC, V. Mon–Fri noon–3pm and 6–10pm. Tube: Oxford Circus or Goodge St.

North Sea Fish Restaurant ✦ *Value* SEAFOOD   The fish served in this bright, clean restaurant is fresh every day; the quality is high, and the prices low. In the view of London's diehard chippie devotees, it's the best in town. The fish is most often served battered and deep-fried, but you can also order it grilled. The menu is wisely limited. Students from the Bloomsbury area flock to the place.

7–8 Leigh St., WC1. ✆ 020/7387-5892. Reservations recommended. Fish platters £8–£17 ($12–$25.50). AE, DC, MC, V. Mon–Sat noon–2:30pm and 5:30–10:30pm. Tube: King's Cross, St. Pancras, or Russell Sq.

Townhouse Brasserie ✦ FRENCH/INTERNATIONAL   Near the British Museum, this Georgian town house is one of the up-and-coming restaurants in Bloomsbury. The ground floor is decorated with contemporary art, and upstairs is a traditional English dining room, with an infusion of Peruvian art. The frequently changing menu is a culinary tour de force, drawing inspiration from around the world. Ingredients are fresh, and are deftly handled by a skilled kitchen staff. Launch your repast with cream of leek soup or sweet potato soup with basil. Then it's on to a delectable charcoal-grilled duck breast with an Asian-style salad. Especially pleasing is a fresh seafood pasta flavored with chives, thick cream, and white wine. Save room for one of the tempting desserts made fresh daily.

24 Coptic St., WC1. ✆ 020/7636-2731. Reservations recommended. Main courses £10–£17.95 ($15–$26.90). AE, DC, MC, V. Mon–Sat 11am–11pm; Sun 10am–6pm. Tube: Tottenham Court Rd. or Holborn.

Wagamama JAPANESE   This noodle joint, in a basement just off New Oxford Street, is noisy and overcrowded, and you'll have to wait in line for a table. It calls itself a "non-destination food station" and caters to some 1,200 customers a day. Many dishes are built around ramen noodles with your choice of chicken, beef, or salmon. Try the tasty gyoza, light dumplings filled with vegetables or chicken. Vegetarian dishes are available, but skip the so-called Korean-style dishes.

4 Streatham St., WC1. ✆ 020/7323-9223. Reservations not accepted. Main courses £5.25–£11 ($7.90–$16.50). AE, MC, V. Mon–Sat noon–11pm; Sun 12:30–10pm. Tube: Tottenham Court Rd.

INEXPENSIVE

British Museum Restaurant TRADITIONAL BRITISH   This is the best place for lunch if you're exploring the wonders of this world-renowned museum.

It's on the lobby level of the West Wing and is decorated with full-size copies of the bas-reliefs from a temple in the town of Nereid in ancient Greece (you'll find the originals in nearby galleries.) The format is self-service. A few hot specials (including a vegetarian selection) and crisp salads are made fresh every day, and there's a good selection of fish and cold meat dishes. Try the soup and baguette special, changed daily. Desserts include pastries and cakes. There's also a cafe offering coffee, sandwiches, pastries, and soup.

Great Russell St., WC1. ⓒ 020/7323-8256. Main courses £7.25 ($10.90); soup and baguette special £5.75 ($8.65). MC, V. Cold food Mon–Wed 10am–5pm, Thurs–Fri 10am–7:45pm, Sat–Sun 10am–5pm. Hot food daily 10am–5pm. Tube: Russell Sq., Holborn, or Tottenham Court Rd.

COVENT GARDEN & THE STRAND

The restaurants in and around Covent Garden and the Strand are most convenient choices when attending theaters in the West End. For more detailed locations of restaurants close to the theaters, refer to the map "Where to Dine in the Theater District" (p. 165).

EXPENSIVE

Neal Street Restaurant ⭐ ITALIAN This stylish restaurant offers an extravagant variety of mushrooms, truffles, and other fungi. It's operated by Turin-born Antonio Carluccio, an authority on the use of mushrooms from around the world. The brick walls of a turn-of-the-20th-century warehouse are hung with the works of such modern masters as Frank Stella and David Hockney. The restaurant operates an aperitif bar in the cellar, where prospective diners sometimes wait for a table. Between 10 and 20 of the world's most exotic mushrooms are available at any time, including an assortment of truffles. Imported seasonally from China, Tibet, Japan, France, and California, they pop up in such recipes as *foie gras* with balsamic sauce; wild mushroom soup; pheasant consommé with morels and port; and tagliolini with truffle sauce. Equally appealing—but less expensive—are the venison ravioli with butter and sage; pappardelle pasta with mixed fungi; truffled egg tagliolini; or black angel-hair pasta with seafood and bottarga (dried tuna roe). Service is attentive and polite and the ambience agreeable. The tiramisu is justifiably popular.

26 Neal St., WC2. ⓒ 020/7836-8368. Reservations recommended. Main courses £18–£22 ($27–$33). AE, DC, MC, V. Mon–Sat noon–2:30pm and 6–11pm. Tube: Covent Garden.

Rules ⭐ TRADITIONAL BRITISH If you're looking for London's most quintessentially British restaurant, eat here. London's oldest restaurant was established in 1798 as an oyster bar; today, the antler-filled Edwardian dining rooms exude nostalgia. You can order such classic dishes as Irish or Scottish oysters, jugged hare, and mussels. Game dishes are offered from mid-August to February or March: wild Scottish salmon or wild sea trout; wild Highland red deer; and game birds like grouse, snipe, partridge, pheasant, and woodcock. As a finale, the "great puddings" continue to impress.

35 Maiden Lane, WC2. ⓒ 020/7836-5314. Reservations recommended. Main courses £16.95–£19.95 ($25.40–$29.90). AE, DC, MC, V. Daily noon–11:30pm. Tube: Covent Garden.

Simpson's-in-the-Strand ⭐ *Kids* TRADITIONAL AND MODERN BRITISH Simpson's is more of an institution than a restaurant. It's been in business since 1828, and as a result of a recent £2-million renovation, it's now better than ever with Adam paneling, crystal, and an army of formal waiters serving up the traditional British fare. Most agree that Simpson's serves the best roasts in London, an array including roast sirloin of beef, roast saddle of mutton with red-currant jelly, roast Aylesbury duckling, and steak-kidney-and-mushroom pie. (Remember to tip the tail-coated carver.) For a pudding, you might order the treacle roll and custard, or Stilton with vintage port.

Simpson's also serves traditional breakfasts. The most popular one, despite the £15.95 ($23.90) price, is "The Ten Deadly Sins": sausage, fried egg, streaky and back bacon, black pudding, lamb's kidneys, bubble-and-squeak (fried cabbage and potatoes), baked beans, lambs' liver, and fried bread, mushrooms, and tomatoes. That will certainly fortify you for the day.

Jacket and tie are no longer essential; we do recommend smart casual attire.

100 The Strand (next to the Savoy Hotel), WC2. ✆ 020/7836-9112. Reservations required. Main courses £22–£30 ($33–$45); fixed-price pre-theater dinner £15.50–£19.95 ($23.25–$29.90); breakfast from £15.95 ($23.90). AE, DC, MC, V. Mon–Fri 7:15–10am; Mon–Sat 12:15–2:15pm and 5:30–10:30pm; Sun noon–2pm and 6–9pm. Tube: Charing Cross or Embankment.

MODERATE

Porter's English Restaurant ✦ (Kids) TRADITIONAL BRITISH   The 7th Earl of Bradford serves "real English food at affordable prices" at this restaurant. He succeeds notably—and not just because Lady Bradford turned over her carefully guarded recipe for banana-and-ginger pudding. This comfortable, two-story restaurant is family friendly, informal, and lively. Porter's specializes in classic English pies, including Old English fish pie; lamb and apricot; ham, leek, and cheese; and, of course, bangers and mash. Main courses are so generous—and accompanied by vegetables and side dishes—that you hardly need appetizers. They have also added grilled English fare to the menu, with sirloin, lamb steaks and pork chops. The puddings, including bread-and-butter pudding and steamed syrup sponge, are served hot or cold, with whipped cream or custard. The bar does quite a few exotic cocktails, as well as beers, wine, or English mead. A traditional English tea is also served from 2:30 to 5:30pm for £3.95 ($5.95) per person.

17 Henrietta St., WC2. ✆ 020/7836-6466. Reservations recommended. Main courses £8.95–£12.95 ($13.40–$19.40); fixed-price menu £17.75 ($26.65). AE, DC, MC, V. Mon–Sat noon–11:30pm; Sun noon–10:30pm. Tube: Covent Garden or Leicester Sq.

INEXPENSIVE

The George TRADITIONAL BRITISH   Go here for the atmosphere of old England. Although its half-timbered facade would have you believe it's older than it is, this pub has been around *only* since 1723, when it was built as a coffeehouse. Set on the Strand, at the lower end of Fleet Street opposite the Royal Courts of Justice, the George is a favorite of barristers, their clients, and the handful of journalists who haven't moved to other parts of London. The pub's illustrious history saw Samuel Johnson having his mail delivered here and Oliver Goldsmith enjoying many tankards of what eventually became draught Bass. Today, the setting seems only slightly changed; much of the original architecture is still intact. Hot and cold platters, including bangers and mash, fish and chips, steak-and-kidney pie, and lasagna, are served from a food counter at the back of the pub. Additional seating is available in the basement, where a headless cavalier is said to haunt the same premises where he enjoyed his liquor in an earlier day.

213 The Strand, WC2. ✆ 020/7427-0941. Main courses £5.75–£7.25 ($8.65–$10.90). AE, MC, V. Mon–Fri 11am–11pm; Sat noon–3pm. Tube: Temple.

Sarastro ✦ TURKISH/CYPRIOT   The setting makes you feel like you're in the prop room of an opera house. As the manager says, "We're the show after the show." The decor is sort of neo-Ottoman, and the cuisine celebrates the bounty

Where to Dine in the Theater District

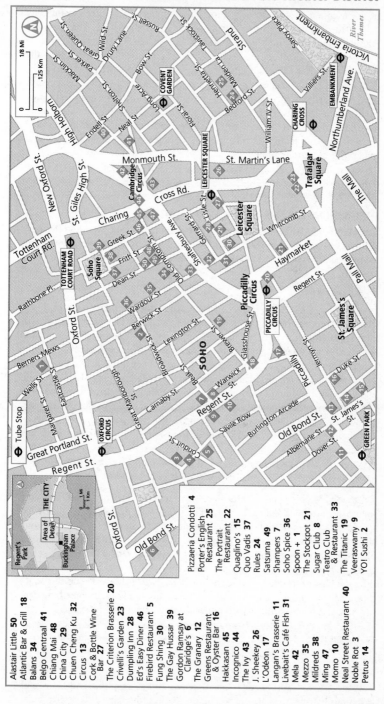

Φ Tube Stop

River Thames

Victoria Embankment

EMBANKMENT

CHARING CROSS

COVENT GARDEN

Russell St.

Wild St.

Drury Lane

Bow St.

Great Queen St.

Parker St.

Macklin St.

High Holborn

New Oxford St.

St. Giles High St.

Endell St.

Shelton St.

Neal St.

Long Acre

Floral St.

Henrietta St.

Maiden Lane

Bedford St.

Tavistock St.

Strand

Villiers St.

Savoy Place

Northumberland Ave.

William IV St.

Monmouth St.

St. Martin's Lane

Trafalgar Square

LEICESTER SQUARE

Cambridge Circus

Charing Cross Rd.

Lisle St.

Gerrard St.

Leicester Square

Whitcomb St.

The Mall

Tottenham Court Rd.

TOTTENHAM COURT ROAD

Greek St.

Frith St.

Dean St.

Old Compton St.

Shaftesbury Ave.

Soho Square

Rathbone Pl.

Oxford St.

Wardour St.

Berwick St.

Brewer St.

SOHO

Lexington St.

PICCADILLY CIRCUS

Piccadilly Circus

Haymarket

Regent St.

St. James's Square

Berners Mews

Wells St.

Eastcastle St.

Margaret St.

Great Marlborough St.

Broadwick St.

Beak St.

Carnaby St.

Warwick St.

Regent St.

Savile Row

Burlington Arcade

Glasshouse St.

Piccadilly

Jermyn St.

Duke St.

St. James's St.

Pall Mall

OXFORD CIRCUS

Great Portland St.

Oxford St.

Great Marlborough St.

Conduit St.

Old Bond St.

New Bond St.

Albemarle St.

Dover St.

GREEN PARK

Regent St.

Old Bond St.

Buckingham Palace

Regent's Park

THE CITY

Area of Detail

Alastair Little **50**
Atlantic Bar & Grill **18**
Balans **34**
Belgo Centraal **41**
Chiang Mai **48**
China City **29**
Chuen Cheng Ku **32**
Circus **13**
Cork & Bottle Wine Bar **27**
The Criterion Brasserie **20**
Crivelli's Garden **23**
Dumpling Inn **28**
Ed's Easy Diner **46**
Firebird Restaurant **5**
Fung Shing **30**
The Gay Hussar **39**
Gordon Ramsay at Claridge's **6**
The Granary **12**
Greens Restaurant & Oyster Bar **16**
Hakkasan **45**
Incognico **44**
The Ivy **43**
J. Sheekey **26**
L'Odéon **17**
Langan's Brasserie **11**
Livebait's Café Fish **31**
Mela **42**
Mezzo **35**
Mildreds **38**
Ming **47**
Momo **10**
Neal Street Restaurant **40**
Noble Rot **3**
Petrus **14**

Pizzaeria Condotti **4**
Porter's English Restaurant **25**
The Portrait Restaurant **22**
Quaglino's **15**
Quo Vadis **37**
Rules **24**
Satsuma **49**
Shampers **7**
Soho Spice **36**
Spoon + 1
The Stockpot **21**
Sugar Club **8**
Teatro Club & Restaurant **33**
The Titanic **19**
Veeraswamy **9**
YOI Sushi **2**

165

of the Mediterranean, especially Turkey and Cyprus. In a Victorian building behind the Theater Royal, the restaurant is decorated with battered urns, old lamps, fading lampshades, and knickknacks—an old Turkish curiosity shop look. Ten opera boxes adorn three sides of the restaurant; the royal box is the most desired. The restaurant takes its name from a character in Mozart's *The Magic Flute*. Live opera performances are staged from time to time. Launch your meal with delights like asparagus in red wine sauce or fresh grilled sardines. Fresh fish is the way to go, especially river trout or grilled halibut. A zesty favorite is lamb Anatolian style (with eggplant and zucchini). We're also fond of the well-seasoned lamb meatballs. A good tasting specialty is chicken Sarastro, made with walnuts and raisins.

126 Drury Lane, WC2. ℂ 020/7836-0101. Reservations required. Main courses £8.50–£15 ($12.75–$22.50). Fixed-price menu £10–£20 ($15–$30); pre-theater menu £10 ($15). AE, DC, MC, V. Daily noon–midnight. Tube: Covent Garden.

PICCADILLY CIRCUS & LEICESTER SQUARE

Piccadilly Circus & Leicester Square lie at the doorstep of the West End theaters. All the choices below are good candidates for dining before or after a show. For more detailed locations, refer to the map "Where to Dine in the Theater District" (p. 165).

EXPENSIVE

Fung Shing ✪ CANTONESE   In a city where the competition is stiff, Fung Shing emerges as London's finest Cantonese restaurant. Firmly established as a culinary landmark, it dazzles with classic and nouvelle Cantonese dishes. Look for the seasonal specials. Some of the dishes may be a bit experimental, notably stir-fried fresh milk with scrambled egg white, but you'll feel at home with the soft-shell crab sautéed in a light batter and served with tiny rings of red-hot chili and deep-fried garlic. Chinese gourmets come here for the fried intestines, but you may prefer the hotpot of stewed duck with yam, or the tender ostrich with yellow bean sauce. The spicy sea bass and the stir-fried crispy chicken are worthy choices. There are some 150 dishes from which to choose and most are moderate in price.

15 Lisle St., WC2. ℂ 020/7437-1539. Reservations required. Main courses £10–£26 ($15–$39); fixed-price menus £26–£34 ($39–$51). AE, DC, MC, V. Daily noon–11:30pm. Tube: Leicester Sq.

J. Sheekey ✪ SEAFOOD   British culinary tradition lives on in this fish joint, long a favorite of West End actors. The jellied eels that delighted Laurence Olivier and Vivien Leigh are still here, along with an array of fresh oysters from the coasts of Ireland and Brittany, plus that Victorian favorite, fried whitebait. Sheekey's fish pie is still on the menu, as is Dover sole, and a Cornish fish stew that's quite savory. The old "mushy" vegetables still appear, but the chefs also offer the likes of steamed organic sea beet. The double chocolate pudding soufflé is a delight, and many favorite puddings remain. But look for something daring now and then—perhaps fried plum ravioli with yogurt ice cream.

28–32 St. Martin's Court, WC2. ℂ 020/7240-2565. Reservations recommended. Main courses £9.75–£29.75 ($14.65–$44.65). AE, DC, DISC, MC, V. Daily noon–3pm and 7:30pm–midnight. Tube: Charing Cross.

MODERATE

Belgo Centraal BELGIAN   Chaos reigns supreme in this audacious and cavernous basement, where mussels mariniére plus frites, and 100 Belgian beers are the *raison d'être*. Take a freight elevator past the busy kitchen and into a converted cellar, divided into two large eating areas. One is a beer hall seating about 250; the menu here is the same as in the restaurant, but you don't need reservations. The restaurant side has three nightly seatings: 5:30, 7:30, and 10pm. Between 5:30 and 8pm you can choose one of three fixed-price menus, and you pay based on the time of your order: the earlier you order, the less you pay. Although heaps of fresh mussels are the big attraction, you can opt for fresh Scottish salmon, roast chicken, a perfectly done steak, or one of the vegetarian specialties. Gargantuan plates of wild boar sausages arrive with *stoemp*, Belgian mashed spuds and cabbage. Belgian stews called *waterzooï* are also served. With waiters in maroon monk's habits with black aprons, barking orders into headset microphones, it's all a bit bizarre.

50 Earlham St., WC2. ℭ 020/7813-2233. Reservations required for the restaurant. Main courses £9–£22 ($13.50–$33); fixed-price menus £7–£27 ($10.50–$40.50). AE, DC, MC, V. Mon–Sat noon–11:30pm; Sun noon–10:30pm. Closed Christmas. Tube: Covent Garden.

China City *Value* CANTONESE   This gigantic Chinese hash house feeds 500 at once and does so admirably well, and for a reasonable price (unless you start ordering lobster). Take a seat on one of two glass-fronted floors, furnished in a vaguely Oriental style, and study the huge menu. Both modern and classic Chinese dishes appear. This eatery is a good address to know about because it's not only central, but you can have lunch or dinner at any time during the afternoon or evening. Many opt for dim sum during the day, but in the evening select more elaborate dishes like eel fried in batter with chili, crab with glass noodles, crispy duck with pancakes, and, if you want to go native, crispy pork belly.

White Bear Yard, 25A Lisle St., WC2. ℭ 020/7734-3388. Reservations recommended. Main courses £7–£22.50 ($10.50–$33.75); fixed-price menus from £19 ($28.50). AE, MC, V. Daily noon–11:30pm. Tube: Leicester Sq.

Dumpling Inn CHINESE   Despite its cutesy name, this cool, elegant restaurant serves a delectable brand of Peking Mandarin cuisine that dates back almost 3,000 years. It owes some of its piquancy to various Mongolian ingredients, which are well represented in the restaurant's savory stew called "hotpot." Regulars come for the shark's-fin soup; the beef in oyster sauce; the seaweed; the sesame-seed prawns on toast; the duck with chili and black-bean sauce, and the fried sliced fish. The specialty is dumplings, and you can make a meal from the dim sum list. Portions aren't large, so order as many dishes as you'd like to sample. Chinese tea is extra. Service is leisurely so don't dine here before a theater date.

15a Gerrard St., W1. ℭ 020/7437-2567. Reservations recommended. Main courses £7–£17 ($10.50–$25.50); fixed-price lunch or dinner £15–£30 ($22.50–$45). AE, MC, V. Sun–Thurs noon–11:30pm; Fri–Sat 11:30am–10:30pm. Tube: Leicester Sq.

Incognico ★★ FRENCH/ECLECTIC   Michelin's three-star chef, Nico Ladenis, is firmly entrenched in Theaterland, which makes Incognico perfect for a pre-theater meal. A modern brasserie with dark-wood paneling and leather banquettes, Incognico offers even better food than the traditional area favorite, the long-running Ivy. Some items on the menu evoke the more famous Chez Nico, but most of the food is straightforward though not simplistic. The virtually faultless cuisine makes for a superlative dining experience, especially if you opt for such delights as filet of salmon with ginger, accompanied by a delicate plum sauce. The chef isn't afraid of the oldies, as exemplified by the marvelous veal kidneys in a mustard sauce. Our favorites are the seared filet of cod and the breast of guinea fowl with lentils. Here is Theaterland's best osso buco. You might also enjoy the artichokes with mushrooms and a sensuous hollandaise. One of the most contemporary dishes is open ravioli with goat's cheese.

117 Shaftesbury Ave., WC2. ✆ **020/7836-8866**. Reservations required. Lunch or pre-theater menu £12.50 ($18.75); main courses £12.50–£18.50 ($18.75–$27.75). AE, MC, V. Mon–Sat noon–3pm and 5:30pm–midnight. Tube: Leicester Sq.

The Ivy ✪ MODERN BRITISH/INTERNATIONAL   Effervescent and sophisticated, The Ivy is the choice of visiting theatrical luminaries. It has been intimately associated with the theater district since it opened in 1911. With its ersatz 1930s look and tiny bar near the entrance, this place is fun, and hums with the energy of London's glamour scene. The menu may seem simple, but the kitchen has a solid appreciation for fresh ingredients and a talent for preparation. Favorite dishes include white asparagus with sea kale and truffle butter; seared scallops with spinach, sorrel, and bacon; and salmon fishcakes. There's also Thai-spiced chicken soup with coconut cream; a great mixed grill; and such English desserts as sticky toffee (sponge cake soaked in a think caramelized syrup) and caramelized bread-and-butter pudding. Meals are served quite late to accommodate the post-theater crowd.

1–5 West St., WC2. ✆ **020/7836-4751**. Reservations required. Main courses £9–£35 ($13.50–$52.50); Sat–Sun fixed-price 3-course lunch £17.50 ($26.25). AE, DC, MC, V. Daily noon–3pm and 5:30pm–midnight (last order). Tube: Leicester Sq.

Livebait's Café Fish ✪ SEAFOOD   Don't you love the name of award-winning chef Andrew Magson's Soho eatery? The catch of the day can be chargrilled or pan-fried as you desire. We know of no better place in London to sample seafood favorites enjoyed by Brits back in the days of Sir Winston Churchill—we're talking smoked haddock kedgeree (a mixture of fish, rice, and hard-boiled eggs), cockles, whelks, steamed mussels, smoky grilled sardines, and the like. We like to go when the Dover sole is brought in. This eclectic menu includes fish flown all the way from the U.S. and Australia. Unlike some soggy chips (fries) at nearby dives, the ones here are crisp and fluffy. Our moist-fleshed sea bream, served with a crisp skin, made us want to "hasten ye back" to the restaurant the next night. From grandma's pantry comes a warm chocolate brownie to finish off the meal. Was that Tony Blair we spotted ten tables down, holding up a London tabloid with a caricature of President George W. Bush? Surely not.

36–40 Rupert St., W1. ✆ **020/7287-8989**. Reservations required. Main courses £10–£16.95 ($15–$25.40); set dinner £25.95 ($38.90). AE, MC, V. Mon–Fri noon–3pm and 5:30–11:30pm; Sat noon–11:30pm; Sun noon–10:30pm. Tube: Piccadilly Circus.

INEXPENSIVE

Cork & Bottle Wine Bar ✪ *Value* INTERNATIONAL   Don Hewitson, a connoisseur of fine wines for more than 30 years, presides over this treasure trove of blissful fermentations. The ever-changing wine list features an excellent selection of Beaujolais *crus* from Alsace, 30 choices from Australia, 30 champagnes, and a good selection of California labels. The most successful dish on the menu is a yeast-raised cheese-and-ham pie, with a cream cheese-like filling and crisp well-buttered pastry—not your typical quiche. There's also chicken and apple salad; Lancashire hotpot; Mediterranean prawns with garlic and asparagus; lamb in ale; and tandoori chicken.

44–46 Cranbourn St., WC2. ✆ **020/7734-7807**. Reservations not accepted after 6:30pm. Main courses £6.50–£11.95 ($9.75–$17.90); glass of wine from £3.50 ($5.25). AE, DC, MC, V. Mon–Sat 11am–11:30pm; Sun noon–10:30pm. Tube: Leicester Sq.

The Stockpot *Value* TRADITIONAL BRITISH/CONTINENTAL Pound for pound (British pounds, that is), we'd hazard a guess that this cozy little restaurant offers one of the best dining bargains in London. Meals might include a bowl of minestrone, spaghetti Bolognese, a plate of braised lamb, and apple crumble (or another dessert), among other items. At these prices, the food is hardly refined, but it's filling and satisfying nonetheless. During peak hours, the Stockpot has a share-the-table policy in its two-level dining room.

38 Panton St. (off Haymarket, opposite the Comedy Theatre), SW1. ℂ 020/7839-5142. Reservations accepted for dinner. Main courses £2.60–£5.90 ($3.90–$8.85); fixed-price 2-course lunch £3.90 ($5.85); fixed-price 3-course dinner £6.40 ($9.60). No credit cards. Mon–Sat 7am–11pm; Sun 7am–9:30pm. Tube: Piccadilly Circus or Leicester Sq.

SOHO

The restaurants of Soho are conveniently located for those rushing to have dinner and then an evening at one of the West End theaters. For more exact locations of the following restaurants, refer to the map "Where to Dine in the Theater District" (p. 165).

VERY EXPENSIVE

Spoon+ ✦ AMERICAN In Ian Schrager's hot new Sanderson Hotel, this is a branch of the Spoon that master chef Alain Ducasse lures *tout Paris* with. Like its Paris namesake, this is Monsieur Ducasse's take on American fusion cuisine. A waiter told us, "We prefer to cater mainly to bright young things, but try to be democratic as well." This is the only place you can go in London to eat a French version of that American classic—macaroni and cheese. Of course, there's also lobster in banana leaves if you want to go native. And who can beat Spoon+ when it comes to dishing up the best bubble-gum ice cream in London? We don't mean to make a caricature of the food, although some items seemed designed to shock. Much of what is offered, though, is really good, especially the crab ceviche, and the iced tomato soup. Spoon+ chefs allow you to compose your own meal or at least pair up ingredients—perhaps a beautiful sole with a crushed lemon confit, or do you prefer it with satay sauce? You choose from a trio of columns—main course, sauce, and accompanying side dish. On our last visit we found the restaurant ridiculously overpriced, but reconsidered when the entertainment of the evening arrived. Our fellow diners turned out to be none other than Madonna and her young groom, Guy Ritchie.

50 Berners St., W1. ℂ 020/7300-1400. Reservations required. Main courses £17–£30 ($25.50–$45). AE, DC, MC, V. Daily noon–3pm and 6–11:30pm (till 10:30pm Sun). Tube: Leicester Sq. or Covent Garden.

EXPENSIVE

Alastair Little ✦ MODERN BRITISH/CONTINENTAL In a brick-fronted town house (ca. 1830)—which, for a brief period supposedly housed John Constable's art studio—this informal, cozy restaurant is a pleasant place to enjoy a well-prepared lunch or dinner. Some critics claim that Alastair Little is the best chef in London, but lately he's been buried under the avalanche of new talent. Actually, Little is not often here; he spends a good deal of time at other enterprises. The talented James Rix is usually in charge. Style is modern European with a slant toward Italian. The menu changes daily. Starters might include a salad of winter leaves with crispy pork or chicken livers in Vin Santo (a sweet wine), flavored with fresh tomatoes and basil. The terrine of wild duck and *foie gras* is a surefire pleaser, as are such main-course delights as risotto with both flap and field mushrooms; and salted cod with spicy chickpeas and greens. For dessert, you can select an array of British cheeses or order such classics as a pear-and-red-wine tart. Ever have olive oil cake? It's served here with a winter fruit compote.

49 Frith St., W1. ℂ 020/7734-5183. Reservations recommended. Fixed-price dinner £35 ($52.50); fixed-price 3-course lunch £27 ($40.50). AE, DC, MC, V. Mon–Fri noon–3pm; Mon–Sat 6–11pm. Tube: Leicester Sq. or Tottenham Court Rd.

The Criterion Brasserie ✿ MODERN BRITISH/FRENCH   Designed by Thomas Verity in the 1870s, this palatial neo-Byzantine mirrored marble hall is a glamorous backdrop for superb cuisine, served under a golden ceiling with peacock-blue draperies, by a mainly French staff. The menu is wide ranging, offering everything from Paris brasserie food to "nouvelle-classical," a combination of classic French cooking techniques with some of the lighter, more experimental leanings of modern French cuisine. The food is excellent, but falls short of sublime. The roast skate wing with deep-fried snails is delectable, as is the roast saddle of lamb stuffed with mushrooms and spinach.

224 Piccadilly, W1. ℂ 020/7930-0488. Main courses £13.95–£21.50 ($20.90–$32.25); fixed-price 2-course lunch £15 ($22.50); fixed-price 3-course lunch £18 ($27). AE, MC, V. Daily noon–2:30pm and 5:30–11:30pm. Tube: Piccadilly Circus.

L'Odéon ✿ FRENCH   When the renowned chef Bruno Loubet opened this chic 1930s-style brasserie, headlines read "Loubet Cooks for the Masses." And the place is indeed massive: In all, some 250 diners can pack this place. (Opt for a table looking out on Regent Street and its bright-red double-decker buses.)

Loubet is no longer here, but his sous chef, Colin Layfield, carries on, with a menu rooted in the Loubet repertoire. However, the culinary style isn't as daring or provocative, and has switched to a more classic French cuisine. Opt for the pan-fried sea bream with a peppery butter sauce, or roast farmhouse chicken with Parmesan, served with basmati rice. For starters, try a light mussel-saffron mousse or a risotto of mushrooms with Parmesan shavings. For dessert, the poached apple in saffron with dried-fig ice cream or the roast papaya with whiskey-and-caramel ice cream will dazzle the palate.

65 Regent St., W1. ℂ 020/7287-1400. Reservations required. Main courses £12.50–£25 ($18.75–$37.50); fixed-price lunch £16 ($24) for 2 courses, £20 ($30) for 3 courses. AE, DC, MC, V. Mon–Sat and Sun noon–2:30pm; Mon–Sat 5:30–11pm. Tube: Piccadilly Circus.

The Sugar Club ✿ PACIFIC RIM   This restaurant comes from the land Down Under, with an adventurous menu. Ashley Sumner and Vivienne Hayman originally launched their restaurant in New Zealand in the mid-1980s. Now they have moved into Soho with their original chef, the talented Peter Gordon, known for attracting homesick Aussies with the best loin of grilled kangaroo in London. The setting is inviting, with soft textures, pale cream colors, and wooden floors. The restaurant is elegant and spacious, offering a bar waiting area for diners, a separate nonsmoking floor, and an open kitchen.

The flavors are often stunning—a good example is the sashimi of Iki Jimi yellowtail with a black bean-and-ginger salsa. The fish tastes amazingly fresh, and flavors surprise the palate in the most exciting ways. You might dig into the duck leg braised in tamarind and star anise, with coconut rice, or try the pan-fried turbot with spinach, sweet potato, and red curry sauce. Many of the starters are vegetarian and can be upgraded to a main course. For dessert, the blood-orange curd tart with crème fraîche is devastatingly delicious.

21 Warwick St., W1. ℂ 020/7437-7776. Main courses £14–£22 ($21–$33). AE, DC, MC, V. Daily noon–3pm and 6–11pm. Tube: Piccadilly Circus or Oxford Circus.

Teatro Club & Restaurant ✮ MODERN BRITISH   This is still called London's restaurant of the moment even though it's been around since 1998, when it was acclaimed for its contemporary British fare. Having Gordon Ramsay, one of London's top chefs, as its consultant helped. The minimalist chic decor is the creation of Lee Chapman, a footballer, and his wife, actress Leslie Ash. The chef is John Newton, an artist who cooks with precision and skill.

The cuisine is richer than the interior, beginning with such starters as warm carpaccio of monkfish and squid with herb and chili dressing. The crab bisque is velvety smooth, as is the *foie gras* du jour. Salmon appears with a lemony couscous. You can delve into the roast filet of cod with girolle mushrooms, peas, and spinach; or perhaps the leg of Barbary duck with wild mushrooms, borlotti beans, and basil. Horseradish butter gives added zest to the grilled halibut. Desserts are a journey into nostalgia: fresh plum tartlet with custard, banana sticky toffee, and the like. The best deal is the £13.50 ($20.25) fixed-price dinner.

93–107 Shaftesbury Ave., W1. ✆ 020/7494-3040. Fax 020/7494-3050. Reservations required. Main courses £16.95–£35 ($25.40–$52.50); fixed-price menus (lunch or dinner) £14–bp]16.95 ($21–$25.40). AE, DC, MC, V. Mon–Fri noon–3pm; Mon–Sat 6–11:30pm. Tube: Piccadilly Circus.

MODERATE

Atlantic Bar & Grill MODERN BRITISH   A titanic restaurant in a former Art Deco ballroom off Piccadilly Circus, this 160-seat locale draws a trendy crowd to London's heart. The restaurant is cosmopolitan, and it's one of the best choices for the after-theater crowd because it closes at 3am most nights. It doesn't attract celebrities as it did back in 1994, but it's still going strong. Chef Steve Carter is doing much to recapture the restaurant's mid-1990s chic. He turns out a new menu every 2 months with emphasis on organic and home-grown produce, seafood, and meats. Some dishes are quite complicated and taste as good as they sound: swordfish dumplings with a salsa of plum tomatoes, fresh cilantro, seated shiitake, soy-infused ginger, and fresh wilted spinach.

For a starter, we recommend the smoked-chicken Caesar club salad. Also memorable is the loin of yellowfin tuna served with a wild parsley-and-eggplant relish and a roasted red bell pepper pesto. The desserts are purposefully unsophisticated: Rice pudding or poached pears are standards. If you're rushed, you can drop into Dick's Bar for a quick bite. The offerings at Dick's include everything from lamb burgers sparked with yogurt and fresh mint, to Cashel blue cheese and pumpkin seeds on ciabatta bread. Most dishes are at the low end of the price scale.

20 Glasshouse St., W1. ✆ 020/7734-4888. Reservations required. Main courses £12.50–£21.50 ($18.75–$32.25); fixed-price 3-course lunch £16.50 ($24.75). AE, DC, MC, V. Mon–Fri noon–3pm; Mon–Sat 6pm–3am; Sun 6–10:30pm. Tube: Piccadilly Circus.

Bam-Bou ✮ VIETNAMESE/FRENCH   London's best Vietnamese-inspired eatery is spread over a series of dining rooms, alcoves, and bars in a town house with tattered French colonial decor. A favorite of young London, the restaurant is so popular that you may have to wait for 30 minutes to an hour for a table. The smell of lime and lemon grass lures you to the table—this combination is married perfectly in the chicken in lemon grass dish. Equally worthy is the caramelized ginger chicken. One of our party ordered tempura of softshell crab with a pemlo citrus and mizuna leaf lettuce salad, and fellow diners nibbled so much that he had to order another helping. Lemon grass and chicken are wed again, very effectively, in a brochette with peanuts. The stuffed cod with tamarind is aromatically appealing, as is the monkfish flavored with an exotic turmeric and onion. Our favorite starter is spicy raw beef with aromatic basil, lime, and chili, or fried marinated squid. A winner for dessert is the sweet banana rolls with chocolate sauce.

1 Percy St., W1. © 020/7323-9130. Reservations required. Main courses £8.50–£13.75 ($12.75–$20.65). AE, DC, MC, V. Mon–Fri noon–11:15pm; Sat 6–11:15pm. Tube: Tottenham Court Rd.

Chuen Cheng Ku CHINESE   This is one of the finest places in Soho's New China. Taking up several floors, Chuen Cheng Ku has the longest, most interesting Cantonese menu in town. Specialties of the house are paper-wrapped prawns; rice in lotus leaves; steamed spareribs in black-bean sauce; and shredded pork with cashew nuts—all served in generous portions. Other featured dishes include lobster with ginger and spring onion, sliced duck in chili and black-bean sauce; and Singapore noodles (thin, rich noodles, sometimes mixed with curry and pork, and sometimes with shrimp with red and green pepper). Dim sum is served from 11am to 5:30pm. We note, however, that the standard of service has slipped over the years.

17 Wardour St., W1. © 020/7437-1398. Reservations recommended on weekend afternoons. Main courses £5.50–£16 ($8.25–$24); fixed-price menus £8.50–£25 ($12.75–$37.50). AE, DC, MC, V. Daily 11am–11:45pm. Closed Dec 24–25. Tube: Piccadilly Circus or Leicester Sq.

The Gay Hussar ★ HUNGARIAN   Is it still the best Hungarian restaurant in the world? That's what some say. We can't agree until we've sampled every Hungarian restaurant in the world, but we're certain Gay Hussar would be near the top. Since 1953, it's been an intimate place with authentic cuisine, a loyal clientele of politicians, and a large international following, especially among visiting Hungarians. You can begin with a chilled wild-cherry soup or mixed Hungarian salami. Gutsy main courses might include cabbage stuffed with minced veal and rice, half a perfectly done chicken in mild paprika sauce with cucumber salad and noodles, excellent roast duck with red cabbage and Hungarian-style caraway potatoes, and, of course, veal goulash with egg dumplings. Expect gigantic portions. For dessert, go with either the poppy seed strudel or walnut pancakes.

2 Greek St., W1. © 020/7437-0973. Reservations recommended. Main courses £10–£17 ($15–$25.50); fixed-price lunch £15.50 ($23.25) for 2 courses, £18.50 ($27.75) for 3 courses. AE, DC, DISC, MC, V. Mon–Sat 12:30–2pm and 5:30–10:30pm. Tube: Tottenham Court Rd.

Hakkasan ★ *(Finds)* CHINESE   Asian mystique and pastiche are found in this offbeat place, lying in a seedy alley off Tottenham Court Road. This is another London venture created by Alan Yau, who became a city-wide dining legend because of his Wagamama noodle bars. For his designer, he obtained Christian Liaigre, who created a dining room encapsulated in a lattice wood "cage" evocative of antique Chinese doors. The leather sofas are emblazoned with dragons, and a bar runs the length of the restaurant. Come here for great dim sum and tantalizing cocktails. Feast on such dishes as *har gau* (steamed prawn dumplings) and strips of tender barbecued pork. The spring roll is refreshing with the addition of fried mango, and a delicate prawn and scallop filling. Steamed scallop shumai (dumplings) with tobiko caviar are fresh and meltingly soft. You may want to sample such delights as the steamed asparagus with bamboo pith and dried shiitake, or the fried taro croquettes. Desserts in most of London's Chinese restaurants are hardly memorable, but the offerings here are an exception to that rule, especially the layered banana sponge with chocolate cream.

8 Hanway Pl. © 020/7907-1888. Reservations recommended. Main courses £8.50–£28 ($12.75–$42). AE, MC, V. Daily noon–2:30pm and 6–11pm. Tube: Tottenham Court Rd.

Mela ⭐ *Value* INDIAN   Serious foodies know that you'll likely be served some of London's finest Indian cuisine at this address. Both Carlton Television and the London Evening Standard named this the best Indian restaurant in Britain in 2001. Expect robust aromas and earthy flavors. Our spiced duck flavored with spring onions, ginger, and coriander evoked some of the best country dining in India. Eggplant came stuffed with a spicy lamb mince, and was superb, as was the whole fresh fish of the day in a spicy marinade flavored with saffron and cooked whole in a charcoal oven. Some of the best curries in the city are served here. Tawa cookery (which in India is street cookery on a hot plate) is a specialty. At Mela, the fresh meats and other ingredients are cooked straight on a hot plate. Look for the chef's special Tawa dish of the day, perhaps succulent queen prawns cooked with onions and fresh tomatoes. Save room for a very special dessert—Sheer Birinj, a rice pudding better than mom made, with such ingredients as milk-ghee (butter), cream, and almonds, pistachio, and cashews.

152–156 Shaftesbury Ave., WC2. ℂ 020/7836-8635. Reservations required. Main courses £8–£14 ($12–$21). Set lunch £5.95 ($8.95); set dinner (5:30–7pm) £10.95 ($16.40). AE, MC, V. Daily noon–11:45pm. Tube: Tottenham Court Rd. or Leicester Sq.

Mezzo MODERN EUROPEAN/ASIAN   This blockbuster 750-seat Soho spot—the creation of Sir Terence Conran—is the biggest restaurant in London. The mammoth space, the former site of rock's legendary Marquee club, is actually composed of several restaurants: **Mezzonine** upstairs, serving a Thai/Asian cuisine with European flair (deep-fried salt-and-pepper squid flavored with garlic, and coriander; and roast duck with Thai red curry and fragrant rice); swankier **Mezzo** downstairs, offering a modern European cuisine in an atmosphere of 1930s Hollywood; and **Mezzo Cafe,** where you can stop in for a simple sandwich and a drink.

The food is at its most ambitious downstairs at Mezzo, where 100 chefs work behind glass to feed up to 400 diners at a time. This is dinner-as-theater. Not surprisingly for this size restaurant, the cuisine tends to be uneven. We suggest the rotisserie rib of beef with red wine and creamed horseradish, or the roast cod, which is crisp-skinned and cooked to perfection. For dessert, you can't beat the butterscotch ice cream with a pitcher of hot fudge. A live jazz band entertains after 10pm from Wednesday to Saturday, and the world of Marlene Dietrich and Noël Coward comes alive again.

100 Wardour St., W1. ℂ 020/7314-4000. Reservations accepted. Mezzo 3-course fixed-price dinner £16.50 ($24.75); Mezzonine 3-course dinner £14.50 ($21.75). AE, DC, MC, V. Mezzo: Wed–Fri noon–3pm; Sun 12:30–3pm; Mon–Thurs 6pm–midnight; Fri–Sat 6pm–3am; Sun 6–11pm. Mezzonine: Mon–Fri noon–3pm; Sat noon–4pm; Mon–Thurs 5:30pm–1am; Fri–Sat 5:30pm–3am. Mezzo Cafe: Mon–Sat 8am–11pm. Tube: Piccadilly Circus.

Ming CANTONESE/PEKINESE   This winning restaurant is located on Shaftesbury Avenue behind the Palace Theatre. The chefs, Mr. Bib and Mr. Bun, welcome you to their gaily decorated green and pink Far East outpost. This is no chop suey joint; many of the recipes have real flair. One dish is described as an 18th-century recipe from the Emperor Qian Long's head chef. What dazzled the emperor? Lean pieces of tender lamb with a slightly sweetened soy sauce. Fish, especially prawns and squid, are prepared in delectable ways, as are a number of tofu combinations. Cauliflower, sautéed in butter and flavored with bits of chili and slivers of spring onions, is an unusual appetizer. You might follow with spiced and peppered duck breast, or simmered chicken with ginger and orange. White fish rolls are intriguing, wrapped in a bean "skin." Mussels in black bean sauce are worth a return visit, as is a whole sea bass cooked Thai style.

However, you're better off skipping the "Chiu Yim sliced eel-and-sea spice shredded pork." We weren't sure what we were eating!

35–36 Greek St., W1. ✆ **020/7734-2721.** Main courses £7.50–£18 ($11.25–$27); fixed-price 2-course dinner £10 ($15); fixed-price 3-course dinner £20 ($30). AE, DC, MC, V. Mon–Sat noon–11:45pm. Tube: Leicester Sq. or Piccadilly Circus.

Quo Vadis ⭐ MODERN BRITISH   This hyper-trendy restaurant occupies the former apartment house of Karl Marx, who would never recognize it nowadays. It was an Italian restaurant from 1926 until the mid-1990s, when its interior was transformed into the stylish postmodern place you'll find today. The stark street-level dining room is a showcase for the ultra-modern paintings of the controversial Damien Hirst and other contemporary artists. Many bypass the restaurant for the upstairs bar, where Hirst has put a severed cow's head and a severed bull's head on display in separate aquariums. Why? They're catalysts to conversation, satirical odes to the destructive effects of mad cow disease, and perhaps tongue-in-cheek commentaries on the flirtatious games that patrons conduct here.

Quo Vadis is associated with Marco Pierre White, but don't expect to see the culinary superstar; he functions as a consultant. Also, don't expect the over-burdened staff to pamper you; they're preoccupied dealing with the glare of publicity. And the food? It's well presented and very good, but not as artful or innovative as the setting might lead you to believe. We suggest the tomato and red mullet broth perfumed with basil, or the terrine of *foie gras* and duck confit. Then try the escallop of tuna with tapenade (olive spread) and eggplant "caviar" (actually eggplant and black olives puréed and seasoned, which gives it the look of caviar) or the breast of chicken *Quo Vadis*, which is stuffed with Gallego cheese, parma ham, and black truffles, and served with mashed potatoes and sautéed mushrooms.

26–29 Dean St., W1D. ✆ **020/7437-9585.** Reservations required. Main courses £12.50–£27.50 ($18.75–$41.25); fixed-price lunches and pre- and post-theater £14.95–£17.95 ($22.40–$26.90). AE, MC, V. Mon–Fri noon–3pm; Mon–Sat 6–11pm. Tube: Leicester Sq. or Tottenham Court Rd.

Rasa Samundra ⭐ *Value* INDIAN/KERALAN   This outpost offers the best southern Indian cuisine in town. While most London Indian restaurants specialize in the cuisine of the north, Rasa Samundra features cookery of the southern state of Kerala, with specialties from the sea. Owner Das Sreedharan's mother has trained all the chefs and the results are delectable. Try *malslam pattichathu* (kingfish cooked in fresh spices, with green chile and coconut paste), *para konju nirachathu* (lobster cooked with black pepper, garlic, and Indian shallots, and served with whole lemon and beet root curry), *masala dosa* (paper-thin rice and black grain pancakes filled with potato and ginger masala) and *moru kachlathu* (green bananas and mangoes cooked in a yogurt sauce with turmeric and onions). Rasa also offers a range of appetizers, side orders, breads, rice, and desserts. Most dishes are at the lower end of the price scale.

5 Charlotte St., W1. ✆ **020/7637-0222.** Reservations required. Main courses £10–£30 ($15–$45); fixed-price lunch £20 ($30); fixed-price dinner £30 ($45). AE, DC, MC, V. Daily noon–11pm. Tube: Tottenham Court Rd.

Satsuma JAPANESE   This funky Japanese canteen is all the rage in London. Clean lines, stark white walls, and long wooden tables might suggest an upmarket youth hostel. But patrons come for good food at reasonable prices. It's ideal for a pre-theater visit. Your meal comes in a lacquered bento box on a matching tray. Try the chicken teriyaki or fresh chunks of tuna and salmon. The dumplings are excellent, as is the miso soup. A specialty is a large bowl of seafood ramen, noodles swimming in a well-seasoned broth studded with mussels, scallops, and prawns. Tofu steaks are a delight, as are udon noodles with wok-fried chicken and fresh vegetables. You can finish with deep-fried tempura ice cream.

56 Wardour St., W1. ✆ 020/7437-8338. Reservations recommended. Main courses £3.90–£15 ($5.85–$22.50). AE, MC, V. Mon–Tues noon–11pm; Wed–Thurs noon–11:30pm; Fri–Sat noon–midnight; Sun noon–10:30pm. Tube: Piccadilly Circus.

Shampers CONTINENTAL   This is a favorite of West End wine-bar aficionados. In addition to the street-level wine bar serving snacks, there's a more formal basement-level restaurant. In either venue, you can order such main dishes as grilled calves' liver with bacon, chips, and salad; pan-fried large prawns with ginger, garlic, and chili; and platters of cheeses. Salads are popular, including grilled eggplant salad with tomato, avocado, buffalo mozzarella, and pesto; and spicy chicken salad. The platter of Irish mussels cooked in a cream-and-tarragon sauce is everybody's favorite. The restaurant is closed in the evening, but the bar serves an extended menu, incorporating such dishes as fresh squid, tuna steak, pan-fried tiger prawns, free-range chicken, and a variety of other offerings.

4 Kingly St. (between Carnaby and Regent sts.), W1. ✆ 020/7437-1692. Reservations recommended. Main courses £8.75–£13.50 ($13.15–$20.25). AE, DC, MC, V. Mon–Sat noon–11pm. Wine bar open at the same times. Closed Easter and Christmas. Tube: Oxford Circus.

Soho Spice SOUTH INDIAN   One of central London's most stylish Indian restaurants combines a sense of media and fashion hip with the flavors and scents of southern India. You might opt for a drink at the cellar bar before heading to the street-level dining room, decorated in saffron, cardamom, bay, and pepper hues. A staff member dressed in similarly vivid apparel will propose a wide array of choices, including slow-cooked Indian tikkas that feature combinations of spices with lamb, chicken, fish, or vegetables. The a la carte menu offers a variety of courses, including *Jhinga Hara Pyaz*, spicy queen prawns with fresh spring onions, and *Paneer Pasanda*, cottage cheese slices stuffed with spinach and served with almond sauce. The cuisine will satisfy traditionalists, but has a modern flair. The presentation takes it a step above typical Indian restaurants.

124–126 Wardour St., W1. ✆ 020/7434-0808. Reservations recommended. Main courses £9.95–£14.95 ($14.90–$22.40); set dinner £14.95 ($22.40). AE, V. Mon–Thurs 11:30am–12:30am; Fri–Sat 11:30am–3am; Sun 12:30–10:30pm. Tube: Tottenham Court Rd.

The Titanic MODERN BRITISH   Although the phone number (1912 is the year the Titanic went down) and the restaurant name suggest a different ship, the staff points out that the nautical Art Deco decor is modeled after the *Queen Mary*. Expect a large, crowded venue where tables turn over several times during the course of a night (not literally, thankfully). Our favorite menu items include *bresaola* (Scottish beef cured in the Mediterranean style with olive oil and herbs); snails in garlic butter; oysters; mussels in white wine; Caesar salads; fish and chips with mushy peas; brochettes of lamb Provençal; and caramelized skate. After 11:30pm, the focus moves to breakfast, presumably for night owls who have worked up an appetite, or for any transatlantic flyer suffering from jet lag and a hankering for eggs Benedict, an omelet, kippers, or shirred eggs with calves' liver.

In the Regent Palace Hotel, 12 Sherwood St., near Piccadilly Circus, W1A. ✆ 020/7437-1912. Reservations required. Main courses £13–£27 ($19.50–$40.50). AE, DC, MC, V. Daily 5:30–11:30pm; breakfast daily 11:30pm–3am. Tube: Piccadilly.

YO! Sushi *(Kids* SUSHI This is London's sushi Disneyland, with high-tech gadgets, gimmicks, and surprisingly good sushi. If you've got a kid, and you want to indoctrinate him or her into the ways of raw fish, this is the place to go. YO! Sushi has the longest sushi bar in the world, with a *kaiten* (conveyor belt) serving 130 guests. You're allowed to choose two pieces of sushi from five price categories. Plates have five colors that match the prices. Lime is the cheapest, pink the most expensive. Service robots move around and take your drink orders. Some of the chefs are actual human beings, although they turn out sushi at automated speeds. They stand behind a counter where you can order everything from fresh clams to avocado-and-salmon hand rolls. You can have your fill of cuttlefish, eel, shrimp, salmon roe, octopus, whatever. Vegetarian sushi includes pickled turnip and cucumber. Wash it all down with Sapporo beer, Japanese tea, or iced or hot sake. Live footage from Japan on Sony wide-screen TVs keeps you amused.

52 Poland St., W1. ℂ 020/7287-0443. Reservations recommended. Sushi £1.50–£3.50 ($2.25–$5.25). AE, DC, MC, V. Daily noon–midnight. Tube: Oxford Circus.

INEXPENSIVE

Balans MODERN BRITISH On one of the gayest streets in London, Old Compton Street, Balans is the best known gay restaurant in London, and has been since its inauguration in 1993. Some of its diehard fans take all their meals here. Its hours of service are almost without equal in London. Although the food is British, it is an eclectic cuisine, borrowing freely from whatever kitchen it chooses, from the Far East to America. You can fill up on one of the succulent pastas, especially the black-ink tortellini sprinkled with scallops. Grills delight the mostly male patrons, especially the tuna teriyaki or the charred roast chicken. Balans has a party pub atmosphere and is a good place to meet people.

60 Old Compton St., W1. ℂ 020/7437-5212. Reservations recommended. Main courses £6–£14 ($9–$21). AE, MC, V. Mon–Sat 8am–5am; Sun 8am–2am. Tube: Piccadilly Circus or Leicester Sq.

Chiang Mai THAI This restaurant, in the center of Soho, is named after the ancient northern capital of Thailand, a region known for its rich, spicy foods. Try the hot-and-sour dishes or vegetarian meals. It's located next door to Ronnie Scott's, the most famous jazz club in England, so it's a good stop for an early dinner before a night on the town. Children's specials are available.

48 Frith St., W1. ℂ 020/7437-7444. Reservations recommended. Main courses £6.95–£12.50 ($10.45–$18.75); 2-course set lunch £10 ($15). AE, MC, V. Mon–Sat noon–3pm and 6–11pm; Sun 6–10:30pm. Tube: Leicester Sq. or Tottenham Court Rd.

Ed's Easy Diner AMERICAN This is one of four branches of the popular retro American diner. It's the kind of place Michael J. Fox might have walked into in *Back to the Future*. Featuring 1950s and 1960s rock-and-roll on the jukebox, a horseshoe-shaped counter with the kitchen in the middle, and a staff that fits the theme, the restaurant offers not only good diner staples such as burgers, onion rings, waffles, hash, and cheesecake, but also good people-watching, with a broad cross-section of fashion trends on parade around the counter.

12 Moor St., W1. ℂ 020/7439-1955. Reservations not accepted. Main courses £3.95–£6 ($5.95–$9). MC, V. Sun–Thurs 11:30am–11pm; Fri–Sat 11:30am–1am. Closed Christmas. Tube: Leicester Sq. and Tottenham Court Rd.

Mildreds *(Finds* VEGETARIAN Mildreds may sound like a 1940s Joan Crawford movie, but it's one of London's most enduring vegetarian and vegan dining spots. It was vegetarian long before such restaurants became trendy. Jane

Muir and Diane Thomas worked in various restaurants together before opening their own place. Today they run a busy, bustling diner with casual, friendly service. Sometimes it's a bit crowded and tables are shared. They do a mean series of delectable stir-fries. The ingredients in their dishes are naturally grown, and they strongly emphasize the best seasonal produce. The menu changes daily, but features an array of homemade soups, casseroles, and salads. Organic wines are served, and portions are very large. Save room for their desserts, especially the nutmeg-and-mascarpone ice cream or the chocolate, rum, and amaretto pudding.

45 Lexington St., W1. ℂ **020/7494-1634.** Reservations not accepted. Main courses £5.30–£7 ($7.95–$10.50). No credit cards. Mon–Sat noon–11pm. Tube: Tottenham Court Rd.

Veeraswamy *Value* INDIAN   The oldest Indian restaurant in England, originally established in the 1920s, has been restyled and rejuvenated and is looking better than ever, its menu redone. Today, it serves some of the most affordable fixed-price menus in Central London, lying in the heart of the city off Piccadilly Circus. Shunning the standard fare offered in most London-based Indian restaurants, Veeraswamy features dishes prepared authentically and freshly, as in a private Indian home. Try almost anything: spicy oysters, brochette of monkfish, chicken curry with almonds, succulent Tandoori chicken, tender, flavorful lamb curry. One of our favorite dishes is lamb with turnips from Kashmir, flavored with large black cardamons, powdered fennel, and a red chili powder giving the dish a savory red color and flavor.

Victory House, 99 Regent St., W1 ℂ **020/7734-1401.** Reservations recommended. Lunch and pre/post theater menu £12.50–£14.75 ($18.75–$22.15). Sun menu £15 ($22.50). Main courses £13–£21 ($19.50–$31.50). AE, DC, MC, V. Mon–Fri noon–2:30pm; Sat–Sun 12:30–3pm. Daily 5:30–11pm. Tube: Picadilly Circus.

TRAFALGAR SQUARE
MODERATE

Crivelli's Garden ⚜ ITALIAN/FRENCH   In the National Gallery, at Trafalgar Square, this hot new dining choice lies over the foyer of the Sainsbury Wing, providing a panoramic view of this fabled square. The view's a bonus—it's the

---

  Après-Theater Dining

For years, lower-priced menus and a lack of late-night eateries convinced most theatergoers to dine before the show. But recently, the city has begun to accommodate those who prefer dining after the theater. **Quaglino's** (p. 185) is a vast establishment that stays open until midnight or 1am. If a hamburger or steak will do, head for the **Hard Rock Cafe** (p. 181), or if you crave pizza, go to **Pizzeria Condotti** (p. 183).

At the heart of Piccadilly Circus, the **Atlantic Bar & Grill** (p. 171) offers its modern British cuisine until 3am. Nearby, you can make it to **Circus** (p. 184) before the last orders go in at midnight or order from the bar menu until 1:30am. **Balans** (p. 176), which caters to a gay crowd, serves until the wee hours. In Soho, **Mezzo** (p. 173) seats 750 so you're also guaranteed a table. It stays open to either 1am or 3am, depending on the day.

cuisine that attracts visitors. The restaurant is named for a striking mural by Paulo Rego that is painted on one side of a wall. The chefs are equally at home with both French and Italian dishes, offering wood-fired pizzas and bruschetta, or more imaginative choices, such as gnocchi with rocket and wild mushrooms. Try the grilled rib of pork, marinated and served with baby artichokes. The lightly batter-fried sole is a worthy choice as well. The steamed salmon with leeks, cilantro, and ginger is an excellent dish, as is the red pepper ravioli in a chive sauce. There is cafe in the basement of the main building, which is a good choice for sandwiches, pastas, soups, and pastries.

In the National Gallery, Trafalgar Square, WC2. ℂ 020/7747-2869. Reservations required. Fixed-price lunch and Wed dinner £15–£20 ($22.50–$30). AE, DC, MC, V. Daily noon–3pm and Wed 6–8pm. Tube: Charing Cross.

The Portrait Restaurant ✿ MODERN BRITISH   If anything, tables here open onto a better view than those at the National Gallery's restaurant (see above). Along with the view (Nelson's Column, the London Eye, Big Ben, and the like), you get superb meals. This rooftop restaurant is a sought-after dining ticket on the fifth floor of the Gallery's Ondaatje Wing. Patrons usually go for lunch, not knowing that the chefs also cook on Thursday and Friday nights. Start with goat cheese fritters with tomato and fennel, or grilled baby leeks. In spring there's nothing finer than the green English asparagus. All the main courses are filled with flavor, but the natural quality of the food especially shines in such dishes as grilled baby chicken, or peppered rump of lamb with a summer bean cassoulet. Chefs aren't afraid of simple preparations mainly because they are assured of the excellence of their products. The wine list features some organic choices.

In the National Portrait Gallery, Trafalgar Square, WC2. ℂ 020/7313-2490. Reservations recommended. Main courses £12–£18 ($18–$27). AE, DC, MC, V. Daily 11:45am–2:45pm; Thurs–Fri 5:30–8:30pm. Tube: Leicester Sq.

MAYFAIR
VERY EXPENSIVE

Gordon Ramsay at Claridge's ✿✿✿ EUROPEAN   Gordon Ramsay is the hottest chef in London today. He races back and forth between this restaurant and his Chelsea restaurant, called Gordon Ramsay (p. 193). He now rules at the staid, traditional Claridge's hotel, which has been legendary ever since 1860, when Queen Victoria stopped by for tea with the Empress Eugenie. The famed Art Deco dining room still retains many of its original architectural features, but the cuisine is hardly the same. Victoria most definitely wasn't served an *amuse-bouche* of pumpkin soup dribbled with truffle oil and studded with truffles, which you can enjoy. When we recently visited for lunch, we were dazzled by the set menu, which is relatively reasonably priced.

Although the menu changes frequently, memorable culinary highlights include filets of baby red mullet on a juniper-flavored sauerkraut, a breast and confit leg of guinea fowl with vegetables and foie gras, and a rum-baba with glazed oranges and crème fraîche. The three-course dinner was even more spectacular, featuring such delights as filet of sea bass wrapped in fresh basil leaves and served with a caviar sauce, and roast Scottish baby lobster cooked slowly in lime butter and served with tomato couscous. The desserts are among our favorite in London, including the likes of a bread and butter brioche pudding with clotted cream ice cream or a prune and Armagnac vanilla tart with *fromage blanc* in cream.

Brook St., W1. © 020/7499-0099. Reservations required as far in advance as possible. Fixed-price lunch £25 ($37.50); fixed-price dinner £45 ($67.50). AE, DC, MC, V. Mon–Sat noon–3pm and 5:45–11:30pm; Sun 6–10:30pm. Tube: Bond St.

Le Gavroche ✪✪✪ CLASSICAL FRENCH   Although challengers come and go, this *luxe* dining room still remains the number-one choice in London for classical French cuisine. The service is faultless and the ambience is chic without being stuffy. There's always something special coming out of the kitchen of Burgundy-born Michel Roux. The menu changes constantly, depending on the fresh produce available and the whims of the chef. But it always remains classically French, although not of the "essentially old-fashioned bourgeois repertoire" as some critics suggest. Try some of the signatures: soufflé Suissesse, *papillote* of smoked salmon, or whole Bresse chicken with truffles and a Madeira cream sauce. Game is often served, depending on availability. New menu options include cassoulet of snails with frog thighs, seasoned with herbs; mousseline of lobster in champagne sauce; pavé of braised turbot with red Provençal wine and smoked bacon; and filet of red snapper with caviar and oyster-stuffed tortellini.

Desserts, including the sablé of pears and chocolate, are sublime. The wine cellar is among the most interesting in London, with many Burgundies and Bordeaux. The *menu exceptionnel* is, in essence, a tasting menu for the entire table. It usually consists of four to five smaller courses, followed by one or two desserts and coffee.

43 Upper Brook St., W1. © 020/7408-0881. Fax 020/7491-4387. Reservations required as far in advance as possible. Main courses £27–£38 ($40.50–$57); fixed-price lunch £40 ($60); menu exceptionnel for entire table £80 ($120) per person. AE, MC, V. Mon–Fri noon–2pm and 7–11pm. Tube: Marble Arch.

Nobu ✪ JAPANESE   London's innovative Japanese restaurant owes much to its founders, actor Robert de Niro and chef Nobu Matsuhisa. The kitchen staff is brilliant and as finely tuned as their New York cousins. The sushi chefs create gastronomic pyrotechnics. Those on the see-and-be-seen circuit don't seem to mind the high prices that go with these incredibly fresh dishes. Elaborate preparations lead to perfectly balanced flavors. Where else can you find an excellent sea urchin tempura? Salmon tartare with caviar is a brilliant appetizer. Follow with a perfectly done filet of sea bass in a sour bean paste or softshell crab rolls. The squid pasta is sublime, as is the black cod with miso; the latter dish is incredibly popular and with good reason. Cold sake arrives in a green bamboo pitcher. If it's featured, finish with the savory ginger crème brûlée.

In the Metropolitan Hotel, 19 Old Park Lane, W1. © 020/7447-4747. Reservations required. Main courses £15–£28.50 ($22.50–$42.75); sushi and sashimi £3–£4.75 ($4.50–$7.15) per piece; fixed-price menu £60 ($90). AE, DC, MC, V. Mon–Fri noon–2:15pm; Mon–Thurs 6–10:15pm; Fri–Sat 6–11pm; Sun 6–9:30pm. Tube: Hyde Park Corner.

Petrus ✪✪ MODERN FRENCH   Clubby and not at all stuffy, this is the domain of chef Marcus Wareing, a former boxer from Lancashire. The restaurant serves nouvelle French food in the grand tradition of Wareing's mentor, Gordon Ramsay, who is London's hottest chef. In a sleek, opulent setting, you get reasonably priced food prepared with technical precision and a touch of whimsy. It's best to order the chef's six-course tasting menu to appreciate his culinary ambitions. You'll be dazzled with everything from marinated *foie gras* to an apple and artichoke salad, from Bresse pigeon in a truffle confit to a Valhrona chocolate fondant. We've delighted in all the dishes we've sampled here, from the eggplant caviar to crisp roast sea bass paired with caramelized endive and plump oysters.

33 St. James's St., SW1. ⓒ 020/7930-4272. Reservations required. Fixed-price menu £26–£50 ($39–$75) for 3 courses; £60 ($90) for 6-course tasting menu. AE, DC, MC, V. Mon–Fri noon–2:30pm; Mon–Sat 6:45–10:45pm. Tube: Green Park.

The Square ✹✹✹ CONTINENTAL Hip, chic, casual, sleek, and modern, this restaurant still doesn't scare Le Gavroche as a competitor for first place on London's restaurant circuit, but The Square has emerged as a great London restaurant. Chef Philip Howard delivers the goods and this is certainly a restaurant to visit on a serious London gastronomic tour. You get immaculate food in a cosseting atmosphere with abstract modern art on the walls. Howard has a magic touch with pasta—it appears as a bulging roll of cannelloni stuffed with shredded trout and green leeks, or as ravioli of partridge on a pool of creamy game-flavored sauce with finely shredded cabbage. Surprise dishes await in every corner of the menu—for example, the risotto of calves' tail with filet of veal and butternut squash. Fish is stunningly fresh, and the Bresse pigeon is as good as it is in its hometown in France. If you're a vegetarian, stay clear of this place, as many dishes are aimed at the true carnivore, who loves to dig into a gamy mixture of sautéed liver and other organ meats. For dessert, try the shortbread sandwich filled with strawberries and a crème fraîche, and served with a velvety vanilla ice cream.

6–10 Bruton St., W1. ⓒ 020/7495-7100. Reservations required. Main courses £17–£24 ($25.50–$36). Fixed-price dinner £55–£75 ($82.50–$112.50). AE, DC, MC, V. Mon–Fri noon–3pm; Mon–Sat 6:30–11pm. Tube: Bond St.

EXPENSIVE

Firebird Restaurant ✹ RUSSIAN Tsarist Russia lives again! Until now, you couldn't get a good bowl of borscht in Mayfair. And you might have had a problem getting grilled sturgeon, although sevruga, oscietra, or beluga caviar were always staples. New York's Firebird is even better, but what you get here is generally a delight. Start with the soft poached oysters with a dollop of caviar and go on to roast venison with apples and beets accompanied by mashed pumpkin and rutabaga with sour berries. Uzbek-style squab is a specialty, and we found it a real delicacy. The braised veal dumplings were a bit heavy, but filled with flavor, as was a perfectly roasted quail with grapes, orange segments, and walnuts. For dessert? The bol'shoi chocolate cake, of course.

23 Conduit St., W1. ⓒ 020/7493-7000. Reservations required. Main courses £15–£25.50 ($22.50–$38.25); fixed-price lunch £15–£18.95 ($22.50–$28.40). AE, DC, MC, V. Daily 12:15–2:45pm and 7–11pm. Tube: New Bond Street or Green Park.

Mirabelle ✹ MODERN BRITISH/FRENCH From Marlene Dietrich and Noel Coward, to Princess Margaret and Aristotle Onassis, to Johnny Depp and the tabloid stars of today, this place in the heart of Mayfair, attracts the rich and famous and the paparazzi who follow them. The interior is Art Deco, with a sexy red leather floor, and a little English garden. On the menu, the chefs remain French classicists. For starters, *foie gras* terrine appears with wine and herb-flavored aspic. For a more daring dish, opt for the pork cheeks flavored with ginger and spices. The squid ink risotto with calamari is a familiar feature, and the sea bass with fennel and béarnaise is worth traveling through the Chunnel from France. The boneless oxtail, topped by a filigree potato galette, is the finest we've sampled. Save room for dessert, especially the bitter-chocolate tart with ice cream.

56 Curzon St., W1. ⓒ 020/7499-4636. Reservations required. Main courses £14.50–£28.50 ($21.75–$42.75); set lunch £17.50–£19.95 ($26.25–$29.90). AE, MC, V. Mon–Sat noon–2:30pm and 6–11:30pm; Sun noon–3pm and 6–10:30pm. Tube: Green Park.

Noble Rot ⭑ CONTINENTAL   Danish-born Soren Jesson, perhaps the only restaurateur in London who uses "rot" as part of the name of his restaurant, strikes again with this modern European venue. Ladies-who-lunch and shoppers drop in during the day, but at night the lighting is lowered and the atmosphere becomes romantic. Some of the best regional specialties of the continent are prepared in lighter variations here, with imaginative culinary twists. Instead of the classic Andalusian gazpacho, you are likely to be served snow crab and lobster gazpacho. Tea-smoked halibut is a specialty, as is the eggplant parfait flavored with aromatic cumin oil. Sea bass comes with a lemon-flavored couscous, and the rack of lamb is perfection under a grain mustard and parsley crust, served with a shallot purée and a red currant sauce. Our favorite dessert? The orange soufflé with orange sauce, accompanied by a rhubarb compote.

3–5 Mill St., W1. ☎ 020/7629-8877. Reservations required. Main courses £16–£22 ($24–$33). Fixed-price lunch £15–£22 ($22.50–$33). AE, MC, V. Mon–Fri noon–3pm and 6–11pm. Tube: Oxford Circus.

MODERATE

Greenhouse MODERN BRITISH   Head chef Paul Merrett is quite inspired by modern British food. Dishes from the heart of England include a roast breast of pheasant that Henry VIII would have loved, and grilled farmhouse pork. We're also fond of the wilted greens wrapped in bacon. The menu is backed up by a well-chosen wine list with some 20 selections. Some of the delightfully sticky desserts, including a moist bread-and-butter pudding and a baked ginger loaf with orange marmalade, would please a Midlands granny. Simply conceived dishes with a resolutely British slant draw a never-ending line of satisfied customers. The ingredients are first-class and beautifully prepared, without ever destroying the natural flavor of a dish.

27A Hays Mews, W1. ☎ 020/7499-3331. Reservations required. Main courses £10–£23 ($15–$34.50). Fixed-price lunch £14–£22 ($21–$33). AE, DC, MC, V. Mon–Fri noon–2:30pm and 6:30–11pm; Sat 6:30–11pm; Sun 12:30–2:30pm and 6:30–11pm. Closed Christmas and bank holidays. Tube: Green Park.

Hard Rock Cafe (Kids) AMERICAN   This is the original Hard Rock. Since it was established in 1971, more than 12 million people have eaten here. Just like every other Hard Rock Cafe, there's usually a line (or in this case, a queue) waiting to get in, an equally long line of people buying T-shirts, better-than-average burgers, and a good selection of beers. The collection of rock memorabilia at the original is a far sight better than at later facsimiles.

150 Old Park Lane, W1. ☎ 020/7629-0382. Reservations not accepted. Main courses £9–£16 ($13.50–$24). AE, DC, MC, V. Mon–Thurs and Sun 11:30am–12:30am; Fri–Sat 11:30am–1am. Closed Dec 25–26. Tube: Green Park or Hyde Park Corner.

Langan's Brasserie TRADITIONAL BRITISH/FRENCH   In its heyday in the early 1980s, this was one of the hippest restaurants in London, and the upscale brasserie still welcomes an average of 700 diners a day. The 1976 brainchild of actor Michael Caine and chef Richard Shepherd, Langan's sprawls over two noisy floors filled with potted plants and ceiling fans that create a 1930s feel. The menu is "mostly English with a French influence" and includes spinach soufflé with anchovy sauce; quail eggs in a pastry case served with a sautéed hash of mushrooms and hollandaise sauce; and roast crispy duck with applesauce and sage-lemon stuffing. There's always a selection of English fare, including bangers and mash and fish and chips. The dessert menu is a journey into nostalgia: bread-and-butter pudding, treacle tart with custard, apple pie with clotted cream. Wait, how did mango sorbet slip in here?

Stratton St., W1. © 020/7491-8822. Reservations recommended. Main courses £12.50–£18.95 ($18.75–$28.40). AE, DC, MC, V. Mon–Fri 12:15pm–midnight; Sat 7pm–midnight. Tube: Green Park.

Momo MOROCCAN/NORTH AFRICAN   You'll be greeted by a friendly, casual staff member clad in a black-and-white T-shirt and fatigue pants. The setting is like Marrakesh, with stucco walls, a wood-and-stone floor, patterned wood window shades, burning candles, and banquettes. You can fill up on the freshly baked bread along with appetizers such as garlicky marinated olives and pickled carrots spiced with pepper and cumin. These starters are a gift from the chef. Other appetizers are also tantalizing, especially the *briouat:* paper-thin and very crisp triangular packets of puffed pastry filled with saffron-flavored chicken and other treats. One of the chef's specialties is *pastilla au pigeon,* a traditional poultry pie with almonds. Many diners visit for the *couscous maison,* among the best in London. Served in a decorative pot, this aromatic dish of raisins, meats (including merguez sausage), chicken, lamb, and chickpeas is given added flavor with a powerful hot sauce of the Middle East, *marissa.* After all this, the refreshing cinnamon-flavored orange slices are a tempting treat for dessert.

25 Heddon St., W1. © 020/7434-4040. Reservations required 2 weeks in advance. Main courses £10.50–£19.50 ($15.75–$29.25); fixed-price 2-course lunch £17 ($25.50). AE, DC, MC, V. Daily noon–2:30pm; Mon–Sat 7–11pm; Sun 6:30–10pm. Tube: Piccadilly Circus or Oxford Circus.

Tamarind INDIAN   In favor with critics as well as the lunchtime business crowd, Tamarind is the most popular Indian restaurant in Mayfair. The basement dining room has gold pillars and a tandoor window so that you can watch the chefs pull their flavorful dishes from the ovens. Chef Atul Kochhar leads a culinary brigade from Delhi that maintains the style of cooking they knew at home; and the team selects the best, freshest ingredients in the markets each day. The kitchen prides itself on nouvelle dishes, but also excels at traditional Indian fare. The monkfish marinated in saffron and yogurt is delectable, and the mixed kebab platter, cooked in a charcoal-fired tandoor is extraordinary—these chefs are kings of kebabs. Your best bet for a curry? Opt for the prawns in a five-spice mixture. Vegetarians will find refuge here, especially if they go for the Dal Bukhari, a black-lentil specialty of northwest India.

20 Queen St., W1. © 020/7629-3561. Reservations required. Main courses £10.50–£28 ($15.75–$42); 3-course set menu £30–£40 ($45–$60). AE, DC, DISC, MC, V. Mon–Fri noon–3pm; Mon–Sat 6–11:15pm; Sun noon–2:15pm and 6–10:15pm. Tube: Green Park.

Zen Central SZECHUAN   Movie stars always seem to have an advance scouting party informing them of the best places to dine in a foreign city. When we heard Eddie Murphy and Tom Cruise were heading here, we followed. We didn't spot any stars, but found a designer-chic Mayfair restaurant with a cool, dignified decor in black and white. Mirrors cover much of the interior (maybe that's why movie stars like it?).

Served by a competent staff, the cuisine is first-rate. Start with the coriander and crabmeat croquettes or the soft-shelled crabs cooked in a crust of salt. The steamed sea bass is perfectly cooked and, for extra flavor, served with a black bean sauce. Pork chops with lemon grass have a Thai flavor, and the baked lobster with crushed roast garlic and slivers of tangerine peel is worth the trip from anywhere. Habitués praise the cold pigs' trotter, though this is an acquired taste for some. Vegetarian meals are also available. The chef's braised fish cheek, sharks' fin, and bird's nest soup serves up flavors enjoyed in China. There is little catering to conventional western palates. Most dishes are at the lower end of the price scale.

20–22 Queen St., W1. ☎ 020/7629-8103. Reservations recommended. Main courses £12–£40 ($18–$60).
AE, DC, MC, V. Mon–Sat 12:15–2:30pm and 6:15–11pm; Sun 12:15–2:30pm and 6:30–11pm. Tube: Green
Park.

INEXPENSIVE

The Granary *Value* TRADITIONAL BRITISH   This family-operated country-style restaurant serves a simple flavor-filled array of home-cooked dishes,
listed on a blackboard. These might include lamb casserole with mint and
lemon; pan-fried cod; or avocado stuffed with prawns, spinach, and cheese. Vegetarian meals include mushrooms stuffed with mixed vegetables, stuffed eggplant with curry sauce, and vegetarian lasagna. Tempting desserts are
bread-and-butter pudding and apple brown Betty (both served hot). The large
portions guarantee you won't go hungry. The cooking is standard, but quite
good for the price.

39 Albemarle St., W1. ☎ 020/7493-2978. Main courses £8–£11 ($12–$16.50). MC, V. Mon–Fri 11:30am–
7:30pm; Sat 11:30am–3:30pm. Tube: Green Park.

Pizzeria Condotti *Kids* ITALIAN/AMERICAN   There can never be any final
agreement on pizza, but many aficionados claim that this is London's best
(frankly, we think dozens of New York spots have it beat). Tastefully decorated
with fresh flowers and art from the 1970s, this spot, just off Regent Street, looks
more costly than it is. For years, the joint has been a favorite of visiting American families.

Pizzas are light and crisp, and arrive at your table bubbling hot. They range
from a simple margherita (mozzarella cheese and tomato sauce) to the sublime
King Edward, with potato, four cheeses, and tomato. Dare to try the "American
Hot," with mozzarella, pepperoni, sausages, and hot peppers. There are also
freshly made salads. Only two pastas are featured, savory versions of lasagna and
cannelloni. The wine list is impressive and reasonable. Finish off with a scoop of
creamy ice cream made with chocolate liqueur, which may evoke a memory of
a visit to Rome.

4 Mill St., W1. ☎ 020/7499-1308. Pizzas £7–£9 ($10.50–$13.50); pastas £8 ($12); salads £7–£10 ($10.50–
$15). AE, DC, MC, V. Mon–Sat 10am–midnight. Tube: Oxford Circus.

Suze PACIFIC RIM   This interesting wine bar lies between Upper Brook
Street and Oxford Street. The owners attach equal importance to their food and
to their impressive wine list (some wines are sold by the glass). On the ground
floor, you can enjoy fine wines along with a well-chosen selection of bar food.
The menu has been upgraded and made more sophisticated and appealing. A
basket of homemade bread is placed before you with olives, goat cheese, salami,
and roasted peppers. Begin perhaps with the zesty tandoori prawns, and follow
with such delights as a Japanese mirin rice wine omelet with pickled vegetables
and a sweet ginger mayonnaise, or duck breast served on parsnip mash with a
tamarillo (a type of chile pepper) sauce.

41 N. Audley St., W1. ☎ 020/7491-3237. Reservations recommended. Main courses £8.95–£13.50
($13.40–$20.25); vegetarian main courses £8–£12 ($12–$18). AE, MC, V. Mon–Sat 11am–9:30pm. Tube:
Bond St.

ST. JAMES'S
EXPENSIVE

L'Oranger ✿ CONTINENTAL   This bistro-cum-brasserie occupies a high-
ceilinged space in an affluent neighborhood near the bottom of St. James's
Street. Amid paneling, burnt-orange paint, patterned carpeting, immaculate

linens, flowers, and uniformed waiters, you'll appreciate the choreographed set menus of executive chef Kamel Benamar. His arrangement of flavors has been praised by a clientele that pundits call "people who have made it." All menus are fixed-price: Depending on the chef's inspiration, they may include *foie gras* poached in a red Pessac wine sauce, or pan-fried filet of sea bass with zucchini, tomatoes, basil, and a black-olive vinaigrette. Other staples include crispy filets of cod with bouillabaisse sauce and new potatoes; braised leg of rabbit in Madeira sauce with whole cloves of yellow garlic *en confit*, served with braised cabbage. Starters include a terrine of ham and tongue served with gherkins and parsley, bound with a layer of spinach and served on a bed of choron sauce, which is a tomato-enriched béarnaise.

5 St. James's St., SW1A. ✆ 020/7839-3774. Reservations recommended. Fixed-price lunches £20–£24 ($30–$36); fixed-price dinner £39.50 ($59.25). AE, DC, MC, V. Mon–Fri noon–2:30pm; Mon–Sat 6–11:15pm. Tube: Green Park.

MODERATE

Circus *Value* MODERN BRITISH/INTERNATIONAL   This place buzzes during pre- and post-theater hours with foodies anxious to sample the wares of chef Richard Lee, which range from oysters to ostrich. Artfully spartan, with the kind of ultra-modern, angular, and minimalist design you might expect in a stylish restaurant in Milan, this restaurant would be a good side for lunch or dinner between avant-garde media moguls. Because of its location in the Granada Television building, meetings like that often occur.

The place evokes a London version of a Left Bank Parisian brasserie and its decor is a bit drab, hardly living up to its namesake. For some country cousins from the north of England who missed the food, Lee offers braised faggot with bubble-and-squeak (bubble-and-squeak is cabbage and potatoes, and faggots are highly seasoned squares of pigs' liver, pork, onion, herbs, and nutmeg—bound with an egg and baked wrapped in a pig's caul). You might taste the divine skate wing with crushed new potatoes accompanied by a thick pesto-like medley of rocket blended with black olives. Or try the tasty sautéed chili-flavored squid with bok choi, made heavenly with a tamarind dressing. The sorbets are a nice finish to a meal, especially the mango and pink grapefruit version. Of course, if you're ravenous, there's the velvety-smooth amaretto cheesecake with a coffee sauce. Service is a delight, and the set lunch and pre- and post-theater fixed-price menus offer incredible value.

1 Upper James St., W1. ✆ 020/7534-4000. Reservations required. Main courses £11.50–£18.50 ($19.55–$31.45); fixed-price menus 5:45–7:15pm and 10:30pm–midnight £10.50–£12.50 ($17.85–$21.25). AE, DC, MC, V. Daily noon–2:30pm; Mon–Sat 6pm–midnight. Bar menu daily noon–1:30am. Tube: Piccadilly Circus.

Greens Restaurant & Oyster Bar SEAFOOD   Critics say it's a triumph of tradition over taste, but as far as seafood in London goes, this is a tried-and-true favorite, thanks to an excellent menu with moderately priced dishes, a central location, and a charming staff. This place has a cluttered entrance leading to a crowded bar where you can sip fine wines and, from September to April, enjoy oysters. In the faux-Dickensian dining room, you can choose from a long menu of fresh seafood dishes, which changes monthly depending on what is in season. The standard menu ranges from fishcakes with roast peppers and tomato sauce to a whole Scottish lobster. For zesty starters, try either the smoked eel filets or the avocado-and-bacon salad with baby-leaf spinach. Desserts include bread-and-butter pudding. The menu changes monthly, but it's always based on the freshest ingredients, deftly prepared by the kitchen staff. (Note that London has two different Duke streets. Greens is on the one in St. James's.)

36 Duke St., St. James's, SW1. ℂ 020/7930-4566. Reservations recommended. Main courses £11–£37 ($16.50–$55.50); most dishes moderately priced. AE, DC, MC, V. Restaurant daily 11:30am–3pm; Mon–Sat 5:30–11pm. Oyster Bar Mon–Sat 11:30am–3pm and 5:30–11pm; Sun 12:30–3pm and 5:30–9pm. Tube: Green Park.

Quaglino's ✿ CONTINENTAL It's vast, it's convivial, and it's fun. Giovanni Quaglino, from Italy's Piedmont, established a restaurant here in 1929, and the personalities who paraded through in ermine and pearls could fill a between-the-wars roster of who's who in Europe. In 1993, restaurateur and designer Sir Terence Conran brought the place into the postmodern age with a vital new decor—eight artists were commissioned to decorate the massive columns supporting the soaring ceiling. A mezzanine with a bar features live jazz on Friday and Saturday nights and live piano music the rest of the week. An altar in the back is devoted to the most impressive display of crustaceans and shellfish in Britain.

Everything seems to be served in bowls. Menu items have been criticized for their quick preparation and standard format. But considering that on some nights up to 800 people might show up, the marvel is that this place functions as well as it does. That's not to say there isn't an occasional delay. Come for fun, not for culinary subtlety and finesse. The menu changes often, but your choices might include a goat cheese and caramelized onion tart; seared salmon with potato pancakes; crab tartlet with saffron; and roasted cod and ox cheek with chargrilled vegetables. The prawns and oysters—delectable and fresh—are the most popular items.

16 Bury St., SW1. ℂ 020/7930-6767. Reservations recommended. Main courses £9.95–£18.50 ($14.90–$27.75); fixed-price menu (available only for lunch and pre-dinner theater between 5:30 and 6:30pm) 2-courses £14 ($21), 3 courses £17 ($25.50). AE, DC, MC, V. Daily noon–2:30pm; Mon–Thurs 5:30–11:30pm; Fri–Sat 5:30pm–12:30am; Sun 5:30–11pm. Tube: Green Park.

4 Westminster & Victoria

Nahm ✿✿ THAI The cookery here is extraordinary, and we like that the chef makes few, if any, concessions to Western palates. David Thompson even purchases rare books on Thai cookery and re-creates dishes that may have been lost for centuries. Take, for example, the salmon roe and fresh seafood mixed with spices and served in a fresh betel leaf, all of it garnished with watermelon. It sounds off-putting but is actually a taste sensation. The chef is against the "fusion fad," even though he's a Westerner himself (Australian), and is instead dedicated to the tenets of Thai cuisine. He's considered such an expert that even some of the citadels of haute Thai cuisine in Thailand seek his advice. Try the crisp salted trout in a tangy salad or the salted duck eggs with crisp fish cakes and irresistible sweet pork, or perhaps a stir fry of scallops with deep-fried galangal, flavored with lemon grass and garlic. For dessert, try the addictive black sticky rice and coconut. One critic summed up the chef's cuisine this way: "David Thompson produces dishes more sagacious, undulating, bewitching, and boisterous than any one you will find even in Thailand, unless, perhaps, you are a guest of the royal family."

In the Halkin Hotel, Halkin St., SW1. ℂ 020/7333-1234. Reservations required. Main courses £9–£27 ($13.50–$40.50). Fixed-price lunch £22.50 ($33.75). Fixed-price dinner £27 ($40.50). AE, DC, MC, V. Mon–Fri noon–2pm and 7–11pm; Sat–Sun 7–10pm. Tube: Hyde Park Corner.

EXPENSIVE

Rhodes in the Square ★★★ MODERN BRITISH   In this discreet residential district, super-chef and media darling Gary Rhodes strikes again. Rhodes is known for taking traditional British cookery and giving it daring twists and new flavors. You can count on delightful surprises from this major talent. The glitterati can be seen nightly in the apartment-block-cum-hotel, sampling his offerings in an elegant high-ceilinged room done in midnight blue. You never know what's available—maybe a whole red mullet stuffed with a delectable medley of eggplant, anchovies, fresh garlic, and peppers, appearing with a cream-laced sauce flavored with fennel. Start, perhaps, with chicken liver parfait with *foie gras,* and go on to an open omelet topped with chunky bits of lobster and a Thermidor sauce and cheese crust. His glazed duck served with bitter orange jus is how this dish is supposed to taste. For dessert, make your selection from the British pudding plate that offers everything from a lemon meringue tart to a simple seared carpaccio of pineapple, oozing with flavor.

Dolphin Sq., Chichester St., SW1. ✆ 020/7798-6767. Reservations required. Fixed-price meals £28.50 ($42.75) for 2 courses, £36.50 ($54.75) for 3 courses. AE, DC, MC, V. Tues–Fri noon–2:30pm; Tues–Sat 7–10pm. Tube: Pimlico.

Shepherd's TRADITIONAL BRITISH   Some observers claim that many of the inner workings of the British government operate from the precincts of this conservative, likable restaurant. Set in the shadow of Big Ben, it enjoys a regular clientele of barristers, members of Parliament, and their constituents from far-flung districts. Don't imagine that the intrigue occurs only at lunchtime; evenings seem just as ripe an hour for negotiations, particularly over the restaurant's roast rib of Scottish beef served with (what else?) Yorkshire pudding. So synchronized is this place to the goings-on at Parliament that a Division Bell rings in the dining room, calling MPs back to the House of Commons when it's time to vote. Even the decor is designed to make them feel at home, with leather banquettes, sober 19th-century accessories, and a worthy collection of English portraits and landscapes.

The menu reflects years of British culinary tradition, and dishes are prepared intelligently, with fresh ingredients. In addition to the classic roast, dishes include a cream-based mussel stew; hot salmon and potato salad with dill dressing; salmon and prawn fishcakes in spinach sauce; roast leg of lamb with mint sauce; wild rabbit; marinated venison with braised red cabbage in juniper sauce; and the English version of crème brûlée, known as "burnt Cambridge cream."

Marsham Court, Marsham St., at the corner of Page St., SW1. ✆ 020/7834-9552. Reservations recommended. Fixed-price meals £25 ($37.50) for 2 courses, £28 ($42) for 3 courses. AE, DC, MC, V. Mon–Fri 12:30pm–2:45pm and 6:30–11:30pm (last order at 11pm). Tube: St. James's.

Simply Nico ★ *Value* FRENCH   Simply Nico is the brainchild of master chef Nico Ladenis, of Incognico (see earlier in this chapter). Simply Nico is run by Ladenis' sous chef. We think it's the best value in town. In Nico's own words, it's "cheap and cheerful." The wood floors reverberate with the din of contented diners, who pack in daily at snug tables to enjoy the simply prepared food. The fixed-price menu changes frequently, but options might include pan-fried *foie gras* followed by shank of lamb with parsnips, or the ever-popular monkfish.

48A Rochester Row, SW1. ✆ 020/7630-8061. Reservations required. Fixed-price 2-course lunch £22 ($33); fixed-price 3-course lunch £25 ($37.50); fixed-price 3-course dinner £28 ($42). AE, DC, MC, V. Mon–Fri noon–2pm; Mon–Sat 6–10pm. Tube: Victoria or St. James's Park.

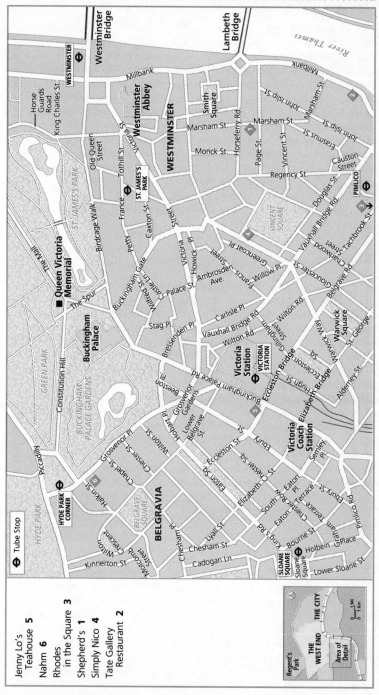

River Thames

Westminster Bridge

Lambeth Bridge

WESTMINSTER

Horse Guards Road

King Charles St.

Millbank

Westminster Abbey

Smith Square

Marsham St.

Marsham St.

John Islip St.

Marsham St.

Erasmus St.

John Islip St.

Millbank

Old Queen Street

Tothill St.

Victoria St.

WESTMINSTER

Monck St.

Horseferry Rd.

Page St.

Vincent St.

Caxton St.

Regency St.

Douglas St.

Causton Street

PIMLICO

ST. JAMES'S PARK

ST. JAMES'S PARK

France

Birdcage Walk

Petty

St. James's Park

Victoria

Street

Greencoat Pl.

Gloucester St.

Charlwood

Vauxhall Bridge Rd.

Tachbrook St.

VINCENT SQUARE

The Mall

Queen Victoria Memorial

The Spur

Buckingham Gate

Castle Ln.

Wilfred St.

Palace St.

Howick Pl.

Francis Street

Willow Pl.

Ambrosden Ave.

Belgrave Rd.

GREEN PARK

Constitution Hill

Buckingham Palace

Stag Pl.

Bressenden Pl.

Carlisle Pl.

Vauxhall Bridge Rd.

Wilton Rd.

Gillingham Street

Wilton Rd.

Warwick Square

St. George's

BUCKINGHAM PALACE GARDENS

Beeston Pl.

Grosvenor Gardens

VICTORIA STATION

Victoria Station

Eccleston Bridge

Elizabeth Bridge

Hugh St.

Warwick Way

Alderney St.

Piccadilly

HYDE PARK CORNER

Grosvenor Pl.

Chester St.

Chapel St.

Wilton St.

Hobart Pl.

Lower Belgrave St.

Victoria Coach Station

Semley Pl.

Eaton Sq.

Eccleston St.

Chester St.

Ebury St.

Eaton Pl.

Ebury St.

Pimlico Rd.

HYDE PARK

Halkin St.

BELGRAVE SQUARE

BELGRAVIA

Lyall St.

Chesham St.

Eaton Sq.

Elizabeth St.

South Eaton Pl.

Chester Row

Eaton Terrace

Bourne St.

Holbein Pl.

Grahame Place

Wilton Crescent

Motcomb Street

Chesham St.

King's Rd.

Sloane Square

SLOANE SQUARE

Lower Sloane St.

Kinnerton St.

Cadogan Ln.

⊕ Tube Stop

Jenny Lo's
Teahouse **5**
Nahm **6**
Rhodes
  in the Square **3**
Shepherd's **1**
Simply Nico **4**
Tate Gallery
  Restaurant **2**

Regent's Park

THE WEST END

THE CITY

Area of Detail

0   1 Mi
0 1 Km

MODERATE

Tate Gallery Restaurant ⭐ *Value* MODERN BRITISH   This restaurant is particularly attractive to wine fanciers. It offers what may be the best bargains for superior wines anywhere in Britain. Bordeaux and burgundies are in abundance, and the management keeps the markup between 40% and 65%, rather than the 100% to 200% added in most restaurants. In fact, the prices here are lower than they are in most wine shops. Wine begins at £13.50 ($20.25) per bottle, or £4.95 ($7.45) per glass. Oenophiles frequently come for lunch. The restaurant specializes in an English menu that changes about every month. Dishes might include pheasant casserole, Oxford sausage with mashed potatoes, pan-fried skate with black butter and capers, and a selection of vegetarian dishes. One critic found the staff and diners as traditional "as a Gainsborough landscape." Access to the restaurant is through the museum's main entrance on Millbank.

Millbank, SW1. ⓒ 020/7887-8877. Reservations recommended. Main courses £10–£17 ($15–$25.50); fixed-price 2-course lunch £18 ($27); fixed-price 3-course lunch £21 ($31.50). Minimum charge £17 ($25.50). AE, DC, MC, V. Mon–Sat noon–3pm; Sun noon–4pm. Tube: Pimlico. Bus: 77 or 88.

INEXPENSIVE

Jenny Lo's Teahouse CANTONESE/SZECHUAN   London's noodle dives don't get much better than this. Before its decline, Ken Lo's restaurant, Memories of China, was the best Chinese dining in London. Ken's grandfather was the Chinese ambassador to the Court of St. James, and the late Ken Lo went on to make a reputation as a cookbook author. Jenny Lo is Ken's daughter, and her father taught her many of his culinary secrets. Belgravia matrons and young professionals come here for perfectly prepared, reasonably priced fare. Ken Lo cookbooks contribute to the dining room decor of black refectory tables set with paper napkins and chopsticks. Opt for such fare as a vermicelli rice noodle dish (a large plate of noodles topped with grilled chicken breast and Chinese mushrooms) or white noodles with minced pork. Rounding out the menu are stuffed Peking dumplings, chili-garnished spicy prawns, and wonton soup with dumplings that glide into your mouth. The black bean–seafood noodle dish is a delight, as is the chili beef soup.

14 Eccleston St., SW1. ⓒ 020/7259-0399. Reservations not accepted. Main courses £6–£9.50 ($9–$14.25). No credit cards. Mon–Fri 11:30am–3pm; Sat noon–3pm; Mon–Sat 6–10pm. Tube: Victoria Station.

5 Knightsbridge to South Kensington

KNIGHTSBRIDGE
VERY EXPENSIVE

La Tante Claire ⭐⭐⭐ FRENCH   Re-settled in swanky new digs, "Aunt Claire" is one of the stellar restaurants of London. Pierre Koffmann remains the chef at this fabled spot, which is more interested in turning out culinary fireworks than in creating a media frenzy. Interior designer David Collins designed the restaurant. The lilac walls and soothing green floors are a backdrop to the cuisine, which uses the freshest and best produce in London. The standards of Chef Koffmann are the benchmark that other chefs aspire to. To sample perfection, try his legendary ravioli langoustine or pigs' trotters. Who would have thought that a pig's foot could be transformed into such a sublime concoction? His soup made with truffles makes gourmands cry for joy. His *nage de homard* (lobster), with Sauternes wine and fresh ginger, is a culinary work of art, as is his steamed lamb with a vegetable couscous. Breads are a passion for Mousieur

Koffmann, and the bakery trolley is loaded with almost every variety of bread you can imagine, all created by the chef himself. For dessert, the hot pistachio soufflé served pistachio ice cream will linger in your memory. The service proceeds like a perfectly trained orchestra.

Wilton Place, Knightsbridge, SW1. ✆ 020/7823-2003. Reservations required. Main courses £28–£32 ($42–$48). AE, DC, MC, V. Mon–Fri 12:30–2pm; Mon–Sat 7–11pm. Tube: Hyde Park Corner or Knightsbridge.

Zafferano ✪ ITALIAN There's something honest and satisfying about this restaurant, where decor consists of little more than ochre-colored walls, immaculate linens, and a bevy of diligent staff members. A quick review of past clients includes Margaret Thatcher, Richard Gere, Princess Margaret, and Eric Clapton. The modernized interpretation of Italian cuisine features such dishes as ravioli of pheasant with black truffles; rabbit with Parma ham and polenta; sea bream with spinach and balsamic vinegar; and monkfish with almonds. Joan Collins claimed that the chefs produce culinary fireworks, but found the bright lighting far too harsh. The owners pride themselves on one of the most esoteric and well-rounded collections of Italian wine in London: You'll find as many as 20 different vintages each of Brunello and Barolos and about a dozen vintages of Sassecaia.

15 Lowndes St., SW1. ✆ 020/7235-5800. Reservations required. Set menus £19.50–£41.50 ($29.25–$62.25). AE, MC, V. Daily noon–2:30pm and 7–11pm. Tube: Knightsbridge.

EXPENSIVE

The Collection ✪ INTERNATIONAL/MODERN BRITISH This is a temple to voyeurism and the vanities, catering to the aesthetics and preoccupations of the fashion industry. It occupies an echoing warehouse; the only access is by a 30-foot catwalk that feels like it should have couture models striding along it. Don't worry about a snobbish chill: Manager Julian Shaw is one of the most adept and humorous in London, a celebrity in his own right because of his skill at dealing with big-ticket, big-ego fashion moguls. Yummy menu items include crispy duck with *yaki soba* noodles; sesame-crusted tuna steak with sweet potatoes and bok choi; sea bream with cilantro; and pan-fried calves' liver with sage and onions. Don't overlook this site as a stop on your after-dark bar-hop.

264 Brompton Rd., SW3. ✆ 020/7225-1212. Reservations recommended. Main courses £11.25–£21.50 ($16.90–$32.25); fixed-price menu £35 ($52.50). AE, DC, MC, V. Mon–Fri 6:30–11:30pm; Sat noon–4pm and 6:30–11:30pm; Sun noon–4pm and 6:30–10:30pm. Tube: South Kensington.

Floriana ✪ ITALIAN Shoppers along Knightsbridge Street, where Princess Di used to go for her Italian meal fix, flock to this dining room. The decor is smart and modern, with marble, mirrors, and an atrium roof. Chef Luigi Penna prepares his food with love, and knows the classics but can be inventive. His gold and saffron risotto is as good as in a *luxe* restaurant in Milano, and his steam-roasted Landais chicken with a green sauce will make you swoon. His minestrone with fruits of the sea is one of central London's best, and his steamed sea bass with fresh sea urchins is our favorite menu delight, although the glazed rack of veal with pan-fried artichoke is a close contender. Especially delectable is the chef's version of ravioli, stuffed with Scottish lobster, artichoke hearts, and sage.

18 Beauchamp Place, SW3. ✆ 020/7838-1500. Reservations required. Main courses £14.50–£23 ($21.75–$34.50); Fixed-price lunch £15 ($22.50). AE, DC, MC, V. Mon–Sat 12:30–3pm and 7–10:45pm. Tube: Knightsbridge.

Where to Dine from Knightsbridge to South Kensington

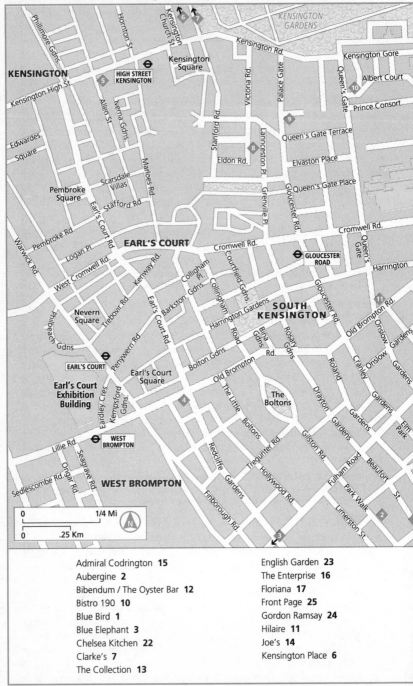

Admiral Codrington **15**
Aubergine **2**
Bibendum / The Oyster Bar **12**
Bistro 190 **10**
Blue Bird **1**
Blue Elephant **3**
Chelsea Kitchen **22**
Clarke's **7**
The Collection **13**

English Garden **23**
The Enterprise **16**
Floriana **17**
Front Page **25**
Gordon Ramsay **24**
Hilaire **11**
Joe's **14**
Kensington Place **6**

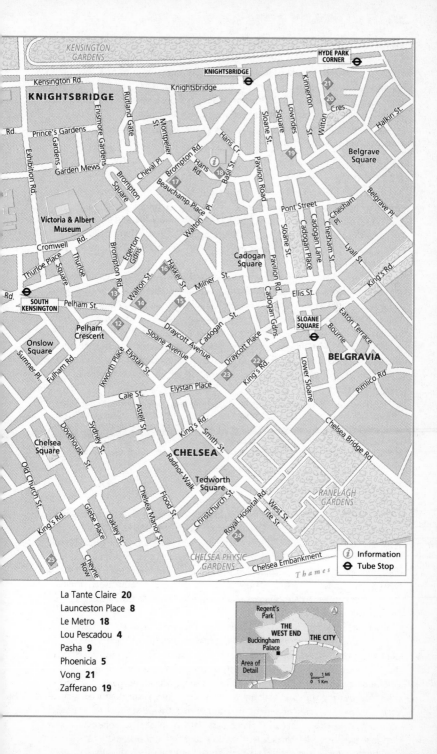

INEXPENSIVE

Le Metro INTERNATIONAL   Located just around the corner from Harrods, Le Metro draws a fashionable crowd to its basement precincts. The place serves good, solid, reliable food prepared with flair. The menu changes frequently, but try the mushroom risotto or confit of duck with lentils, garlic, and shallots if you can. You can order special wines by the glass.

28 Basil St., SW3. ⓒ 020/7589-6286. Main courses £7.50–£12.50 ($11.25–$18.75). AE, DC, MC, V. Mon–Sat 7:30am–10:30pm. Tube: Knightsbridge.

BELGRAVIA
EXPENSIVE

Vong ⓡ FRENCH/THAI   Just yards from Harrods, this modern restaurant on three levels is one of the most chic rendezvous points in London. Jean-Georges Vongerichten has brought his award-winning French/Thai menu to town, stating that the superior Thai ingredients in London will make the offspring even better than the parent in New York. The results are subtle, innovative, and inspired.

In a minimalist setting, you can partake of the "Black Plate," featuring samples of six starters, for a taste of everything. Other options are a perfectly roasted halibut, or a lobster and daikon roll, the latter served with rosemary and ginger sauce. Virtually everything on the menu is cause for wonder and admiration, especially the crab spring roll with a vinegary tamarind dipping sauce. The sautéed *foie gras* with ginger and mango literally melts in the mouth. The spiced cod with curried artichokes is well worth a try. Desserts are equally exotic, especially the salad of banana and passion fruit with white-pepper ice cream (yes, you heard right).

In the Berkeley Hotel, Wilton Place, SW1. ⓒ 020/7235-1010. Reservations recommended. Main courses £18–£33 ($27–$49.50); tasting menu £80 ($120); 3-course lunch £21.50 ($32.25); fixed-price 3-course dinner £30–£43 ($45–$64.50); pre- and post-theater dinner £21 ($31.50). AE, DC, DISC, MC, V. Mon–Sat noon–2:30pm and 6–11:30pm; Sun 11:30am–2pm and 6–10:30pm. Dim sum available Sat–Sun 11:30am–2:30pm from £2.50 ($3.75) per plate. Pre- and post-theater dinner available 6–7pm and 10:30–11:30pm. Tube: Hyde Park.

CHELSEA
VERY EXPENSIVE

Aubergine ⓡⓡ FRENCH   This restaurant ("eggplant") is luring savvy diners down to the lower reaches of Chelsea where chef Williams Drabble takes over from the renowned Gordon Ramsay. Drabble, who earned his first Michelin star in 1998, has remained true to the style and ambience of this establishment. Although popular with celebrities, the restaurant remains unpretentious and refuses to pander to fame. (When Princess Margaret complained the air-conditioning was too cold, she was lent a cardigan; and Madonna was refused a late-night booking!)

Every dish is satisfyingly flavorsome, from the warm salad of vegetables with shaved truffles and asparagus purée, to the roasted monkfish served with crushed new potatoes, roasted leeks, and a red-wine sauce. Starters also charm and delight palates, ranging from the ravioli of crab with mussels, chili, ginger, and coriander, to the terrine of *foie gras* with confit of duck and pears poached in port. Also resting on your Villeroy & Boch aubergine plate might be mallard with a celeriac fondant or assiette of lamb with a thyme-scented jus. Another stunning main course is a slice of sea bass with bouillabaisse potatoes. A new dish is roasted veal sweetbreads with caramelized onion purée and a casserole of flap mushrooms. There are only 14 tables, so bookings are imperative.

11 Park Walk, SW10. © 020/7352-3449. Reservations required and accepted up to 4 weeks in advance. Fixed-price 2-course lunch £20 ($30), 3-course lunch £25 ($37.50); fixed-price 3-course dinner £48 ($72); menu gourmand £65 ($97.50); truffle menu £90 ($135). AE, DC, MC, V. Mon–Fri noon–3:30pm; Mon–Sat 6:45–11pm. Tube: South Kensington.

Gordon Ramsay ★★★ FRENCH Gordon Ramsay is one of the city's most innovative and talented chefs. He has taken over the former location of La Tante Claire (see above), and serves a cuisine even more innovative and exciting than the long-established La Tante herself. London is rushing to sample Mr. Ramsay's wares. Lord Andrew Lloyd Webber has visited and acclaimed Ramsay as one of Europe's grandest chefs, saying "you can get better food here than anywhere else in London." There may be no restaurant in London with more myths spinning around it. One legend is that serious gourmets fly across the Atlantic nightly to dine here. Another is that you need to book years ahead. Finally, it's been said that the excitement of the evening might be when Gordon rushes out of the kitchen wielding a meat cleaver.

Every dish from this kitchen is gratifying, reflecting subtlety and delicacy without any sacrifice to the food's natural essence. Try, for example, Ramsay's celebrated cappuccino of white beans with grated truffles. His appetizers are likely to dazzle: a salad of crispy pigs' trotters with calves' sweetbreads, fried quail eggs, and a cream-flavored vinaigrette; or *foie gras* three ways—sautéed with quince, *mi-cuit* with an Earl Grey consommé, or pressed with truffle peelings. From here, you can grandly proceed to filet of brill poached in red wine, grilled filet of red mullet on a bed of caramelized endives, or caramelized Challandaise duck cooked with dates. Desserts are equally stunning, especially the pistachio soufflé with chocolate sorbet or the passion fruit and chocolate parfait. You can also sample Ramsay's extraordinary fare at Gordon Ramsay's at Claridge's (listed earlier in this chapter).

68 Royal Hospital Rd., SW3. © 020/7352-4441. Reservations required (1 month in advance). Fixed-price lunch £35 ($52.50) for 3 courses; fixed-price dinner £65 ($97.50) for 3 courses, £80 ($120) for 7 courses. AE, DC, MC, V. Mon–Fri noon–2:30pm and 6:45–11pm. Tube: Sloane Sq.

EXPENSIVE

Blue Bird ★ MODERN CONTINENTAL This enormous space resounds with clinking silverware and peals of laughter from a loyal clientele. Locals and staff alike refer to it as a *restaurant de gare*—a railway station restaurant. Although there's a cafe and an upscale delicatessen and housewares store on the street level, the heart and soul is above in the restaurant. It holds up to 275 diners at a time, and you'll find a color scheme of red and blue canvas cutouts that replicate birds in flight. Tables are close together, but the scale of the place makes dining private and intimate. The massive menu emphasizes savory, precisely cooked cuisine, some emerging from a wood-burning stove used to roast everything from lobster to game. An immense shellfish bar stocks every crustacean you can think of, and a bar does a thriving business with the Sloane Square subculture. Perennial favorites include the marinated lamb with baked beans and aioli, as well as pasta and fresh fish.

Oh, the name: Before it was a restaurant, the site was a garage that repaired the legendary Bluebird, an English sports car that is, alas, no longer produced.

350 King's Rd., SW3. © 020/7559-1000. Reservations recommended. Main courses £11.50–£19.25 ($17.25–$28.90). AE, DC, MC, V. Mon–Fri noon–3pm and 6–10:30pm; Sat noon–3:30pm and 6–11pm; Sun noon–3:30pm and 6–10:30pm. Tube: Sloane Sq.

English Garden ★ BRITISH   This is a metropolitan restaurant par excellence. The decor in this historic town house is pretty and lighthearted: The Garden Room is whitewashed brick with a domed conservatory roof; vivid florals, rattan chairs, banks of plants, and candy-pink linens to complete the scene. Every component of a meal is carried out perfectly. Launch into a fine repast with a caramelized red onion-and-cheddar cheesecake or mussel-and-watercress soup. For a main course, opt for such delights as roast baron of rabbit with oven-dried tomato, prunes, and olive oil mash; or saddle of venison with potted cabbage. Some of the dishes sound as if they were copied directly from an English cookbook of the Middle Ages—and are they ever good. Desserts, especially the rhubarb and cinnamon ice cream or the candied orange tart with orange syrup, would've pleased Miss Marple.

10 Lincoln St., SW3. ℂ 020/7584-7272. Reservations required. Fixed-price lunch £19.50 ($29.25); fixed-price dinner £27.50 ($41.25). AE, DC, MC, V. Mon–Sat noon–3pm; Sun 12:30–2pm; Mon–Sat 6:30–11pm; Sun 6:30–10:30pm. Tube: Sloane Sq.

INEXPENSIVE

Chelsea Kitchen INTERNATIONAL   This simple restaurant feeds large numbers of Chelsea residents in a setting that's little-changed since 1961. The food and the clientele move fast, almost guaranteeing that the entire inventory of ingredients is sold out at the end of each day. Menu items usually include leek-and-potato soup, chicken Kiev, chicken parmigiana, steaks, sandwiches, and burgers. The clientele includes a broad cross-section of Londoners—all having a good and cost-conscious time.

98 King's Rd., SW3. ℂ 020/7589-1330. Reservations recommended. Main courses £4–£6 ($6–$9); fixed-price menu £7 ($10.50). No credit cards. Daily 8am–11:45pm. Tube: Sloane Sq.

Front Page MODERN EUROPEAN   Front Page is favored by young professionals who like the atmosphere of wood paneling, wooden tables, and pews and benches. On cold nights, an open fire burns. The pub stands in a residential section of Chelsea and is a good place to go for a drink or some pub grub. Check the chalkboard for the daily specials, which might include hot chicken salad, fishcakes, and smoked salmon with cream cheese on a bagel.

35 Old Church St., SW3. ℂ 020/7352-0648. Main courses £4.25–£10 ($6.40–$15). AE, DISC, MC, V. Restaurant Mon–Fri noon–2:30pm; Sat–Sun 12:30–3pm; Mon–Sat 7–10pm; Sun 7–9:30pm. Pub Mon–Sat 11am–11pm; Sun noon–10:30pm. Tube: Sloane Sq.

KENSINGTON & SOUTH KENSINGTON
EXPENSIVE

Bibendum/The Oyster Bar ★ FRENCH/MEDITERRANEAN   In trendy Brompton Cross, this still-fashionable restaurant occupies two floors of a garage that's now an Art Deco masterpiece. Though its heyday came in the early 1990s, the white-tiled room, with stained-glass windows, sunlight, and a chic clientele, is still an extremely pleasant place. The eclectic cuisine, known for its freshness and simplicity, is based on what's available seasonally. Dishes might include roast pigeon with celeriac purée and apple sauté; rabbit with anchovies, garlic, and rosemary; or grilled lamb cutlets with a delicate sauce. Some of the best dishes are for dining à deux, including Bresse chicken flavored with fresh tarragon, or grilled veal chops with truffle butter.

Simpler meals and cocktails are available in the **Oyster Bar** on the building's street level. The bar-style menu stresses fresh shellfish presented in the traditional French style, on ice-covered platters adorned with strands of seaweed. It's a crustacean-lover's dream.

81 Fulham Rd., SW3. ℂ 020/7581-5817. Reservations required in Bibendum; not accepted in Oyster Bar. Main courses £15–£25 ($22.50–$37.50); fixed-price 3-course lunch £28 ($42); cold seafood platter in Oyster Bar £45 ($67.50) for 2. AE, DC, MC, V. Bibendum Mon–Fri noon–2:30pm and 7–11:15pm; Sat 12:30–3pm and 7–11:15pm; Sun 12:30–3pm and 7–10:15pm. Oyster Bar Mon–Sat noon–10:30pm; Sun noon–3pm and 7–10pm. Tube: South Kensington.

Clarke's ✿ MODERN BRITISH   Sally Clarke is one of the finest chefs in London, and this is one of the hottest restaurants around. *Still.* She opened it in the Thatcher era and it's still going strong. Clarke honed her skills at Michael's in Santa Monica and the West Beach Cafe in Venice (California) before heading back to her native land. In this excellent restaurant, everything is bright and modern, with wood floors, discreet lighting, and additional space in the basement where tables are more spacious and private. Some people are put off by the fixed-price menu, but the food is so well prepared that diners rarely object to what ends up in front of them. The menu, which changes daily, emphasizes chargrilled foods with herbs and seasonal veggies. You might begin with an appetizer salad of blood orange with red onion, watercress, and black olive-anchovy toast, then follow with grilled breast of chicken with black truffle, crisp polenta, and arugula. Desserts are likely to include a warm pear-and-raisin puff pastry with maple syrup ice cream. Just put yourself in Clarke's hands—you'll be glad you did.

124 Kensington Church St., W8. ℂ 020/7221-9225. Reservations recommended. Fixed-price lunches £10–£15 ($15–$22.50); fixed-price 4-course dinner £48 ($72). AE, DC, MC, V. Mon–Fri 12:30–2pm and 7–10pm. Tube: High St. Kensington.

Hilaire ✿ CONTINENTAL   After this Victorian storefront was refurbished following a fire, it became one classy joint, an elegant restaurant like you might find in the heart of France. With its vases of flowers and shiny mirrors, it is a fitting ambience for fine food. Chef Bryan Webb offers a mixture of classical French and *cuisine moderne,* following his own impulses and good culinary sense and style. The menu reflects the best of the season's offerings. A typical lunch might begin with a red-wine risotto with radicchio and sun-dried tomato pesto, followed with sautéed scallops with creamed chicory, and ending with rhubarb sorbet. At dinner, main courses might include rack of lamb with tapenade and wild garlic; saddle of rabbit; or grilled tuna with Provençal vegetables. An aperitif bar, extra tables, and a pair of semi-private alcoves make up the lower dining room.

68 Old Brompton Rd., SW7. ℂ 020/7584-8993. Reservations recommended. Fixed-price 2-course lunch £21 ($31.50), 3-course lunch £25 ($37.50); fixed-price 3-course dinner £45 ($67.50); dinner main courses £14–£22 ($21–$33). AE, DC, MC, V. Mon–Fri 12:30–2:30pm; Mon–Sat 6:30–11pm. Closed bank holidays. Tube: South Kensington.

Launceston Place ✿ MODERN BRITISH   Launceston Place is in an almost village-like neighborhood where many Londoners would like to live, if only they could afford it. This stylish restaurant lies within a series of uncluttered Victorian parlors, the largest of which is illuminated by a skylight. Each room contains a collection of Victorian-era oils and watercolors, as well as contemporary paintings. Since 1986, it has been known for its new British cuisine. The menu changes every 6 weeks, but you're likely to be served such appetizers as smoked salmon with horseradish crème fraîche or seared *foie gras* with lentils and vanilla dressing. For a main dish, perhaps it'll be roast partridge with bacon, onions, and parsnip mash, or grilled sea bass with tomato and basil cream.

1A Launceston Place, W8. © 020/7937-6912. Reservations required. Main courses £16–£18 ($24–$27); fixed-price menu for lunch and early dinner until 8pm £15.50 ($23.25) for 2 courses, £18.50 ($27.75) for 3 courses. AE, MC, V. Mon–Fri 12:30–2:30pm; Sun 12:30–3pm; Mon–Sat 7–11:30pm. Tube: Gloucester Rd. or High St. Kensington.

MODERATE

Bistro 190 MEDITERRANEAN   In the airy front room of The Gore hotel (p. 123), this restaurant features a light Mediterranean cuisine appreciated by the music and media crowd that keeps the place hopping. In an artfully simple setting of wood floors, potted plants, and framed art, you can dine on such dishes as scallop and tiger prawn kebabs with cumin pilaf and oregano-and-lemon dressing; leek cannelloni with wild mushroom and barley stuffing; rare peppered tuna with apple and herb salad; and, if available, a rhubarb crumble based loosely on an old-fashioned British dessert. Service isn't particularly fast, and if you're not a member of the club (or a guest at the hotel), you'll have to reserve 24 hours in advance. In the crush of peak dining hours, your waiter may not remember the nuances of your order, but the restaurant is memorable. Go down to Downstairs 190 for a seafood or vegetarian meal.

In the Gore Hotel, 190 Queen's Gate, SW7. © 020/7581-5666. Main courses £10–£15 ($15–$22.50). AE, DC, MC, V. Mon–Fri 7am–midnight; Sat 7:30am–midnight; Sun 7:30am–11:30pm. Tube: Gloucester Rd.

Blue Elephant ⭐ THAI   This is the counterpart of the famous **L'Éléphant Bleu** in Brussels. Located in a converted factory building in West Brompton, the Blue Elephant has been all the rage since 1986. It remains the leading Thai restaurant in London, where the competition seems to grow daily. In an almost magical garden setting of tropical foliage, diners are treated to an array of MSG-free Thai dishes. You can begin with a "Floating Market" (shellfish in clear broth, flavored with chile paste and lemon grass), then go on to a splendid selection of main courses, for which many of the ingredients have been flown in from Thailand. We recommend the roasted duck curry served in a clay cooking pot.

3–6 Fulham Broadway, SW6. © 020/7385-6595. Reservations required. Main courses £10–£25 ($15–$37.50); Royal Thai banquet £32–£36 ($48–$54); Sun buffet £19.50 ($29.25). AE, DC, MC, V. Mon–Fri noon–2:30pm; Mon–Sat 6:30pm–12:30am; Sun noon–3pm and 6:30–10:30pm. Tube: Fulham Broadway.

The Enterprise TRADITIONAL BRITISH/EUROPEAN   The Enterprise's proximity to Harrods attracts both regulars and out-of-town shoppers. Although the joint swarms with singles at night, during the day it attracts the ladies who lunch. With banquettes, white linen, and fresh flowers on the tables, you won't mistake it for a lowly boozer. The kitchen serves respectable traditional English fare as well as European favorites, all prepared with fresh ingredients. Featured dishes include fried salmon cakes with perfectly done fries, and grilled steak with fries and salad. They're not so grand that they won't prepare an entrecôte with frites if that's what pleases you—actually, the juicy, properly aged, flavorful and thin French-style slice of beef is about the best you can have in London.

35 Walton St., SW3. © 020/7584-3148. Reservations accepted only for lunch. Main courses £9.65–£14 ($14.50–$21). AE, MC, V. Daily 12:30–2:30pm; Sat–Sun 12:30–3:30pm; Mon–Sat 7–11pm; Sun 7–10:20pm (the bar is open all day). Tube: South Kensington.

Joe's ⭐ (Finds MODERN BRITISH   This is one of three London restaurants established by fashion designer Joseph Ettedgui. Thanks to its sense of glamour and fun, it's often filled at breakfast and lunch with well-known names from the British fashion, music, and entertainment industries. You can enjoy such dishes as spiced venison strips and vegetables, roast cod in a champagne crab sauce, charcoal grilled swordfish with cracked wheat and salsa verde, or fresh lobster lasagna. It's all safe, but unexciting. No one will mind if your meal is composed exclusively of appetizers. There's a bar near the entrance, a cluster of tables for quick meals near the door, and more leisurely (and gossipy) dining available in an area a few steps up. The atmosphere remains laid back and unstuffy, just like trendsetters in South Ken prefer it. With a name like Joe's, what else could it be?

126 Draycott Ave., SW3. ℂ 020/7225-2217. Reservations required. Main courses £11–£18 ($16.50–$27). AE, DC, MC, V. Mon–Sat 9am–6pm; Sun 10am–5pm. Tube: South Kensington.

Kensington Place MODERN EUROPEAN   Rowley Leigh, the chef here, has attracted a devoted following of regulars. But now, word of his cuisine is spreading and more and more visitors are rushing here to sample some of his signature dishes, such as griddled *foie gras* on a sweetcorn pancake, or scallops with pea purée and mint vinaigrette. His slow-braised lamb shank is one of the best dishes of its kind. Also look for his seasonal and innovative dishes. The chef has a marvelous way with grouse, venison, roast partridge, and sea bass. He grills scallops to golden perfection, and even a simple chicken dish is enhanced by a goat cheese mousse and olives. Everybody from pop stars to Kensington dowagers flock to this animated, noisy bistro. The set lunch is one of the best values in the area. Save room for the steamed chocolate pudding with custard. Harking back to olde England, the chef still serves rhubarb fool or a summer trifle flavored with red fruits and liqueur.

201 Kensington Church St., W8. ℂ 020/7727-3184. Reservations required. Main courses £13.50–£18.50 ($20.25–$27.75); fixed-price lunch £18 ($27). AE, DC, MC, V. Mon–Sat noon–3:30pm and 6:30–11:45pm; Sun noon–3:30pm and 6:30–10:45pm. Tube: Notting Hill Gate.

Pasha MOROCCAN   You'll find virtually every kind of ethnic restaurant within London, but few equal the zest and stylishness of this re-creation of a palace within the medina at Marrakesh. Within the two dining rooms, each outfitted with Bedouin colors, rich upholsteries, flickering candles, and belly-dancing music, you'll enjoy regional specialties that were once sampled only by cherished royal family guests. Examples include a crispy lamb salad with pomegranate and mint; grilled sea bass with warm hummus and parsley salad; chicken *merguez* (spicy sausage) with a coriander tagine; and chargrilled skewered chicken with green chile salsa. And if you have a fondness for couscous, you'll have at least three different kinds from which to choose.

1 Gloucester Rd., SW7. ℂ 020/7589-7969. Reservations recommended. Main courses £10–£20 ($15–$30). AE, DC, MC, V. Mon–Sat noon–3pm and 7–11:30pm; Sun 7–10:30pm. Tube: Gloucester Rd.

Phoenicia *Value* LEBANESE   Phoenicia is highly regarded for its Lebanese cuisine—outstanding in presentation and freshness—and for its moderate prices. For the best value, go for lunch, and enjoy a buffet of more than two dozen *meze* (appetizers), in little pottery dishes. Each day at lunch, the chef prepares two or three home-cooked dishes to tempt you, including chicken in garlic sauce or stuffed lamb with vegetables. Many Lebanese patrons begin their meal with the *aperitif arak,* a liqueur some compare to the Greek anise-flavored liqueur ouzo. To start, you can select from such classic Middle Eastern dishes as hummus or stuffed vine leaves. The chefs bake fresh bread and two types of pizza daily. Minced lamb, spicy and well flavored, is an eternal favorite. Charcoal-grilled dishes are also offered.

11–13 Abingdon Rd., W8. ℂ 020/7937-0120. Reservations required. Main courses £10.90–£15 ($16.35–$22.50); buffet lunch £12.95–£14.95 ($19.40–$22.40); fixed-price dinner £16.80–£30.95 ($25.20–$46.45). AE, DC, MC, V. Daily 12:15pm–midnight; buffet lunch daily 12:15–3:30pm. Tube: High St. Kensington.

INEXPENSIVE

Admiral Codrington ⭐ *Finds* MODERN BRITISH/CONTINENTAL
Once a lowly pub, this stylish bar and restaurant is all the rage nowadays. The old "Cod," as it is affectionately known, offers plush dining with a revitalized decor by Nina Campbell, and a glass roof that rolls back on sunny days. The bartenders still offer a traditional pint, but the sophisticated menu features such delectable fare as linguine with zucchini, crab, and chile peppers, or rib eye steak with slow-roasted tomatoes. Opt for the grilled breast of chicken salad with bean sprouts, apple, and cashews, or the grilled tuna with a couscous salad and eggplant "caviar."

17 Mossop St., SW3. ℂ 020/7581-0005. Reservations recommended. Main courses £9.75–£13.75 ($14.65–$20.65). MC, V. Mon–Sat noon–11:30pm; Sun noon–10:30pm. Tube: South Kensington.

Lou Pescadou *Value* SEAFOOD Most London Seafood restaurants are expensive. This one isn't, probably because it's located in unfashionable Earl's Court. Partly because of its friendly waiters, it draws a large repeat business from local residents, but mainly because of its generous and affordably-priced set menus (see below). The very fresh-tasting and most popular dishes are concocted from squid, prawns, lobster, clams, or oysters. You'll think, from the taste of that food, that you've arrived just as the fish boats have come into a Breton port. We're fond of braised Scottish salmon with fresh vegetables or the catch of the day poached to perfection and served with a velvet-smooth mayonnaise that's evocative of the French Riviera. Tables spill out onto the sidewalk whenever the weather is fair, which a waiter facetiously suggested, "is at least on ten days a year in London."

241 Old Brompton Rd., SW5 ℂ 020/7370-1057. Reservations required. Main courses £7–£14.80 ($10.50–$22.20); Mon–Fri set menu £9.90 ($14.85); Sat–Sun set menu £13.50 ($20.25). AE, DC, MC, V. Daily noon–3pm; Mon–Fri 7pm–midnight; Sat–Sun 6:30pm–midnight. Tube: Earl's Court.

6 Marylebone to Notting Hill Gate

MARYLEBONE
VERY EXPENSIVE

John Burton—Race at the Landmark ⭐⭐ FRENCH Immaculately operated, this remarkable restaurant blends the very finest ingredients with the razor-sharp skills of one of England's most brilliant chefs, John Burton-Race. Just across from Marylebone Station, the elegant restaurant has 20-foot high ceilings and floor-to-ceiling windows—real Grand Hotel style. Burton-Race is passionate about cuisine and proud of his French culinary heritage, having been heavily influenced by haute cuisine in the Escoffier style, although he makes the menu his own with a lighter, healthier approach to cooking. Dining here can range from a light, three-course lunch to a seven-course menu gourmand.

The hors d'oeuvres are superb concoctions, such as a smoked salmon terrine layered with curry butter and served with a mint yogurt, or a confit of duck and foie gras with seasonal greens bound with hazelnut vinaigrette. For the main courses, expect a daily changing menu of seasonal delights. Inventiveness and a solid technique are reflected in such dishes as a risotto of wild mushrooms or filet of pan-fried sea bream nestling on a fricassée of baby squid. For dessert, how can you resist the chocolate and banana parfait studded with pistachios between leaves of lacquered chocolate puff pastry?

222 Marylebone Rd., NW1. ℂ 022/7723-7800. Reservations required. Main courses £32–£38 ($48–$57). Fixed-price lunch £28 ($42), fixed-price dinner £46 ($69). AE, DC, MC, V. Sun–Fri noon–2:15pm; Mon–Sat 7–10:30pm. Tube: Marylebone.

EXPENSIVE

Assaggi ★★ *Finds* ITALIAN   Some of London's finest Italian cuisine is served in this room above a pub. The place is a real discovery, and completely unpretentious. The relatively simple menu points up the creative, outstanding cookery. All the ingredients are fresh and deftly handled by a skilled kitchen staff. The appetizers such as asparagus with poached egg and pancetta (cured bacon), or beef carpaccio, are so truly sublime you'll want to make a meal entirely of them. Simplicity and flavor reign throughout. At least three freshly made pastas are featured nightly. The tortelloni (pocket-shaped noodles filled with cheese) with pork and a zesty tomato sauce is especially delicious. For a main course, opt for such delights as the thick, juicy, tender grilled veal, flavored with fresh rosemary, or filet of brill with saffron-infused semolina dumplings. Another savory choice is a plate of lamb cutlets (without any fat) with eggplant and a raisin salad. The chocolate truffle cake is the finest you'll find this side of northern Italy.

39 Chepstow Place, W2. © **020/7792-5501**. Reservations required (as far in advance as possible). Main courses £16.50–£20 ($24.75–$30). AE, DC, MC, V. Mon–Sat 12:30–2:30pm and 7:30–11pm. Closed 2 weeks at Christmas. Tube: Notting Hill Gate.

Odin's ★ INTERNATIONAL   This elegant restaurant is one of at least four in London owned by chef Richard Shepherd and actor Michael Caine. Set adjacent to its less expensive twin, Langan's Bistro (see below), it features ample space between tables and an eclectic decor that includes paintings and theatrical memorabilia from West End plays. As other restaurants come and go, the cookery here remains solid and reliable, served in an atmosphere that is arty, cozy, intimate, and urbane. The standard of fresh ingredients and well-prepared dishes is always maintained. The menu changes with the seasons: Typical fare might include forest mushrooms in brioche; braised leeks glazed with mustard and tomato sauce; roast duck with applesauce and sage-and-onion stuffing; or roast filet of sea bass with a juniper cream sauce.

27 Devonshire St., W1. © **020/7935-7296**. Reservations required. Fixed-price 2-course lunch or dinner £26 ($39); fixed-price 3-course lunch or dinner £29 ($43.50). AE, DC, MC, V. Mon–Fri 12:30–2:30pm and 6:30–11pm. Tube: Regent's Park.

Orrey ★★ INTERNATIONAL/CLASSICAL FRENCH   With ingredients imported from France, this is one of London's classic French restaurants. Sea bass from the shores of Montpellier, olive oil from Maussane-les-Alpilles, mushrooms from the fields of Calais, and poultry from Bresse—it all turns up on this highly refined menu, the creation of chef Chris Galvin, who is enjoying his first Michelin star. On the second floor of The Conran Shop in Marylebone, the restaurant changes its menu seasonally to take advantage of the best produce. Galvin is a purist in terms of ingredients. Our favorites among his first-rate dishes are Bresse pigeon with savoy cabbage and mushroom ravioli; and duckling with an endive tatin and cepe (flap mushrooms) sauce. Where but here can you get a good caramelized calves' sweetbread salad in a truffle vinaigrette? All the dishes have a brilliant, often whimsical, touch as exemplified by the sautéed leeks in pumpkin oil. A wild mushroom consommé arrives with a medley of such fungi as *pieds de bleu, pieds de mouton,* chanterelles, and *trompettes de morte,* all from French forests. Skipping the blueberry soufflé, we ended with a cheese plate that featured a Banton goat cheese from Provence that was so fresh that it oozed onto the plate. Lazy summer evenings are to be enjoyed on a fourth-floor terrace, where you can drink and order light fare from the bar menu.

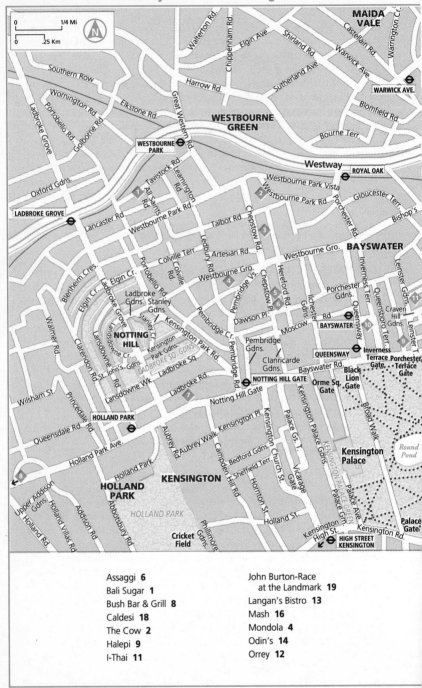

Assaggi **6**
Bali Sugar **1**
Bush Bar & Grill **8**
Caldesi **18**
The Cow **2**
Halepi **9**
I-Thai **11**

John Burton-Race
  at the Landmark **19**
Langan's Bistro **13**
Mash **16**
Mondola **4**
Odin's **14**
Orrey **12**

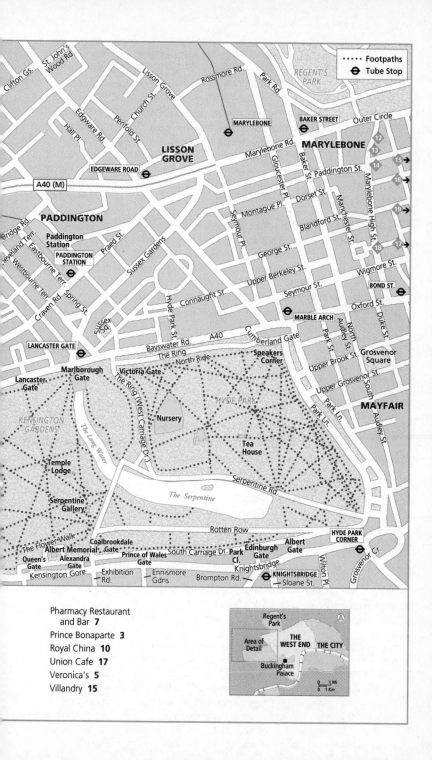

Pharmacy Restaurant
  and Bar **7**
Prince Bonaparte **3**
Royal China **10**
Union Cafe **17**
Veronica's **5**
Villandry **15**

55 Marylebone High St., W1. ℂ 020/7616-8000. Reservations required. Main courses £15.50–£25 ($23.25–$37.50). Fixed-price 3-course menu £24 ($36), fixed price 5-course menu £50 ($75). AE, DC, MC, V. Daily noon–3pm, Mon–Sat 7–1pm, Sun 7–10:30pm. Tube: Baker St.

MODERATE

Bush Bar & Grill ★ *Finds* TRADITIONAL BRITISH /FRENCH   Hip, light-hearted, and sought after by the quasi-celebrities of London's world of media and entertainment, this bar and brasserie was established in 2000 by the owners of two of the city's most desirable private clubs, Woody's and The Groucho Club. Both of these are membership-only venues in other parts of town, but at the tables near you at this spinoff restaurant, you're likely to see members of those clubs dining with the likes of Jerry Hall, Kate Moss, cookbook author Nigella Lawson, pop singer Kylie Minogue, and writers from such publications as *British Vogue* and *Tatler*. The setting was originally conceived as a milk-bottling plant, but since a team of decorators revamped it, it evokes an arts-conscious Manhattan bistro with a neo-industrial decor, exposed air ducts, and a busy kitchen that's open to view. Chefs here place an emphasis on organic pro-duce, preparing dishes that include French onion soup; marinated mussels; rémoulade of celeriac; roasted rib of beef, served with Béarnaise and french fries, and prepared for only two diners at a time; and roasted duck with mashed pota-toes and black peppercorn sauce. Grilled squid, roasted lamb, and cod-and-haddock pie are always tempting as well.

45 Goldhawk Rd. ℂ 020/8746-2111. Reservations required. Main courses £9.50[nd£17 ($14.25–$25.50); fixed-price menus, served only at lunch and at dinner till 7:30pm £10.50–£12 ($15.75–$18). AE, MC, V. Mon–Sat noon–3pm and 7–10:30pm. Tube: Goldhawk Road.

Caldesi ITALIAN/TUSCAN   Good food, reasonable prices, fresh ingredi-ents, and authentic Tuscan family recipes attract a never-ending stream to this eatery founded by owner and head chef Giancarlo Caldesi. The extensive menu includes a wide array of pasta, antipasti, fish, and meat dishes. Start with the excellent *insalata Caldesi,* made with tomatoes slow-roasted in garlic and rose-mary oil, and served with mozzarella flown in from Tuscany. Pasta dishes include an especially flavor-filled homemade tortelloni stuffed with salmon and ricotta and served with a creamy spinach sauce. Monkfish and prawns are flavored with wild fennel and fresh basil, or you might sample the tender duck breast with fresh peaches, steeped in white wine, honey, thyme, and rosemary.

15–17 Marylebone Lane, W1. ℂ 020/7935-9226. Reservations required. Main courses £7–£16.50 ($10.50–$24.75). AE, MC, V. Mon–Fri noon–2:30pm and 6–11pm; Sat 6–11pm. Tube: Bond St.

Langan's Bistro TRADITIONAL BRITISH/FRENCH   This unpretentious bistro is still around—although perhaps not quite the happening scene it was when Michael Caine founded it back in the 1960s. Of the restaurants in this chain (see Langan's Brasserie, earlier in this chapter, and Odin's, above), it's the least expensive, but the most visually appealing. Set behind a brightly colored storefront, the dining room is decorated with clusters of Japanese parasols, mir-rors, surrealistic paintings, and old photographs. The menu is "mostly English with a French influence"; it changes with the seasons but might include red pep-per and Brie tartlets or grilled goat cheese with rocket salad. Longtime brasserie favorites like onion soup, pepper steak and braised calves' liver with onion, are reassuringly familiar and as good as they ever were. Check out the dish of the day or opt for the chargrilled tuna Niçoise or the cod with an herb crust. Chocoholics should finish off with the extravaganza known as "Mrs. Langan's Chocolate Pudding."

26 Devonshire St., W1. © 020/7935-4531. Reservations recommended. Fixed-price 2-course lunch or dinner £18 ($27); fixed-price 3-course lunch or dinner £20 ($30). AE, DC, MC, V. Mon–Fri 12:30–2:30pm; Mon–Sat 6:30–11pm. Tube: Regent's Park.

Mash ⭐ *Finds* MODERN CONTINENTAL   What is it, you ask? A bar? A deli? A microbrewery? Actually, it's all of the above, plus a restaurant. Breakfast and weekend brunch are the highlights, but don't ignore dinner. The novelty decor includes curvy sci-fi lines that might remind you of a *Star Trek* set, and lizard-eye lighting fixtures, but ultimately the food is the attraction. The owners of the hot Atlantic Bar & Grill and the Coast restaurant have opened this "sunken chill-out zone" created by leading designer John Currin. The atmosphere is trendy, hip, breezy, and arty.

Suckling pig with spring cannellini stew made us forget all about the trendy mirrored bathrooms. So did the terrific pizzas emerging from the wood-fired oven. On another occasion, we returned for the fish freshly grilled over wood. It was sea bass and was presented enticingly with grilled artichoke. Try also the chargrilled tuna with sautéed new potatoes, wilted spinach, and puttanesca dressing.

19–21 Great Portland St., W1. © 020/7637-5555. Reservations required. Main courses £10–£17 ($15–$25.50); fixed-price lunch £10 ($15). AE, DC, MC, V. Mon–Sat 7:30am–11pm. Tube: Oxford Circus.

Union Cafe CONTINENTAL   After shopping along Oxford Street, restore your spirits with the quality ingredients and exceptional food served at this sleek spot. The mainly female chefs use the finest ingredients in any season. Everything from farmhouse English cheeses to free-range meat will tempt you. Rarely is any item over-sauced. Natural, fresh flavors come to the fore. In most cases, the fresh fish and meat are chargrilled to perfection. The pepper tuna steaks, served rare, are an exceptional taste sensation, as is the oak-smoked salmon with fresh horseradish sauce, and the wild boar-and-apple sausage. A daily vegetarian pizza is offered, including one filled with mozzarella, spinach, tomatoes, and eggplant. If you don't want wine, you can choose some homemade drinks that might have delighted Dickens, including, for example, elderflower cordial. Desserts such as caramelized pear cake or blood orange sorbet are worth the trek across town.

96 Marylebone Lane, W1. © 020/7486-4860. Reservations recommended. Main courses £10–£16 ($15–$24). AE, MC, V. Mon–Sat 12:30–10:30pm. Tube: Bond St.

Villandry ⭐ INTERNATIONAL/CONTINENTAL   Food lovers and gourmands flock to this food store, delicatessen, and restaurant, where racks of the finest meats, cheese, and produce in the world are displayed and changed virtually every hour. Some of the best of the merchandise is quickly and whimsically transformed into the restaurant's menu choices. The setting is an oversize Edwardian-style storefront north of Oxford Circus. The inside is a kind of minimalist temple dedicated to the glories of fresh produce and esoteric foodstuffs. Ingredients here change so frequently that the menu is rewritten twice a day—during our latest visit, it proposed such perfectly crafted dishes as breast of duck with fresh spinach and a gratin of baby onions; boiled haunch of pork with blood sausages, mashed potatoes, kale, and mustard sauce; and pan-fried turbot with deep-fried celery, artichoke hearts, and hollandaise sauce.

170 Great Portland St., W1. © 020/7631-3131. Reservations recommended. Main courses £12–£20 ($18–$30). AE, MC, V. Mon–Sat noon–3pm and 7–10pm. Food store Mon–Sat 8am–10pm; Sun 10am–4pm. Tube: Great Portland St.

PADDINGTON & BAYSWATER
VERY EXPENSIVE

I-Thai ★ ITALIAN/THAI/JAPANESE   Part of the aggressively minimalist Hempel Hotel (p. 133), this spot specializes in upscale clients, upscale Thai and Italian food, and upscale prices. The antithesis of the showy, lushly decorated restaurants of the 1980s, I-Thai prides itself on a Zen-like calm. The sparse but innovative menu is expensive, so dining here is more fun if you're on an expense account. We suggest beginning with one of the soups, either the spicy squid-ink soup with lemon grass and coconut cream, or the chicken, coconut, and *foie gras* soup flavored with Thai basil. Main dishes are prepared exquisitely; we loved the truffle and mascarpone risotto as well as the stir-fried cellophane noodles with tiger prawns in a black-ink parcel. On our most recent trip, we enjoyed the red chicken and gingko-nut curry served with sweet Thai basil. For dessert, try almost anything, especially the steamed Pandan pudding garnished with a warm coconut-and-blueberry sauce.

In The Hempel Hotel, Hempel Sq., 31–35 Craven Hill Gardens, W2. ℭ 020/7298-9000. Reservations required. Main courses £16–£29.50 ($24–$44.25). AE, DC, MC, V. Daily noon–2:30pm and 7–11pm. Tube: Lancaster Gate.

EXPENSIVE

Royal China ★ *Kids* CANTONESE/SZECHUAN   Unexpectedly delightful Szechuan and Cantonese specialties lure you to this popular eatery, a family favorite. Come here for the best dim sum in London. You might have to go to Hong Kong to find Chinese cooking as authentic as this. Forget the garish decor and concentrate on what's on your plate. The eight-page menu is overwhelming in its choices, and many of the classic dishes are only known to true students of Chinese cuisine. We were delighted by the Shanghai dumplings, steamed on one side and sautéed on the other. Various whole ducks and chickens are prepared with skill passed down through centuries. We noticed a table of London Chinese raving about the jellyfish with sesame oil, although we opted for the steamed eel with black-bean sauce.

13 Queensway, W2. ℭ 020/7221-2535. Reservations recommended. Main courses £6–£70 ($9–$105); fixed-price dinner £23–£29 ($34.50–$43.50). AE, DC, MC, V. Mon–Sat noon–11:30pm; Sun 11am–10pm. Tube: Bayswater or Queensway.

MODERATE

Halepi ★ *Finds* GREEK/CYPRIOT   Run by the Kazolides family since 1966, this establishment is hailed by the *Automobile Association of America Guide* as the best Greek restaurant in the world. Despite its reputation, the atmosphere is informal, with rows of brightly clothed tables, *bouzouki* background music, and a large native clientele.

Portions are generous. Menu items rely heavily on lamb and include kebabs, *klefticon* (baby lamb prepared with aromatic spices), moussaka (minced lamb and eggplant with bechamel sauce), and *dolmades* (vine leaves stuffed with lamb and rice). Other main courses include scallops; sea bass; Scotch halibut; huge Indonesian shrimp with lemon juice, olive oil, garlic, and spring onion sauce; and *afelia* (filet of pork cooked with wine and spices, served with potatoes and rice). The homemade baklava is recommended for dessert, and the wine list features numerous selections from Greece and Cyprus. Most dishes are moderate in price.

18 Leinster Terrace, W2. ℭ 020/7262-1070. Reservations required. Main courses £9.50–£28 ($14.25–$42). AE, DC, MC, V. Daily noon–midnight. Closed Dec 25–26. Tube: Queensway.

Veronica's ★ *Finds* TRADITIONAL BRITISH   Called the "market leader in cafe salons," Veronica's offers traditional—and historical—fare at prices you won't mind paying. It's a celebration of British cuisine over a 2,000-year period, with dishes based on medieval, Tudor, and even Roman-age recipes, given an imaginative modern twist by owner Veronica Shaw. One month she'll focus on Scotland, another month on Victorian foods, yet another on Wales, and the next on Ireland. Your appetizer might be a salad called *salmagundy*, made with crunchy pickled vegetables, that Elizabeth I enjoyed in her day. Another concoction might be "Tweed Kettle," a 19th-century salmon stew recipe. Many dishes are vegetarian, and everything tastes better when followed with a British farmhouse cheese or a pudding. The restaurant offers a moderated menu to help keep cholesterol down. The restaurant is brightly and attractively decorated, and the service warm and ingratiating.

3 Hereford Rd., W2. ℂ 020/7229-5079. Reservations required. Main courses £10–£17.25 ($15–$25.90); fixed-price meals £8.50–£15.50 ($12.75–$23.25). AE, DC, MC, V. Tues–Fri and Sun 12:30–3pm; Mon–Sat 6–11pm. Tube: Bayswater.

NOTTING HILL GATE
EXPENSIVE

Bali Sugar ★ PACIFIC RIM   Chef David Selex brings an exotic, bold, and extraordinary new look to fusion cuisine, which has been labeled "Southern Hemisphere Pacific Rim Modern Mediterranean Cosmopolitan British cookery"—whatever. Selex has created a menu using Japanese and South American ingredients to great effect. For starters, dig into his Peruvian ceviche with king prawn, coconut, lime, and sweet potato, followed by rare tuna. The tastes are magical. His cured salmon is perfect and wonderfully accompanied by a side order of wasabi-flavored mashed potatoes. The overall effect, in the words of one diner, is a meeting of the Pacific Rim with Nuevo Latino. Try also the breast of chicken integrated with an irresistibly rich tofu. The two-floor eatery is a delight with a sunken garden. Chic London goes here. There's a separate nonsmoking floor.

33A All Saints Rd., W11. ℂ 020/7221-4477. Main courses £11–£22 ($16.50–$33); brunch from £9 ($13.50). AE, DC, MC, V. Daily 6–11pm; brunch Sat–Sun 11:30am–3:30pm. Tube: Westbourne Park.

Pharmacy Restaurant and Bar ★ MODERN EUROPEAN   The theme of this medical-chic restaurant evokes all sorts of drug-related venues, from a harmless small-town pharmacy to a drug lord's secret stash of mind-altering pills. This ambiguity is appreciated by the arts-conscious crowd that flocks here, partly because they're interested in what Damien Hirst (*enfant terrible* of London's art world) has created, and partly because the place can be a lot of fun. You'll enter the street-level bar, where a drink menu lists lots of highly palatable martinis as well as a somewhat icky concoction known as a Cough Syrup (cherry liqueur, honey, and vodka that's shaken, not stirred, over ice). Bottles of pills, bar stools with seats shaped like aspirins, and painted representations of fire, water, air, and earth decorate the area. Upstairs in the restaurant, the pharmaceutical theme is less pronounced but subtly omnipresent. Menu items include trendy but comforting food items such as carpaccio of whitefish; lamb cooked with Provençal vegetables; pan-fried cod in red wine with Jerusalem artichokes and shallots; and roast saddle of hare in pear sauce.

150 Notting Hill Gate, W11. ℂ 020/7221-2442. Reservations required Fri–Sat, strongly recommended other nights. Main courses £11.50–£24 ($17.25–$36). AE, DC, DISC, MC, V. Daily noon–2:45pm and 6:45–10:45pm. Tube: Notting Hill Gate.

MODERATE

The Cow *★ Finds* MODERN BRITISH   You don't have to be a young fashion victim to enjoy the superb cuisine served here (although many of the diners are). Tom Conran (son of entrepreneur Sir Terence Conran) holds forth in this increasingly hip Notting Hill watering hole. It looks like an Irish pub, but the accents you'll hear are trustafarian rather than street-smart Dublin. With a pint of Fuller's or London Pride, you can linger over the modern European menu, which changes daily but is likely to include ox tongue poached in milk; mussels in curry and cream; or a mixed grill of lamb chops, calves' liver, and sweetbreads. The seafood selections are delectable. "The Cow Special"—a half-dozen Irish rock oysters with a pint of Guinness or a glass of wine for £8.50 ($12.75)—is the star of the show. A raw bar downstairs serves other fresh seafood choices. To finish, skip the filtered coffee served upstairs (it's wretched), and opt for an espresso downstairs.

89 Westbourne Park Rd., W2. ✆ 020/7221-0021. Reservations required. Main courses £13.50–£16 ($20.25–$24). MC, V. Mon–Sat 6–11pm; Sun 12:30–4pm (brunch) and 6:30–10:30pm; bar daily noon–11pm. Tube: Westbourne Grove.

INEXPENSIVE

Mondola SUDANESE   Of all the African restaurants in London, this is the only one that specializes in the spicy cuisine of the Sudan. Very small and intimate, on the fringe of trendy Notting Hill, this bohemian hangout is far from trendy itself. It doesn't have a liquor license, but you're free to BYOB. A Moorish archway and various photos and artifacts give the place a North African atmosphere.

The food is a blend of various cuisines. The chefs borrow ideas for their eclectic and inexpensive fare from the various kitchens of North Africa, Ethiopia, and even the Middle East. Begin with the classic soup of the region, made with meat and peanuts. Although the menu is limited, the dishes are well prepared from fresh ingredients. Opt for lamb, especially the tasty chops marinated in African spices. Ground red chiles add zest to any dish. Lentils with caramelized garlic are another treat, and there's a generous salad bar costing £10.50 ($15.75) for two persons. Skip the desserts and ask for a traditional African coffee. The place is a dining oddity for London and a bit of a culinary adventure.

139 Westbourne Grove, W11. ✆ 020/7229-4734. Reservations recommended. Main courses £10–£12 ($15–$18). Fixed-price meals £17 ($25.50). MC, V. Daily 11am–11pm. Tube: Notting Hill Gate.

Prince Bonaparte INTERNATIONAL   This offbeat restaurant serves great pub grub in what used to be a grungy boozer in the days before Notting Hill Gate became fashionable. Now pretty young things show up, spilling onto the sidewalk when the evenings are warm. The pub is filled with mismatched furniture from schools and churches; and CDs of jazz and lazy blues fill the air, competing with the babble. It may seem at first that the staff doesn't have its act together, but once the food arrives, you won't care: It's very good. The menu roams the world for inspiration: Moroccan chicken with couscous is as good or better than any you'll find in Marrakesh; seafood risotto is delicious, as is the salad of beet root, new potatoes, walnuts, and eggplant. Roast lamb, tender and juicy, appears on the traditional Sunday menu. We recommend the London Pride or Grolsch to wash it all down.

80 Chepstow Rd., W2. ✆ 020/7313-9491. Reservations required. Main courses £8.50–£14 ($12.75–$21). MC, V. Mon–Sat noon–11pm; Sun 12:30–10pm. Tube: Notting Hill Gate or Westbourne Park.

7 A Bit Farther Afield

HAMMERSMITH

To see where Hammersmith lies in relation to central London, refer to the map "Guide to London Restaurant Maps" (p. 146).

VERY EXPENSIVE

The River Café ★★ ITALIAN   For the best Italian cuisine in London, head to this Thames-side bistro operated by Ruth Rogers and Rose Gray. The charmingly contemporary establishment, with a polished steel bar, was designed by Ruth's husband, Richard, who also designed the Pompidou Centre in Paris. The cafe attracts a trendy crowd that comes to see and be seen, and to eat fabulous food. The menu changes regularly. The owners' goal was to recreate the kind of cuisine they'd enjoyed in private homes in the Italian countryside, and they've succeeded. Some chefs can be seen shopping in London's markets—but not these chefs. The market comes to them: first-spring asparagus harvested in Andalusia and arriving in London within the day; live scallops and langoustines taken by divers in the icy North Sea; and a daily shipment of the finest harvest of Italy, ranging from radicchio to artichokes. Even tiny bulbs of fennel are zipped across the Channel from France. Britain's own rich bounty appears in pheasant and wild salmon. The best dishes are either slowly roasted or quickly seared.

Thames Wharf, Rainville Rd., W6. ℂ 020/7386-4200. Reservations required. Main courses £11–£28 ($16.50–$42). AE, DC, MC, V. Mon–Sat 12:30–3:30pm and 7–11pm; Sun 12:30–3:30pm. Tube: Hammersmith.

CAMDEN TOWN
MODERATE

The Engineer ★ (Finds) MODERN EUROPEAN/THAI   This castle of north London chic is another one of our favorites. The stylishly converted pub is owned by Abigail Osborne and Tamsin Olivier, daughter of Lord Olivier (or "Larry's Daughter," as she's called locally), and is named for Victorian bridge, tunnel, and railway builder Isambard Kingdom Brunel. It sits beside Regent's Canal, one of Brunel's creations. The pub is divided into a bar, a dining room, and a garden area for warm days. The decor is light and modern. The cuisine is modern European with a Thai influence and relies on seasonal produce and organic meat and eggs. Choices include Thai fishcakes, crispy duck confit with roasted sweet potatoes; and a warm salad of shiitake mushrooms with celeriac and red onion confit. A tantalizing appetizer is the deep-fried Camembert with kiwi-fruit relish. Desserts change nightly and might include an orange and cardamom pudding. From the tap, go with the Caffrey's or a Guinness.

65 Gloucester Ave., NW1. ℂ 020/7722-0950. Reservations recommended. Main courses £9.50–£15 ($14.25–$22.50). MC, V. Daily 9am–11pm. Tube: Chalk Farm or Camden Town.

8 Teatime

Everyone should indulge in a formal afternoon tea at least once while in London. It's a relaxing, drawn-out, civilized affair that usually consists of three courses, all elegantly served on delicate china: first, dainty finger sandwiches (with the crusts cut off, of course), then fresh-baked scones served with jam and deliciously decadent clotted cream (Devonshire cream), and then an array of bite-size sweets. All the while, an indulgent server keeps the pot of tea of your choice fresh at hand. Sometimes ports and aperitifs are on offer to accompany your final course. It's a quintessential British experience, and we've listed our favorite tea venues below. Note that for the most popular hotels (especially the Ritz), you should make reservations as far in advance as possible. If you go to a place that doesn't take reservations, show up at least half an hour early, especially between April and October. Jacket and tie are often required for gentlemen, and jeans and sneakers are usually frowned upon.

The British Empire no longer comes to a grinding halt at 4pm with all of England rushing for their cuppa. The English still like a cup of tea in the afternoon, but in workaday London that tea is often consumed at desks piled high with papers. A proper sit-down tea is reserved mainly for those ladies-who-lunch who like to follow lunch with fattening but delectable pastries in the late afternoon. Visitors also are fond of participating in this ritual.

London is awash in coffee-bar chains, and many have abandoned the time-honored custom of afternoon tea altogether, but not all. Some Londoners are returning to this quaint custom and finding a revival of tea-drinking.

There are variations in tea-drinking, as today's London is a rainbow-hued city. Take **Mô** at 23 Heddon St. (© **020/7434-4040**). At this offshoot of a North African restaurant, you'll think you're in Morocco as you're served mint tea in gold-encrusted glasses against a backdrop of hanging lanterns and embroidered cushions. Queen Victoria might be horrified at the changes occurring with her traditional afternoon tea.

If drinking tea with your pinky extended just isn't your style, we've also included a handful of less formal (and less expensive) alternatives. A full high tea costs more than £20 ($30) at the finest hotels.

Be careful when you make reservations that you are reserving at the right "Palm Court," as there are several of them.

HIGH TEA
COVENT GARDEN & THE STRAND

Palm Court at the Waldorf Meridien   The Waldorf's Palm Court combines afternoon tea with afternoon dancing (the fox trot, quickstep, and the waltz). The Palm Court is often compared to a 1920s movie set (which it has served as several times in its long life). You can order tea on a terrace or in a pavilion the size of a ballroom lit by skylights. On tea-dancing days, the orchestra leader will conduct such favorites as "Ain't She Sweet" and "Yes, Sir, That's My Baby," as a butler in a cutaway asks if you want a cucumber sandwich.

In the Waldorf Hotel, Aldwych, WC2. © **020/7836-2400**. Reservations required for tea dance. Jacket and tie required for men at tea dance. Afternoon £14 ($21); tea dance £25–£28 ($37.50–$42). AE, DC, MC, V. Afternoon tea Mon–Fri 3–5:30pm; tea dance Sat 3–5:30pm, Sun 4–6:30pm. Tube: Covent Garden or Temple.

MAYFAIR

Brown's Hotel ★   Along with the Ritz, Brown's ranks as one of the most chic venues for tea in London. Tea is served in the drawing room; done in English antiques, oil paintings, and floral chintz—much like the drawing room of a country estate. Give your name to the concierge upon arrival; he'll seat you at one of the sofas and settees or at low tables. There's a choice of 10 teas, plus sandwiches, scones, and pastries (all made in the hotel kitchens) rolled around on a trolley for your selection.

29–34 Albemarle St., W1. © **020/7518-4108**. Reservations not accepted. Afternoon tea £24 ($36). AE, DC, MC, V. Daily 2–5:45pm. Tube: Green Park.

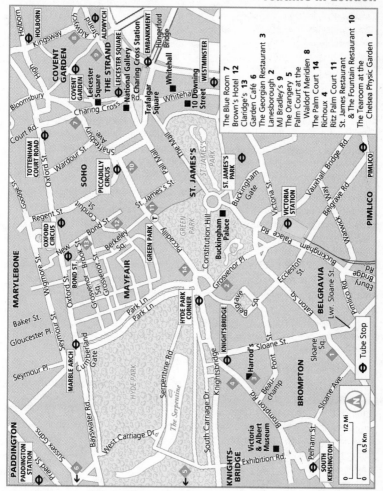

The Blue Room 7
Brown's Hotel 12
Claridge's 13
Garden Café 6
The Georgian Restaurant 3
Lanesborough 2
MJ Bradley's 9
The Orangery 5
Palm Court at the
   Waldorf Méridien 8
The Palm Court 14
Richoux 4
Ritz Palm Court 11
St. James Restaurant
   & The Fountain Restaurant 10
The Tearoom at the
   Chelsea Physic Garden 1

Claridge's ✪ Claridge's teatime rituals have managed to persevere through the years with as much pomp and circumstance as the British Empire itself. It's never stuffy, though; you'll feel very welcome. Tea is served in the Reading Room. A portrait of Lady Claridge gazes from above as a choice of 17 kinds of tea is served ever so politely. The courses are served consecutively, including finger sandwiches with cheese savories, apple and raisin scones, and yummy pastries.

Brook St., W1. ☎ **020/7629-8860.** Reservations recommended. Jacket and tie required for men. High tea Mon–Fri £26 ($39), Sat–Sun £35 ($52.50) including champagne. AE, DC, MC, V. Daily 3–5:30pm. Tube: Bond St.

The Palm Court This is one of the great London favorites for tea. Restored to its former charm, the lounge has an atmosphere straight from 1927, with a domed yellow-and-white glass ceiling, *torchères,* and palms in Compton stoneware *jardinières.* A delightful afternoon repast that includes a long list of different teas is served daily. A harpist plays every weekend afternoon.

In the Sheraton Park Lane Hotel, Piccadilly, W1. ✆ 020/7290-7328. Reservations recommended. Afternoon tea £19 ($28.50); with a glass of Park Lane champagne £25 ($37.50). AE, DC, MC, V. Daily 3–6pm. Tube: Hyde Park Corner or Green Park.

ST. JAMES'S

Ritz Palm Court ★★★ This is the most fashionable place in London to order afternoon tea—and the hardest to get into without reserving way in advance. Its spectacular setting is straight out of *The Great Gatsby,* complete with marble steps and columns, and a baroque fountain. You have your choice of a long list of teas served with delectable sandwiches and luscious pastries.

In The Ritz Hotel, Piccadilly, W1. ✆ 020/7493-8181. Reservations required at least 8 weeks in advance. Jeans and sneakers not acceptable. Jacket and tie required for men. Afternoon tea £27 ($40.50). AE, DC, MC, V. 3 seatings daily at 12:30pm, 3:30 and 5:30pm. Tube: Green Park.

St. James Restaurant & The Fountain Restaurant This pair of tea salons function as a culinary showplace for London's most prestigious grocery store, Fortnum & Mason. The more formal of the two, the St. James, on the store's fourth floor, is a pale green and beige homage to formal Edwardian taste. More rapid and less formal is The Fountain Restaurant, on the street level, where a sense of tradition and manners is very much a part of the teatime experience, but in a less opulent setting. The quantities of food served in both venues are usually ample enough to be defined as full-fledged early suppers for most theatergoers.

In Fortnum & Mason, 181 Piccadilly, W1. ✆ 020/7734-8040. In the St. James, full tea £18.95 ($28.40); in The Fountain, full tea £11.95 ($17.90). AE, DC, MC, V. St. James, Mon–Sat 3–5pm; The Fountain, Mon–Sat 3–6pm. Tube: Piccadilly Circus.

KNIGHTSBRIDGE

The Georgian Restaurant For as long as anyone can remember, teatime at Harrods has been a distinctive feature of Europe's most famous department store. A flood of visitors is gracefully herded into a high-volume but elegant room. Many come here for the ritual of the tea service, where staff members haul silver pots and trolleys laden with pastries and sandwiches through the cavernous dining hall. Most exotic is Betigala tea, a rare blend from China, similar to Lapsang Souchong.

On the 4th floor of Harrods, 87–135 Brompton Rd., SW1. ✆ 020/7225-6800. High tea £18.50 ($27.75) or £25.50 ($38.25) with Harrods champagne per person. AE, DC, MC, V. Mon–Sat 3–5:15pm (last order). Tube: Knightsbridge.

The Lanesborough You'll suspect that many of the folks sipping exotic teas here have dropped in to inspect the public areas of one of London's most expensive hotels. The staff offers a selection of seven teas that include the Lanesborough special blend and herbal esoterica like Rose Cayou. The focal point for this ritual is the Conservatory, a glass-roofed Edwardian fantasy filled with potted plants and a sense of the long-gone majesty of empire. The finger sandwiches, scones, and sweets are all appropriately lavish and endlessly correct.

Hyde Park Corner, SW1. ✆ 020/7259-5599. Reservations required. High tea £24.50 ($36.75); high tea with strawberries and champagne £29.50 ($44.25); pot of tea £4.90 ($7.35). AE, DC, MC, V. Daily 3:30–6pm. Tube: Hyde Park Corner.

Richoux Try the old-fashioned atmosphere of Richoux, established in the 1920s. You can order four hot scones with strawberry jam and whipped cream or choose from a selection of pastries. Of course, tea is obligatory; always specify lemon or cream, one lump or two. A full menu, with fresh salads, sandwiches, and burgers, is served all day. There are three other locations, open Monday through Saturday from 8am to 11pm, Sunday from 9am to 10:30pm. There's a branch at the bottom of Bond Street, 172 Piccadilly (© **020/ 7493-2204;** Tube: Piccadilly Circus or Green Park); one at 41A S. Audley St. (© **020/7629-5228;** Tube: Green Park or Hyde Park Corner); and one at 3 Circus Rd. (© **020/7483-4001;** Tube: St. John's Wood).

86 Brompton Rd. (opposite Harrods), Knightsbridge, SW3. © 020/7584-8300. Full tea £12.50 ($18.75). AE, MC, V. Mon–Sat 8am–8pm; Sun 9am–8pm. Tube: Knightsbridge.

KENSINGTON

The Orangery ★ *Finds*   In its way, the Orangery is the most amazing place for afternoon tea in the world. Set 50 yards north of Kensington Palace, it occupies a long narrow garden pavilion built in 1704 by Queen Anne. In homage to her original intentions, rows of potted orange trees bask in sunlight from soaring windows, and tea is served amid Corinthian columns, ruddy-colored bricks, and a pair of Grinling Gibbons woodcarvings. There are even some urns and statuary that the royal family imported from Windsor Castle. The menu includes soups and sandwiches, with a salad and a portion of upscale potato chips known as kettle chips. There's an array of different teas, served with high style, accompanied by fresh scones with clotted cream and jam, and Belgian chocolate cake.

In the gardens of Kensington Palace, W8. © 020/7376-0239. Reservations not accepted. Pot of tea £1.95 ($2.95); summer cakes and puddings £1.95–£4.25 ($2.95–$6.40); sandwiches £5.25 ($7.90). MC, V. Daily 10am–6pm. Tube: High St. Kensington or Queensway.

CASUAL TEAROOMS
COVENT GARDEN & THE STRAND

MJ Bradley's   Although it defines itself as a coffeehouse, many of MJ Bradley's fans resolutely drop in for a cup of one of the 20 different kinds of tea, everything from Earl Grey and Assam to such herbal brews as peppermint. Outfitted like a brasserie, it manages to mingle nostalgia with modern wall sculptures. If you're hungry, consider one of the imaginative sandwiches with fillings of herb-flavored cream cheese with sun-dried tomatoes.

9 King St., WC2. © 020/7240-5178. Cup of tea £1.40 ($2.10); sandwiches £2.85–£4.95 ($4.30–$7.45) each. AE, DC, DISC, MC, V. Daily 8am–11pm. Tube: Covent Garden or Charing Cross.

SOHO

The Blue Room   Nothing about this place has been patterned on the grand tearooms above, where tea-drinking is an intricate and elaborate social ritual. What you'll find here is a cozy, eccentric enclave lined with the artworks of some of the regular patrons, battered sofas that might have come out of a college dormitory, and a gathering of likable urban hipsters to whom very little is sacred. You can enjoy dozens of varieties of tea, including herbals, served in steaming mugs. Lots of arty types gather here during the late afternoon, emulating some of the rituals of the old-fashioned tea service but with absolutely none of the hauteur.

3 Bateman St., W1. © 020/7437-4827. Reservations not accepted. Cup of tea £1.20 ($1.80); cakes and pastries £1–£2.50 ($1.50–$3.75); sandwiches £3–£5 ($4.50–$7.50). No credit cards. Mon–Sat 8am–10:30pm; Sun noon–11pm. Tube: Leicester Sq.

CHELSEA

The Tearoom at the Chelsea Physic Garden   The garden encompasses a small area, crisscrossed with gravel paths and ringed with a high brick wall that shuts out the roaring traffic of Royal Hospital Road. These few spectacular acres, however, revere the memory of industries that were spawned from seeds developed and tested within its walls. Founded in 1673 as a botanical education center, the Chelsea Physic Garden's list of successes includes the exportation of rubber from South America to Malaysia and tea from China to India.

On the 2 days a week that it's open, the tearoom is likely to be filled with botanical enthusiasts sipping cups of tea as fortification for their garden treks. The setting is a banal-looking Edwardian building. Since the tearoom is only an adjunct to the garden itself, don't expect the lavish pomp of some other teatime venues. But you can carry your cakes and cups of tea out into a garden that, despite meticulous care, always looks a bit unkempt. (Herbaceous plants within its hallowed precincts are left untrimmed to encourage bird life and seed production.) Botanists and flower lovers in general find the place fascinating.

66 Royal Hospital Rd., SW3. ✆ **020/7352-5646.** Tea with cake £4 ($6). MC, V (in shop only). Wed noon–5pm; Sun 2–6pm. Closed Nov–Mar. Tube: Sloane Sq.

NOTTING HILL

The Garden Café   This is the most unusual of the places we recommend, and one of the most worthwhile. The Garden Cafe is in The Lighthouse, the largest center in Europe for people with HIV and AIDS. Princess Diana made the organization one of her projects. The cafeteria is open to the public and is less institutional looking than you might expect; French doors open onto a garden with fountains and summertime tables. Tea is available throughout the day, although midafternoon, between 3:30 and 5:30pm, seems to be the most convivial time. The Notting Hill location is a short walk from Portobello Road.

London Lighthouse, 111–117 Lancaster Rd., W11. ✆ **020/7792-1200.** Cup of tea 70p ($1.05); platter of food £2–£5 ($3–$7.50). No credit cards. Mon–Fri 9am–5pm; Sat 10am–5pm. Tube: Ladbroke Grove.

Exploring London

Dr. Samuel Johnson said, "When a man is tired of London, he is tired of life, for there is in London all that life can afford." It would take a lifetime to explore every alley, court, street, and square in this city, and volumes to discuss them. Since you don't have a lifetime to spend, we've chosen the best that London has to offer.

For the first-time visitor, the question is never what to do, but what to do first. The "Suggested Itineraries" and "The Top Attractions" should help.

A note about admission and open hours: In the listings below, children's prices generally apply to those 16 and under. To qualify for a senior discount, you must be 60 or older. Students must present a student ID to get discounts, where available. In addition to closing on bank holidays, many attractions close around Christmas and New Year's (and, in some cases, early in May), so always call ahead if you're visiting in those seasons.

SUGGESTED ITINERARIES

If You Have 1 Day

No first-time visitor should leave London without a visit to **Westminster Abbey,** with its Poet's Corner (where Browning, Dickens, and Chaucer, among others, are buried) and royal tombs. Also see the **Changing of the Guard** at Buckingham Palace if it's on, and walk to **10 Downing Street,** home of the prime minister. After lunch, see **Big Ben** and the **Houses of Parliament.** Dine at one of the little restaurants in **Covent Garden** such as **Porter's,** owned by the Earl of Bradford (p. 164). Try one of their classic English pies (maybe lamb and apricot). For a pre-theater drink, head over to the ultimate Victorian pub, the Red Lion in Mayfair; it's the kind of place Oscar Wilde might have chosen for a brandy. If you're so inclined, head for a play, musical, or drama in the West End. London has the best English language theater in the world, and the offerings are even greater than that of New York.

If You Have 2 Days

Day 1 Spend Day 1 as above.

Day 2 Devote a good part of the day to exploring the **British Museum,** one of the world's best. In the afternoon, visit the **Tower of London** and see the **Crown Jewels** (expect slow-moving lines). Later, go to a local place for dinner, such as Shepherd's in Westminster, where you can dine alongside MPs from the House of Commons. Perhaps you'll catch another play this evening or head for one of London's nightclubs to dance the night away.

If You Have 3 Days

Days 1–2 Spend Days 1 and 2 as above.

Day 3 In the morning take in the masterworks at the **National Gallery.** For a change of pace in the afternoon, head to **Madame Tus-saud's** waxworks if you have kids in tow. Take a walking tour of **St. James's** (see below). In the evening, take in a **West End** play or a performance at the **National Theatre** or at Queen Elizabeth Hall at South Bank Centre.

If You Have 4 or 5 Days

Days 1–3 Spend Days 1, 2, and 3 as above.

Day 4 In the morning, head for the **City,** London's financial district. Your major sightseeing here will be Sir Christopher Wren's **St. Paul's Cathedral.** In the afternoon, head for **King's Road** in Chelsea for boutique hopping and to dine at

one of **Chelsea's** restaurants. Later, take in a show at a **Soho** nightclub, such as Ronnie Scott's, which features some of the city's best jazz.

Day 5 Explore the **Victoria and Albert Museum** in the morning. Then go to the **Tate Britain Gallery** for a look at some of its masterpieces, and have lunch at its restaurant, which offers some of the best values on wine in Britain. For a glimpse of the dark days of World War II, visit the **Cabinet War Rooms** at Clive Steps, where Churchill directed British operations in the war against the Nazis. Spend the evening at the theater, or take a themed walking tour.

1 Sights & Attractions by Neighborhood

BELGRAVIA
Apsley House, The Wellington
Museum ✧ (p. 251)

BLOOMSBURY
British Library ✧✧ (p. 254)
British Museum ✧✧✧ (p. 221)
Dickens House (p. 250)
Percival David Foundation of
Chinese Art ✧ (p. 261)
St. Pancras Station (p. 247)

CAMDEN TOWN
Jewish Museum (p. 258)

CHELSEA
Carlyle's House (p. 249)
Chelsea Physic Garden (p. 265)
Chelsea Royal Hospital ✧✧
(p. 246)
National Army Museum ✧
(p. 260)

THE CITY
All Hallows Barking-by-the-Tower
(p. 238)
Guildhall Art Gallery ✧ (p. 256)
London Bridge (p. 216)
Museum of London ✧✧ (p. 260)
Old Bailey (p. 248)

Samuel Johnson's House ✧
(p. 250)
St. Bride's ✧ (p. 239)
St. Giles Cripplegate ✧ (p. 242)
St. Mary-le-Bow ✧✧ (p. 243)
St. Paul's Cathedral ✧✧✧ (p. 230)
Temple Church ✧✧ (p. 243)
Tower Bridge ✧✧ (p. 233)
Tower of London ✧✧✧ (p. 233)

CLERKENWELL
St. Etheldreda's (p. 239)
Wesley's Chapel, House &
Museum of Methodism (p. 244)

COVENT GARDEN & THE STRAND
Courtauld Gallery ✧✧ (p. 255)
Gilbert Collection at Somerset
House (p. 256)
The Hermitage Rooms at Somerset
House ✧✧✧ (p. 257)
London Transport Museum ✧
(p. 259)
St. Paul's Church (the Actors'
Church) ✧ (p. 243)
Theatre Museum (p. 263)

DOCKLANDS
Butler's Wharf (p. 268)

WALKING TOUR	**WHERE LONDON WAS BORN: "THE CITY"**

The best way to discover London is on foot. A jumble of ancient mews and antiques-filled alleyways, it's a city that's easy and fun to get lost in. Since many of the major sights are concentrated in specific areas of the city—historic and financial London in the City; gentlemanly London in St. James's, and so on—walking is a good way to take in a number of London sights at one time.

For more walking tours showcasing different parts of London (Royal London, Chelsea), visit the Frommer's website at www.frommers.com.

Start:	The southern terminus of London Bridge. Tube: Northern Line to London Bridge; Northern, District, or Circle Lines to Monument.
Finish:	St. Paul's Cathedral. Tube: Central Line to St. Paul's.
Time:	About 3 hours, excluding interior visits.
Best Times:	Weekday mornings, when the financial district is functioning, but churches aren't crowded.
Worst Times:	Weekends, when the district is almost deserted.

The area known as the City—the original square mile that the Romans lived in and called "Londinium"—offers the densest concentration of historic and cultural monuments in Britain. It's also one of the financial capitals of the world—Britain's Wall Street, as it were.

Our tour begins on the southern edge of the Thames, directly west of London Bridge, one of the world's most famous bridges. Facing the Thames rises:

① Southwark Cathedral

When it was built in the 1200s, the cathedral was an outpost of the far-away diocese of Winchester. Deconsecrated after Henry VIII's Reformation, it later housed bakeries and pigpens. Much of what you see is a result of a sorely needed 19th-century rebuilding, but its Gothic interior, with its many commemorative plaques, gives an idea of the religious power of the medieval church.

After your visit, walk across the famous:

② London Bridge

Originally designed by Peter de Colechurch in 1176, under the patronage of Henry II, this famous bridge has been replaced several times since. Until 1729, London Bridge was the only bridge across the Thames. During the Middle Ages, the bridge was lined with shops, and houses crowded its edges. The bridge served as the showplace of severed heads—preserved in tar—of enemies of the British monarchs. (The most famous of these was Sir Thomas More, the highly vocal Lord Chancellor, beheaded in 1535.) The 1825 to 1831 version of the bridge was moved to the United States and is now located in Lake Havasu, Arizona. The current bridge was completed in 1973, and is not falling down.

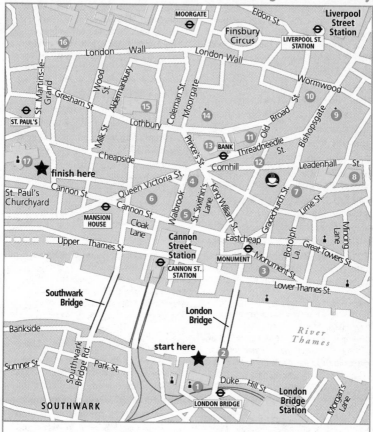

1   Southwark Cathedral
2   London Bridge
3   Monument
4   Mansion House
5   St. Stephen Walbrook
6   The Temple of Mithras
7   Leadenhall Market
8   Lloyd's of London Building
9   St. Helen Bishopsgate

10 NatWest Tower
11 London Stock Exchange
12 Royal Exchange
13 Bank of England
14 St. Margaret Lothbury
15 Guildhall
16 Museum of London
17 St. Paul's Cathedral

✝ Church
🥣 "Take a Break" stop
⊖ Tube Station

After crossing the river, head east along Monument Street, the steep cobbled street that descends to the right. Detour down it a short distance to read the commemorative plaques attached to the:

❸ Monument

Commemorating the Great Fire of 1666, this soaring Doric column is appropriately capped with a carved depiction of a flaming urn. The disastrous fire that it memorializes started in a bakery in nearby Pudding Lane, and raged for 4 days and nights, destroying 80% of the City. A cramped and foreboding set of stairs spirals up to the top of the monument. It's a tough climb, but the view of the cityscape, so heavily influenced after the fire by architect Sir Christopher Wren (who also designed the Monument), is worth it.

Retrace your steps toward London Bridge, but this time head northwest (right) along King William Street until you reach the Bank Underground station, within a stone's throw of some of England's most powerful financial institutions. As you reach Mansion House Place, make a left, looking right to:

❹ Mansion House

This is the official residence of the Lord Mayor, built between 1739 and 1752 and designed by George Dance the Elder. A rather optimistic pediment frieze depicts London defeating Envy and ushering in Plenty. The mansion's architectural gem is the Egyptian Hall. Official banquets are staged here, but unless you get an invitation, you'll have to confine your viewing to the exterior.

From the mansion, proceed into a small passageway, St. Stephen's Row, and at the end take a left into Walbrook, the site of a brook that was paved over in medieval times. On the left is the entrance to:

❺ St. Stephen Walbrook

One of Sir Christopher Wren's finest works, the splendid dome of this church served as a model for St. Paul's Cathedral. British sculptor Henry Moore carved the travertine altar under the dome in 1986.

Now walk across Walbrook and head into Bucklersbury, continuing until you reach Queen Victoria Street. Turn left on Queen Victoria Street, walk 1 block, make another left, and climb the steps outside the major entrance to Temple Court. Here on your left you can peer over the railings at:

❻ The Temple of Mithras

This is London's archaeological jewel. Although it's shaped like a miniature Christian church, the temple was held sacred by the Mithraic cult, which had its origins in Iran and reached the Roman Empire prior to Christianity. The temple was built in A.D. 2nd century. Artifacts removed from the site are now in the Museum of London.

After you've looked around, walk back to the Bank Underground. Here, head east along Cornhill, which becomes Leadenhall Street. Just after the intersection with Gracechurch Street, behind Lloyd's of London, you'll come upon:

❼ Leadenhall Market

Horace Jones designed the curved arcades on The City's central (and conspicuously non-financial) market in 1881. Since then, the market has housed a colorful collection of butchers, fishmongers, cheesemongers, and flowermongers, as well as pubs and restaurants.

Once you're finished buying or browsing, return to Gracechurch Street and walk north, and then right (east) on Leadenhall Street. Take the second right (south) on Lime Street, where you can admire the soaring and iconoclastically modern:

❽ Lloyd's of London Building

Designed by Richard Rogers in 1986, this striking glass, steel, and concrete structure in the heart of ancient Roman London is the company's newest home. Lloyd's was founded in the 1680s as a marine insurer; today it is perhaps the most famous—and financially troubled—insurer in the world. Immense underwriting losses in the early 1990s threatened the company's survival.

Nearby are the London Metal Exchange, the London Futures and Options Exchange, and other financial institutions with worldwide clout.

Next follow Lime Street back to Leadenhall and turn left. Take the first right on Bishopsgate, and then the second right, and turn into an alleyway known as Great St. Helen's. Toward the end, you'll find the largest surviving medieval church in London:

9 St. Helen Bishopsgate

Built in the 1400s and dedicated to St. Helen, the British mother of the legendary Roman emperor Constantine, St. Helen was fashionable during the Elizabethan and Jacobean periods. The interior monuments, memorials, and grave markers are of special interest.

Exit back onto Bishopsgate and turn right (north). Two short blocks later, turn left onto Wormwood Street. Then take the first left onto Old Broad Street. Towering above you rises the modern bulk of the tallest building in Britain and the second-highest in Europe, the:

10 NatWest Tower

Richard Seifert designed the headquarters of National Westminster Bank in 1981. Its massive concrete foundations are built on top of mostly impervious clay, allowing the building to sway gently in the wind. Unfortunately, since it doesn't have an observation tower open to the public, you'll have to admire it from afar.

Continue south along Old Broad Street, noticing on your right the imposing headquarters of the:

11 London Stock Exchange

Built in the early 1960s to replace the exchange's outmoded original quarters, this institution has become much less boisterous since most of the City's financial operations went modern in 1986, transforming from face-to-face agreements between brokers to computerized deal making, with the exchange functioning as an electronic clearinghouse.

TAKE A BREAK
Continue southwest along Old Broad Street until it merges with Threadneedle Street. Cross Threadneedle Street, walk a few paces to your left, and head south along the narrow confines of Finch Lane. Cross busy Cornhill to the south side of the street. Follow it east to St. Michael's Alley to **Jamaica Wine House**, St. Michael's Alley, EC3 (② 020/7626-9496), one of Europe's oldest coffeehouses. Once a favorite hangout of London merchants and sea captains, today it dispenses ale, lager, wine, and bar snacks.

After tippling, take time to explore the medieval maze of narrow alleyways that provide shelter from roaring weekday traffic. Then head back to the major boulevard, Cornhill, just north of your refueling stop. Here, near the junction of five major streets, rises the:

12 Royal Exchange

Designed by William Tite in the early 1840s, the Royal Exchange's imposing neoclassical pediment is inset with Richard Westmacott's sculpture of *Commerce*. Launched by a partnership of merchants and financiers during the Elizabethan Age, the Royal Exchange was an attempt to lure European banking and trading functions from Antwerp (then the financial capital of northern Europe) to London. Frenzied trading and auctioning of raw materials continued here until 1982, when the building became the headquarters of the London International Financial Futures Exchange (LIFFE). If you want to see the excitement of live trading, get thee to the London Stock Exchange on Old Broad St., EC2.

On the opposite side of Threadneedle Street rises the massive bulk of the:

13 Bank of England

Originally established "for the Public Good and Benefit of Our People" in a charter granted in 1694 by William and Mary, this is a treasure trove of gold bullion, British banknotes, and historic archives. The only part of this massive building open to the public is the Bank of England Museum, whose entrance is on a narrow side street, Bartholomew Lane (☎ 020/7601-5793); it's open Monday through Friday from 10am to 5pm; free admission.

From the Bank of England, walk northwest along Prince's Street to Lothbury. On the northeast corner of the intersection rises yet another church by Sir Christopher Wren, this one completed in 1690:

⑭ St. Margaret Lothbury

Filled with statues of frolicking cupids, elaborately carved screens, and a soaring eagle near the altar, the interior is well worth a visit.

Now walk west on Lothbury, which will become Gresham Street. After passing a handful of alleyways, on your right you'll see the gardens and the grand historic facade of the:

⑮ Guildhall

The power base for the Lord Mayor of London since the 12th century (and continually rebuilt and enlarged since), Guildhall was the site of endless negotiations throughout the Middle Ages between the English kings (headquartered outside the City at Westminster) and the guilds, associations, and brotherhoods of the City's merchants and financiers. Today, the rituals associated with the Lord Mayor are almost as elaborate as those of the monarchy itself. The Guildhall's medieval crypt is the largest in London; Sir Christopher Wren rebuilt its east facade after the Great Fire of 1666.

Continue westward on Gresham and turn right onto Wood Street. Walk north to London Wall, and then left for about a block. On the right you'll see the modern:

⑯ Museum of London

Located in new quarters built in 1975, the Museum of London contains London memorabilia gathered from several earlier museums, and one of the best collections of period costumes in the world. Built on top of the western gate of the ancient Roman colony of Londinium, the museum has a strong collection of archaeological remnants unearthed during centuries of City construction, as well as dioramas portraying the Great Fire and Victorian prison cells.

Now head south on Aldersgate, which quickly becomes St. Martins-le-Grand. After you merge with Newgate Street, the enormous stately dome of one of Europe's most important churches slowly appears in front of you:

⑰ St. Paul's Cathedral

Sir Christopher Wren's masterpiece is known to many as the site of the wedding of Prince Charles and Princess Diana. St. Paul's also held the state funerals of Nelson, Wellington, and Churchill, and served as an inspiration to a generation of Londoners who survived the bombings of World War II. The only cathedral in England constructed with a dome, and the country's only church built in the English baroque style, St. Paul's was also the first English cathedral designed and built by a single architect.

From St. Paul's, you can catch the Underground's Central Line to your next destination.

2 The Top Attractions

One of Britain's greatest private art collections, **The Saatchi Gallery,** is currently floating around without a permanent home. Check with the London Tourist Board to see if this collection—or at least a part of it—is on view somewhere in London at the time of your visit.

TIMESAVER

With 4km (2½ miles) of galleries, the British Museum can be overwhelming. To get a handle on it, we recommend taking a 1½-hour overview tour for £7

($10.50). Tours are Monday through Saturday at 10:30am and 1pm or Sunday at 11am, 1:30pm, 2:30pm, and 4pm. After, you can return to the galleries that most interested you. If you have limited time at the museum, concentrate on the Greek and Roman rooms (1–15), which hold the golden hoard of booty both bought and stolen from the Empire's once far-flung colonies.

British Museum ★★★ Set in scholarly Bloomsbury, this immense museum grew out of a private collection of manuscripts purchased in 1753 with the proceeds of a lottery. It grew and grew, fed by legacies, discoveries, and purchases, until it became one of the most comprehensive collections of art and artifacts in the world. It's impossible to take in this museum in a day.

The overall storehouse splits basically into the national collections of antiquities; prints and drawings; coins, medals, and banknotes; and ethnography. Even on a cursory first visit, be sure to see the Asian collections (the finest assembly of Islamic pottery outside the Islamic world), the Chinese porcelain, the Indian sculpture, and the Prehistoric and Romano-British collections. Special treasures you might want to seek out on your first visit include the **Rosetta Stone,** in the Egyptian Room, whose discovery led to the deciphering of hieroglyphics; the **Elgin Marbles,** a series of pediments, metopes, and friezes from the Parthenon in Athens, in the Duveen Gallery; and the legendary **Black Obelisk,** dating from around 860 B.C., in the Nimrud Gallery. Other treasures include the contents of Egyptian royal tombs (including mummies); fabulous arrays of 2,000 year-old jewelry, cosmetics, weapons, furniture, and tools; Babylonian astronomical instruments; and winged lion statues (in the Assyrian Transept) that guarded Ashurnasirpal's palace at Nimrud. The exhibits change throughout the year, so if your heart is set on seeing a specific treasure, call to make sure it's on display.

Insider's Tip: If you're a first-time visitor, you will, of course, want to concentrate on some of the fabled treasures previewed above. But what we do is duck into the British Museum several times on our visits to London, even if we have only an hour or two, to see the less heralded but equally fascinating exhibits. We recommend wandering rooms 33 and 34 and 91 to 94 to take in the glory of the Orient, covering Taoism, Confucianism, and Buddhism. The Chinese collection is particularly strong. Sculpture from India is as fine as anything at the Victoria and Albert. The ethnography collection is increasingly beefed up, especially the Mexican Gallery in room 33C, which traces that country's art from the 2nd millennium B.C. to the 16th century A.D. A gallery for the North American collection is also open nearby. Another section of the museum is devoted to the **Sainsbury African Galleries** ★, one of the finest collections of African art and artifacts in the world, featuring changing displays selected from more than 200,000 objects. Finally, the museum has opened a new Money Gallery in room 68, tracing the story of money. You'll learn that around 2000 B.C. in Mesopotamia, money was grain, and that printed money came into being in the 10th century in China.

During the year 2000, the "Great Court" project was completed. The museum's inner courtyard is now canopied by a lightweight, transparent roof, transforming the area into a covered square that houses a Centre for Education, exhibition space, bookshops, and restaurants. The center of the Great Court features the Round Reading Room, which is famous as the place where Karl Marx hung out while formulating his ideas on Communism and writing *Das Kapital.* Visitors are free to wander through, although there's little to see that you can't view from the doorway.

The Top Attractions

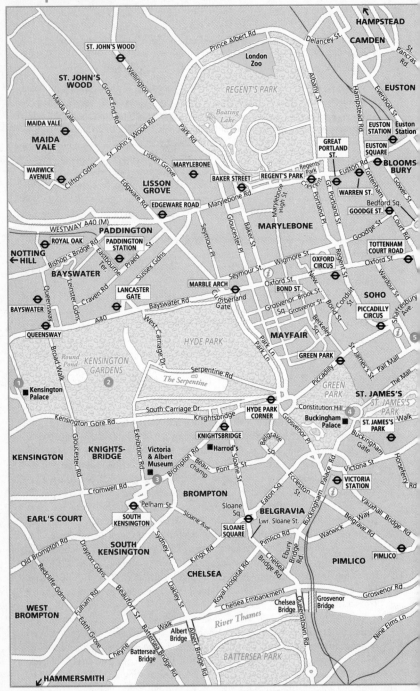

HAMPSTEAD
CAMDEN

ST. JOHN'S WOOD

Prince Albert Rd.

London Zoo

REGENT'S PARK

Boating Lake

ST. JOHN'S WOOD

Wellington Rd.

Grove End Rd.

St. John's Wood Rd.

MAIDA VALE

MAIDA VALE

Maida Vale

Clifton Gdns.

WARWICK AVENUE

Edgware Rd.

Lisson Grove

LISSON GROVE

EDGEWARE ROAD

Marylebone Rd.

MARYLEBONE

MARYLEBONE

BAKER STREET

REGENT'S PARK

Baker St.

Park Rd.

Regents Park Crescent

Albany St.

Hampstead Rd.

EUSTON

EUSTON STATION Euston Station

EUSTON SQUARE

GREAT PORTLAND ST.

WARREN ST.

BLOOMS BURY

GOODGE ST.

Bedford Sq.

Gower St.

Court Rd.

St. Pancras Rd.

Delancey St.

Eversholt St.

Euston Rd.

Tottenham Court Rd.

Goodge St.

TOTTENHAM COURT ROAD

WESTWAY A40 (M)

PADDINGTON

ROYAL OAK

PADDINGTON STATION

NOTTING HILL

BAYSWATER

Bishop's Bridge Rd.

Eastbourne Ter.

Praed St.

Sussex Gdns.

Leinster Gdns.

Craven Rd.

Gloucester Pl.

Seymour Pl.

Seymour St.

Wigmore St.

OXFORD CIRCUS

Oxford St.

BOND ST.

Regent St.

Wardour St.

Shaftesbury Ave.

SOHO

PICCADILLY CIRCUS

MARBLE ARCH

Cumberland Gate

Oxford St.

Grosvenor Sq.

Brook St.

Grosvenor St.

Bond St.

New Bond St.

Conduit St.

Berkeley St.

BAYSWATER

Queensway

QUEENSWAY

Bayswater Rd.

LANCASTER GATE

A40

West Carriage Dr.

HYDE PARK

Broad Walk

Round Pond

KENSINGTON GARDENS

The Serpentine

Serpentine Rd.

Park Ln.

Park Ln.

MAYFAIR

GREEN PARK

Piccadilly

GREEN PARK

St. James's St.

Pall Mall

The Mall

ST. JAMES'S

ST. JAMES'S PARK

Kensington Palace

South Carriage Dr.

Kensington Gore Rd.

Knightsbridge

HYDE PARK CORNER

Constitution Hill

Grosvenor Pl.

Buckingham Palace

ST. JAMES'S PARK

Buckingham Gate

Walk

Horseferry Rd.

KNIGHTSBRIDGE

KNIGHTS-BRIDGE

Gloucester Rd.

Exhibition Rd.

Victoria & Albert Museum

Harrod's

Brompton Rd.

Beau-champ

Pont St.

Sloane St.

Belgrave Sq.

Eccleston St.

Victoria St.

VICTORIA STATION

KENSINGTON

Cromwell Rd.

BROMPTON

Eaton Sq.

BELGRAVIA

Buckingham Palace Rd.

EARL'S COURT

Old Brompton Rd.

SOUTH KENSINGTON

SOUTH KENSINGTON

Pelham St.

Sloane Ave.

Sydney St.

Sloane Sq.

SLOANE SQUARE

Lwr. Sloane St.

Pimlico Rd.

Ebury Bridge Rd.

Warwick Way

Belgrave Rd.

Vauxhall Bridge Rd.

PIMLICO

PIMLICO

WEST BROMPTON

Drayton Gdns.

Redcliffe Gdns.

Fulham Rd.

Beaufort St.

CHELSEA

Oakley St.

Kings Rd.

Royal Hospital Rd.

Chelsea Embankment

Chelsea Bridge

Queenstown Rd.

Grosvenor Bridge

Grosvenor Rd.

Nine Elms Ln.

Edith Grove

Cheyne Walk

Battersea Bridge

Albert Bridge

Albert Bridge Rd.

Battersea Bridge Rd.

River Thames

BATTERSEA PARK

HAMMERSMITH

222

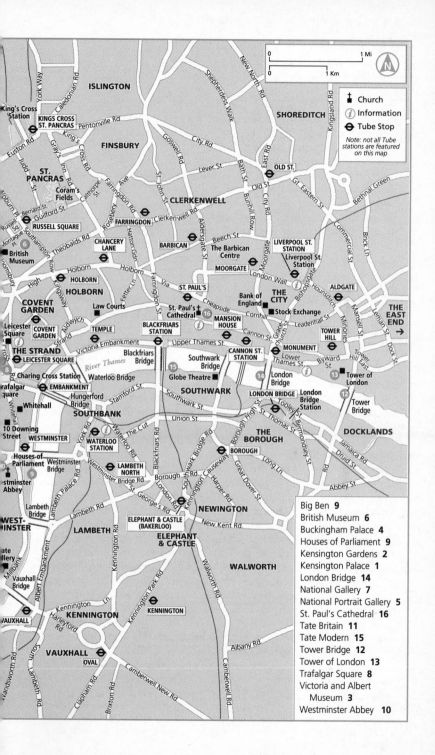

Map legend / Key

† Church
ⓘ Information
⊖ Tube Stop

Note: not all Tube stations are featured on this map

ISLINGTON
SHOREDITCH
King's Cross Station
KINGS CROSS ST. PANCRAS
Pentonville Rd.
OLD ST.
FINSBURY
ST. PANCRAS
Euston Rd.
Coram's Fields
CLERKENWELL
RUSSELL SQUARE
FARRINGDON
CHANCERY LANE
British Museum
BARBICAN
The Barbican Centre
LIVERPOOL ST. STATION
Liverpool St. Station
MOORGATE
HOLBORN
HOLBORN
ST. PAUL'S
London Wall
THE CITY
ALDGATE
COVENT GARDEN
Law Courts
Bank of England
Stock Exchange
THE EAST END →
Leicester Square
COVENT GARDEN
TEMPLE
BLACKFRIARS STATION
St. Paul's Cathedral
MANSION HOUSE
CANNON ST. STATION
TOWER HILL
THE STRAND
LEICESTER SQUARE
Charing Cross Station
EMBANKMENT
Blackfriars Bridge
MONUMENT
Tower of London
Trafalgar Square
Whitehall
Waterloo Bridge
Southwark Bridge
London Bridge
Tower Bridge
Hungerford Bridge
SOUTHBANK
Globe Theatre
SOUTHWARK
LONDON BRIDGE
London Bridge Station
DOCKLANDS
10 Downing Street
WESTMINSTER
WATERLOO STATION
THE BOROUGH
Houses of Parliament
Westminster Bridge
LAMBETH NORTH
BOROUGH
Westminster Abbey
NEWINGTON
WEST MINSTER
Lambeth Bridge
ELEPHANT & CASTLE (BAKERLOO)
ELEPHANT & CASTLE
LAMBETH
WALWORTH
Tate Gallery
Vauxhall Bridge
KENNINGTON
VAUXHALL
OVAL

River Thames

Big Ben **9**
British Museum **6**
Buckingham Palace **4**
Houses of Parliament **9**
Kensington Gardens **2**
Kensington Palace **1**
London Bridge **14**
National Gallery **7**
National Portrait Gallery **5**
St. Paul's Cathedral **16**
Tate Britain **11**
Tate Modern **15**
Tower Bridge **12**
Tower of London **13**
Trafalgar Square **8**
Victoria and Albert Museum **3**
Westminster Abbey **10**

223

For information on the British Library, see p. 254.

Great Russell St., WC1. © 020/7323-8299 or 020/7636-1555 for recorded information. www.thebritishmuseum.ac.uk. Free admission. Sat–Wed 10am–5:30pm; Thurs–Fri 10am–8:30pm. Tube: Holborn, Tottenham Court Rd., or Goodge St.

Buckingham Palace ★★ *Kids* This massive, graceful building is the official residence of the queen. The redbrick palace was built as a country house for the notoriously rakish duke of Buckingham. In 1762, King George III, who needed room for his 15 children, bought it. It didn't become the official royal residence, though, until Queen Victoria took the throne; she preferred it to St. James's Palace. From George III's time, the building was continuously expanded and remodeled, faced with Portland stone, and twice bombed (during the Blitz). Located in a 40-acre garden, it's 108m (360 ft.) long and contains 600 rooms. You can tell whether the queen is at home by whether the Royal Standard is flying from the mast outside. For most of the year, you can't visit the palace without an official invitation. Since 1993, though, much of it has been open for tours during an 8-week period in August and September, when the royal family is usually vacationing outside London. Elizabeth II agreed to allow visitors to tour the State Room, the Grand Staircase, the Throne Room, and other areas designed by John Nash for George IV, as well as the Picture Gallery, which displays masterpieces by Van Dyck, Rembrandt, Rubens, and others. The admission charges help pay for repairs to Windsor Castle, damaged by fire in 1992. You have to buy a timed-entrance ticket the same day you tour the palace. Tickets go on sale at 9am, but rather than lining up at sunrise with all the other tourists—this is one of London's most popular attractions—book by phone with a credit card and give yourself a few more hours of sleep.

During the 8 weeks of summer, visitors are also allowed to stroll through the royal family's garden, along an 4,455m (1,485-ft.) walk on the south side of the grounds, with views of a lake and the usually off-limits west side of the palace. The garden is home to 30 types of birds, including the great crested grebe, plus 350 types of wildflowers.

Buckingham Palace's most famous spectacle is the vastly overrated **Changing of the Guard** (daily Apr–July and every other day the rest of the year). The new guard, marching behind a band, comes from either the Wellington or Chelsea barracks and takes over from the old guard in the forecourt of the palace. The ceremony begins at 11:30am, although it's frequently canceled for bad weather, state events, and other harder-to-fathom reasons. We like the changing of the guards at Horse Guards better (p. 246), where you can actually see the men marching and don't have to battle such tourist hordes. However, few first-time visitors can resist the Buckingham Place changing of the guard. If that's you, arrive as early as 10:30am and claim territorial rights to a space in front of the palace. If you're not firmly anchored here, you'll miss much of the ceremony. *Insider's Tip:* You can avoid the long queues for Buckingham Palace tours by purchasing tickets before you go, through **Global Tickets,** 234 West 44th St., Suite 1000, New York, NY 10034 (© **800/223-6108** or 212/332-2435). You'll have to pick the exact date on which you'd like to go. Visitors with disabilities can reserve tickets directly through the palace by calling © **020/7930-5526.**

At end of The Mall (on the road running from Trafalgar Sq.). © **020/7839-1377** or 020/7321-2233. www.royal.gov.uk. Palace tours £11.50 ($17.25) adults, £9.50 ($14.25) seniors, £6 ($9) children under 17. Changing of the Guard free. Palace open for tours Apr 8–Sept 30 daily 9:30am–4:30pm. Changing of the guard daily from Apr–July at 11am, and every other day for the rest of the year at 11am. Tube: St. James's Park, Green Park, or Victoria.

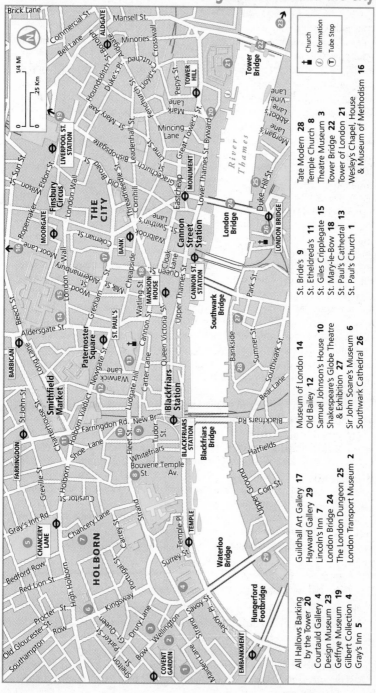

Church
Information
Tube Stop

All Hallows Barking
by the Tower **20**
Courtauld Gallery **4**
Design Museum **23**
Geffrye Museum **19**
Gilbert Collection **4**
Gray's Inn **5**

Guildhall Art Gallery **17**
Hayward Gallery **29**
Lincoln's Inn **7**
London Bridge **24**
The London Dungeon **25**
London Transport Museum **2**

Museum of London **14**
Old Bailey **12**
Samuel Johnson's House **10**
Shakespeare's Globe Theatre
& Exhibition **27**
Sir John Soane's Museum **6**
Southwark Cathedral **26**

St. Bride's **9**
St. Etheldreda's **11**
St. Giles Cripplegate **15**
St. Mary-le-Bow **18**
St. Paul's Cathedral **13**
St. Paul's Church **1**

Tate Modern **28**
Temple Church **8**
Theatre Museum **3**
Tower Bridge **22**
Tower of London **21**
Wesley's Chapel, House
& Museum of Methodism **16**

Houses of Parliament ★★ The Houses of Parliament, along with their trademark clock tower, are the ultimate symbol of London. They're the strongholds of Britain's democracy, the assemblies that effectively trimmed the sails of royal power. Both the House of Commons and the House of Lords are in the former royal Palace of Westminster, the king's residence until Henry VIII moved to Whitehall. The current Gothic Revival buildings date from 1840 and were designed by Charles Barry. (The earlier buildings were destroyed by fire in 1834.) Assisting Barry was Augustus Welby Pugin, who designed the paneled ceilings, tiled floors, stained glass, clocks, fireplaces, umbrella stands, and even the inkwells. There are more than 1,000 rooms and 3km (2 miles) of corridors. The clock tower at the eastern end houses the world's most famous timepiece. **"Big Ben"** refers not to the clock tower itself, but to the largest bell in the chime, which weighs close to 14 tons and is named for the first commissioner of works, Sir Benjamin Hall.

You may observe debates from the **Stranger's Galleries** in both houses. Sessions usually begin in mid-October and run to the end of July, with recesses at Christmas and Easter. Although we can't promise you the oratory of a Charles James Fox or a William Pitt the Elder, the debates in the House of Commons are often lively and controversial (seats are at a premium during crises). The chances of getting into the House of Lords when it's in session are generally better than for the more popular House of Commons.

For years London tabloids have portrayed members of the House of Lords as a bunch of "Monty Pythonesque upper-class wits," with one foreign secretary calling the House of Lords "medieval lumber." Today, under Tony Blair's Labour government, the House of Lords is being shaken up as lords lose their inherited posts. Panels are studying what to do with this largely useless house, its members often descendants of royal mistresses and ancient landowners.

Those who'd like to book a tour can do so, but it takes a bit of work. Both houses are open to the general public for guided tours only during August and September. During those times, the palace is open Monday through Saturday from 9:30am, with the last entry at 4:15pm. All tour tickets cost £6 ($9) per person. You need to send a written request for a tour to the Public Information Office, 1 Derby Gate, Westminster, London SW1A 2TT. The staff is prompt in replying but only if you include a stamped return address (international postage only). Tickets can also be booked through London's Ticketmaster (© 020/ 7344-9966; www.ticketmaster.co.uk).

You can attend a session for free. You line up at Stephen's Gate, heading to your left for the entrance into the Commons or to the right for the Lords. The London daily newspapers announce sessions of Parliament.

> ⌐*Tips* **The Guard Doesn't Change Every Day**
>
> The schedule for the Changing of the Guard ceremony is variable at best. In theory at least, the guard is changed daily from some time in April to mid-July, at which time it goes on its "winter" schedule—that is, every other day. Always check locally with the tourist office to see if it's likely to be staged at the time of your visit. The ceremony has been cut at the last minute, leaving thousands of tourists feeling they have missed out on a London must-see.

Insider's Tip: The hottest ticket and the most exciting time to visit is during "Prime Minister's Question Time" on Wednesdays, which is only from 3 to 3:30pm but which must seem like hours to Tony Blair who is on the hot seat. It's not quite as thrilling as it was back when Margaret Thatcher exchanged barbs with the MPs (members of Parliament), but Blair holds his own admirably against any and all who are trying to embarrass him and his government. He is given no mercy from these MPs, especially those who oppose his policies. Typical question put to Blair: "Is George Bush the idiot the press has made him out to be?"

Westminster Palace, Old Palace Yard, SW1. House of Commons (✆ 020/7219-4272. House of Lords (✆ 020/7219-3107. www.parliament.uk. Free admission to sessions. £6 ($9) for all tours (only during Aug and Sept). House of Lords open mid-Oct to Aug Mon–Wed from 2:30pm, Thurs from 11:30am, and sometimes Fri (check by phone). House of Commons open mid-Oct to Aug Mon–Tues 2:30–10:30pm, Wed 9:30am–10:30pm, Thurs 11:30am–7pm, Fri call ahead—not always open. Both houses are open for tours during Aug and Sept, from 9:15am–4:15pm. Join line at St. Stephen's entrance. Tube: Westminster.

Kensington Palace 𝆏 *Kids*   Once the residence of British monarchs, Kensington Palace hasn't been the official home of reigning kings since George II. It was acquired in 1689 by William III and Mary II as an escape from the damp royal rooms along the Thames. Since the end of the 18th century, the palace has housed various members of the royal family, and the State Apartments are open for tours.

It was here in 1837 that a young Victoria was awakened with the news that her uncle, William IV, had died and she was queen of England. You can view a collection of Victoriana, including some of her memorabilia. In the apartments of Queen Mary II is a striking 17th-century writing cabinet inlaid with tortoiseshell. Paintings from the Royal Collection line the walls. A rare 1750 lady's court dress and splendid examples of male court dress from the 18th century are on display in rooms adjacent to the State Apartments, as part of the Royal Ceremonial Dress Collection, featuring royal costumes dating as far back as 200 years.

Kensington Palace was the London home of the late Princess Margaret, and is current home to the Duke and Duchess of Kent. It was also the home of Diana, Princess of Wales, and her two sons. (Harry and William now live with their father at St. James's Palace.) The palace is probably best known for the millions of flowers placed in front of it during the days following Diana's death.

Warning: You don't get to see the apartments where Princess Di lived or where both Di and Charles lived until they separated. Many visitors think they'll get to peek at these rooms and are disappointed. Charles and Di lived on the west side of the palace, still occupied today by minor royals.

The **Kensington Gardens** are open to the public for leisurely strolls through the manicured grounds and around the Round Pond. One of the most famous sights is the controversial Albert Memorial, a lasting tribute not only to Victoria's consort, but also to the questionable artistic taste of the Victorian era. There's a wonderful afternoon tea offered in The Orangery (p. 211).

The Broad Walk, Kensington Gardens, W8. (✆ 020/7937-9561. www.hrp.org.uk. Admission £9 ($13.50) adults, £7 ($10.50) seniors/students, £6.50 ($9.75) children, family £28 ($42). June–Sept daily 10am–5pm; off-season daily 10am–4pm. Tube: Queensway or Notting Hill Gate; High St. Kensington on south side.

National Gallery 𝆏𝆏𝆏   This stately neoclassical building contains an unrivaled collection of Western art spanning 7 centuries—from the late 13th to the early 20th—and covers every great European school. For sheer skill of display

Trafalgar: London's Most Famous Square

London is a city full of landmark squares. Without a doubt, the best-known is **Trafalgar Square** 🏵🏵 (Tube: Charing Cross), which honors one of England's great military heroes, Horatio Viscount Nelson (1758–1805). Although he suffered from seasickness all his life, he went to sea at the age of 12 and was an admiral at 39. Nelson was a hero of the Battle of Calvi in 1794, where he lost an eye; the Battle of Santa Cruz in 1797, where he lost an arm; and the Battle of Trafalgar in 1805, where he lost his life. He is also famous for his affair with Lady Hamilton, the subject of books and films (including *That Hamilton Woman,* with Laurence Olivier and Vivien Leigh).

The square is dominated by the 44m (145-ft.) granite *Nelson's Column,* built by E. H. Baily in 1843. The column looks down Whitehall toward the Old Admiralty, where Lord Nelson's body lay in state. The figure of the naval hero towers 5m (17 ft.) high—not bad for a man who stood 5'4" in real life. The capital is of bronze cast from cannons recovered from the wreck of the *Royal George,* which sank in 1782. Queen Victoria's favorite animal painter, Sir Edward Landseer, added the four lions at the base of the column in 1868. The pools and fountains weren't added until 1939; they were the last work of Sir Edwin Lutyens.

Political demonstrations still take place in the square and around the column, which has the most aggressive pigeons in London.

Much of the world focuses on the square via TV cameras on New Year's Eve, watching crazy revelers jumping into the chilly waters of the fountains. The giant Christmas tree that's installed here every December is an annual gift from Norway to the British people, in appreciation of Britain's sheltering their royal family during World War II. The tree is surrounded by carolers most December evenings. Year-round, street performers (now officially licensed) will entertain you in hopes of receiving a token of appreciation for their efforts.

To the southeast of the square, at 36 Craven St., stands a house that was occupied by Benjamin Franklin from 1757 to 1774. On the north side of the square rises the National Gallery, constructed in the 1830s. In front of the building is a copy of a statue of George Washington by J. A. Houdon.

To the left of St. Martin's Place is the National Portrait Gallery, a collection of portraits of famous Brits—from Chaucer and Shakespeare to Nell Gwynne, Margaret Thatcher, and The Who's Pete Townshend. Also on the square is the steeple of St. Martin-in-the-Fields, the final resting place of Sir Joshua Reynolds, William Hogarth, and Thomas Chippendale.

and arrangement, it surpasses its counterparts in Paris, New York, Madrid, and Amsterdam.

The largest part of the collection is devoted to the Italians, including the Sienese, Venetian, and Florentine masters. They're now housed in the Sainsbury

Wing, which was designed by noted Philadelphia architects Robert Venturi and Denise Scott Brown and was opened by Elizabeth II in 1991. On display are such works as Leonardo's *Virgin of the Rocks;* Titian's *Bacchus and Ariadne;* Giorgione's *Adoration of the Magi;* and unforgettable canvases by Bellini, Veronese, Botticelli, and Tintoretto. Botticelli's *Venus and Mars* is eternally enchanting. (The Sainsbury Wing is also used for large temporary exhibits.)

Of the early Gothic works, the Wilton Diptych (French or English school, late 14th century) is the rarest treasure; it depicts Richard II being introduced to the Madonna and Child by John the Baptist and the Saxon kings, Edmund and Edward the Confessor. Then there are the Spanish giants: El Greco's *Agony in the Garden* and portraits by Goya and Velázquez. The Flemish-Dutch school is represented by Brueghel, Jan van Eyck, Vermeer, Rubens, and de Hooch; the Rembrandts include two of his immortal self-portraits. There's also an immense French Impressionist and post-Impressionist collection that includes works by Manet, Monet, Degas, Renoir, and Cézanne. Particularly charming is the peep-show cabinet by Hoogstraten in one of the Dutch rooms: It's like spying through a keyhole.

British and modern art are the specialties of the Tate Modern (see below), but the National Gallery does have some fine 18th-century British masterpieces, including works by Hogarth, Gainsborough, Reynolds, Constable, and Turner.

Guided tours of the National Gallery are offered daily at 11:30am and 2:30pm. The Gallery Guide Soundtrack is also available. A portable CD player provides audio information on paintings of your choice with the mere push of a button. Although this service is free, voluntary contributions are appreciated.

Insider's Tip: The National Gallery has a computer information center where you can design your own personal tour map for free. The computer room, located in the Micro Gallery, includes a dozen hands-on workstations. The online system lists 2,200 paintings and has background notes for each work. Using a touch-screen computer, you design your own personalized tour by selecting a maximum of 10 paintings you would like to view. Once you have made your choices, you print a personal tour map with your selections.

North side of Trafalgar Sq., WC2. (*C*) 020/7747-2885. www.nationalgallery.org.uk. Free admission. Thurs–Tues 10am–6pm; Wed 10am–9pm. Tube: Charing Cross, Embankment, Leicester Sq., or Piccadilly Circus.

National Portrait Gallery ★★ In a gallery of remarkable and unremarkable pictures (they're collected for their subjects rather than their artistic quality), a few paintings tower over the rest, including Sir Joshua Reynolds's first portrait of Samuel Johnson ("a man of most dreadful appearance"), Nicholas Hilliard's miniature of handsome Sir Walter Raleigh, and a full-length Elizabeth I, along with the Holbein cartoon of Henry VIII. There's also a portrait of William Shakespeare (with a gold earring) by an unknown artist that bears the claim of being the "most authentic contemporary likeness" of its subject. One of the most famous pictures in the gallery is the group portrait of the Brontë sisters (Charlotte, Emily, and Anne) by their brother, Bramwell. An idealized portrait of Lord Byron by Thomas Phillips is also on display.

The galleries of Victorian and early-20th-century portraits were radically redesigned recently. Occupying the whole of the first floor, they display portraits from 1837 (when Victoria took the throne) to the present day. The later 20th-century portraiture includes major works by such artists as Warhol and Hambling. Some of the more flamboyant personalities of the past 2 centuries are on show: T. S. Eliot; Disraeli; Macmillan; Sir Richard Burton (the explorer, not the actor); Elizabeth Taylor; and our two favorites, G. F. Watts' famous portrait of his great actress wife, Ellen Terry, and Vanessa Bell's portrait of her sister, Virginia Woolf. The late Princess Diana is on the Royal Landing, and this portrait seems to attract the most viewers. The Gallery has recently opened a new cafe and art bookshop.

In 2000, Queen Elizabeth opened the Ondaatje Wing of the gallery, increasing the gallery's exhibition space by over 50 percent. The most intriguing new space is the splendid Tudor Gallery, featuring portraits of Richard III and Henry II, Richard's conqueror in the Battle of Bosworth in 1485. There's also a portrait of Shakespeare that the gallery acquired in 1856. Rooms lead through centuries of English monarchs, with literary and artistic figures thrown in. A Balcony Gallery displays more recent figures whose fame has lasted longer than Warhol's 15 minutes. These include everybody from Mick Jagger to Joan Collins, and of course, the Baronness Thatcher. This new wing certainly taps into the cult of the celebrity.

St. Martin's Place, WC2. © 020/7306-0055. www.npg.org.uk. Free admission; fee charged for certain temporary exhibitions. Mon–Wed 10am–6pm; Thurs–Fri 10am–9pm; Sat 10am–6pm; Sun 10am–6pm. Tube: Charing Cross or Leicester Sq.

St. Paul's Cathedral ★★★   During World War II, newsreel footage reaching America showed St. Paul's Cathedral standing virtually alone among the rubble of the City, its dome lit by fires caused by bombings all around it. That the cathedral survived at all is a miracle, since it was badly hit twice during the early years of the bombardment of London during World War II. But St. Paul's is accustomed to calamity, having been burned down three times and destroyed once by invading Norsemen. It was during the Great Fire of 1666 that the old St. Paul's was razed, making way for a new structure designed by Sir Christopher Wren and built between 1675 and 1710. It's architectural genius Wren's ultimate masterpiece.

The classical dome of St. Paul's dominates the City's square mile. The golden cross surmounting it is 110m (365 ft.) above the ground; the golden ball on which the cross rests measures 2m (6 ft.) in diameter, though it looks like a marble from below. In the interior of the dome is the Whispering Gallery, an acoustic marvel in which the faintest whisper can be heard clearly on the opposite side. Sit on one side, have your traveling companions sit on the opposite side, and whisper away. You can climb to the top of the dome for a 360-degree view of London. From the Whispering Gallery a second steep climb leads to the **Stone Gallery,** opening onto a panoramic view of London. Another 153 steps takes you to the **Inner Golden Gallery,** situated at the top of the inner dome. Here an even more panoramic view of London unfolds. These combine to form "the galleries."

St. Paul's Churchyard, EC4. © 020/7236-4128. www.stpauls.co.uk. Cathedral and galleries £5 ($7.50) adults, £2.50 ($3.75) children 6–16. Guided tours £2.50 ($3.75) adults, £2 ($3) students and seniors, £1

Moments **Roses Are Red**

One of the most enjoyable aspects of a spring visit to London is sauntering through the gardens of St. Paul's when the roses are in bloom.

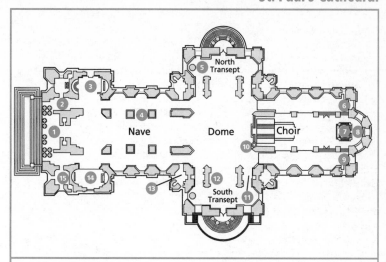

Nave

Dome

Choir

North Transept

South Transept

All Souls' Chapel **2**
American Memorial Chapter **8**
Anglican Martyr's Chapel **6**
Chapel of St. Michael
  & St. George **14**
Dean's Staircase **15**
Entrance to Crypt
  (Wren's grave) **11**
Font **5**

High Altar **7**
Lady Chapel **9**
Nelson Monument **12**
Pulpit **10**
St. Dunstan's Chapel **3**
Staircase to Library,
  Whispering Gallery & Dome **13**
Wellington Monument **4**
West Doorway **1**

($1.50) children; recorded tours £3.50 ($5.25). Free for children 5 and under. Sightseeing Mon–Sat 8:30am–4pm; galleries Mon–Sat 9:30am–4pm. No sightseeing Sun (services only). Tube: St. Paul's.

Tate Britain ⭐⭐⭐   Fronting the Thames near Vauxhall Bridge in Pimlico, the Tate looks like a smaller and more graceful relation of the British Museum. The most prestigious gallery in Britain, it houses the national collections, covering British art from the 16th century to the present day, as well as an array of international artists. In spring of 2000, the Tate moved its collection of 20th- and 21st-century art to the **Tate Modern** (see below). This split helped to open more space at the Tate Britain, but the collection here is still much too large to be displayed at once, so the works on view change from time to time.

The older works include some of the best of Gainsborough, Reynolds, Stubbs, Blake, and Constable. William Hogarth is well represented, particularly by his satirical *O the Roast Beef of Old England* (known as *The Gate of Calais*). The illustrations of William Blake, the incomparable mystical poet, are here— including such works as *The Book of Job*, *The Divine Comedy*, and *Paradise Lost*. The collection of works by J. M. W. Turner is the Tate's largest collection of works by a single artist; Turner himself willed most of the paintings and water-colors to the nation.

Also on display are the works of many major 19th- and 20th-century painters, including Paul Nash, Matisse, Dalí, Modigliani, Munch, Bonnard, and Picasso. Truly remarkable are the several enormous abstract canvases by Mark Rothko,

The Wren Style

One of the great geniuses of his age, Sir Christopher Wren (1632–1723) was a professor of astronomy at Oxford before becoming an architect. After the Great Fire of London in 1666, Wren was chosen to rebuild the devastated city and its many churches, including St. Paul's, on which work began in 1675. His designs had great originality, and he became known for his spatial effects in his impressive fusion of classical and baroque. He believed in classical stability and repose, yet liked to enliven his churches with baroque whimsy and fantasy.

In our view, his crowning glory is the dome over St. Paul's, which is celebrated for the beauty of its proportions. Surely Michelangelo would have patted Wren on the back. If, during his stay in France, Wren stole an idea or two from the Invalides in Paris, so what? We'll never tell.

Nothing better represents the Wren style than the facade of St. Paul's, for which he combined classical columns, reminiscent of Greek temples, with baroque decorations and adornments. Regrettably, the town plan that Wren conceived for rebuilding London was rejected, and the city was reconstructed piecemeal. Could you imagine what London would look like if Wren had been turned loose? Surely Prince Charles would no longer go around denouncing the architecture of London, but praising it.

the group of paintings and sculptures by Giacometti, and the paintings of one of England's best-known modern artists, Francis Bacon. Sculptures by Henry Moore and Barbara Hepworth are also occasionally displayed.

Insider's Tip: After you've seen the grand art, don't hasten away. Drop in to the Tate Gallery Shop for some of the best art books and postcards in London. The gallery sells whimsical T-shirts with art masterpieces on them. Those ubiquitous Tate Gallery canvas bags seen all over London are sold here, as are the town's best art posters. Invite your friends for tea at the Coffee Shop with its excellent cakes and pastries, or lunch at the Tate Gallery Restaurant (p. 188). You get to enjoy good food, Rex Whistler art, and the best and most reasonably priced wine list in London.

Millbank, SW1. © 020/7887-8000. www.tate.org.uk. Free admission; special exhibitions sometimes incur a charge varying from £3–£8.50 ($4.50–$12.75). Daily 10:30am–5:40pm. Tube: Pimlico.

Tate Modern ★★★   Located in n a transformed Bankside Power Station in Southwark, this museum, which opened in 2000, draws some 2 million visitors a year to see the greatest collection of international 20th-century art in Britain. It is one of the three or four most important modern art galleries in the world. How would we rate the collection? At the same level of the Pompidou in Paris, and with a slight edge over New York's Guggenheim. Of course, New York's Museum of Modern Art remains in a class of its own. Tate Modern is viewer friendly with eye-level hangings. All the big painting stars are here, a whole galaxy ranging from Dalí to Duchamp, from Giacometti to Matisse and Mondrian, from Picasso and Pollock to Rothko and Warhol. The Modern is also a gallery of 21st-century art, displaying new and exciting recently created art.

You can cross the Millennium Bridge, a pedestrian-only walk from the steps of St. Paul's, over the Thames to the gallery. The Tate Modern makes extensive use of glass for its exterior and interior, offering panoramic views. Galleries are arranged over three levels and provide different kinds of space. Instead of exhibiting art chronologically and by school, the Tate Modern takes a thematic approach, so displays cut across movements.

Bankside, SE1. ℂ 020/7887-8008. www.tate.org.uk. Free admission. Sun–Thurs 10am–6pm; Fri–Sat 10am–10pm. Tube: Southwark.

Tower Bridge ✦✦

One of the world's most celebrated landmarks, and possibly the most photographed and painted bridge on earth. (Presumably, this is the one the Arizona businessman thought he was getting, instead of the London Bridge.) Despite of its medieval appearance, Tower Bridge was built in 1894.

In 1993, an exhibition opened inside the bridge to commemorate its century-old history; it takes you up the north tower to high-level walkways between the two towers with spectacular views of St. Paul's, the Tower of London, and the Houses of Parliament. You're then led down the south tower and into the bridge's original engine room, with the Victorian boilers and steam engines that used to raise and lower the bridge for ships to pass. Exhibits in the bridge's towers use advanced technology, including animatronic characters, video, and computers to illustrate the history of the bridge. Admission to the **Tower Bridge Experience** (ℂ **020/7403-3761**) is £4.50 ($6.75) for adults and £3 ($4.50) for children 5 to 15, students, and seniors; family tickets start at £18.25 ($27.40); it's free for children 4 and under. Open April through October daily from 10am to 6:30pm; November through March daily from 9:30am to 6pm; last entry is 1¼ hours before closing. Closed Good Friday and from January 1 to 28 as well as a few days around Christmas.

At Tower Bridge, SE1. ℂ 020/7403-3761. Tube: Tower Hill.

Tower of London ✦✦✦ Kids

This ancient fortress continues to pack in the crowds with its macabre associations with the legendary figures imprisoned and/or executed here. There are more spooks here per square foot than in any other building in the whole of haunted Britain. Headless bodies, bodiless heads, phantom soldiers, icy blasts, clanking chains—you name them, the Tower's got them. Centuries after the last head rolled on Tower Hill, a shivery atmosphere of impending doom still lingers over its mighty walls. Plan on spending a lot of time here.

The Tower is actually an intricately patterned compound of structures built throughout the ages for varying purposes, mostly as expressions of royal power. The oldest is the **White Tower,** begun by William the Conqueror in 1078 to keep London's native Saxon population in check. Later rulers added other towers, more walls, and fortified gates, until the buildings became like a small town within a city. Until the reign of James I, the Tower was also one of the royal residences. But above all, it was a prison for distinguished captives.

Every stone of the Tower tells a story—usually a gory one. In the **Bloody Tower,** according to Shakespeare, the two little princes (the sons of Edward IV) were murdered by henchmen of Richard III. Richard knew that his position as king could not be secure as long as his nephews were alive. There seems no reasonable doubt that the little princes were murdered in the Tower on orders of their uncle. Attempts have been made by some historians to clear Richard's name, but Richard remains the chief suspect, and his deed caused him to lose the "hearts of the people" according to the *Chronicles of London* at the time.

Sir Walter Raleigh spent 13 years in the Bloody Tower before his date with the executioner. On the walls of the **Beauchamp Tower,** you can still read the last messages scratched by despairing prisoners. Through **Traitors' Gate** passed such ill-fated, romantic figures as Robert Devereux, the second Earl of Essex, and a favorite of Elizabeth I. A plaque marks the eerie place at **Tower Green** where two wives of Henry VIII, Anne Boleyn and Catherine Howard, Sir Thomas More, and the 4-day queen, Lady Jane Grey, all lost their lives.

The Tower, besides being a royal palace, a fortress, and a prison, was also an armory, a treasury, a menagerie, and in 1675, an astronomical observatory. Reopened in 1999, the White Tower holds the **Armouries,** which date from the reign of Henry VIII, as well as a display of instruments of torture and execution that recall some of the most ghastly moments in the Tower's history. In the Jewel House, you'll find the tower's greatest attraction, the **Crown Jewels.** Here, some of the world's most precious stones are set into robes, swords, scepters, and crowns. The Imperial State Crown is the most famous crown on earth; made for Victoria in 1837, it's worn today by Queen Elizabeth II when she opens Parliament. Studded with some 3,000 jewels (principally diamonds), it includes the Black Prince's Ruby, worn by Henry V at Agincourt. The 530-carat Star of Africa, a cut diamond on the Royal Sceptre with Cross, would make Harry Winston turn over in his grave. You'll have to stand in long lines to catch just a glimpse of the jewels as you and hundreds of others scroll by on moving sidewalks, but the wait is worth it.

In the latest development here, the presumed prison cell of Sir Thomas More opened to the public in 2000. More left this cell in 1535 to face his executioner after he'd fallen out with King Henry VIII over the monarch's desire to divorce Catherine of Aragon, the first of his six wives. More is believed to have lived in the lower part of the Bell Tower, here in this whitewashed cell, during the last 14 months of his life, although some historians doubt this claim.

A **palace** once inhabited by King Edward I in the late 1200s stands above Traitors' Gate. It's the only surviving medieval palace in Britain. Guides are dressed in period costumes. Reproductions of furniture and fittings, including Edward's throne, evoke the era, along with burning incense and candles.

Oh, yes—don't forget to look for the ravens. Six of them (plus 2 spares) are all registered as official Tower residents. According to a legend, the Tower of London will stand as long as those black, ominous birds remain, so to be on the safe side, one of the wings of each raven is clipped.

A 21st-century addition to the Tower complex is the New Armories restaurant, offering a range of snacks and meals, including the traditional cuppa for people about to lose their heads from too many attractions and not enough to eat.

One-hour guided tours of the entire compound are given by the Yeoman Warders (also known as "Beefeaters") every half-hour, starting at 9:25am from

---

Tips Tower Tips

You can spend the shortest time possible in the Tower's long lines if you buy your ticket in a kiosk at any Tube station before emerging above ground. Even so, choose a day other than Sunday—crowds are at their worst then, and arrive as early as you can in the morning.

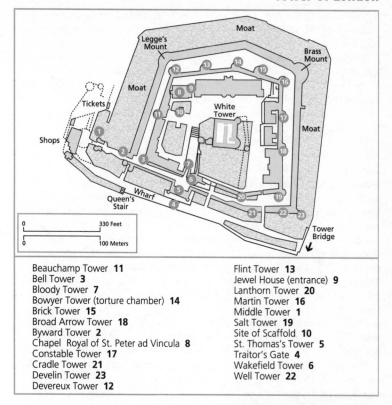

Beauchamp Tower **11**
Bell Tower **3**
Bloody Tower **7**
Bowyer Tower (torture chamber) **14**
Brick Tower **15**
Broad Arrow Tower **18**
Byward Tower **2**
Chapel Royal of St. Peter ad Vincula **8**
Constable Tower **17**
Cradle Tower **21**
Develin Tower **23**
Devereux Tower **12**

Flint Tower **13**
Jewel House (entrance) **9**
Lanthorn Tower **20**
Martin Tower **16**
Middle Tower **1**
Salt Tower **19**
Site of Scaffold **10**
St. Thomas's Tower **5**
Traitor's Gate **4**
Wakefield Tower **6**
Well Tower **22**

the Middle Tower near the main entrance. The last guided walk starts about 3:25pm in summer, 2:25pm in winter, weather permitting, of course.

You can attend the nightly **Ceremony of the Keys,** the ceremonial locking-up of the Tower by the Yeoman Warders. For free tickets, write to the Ceremony of the Keys, Waterloo Block, Tower of London, London EC3N 4AB, and request a specific date, but also list alternate dates. At least 6 weeks' notice is required. All requests must be accompanied by a stamped, self-addressed envelope (British stamps only) or two International Reply Coupons. With ticket in hand, you'll be admitted by a Yeoman Warder at 9:35pm. Frankly, we think it's not worth the trouble you go through to see this rather cheesy ceremony, but we know some who disagree with us.

Tower Hill, EC3. © 020/7709-0765. www.hrp.org.uk. Admission £11.30 ($16.95) adults, £8.50 ($12.75) students and seniors, £7.50 ($11.25) children, free for children under 5, £34 ($51) family ticket for 5 (but no more than 2 adults). Mar–Oct Mon–Sat 9am–6pm, Sun 10am–6pm; off-season Tues–Sat 9am–5pm, Sun–Mon 10am–5pm. Tube: Tower Hill.

Victoria and Albert Museum ★★★ The Victoria and Albert is the greatest decorative arts museum in the world. It's also one of the liveliest and most imaginative museums in London—where else would you find the quintessential "little black dress" in the permanent collection?

The medieval holdings include such treasures as the early-English Gloucester Candlestick; the Byzantine Veroli Casket, with its ivory panels based on Greek plays; and the Syon Cope, a unique embroidery made in England in the early 14th century. An area devoted to Islamic art houses the Ardabil Carpet from 16th-century Persia.

The V&A houses the largest collection of Renaissance sculpture outside Italy. A highlight of the 16th-century collection is the marble group *Neptune with Triton* by Bernini. The cartoons by Raphael, which were conceived as designs for tapestries for the Sistine Chapel, are owned by the queen and on display here. A most unusual, huge, and impressive exhibit is the Cast Courts, life-size plaster models of ancient and medieval statuary and architecture.

The museum has the greatest collection of Indian art outside India, plus Chinese and Japanese galleries as well. In complete contrast are suites of English furniture, metalwork, and ceramics, and a superb collection of portrait miniatures, including the one Hans Holbein the Younger made of Anne of Cleves for the benefit of Henry VIII, who was again casting around for a suitable wife. The Dress Collection includes a collection of corsets through the ages that's sure to make you wince. There's also a remarkable collection of musical instruments.

V&A has recently opened 15 new galleries—the British Galleries—telling the story of British design from 1500 to 1900. No other museum in the world houses such a diverse collection of British design and decorative art. From Chippendale to Morris, all of the top British designers are featured in some 3,000 exhibits, ranging from the 5m (17 ft.) high Melville Bed (1697) with its luxurious wild silk damask and red silk velvet hangings, to 19th-century classics such as furniture by Charles Rennie Mackintosh. One of the most prized possessions is the "Great Bed of Ware," mentioned in Shakespeare's *Twelfth Night* and the wedding suite of James II. And don't miss the V&A's most bizarre gallery, Fakes and Forgeries. The impostors here are amazingly authentic—in fact, we'd judge some of them as better than the old masters themselves.

Cromwell Rd., SW7. © 020/7942-2000. www.vam.ac.uk. Free admission. Daily 10am–5:45pm (Wed until 10pm). Tube: South Kensington.

Westminster Abbey ✪✪✪   With its identical square towers and superb archways, this early-English Gothic abbey is one of the greatest examples of ecclesiastical architecture on earth. But it's far more than that: It's the shrine of a nation, the symbol of everything Britain has stood for and stands for, the place in which most of its rulers were crowned and where many lie buried.

Nearly every figure in English history has left his or her mark on Westminster Abbey. Edward the Confessor founded the Benedictine abbey in 1065 on this spot overlooking Parliament Square. The first English king crowned in the abbey was Harold, in January 1066. The man who defeated him at the Battle of Hastings later that year, William the Conqueror, was also crowned here. The coronation tradition has continued to the present day, broken only twice (Edward V and Edward VIII). The essentially early-English Gothic structure existing today owes more to Henry III's plans than to those of any other sovereign, although many architects, including Wren, have contributed to the abbey.

⌐ **Finds**   **All That Jazz at the V&A**

The museum hosts a jazz brunch on Sunday from 11am to 3pm. You can hear some of the hottest jazz in the city, accompanied by a full English brunch for only £8.50 ($12.75).

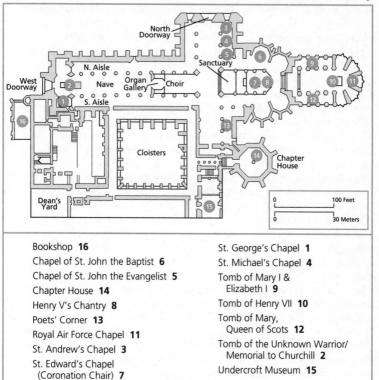

Bookshop **16**
Chapel of St. John the Baptist **6**
Chapel of St. John the Evangelist **5**
Chapter House **14**
Henry V's Chantry **8**
Poets' Corner **13**
Royal Air Force Chapel **11**
St. Andrew's Chapel **3**
St. Edward's Chapel
  (Coronation Chair) **7**

St. George's Chapel **1**
St. Michael's Chapel **4**
Tomb of Mary I &
  Elizabeth I **9**
Tomb of Henry VII **10**
Tomb of Mary,
  Queen of Scots **12**
Tomb of the Unknown Warrior/
  Memorial to Churchill **2**
Undercroft Museum **15**

Built on the site of the ancient Lady Chapel in the early 16th century, the **Henry VII Chapel** is one of the loveliest in Europe, with its fan vaulting, Knights of Bath banners, and Torrigiani-designed tomb for the king himself, over which hangs a 15th-century Vivarini painting, *Madonna and Child.* Also here, ironically buried in the same tomb, are Catholic Mary I and Protestant Elizabeth I (whose archrival, Mary Queen of Scots, is entombed on the other side of the Henry VII Chapel). In one end of the chapel, you can stand on Cromwell's memorial stone and view the **Royal Air Force Chapel** and its Battle of Britain memorial window, unveiled in 1947 to honor the Royal Air Force.

You can also visit the most hallowed spot in the abbey, the **shrine of Edward the Confessor** (canonized in the 12th century). In the chapel is the Coronation Chair, made at the command of Edward I in 1300 to display the mystical Stone of Scone (which some think is the sacred stone mentioned in Genesis and known as Jacob's Pillar). Scottish kings were once crowned on the stone (it has since been returned to Scotland).

When you enter the transept on the south side of the nave and see a statue of the Bard, with one arm resting on a stack of books, you've arrived at **Poets' Corner.** Shakespeare himself is buried at Stratford-upon-Avon, but resting here are Chaucer, Ben Jonson, Milton, Shelley, and many others; there's even an American, Henry Wadsworth Longfellow, as well as monuments to just about everybody: Chaucer, Shakespeare, "O Rare Ben Johnson" (his name misspelled),

Samuel Johnson, George Eliot, Charles Dickens, and others. The most stylized monument is Sir Jacob Epstein's sculptured bust of William Blake. More recent tablets commemorate poet Dylan Thomas and Lord Laurence Olivier.

Statesmen and men of science—Disraeli, Newton, Charles Darwin—are also interred in the abbey or honored by monuments. Near the west door is the 1965 memorial to Sir Winston Churchill. In the vicinity of this memorial is the tomb of the **Unknown Warrior,** commemorating the British dead of World War I.

Although most of the Abbey's statuary commemorates notable figures of the past, ten new statues were unveiled in July 1998. Placed in the Gothic niches above the West Front door, these statues honor ten modern-day martyrs drawn from every continent and religious denomination. Designed by Tim Crawley and carved under his general direction from French Richemont limestone, the sculptures include Elizabeth of Russia, Janani Luwum, and Martin Luther King, representatives of those who have sacrificed their lives for their beliefs.

Off the Cloisters, the **College Garden** is the oldest garden in England, under cultivation for more than 900 years. Established in the 11th century as the abbey's first infirmary garden, this was once a magnificent source of fruits, vegetables, and medicinal herbs. Five trees in the garden were planted in 1850 and continue to thrive today. Surrounded by high walls, flowering trees dot the lawns, and park benches provide comfort where you can hardly hear the roar of passing traffic. It's open only on Tuesday and Thursday, April through September from 10am to 6pm and October through March from 10am to 4pm.

Insider's Tip: Far removed from the pomp and glory is the **Abbey Treasure Museum,** which displays a real bag of oddities in the undercroft, or crypt, part of the monastic buildings erected between 1066 and 1100. You'll find royal effigies that were used instead of the real corpses for lying-in-state ceremonies because they smelled better. You'll see the almost lifelike effigy of Admiral Nelson (his mistress arranged his hair) and even that of Edward III, his lip warped by the cerebral hemorrhage that felled him. Other oddities include a Middle English lease to Chaucer, Henry VI's much-used sword, and the Essex Ring that Elizabeth I gave to her favorite (Robert Dudley, who was the Earl of Leicester) when she was feeling good about him.

On Sunday, the Royal Chapels are closed, but the rest of the church is open unless a service is being conducted. For times of services, phone the **Chapter Office** (© 020/7222-5152).

Broad Sanctuary, SW1. © 020/7222-7110. www.westminster-abbey.org. Admission £6 ($9) adults, £3 ($4.50) for students, seniors, and children 11–18, free for children under 11, family ticket £12 ($18). Mon–Fri 9:30am–3:45pm; Sat 9:30am–1:45pm. Tube: Westminster or St. James's Park.

3 More Central London Attractions

See the "Sights & Attractions by Neighborhood," list on p. 214 for more information on which attraction is in which neighborhood.

CHURCHES & CATHEDRALS

Many of London's churches offer free lunchtime concerts; a full list is available from the London Tourist Board. It's customary to leave a small donation.

All Hallows Barking-by-the-Tower The brass-rubbing center at this fascinating church, located next door to the Tower, has a crypt museum, Roman remains, and traces of early London, including a Saxon arch predating the Tower. Samuel Pepys, the famed diarist, climbed to the spire to watch the raging fire of London in 1666. In 1644, William Penn was baptized here, and in

---

(Fun Fact American Woman

The parents of Virginia Dare, the first English child born in America (at Roanoke in 1587) were married in St. Bride's. An effigy of Virginia can be seen over the baptismal font.

1797, John Quincy Adams was married here. Bombs destroyed the church in 1940, leaving only the tower and walls standing. The church was rebuilt from 1949 to 1958.

Byward St., EC3. ✆ 020/7481-2928. Free admission; crypt museum tour £2.50 ($3.75). Museum Mon–Fri 11am–4pm, Sat 10am–5pm, Sun 2–4:30pm; church Mon–Fri 9am–6pm, Sat–Sun 10am–5pm. Tube: Tower Hill.

Southwark Cathedral ★★   There's been a church on this site, in the heart of London's first theater district, for more than a thousand years. The present one dates from the 15th century, and was partly rebuilt in 1890. The previous one was the first Gothic church (1106) to be constructed in London. Shakespeare and Chaucer worshipped here; a Shakespeare birthday service is held annually, and inside is a memorial to the playwright. A wooden effigy of a knight dates from 1275. In 1424, James I of Scotland married Mary Beaufort here. During the reign of Mary Tudor, Stephen Gardiner, the Bishop of Winchester, held a consistory court in the retro choir that condemned seven Protestants, the Marian martyrs, to death. Later, the same retro choir was rented to a baker and even used to house pigs. Lunchtime concerts are regularly given on Monday and Tuesday; call for exact times and schedules.

Montague Close, London Bridge, SE1. ✆ 020/7367-6734. www.southwark.gov.uk. Free admission; suggested donation £3 ($4.50). Mon–Fri 8am–6pm. Tube: London Bridge.

St. Bride's ★   Known as the "the church of the press," thanks to its location at the end of Fleet Street, St. Bride's is a remarkable landmark. The current church is the eighth one that has stood here. After it was bombed in 1940, an archaeologist excavated the crypts and was able to confirm much of the site's legendary history: A Roman house was discovered, and it was established that St. Brigit of Ireland had founded the first Christian church that was built here, in the sixth century. In addition, a crypt with evidence of six subsequent churches was discovered. Among the famous parishioners have been writers John Dryden, John Milton, Richard Lovelace, and John Evelyn. The diarist Samuel Pepys was baptized here, and novelist Samuel Richardson and his family are buried here. After the Great Fire destroyed it, Christopher Wren rebuilt the church with a spire that's been described as a "madrigal in stone." The crypt was a burial chamber and charnel house for centuries; today, it's a museum. Choral concerts are given on Tuesday, Wednesday and Friday. Concerts are often suspended during Lent and Christmas.

Fleet St., EC4. ✆ 020/7427-0133. Free admission. Mon–Fri 8am–4:45pm; Sat 10am–4pm; Sun 10am–12:30pm and 5:30–7:30pm. Choral concerts at 1:15pm Tues, Wed, and Fri. Tube: Blackfriars.

St. Etheldreda's   The oldest Roman Catholic church in London, St. Etheldreda's stands on Ely Place, off Charterhouse Street, at Holborn Circus. Built in 1251, it was mentioned by the Bard in both Richard II and Richard III. A survivor of the Great Fire of 1666, the church and the area surrounding it were the property of the diocese of the city of Ely, in the days when many bishops had

West End Sights

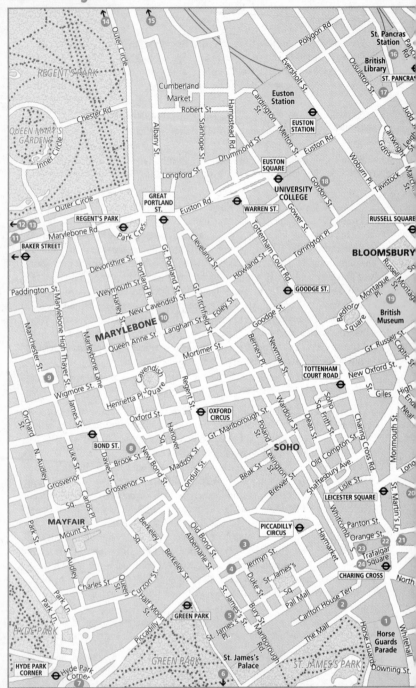

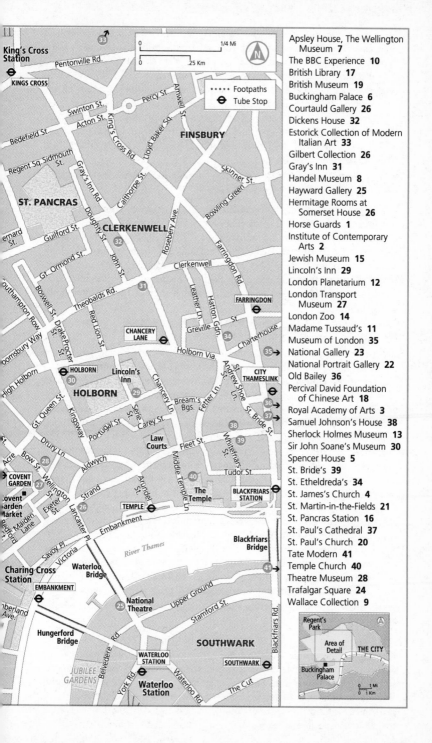

King's Cross Station

KINGS CROSS

Pentonville Rd.

Swinton St.

Acton St.

Bedefield St.

Regent Sq. Sidmouth St.

FINSBURY

Percy St.

Amwell St.

King's Cross Rd.

Lloyd Baker St.

Skinner St.

Bowling Green

Gray's Inn Rd.

Calthorpe St.

Rosebery Ave.

ST. PANCRAS

ernard St.

Guilford St.

Doughty St.

John St.

CLERKENWELL

Gt. Ormond St.

outhampton Row

Boswell St.

Drake Procter St.

Theobalds Rd.

Red Lion St.

Leather Ln.

Hatton Gdn.

Greville St.

Farringdon Rd.

Clerkenwell

FARRINGDON

oomsbury Way

CHANCERY LANE

Holborn Via.

Charterhouse

St.

Chancery Ln.

Andrew Shoe Ln.

CITY THAMESLINK

High Holborn

HOLBORN

Lincoln's Inn

HOLBORN

Gt. Queen St.

Kingsway

Serle St.

Bream's Bgs.

Fetter Ln.

St. Bride St.

Old Bailey

Drury Ln.

Portugal St.

Carey St.

Fleet St.

St. Paul's Cathedral

Acre

Bow St.

Aldwych

Law Courts

Middle Temple Ln.

Whitefriars St.

St. Bride's

COVENT GARDEN

Wellington St.

Strand

Tudor St.

ovent arden arket

Exeter St.

Maiden Lane

Lancaster Pl.

Arundel St.

The Temple

BLACKFRIARS STATION

Savoy Pl.

Embankment

TEMPLE

Temple Church

Blackfriars Bridge

Charing Cross Station

EMBANKMENT

Victoria

Waterloo Bridge

River Thames

Blackfriars Rd.

Blackfriars Bridge

berland Ave.

National Theatre

Upper Ground

Hungerford Bridge

Belvedere Rd.

Stamford St.

SOUTHWARK

JUBILEE GARDENS

WATERLOO STATION

York Rd.

Waterloo Rd.

SOUTHWARK

Waterloo Station

The Cut

0 .... 1/4 Mi
0 .... .25 Km

•••• Footpaths
Ⓣ Tube Stop

Apsley House, The Wellington Museum **7**
The BBC Experience **10**
British Library **17**
British Museum **19**
Buckingham Palace **6**
Courtauld Gallery **26**
Dickens House **32**
Estorick Collection of Modern Italian Art **33**
Gilbert Collection **26**
Gray's Inn **31**
Handel Museum **8**
Hayward Gallery **25**
Hermitage Rooms at Somerset House **26**
Horse Guards **1**
Institute of Contemporary Arts **2**
Jewish Museum **15**
Lincoln's Inn **29**
London Planetarium **12**
London Transport Museum **27**
London Zoo **14**
Madame Tussaud's **11**
Museum of London **35**
National Gallery **23**
National Portrait Gallery **22**
Old Bailey **36**
Percival David Foundation of Chinese Art **18**
Royal Academy of Arts **3**
Samuel Johnson's House **38**
Sherlock Holmes Museum **13**
Sir John Soane's Museum **30**
Spencer House **5**
St. Bride's **39**
St. Etheldreda's **34**
St. James's Church **4**
St. Martin-in-the-Fields **21**
St. Pancras Station **16**
St. Paul's Cathedral **37**
St. Paul's Church **20**
Tate Modern **41**
Temple Church **40**
Theatre Museum **28**
Trafalgar Square **24**
Wallace Collection **9**

Regent's Park

Area of Detail

THE CITY

Buckingham Palace

0 ___ 1 Mi
0 ___ 1 Km

Episcopal houses in London, as well as in the cathedral cities in which they held their sees. The property still has a private road, with impressive iron gates and a lodge for the gatekeeper, and it is administered by six elected commissioners.

St. Etheldreda, whose name is sometimes shortened to St. Audrey, was a 7th-century king's daughter who left her husband and established an abbey on the Isle of Ely. St. Etheldreda's has a distinguished musical tradition, with the 11am mass on Sunday sung in Latin. Other masses are on Sunday at 9am, Monday through Friday at 8am and 1pm, and on Saturday at 9:30am. Lunch, with a varied choice of hot and cold dishes, is served Monday through Friday from 11:30am to 2pm in the Pantry.

Ely Place, Holborn Circus, EC1. © 020/7405-1061. Free admission. Daily 7:30am–6:30pm; Sun masses 9 and 11am, weekday masses Mon–Fri 8am and 1pm. Tube: Farringdon or Chancery Lane.

St. Giles Cripplegate ✸ Named for the patron saint of cripples, St. Giles was founded in the 11th century. The church survived the Great Fire, but the Blitz left only the tower and walls standing. In 1620, English revolutionary Oliver Cromwell was betrothed to Elizabeth Bourchier here, and in 1674, John Milton, author of *Paradise Lost*, was buried here. More than a century later, someone opened the poet's grave, knocked out his teeth, stole a rib bone, and tore hair from his skull. Guided tours are available on most Tuesday afternoons. Call to confirm.

At Fore and Wood sts., London Wall, EC2. © 020/7638-1997. www.stgilescripplegate.com. Free admission. Mon–Fri 11am–4pm; Sat–Sun 9am–noon for services. Tube: Moorgate or St. Paul's.

St. James's Church ✸ When the aristocratic area known as St. James's was developed in the late 17th century, Sir Christopher Wren was commissioned to build its parish church. Diarist John Evelyn wrote of the interior, "There is no altar anywhere in England, nor has there been any abroad, more handsomely adorned." The reredos (a screen decorated with religious icons placed behind the altar), organ case, and font were all carved by Wren's master carver Grinling Gibbons. As might be expected, this church has rich historical associations: The poet William Blake was baptized here, as was William Pitt, the first Earl of Chatham, who became England's youngest prime minister at age 24. Caricaturist James Gillray, auctioneer James Christie, and coffeehouse founder Francis White are all buried here. One of the more colorful marriages celebrated here was that of explorer Sir Samuel Baker and the woman he had bought at a slave auction in a Turkish bazaar. St. James's Church is a radical, inclusive Anglican church. It's also the Centre for Health and Healing and holds seminars on New Age and Creation Spirituality. There's a Bible Garden and a crafts market in the courtyard. The Wren Cafe is open daily, and lunchtime and evening concerts are held. There is an antiques market at St. James's on Tuesday from 10 am to 7pm, and a crafts market Wednesday through Saturday from 10am to 7pm.

197 Piccadilly, W1. © 020/7734-4511. Free admission. Recitals on Mon, Wed, and Fri 1:10pm. Tube: Piccadilly Circus or Green Park.

St. Martin-in-the-Fields ✸ Designed by James Gibbs, a disciple of Christopher Wren, and completed in 1726, this classical church stands at the northeast corner of Trafalgar Square, opposite the National Gallery. Its spire, added in 1824, towers 56m (185 ft., taller than Nelson's Column, which also rises on the square). The steeple became the model for many churches in colonial America. Since the first year of World War I (1914), the homeless have sought "soup and shelter" at St. Martin, a tradition that continues.

At one time, the crypt held the remains of Charles II (he's in Westminster Abbey now), who was christened here, giving St. Martin a claim as a royal parish church. His mistress, Nell Gwynne, and the highwayman Jack Sheppard are both interred here. The floors of the crypt are actually gravestones, and the walls date from the 1500s. The little restaurant, **Café in the Crypt,** is still called "Field's" by its devotees. Also in the crypt is **The London Brass Rubbing Centre** (© **020/7930-9306**) with 88 exact copies of bronze portraits ready for use. Paper, rubbing materials, and instructions on how to begin are furnished, and there's classical music for you to enjoy as you proceed. The charges to make the rubblings range from £3 to £16 ($4.50–$24), the latter price for the largest, a life-size Crusader knight. There's also a gift shop with brass-rubbing kits for children, budget-priced ready-made rubbings, Celtic jewelry, miniature brasses, and model knights. The center is open Monday through Saturday from 10am to 6pm and Sunday from noon to 6pm.

Insider's Tip: In back of the church is a crafts market. Lunchtime and evening concerts are staged Monday, Tuesday, and Friday at 1:05pm, and Thursday through Saturday at 7:30pm. Tickets cost £6.50 to £15.50 ($9.75–$23.25).

Trafalgar Sq., WC2. © **020/7766-1100.** Mon–Fri 7:45am–6pm; Sat–Sun 8:45am–7pm as long as no service is taking place. Tube: Charing Cross.

St. Mary-le-Bow ★★   It's said that a true Cockney must be born within the sound of this church's famous Bow bells. The church has a sometimes-gruesome history. In 1091, its roof was ripped off in a storm; the church tower collapsed in 1271 and 20 people were killed; in 1331, Queen Philippa and her ladies-in-waiting fell to the ground when a balcony collapsed during a joust celebrating the birth of the Black Prince. The church was rebuilt by Wren after being engulfed by the Great Fire in 1666. The original "Cockney" Bow bells were destroyed in the Blitz, but have been replaced. The church was rededicated in 1964 after extensive restoration work.

Cheapside, EC2. © **020/7248-5139.** Free admission. Mon–Thurs 6:30am–5:30pm; Fri 6:30am–4pm. Tube: St. Paul's or Bank.

St. Paul's Church (the Actors' Church) ★   With the Drury Lane Theatre, the Royal Opera House, and many other theaters within its parish, St. Paul's has long been associated with the theatrical arts. Inside you'll find scores of memorial plaques dedicated to such luminaries as Vivien Leigh, Boris Karloff, Margaret Rutherford, and Noel Coward, to name only a few. Designed by Inigo Jones in 1631, this church has been substantially altered over the years, but has retained a quiet garden-piazza in the rear. Among the famous buried here are woodcarver Grinling Gibbons, writer Samuel Butler, and actress Ellen Terry. Landscape painter J. M. W. Turner and librettist W. S. Gilbert were both baptized here. The church still draws members of the entertainment world.

Bedford St., Covent Garden, WC2. © **020/7836-5221.** Free admission. Tues–Fri 9:30am–4:30pm; Sun service 11am. Tube: Covent Garden.

Temple Church ★★   One of three Norman "round churches" left in England, this one was first completed in the 12th century. Not surprisingly, it has been restored. Look for the knightly effigies and the Norman door, and take note of the circle of grotesque portrait heads, including a goat in a mortarboard. On Inner Temple Lane, about where the Strand becomes Fleet Street going east, you'll see the memorial pillar called **Temple Bar,** which marks the boundary of the City of London.

The Temple (within the Inner Temple), King's Bench Walk, EC4. ℂ 020/7353-1736. Free admission. Wed–Sat 10am–4pm; Sun 1–4pm. Tube: Temple.

Wesley's Chapel, House & Museum of Methodism   John Wesley, the founder of Methodism, established this church in 1778 as his London base. Wesley, who rode on horseback throughout the English countryside and preached in the open air, lived at no. 47, next door to the chapel. He's buried in a grave behind the chapel. The house contains many of Wesley's belongings, including his "electrical machine" (a contraption that he claimed was successful in treating melancholy) and his study chair. While it survived the Blitz, the church later fell into disrepair; major restoration was completed in the 1970s. In the crypt, a museum traces the history of Methodism to present times.

Across the road in Bunhill Fields is the **Dissenters Graveyard,** where Daniel Defoe, William Blake, and John Bunyan are buried.

49 City Rd., EC1. ℂ 020/7253-2262. Chapel free. House and museum £4 ($6) adults; £2 ($3) seniors, students, and children 5–17. House and museum Mon–Sat 10am–4pm. Both free on Sun after service, between noon and 2pm. Tube: Old St. or Moorgate.

Westminster Cathedral ☆   This spectacular brick-and-stone church (1903) is the headquarters of the Roman Catholic Church in Britain. Adorned in early-Byzantine style, it's massive: 108m (360 ft.) long and 47m (156 ft.) wide. One hundred different marbles compose the richly decorated interior, and eight marble columns support the nave. The huge canopy over the high altar is held up by eight yellow marble columns. Mosaics emblazon the chapels and the vaulting of the sanctuary. If you take the elevator to the top of the 82m (273 ft.) campanile, you're rewarded with sweeping views that take in Buckingham Palace, Westminster Abbey, and St. Paul's Cathedral. There is a cafe serving light snacks and soft drinks from 9am to 5pm and a gift shop open from 9:30am to 5:15pm.

Ashley Place, SW1. ℂ 020/7798-9055. www.westminstercathedral.org.uk. Cathedral free. Audio tours £2.50 ($3.75). Tower £2 ($3). Cathedral, daily 7am–7pm. Tower, May–Nov daily 9am–12:30pm and 1–5pm; otherwise, Thurs–Sun only. Tube: Victoria.

HISTORIC BUILDINGS

Banqueting House ☆☆   The feasting chamber in Whitehall Palace is probably the most sumptuous dining hall on earth. (Unfortunately, you can't dine here unless you're a visiting head of state.) Designed by Inigo Jones and decorated with, among other things, original ceiling paintings by Rubens, the hall is dazzling enough to make you forget food altogether. Among the historic events that took place here were the beheading of King Charles I, who stepped through

---

Finds   **Drake's Long Voyage**

As you're strolling along the riverside, you'll come upon the old dock of St. Mary Overie, SE1. Here, delightfully, is an exact replica of the *Golden Hinde,* the ship in which **Sir Francis Drake** circumnavigated the globe. It's amazingly tiny for an around-the-world voyage. This actual ship has sailed around the world some two dozen times, exploring both the Atlantic and Pacific oceans, and the American coast. Visits are daily from 9:30am to 4:30pm, costing £2.50 ($3.75). For information, call ℂ 020/7403-0123.

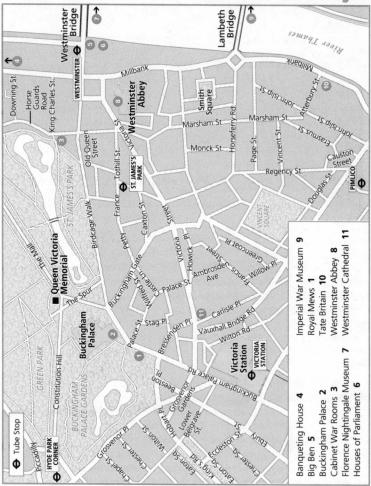

Imperial War Museum **9**
Royal Mews **1**
Tate Britain **10**
Westminster Abbey **8**
Westminster Cathedral **11**

Banqueting House **4**
Big Ben **5**
Buckingham Palace **2**
Cabinet War Rooms **3**
Florence Nightingale Museum **7**
Houses of Parliament **6**

a window onto the scaffold outside, and the restoration ceremony of Charles II, marking the return of monarchy after Cromwell's brief Puritan Commonwealth.

Whitehall Palace, Horse Guards Ave., SW1. © **020/7930-4179**. www.hrp.org.uk/bh. Admission £3.90 ($5.85) adults, £3.10 ($4.65) seniors and students, £2.30 ($3.45) children. Mon–Sat 10am–5pm (last admission 4:30pm). Tube: Westminster, Charing Cross, or Embankment.

Cabinet War Rooms   This is the bombproof bunker from which Sir Winston Churchill and his government ran the nation during World War II. Many of the rooms are exactly as they were in September 1945: Imperial War Museum curators studied photographs to put notepads, files, typewriters, even pencils, pins, and clips, in their correct places.

Along the tour, you'll have a personal sound guide that provides a detailed account of the function and history of each room of this nerve center. They include the Map Room, with its huge wall maps, Churchill's bedroom/office,

⟨ **Finds** A City of Wine

At **Vinopolis**, 1 Bank End, Park St., SE1 (✆ **020/7288-6005**) you can partake of London's largest selection of wine sold by the glass. On the South Bank, this "city of wine" lies under cavernous railway arches created in Victoria's era. The bacchanalian attraction was created in a multimedia format, at the cost of £23 million. You can journey virtually through some of the earth's most prestigious wine regions, driving a Vespa through the Tuscan countryside or taking a "flight" over the vineyards of Australia. The price of entrance includes free tastings of five premium wines, and an on-site shop sells almost any item related to the grape. The site also boasts a good restaurant (see "Cantina Vinopolis," p. 158). Admission is £11.50 ($17.25) for adults, £5 ($7.50) for ages 5 to 14, and £10.50 ($15.75) for seniors.

with a basic bed and a desk with two BBC microphones for those famous broadcasts that stirred the nation. The Transatlantic Telephone Room is little more than a closet, but it held the extension linked to the special scrambler phone (called "Sig-Saly") on which Churchill conferred with Roosevelt. (The scrambler equipment itself was actually too large to house in the bunker, so it was placed in the basement of Selfridges department store on Oxford Street.)

Clive Steps, at end of King Charles St. (off Whitehall near Big Ben), SW1. ✆ 020/7930-6961. www.iwm. org.uk. Admission £5.80 ($8.70) adults, £4.20 ($6.30) seniors and students, free for children 16 and under. Apr–Sept daily 9:30am–6pm (last admission at 5:15pm); Oct–Mar daily 10am–6pm. Tube: Westminster or St. James's.

Chelsea Royal Hospital ✮✮ This dignified institution, founded by Charles II in 1682 as a home for veterans, was designed and completed by Sir Christopher Wren in 1692. It consists of a main block containing the hall and the chapel, flanked by east and west wings. There's been little change to Wren's design, except for minor work done by Robert Adam in the 18th century and the addition of stables by Sir John Soane in 1814. The duke of Wellington lay in state here from November 10–17, 1852. So many people thronged to see him that two were crushed to death. Today, the hospital is home to bachelor pensioners who fought in World War II or other conflicts.

If you want a tour, apply in writing to Adjutant, Royal Hospital Chelsea, London, SW3 4SR. Guided tours are free, but donations are gratefully accepted. Otherwise, you are welcome to explore on your own.

Royal Hospital Rd., SW3. ✆ 020/7881-5244. www.chelseapensioner.org.uk. Free admission. Mon–Sat 10am–noon and 2–4pm; Sun 2–4pm. Museum and shop closed Sun Oct–Mar. Tube: Sloane Sq.

Horse Guards ✮ North of Downing Street, on the west side of Whitehall, is the building of the Horse Guards, which is the headquarters of the British Army. The building was designed by William Kent, chief architect to George II. The real draw here is the Horse Guards themselves: the Household Cavalry Mounted Regiment, a combination of the oldest and most senior regiments in the British Army—the Life Guards and the Blues and Royals. In theory, their duty is to protect the sovereign. Life Guards wear red tunics and white plumes and Blues and Royals are attired in blue tunics with red plumes. Two much-photographed mounted members of the Household Cavalry keep watch daily from 10am to 5pm. The mounted sentries change duty every hour as a benefit to the horses.

Foot sentries change every 2 hours. The chief guard rather grandly inspects the troops here daily at 4pm. The guard, with flair and fanfare, dismounts at 5pm.

We prefer the **changing of the guards** here to the more famous ceremony at Buckingham Palace. Beginning around 11am Monday through Saturday and 10:30am on Sunday, a new guard leaves the Hyde Park Barracks, rides down Pall Mall, and arrives at the Horse Guards building, all in about 30 minutes. The old guard then returns to the barracks.

If you pass through the arch at Horse Guards, you'll find yourself at the **Horse Guards Parade,** which opens onto St. James's Park. This spacious court provides the best view of the various architectural styles that make up Whitehall. Regrettably, the parade ground itself is now a parking lot.

The military pageant—the most famous in Britain—known as **Trooping the Colour,** celebrating the queen's birthday, takes place in June at the Horse Guards Parade (see "London Calendar of Events," in chapter 3). The "Colour" refers to the flag of the regiment. For devotees of pomp and circumstance, "Beating the Retreat" is staged here 3 or 4 evenings a week during the first 2 weeks of June. It's only a dress rehearsal, though, for Trooping the Colour.

Whitehall, SW1. ✆ 020/7414-2396. www.army.mod.uk. Tube: Charing Cross, Westminster, or Embankment.

Spencer House ★★ This is one of the city's most beautiful buildings. It was constructed in 1766 for the first Earl Spencer, who intended it as a shrine to Georgiana Poyntz, his childhood sweetheart whom he had secretly married the year before. It hasn't been a private residence since 1927, and had something of a checkered history until it was restored and opened as a museum in 1990. Rooms are filled with period furniture and art, some even loaned by the queen herself. The most spectacular salon is the Palm Room, all in white, gold, and green.

27 St. James's Place, SW1. ✆ 020/7499-8620. www.spencerhouse.co.uk. Admission £6 ($9) adults, £5 ($7.50) children 10–16; children under 10 not allowed. Sun 10:30am–4:45pm. Closed Jan and Aug. Tube: Green Park.

St. Pancras Station The London terminus for the Midland Railway, St. Pancras Station (1863–67) is a masterpiece of Victorian engineering. Designed by W. H. Barlow, the 207m (689-ft.) long glass-and-iron train station spans

Legal London

The smallest borough in London, bustling **Holborn** (*ho*-burn) is often referred to as "Legal London." It's home to the majority of the city's barristers, solicitors, and law clerks, as well as the ancient **Inns of Court** (Tube: Holborn or Chancery Lane), the beautiful complexes where barristers have their chambers and law students perform their apprenticeships. All barristers (litigators) must belong to one of these institutions, and many work from their dignified ancient buildings: **Gray's Inn, Lincoln's Inn** (the best preserved of the three), and the **Middle and Inner Temple** (just over the line inside the City). They were severely damaged during World War II, and some razed buildings were replaced with modern offices, but the borough still retains pockets of architecture of former days.

72m (240 ft.) in width and rises to a peak of 30m (100 ft.) above the rails. The platforms were raised 6m (20 ft.) above the ground because the tracks ran over the Regent's Canal before entering the station. The pièce de résistance, though, is Sir George Gilbert Scott's fanciful Midland Grand Hotel: Done in high Gothic style; it's graced with pinnacles, towers, and gables; it now functions as office space. The facade runs 170m (565 ft.) and is flanked by a clock tower and a west tower.

Euston Rd., NW1. Tube: King's Cross/St. Pancras.

Gray's Inn ★   Gray's Inn is one of four ancient Inns of Court still in opera-tion. As you enter, you'll see a late-Georgian terrace lined with buildings that, like many of the other houses in the inns, serve as both residences and offices. Gray's was restored after suffering heavy damage in World War II. It contains a rebuilt Tudor Hall, but its greatest attraction is the tree-shaded lawn and hand-some gardens. The 17th-century atmosphere exists today in the square. Scientist-philosopher Francis Bacon (1561–1626) was the inn's most eminent tenant.

Gray's Inn Rd. (north of High Holborn; entrance on Theobald's Rd.), 8 South Sq., WC1. © 020/7458-7800. www.online-law.co.uk. Free admission to squares and gardens. Gardens Mon–Fri 9am–2:30pm; squares Mon–Fri 9am–5pm. Tube: Chancery Lane.

Lincoln's Inn ★★   Lincoln's Inn is the oldest of the four Inns of Court. Between the City and the West End, Lincoln's Inn comprises 4.4 hectares (11 acres), including lawns, squares, gardens, a 17th-century chapel (open Mon–Fri noon–2pm), a library, and two halls. One of these, Old Hall, dates from 1490 and has remained almost unaltered with its linenfold paneling, stained glass, and wooden screen by Inigo Jones. It was once the home of Sir Thomas More, and it was where barristers met, ate, and debated 150 years before the *Mayflower* sailed on its epic voyage. Old Hall is the scene for the opening chapter of Charles Dickens's *Bleak House*. The other hall, Great Hall, remains one of the finest Tudor Revival buildings in London and was opened by Queen Victoria in 1843. It's now the center of the inn and is used for the formal ceremony of call-ing students to the bar.

Lincoln's Inn Fields, WC2. © 020/7405-1393. www.lincolnsinn.org.uk. Free admission to grounds. Mon–Fri 9am–6pm. Tube: Holborn or Chancery Lane.

Old Bailey   This courthouse replaced the infamous Newgate Prison, once the scene of hangings and other forms of "public entertainment." It's affectionately known as the "Old Bailey" after a street that runs nearby. It's fascinating to watch the bewigged barristers presenting their cases to the high-court judges. Entry is strictly on a first-arrival basis, and guests line up outside; security will then direct you to one of the rooms where cases are being tried. It's impossible to predict how long a line you might face. If there's a London equivalent of the O.J. Simpson trial, forget about it. You'll never get in. On a day with trials attracting little attention, you can often enter after only 15 minutes or so. You never know until you show up. The best time to line up is 10am. You enter courts 1 to 4, 17, and 18 from Newgate Street, and the others from Old Bailey Street.

Newgate St., EC4. To get here from the Temple, travel east on Fleet St., which becomes Ludgate Hill; cross Ludgate Circus and turn left at the Old Bailey, a domed structure with the figure of *Justice* atop it. © 020/7248-3277. Free admission. Court in session Mon–Fri 10:30am–1pm and 2–4pm. Children under 14 not admitted; those 14–16 must be accompanied by a responsible adult. No cameras, tape recorders, or cell-phones (and there are no coat-checking facilities). Tube: St. Paul's.

A Neighborhood of One's Own: The Homes of Virginia Woolf

Born in London in 1882, author and essayist Virginia Woolf used the city as the setting of many of her novels, including *Jacob's Room* (1922). The daughter of Sir Leslie Stephen and his wife Julia Duckworth, Virginia spent her formative years at **22 Hyde Park Gate,** off Kensington Road, west of Royal Albert Hall. Her mother died in 1895 and her father in 1904.

After the death of their father, Virginia and her sister Vanessa left Kensington for Bloomsbury, settling near the British Museum. It was an interesting move, as Bloomsbury was a neighborhood that upper-class Victorians didn't view as "respectable." But Virginia was to make it her own, and in the process, make the district world-famous as the hub of literary London. From 1905, the Stephens lived at **46 Gordon Square,** east of Gower Street and University College. It was here that the celebrated circle known as the "Bloomsbury Group" came into being. In time, the group would embrace art critic Clive Bell and author Leonard Woolf, future husbands of Vanessa and Virginia, respectively. Later, Virginia went to live at **29 Fitzroy Sq.,** west of Tottenham Court Road, in a house once occupied by Bernard Shaw.

During the next 2 decades, Virginia resided at several more Bloomsbury addresses, including **Brunswick Square, Tavistock Square,** and **Mecklenburg Square.** These homes have disappeared or been altered beyond recognition. During this time, the Bloomsbury Group reached out to include the artists Roger Fry and Duncan Grant, and Virginia became a friend of economist John Maynard Keynes and author E. M. Forster (*A Passage to India*). At Tavistock Square (1924–39) and at Mecklenburg Square (1939–40), she operated the Hogarth Press with Leonard. She published her own early work here, as well as T. S. Eliot's *The Waste Land.*

LITERARY AND MUSICAL LANDMARKS

Besides the home of the authors and composers listed below, you can also visit the abodes of other celebrated Londoners, including Apsley House, the former mansion of the duke of Wellington (p. 251). The homes of John Keats and Sigmund Freud are also open to the public; both are north of London in Hampstead (p. 268). Finally, the fascinating home of legendary architect Sir John Soane (p. 263), is open to the public and now houses a museum about Soane.

Carlyle's House From 1834 to 1881, Thomas Carlyle, author of *The French Revolution,* and Jane Baillie Welsh Carlyle, his noted letter-writing wife, resided in this modest 1708 terraced house. Furnished essentially as it was in Carlyle's day, the house is located about half a block from the Thames, near the Chelsea Embankment, along King's Road. It was described by his wife as being "of most antique physiognomy, quite to our humour; all wainscotted, carved, and queer-looking, roomy, substantial, commodious, with closets to satisfy any Bluebeard."

The second floor contains Mrs. Carlyle's drawing room, but the most interesting chamber is the not-so-soundproof "soundproof" study in the skylit attic. Filled with Carlyle memorabilia—his books, a letter from Disraeli, personal effects, a writing chair, even his death mask—this is where the author did his work.

24 Cheyne Row, SW3. ☎ 020/7352-7087. Admission £3.60 ($5.40) adults, £1.80 ($2.70) children 5–16 (4 and under free). Wed–Sun 11am–5pm. Closed Nov–Mar. Tube: Sloane Sq.

Dickens House   Here in Bloomsbury stands the simple abode in which Charles Dickens wrote *Oliver Twist* and finished *The Pickwick Papers* (his American readers actually waited at the dock for the ship that brought in each new installment). The place is almost a shrine: It contains his study, manuscripts, and personal relics, as well as reconstructed interiors. During Christmas week (including Christmas day), the museum is decorated in the style of Dickens's first Christmas there. During Christmas, the raised admission prices of £10 ($15) for adults and £5 ($7.50) for children include hot mince pies and a few glasses of "Smoking Bishop," Dickens's favorite hot punch, as well as a copy of the museum's guidebooks.

48 Doughty St., WC1. ☎ 020/7405-2127. www.dickensmuseum.com. Admission £4 ($6) adults, £3 ($4.50) students, £2 ($3) children, £9 ($13.50) families. Mon–Sat 10am–5pm. Tube: Russell Sq.

Handel Museum   This is the first composer museum to open in London. George Frederic Handel lived in this town house until his death in 1759, and it was here that he composed "Messiah." Most of his organ concerts were written here, as well as "Israel in Egypt" and "Coronation Anthems." Handel settled in London in 1710 but didn't move to this Georgian house until 1723. The house has been restored to its original 18th-century styling, with furniture and fabrics accurate to the time Handel lived here (not the originals, though). The museum is hung with portraits and prints of Handel, his colleagues, and patrons.

On display are two harpsichords, which are played frequently by professionals and harpsichord students when the museum is open. Precious objects include Mozart's handwritten arrangement of a Handel fugue, and furnishings such as a canopied bedroom from 1720 on loan from the Victoria and Albert Museum.

25 Brook St., W1. ☎ 020/7495-1685. Admission £4.50 ($6.75) adults, £3.50 ($5.25) students, and £2 ($3) children 12 and under. Tues–Sat 10am–6pm (until 8pm Thurs); Sun noon–6pm. Tube: Bond Street.

Samuel Johnson's House ✦   Dr. Johnson and his copyists compiled his famous dictionary in this Queen Anne house, where the lexicographer, poet, essayist, and fiction writer lived from 1748 to 1759. Although Johnson also lived at Staple Inn in Holborn and at a number of other places, the Gough Square house is the only one of his residences remaining in modern London. The 17th-century building has been painstakingly restored, and it's well worth a visit.

After you're done touring the house, you might want to stop in at **Ye Olde Cheshire Cheese,** Wine Court Office Court, 145 Fleet St. (☎ **020/7353-6170**), Johnson's favorite locale. He must have had some lean nights at the pub because by the time he had compiled his dictionary, he'd already spent his advance of 1,500 guineas. G. K. Chesterton, author of *What's Wrong with the World* (1910) and *The Superstition of Divorce* (1920), was also a familiar patron at the pub.

17 Gough Sq., EC4. Walk up New Bridge St. and turn left onto Fleet; Gough Sq. is tiny and hidden, north of Fleet St. ☎ 020/7353-3745. www.drjh.dircon.co.uk. Admission £4 ($6) adults, £3 ($4.50) students and seniors, £1 ($1.50) children, free for children 10 and under. Oct–Apr Mon–Sat 11am–4:45pm; May–Sept Mon–Sat 11am–5:15pm. Tube: Blackfriars or Chancery Lane.

MUSEUMS & GALLERIES

Apsley House, The Wellington Museum ⋆   This was the mansion of the duke of Wellington, the "Iron Duke," one of Britain's greatest generals, who defeated Napoleon at Waterloo. Later, for a short period while he was prime minister, the duke had to have iron shutters fitted to his windows to protect him from a mob outraged by his autocratic opposition to reform. (His unpopularity soon passed, however.)

The house is crammed with art treasures, including three original Velázquez paintings, and military mementos that include the duke's medals and battlefield orders. Apsley House also holds some of the finest silver and porcelain pieces in Europe, displayed in the Plate and China Room. Grateful to Wellington for saving their thrones, European monarchs endowed him with treasures. The collection includes a Sèvres Egyptian service that was intended as a divorce present from Napoléon to Josephine (but she refused it); Louis XVIII eventually presented it to Wellington. The Portuguese Silver Service, created between 1812 and 1816, has been hailed as the single greatest artifact of Portuguese neoclassical silver.

149 Piccadilly, Hyde Park Corner, SW1. ✆ 020/7499-5676. www.vam.ac.uk/collections/apsley. Admission £4.50 ($6.75) adults, £3 ($4.50) seniors, free for children under 18. Tues–Sun 11am–5pm. Tube: Hyde Park Corner.

The BBC Experience   Opened by the queen in 1997, on the 75th anniversary of the BBC, this attraction gives visitors a behind-the-scenes look at "The Beeb."

⟨*Value* Money-Saving Passes

If you're coming to London to pubcrawl, forget doing it cheaply, but if you plan to visit a lot of museums, you can save a lot of money with the **London GoSee Card.** It's valid for admission at many of London's major attractions, including the Apsley House, Barbican Art Gallery, the Shakespeare Globe Theatre, and the Design Museum, plus a lot more. Validity ranges from 3 to 7 days. An adult 3-day card costs £16 ($24), and a 7-day card goes for £26 ($39). Families of two adults and up to four children can purchase a 3-day card for £32 ($48) or a 7-day card for £50 ($75). Cards are sold at British tourist information centers, London Transport centers, airports, and various attractions. For more details, call ✆ 800/223-6108 in the U.S. or ✆ 020/8995-4007 in the UK. or try the Web: www.visitbritain.com.

The **London Pass** provides admission to 60 attractions in and around London, £5 worth of phone calls, "timed" admission at some attractions (bypassing the queues), plus free travel on public transport (buses, tubes, and trains), and a pocket guidebook. It costs £22 ($33) for 1 day, £49 ($73.50) for 3 days or £79 ($118.50) for 6 days (children pay £14/$21, £30/$45, or £42/$63) and includes admission to St. Paul's Cathedral, *HMS Belfast,* the Jewish Museum, and the Thames Barrier Visitor Centre—and many more. Visit the website at www.londonpass. com or call ✆ 870/242-9988. *Tip:* Purchase the pass before you go because passes purchased in London do not include free transportation.

Sights from Knightsbridge to Kensington

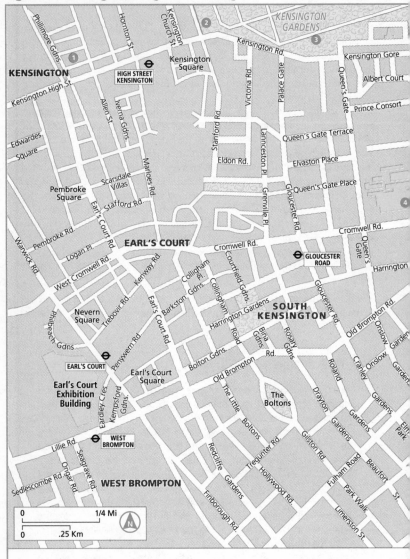

Apsley House, The Wellington Museum **7**

Carlyle's House **11**

Chelsea Physic Garden **10**

Chelsea Royal Hospital **8**

Kensington Gardens **3**

Kensington Palace **2**

Linley Sambourne House **1**

National Army Museum **9**

Natural History Museum **4**

Science Museum **5**

Victoria & Albert Museum **6**

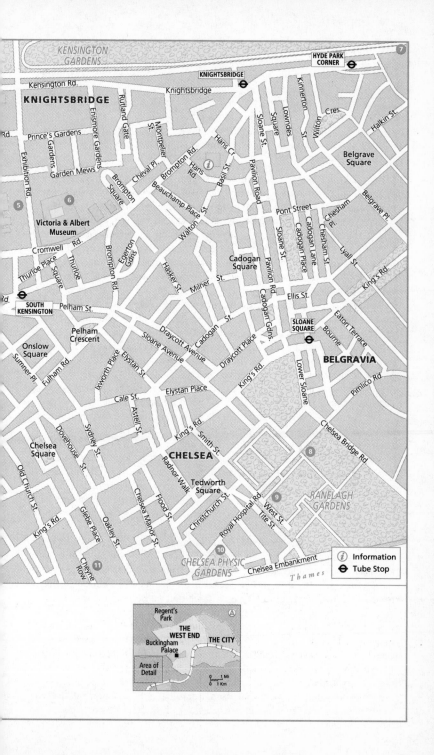

You can go inside the studio to relive important events of the century, make a radio drama in a studio, test your abilities as a sports commentator, watch yourself on television, and edit a scene from the soap opera "EastEnders." Visitors are also taken on a backstage tour, including the news studio, the prop storehouse, and the production galleries. Those looking for souvenirs, books, or videos will find an on-site shop. There is also a lunch cafe.

Television Centre, Wood Lane, W12. ℂ **0870/603-0304.** www.bbc.co.uk/experience. Admission £7.95 ($11.95) adults, £6.95 ($10.45) seniors, £5.95 ($8.95) students, £4.95 ($7.45) children, £21.95 ($32.95) family ticket. Tues–Sun 10am–4:30pm; Mon 11am–4:30pm. Tube: Oxford Circus.

British Library ★★   In December 1996, one of the world's great libraries began moving its collection of some 12 million books, manuscripts, and other items from the British Museum to its very own home in St. Pancras. In the new building, you get modernistic beauty rather than the fading glamour and the ghosts of Karl Marx, Thackeray, and Virginia Woolf of the old library at the British Museum. You are also likely to get the book you want within an hour instead of 3 days. Academics, students, writers, and bookworms from the world over come here. On a recent visit, we sat next to a student researching the history of pubs.

The bright, roomy interior is far more inviting than the rather dull red brick exterior suggests. The writer Alain de Botton likened the exterior to a supermarket, and Prince Charles made it the subject of one of his screeds against modern architecture (he has since taken a private tour, and was much more encouraged, although he did not air these comments as publicly). Still, Colin St. John Wilson, the architect, says he has been delighted by the positive response to his building. The most spectacular room is the Humanities Reading Room, constructed on three levels with daylight filtered through the ceiling.

The fascinating collection includes such items of historic and literary interest as two of the four surviving copies of the Magna Carta (1215), a Gutenberg Bible, Nelson's last letter to Lady Hamilton, and the journals of Captain Cook. Almost every major author—Dickens, Jane Austen, Charlotte Brontë, Keats, and hundreds of others—is represented in the section devoted to English literature. Beneath Roubiliac's 1758 statue of Shakespeare stands a case of documents relating to the Bard, including a mortgage bearing his signature and a copy of the First Folio of 1623. There's also an unrivaled collection of stamps and stamp-related items.

Visitors can view the Diamond Sutra, dating from 868, and said to be the oldest surviving printed book. Using headphones set around the room, you can also hear thrilling audio snippets such as James Joyce reading a passage from *Finnegans Wake.* Curiosities include the earliest known tape of a birdcall, dating from 1889. Particularly intriguing is an exhibition called "Turning the Pages." You can, for example, electronically read a complete Leonardo da Vinci notebook, putting your hands on a special computer screen that flips from one page to another. There is a copy of *The Canterbury Tales* from 1410, and even manuscripts from *Beowulf* (ca. 1000). Illuminated texts from some of the oldest known Biblical displays include the Codex Sinaitticus and Codex Alexandrius, 3rd-century Greek gospels. In the Historical Documents section are letters by everybody from Henry VIII to Napoleon, from Elizabeth I to Churchill. In the music displays, you can seek out original sheet music by Beethoven, Handel, Stravinsky, and Lennon and McCartney. An entire day spent here will only scratch the surface.

Walking tours of the library cost £5 ($7.50) for adults and £4 ($6) for seniors, students, and children. They are conducted Wednesday through Monday at 3pm, Tuesday at 6:30pm, with an extra tour on Sunday at 3pm. Reservations are advised 3 weeks in advance.

96 Euston Rd., NW1. © 020/7412-7332. www.bl.uk. Free admission. Mon and Wed–Sat 9:30am–6pm; Tues 9:30am–8pm; Sun 11am–5pm. Tube: King's Cross/St. Pancras, or Euston.

Courtauld Gallery ★★ Although surprisingly little known, the Courtauld contains a fabulous wealth of paintings. It has one of the world's greatest collections of Impressionist works outside Paris. There are French Impressionists and post-Impressionists, with masterpieces by Monet, Manet, Degas, Renoir, Cézanne, van Gogh, and Gauguin. The gallery also has a superb collection of old-master paintings and drawings, with works by Rubens, Michelangelo, and Tiepolo; plus early-Italian paintings, ivories, and majolica; the Lee collection of old masters; and early-20th-century English and French paintings, as well as 20th-century British paintings.

Like the Frick Collection in New York, it's a superb display, a visual feast in a jewel-like setting. We come here at least once every season to revisit one painting in particular: Manet's exquisite *A Bar at the Folies-Bérgere*. Many paintings are displayed without glass, giving the gallery a more intimate feel than most.

The Hermitage of St. Petersburg is opening a series of eight rooms here for rotating exhibits from its vast collections, opening with the treasures of Catherine the Great, including some of her jewels, furniture, and portraits.

Somerset House, The Strand, WC2. © 020/7848-2526. www.courtauld.ac.uk. Admission £4 ($6) adults, £3 ($4.50) students, free for children under 18. Daily 10am–6pm; last admission 5:15pm. Tube: Temple or Covent Garden.

Design Museum The Design Museum is a showcase of modern design—kind of like Pottery Barn without the price tags. It's the only museum in Europe that explains why and how mass-produced objects work and look the way they do, and how design contributes to the quality of our lives. The collection of objects includes cars, furniture, domestic appliances, graphics, and ceramics, as well as changing displays of new products and prototypes from around the world. The cafe offers panoramic views of Tower Bridge and the Thames.

28 Shad Thames, SE1. © 020/7940-8790. Admission £6 ($9) adults, £4 ($6) children, £16 ($24) family ticket. Daily 10am–6pm. Tube: Tower Bridge or London Bridge.

Estorick Collection of Modern Italian Art Long dismissed as "unfashionable," early-20th-century Italian art is given a showcase in London. Eric Estorick (1913–93) was an American political scientist and writer who was a passionate collector. The year he died, he established a foundation to display his collection and to stage temporary loan exhibitions. His collection has been hailed as one of the finest of early-20th-century Italian art anywhere in the world. Estorick had a remarkable eye and prophetic judgment in art when he began his collection, although his treasure trove was dismissed by the art snobs of his day. Powerful images by the main protagonists of the early 20th century Italian avant-garde Futurist movement, including Balla, Boccioni, Carrá, Serverini, and Russolo, are on permanent view. The collection includes works by figurative artists like Modigliani, Sironi, and Campigli, plus the metaphysical painter de Chirico.

39A Canonbury Sq., N1. © 020/7704-9522. www.estorickcollection.com. Admission £3.50 ($5.25) adults, £2.50 ($3.75) seniors and children. Wed–Sat 11am–6pm; Sun noon–5pm. Tube: Victoria Line to Highbury and Islington.

Florence Nightingale Museum   The life and work of one of England's most influential women of the 1800s is celebrated here. You learn that her most famous accomplishment—nursing soldiers during the Crimean War—was only a part of a career spanning half a century. Nightingale did everything from raise the image of the British soldier (from a brawling lowlife to a heroic working man) to making nursing a respectable profession. Before the "Lady with the Lamp," nursing was seen as a job fit only for prostitutes.

In 1896 Nightingale "retired to her bed," but didn't slow down. She continued to write on public health. Much of her advice is still valid today. When she died in 1910 at the age of 90, she had become so reclusive that the general public assumed she was already dead.

St. Thomas' Hospital, 2 Lambeth Palace Rd., SE1. ℂ 020/7620-0374. www.florence-nightingale.co.uk. Admission £4.80 ($7.20) adults, £3.60 ($5.40) seniors, children, and persons with disabilities. Mon–Fri 10am–5pm; Sat–Sun 11:30am–4:30pm. Tube: Westminster.

Geffrye Museum ★   Those who'd like a preview of British interiors and lifestyles of the past 4 centuries, head here to a series of restored 18th-century almshouses that escaped Hitler's Blitz. Period rooms are arranged chronologically, allowing you to follow changing tastes in the days of the Empire. You'll see the development of furnishings and objets d'art in English middle-class homes. The collection is rich in Jacobean and Georgian interiors and strongest in the Victorian period. In the 20th century, you'll see the richness of Art Deco and the bleakness of the utilitarian designs that followed in the aftermath of World War II. Newer galleries showcase the decor of the latter 20th century.

Originally, in 1715, these almshouses belonged to the Ironmongers' Company. The architecture alone is worth a visit. Gardens in front attract much attention, especially the herb garden. There is also a design center and a cafe/restaurant.

Kingsland Rd., Shoreditch E2. ℂ 020/7739-9893. www.geffrye-museum.org.uk. Free admission. Tues–Sat 10am–5pm; Sun and bank holidays noon–5pm. Closed Good Friday, Dec. 24–26, New Year's Day. Gardens open Apr–Oct. Tube: Liverpool St. then bus 149 or 242. Old St. then bus 243.

Gilbert Collection   One of the most important bequests ever made to England went on view in a new museum in 2000. Somerset House has become the permanent home for the Gilbert Collection of decorative arts. Sir Arthur Gilbert made his gift of gold, silver, mosaics, and gold snuffboxes to the nation in 1996, at which time the value was estimated at £75 million. The collection of some 800 objects in each of three fields (gold and silver, mosaics, and gold snuffboxes) is among the most distinguished in the world. The array of mosaics is among the most comprehensive ever gathered, with Roman and Florentine examples dating from the 16th to the 19th centuries. The gold and silver collection has exceptional breadth, ranging from the 15th to the 19th centuries, spanning India to South America. It is strong in masterpieces of great 18th-century silversmiths, such as Paul de Lamerie. The gallery also displays one of the most representative collections of gold snuffboxes in the world, with some 200 examples. Some of the snuffboxes were owned by Louis XV or Napoleon.

Somerset House, The Strand WC2. ℂ 020/7240-9400. Admission £5 ($7.50) adults, £4 ($6) seniors, under 18 free. Daily 10am–6pm. Tube: Temple, Covent Garden, or Charing Cross.

Guildhall Art Gallery ★   In 1999, Queen Elizabeth opened a new £70 million gallery in the City, a continuation of the original gallery, launched in 1886, that was burned down in a severe air raid in May 1941. Many famous and much-loved pictures, which for years were known only through temporary exhibitions and reproductions, are again available for the public to see in a permanent setting. The new gallery can display only 250 of the 4,000 treasures it owns. The art ranges from classical to modern. A curiosity is the huge double-height wall built to accommodate Britain's largest independent oil painting, John Singleton Copley's *The Defeat of the Floating Batteries at Gibraltar, September 1782*. The Corporation of London in the City owns these works and has been collecting them since the 17th century. The most popular art is in the Victorian collection, including such well-known favorites as Millais's *My First Sermon* and *My Second Sermon*, and Landseer's *The First Leap*. There is also a landscape of Salisbury Cathedral by John Constable. Since World War II, all paintings acquired by the gallery concentrate on London subjects.

Guildhall Yard, EC ℭ 020/7332-3700. www.cityoflondon.gov.uk. Admission £2.50 ($3.75). Mon–Sat 10am–5pm; Sun noon–4pm. Tube: Bank, St. Paul's, Mansion House, or Moorgate.

Hayward Gallery   Opened by Elizabeth II in 1968, this gallery presents a changing program of major contemporary and historic exhibits. It's managed by the South Bank Board, which also operates the Royal Festival Hall, the Queen Elizabeth Hall, and the Purcell Room. Each exhibition is accompanied by a variety of activities, including tours, workshops, lectures, and publications. The gallery closes between exhibitions, so call before crossing the Thames.

On the South Bank, SE1. ℭ 020/7960-4242, or 020/7261-0127 for recorded information. www.hayward gallery.org.uk. Admission £6–£8 ($9–$12) adults, £4–£5 ($6–$7.50) students, seniors, and children, free for children under 12, £14 ($21) family ticket. Fee varies according to exhibitions; children often admitted half price. Thurs–Mon 10am–6pm; Tues–Wed 10am–8pm. Tube: Waterloo or Embankment.

Hermitage Rooms at Somerset House ★★★   This is a virtual outstation of St. Petersburg's State Hermitage Museum, which owns a great deal of the treasure trove left over from the czars, including possessions of art-collecting Catherine the Great. Now you don't have to journey all the way to Russia to see some of Europe's great treasures, acquired over a period of 3 centuries by Russian czars. The exhibitions will rotate, and you'll get to see such treasures as medals, jewelry, portraits, porcelain, clocks, and furniture from the Hermitage Museum in St. Petersburg. There will be a rotating "visiting masterpiece" in addition to the other collections. Some items that amused us on our first visit (and you are likely to see similar novelties) was a wig made entirely out of silver thread for Catherine the Great; a Wedgwood "Green Frog" table service, and two Chinese silver filigree toilet sets. The rooms themselves have been designed in the style of the Winter Palace at St. Petersburg. Because this exhibit attracts so much interest, tickets should be purchased in advance. Tickets are available from Ticketmaster at ℭ **020/7413-3398** (24 hr.). You can book online at www.ticketmaster.co.uk. Somerset House also contains the priceless Gilbert Collection (p. 256).

The Strand, WC2. ℭ 020/7845-4600. Admission £6 ($9) adults, £4 ($6) students and seniors. Mon–Sat 10am–6pm; Sun noon–6pm. Tube: Temple, Covent Garden, or Charing Cross.

Imperial War Museum ☆   One of the few major sights south of the Thames, this museum occupies 1 city block the size of an army barracks, greeting you with 38cm (15-in.) guns from the battleships *Resolution* and *Ramillies*. The large domed building, constructed in 1815, was the former Bethlehem Royal Hospital for the insane, known as "Bedlam."

A wide range of weapons and equipment is on display, along with models, decorations, uniforms, posters, photographs, and paintings. You can see a Mark V tank, a Battle of Britain Spitfire, and a German one-man submarine, as well as a rifle carried by Lawrence of Arabia. In the Documents Room, you can view the self-styled "political testament" that Hitler dictated in the chancellery bunker in the closing days of World War II, witnessed by henchmen Joseph Goebbels and Martin Bormann, as well as the famous "peace in our time" agreement that Neville Chamberlain brought back from Munich in 1938. (Of his signing the agreement, Hitler later said, "[Chamberlain] was a nice old man, so I decided to give him my autograph.") It's a world of espionage and clandestine warfare in the major new permanent exhibit known as the "Secret War Exhibition," where you can discover the truth behind the image of James Bond—and find out why the real secret war is even stranger and more fascinating than fiction. Displays include many items never before seen in public: coded messages, forged documents, secret wirelesses, and equipment used by spies from World War I to the present day.

Public film shows take place on weekends at 3pm and on certain weekdays during school holidays and on public holidays.

One of the latest additions opened in June 2000. Supported by a £12.6 million grant from the Heritage Lottery Fund, a permanent Holocaust exhibition occupies two floors. Through original artifacts, documents, film, and photographs, some lent to the museum by former concentration camps in Germany and Poland, the display poignantly relates the story of Nazi Germany and the persecution of the Jews. In addition, the exhibition brings attention to the persecution of other groups under Hitler's regime, including Poles, Soviet prisoners of war, people with disabilities, and homosexuals. Among the items on display are a funeral cart used in the Warsaw Ghetto, a section of railcar from Belgium, a sign from the extermination camp at Belzec, and the letters of an 8-year old French Jewish boy who hid in an orphanage before being sent to Auschwitz.

Lambeth Rd., SE1. ℂ 020/7416-5000. www.iwm.org.uk. Free admission. Daily 10am–6pm. Tube: Baker Line to Lambeth North or Elephant and Castle.

Institute of Contemporary Arts   London's liveliest cultural program takes place in this temple to the avant-garde, launched in 1947. It keeps Londoners and others up-to-date on the latest in the worlds of cinema, theater, photography, painting, sculpture, and other visual and performing arts. Foreign or experimental movies are shown, and special tributes—perhaps a retrospective of the films of Rainer Werner Fassbinder—are often the order of the day. The classics and cult favorites are frequently dusted off here. On Saturday and Sunday at 3pm, the cinema offers screenings for kids. Sometimes well-known writers and artists speak here, which makes the low cost of membership even more enticing. Experimental plays are also presented. Sun Microsystems, the American Internet pioneer, donated £2 million to build a state-of-the-art New Media Centre in 1998. The photo galleries, showing the latest from British and foreign photographers, probably wouldn't win the approval of people who set up "decency" panels for the arts.

The Mall, SW1. ℂ 020/7930-3647. www.ica.org.uk. Admission £1.50 ($2.25) Mon–Fri, £2.50 ($3.75) Sat–Sun adults; £1.50 ($2.25) Mon–Fri, £1 ($1.50) Sat–Sun students. Galleries daily noon–7:30pm; bookstore daily noon–9pm. Film screenings daily. Tube: Piccadilly Circus or Charing Cross.

Jewish Museum   This museum tells the story of Jewish life in Britain. Arriving at the time of the Norman Conquest, Jews survived in England until King Edward I forced them out in 1290. From that time, no Jews (or at least no known Jews) lived in Britain until a small community returned in 1656 during the reign of Elizabeth I. The museum has recently been awarded designated status by the Museums and Galleries Commission for its outstanding collection of Jewish ceremonial art. On display are silver Torah bells made in London and two loving cups presented by the Spanish and Portuguese Synagogue to the lord mayor in the 18th century. The museum also sponsors **walking tours of Jewish London.**

The Jewish Museum has another location in Finchley, which focuses attention on Jewish immigration and settlement in London. On display are reconstructions of East End tailoring and furniture workshops. Holocaust education is also a fundamental feature of this museum. The Finchley branch is open Monday through Thursday and Sunday from 10:30am to 5pm, admission is £2 ($3) adults, £1 ($1.50) seniors and students. For further information, call ℂ **020/8349-1143.**

129-131 Albert St., Camden Town, NW1. ℂ 020/7284-1997. www.jewmusm.ort.org. Main branch admission £3.50 ($5.25) adults, £2.50 ($3.75) seniors, £1.50 ($2.25) children. Main branch: Sun 10am–5pm, Mon–Thurs 10am–4pm. Closed Fri, Sat, bank holidays, and Jewish festivals. Tube: Camden Town or Mornington Crescent.

Linley Sambourne House ⋆   You'll step back into the days of Queen Victoria when you visit this house, which has remained unchanged for more than a century. Part of a terrace built in the late 1860s, this five-story Suffolk brick structure was the home of Linley Sambourne, a legendary cartoonist for *Punch*. In the entrance hall, you see a mixture of styles and clutter that typifies Victorian decor, with a plush portière, a fireplace valance, stained glass, and a large set of antlers vying for attention. The drawing room alone contains an incredible number of Victorian items.

18 Stafford Terrace, W8. ℂ 020/8994-1019. www.rbkc.gov.uk. Admission £3.50 ($5.25) adults, £2 ($3) children 16 and under, £10 ($15) family ticket. Mar–Oct Wed 10am–4pm (last admission 3:30pm); Sun. guided tours only (2:15, 3:15, and 4:15pm). Closed Nov–Feb. Tube: High St. Kensington.

London Transport Museum ⋆ *Kids*   A collection of nearly 2 centuries of historic vehicles is displayed in a splendid Victorian building that formerly housed the Flower Market at Covent Garden. The museum shows how London's transport system evolved, and a representative collection of road vehicles includes a reconstruction of George Shillibeer's Omnibus of 1829. A steam locomotive that ran on the world's first underground railway, a knifeboard horse bus, London's first trolleybus, and the Feltham tram are also of particular interest.

Originally an operational Tube depot, the Depot at Acton Town is now a branch of the main museum, containing 370,000 items not currently on display at the Covent Garden site, ranging from station signs and posters to transportation memorabilia. Highlights include the first Routemaster bus and a spiral escalator from 1906. The Depot will be open to the public on a limited basis through guided tours. Call ℂ **020/7379 6344** to find out when the Depot is open, and to book a tour. The Depot is located at Gunnersbury Road, Acton Town. The Tube stop is Acton Town.

The Piazza, Covent Garden, WC2. ℂ 020/7379-6344, or 020/7565-7299 for recorded info. www.ltmuseum. co.uk. Admission £5.95 ($8.95) adults, children under 16 accompanied by an adult admitted free. Sat–Thurs 10am–6pm; Fri 11am–6pm (last entrance at 5:15pm). Tube: Covent Garden.

Madame Tussaud's ⋆ *Kids*   Madame Tussaud's is not so much a wax museum as an enclosed amusement park. A weird, moving, sometimes terrifying (to children) collage of exhibitions, panoramas, and stage settings, it manages to be many things to many people, most of the time.

Madame Tussaud attended the court of Versailles and learned her mask-making craft in France. She personally took the death masks from the guillotined heads of Louis XVI and Marie Antoinette (still among the exhibits). She moved her museum from Paris to England in 1802. Her exhibition has been imitated, but never with the realism and imagination on hand here. Madame herself molded the features of Benjamin Franklin, whom she met in Paris. All the rest—from George Washington to John F. Kennedy, Mary Queen of Scots to Sylvester Stallone—have been subjects for the same painstaking (and breathtaking) replication.

In the well-known Chamber of Horrors—a kind of underground dungeon—are all kinds of instruments of death, along with figures of their victims. The shadowy presence of Jack the Ripper lurks in the gloom as you walk through a Victorian London street. Present-day criminals are portrayed within the confines of prison. The latest attraction to open here is "The Spirit of London," a musical ride that depicts 400 years of London's history, using special effects that include audio-animatronic figures. Visitors take "time-taxis" that allow them to see and hear "Shakespeare" as he writes and speaks lines, be received by Queen Elizabeth I, and feel and smell the Great Fire of 1666 that destroyed London.

We've seen these exhibitions so many times that we're well over them, but we still remember how fascinated we were the first time we were taken here as kids.

Insider's Tip: To avoid the long lines, sometimes more than an hour in summer, call in advance and reserve a ticket for fast pickup at the entrance. If you don't want to bother with that, be aggressive and form a group of 9 people waiting in the queue. With 9, you constitute a group and can go in almost at once through the "group door." Otherwise, go when the gallery first opens or late in the afternoon when crowds have thinned.

Marylebone Rd., NW1. ℂ 0870/400-30000. www.madame-tussauds.com. Admission £11.50 ($17.25) adults, £9 ($13.50) seniors, £8 ($12) children under 16, free for children under 5. Combination tickets including the new planetarium £13.95 ($20.95) adults, £10.80 ($16.20) seniors, £8 ($12) children under 16. Mon–Fri 10am–5:30pm; Sat–Sun 9:30am–5:30pm. Tube: Baker St.

Museum of London ★★ In London's Barbican district, near St. Paul's Cathedral and overlooking the city's Roman and medieval walls, this museum traces the history of London from prehistoric times to the 20th century through archeological finds; paintings and prints; social, industrial, and historic artifacts; and costumes, maps, and models. Exhibits are arranged so that you can begin and end your chronological stroll through 250,000 years at the main entrance to the museum. The museum's pièce de résistance is the Lord Mayor's Coach, a gilt-and-scarlet fairy-tale coach built in 1757 and weighing in at 3 tons, but you can also see the Great Fire of London in living color and sound; the death mask of Oliver Cromwell; cell doors from Newgate Prison, made famous by Charles Dickens; and most amazing of all, a shop counter showing pre–World War II prices. Early in 2002, the museum unveiled its latest permanent gallery, occupying an entire floor. Called the World City Gallery, the exhibit examines life in London between 1789 and 1914, the beginning of World War I. Some 2,000 objects are on view.

150 London Wall, EC2. ℂ 020/7600-3699. www.museumoflondon.org.uk. Free admission. Mon–Sat 10am–5:50pm; Sun noon–5:50pm. Tube: St. Paul's or Barbican.

National Army Museum ★ *Kids* The National Army Museum occupies a building adjoining the Royal Hospital, a home for retired soldiers. Whereas the Imperial War Museum is concerned with wars of the 20th century, the National

Army Museum tells the colorful story of British armies from 1485 on. Here you'll find uniforms worn by British soldiers in every corner of the world, plus weapons and other gear, flags, and medals. Even the skeleton of Napoleon's favorite charger is here. Also on display are Florence Nightingale's jewelry, the telephone switchboard from Hitler's headquarters (captured in 1945), and Orders and Medals of HRH Duke of Windsor. A more recent gallery, "The Rise of the Redcoats," contains exhibitions detailing the life of the British soldier from 1485 to 1793. Included in the exhibit are displays on the English Civil War and the American War of Independence.

Royal Hospital Rd., SW3. ✆ 020/7730-0717. www.national-army-museum.ac.uk. Free admission. Daily 10am–5:30pm. Closed Good Friday, first Mon in May, and Dec 24–26. Tube: Sloane Sq.

Natural History Museum ✮✮ Kids
This is the home of the national collections of living and fossil plants, animals, and minerals, with many magnificent specimens on display. Exciting exhibits designed to encourage people of all ages to learn about natural history include "Human Biology—An Exhibition of Ourselves," "Our Place in Evolution," "Origin of the Species," "Creepy Crawlies," and "Discovering Mammals." The Mineral Gallery displays marvelous examples of crystals and gemstones. Visit the Meteorite Pavilion, which exhibits fragments of rock that have crashed into the earth, some from the farthest reaches of the galaxy. What attracts the most attention is the dinosaur exhibit, displaying 14 complete skeletons. The center of the show depicts a trio of full-size robotic Deinonychus enjoying a freshly killed Tenontosaurus. The latest addition is "Earth Galleries," an exhibition outlining humankind's relationship with planet Earth. Here, in the exhibition "Earth Today and Tomorrow," visitors are invited to explore the planet's dramatic history from the big bang to its inevitable death.

Cromwell Rd., SW7. ✆ 020/7942-5000. www.nhm.ac.uk. Free admission. Mon–Sat 10am–5:50pm; Sun 11am–5:50pm. Tube: South Kensington.

Percival David Foundation of Chinese Art ✮
This foundation displays the greatest collection of Chinese ceramics outside China. Approximately 1,700 ceramic objects reflect Chinese court taste from the 10th to 18th centuries. Many pieces of exceptional beauty are included. An extraordinary collection of stoneware from the Song (960–1279) and Yuan (1279–1368) dynasties includes examples of rare Ru and Guan wares. Among the justifiably famous blue and white porcelains are two unique temple vases, dated by inscription to A.D. 1351. A wide variety of polychrome wares are also represented; they include examples of the delicate doucai wares from the Chenghua period (1465–87) as well as a remarkable group of 18th-century porcelains.

53 Gordon Sq., WC1. ✆ 020/7387-3909. Free admission; donations encouraged. £5 ($7.50) per person for a guided tour of 10–20 people. Admission to the library must be arranged with the curator ahead of time. There is a charge for use of the library. Mon–Fri 10:30am–5pm. Tube: Russell Sq. or Euston Sq.

Royal Academy of Arts
Established in 1768, this organization included Sir Joshua Reynolds, Thomas Gainsborough, and Benjamin West among its founding members. Since its beginning, each member has had to donate a work of art, and so over the years the academy has built up a sizable collection. The outstanding treasure is Michelangelo's beautiful relief of *Madonna and Child.* The annual Summer Exhibition has been held for more than 200 years; see the "London Calendar of Events" in chapter 3 for details.

Burlington House, Piccadilly, W1. ✆ 020/7300-8000. www.royalacademy.org.uk. Admission varies, depending on the exhibition. Sat–Thurs 10am–6pm (last admission 5:30pm); Fri 10am–10pm (last admission 9:30pm). Tube: Piccadilly Circus or Green Park.

Royal Mews ★★   This is where you can get a close look at Her Majesty's State Coach, built in 1761 to the designs of Sir William Chambers and decorated with paintings by Cipriani. Traditionally drawn by eight gray horses, it was formerly used by sovereigns when they traveled to open Parliament and on other state occasions; Queen Elizabeth traveled in it to her 1953 coronation and in 1977 for her Silver Jubilee Procession. The queen's carriage horses are also housed here, as well as other state coaches, and you can pay a visit to the royal horses.

Buckingham Palace, Buckingham Palace Rd., SW1. ℂ 020/7839-1377. www.royal.gov.uk. Admission £5 ($7.50) adults, £4 ($6) seniors, £2.50 ($3.75) children 5–17, free for children under 5. Daily 11am–3:15pm. Tube: Green Park or Victoria.

Science Museum ★★★ *Kids*   This museum traces the development of science and industry and their influences on everyday life. These collections are among the largest, most comprehensive, and most significant anywhere. On display are Stephenson's original rocket and the tiny prototype railroad engine. You can also see Whittle's original jet engine and the Apollo 10 space module. The King George III Collection of scientific instruments is the highlight of a gallery on science in the 18th century. Health Matters is a permanent gallery on modern medicine. The museum has two hands-on galleries, as well as working models and video displays.

Insider's Tip: A large addition to this museum explores such topics as genetics, digital technology, and artificial intelligence. Four floors of a new Welcome Wing shelter half a dozen exhibition areas and a 450-seat Imax theater. One exhibition explores everything from the use of drugs in sports to how engineers observe sea life with robotic submarines. On an upper floor, visitors can learn how DNA was used to identify living relatives of the Bleadon Man, a 2,000-year-old Iron Age Man. On the third floor is the computer that Tim Berners-Lee used to design the World Wide Web outside Geneva, writing the first software for it in 1990.

Exhibition Rd., SW7. ℂ 020/870-4868. www.sciencemuseum.org.uk. Free admission. Daily 10am–6pm. Tube: South Kensington.

Shakespeare's Globe Theatre & Exhibition ★   This is a recent recreation of what was probably the most important public theater ever built, Shakespeare's Globe—on the exact site where many of Shakespeare's plays opened. The late American filmmaker Sam Wanamaker worked for some 20 years to raise funds to re-create the theater as it existed in Elizabethan times, thatched roof and all. A fascinating exhibit tells the story of the Globe's construction, using the material (including goat hair in the plaster), techniques, and craftsmanship of 400 years ago. The new Globe isn't an exact replica: It seats 1,500 patrons, not the 3,000 who regularly squeezed in during the early 1600s, and this thatched roof has been specially treated with a fire retardant. Guided tours of the facility are offered throughout the day.

See "The Play's the Thing: London's Theater Scene" in chapter 9, for details on attending a play here.

New Globe Walk, Southwark, SE1. ℂ 020/7902-1500. www.shakespeares-globe.org. Exhibition and tour admission £8 ($12) adults, £5.50 ($8.25) children 15 and under, £6.50 ($9.75) seniors and students. Daily 10am–6pm (guided tours every 30 min. or so). Tube: Mansion House or London Bridge.

Sherlock Holmes Museum   Where but on Baker Street would there be a museum displaying mementos of this famed fictional detective? Museum officials call it "the world's most famous address" (although 10 Downing Street is a rival for the title); it was here that mystery writer Sir Arthur Conan Doyle created a residence for Sherlock Holmes and his faithful Dr. Watson. These sleuths "lived" here from 1881 to 1904. In Victorian rooms, you can examine a range of exhibits, including published Holmes adventures and letters written to Holmes. This is a very commercial and artificial museum, but Holmes buffs don't seem to mind.

221B Baker St., NW1. © 020/7935-8866. www.sherlock-holmes.co.uk. Admission £6 ($9) adults, £4 ($6) children, free for children under 7. Daily 9:30am–6:30pm. Tube: Baker St.

Sir John Soane's Museum ⭐ This is the former home of Sir John Soane (1753–1837), an architect who rebuilt the Bank of England (although not the present structure). With his multiple levels, fool-the-eye mirrors, flying arches, and domes, Soane was a master of perspective and a genius of interior space (his picture gallery, for example, is filled with three times the number of paintings that a room of similar dimensions would be likely to hold). One prize of the collection is William Hogarth's satirical series *The Rake's Progress*, which includes his much-reproduced *Orgy and The Election*, a satire on mid-18th-century politics. Soane also filled his house with classical sculpture: The sarcophagus of Pharaoh Seti I, found in a burial chamber in the Valley of the Kings, is here. Also on display are architectural drawings from Soane's collection of 30,000.

13 Lincoln's Inn Fields, WC2. © 020/7405-2107. Free admission (donations invited). Tues–Sat 10am–5pm; first Tues of each month 6–9pm. Tours given Sat at 2:30pm; £3 ($4.50) tickets distributed at 2pm on a first-come, first-served basis (group tours by appointment only). Tube: Holborn.

Theatre Museum This branch of the Victoria and Albert Museum contains the national collections of the performing arts, encompassing theater, ballet, opera, music hall, pantomime, puppets, circus, and rock and pop music. Daily makeup demonstrations and costume workshops use costumes from the Royal Shakespeare Company and the Royal National Theatre. The museum also has a major Diaghilev archive.

Russell St., WC2. © 020/7943-4700. www.theatremuseum.org. Admission £5 ($7.50) adults, £3 ($4.50) seniors and students, free for children under 16. Tues–Sun 10am–6pm. Tube: Covent Garden or Leicester Sq.

Wallace Collection ⭐⭐ Located in a palatial setting (the modestly described "town house" of the late Lady Wallace), this collection is a contrasting array of art and armaments. The art collection (mostly French) includes works by Watteau, Boucher, Fragonard, and Greuze, as well as such classics as Frans Hals's *Laughing Cavalier* and Rembrandt's portrait of his son Titus. The paintings of the Dutch, English, Spanish, and Italian schools are outstanding. The collection also contains important 18th-century French decorative art, including furniture from a number of royal palaces, Sèvres porcelain, and gold boxes. The European and Asian armaments, on the ground floor, are works of art in their own right: superb inlaid suits of armor, some obviously for parade rather than battle, with more businesslike swords, halberds, and magnificent Persian scimitars. The Heritage Lottery Fund and Christie's in London have awarded a £7.5 million grant to the gallery's Centenary Project for the addition of a museum.

Manchester Sq., W1. © 020/7563-9500. www.the-wallace-collection.org.uk. Free admission. Mon–Sat 10am–5pm; Sun noon–5pm. Tube: Bond St. or Baker St.

PARKS & GARDENS

London's parks are the most advanced system of "green lungs" in any large city on the globe. Although not as rigidly maintained as those of Paris (Britons traditionally prefer a more natural look), they're cared for with a loving and lavishly artistic hand that puts their American equivalents to shame.

The largest of the central London parks is **Hyde Park** ✶✶ (Tube: Marble Arch, Hyde Park Corner, or Lancaster Gate), once a favorite deer-hunting ground of Henry VIII. With the adjoining Kensington Gardens (see below), it covers 246 hectares (615 acres) of central London with velvety lawns interspersed with ponds, flowerbeds, and trees. Running through its width is a 16.5-hectare (41-acre) lake known as the **Serpentine,** where you can row, sail model boats, or swim (provided you don't mind sub-Florida water temperatures). **Rotten Row,** a 2.5km (1½-mile) sand riding track, attracts some skilled equestrians on Sunday. You can rent a paddleboat or a rowboat from the boathouse (open Mar–Oct) on the north side of **Hyde Park's Serpentine** (© 020/7262-1330).

At the northeastern tip, near Marble Arch, is **Speakers' Corner.** Since 1855 (before the legal right to assembly was guaranteed), people have been getting on their soapboxes about any and every subject under the sky. In the past you might have heard Karl Marx, Frederick Engels, or Lenin, certainly William Morris and George Orwell. Hecklers, often aggressive, are part of the fun. Anyone can speak; just don't blaspheme, use obscene language, or start a riot.

Blending with Hyde Park and bordering on the grounds of Kensington Palace, well-manicured **Kensington Gardens** (Tube: High Street Kensington or Queensway) contains the famous statue of Peter Pan, with bronze rabbits that toddlers are always trying to kidnap. It's also home to that Victorian extravaganza, the Albert Memorial. The Orangery is an ideal place to take afternoon tea (p. 211).

East of Hyde Park, across Piccadilly, stretch **Green Park** ✶ (Tube: Green Park) and **St. James's Park** ✶ (Tube: St. James's Park), forming an almost unbroken chain of landscaped beauty. They are ideal for picnics; you'll find it hard to believe that this was once a festering swamp near a leper hospital. There's a romantic lake stocked with ducks and some surprising pelicans, descendants of the pair that the Russian ambassador presented to Charles II in 1662.

Regent's Park ✶✶✶ (Tube: Regent's Park or Baker Street) covers most of the district of that name, north of Baker Street and Marylebone Road. Designed by the 18th-century genius John Nash to surround a palace for the prince regent (the palace never materialized), this is the most classically beautiful of London's parks. Its core is a rose garden planted around a small lake alive with waterfowl and spanned by Japanese bridges; in early summer, the rose perfume in the air is as heady as wine. The park is home to the **Open-Air Theatre** (p. 308) and the **London Zoo** (see "Especially for Kids," below). As at all the local parks, hundreds of chairs are scattered around the lawns, waiting for sunbathers. The deck-

---

⟨Tips⟩ Where to In-Line Skate

London's parks are great places to skate. Rental skates are available at **Slick Willies,** 41 Kensington High Street, W8 (© 020/7937-3824; Tube: High Street Kensington) costing £10 ($15) for skates and wrist guards. A £100 ($150) deposit is required, which can be imprinted on a credit card. Hours are Monday through Saturday from 10am to 6pm, Sunday from noon to 5pm.

chair attendants, who collect a small fee, are mostly college students on break. Rowboats and sailing dinghies are available in **Regent's Park** (© **020/ 7486-4759**). Sailing and canoeing cost around £6 ($9) for 1½ hours.

Chelsea Physic Garden, 66 Royal Hospital Rd., SW3 (© **020/7352-5646;** www.cpgarden.demon.co.uk; Tube: Sloane Square), founded in 1673 by the Worshipful Society of Apothecaries, is the second-oldest surviving botanical garden in England. Sir Hans Sloane, doctor to George II, required the apothecaries of the empire to develop 50 plant species a year for presentation to the Royal Society. The objective was to grow plants for medicinal study. Plant specimens and even trees arrived at the gardens by barge, many to grow in English soil for the first time. Cottonseed from this garden launched an industry in the new colony of Georgia. Some 7,000 plants still grow here, everything from the pomegranate to the willow pattern tree; there's even exotic cork oak, as well as England's earliest rock garden. The garden is open April through November, Wednesday from noon to 5pm and Sunday from 2 to 6pm. Admission is £4 ($6) for adults, £2 ($3) for children 5 to 15 and students. The garden is a perfect setting for a well-recommended afternoon tea—you can carry your cuppa on promenades through the garden (p. 211).

Battersea Park, SW11 (© **020/8871-7530;** Tube: Sloane Square), is a vast patch of woodland, lakes, and lawns on the south bank of the Thames, opposite Chelsea Embankment, between Albert Bridge and Chelsea Bridge. Formerly known as Battersea Fields, the park was laid out between 1852 and 1858 on an old dueling ground. (The most famous duel was between Lord Winchelsea and the Duke of Wellington in 1829.) There's a lake for boating, a deer field with fenced-in deer and wild birds, and tennis and soccer areas. There's a children's zoo, open from Easter to late September, daily from 10am to 5pm and weekends only in winter, from 1 to 3pm. The park's architectural highlight is the Peace Pagoda, built by Japanese craftspeople in cooperation with British architects. The stone and wood pagoda was dedicated in 1986 to the now-defunct Council of Greater London by an order of Japanese monks. The park is open from dawn to dusk. From the Sloane Square Tube stop, it's a brisk 15-minute walk to the park, or you can pick up bus no. 137 (get off at the first stop after the bus crosses the Thames).

The hub of England's—and perhaps the world's—horticulture is in Surrey, at the **Royal Botanic Gardens at Kew** (also known as Kew Gardens). See "Attractions on the Outskirts," below.

4 Exploring London by Boat

All of London's history and development is linked with the River Thames: This winding ribbon of water connects the city with the sea, from which London first drew its wealth and power. The Thames was London's chief commercial thoroughfare and royal highway. Every royal procession was undertaken on gorgeously painted and gilded barges (which you can still see at the National Maritime Museum in Greenwich). Important state prisoners were delivered to the Tower of London by water, eliminating the chance of an ambush in one of the narrow, crooked alleys surrounding the fortress. Much commercial traffic disappeared when London's streets were widened enough for horse-drawn coaches to maintain a decent pace.

RIVER CRUISES ALONG THE THAMES

A trip up or down the river will give you an entirely different view of London from the one you get from land. You'll see how the city grew along and around

Hanging "Around" in London

The world's largest observation wheel, the **Millennium Wheel London Eye** ⊛, Millennium Jubilee Gardens (© 020/7487-0294; www.balondoneye.com), opened in February 2000. It is the fourth tallest structure in London, offering panoramic views that extend for some 40km (25 miles) if the weather's clear. Passengers are carried in 32 "pods" that make a complete revolution every half-hour. Along the way you'll see some of London's most famous landmarks from a bird's-eye view.

Built out of steel by a European consortium, it was conceived and designed by London architects Julia Barfield and David Marks, who claim inspiration from the Statue of Liberty in New York and the Eiffel Tower in Paris. Some 2 million visitors are expected to ride the eye every year.

The eye lies close to the Westminster Bridge (you can hardly miss it). Tickets for the ride are £9.50 ($14.25) for adults, £7.50 ($11.25) for seniors, and £5 ($7.50) for children. Hours are daily from 10am to 7pm November through March; otherwise, daily from 9am to late—depending on the weather. Tube: Embankment or Waterloo.

the Thames and how many of its landmarks turn their faces toward the water. Several companies operate motor launches from the Westminster piers (Tube: Westminster), offering panoramic views of one of Europe's most historic waterways en route.

Westminster-Greenwich Thames Passenger Boat Service, Westminster Pier, Victoria Embankment, SW1 (© **020/7930-4097**), concerns itself with downriver traffic from Westminster Pier to such destinations as Greenwich (see "Attractions on the Outskirts," below). The most popular excursion departs for Greenwich (a 50-min. ride) at half-hour intervals between 10am and 4pm April through October, between 10:30am and 5pm June through August; and from 10am to 3:20pm November through March. One-way fares are £6.30 ($9.45) for adults, £3.30 ($4.95) for children under 16, £5 ($7.50) for seniors. Round-trip fares are £7.60 ($11.40) for adults, £3.80 ($5.70) for children, £6.30 ($9.45) for seniors. A family ticket for two adults and up to three children under 15 costs £16.80 ($25.20) one-way, £20 ($30) round-trip.

Westminster Passenger Association (Upriver) Ltd., Westminster Pier, Victoria Embankment, SW1 (© **020/7930-2062** or 020/7930-4721), offers the only riverboat service upstream from Westminster Bridge to Kew, Richmond, and Hampton Court. There are daily sailings from the Monday before Easter until the end of October on traditional riverboats, all with licensed bars. Trip time can be as little as 1½ hours to Kew and between 2½ to 4 hours to Hampton Court, depending on the tide. Cruises from Westminster Pier to Hampton Court via Kew Gardens leave daily at 10:30am, 11:15am, and noon. Round-trip tickets are £10 to £14.50 ($15–$21.75) adults, £7.50 to £12 ($11.25–$18) seniors, and £4 to £9 ($6–$13.50) children 4 to 14; one child under 4 accompanied by an adult goes free. Evening cruises from May to September are also available, departing Westminster Pier at 7:30 and 8:30pm (9:30pm on demand) for £6.50 ($9.75) adults and £5 ($7.50) children. Prices are less for a trip to Richmond or Kew.

THAMES-SIDE SIGHTS
THE BRIDGES

Some of the Thames bridges are household names. **London Bridge,** contrary to the nursery rhyme, never fell down, but it has been replaced a number of times and is vastly different from the original London Bridge, which was lined with houses and shops. The one that you see now is the ugliest of the versions; the previous incarnation was dismantled and shipped to Lake Havasu, Arizona, in the 1960s.

Also on the Thames, you can visit London's newest park, Thames Barrier Park, SE1, which is the city's first riverside park in years. It lies on the north bank of the Thames alongside the Thames Barrier, that steel and concrete movable flood barrier inaugurated in 1982. The park is spread across 8.8 hectares (22 acres), and has fountains that flow into a channel in the 390m (1,300-ft.) sunken landscaped garden. There's also a riverside promenade and a children's playground. The park is open daily from sunrise to sunset (reached via no. 69 bus from the Canning Town Tube station).

HMS BELFAST

An 11,500-ton cruiser, the **HMS** *Belfast,* Morgan's Lane, Tooley Street, SE1 (© 020/7940-6300; www.lwm.org.uk; Tube: Monument, Tower Hill, or London Bridge), is a World War II ship preserved as a floating museum. It's moored opposite the Tower of London, between Tower Bridge and London Bridge. During the Russian convoy period and on D-day, the *Belfast* saw distinguished service, and in the Korean War it was known as "that straight shootin' ship." You can explore all its decks, right down to the engine room; exhibits above and below show how sailors lived and fought over the past 50 years. It's open daily from 10am with last boarding at 6pm in summer, 5pm in winter. Admission is £5.40 ($8.10) adults, children under 16 free; seniors and students pay £4 ($6) and family admission (2 adults and 2 children) is £12 ($18).

DOCKLANDS ✦

What was a dilapidated wasteland surrounded by water—some 89km (55 miles) of waterfront acreage within a sailor's cry of London's major attractions—has been reclaimed, restored, and rejuvenated. **London Docklands** is coming into its own as a leisure, residential, and commercial lure.

Next to the Tower of London, **St. Katharine's Dock** was the first of the docks to be given an entirely new role. Originally built in 1827 to 1828, this was for many years a leading dock, with the advantage of being closest to the City. Today, as a residential center and yacht marina, St. Katharine's again profits from its proximity to the City. The modern World Trade Centre looks down on the brick-brown sails of barges and gleaming hulls of moored luxury yachts. Blocks of fashionable Manhattan-style loft apartments sit between the docks and the river.

Canary Wharf, on the Isle of Dogs, is the heart of Docklands. This huge site is dominated by a 240m (800-ft.) tower, the tallest building in the United Kingdom, designed by Cesar Pelli. The **Piazza** is lined with shops and restaurants. A visit to the **Exhibition Centre** gives you an overview of the Docklands—past, present, and future. Already, the area has given space to the overflow from the City of London's square mile, and its development is more than promising.

On the south side of the river at Surrey Docks, the Victorian warehouses of **Butler's Wharf** have been converted into offices, houses, shops, and restaurants; it's home to the **Design Museum** (p. 255).

Docklands can be reached via the **Dockland Light Railway,** which links the Isle of Dogs to London Underground's Tower Hill station. To see the whole complex, take the railway at Tower Gateway near Tower Bridge for a short journey through Wapping and the Isle of Dogs. You can get off at Island Gardens and then cross through the 100-year-old Greenwich Tunnel under the Thames to see the attractions at Greenwich (see "Attractions on the Outskirts," below).

EXPLORING LONDON'S CANALS BY BOAT

Boat trips on London's canals, especially Regent's Canal in London's canal-riddled "Little Venice," is becoming an increasingly popular way of seeing the city. London's canals were once the city's major waterways. Bus no. 214 takes you to Little Venice where you can board one of several boats for a tour along the canals. You can return either by boat or from the nearby Underground station at the end of a one-way trip.

Since the Festival of Britain in 1951, some of the traditional painted canal boats have been resurrected for Venetian-style trips through the waterways. One of them is **Jason,** which takes you on a 90-minute trip from Bloomfield Road in Little Venice through the long Maida Hill tunnel under Edgware Road, through Regent's Park, past the Mosque, the London Zoo, and Lord Snowdon's Aviary, and the Pirate's Castle to Camden Lock, and finally back to Little Venice. Passengers making the 45-minute one-way journey disembark at Camden Lock.

The season runs from March 23 to the end of October, with daily trips at 10:30am, and 12:30 and 2:30pm. In June, July, and August, an additional trip on weekends and bank holidays leaves at 4:30pm. A canalside seafood specialty restaurant/café at Jason's moorings offers lunches, dinner, and teas, all freshly made. Advance notice must be made for lunch service on the boat. The round-trip fare is £6.95 ($10.45) for adults and £5.50 ($8.25) for children and seniors.One-way fares are £5.95 ($8.95) for adults and £4.75 ($7.15) for children and seniors. Family tickets cost £20 ($30). For reservations contact **Jason's Trip,** Jason's Wharf, opposite 60 Blomfield Rd., Little Venice, London W9 (© **020/ 7286-3428;** Tube: Warwick Avenue).

5 Attractions on the Outskirts

These sights are perfect for a morning or afternoon jaunt and are easily accessible by Tube, train, boat, or bus.

HAMPSTEAD

About 6.5km (4 miles) north of the center of London is the lovely village of Hampstead (Tube: Northern Line to Hampstead) and scenic Hampstead Heath.

The 320-hectare (800-acre) expanse of high heath known as **Hampstead Heath** is a chain of formal parkland, woodland, heath, meadowland, and ponds. On a clear day you can see St. Paul's Cathedral and even the hills of Kent. Londoners would certainly mount the barricades if Hampstead Heath were imperiled; for years, they've come here to sun worship, fly kites, fish the ponds, swim, picnic, and jog. In good weather, it's also the site of big 1-day fairs. At the shore of Kenwood Lake, in the northern section, is a concert platform devoted to symphony performances on summer evenings. In the northeast corner, in Waterlow Park, ballets, operas, and comedies are staged at the Grass Theatre in June and July.

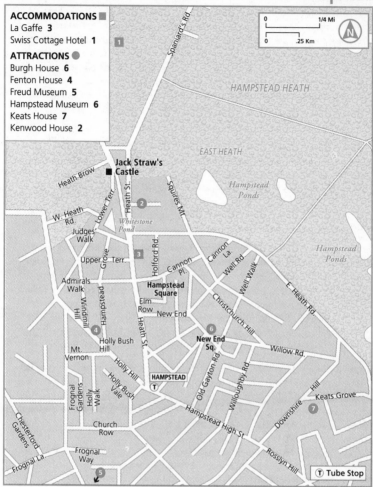

ACCOMMODATIONS ■
La Gaffe **3**
Swiss Cottage Hotel **1**

ATTRACTIONS ●
Burgh House **6**
Fenton House **4**
Freud Museum **5**
Hampstead Museum **6**
Keats House **7**
Kenwood House **2**

Once the Underground came to **Hampstead Village** in 1907, writers, artists, architects, musicians, and scientists were among those who decamped for the leafy village. Keats, D. H. Lawrence, Shelley, Robert Louis Stevenson and Kingsley Amis all once lived here, and John Le Carré still does.

The Regency and Georgian houses of the village and the rolling greens of the heath are just 20 minutes by Tube from Piccadilly Circus. The village has a quirky mix of historic pubs, toyshops, and chic boutiques along **Flask Walk,** a pedestrian mall. The original village, on the side of a hill, still has old alleys, steps, courts, and groves ideal for strolling.

Burgh House   This Queen Anne home (1703) in the center of the village was the residence of the daughter and son-in-law of Rudyard Kipling, who often visited here. It's now used for local art exhibits, concerts, recitals, talks, and public meetings on many subjects. The house is the headquarters of several local societies, including the Hampstead Music Club and the Hampstead Scientific Society.

Hampstead Museum, in Burgh House, illustrates the local history of the area. It has a room devoted to reproductions of works by the great artist John Constable, who lived nearby for many years and is buried in the local parish church. There's also a licensed **buttery** (✆ **020/7431-7401**) that's popular for lunch or tea, with lunches for just £5 ($7.50) (£5.35 [$8.05] on Sat and £5.95 [$8.95] on Sun). In pricey Hampstead, it's a real dining bargain.

New End Sq., NW3. ✆ 020/7431-0144 or 020/7431-2516 for buttery reservations. Free admission. House and museum Wed–Sun noon–5pm, Sat by appt.; buttery Wed–Sun 11am–5:30pm. Tube: Northern Line to Hampstead.

Fenton House   This National Trust property is on the west side of Hampstead Grove, just north of Hampstead Village. Built in 1693, its paneled rooms contain furniture and pictures; 18th-century English, German, and French porcelain; and an outstanding collection of early keyboard musical instruments.

Windmill Hill, NW3. ✆ 020/7435-3471. Admission £4.40 ($6.60) adults, £2.20 ($3.30) children, £11 ($16.50) family ticket. Mar Sat–Sun 2–5pm; Apr–Oct Sat–Sun 11am–5pm, Wed–Fri 2–5pm. Closed Good Friday and Nov–Feb. Tube: Northern Line to Hampstead.

Freud Museum   This is the spacious house in which the founder of psychoanalysis lived, worked, and died after escaping with his family and possessions from Nazi-occupied Vienna. The rooms hold his furniture (including the famous couch), letters, photographs, paintings, and personal effects, as well as those of his daughter, Anna Freud, also a noted psychoanalyst. Temporary exhibitions and an archive film program are also offered.

20 Maresfield Gardens, NW3. ✆ 020/7435-2002. www.freud.org.uk. Admission £4 ($6) adults, £2 ($3) full-time students, free for children under 12. Wed–Sun noon–5pm. Tube: Jubilee Line to Finchley Rd.

Keats House   This was the home of the poet John Keats for only 2 years; but it was here in 1819 that he wrote two of his most famous poems, "Ode to a Nightingale" and "Ode on a Grecian Urn." This Regency house contains some of his manuscripts and letters. Call before coming here, as the house is experiencing ongoing renovation and will be closed at random periods until at least 2003.

Wentworth Place, Keats Grove, NW3. ✆ 020/7435-2062. Free admission; donations welcome. Apr–Oct Mon–Fri 10am–1pm and 2–6pm; Sat 10am–1pm and 2–5pm; Sun and bank holidays 2–5pm. Nov–Mar Mon–Fri 1–5pm; Sat 10am–1pm and 2–5pm; Sun 2–5pm. Tube: Northern Line to Hampstead.

Kenwood House ★★   This structure was built as a gentleman's country home and later enlarged and decorated by the famous Scottish architect Robert Adam, starting in 1764. The house contains period furniture and paintings by Rembrandt, Vermeer, Gainsborough, and Turner, among others. It's also a venue for special visiting exhibitions and evening concerts (at which time admission is charged). In the summer, there are concerts and fireworks displays by the lake.

Hampstead Lane, NW3. ✆ 020/8348-1286. www.keatshouse.org. Admission £3 ($4.50) adults, £1.50 ($2.25) seniors and students. Free 15 and under. Apr–Oct daily 10am–6pm; Nov–Mar daily 10am–4pm. Tube: Northern Line to Golders Green, then Bus 210.

IN NEARBY HIGHGATE

Highgate Cemetery   Described in the British press as everything from "walled romantic rubble" to "an anthology of horror," this 37-acre burial ground is the ideal setting for a fine collection of Victorian sculpture, as well as the graves of Karl Marx and others, including George Eliot, Christina Rossetti, and Elizabeth Siddell, wife of Dante Gabriel Rossetti and the Pre-Raphaelites' favorite model. You must take a tour in order to see the Western cemetery.

However, there are no guided tours of the eastern part of the Cemetery; guests wander about at will. Allow about 30 minutes to reach this attraction.

Swain's Lane, N6. (℗ 020/8340-1834. Western Cemetery guided tour £3 ($4.50). Eastern Cemetery £2 ($3) admission, £1 ($1.50) camera pass charge (no video cameras; hand-held still cameras only). Western Cemetery: Mar–Oct guided tours only Mon–Fri at noon, 2, and 3pm, and Sat–Sun hourly 11am–3pm; Nov–Feb, tours Sat–Sun hourly 11am–3pm. Eastern Cemetery: Apr–Oct daily 10am–5pm; Nov–Feb daily 10am–4pm. Both cemeteries are closed at Christmas and during funerals. Tube: Northern Line to Archway, then walk or take Bus 43 or 134.

GREENWICH ✮✮✮

When London overwhelms you, and you'd like to escape for a beautiful, sunny afternoon on the city's outskirts, make Greenwich your destination.

Greenwich Mean Time is the basis of standard time throughout most of the world, and Greenwich has been the zero point used in the reckoning of terrestrial longitudes since 1884. But this lovely village—the center of British seafaring when Britain ruled the seas—is also home of the Royal Naval College, the National Maritime Museum, and the Old Royal Observatory. In dry dock at Greenwich Pier is the clipper ship *Cutty Sark* (see "River Cruises Along the Thames," earlier in this chapter). Greenwich also has some wonderful shopping, including a famous weekend market (see the "Greenwich Shopping Time" box in chapter 8).

Greenwich was the site of Britain's Millennium Dome, a multimedia extravaganza mixing education and entertainment. Most of the project's cost, estimated at more than $1.3 billion, came from a national lottery. Then, the much-heralded Dome bombed with audiences. The project became a national joke, and finally closed, its future uncertain. Prince Charles ridiculing it as a monstrous *blanc mange,* that unattractive milky gelatin dessert, didn't help it along.

GETTING THERE   The London Underground extended the Jubilee Line to Greenwich in 1999. This Tube follows a new line from Green Park via Westminster, Waterloo, London Bridge, the Docklands, and North Greenwich through to Stratford in East London. Greenwich North is the largest station on the London Underground not connected to the British Rail network.

The Tube is for speed, taking only 15 minutes, but if you'd like to travel the 6.5km (4 miles) to Greenwich the way Henry VIII did, you still can. In fact, getting to Greenwich is still half the fun. The most appealing way involves boarding any of the frequent ferryboats that cruise along the Thames at intervals that vary from every half-hour (in summer) to every 45 minutes (in winter). Boats that depart from Westminster Pier (Tube: Westminster) are maintained by **Westminster Passenger Services, Ltd.** (℗ 020/7930-4097). Boats that leave from Charing Cross Pier (Tube: Embankment) and Tower Pier (Tube: Tower Hill) are run by **Catamaran Cruises, Ltd.** (℗ 020/7987-1185). Depending on the tides and the carrier you select, travel time varies from 50 to 75 minutes each way. Passage is £6 to £10 ($9–$15) round-trip for adults, £4 to £6 ($6–$9) round-trip for children 5 to 12, and it's free for those under 5.

VISITOR INFORMATION   The **Greenwich Tourist Information Centre** is at 46 Greenwich Church St. (℗ 020/8858-6376); open daily from 10am to 5pm. The Tourist Information Centre conducts **walking tours** of Greenwich's major sights. The tours, which cost £4.50 ($6.75), depart daily at 12:15 and 2:15pm and last 1½ to 2 hours. Advance reservations aren't required, but it's a good idea to phone in advance to find out if there have been any last-minute schedule changes.

SEEING THE SIGHTS

Visitors came to visit the Millennium Dome in 2000, but the historic old town of Greenwich was a tourist attraction long before that.

The **National Maritime Museum,** the **Old Royal Observatory,** and the **Queen's House** stand together in a beautiful royal park high on a hill overlooking the Thames. Admission into all three sights is free and they are open daily from 10am to 5pm. For more information, call © **020/8312-6608** or visit www.nmn.ac.uk.

From the days of early seafarers to 20th-century sea power, the **National Maritime Museum** ✶✶ illustrates the glory that was Britain at sea. The cannon, relics, ship models, and paintings tell the story of a thousand naval battles, as well as the price of those battles. Look for some oddities here—everything from the dreaded cat-o'-nine-tails used to flog sailors, to Nelson's Trafalgar coat, with the fatal bullet hole in the left shoulder clearly visible. In time for the millennium, the museum spent £20 million in a massive expansion that added 16 new galleries devoted to British maritime history and improved visitor facilities.

Old Royal Observatory ✶ is the original home of Greenwich Mean Time. It has the largest refracting telescope in the United Kingdom and a collection of historic timekeepers and astronomical instruments. You can stand astride the meridian and set your watch by the falling time-ball. Sir Christopher Wren designed the Octagon Room. Here the first royal astronomer, Flamsteed, made his 30,000 observations that formed the basis of his *Historia Coelestis Britannica.* Edmond Halley of the eponymous Comet succeeded him. In 1833, the ball on the tower was hung to enable shipmasters to set their chronometers accurately.

Designed by Inigo Jones, **Queen's House** ✶✶ (1616) is a fine example of this architect's innovative style. It's most famous for the cantilevered tulip staircase, the first of its kind. Carefully restored, the house contains a collection of royal and marine paintings and other objets d'art.

Nearby is the **Royal Naval College** ✶✶, King William Walk, off Romney Road (© **020/8269-4747**). Designed by Sir Christopher Wren in 1696, it occupies 4 blocks named after King Charles, Queen Anne, King William, and Queen Mary. Greenwich Palace stood here from 1422 to 1640. It's worth stopping in to see the magnificent Painted Hall by Thornhill, where the body of Nelson lay in state in 1805, and the Georgian chapel of St. Peter and St. Paul. Open daily from 2:30 to 4:45pm; admission is free.

KEW ✶✶✶

15km (9 miles) southwest of central London near Richmond, Kew is home to the best-known botanic gardens in Europe. It's also the site of **Kew Palace** ✶✶, the former residence of George III and Queen Charlotte. A dark redbrick structure, characterized by its Dutch gables, it was constructed in 1631. At its rear is the Queen's Garden, a formal design filled with plants thought to have grown here in the 17th century. The interior is an elegant country house of the time, fit for a king, but not as regal as Buckingham Palace. You get the feeling that someone could have actually lived here, as you wander through the dining room, the breakfast room, and go upstairs to the Queen's drawing room where musical evenings were staged. The rooms are wallpapered with designs used at the time. Perhaps the most intriguing exhibits are little possessions once owned by royal occupants here—everything from snuffboxes to listings of Prince Frederick's gambling debts. The most convenient way to get to Kew is to take the **District Line** Tube to the Kew Gardens stop, on the south bank of the Thames. Allow about 30 minutes.

Royal Botanic (Kew) Gardens ★★★   These world-famous gardens offer thousands of varieties of plants. But Kew is no mere pleasure garden—it's essentially a vast scientific research center that happens to be beautiful. The gardens, on a 300-acre site, encompass lakes, greenhouses, walks, pavilions, and museums, along with fine examples of the architecture of Sir William Chambers. Among the 50,000 plant species are notable collections of ferns, orchids, aquatic plants, cacti, mountain plants, palms, and tropical water lilies.

No matter what season you visit Kew, there's always something to see, from the first spring flowers to winter. Gigantic hothouses grow species of shrubs, blooms, and trees from every part of the globe, from the Arctic Circle to tropical rainforests. Other attractions include a newly restored Japanese gateway in traditional landscaping, as well as exhibitions that vary with the season. The newest greenhouse, the Princess of Wales Conservatory (beyond the rock garden), encompasses 10 climatic zones, from arid to tropical, and boasts London's most thrilling collection of miniature orchids. The Marianne North Gallery (1882) is an absolute gem, paneled with 246 different types of wood that the intrepid Victorian artist collected on her world journeys; she also collected 832 paintings of exotic and tropical flora, all of which are displayed on the walls. Afternoon tea is offered at the Orangery, and there's no better place in the gardens to sit and soak in the beauty. The Visitor Centre at Victoria Gate houses an exhibit telling the story of Kew, as well as a bookshop.

Kew. © 020/8940-1171. www.rbgkew.org.uk. Admission £5.85 ($8.80) adults, £4.05 ($6.10) students and seniors, free for children 16 and under, £15 ($22.50) family ticket. Daily 9:30am–5pm. Tube: District Line to Kew Gardens.

KEW FOR TEA

Across the street from the Royal Botanic Gardens is one of the finest tearooms in the area, the **Original Maids of Honour Tearooms,** 288 Kew Rd. (© 020/8940-2752). Oak paneling and old leaded-glass windows give the place a cozy warmth. The homemade cakes are delectable, as are the delightfully light scones. The Maids of Honour (flavored with jam, cottage cheese, golden raisins, almond extract, and almonds) is their pastry specialty, originally baked for Henry VIII, who liked it so much that its secret recipe has been passed along through the centuries. Afternoon tea is £5.25 to £8 ($7.90–$12). The tearoom is open Monday from 9:30am to 1pm and Tuesday through Saturday from 9:30am to 6pm, and tea is served from 2:30 to 5:30pm.

HAMPTON COURT

Hampton Court, on the north side of the Thames, 21km (13 miles) west of London in East Molesey, Surrey, is easily accessible, and one of the great palaces of England. But if you have very limited time, we'd save it for a future visit. If you're going to be in London for perhaps a week, then we'd recommend a visit, but only after you've spent a day at Windsor. Frequent **trains** (© 08457/484-950 in the UK. only or 01603/764-776) run from Waterloo Station (Network Southeast) to Hampton Court Station. **London Transport** (© 020/7730-3466 or 087051/808-080) buses nos. 111, 131, 216, 267, and 461 make the trip from Victoria Coach Station on Buckingham Palace Road (just southwest of Victoria Station). Boat service is offered to and from Kingston, Richmond, and Westminster (see "River Cruises Along the Thames," earlier in this chapter). If you're **driving** from London, take A308 to the junction with A309 on the north side of Kingston Bridge over the Thames.

Hampton Court Palace *Value* Cardinal Wolsey's 16th-century palace can teach us a lesson: Don't try to outdo your boss—particularly if he happens to be Henry VIII. The rich cardinal did just that, and he eventually lost his fortune, power, and prestige, and ended up giving his lavish palace to the Tudor monarch.

Today you can parade through the apartments, filled with porcelain, furniture, paintings, and tapestries. You'll see that Henry outdid Wolsey when he took over the palace. Tudor additions include the **Anne Boleyn Gateway,** with its 16th-century astronomical clock that even tells the high-water mark at London Bridge. From **Clock Court,** you can see one of Henry's major contributions, the aptly named **Great Hall,** with its hammerbeam ceiling. (The Clock Court is also the starting point for costumed guided tours.) Henry cavorted through the various apartments with his wife of the moment, from Anne Boleyn to Catherine Parr (who turned the tables on Henry by outliving him). Later, Charles I was imprisoned here, and temporarily managed to escape his jailers.

Although the palace enjoyed prestige and pomp in Elizabethan days, it owes much of its present look to William and Mary—or rather, to their architect, Sir Christopher Wren, who designed and had built the northern or **Lion Gates,** intended to be the main entrance to the new parts of the palace. **The King's Dressing Room** is graced with some of the best art, mainly paintings by old masters on loan from Queen Elizabeth II. Be sure to inspect the **royal chapel**— Wolsey wouldn't recognize it. To confound yourself totally, get lost in the serpentine shrubbery **maze** in the garden, also the work of Wren. Also in the garden is the Great Vine, thought to be the oldest living vine; it still produces 500 to 700 pounds of grapes every year. The fine wrought-iron screen at the south end of the south gardens was made by Jean Tijou around 1694 for William and Mary. There's a cafe and restaurant in the Tiltyard Gardens.

Surrey, KT8 9AU ℂ 020/8781-9500. www.hrp.org.uk. Admission £10.80 ($16.20) adults, £8.30 ($12.45) students and seniors, £7.20 ($10.80) children 5–15, free for children under 5, £32.20 ($48.30) family ticket. Free admission to all gardens except the Privy Garden (admission £2.80/$4.20 adults, £1.90/$2.85 child) without palace ticket during summer months. Gardens open year-round daily 7am–dusk (no later than 9pm). Cloisters, courtyards, state apartments, great kitchen, cellars, and Hampton Court exhibition open mid-Mar to mid-Oct daily 9:30am–6pm; mid-Oct to mid-Mar Tues–Sun 9am–4:30pm and Mon 10:15am–4:30pm. Tudor tennis court open mid-Mar to mid-Oct.

6 Especially for Kids

London has fun places for kids of all ages. In addition to what's listed below, kids love **Madame Tussaud's,** the **Science Museum,** the **London Transport Museum,** the **Natural History Museum,** the **Tower of London,** and the **National Maritime Museum** in Greenwich, all discussed above.

Bethnal Green Museum of Childhood *Kids* This branch of the Victoria and Albert Museum specializes in toys. The variety of dolls alone is staggering; some have such elaborate period costumes that you don't even want to think of the price tags they would carry today. With the dolls go dollhouses, from simple cottages to miniature mansions, complete with fireplaces, grand pianos, kitchen utensils, household pets, and carriages. There are also optical toys, marionettes, puppets, a considerable exhibit of soldiers and war toys from both World War eras, trains and aircraft, and clothing and furniture relating to the social history of childhood.

Cambridge Heath Rd., E2. ℂ 020/8980-2415. www.vam.ac.uk. Free admission. Sat–Thurs 10am–5:45pm. Tube: Central Line to Bethnal Green.

Little Angel Theatre (*Kids*) Puppetry in all its forms is presented at this charming small theater in Islington, north of the city. There are homegrown shows that tour nationally and internationally as well as the work of a variety of visiting companies. The range of puppetry is wide, from marionettes (string puppets) to rod-and-glove puppets. Most of the work is targeted at children; age limits are stated for every show presented (for example, "no under-3s allowed"); grown-ups will enjoy them, too. There's a coffee bar and an adjacent workshop where the puppets, sets, and costumes are made. One show per season is adult-oriented. Call for information. The theater is accessible to people with disabilities.

14 Dagmar Passage, N1. ℂ 020/7226-1787, or 020/7359-8581. Admission £7 ($10.50) adults, £6 ($9) children. Show times Sat–Sun 11am and 2:30pm; some weekdays. Tube: Northern Line to Angel or Victoria Line to Highbury and Islington.

The London Dungeon (*Kids*) This ghoulish place was designed to chill the blood while reproducing the conditions of the Middle Ages. Under the arches of London Bridge Station, it presents a series of tableaux more grisly than the ones in Madame Tussaud's. The rumble of trains overhead adds to the atmosphere, and tolling bells bring a note of melancholy; dripping water and caged rats make for even more atmosphere. Naturally, there's a burning at the stake and a torture chamber with racking, branding, and fingernail extraction, and a spine-chilling "Jack the Ripper Experience." The special effects were conceived for major film and TV productions. They've recently added a new show called "Judgment Day." You are sentenced to death (by actors) and taken on a boat ride to meet your fate. If you survive, there's a Pizza Hut on the premises and a souvenir shop selling certificates that testify that you made it through Judgment Day.

28-34 Tooley St., SE1. ℂ 020/7403-7221. www.thedungeons.com. Admission £10.95 ($16.45) adults, £9.50 ($14.25) students and seniors, £6.95 ($10.45) children under 15. Admission includes Judgment Day boat ride. Daily 10:30am–5pm during winter; high season 10am–6pm daily. Tube: London Bridge.

London Planetarium (*Kids*) Next-door to Madame Tussaud's, the planetarium explores the mysteries of the stars and the night sky. The most recent show starts with a spaceship of travelers forced to leave their planet when a neighboring star explodes. Accompanying them on their journey, the audience travels through the solar system, visiting its major landmarks and witnessing spectacular cosmic activity. There are also several hands-on exhibits that relate to planets and space. For example, you can see what shape or weight you'd be on other planets, and you can hear a recorded Stephen Hawking talk about mysterious black holes.

Marylebone Rd., NW1. ℂ 020/7935-6861. www.madame-tussauds.com. Admission £6.50 ($9.75) adults, £5.10 ($7.65) seniors, £4.35 ($6.55) children 5–17. Weekdays daily from 10am and Sat–Sun from 9:30am, with shows beginning at 12:20pm (10:20am on weekends) and last show at 5pm. Tube: Baker St.

London Zoo ✪ (*Kids*) One of the greatest zoos in the world, the London Zoo is more than 1½ centuries old. This 15-hectare (36-acre) garden houses about 8,000 animals, including some of the rarest species on earth. There's an insect house (incredible bird-eating spiders); a reptile house (huge dragon-like monitor lizards); and others, such as the Sobell Pavilion for Apes and Monkeys and the Lion Terraces. In the Moonlight World, special lighting simulates night for the nocturnal beasties while rendering them visible to onlookers, so you can see all the night rovers in action.

In 1999, the Millennium Conservation Centre opened, combining animals, visuals, and displays to demonstrate the nature of life on this planet. Many families budget almost an entire day here, watching the penguins being fed, enjoying an animal ride in summer, and meeting elephants on their walks around the zoo.

Especially for Kids

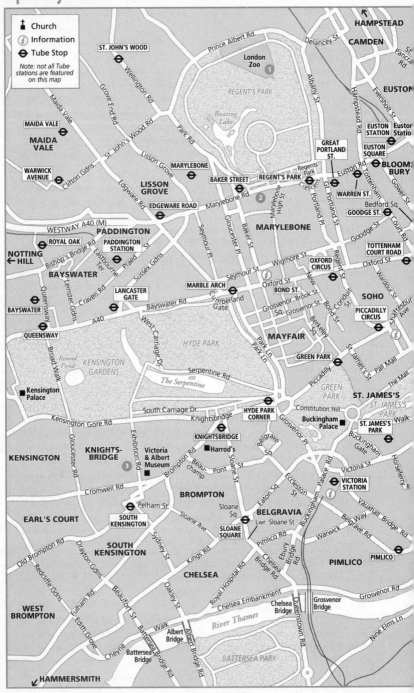

Legend:
- ✝ Church
- ⓘ Information
- 🚇 Tube Stop

Note: not all Tube stations are featured on this map

HAMPSTEAD

CAMDEN

Prince Albert Rd.

Delancey St.

ST. JOHN'S WOOD

London Zoo ❶

EUSTON

REGENT'S PARK

Boating Lake

MAIDA VALE

MAIDA VALE

GREAT PORTLAND ST.

EUSTON STATION

EUSTON SQUARE

BLOOMS-BURY

WARWICK AVENUE

MARYLEBONE

BAKER STREET

REGENT'S PARK

WARREN ST.

GOODGE ST.

LISSON GROVE

Marylebone Rd. ❷

EDGEWARE ROAD

MARYLEBONE

TOTTENHAM COURT ROAD

WESTWAY A40 (M)

PADDINGTON

ROYAL OAK

PADDINGTON STATION

OXFORD CIRCUS

NOTTING
← HILL

BAYSWATER

MARBLE ARCH

BOND ST.

SOHO

LANCASTER GATE

Bayswater Rd.

Cumberland Gate

PICCADILLY CIRCUS

BAYSWATER

HYDE PARK

QUEENSWAY

MAYFAIR

GREEN PARK

KENSINGTON GARDENS

Serpentine Rd.

The Serpentine

GREEN PARK

ST. JAMES'S

Kensington Palace

Round Pond

Broad Walk

ST. JAMES'S PARK

Constitution Hill

Buckingham Palace

ST. JAMES'S PARK

Kensington Gore Rd.

South Carriage Dr.

Knightsbridge

HYDE PARK CORNER

KNIGHTSBRIDGE

KENSINGTON

KNIGHTS-BRIDGE ❸

Victoria & Albert Museum

Harrod's

VICTORIA STATION

Cromwell Rd.

BROMPTON

EARL'S COURT

Pelham St.

SOUTH KENSINGTON

Sloane Sq.

BELGRAVIA

SOUTH KENSINGTON

SLOANE SQUARE

PIMLICO

CHELSEA

PIMLICO

WEST BROMPTON

Chelsea Embankment

Grosvenor Rd.

River Thames

Albert Bridge

Chelsea Bridge

Grosvenor Bridge

Battersea Bridge

BATTERSEA PARK

↙ HAMMERSMITH

276

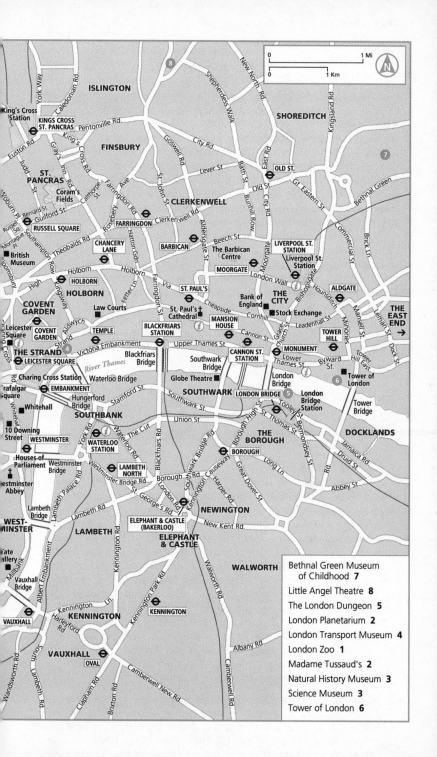

0 | 1 Mi
0 | 1 Km

ISLINGTON

King's Cross Station
KINGS CROSS ST. PANCRAS
Pentonville Rd.
Caledonian Rd.
York Way
Euston Rd.
Judd St.
Gray's Inn Rd.
King's Cross Rd.
FINSBURY
Goswell Rd.
City Rd.
SHOREDITCH
Kingsland Rd.
8

ST. PANCRAS
Woburn Pl.
Bernard St.
Russell Sq.
Guilford St.
Coram's Fields
Calthorpe St.
Farringdon Rd.
St. John St.
Lever St.
Bath St.
Bunhill Row
East Rd.
Old St.
OLD ST.
Gt. Eastern St.
Bethnal Green
7

RUSSELL SQUARE
Montague Pl.
Southampton Row
Theobalds Rd.
CLERKENWELL
FARRINGDON
Clerkenwell Rd.
Aldersgate St.
Beech St.
LIVERPOOL ST. STATION
Liverpool St. Station
Commercial Rd.
Brick Ln.

British Museum
Bloomsbury
High
Kingsway
Holborn
Holborn
HOLBORN
Fetter Ln.
Farringdon St.
CHANCERY LANE
Hatton Gdn.
BARBICAN
The Barbican Centre
MOORGATE
Moorgate
London Wall
Bishopsgate
Houndsditch
ALDGATE
Leman St.

COVENT GARDEN
Leicester Square
COVENT GARDEN
Aldwych
TEMPLE
Law Courts
HOLBORN
Via.
ST. PAUL'S
St. Paul's Cathedral
Cheapside
Bank of England
THE CITY
Cornhill
Stock Exchange
Leadenhall St.
TOWER HILL
Minories
Mansell St.
THE EAST END →

THE STRAND
LEICESTER SQUARE
Charing Cross
Strand
Victoria Embankment
BLACKFRIARS STATION
Upper Thames St.
MANSION HOUSE
Cannon St.
MONUMENT
Grace church St.
King William St.
Lower Thames St.
By Ward St.
Tower Hill East
Dock St.

River Thames
Blackfriars Bridge
Waterloo Bridge
Southwark Bridge
Globe Theatre
CANNON ST. STATION
London Bridge
6
Tower of London

Charing Cross Station
Trafalgar Square
EMBANKMENT
Hungerford Bridge
Stamford St.
SOUTHWARK
LONDON BRIDGE
5
London Bridge Station
Tooley St.
Bermondsey St.
Tower Bridge

Whitehall
10 Downing Street
WESTMINSTER
SOUTHBANK
WATERLOO STATION
York Rd.
Waterloo Rd.
The Cut
Blackfriars Rd.
Union St.
Southwark St.
Borough High St.
St. Thomas St.
DOCKLANDS
Jamaica Rd.
Druid St.

Houses of Parliament
Westminster Bridge
LAMBETH NORTH
Lambeth Palace Rd.
Westminster Bridge Rd.
Borough Rd.
London Rd.
BOROUGH
THE BOROUGH
Long Ln.
Great Dover St.
Abbey St.

Westminster Abbey
Lambeth Bridge
Lambeth Rd.
St. George's Rd.
NEWINGTON
Harper Rd.

WESTMINSTER
Tate Gallery
Millbank
Vauxhall Bridge
Albert Embankment
LAMBETH
Kennington Rd.
ELEPHANT & CASTLE (BAKERLOO)
ELEPHANT & CASTLE
New Kent Rd.
Kennington Park Rd.
WALWORTH
Walworth Rd.

Kennington Ln.
Harleyford Rd.
KENNINGTON
Kennington Park Rd.
KENNINGTON

Wandsworth Rd.
South Lambeth Rd.
VAUXHALL
OVAL
Clapham Rd.
Brixton Rd.
Camberwell New Rd.
Albany Rd.
Camberwell Rd.

Bethnal Green Museum of Childhood 7
Little Angel Theatre 8
The London Dungeon 5
London Planetarium 2
London Transport Museum 4
London Zoo 1
Madame Tussaud's 2
Natural History Museum 3
Science Museum 3
Tower of London 6

277

Regent's Park, NW1. ℂ 020/7722-3333. www.londonzoo.co.uk. Admission £10 ($15) adults, £7 ($10.50) children and students, free for children aged 3–15. Mar–Sept daily 10am–5:30pm; Oct–Feb daily 10am–4pm. Tube: Regent's Park or Camden Town, then Bus C2 or 274.

7 Organized Tours

BUS TOURS

For the first-timer, the quickest and most economical way to bring the big city into focus is to take a bus tour. One of the most popular is the **Original London Sightseeing Tour,** which passes all the major sights in about 1½ hours. The tour, which uses a traditional double-decker bus with live commentary by a guide, costs £14 ($21) for adults, £7.50 ($11.25) for children under 16, free for those under 5. The tour is hop on/hop off at any point. The tour plus admission to Madame Tussaud's is £26 ($39) for adults, £22.50 ($33.75) for children.

Departures are from convenient points within the city; you can choose your departure point when you buy your ticket. Tickets can be purchased on the bus or at a discount from any London Transport or London Tourist Board Information Centre. Most hotel concierges also sell tickets. For information or phone purchases, call ℂ **020/8877-1722.** It's also possible to write for tickets: **London Coaches,** Jews Row, London SW18 1TB.

Big Bus Company Ltd., Waterside Way, London SW17 (ℂ **020/8944-7810** or 0800/169-1365), operates a 2-hour tour in summer, departing frequently between 8:30am and 5pm daily from Marble Arch by Speakers Corner, Green Park by the Ritz Hotel, and Victoria Station (Buckingham Palace Rd. by the Royal Westminster Hotel). Tours cover the highlights—18 in all—ranging from the Houses of Parliament and Westminster Abbey to the Tower of London and Buckingham Palace (exterior looks only), accompanied by live commentary. The cost is £15 ($22.50) for adults, £6 ($9) for children. There's also a 1-hour tour that follows the same route, but covers only 13 sights. Tickets are valid all day; you can hop on and off the bus as you wish.

WALKING TOURS

The Original London Walks 🎯, 87 Messina Ave., P.O. Box 1708, London NW6 4LW (ℂ **020/7624-3978**), the oldest established walking-tour company in London, is run by an Anglo-American journalist/actor couple, David and Mary Tucker. Their hallmarks are variety, reliability, reasonably sized groups, and—above all—superb guides. The renowned crime historian Donald Rumbelow, the leading authority on Jack the Ripper and the author of the classic guidebook *London Walks,* is a regular guide, as are several prominent actors (including classical actor Edward Petherbridge). Walks are regularly scheduled daily and cost £5 ($7.50) for adults, £3.50 ($5.25) for students and seniors; children under 15 go free. Call for schedule; no reservations needed.

Discovery Walks, 67 Chancery Lane, London WC2 (ℂ **020/8530-8443;** www.Jack-the-Ripper-Walk.co.uk), are themed walks, led by Richard Jones, author of *Frommer's Memorable Walks in London.* **Stepping Out** (ℂ **020/ 8881-2933;** www.walklon.ndirect.co.uk) offers a series of offbeat walks led by qualified historians. Tours generally cost £4 to £6 ($6–$9).

8 Spectator Sports

CRICKET In summer, attention turns to cricket, played either at **Lord's,** St. John's Wood Road, NW8 (ℂ **020/7289-1611;** Tube: Jubilee Line to St. John's Wood), in north London, or at the somewhat less prestigious **Oval Cricket**

Ground, The Oval, Kennington, London SE11 (☏ **020/7582-6660;** Tube: Northern Line to The Oval or Vauxhall), in south London. During the international test matches between Britain and Australia, the West Indies, India, or New Zealand (as important as the World Series in the United States), Britons go into a collective trance, with everyone glued to the nearest radio or TV.

FOOTBALL (SOCCER)   The season runs from August to April and attracts fiercely loyal fans. Games usually start at 3pm and are great to watch, but the stands can get very rowdy, so think about reserving seats. Centrally located first-division football clubs include **Arsenal,** Arsenal Stadium, Avenell Road, N5 (☏ **020/7704-4000,** box office 020/7704-4040; Tube: Piccadilly Line to Arsenal); **Tottenham Hotspur,** 748 High Rd., N17 (☏ **020/8365-5000,** box office 087/0011-2222; Tube: Victoria Line to Seven Sisters); and **Chelsea,** Stamford Bridge, Fulham Road, SW6 (☏ **020/7385-5545,** box office 0891/121-011; Tube: District Line to Fulham Broadway). Tickets cost £21 to £40 ($31.50–$60). The country's most visible site of world-class soccer matches is **Wembley Stadium,** Wembley, Middlesex (☏ **020/8902-8833;** Tube: Metropolitan Line to Wembley Park), about 9.5km (6 miles) north of London's center.

HORSE RACING   Within reach of central London are horse-racing tracks at Kempton Park, Sandown Park, and the most famous, Epsom, where the Derby is the main event of early June. Racing takes place midweek and on weekends, but not continuously. Contact **United Racecourses Ltd.** (☏ **01372/470-047**) for information on the next races at one of these tracks.

TENNIS   Fans from around the world focus on **Wimbledon** (Tube: District Line to Southfields). At Wimbledon's All England Lawn Tennis & Croquet Club, you'll see some of the world's best tennis players. The famous annual championships span roughly the last week in June to the first week in July, with matches lasting from about 2pm until dark. (The gates open at 10:30am.) Tickets usually range in price from £15 to £60 ($22.50–$90). Coveted center-court seats are sold by lottery. A limited number of tickets for the outside courts are available at the gate. For recorded ticket information, call ☏ **020/8946-2244,** or send a self-addressed stamped envelope (Aug–Dec) to the **All England Lawn Tennis & Croquet Club,** P.O. Box 98, Church Road, Wimbledon, SW19 5AE.

8

Shopping

When Prussian Field Marshal Blücher, Wellington's stout ally at Waterloo, first laid eyes on London, he allegedly slapped his thigh and exclaimed, "Herr Gott, what a city to plunder!" He was gazing at what, for the early 19th century, was a phenomenal mass of shops and stores. Since those days, other cities may have equaled London as a shopping mecca, but none have surpassed it.

1 Shopping London

Although London is one of the world's best shopping cities, it often seems made for wealthy visitors. To find real values, do what most Londoners do: Wait for sales or search out specialty finds.

American-style shopping has taken Britain by storm, in concept—warehouse stores and outlet malls—and in actual name: One block from Hamleys, you'll find the Disney Store. The Gap is everywhere, and Tiffany sells more wedding gifts than Asprey these days. Your best bet is to concentrate on British goods. You can also do well with French products; values are almost as good as in Paris.

TAXES & SHIPPING   Value-added tax (VAT) is the British version of sales tax. VAT is a whopping 17.5% on most goods, but it's included in the price, so the number you see on the price tag is exactly what you'll pay at the register. Non-EU residents can get back much of the tax by applying for a VAT refund (see "How to Get Your VAT Refund," below).

In Britain, the minimum expenditure needed to qualify for a refund on value-added tax is £50 ($75). Not every single store honors this minimum, but it's far easier to qualify for a tax refund in Britain than almost any other country in the European Union.

Vendors at flea markets might not be equipped to provide the paperwork for a refund, so if you're contemplating a major purchase and are counting on a refund, ask before you buy. Be suspicious of any dealer who tells you there's no VAT on antiques. This was once true, but things have changed—the European Union has made the British add VAT to antiques. Since dealers still have mixed stock, pricing should reflect this. So ask if it's included—before you bargain. Get to the price you're comfortable with first, then ask for the VAT refund.

VAT is not charged on goods shipped out of the country, whether you spend £50 or not. Many London shops will help you beat the VAT by shipping for you. But watch out: Shipping may be even more expensive than the VAT, and you might also have to pay U.S. duties when the goods get to you at home.

You can ship your purchases on your flight home by paying for excess baggage (rates vary by airline) or have your packages shipped independently, which is generally less expensive than shipping it through the airlines. Try **London Baggage,** London Air Terminal, Victoria Place, SW1 (© **020/7828-2400;** Tube: Victoria), which is not in an airport, or **Burns International Facilities,** at

> **Tips   How to Get Your VAT Refund**
>
> You *must* get your VAT refund form from the retailer. Several readers have reported that merchants have told them they can get refund forms at the airport as they leave the country. *This is not true.* Don't leave the store without a form—it must be completed by the retailer on the spot. After you have asked if the store does VAT refunds and determined their minimum, request the paperwork.
>
> Fill out your form and then present it—with the goods—at the Customs office in the airport. Allow a half-hour to stand in line. Remember: You're required to show the goods, so put them in your carry-on.
>
> Once the paperwork has been stamped, you have two choices: You can mail the papers (remember to bring a stamp) and receive your refund as a British check (no!) or a credit-card refund (yes!), or go to the Cash VAT Refund desk at the airport and get your refund in cash. The bad news: If you accept cash other than sterling, you will lose money on the conversion.
>
> Many stores charge a flat fee for processing your refund, so £3 to £5 may be automatically deducted from the total you receive. But since the VAT in Britain is 17.5%, it's worth the trouble to get the money back.
>
> *Note:* If you're heading to other countries in the European Union, you go through this at your final destination in the EU, filing all your VAT refunds at once.

Heathrow Airport Terminal 1 (© **020/8745-5301**) and Terminal 4 (© **020/8745-7460**). You can avoid the VAT up front *only* if you have the store ship directly for you. If you ship via excess baggage or London Baggage, you still have to pay the VAT up front and apply for a refund.

HOURS   London keeps fairly uniform store hours, mostly shorter than American equivalents. The norm is 10am opening and 5:30pm closing, with a late Wednesday or Thursday night until 7pm, maybe 8pm. Some stores in districts such as Chelsea and Covent Garden tend to keep slightly later hours.

Sunday shopping is now legal. Stores are allowed to be open for 6 hours; usually they choose 11am to 5pm. Stores in designated tourist areas and flea markets are exempt from this law and may stay open all day on Sunday. Therefore, Covent Garden, Greenwich, and Hampstead are big Sunday destinations for shoppers.

SALES   Traditionally, stores in Britain held only two sale periods: January and July. Now whenever they need cash, they have a sale. July sales begin in June—or earlier—and promotions are commonplace. The January sale is still the big event of the year. Although a few stores hold their after-Christmas sale on December 27, most usually start after the first week in January, when round-trip airfares are in the low range, and savings on sale items might earn your travel money back if you find enough bargains.

Discounts can range from 25% to 50% at leading department stores. Depending on their inventories and their sense of timing, Harrods produces some very

London Shopping

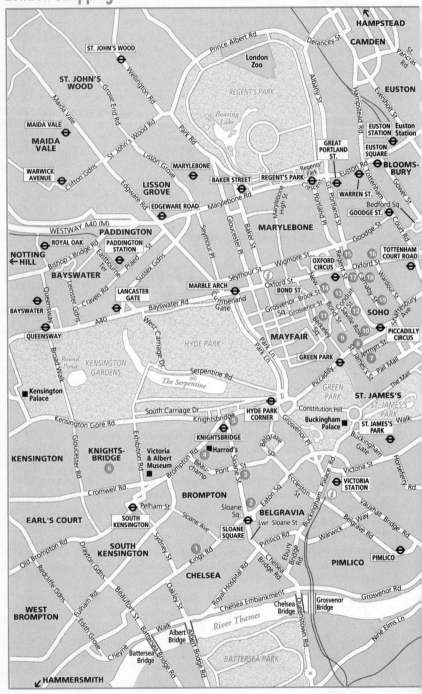

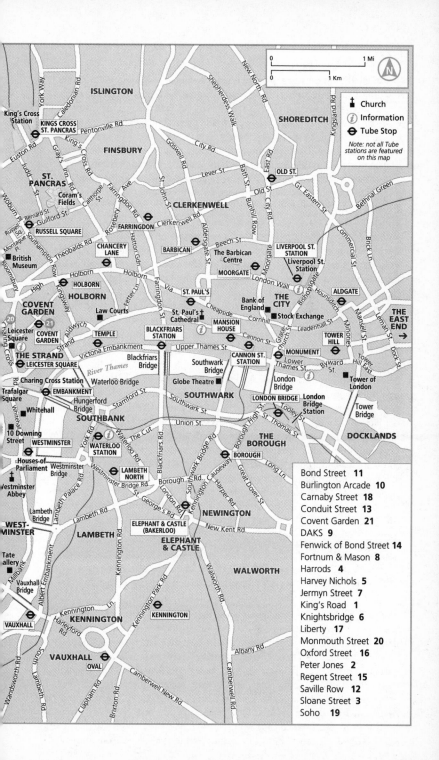

ISLINGTON

SHOREDITCH

King's Cross Station

KINGS CROSS ST. PANCRAS · Pentonville Rd.

York Way

Caledonian Rd.

King's Cross Rd.

Euston Rd.

Gray's Inn Rd.

FINSBURY

Goswell Rd.

City Rd.

Shepherdess Walk

New North Rd.

Kingsland Rd.

Kingsland High St.

Bethnal Green

OLD ST.

ST. PANCRAS

Judd St.

Woburn Pl.

Bernard St.

Russell Sq.

Coram's Fields

Guilford St.

Calthorpe St.

Rosebery Ave.

Farringdon Rd.

St. John St.

Lever St.

Bath St.

City Rd.

Old St.

East St.

Gt. Eastern St.

Commercial St.

Brick Ln.

CLERKENWELL

Clerkenwell Rd.

Beech St.

Aldersgate St.

Moorgate

Bunhill Row

LIVERPOOL ST. STATION

Liverpool St. Station

Bishopsgate

ALDGATE

Mansell St.

Leman St.

THE EAST END →

RUSSELL SQUARE

Southampton Row

Theobalds Rd.

Mortague Pl.

British Museum

Bloomsbury

FARRINGDON

CHANCERY LANE

Hatton Gdn.

BARBICAN

The Barbican Centre

MOORGATE

London Wall

Holborn

Holborn

Holborn

High

Kingsway

Fetter Ln.

Farringdon St.

Via.

ST. PAUL'S

Bank of England

THE CITY

Cornhill

Stock Exchange

Leadenhall St.

Minories

Tower Hill East

Dock St.

HOLBORN

COVENT GARDEN

Law Courts

St. Paul's ✝ Cathedral

Cheapside

MANSION HOUSE

Cannon St.

Grace Church St.

MONUMENT

TOWER HILL

Byward St.

Tower of London

20

Leicester Square

21

COVENT GARDEN

Charing Cross Rd.

Aldwych

Strand

TEMPLE

BLACKFRIARS STATION

Upper Thames St.

CANNON ST. STATION

Lower Thames St.

Tower Hill

LEICESTER SQUARE

THE STRAND

Victoria Embankment

Blackfriars Bridge

Southwark Bridge

London Bridge

Tower Bridge

Charing Cross Station

EMBANKMENT

Waterloo Bridge

Globe Theatre ■

SOUTHWARK

LONDON BRIDGE

London Bridge Station

Tower Bridge

Trafalgar Square

Whitehall

Hungerford Bridge

Stamford St.

Southwark St.

Tooley St.

DOCKLANDS

10 Downing Street

WESTMINSTER

SOUTHBANK

York Rd.

Waterloo Rd.

The Cut

Union St.

Borough High St.

Thomas St.

Houses of Parliament

Westminster Bridge

WATERLOO STATION

THE BOROUGH

Westminster Abbey

LAMBETH NORTH

BOROUGH

Long Ln.

Westminster Bridge

Lambeth Palace Rd.

Westminster Bridge Rd.

Borough Rd.

St. George's Rd.

London Rd.

Blackfriars Rd.

Southwark Bridge Rd.

Kennington Causeway

Harper Rd.

Great Dover St.

WEST-MINSTER

Lambeth Bridge

LAMBETH

Lambeth Rd.

ELEPHANT & CASTLE (BAKERLOO)

NEWINGTON

New Kent Rd.

Tate Gallery

Millbank

Vauxhall Bridge

Albert Embankment

Kennington Rd.

ELEPHANT & CASTLE

WALWORTH

Walworth Rd.

VAUXHALL

Kennington Ln.

Harleyford Rd.

KENNINGTON

Kennington Park Rd.

KENNINGTON

Albany Rd.

Camberwell Rd.

South Lambeth Rd.

Wandsworth Rd.

VAUXHALL

OVAL

Clapham Rd.

Brixton Rd.

Camberwell New Rd.

River Thames

Waterloo Bridge

Blackfriars Bridge

Tips Tax-Free Shopping

Global Refund (www.taxfree.se) is your best bet for getting VAT refunds at the airport. In London, shop where you see the Global Refund Tax-free Shopping sign, and ask for a Global Refund Tax Free check when you purchase your items. When leaving Britain, show your purchases, receipts, and passport to Customs, and have your Global Refund checks stamped. You have several choices—immediate cash at one of Global Refund's offices, crediting to a credit card or bank account, or a bank check sent to a chosen address. Refund offices are situated at all major London exit points such as Gatwick and Heathrow airports.

---

visible events of this nature, spending large amounts on promotions and publicity. Depending on the event, extra discounts might apply to souvenirs with Harrods' logos, furniture and gift items, English china (seconds are trucked in from factories in Stoke-on-Trent), and English designer brands like Jaeger. But while the Harrods sale is the most famous in London, it's not the only game in town. Just about every other store—save Boots—also has a big sale at that time. Beware, though: There's a huge difference in the quality of the finds at genuine sales, when stores are actually clearing the shelves, and the goods bought at "produced" sales, when special merchandise has been hauled in just for the sale.

DUTY-FREE AIRPORT SHOPPING Shopping at airports is big business. Terminal 4 at Heathrow is a virtual shopping mall, but each of the other terminals at Heathrow has a wide range of shopping outlets, with not a lot of crossover between brands. Prices at the airport for items like souvenirs and candy bars are, of course, higher than on the streets of London, but duty-free prices on luxury goods are usually fair. There are often promotions and coupons that allow for pounds off at the time of the purchase. Most of the sales at these airport shops are made for passengers waiting for flights on to other destinations, usually home. Most passengers, by the end of their stay in London, have at least some grasp of what items are available in London shops and at what prices, and therefore have some basis of comparison to prices of equivalent goods outside the airports.

2 Central London Shopping

Thankfully for those pressed for time, several key streets offer some (or even all) of London's best retail stores, compactly located in a niche or neighborhood so you can just stroll and shop.

THE WEST END As a neighborhood, the West End includes Mayfair and is home to the core of London's big-name shopping. Most of the department stores, designer shops, and multiples (chain stores) have their flagships in this area.

The key streets are **Oxford Street** (in either direction) for affordable shopping (start at Marble Arch Tube station if you're ambitious, or Bond Street station if you only care to see some of it), and **Regent Street,** which intersects Oxford Street at Oxford Circus (Tube: Oxford Circus). The Oxford Street flagship (at Marble Arch) of the private-label department store Marks & Spencer ("Marks & Sparks" in the local parlance) is worth visiting for quality goods. Regent Street, which leads all the way to Piccadilly, has more upscale department stores (including the famed Liberty of London), chains (Laura Ashley), and specialty dealers.

Parallel to Regent Street, **Bond Street** (Tube: Bond Street) connects Piccadilly with Oxford Street and is synonymous with the luxury trade. Divided into New and Old, it has experienced a recent revival and is the hot address for international designers; Donna Karan has two shops here. A slew of international hotshots, from Chanel to Ferragamo to Versace, have digs nearby.

Burlington Arcade (Tube: Piccadilly Circus), the famous glass-roofed, Regency-style passage leading off Piccadilly, looks like a period exhibition and is lined with intriguing shops and boutiques. Lit by wrought-iron lamps and decorated with clusters of ferns and flowers, its small, smart stores specialize in fashion, jewelry, Irish linen, cashmere, and more. If you linger there until 5:30pm, you can watch the beadles (the last London representatives of Britain's oldest police force), in their black-and-yellow livery and top hats, ceremoniously place the iron grills that block off the arcade until 9am, at which time they just as ceremoniously remove them to start a new business day. (There are only 3 beadles remaining.) Also at 5:30pm, a hand bell called the Burlington Bell is sounded, signaling the end of trading.

For a total contrast, check out **Jermyn Street** (Tube: Piccadilly Circus), on the far side of Piccadilly, a tiny 2-block-long street devoted to high-end men's haberdashers and toiletries shops; many have been doing business for centuries. Several hold royal warrants, including Turnbull & Asser, where HRH Prince Charles has his P.J.s made. A bit to the northwest, Savile Row (between Regent Street and New Bond Street) is synonymous with the finest in men's tailoring.

Tips **GST: Greenwich Shopping Time**

Though many London shops are now open on Sundays, the best Sunday shopping is in the stalls of the flea and craft markets in the royal city of Greenwich.

The best way to enjoy the trip is to float downstream on a boat from Charing Cross or Westminster pier (service begins at 10:30am on Sun; see "River Cruises Along the Thames," under "Exploring London by Boat," in chapter 7). The trip takes about a half-hour, but you'll get a knowledgeable commentary on the Docklands development and the history of the river, and view the Tower and much of London from the water along the way.

The boat leaves you in the heart of Greenwich, minutes from the craft market held on Saturday and Sunday. Follow the signs—or the crowd. After you're done, follow the crowd again to Greenwich's several antiques markets. First is **Canopy Market,** which isn't under a canopy at all, but sprawls through several parking lots where junk and old books abound, and then onto **High Street,** where the fancier flea market is held. It's possible that there's yet another antiques market at **Town Hall,** across the street, but these shows usually charge an admission fee.

You're only a half block from the Greenwich BritRail station now, which is on Greenwich High Road; and there's a train back to London every half-hour, until about 11:30pm.

The West End theater district borders two more shopping areas: the still-not-ready-for-prime-time **Soho** (Tube: Tottenham Court Road), where the sex shops are slowly converting into cutting-edge designer shops, and **Covent Garden** (Tube: Covent Garden), a shopping masterpiece unto itself. The original Covent Garden marketplace has overflowed its boundaries and eaten up the surrounding neighborhood; it's fun to wander the narrow streets and shop. Covent Garden is mobbed on Sundays.

Just a stone's throw from Covent Garden, **Monmouth Street** is somewhat of a London shopping secret: Londoners know they can find an array of stores in a space of only 2 blocks. Many shops here are outlets for British designers such as Alexander Campbell, who specializes in outfits made of wispy materials. Some shops along this street specialize in both used and new clothing. Besides clothing, stores specialize in everything from musical instruments from the Far East to palm and crystal ball readings.

KNIGHTSBRIDGE & CHELSEA Knightsbridge (Tube: Knightsbridge), the home of Harrods, is the second-most-famous London retail district. (Oxford Street edges it out.) Nearby Sloane Street is chock-a-block with designer shops.

Walk southwest on **Brompton Road** (toward the Victoria and Albert Museum) and you'll find **Cheval Place,** lined with designer resale shops, and Beauchamp (*Bee*-cham) Place. It's only a block long, but it's very "Sloane Ranger" or "Sloanie" (as the Brits would say), featuring the kinds of shops where young British aristocrats buy their clothing for the "season."

If you walk farther along Brompton Road, you connect to **Brompton Cross,** another hip area for designer shops made popular when Michelin House was rehabbed by Sir Terence Conran, becoming the Conran Shop. Seek out **Walton Street,** a tiny snake of a street running from Brompton Cross back toward the museums. Most of the shops along this street specialize in non-essential luxury products, the kind a severe and judgmental Victorian moralist might dismiss as vanities and fripperies. This is where you'll find aromatherapy from Jo Malone, needlepoint, or costume jewelry. **King's Road** (Tube: Sloane Square), the main street of Chelsea, will forever remain a symbol of the Swinging '60s. It's still popular with the young crowd, but there are fewer mohawk haircuts, Bovver boots, and Edwardian ball gowns than before. More and more, King's Road is a lineup of markets and "multi-stores," conglomerations of indoor stands, stalls, and booths within one building or enclosure. About a third of King's Road is devoted to "multi-store" antiques markets; another third houses design-trade showrooms and stores of household wares; and the remaining third is faithful to the area's teenybopper roots.

Finally, don't forget all those museums in nearby **South Kensington**—they all have great gift shops.

KENSINGTON, NOTTING HILL & BAYSWATER **Kensington High Street** (Tube: High Street Kensington) is the hangout of the classier breed of teen, one who has graduated from Carnaby Street and is ready for street chic. While there are a few staples of basic British fashion here, most of the stores feature items that stretch, are very, very short, very, very tight, and very, very black.

From Kensington High Street, you can walk up **Kensington Church Street,** which, like Portobello Road, is one of the city's main shopping avenues for antiques, selling everything from antique furniture to Impressionist paintings.

Kensington Church Street dead-ends at the Notting Hill Gate Tube station, jumping-off point for Portobello Road; the antiques dealers and weekend market are 2 blocks beyond.

Not far from Notting Hill Gate is **Whiteleys of Bayswater,** Queensway, W2 (© **020/7229-8844;** Tube: Bayswater or Queensway), an Edwardian mall whose chief tenant is Marks & Spencer. Whiteleys also contains 75 to 85 shops, mostly specialty outlets and restaurants, cafes, and bars as well as an eight-screen movie theater.

3 The Department Stores

Contrary to popular belief, Harrods is not the only department store in London. The British invented the department store, and they have lots of them, mostly in Mayfair, and each has its own customer profile.

DAKS Opened in 1936 as the home of DAKS clothing, DAKS has been going strong ever since. It's known for menswear—its basement-level men's shoe department is a model of the way quality shoes should be fitted—as well as women's fashions, perfume, jewelry, and lingerie. Many of the clothes are light-hearted, carefully made, and well suited to casual elegance. Solid, reliable and dependant, this is a well-established store whose core market is male and female clients ages 30 to 50. Clothes aren't particularly cutting edge (and indeed, many of the regular clients here aren't necessarily looking for that), except for the clothing from the recently inaugurated youth line "Daks E1." 10 Old Bond St., W1. © 020/7409-4000. Tube: Green Park.

Fenwick of Bond Street Fenwick (the "w" is silent), dating from 1891, is a stylish fashion store that offers an excellent collection of designer womenswear, ranging from moderately priced ready-to-wear items to more expensive designer fashions. An extensive selection of lingerie in all price ranges is also sold. 63 New Bond St., W1. © 020/7629-9161. Tube: Bond St.

Fortnum & Mason Catering to well-heeled clients as a full-service department store that was founded in 1707, Fortnum & Mason recently spent £14 million on an overhaul of its premises and inventories. Inventories include one of the most comprehensive delicatessens and food markets in London, as well as stationery, gift items, porcelain and crystal, and lots and lots of clothing for men, women, and children. 181 Piccadilly, W1. © 020/7734-8040. Tube: Piccadilly Circus.

Harrods Harrods remains an institution, but in the last decade or so it has grown increasingly dowdy and is not as cutting edge as it used to be. For the latest trends, shop elsewhere. We always stop here anyway during our visits to London. As entrenched in English life as Buckingham Palace and the Ascot Races, it's still an elaborate emporium. Goods are spread across 300 departments, and the range, variety, and quality can still dazzle the visiting out-of-towner.

The whole fifth floor is devoted to sports and leisure, with a wide range of equipment and attire. Toy Kingdom is on the fourth floor, along with children's wear. The Egyptian Hall, on the ground floor, sells crystal from Lalique and Baccarat, plus porcelain.

There's also a men's grooming room, a jewelry department, and a fashion department for younger customers. You have a choice of 18 restaurants and bars. Best of all are the **Food Halls,** with a huge variety of foods and several cafes. Harrods began as a grocer in 1849, and that's still the heart of the business. The motto remains, "If you can eat or drink it, you'll find it at Harrods." 87–135 Brompton Rd., Knightsbridge, SW1. © 020/7730-1234. Tube: Knightsbridge.

Harvey Nichols Locals call it "Harvey Nicks." Once a favorite of the late Princess Di, the store is large, but doesn't compete with Harrods because it has a more upmarket, fashionable image. Harvey Nicks has its own gourmet food hall and fancy restaurant, **The Fifth Floor,** and a huge store crammed with the best designer home furnishings, gifts, and fashions for all, although women's clothing is the largest segment of its business. The store carries many American designer brands; avoid them, as they're more expensive in London than they are in the States. 109–125 Knightsbridge, SW1. ℂ 020/7235-5000. Tube: Knightsbridge.

Liberty   This department store is celebrated for its Liberty Prints: top-echelon fabrics, often in floral patterns, prized by decorators for the way they add a sense of English tradition to a room. The front part of the Regent Street store isn't particularly distinctive, but don't be fooled: Other parts of the place have been restored to Tudor-style splendor that includes half-timbering and interior paneling. There are six floors of fashion, china, and home furnishings, the famous Liberty Print fashion fabrics, upholstery fabrics, scarves, ties, luggage, and gifts. 214-220 Regent St., W1. ℂ 020/7734-1234. Tube: Oxford Circus.

Peter Jones   Founded in 1877 and rebuilt in 1936, Peter Jones is known for household goods, household fabrics and trims, china, glass, soft furnishings, and linens. The linen department is one of the best in London. Sloane Sq., SW1. ℂ 020/7730-3434. Tube: Sloane Sq.

4 Goods A to Z

ANTIQUES

Alfie's Antique Market   This is the biggest and one of the best-stocked conglomerates of antique dealers in London, crammed into the premises of a 19th-century store. It has more than 370 stalls, showrooms, and workshops in over 35,000 square feet of floor space. You'll find the biggest Susie Cooper (a well-known designer of tableware and ceramics for Wedgwood) collection in Europe here. A whole antiques district has grown up around Alfie's along Church Street. 13–25 Church St., NW8. ℂ 020/7723-6066. Fax 020/7724-0999. Tube: Marylebone or Edgware Rd.

Antiquarius   The recently redecorated Antiquarius echoes the artistic diversity of King's Road. More than 120 dealers offer specialized merchandise, usually of the small, domestic variety, such as antique and period jewelry, porcelain, silver, first-edition books, boxes, clocks, prints, and paintings, with an occasional piece of antique furniture. You'll find a lot of items from the 1950s. 131–141 King's Rd., SW3. ℂ 020/7969-1500. Tube: Sloane Sq. or South Kensington.

Bond Street Antiques Centre   This place, in the heart of London's finest shopping district, enjoys a reputation for being London's premium center for antique jewelry, silver, watches, porcelain, glass, and Asian antiques and paintings. 124 New Bond St., W1. ℂ 020/7351-5353 or 020/7493-1854. Tube: Bond St. or Green Park.

Grays Antiques and Grays Mews   These markets have been converted into walk-in stands with independent dealers. The term "antique" covers items from oil paintings to, say, the 1894 edition of the *Encyclopedia Britannica.* Also sold are antique jewelry; silver; gold; maps and prints; bronzes and ivories; arms and armor; Victorian and Edwardian toys; furniture; Art Nouveau and Art Deco items; antique lace; scientific instruments; craft tools; and Asian, Persian, and Islamic pottery, porcelain, miniatures, and antiquities. There's a cafe in each building. Check out the 1950s-style **Victory Cafe** on Davies Street for their homemade cakes. 58 Davies St. and 1–7 Davies Mews, W1. ℂ 020/7629-7034. Tube: Bond St.

The Mall at Camden Passage   The mall contains one of Britain's greatest concentrations of antiques dealers. In individual shops, you'll find some 35 dealers offering fine furniture, porcelain, and silver. The area expands into a street market on Wednesday and Saturday. Islington, N1. © 020/7351-5353. Tube: Northern Line to Angel.

ARCHITECTURAL SALVAGE

LASSCO (London Architectural Salvage & Supply Co.)   Established in 1978, this company controls the largest inventories of architectural remnants in the UK, with warehouses chock-full of mantelpieces, stained glass windows, antique doors, statuary, ecclesiastical accessories (including, among others, assorted pews from Victorian-era churches), and garden ornaments. Each piece was rescued during the renovation or demolition of buildings throughout Greater London. Many of them originated within unheralded private homes; others come from public buildings that have included the Palace of Westminster and the Royal Opera House. The company's headquarters and most impressive showroom occupy a deconsecrated Victorian church.

A particularly interesting annex of this outfit (same phone, same tube stop) lies within a 5-minute walk at Britannia Walk, N1. It specializes in antique doors, a resource that building contractors and architects usually find fascinating. Small, easy-to-transport antique items are available, including some charming 19th-century woodworking tools. Any of the large objects available here can be crated and shipped. The address for the headquarters is St. Michael and All Angels, on Mark St., off Paul St., EC2. © 020/7749-9944. Tube: Old St.

ART & CRAFTS

ACAVA *(Finds)*   This London-based visual arts facility provides studios and other services for professional artists, and represents about 250 artists working in spaces around London. Call for individual open-studio schedules, as well as dates for the annual Open Studios weekend. © 020/8960-5015.

Cecilia Colman Gallery   One of London's most established crafts galleries, Cecilia Colman features decorative ceramics, studio glass, jewelry, and metalwork. Among the offerings are glass sculptures by Lucien Simon, jewelry by Caroline Taylor, and pottery by Simon Rich. Exhibitions of contemporary original works in ceramic, glass, and metal are featured. There's also a large selection of mirrors and original-design perfume bottles. 67 St. John's Wood High St., NW8. © 020/7722-0686. Tube: Jubilee Line to St. John's Wood.

Contemporary Applied Arts   This association encourages traditional and progressive contemporary artwork. Many of Britain's best-established craftspeople, as well as promising talents, are represented in galleries that house a diverse retail display of glass, ceramics, textiles, wood, furniture, jewelry, and metalwork—all by contemporary artisans. A program of special exhibitions, including solo and small-group shows, focuses on innovations in craftwork. There are new exhibitions every 6 weeks. 2 Percy St., W1. © 020/7436-2344. Tube: Goodge St.

Crafts Council Gallery   This gallery is run by the Crafts Council, the national body promoting contemporary crafts. You'll discover some of today's most creative work here. There's a shop specializing in craft objects and publications, and a reference library. The gallery is closed on Mondays. 44A Pentonville Rd., Islington, N1. © 020/7278-7700. Tube: Northern Line to Angel.

England & Co.   Under the guidance of Jane England, this gallery specializes in Outsider Art and Art in Boxes, which incorporates a box structure into the

Finds **Go East, Art Lover**

The East End neighborhood of Hoxton used to be a tawdry backwater until artists starting flocking here and opening studios, cleaning up the discarded mattresses and rejuvenating abandoned buildings.

Success was assured with the opening of **White Cube 2**, 48 Hoxton Sq., EC2 (℃ **020/7930-5373**), owned by Jay Jopling, the leading dealer in modern English art, whose artists include Britain's most controversial, Damien Hirst. The other hot gallery is **Victoria Miro Gallery**, 16 Wharf Rd., EC2 (℃ **020/7336-8109**). Some of London's most controversial art appears here. Miro represents Chris Ofili, whose "Madonna and Dung" painting enraged New York mayor and art critic Rudolph Giuliani.

These art dealers and the artists themselves (that is, those who sold a painting) can be found dining at **Cantaloupe**, 35 Charlotte Rd., EC2 (℃ **020/7729-5566**), with its Mediterranean cuisine and great tapas. This informal bar/restaurant, with its wooden tables and industrial fittings, prepares such superb dishes as chargrilled Aberdeen Angus steak with rosemary butter or fried *halloumi* (a white cheese from Cyprus) with olive salsa. Open Monday through Friday from noon to 3pm, and Monday through Saturday from 6 to 11:30pm. Main courses cost from £8.50 to £15 ($12.75–$22.50).

Take the Tube to Old Street to arrive near the doorsteps of all of these establishments.

composition or frame of a three-dimensional work. The gallery focuses attention on neglected post-war British artists such as Tony Stubbings and Ralph Romney. One-person and group shows are mounted frequently, and many young artists get early exposure here. 216 Westbourne Grove, W11. ℃ **020/7221-0417**. Tube: Notting Hill Gate.

Gong One of the best selections of offbeat crafts and jewelry in England awaits you here. The merchandise is the work of both Asian and international artisans. 182 Portobello Rd., W11 ℃ **020/7565-4162**. Tube: Notting Hill Gate.

Whitechapel Art Gallery Since this East End gallery opened its Art Nouveau doors in 1901, collectors have been heading here to find out what's hot. It maintains its cutting edge; to some, it's the incubation chamber for some of the most talented of east London's artists. The collections are fun, hip, often sexy, and in your face. 80–82 Whitechapel High St., E1. ℃ **020/7522-7888** or 020/7522-7878 (recorded). Fax 020/7377-1685. Tube: District or Hammersmith & City Lines to Aldgate East.

BATH & BODY

The Body Shop There's a branch of The Body Shop in every shopping area and tourist zone in London. Some are bigger than others, but all are filled with politically and environmentally aware beauty, bath, and aromatherapy products. Prices are much lower in the UK than they are in the U.S. There's an entire children's line, a men's line, and lots of travel sizes and travel products. 374 Oxford St., W1. ℃ **020/7409-7868**. Tube: Bond St. Other locations throughout London.

Boots the Chemist This store has a million branches; we like the one across the street from Harrods for convenience and size. The house brands of beauty products are usually the best, be they Boots products (try the cucumber facial scrub), Boot's versions of The Body Shop (two lines, Global and Naturalistic), or Boot's versions of Chanel makeup (called No. 7). They also sell film, pantyhose (called tights), sandwiches, and all of life's other little necessities. 72 Brompton Rd., SW3. ℂ 020/7589-6557. Tube: Knightsbridge. Other locations throughout London.

Culpeper the Herbalist This store has another branch in Mayfair, at 21 Bruton St., W1 (ℂ **020/7629-4559**), but the hours are better at Covent Garden, You'll have to put up with the cramped space here to check out all the food, bath, and aromatherapy products, but it's worth it. Stock up on essential oils, or go for the dream pillows, candles, sachets, and many a shopper's fave—the aromatherapy fan, for home and the car. 8 The Piazza, Covent Garden, WC2. ℂ **020/ 7379-6698**. Tube: Covent Garden.

Floris A variety of toilet articles and fragrances fill Floris's floor-to-ceiling mahogany cabinets, which are architectural curiosities in their own right. They were installed relatively late in the establishment's history—that is, 1851—long after the shop had received its royal warrants as suppliers of toilet articles to the king and queen. 89 Jermyn St., SW1. ℂ **020/7930-2885**. Fax 020/7930-1402. Tube: Piccadilly Circus.

Neal's Yard Remedies Noted the world over for their cobalt-blue bottles, these chi-chi bath, beauty, and aromatherapy products are must-haves for those who pooh-pooh The Body Shop as too common. Prices are higher in the United States, so stock up here. 15 Neal's Yard, WC2. ℂ **020/7379-7222**. Tube: Covent Garden.

Penhaligon's This Victorian perfumery, established in 1870, holds royal warrants to HRH Duke of Edinburgh and HRH Prince of Wales. All items sold are exclusive to Penhaligon's. It offers a large selection of perfume, aftershave, soap, and bath oils for women and men. Gifts include antique-silver scent bottles, grooming accessories, and leather traveling goods. Penhaligon's is now in more than 20 Saks Fifth Avenue stores across the United States. 41 Wellington St., WC2. ℂ **020/7836-2150**, or 212/661-1300 in the U.S. for mail order. Tube: Covent Garden.

BOOKS, MAPS & ENGRAVINGS

In addition to the bookstores below, you'll find well-stocked branches of the **Dillon's** chain around town, including one at 82 Gower St. (Tube: Euston Square).

Children's Book Centre With thousands of titles, this is the best place to go for children's books. Fiction is arranged according to age, up to 16. There are also videos and toys for kids. 237 Kensington High St., W8. ℂ **020/7937-7497**. Tube: Kensington.

Foyle's Bookshop Claiming to be the world's largest bookstore, Foyle's has an impressive array of hardcovers and paperbacks, as well as travel maps, new records, CDs, videotapes, and sheet music. They have opened a "hypermarket" where you can buy original artwork off the shelf. Works by some three-dozen Spanish and French artists are for sale at prices beginning at £60 ($90). 113–119 Charing Cross Rd., WC2. ℂ **020/7437-5660**. Tube: Tottenham Court Rd.

Gay's the Word Britain's leading gay and lesbian bookstore offers a large selection of books, as well as magazines, cards, and guides. There's also a used-books section. 66 Marchmont St., WC1. ℂ **020/7278-7654**. Tube: Russell Sq.

Hatchards On the south side of Piccadilly, Hatchards offers a wide range of books on all subjects and is particularly renowned in the areas of fiction, biography, travel, cookery, gardening, art, history, and finance. In addition, Hatchards is second to none in its range of books on royalty. 187 Piccadilly, W1. ✆ 020/7439-9921. Tube: Piccadilly Circus or Green Park.

The Map House of London An ideal place to find an offbeat souvenir. Map House sells antique maps and engravings and a vast selection of old prints of London and England, both original and reproduction. A century-old original engraving costs about £20 ($30). 54 Beauchamp Place, SW3. ✆ 020/7589-4325. Tube: Knightsbridge.

Murder One *Finds* Maxim Jakubowski's bookshop is dedicated to the genres of crime, romance, science fiction, and horror. Crime and science fiction magazines, some of them obscure, are also available. 71–73 Charing Cross Rd., WC2. ✆ 020/ 7734-3483. Tube: Leicester Sq.

Silver Moon Women's Bookshop This place stocks thousands of titles by and about women, plus videos, jewelry, and a large selection of lesbian books. 64–68 Charing Cross Rd., WC2. ✆ 020/7836-7906. Tube: Leicester Sq.

Stanfords Established in 1852, Stanfords is the world's largest map shop. Many maps, which include worldwide touring and survey maps, are unavailable elsewhere. It's also London's best travel bookstore (with a complete selection of Frommer's guides!) 12–14 Long Acre, WC2. ✆ 020/7836-1321. Tube: Covent Garden.

CASHMERE & WOOLENS

Berk This store boasts one of the largest collections of cashmere sweaters in London—at least the top brands. The outlet also carries capes, stoles, scarves, and camelhair sweaters. 46 Burlington Arcade, Piccadilly, W1. ✆ 020/7493-0028. Tube: Piccadilly Circus or Green Park.

Scotch House For top-quality woolen fabrics and garments, go to Scotch House, renowned for its comprehensive selection of cashmere and wool knitwear for men, women, and children. Also available is a wide range of tartan garments and accessories, as well as Scottish tweed classics. 157–165 Regent St., W1. ✆ 020/7734-0203. Tube: Piccadilly Circus.

Westaway & Westaway Stopping here is a substitute for a shopping trip to Scotland. You'll find a range of kilts, scarves, waistcoats, capes, dressing gowns, and rugs in authentic clan tartans. The staff is knowledgeable about the clan symbols. They sell cashmere, camelhair, and Shetland knitwear, plus Harris tweed jackets, Burberry raincoats, and cashmere overcoats for men. 64–65 Great Russell St. (opposite the British Museum), WC1. ✆ 020/7405-4479. Tube: Tottenham Court Rd. or Holborn.

CHINA, GLASS & SILVER

Royal Doulton Founded in the 1930s, this store has one of the largest inventories of china in Britain. A wide range of English bone china, as well as crystal and giftware, is sold. The firm specializes, of course, in Royal Doulton (plus Minton and Royal Crown Derby) china, Lladro figures, Border Fine Arts, and other famous names. The January and June sales are excellent. 154 Regent St., W1. ✆ 020/7734-3184. Tube: Piccadilly Circus or Oxford Circus.

London Silver Vaults *Finds* Don't let the out-of-the-way location or the facade's lack of charm slow you down. Downstairs, you'll enter vaults—40 in all—that are filled with tons of silver and silverplate, plus collections of jewelry. It's a staggering selection of old and new, with excellent prices and friendly dealers. Chancery House, 53–64 Chancery Lane, WC2. ✆ 020/7242-3844. Tube: Chancery Lane.

Reject China Shop   Don't expect too many rejects or too many bargains, despite the name. This shop sells seconds (sometimes) along with first-quality pieces of china with such names as Royal Doulton, Spode, and Wedgwood. You can also find a variety of crystal, glassware, and flatware. If you'd like to have your purchases shipped home for you, the shop can do it for a fee. 183 Brompton Rd., SW3. ✆ 020/7581-0739. Tube: Knightsbridge. Other locations throughout London.

Thomas Goode   This is one of the most famous emporiums in Britain; it's worth visiting for its architectural interest and nostalgic allure alone. Originally built in 1876, Goode's has 14 rooms loaded with porcelain, gifts, candles, silver, tableware, and even a private museum. There's also a tearoom-cum-restaurant tucked into the corner. 19 S. Audley St., W1. ✆ 020/7499-2823. Tube: Bond St., Green Park, or Marble Arch.

CHOCOLATES

Godiva Chocolates   This world-famous chocolate maker has invaded Covent Garden with the tastiest sweets in town. The store offers London's finest selection of chocolates, with some seasonal products. In addition to handcrafted chocolates, the sales people here also hawk the chocolate jam. 17 Russell St., WC2. ✆ 020/7836-5706. Tube: Covent Garden.

FASHION

While every internationally known designer worth his or her weight in shantung has a boutique in London, the best buys are on the sturdy English styles that last forever. See also the separate sections on "Cashmere & Woolens," "Handbags," "Lingerie," and "Shoes."

Austin Reed   Austin Reed has long stood for superior-quality clothing and excellent tailoring. Chester Barrie's off-the-rack suits, for example, are said to fit like tailor-made. The polite employees are unusually honest about telling you what looks good. The store always has a wide variety of top-notch jackets and suits, and men can outfit themselves from dressing gowns to overcoats. For women, there are carefully selected suits, separates, coats, shirts, knitwear, and accessories. 103–113 Regent St., W1. ✆ 020/7734-6789. Tube: Piccadilly Circus.

Beau Monde   This outlet earns its fame selling a chic but affordable "nouvelle couture" for women—fitted and adjusted to your body. All designs are by the locally famous London designer, Sylvia Young. Her design philosophy is that a busy woman should be conscious of fashion, but not a victim of its whims, and that clothes should work for her—not against her. Her women's wear is comfortable to wear and fashionable but not stuffy. 43 Lexington St., W1 ✆ 020/7734-6563. Tube: Piccadilly Circus.

Burberry   The name has been synonymous with raincoats ever since Edward VII ordered his valet to "bring my Burberry" when the skies threatened. An impeccably trained staff sells the famous raincoats, plus excellent men's shirts, sportswear, knitwear, and accessories. Raincoats are available in women's sizes and styles as well. Prices are high, but you get quality and prestige. 18–22 Haymarket, SW1. ✆ 020/7930-3343. Tube: Piccadilly Circus.

Designer Sale Studio   More and more frugal women shoppers from around the world are heading to the city's East End to see what high-fashion clothing bargains are on the racks at this discount sales outlet. All the big British designers have clothing here, including Alexander McQueen. Perhaps you'll even "discover" the controversial dress he designed for Gwyneth Paltrow's appearance at the Oscars, which she presumably dumped right after the negative press began pouring in. Old Truman Brewery Complex, 95A Brick Lane. ✆ **020/7247-8595.** Tube: Aldgate East or Liverpool St.

Dr. Marten's Department Store   Teens come to worship at Doc Marten's because the prices here are better than in the United States or Europe. The shoes have become so popular internationally that they have spawned an entire store, selling dozens of styles of footwear, as well as accessories, gifts, and an ever-expanding range of clothes. 1–4 King St., WC2. ✆ **020/7497-1460.** Tube: Covent Garden.

Gieves & Hawkes   This men's clothing store has a prestigious address and a list of clients that includes the Prince of Wales, yet its prices aren't as lethal as others on this street. They're high, but you get good quality. Cotton shirts, silk ties, Shetland sweaters, and exceptional ready-to-wear and tailor-made ("bespoke") suits are sold. 1 Savile Row, W1. ✆ **020/7434-2001.** Tube: Piccadilly Circus or Green Park.

Hilditch & Key   The finest name in men's shirts, Hilditch & Key has been in business since 1899. The two shops on this street both offer men's clothing (including a custom-made shirt service) and women's ready-made shirts. There's also an outstanding tie collection. Shirts go for half price during the twice-yearly sales; men fly in from all over the world for them. 37 and 73 Jermyn St., SW1. ✆ **020/7734-4707.** Tube: Piccadilly Circus or Green Park.

Jigsaw   Branches of this fashion chain are numerous, but the Long Acre branch features trendy, middle-market womenswear and children's clothing. Around the corner, the Floral Street shop carries menswear, including a wide range of colored moleskin items. 21 Long Acre, WC2. ✆ **020/7240-3855.** Tube: Covent Garden.

Jigsaw Menswear   This store is for the male who wants to be a bit daring in his dress. You've heard of the gray flannel suit, but what about the gray flannel kilt with not a single shred of plaid on it? The wool jumpsuits must have been inspired by the workers at Heathrow. There is also a selection of moleskin suits, black leather pants, and all the latest styles. 126 King's Rd., SW3. ✆ **020/7823-7304.** Tube: Sloane Sq.

Laura Ashley   This is the flagship store of the company whose design ethos embodies the flowery English country look. The store carries a wide choice of women's clothing, plus home furnishings. Prices are lower than in the United States. 256–258 Regent St., W1. ✆ **020/7437-9760.** Tube: Oxford Circus. Other locations around London.

Next   This chain of "affordable fashion" stores saw its heyday in the 1980s, when it was celebrated for its success in marketing avant-garde fashion ideas to a wide spectrum of the British public. No longer at its peak, it still merits a stop. The look is still very contemporary, with a continental flair, and there are clothes for men, women, and kids, too. 15–17 Long Acre, WC2. ✆ **020/7420-8280.** Tube: Covent Garden. Other locations throughout London.

Reiss   In a city where men's clothing often sells at celestial prices, Reiss is a haven of reasonable sporty and casual wear. Take your pick from everything from pullovers to rugged cargo pants. 114 King's Rd., SW3. ✆ **020/7225-4910.** Tube: Sloane Sq.

SU214   If you find $5,000 a bit much for a Savile Row suit, you can buzz over here for a made-to-measure suit that somewhat evokes the same look, with suits beginning at $400. In-house consultants are on hand for fittings, and you'll emerge looking quite English in a three-button pin-striped jacket and narrow pants. Of course, a mauve shirt and a mauve tie will help you top off the look. 214 Oxford St., W1. ℂ 020/7927-0104. Tube: Bond St.

Thomas Pink   This Jermyn Street shirtmaker, named after an 18th-century Mayfair tailor, gave the world the phrase "in the pink." It has a prestigious reputation for well-made cotton shirts, for both men and women. The shirts are created from the finest two-fold Egyptian and Sea Island pure-cotton poplin. Some patterns are classic, others new and unusual. All are generously cut with long tails and finished with a choice of double cuffs or single-button cuffs. A small pink square in the tail tells all. 85 Jermyn St., SW1. ℂ 020/7930-6364. Tube: Green Park.

Turnbull & Asser   Over the years, everyone from David Bowie to Ronald Reagan has been seen in custom-made shirts from Turnbull & Asser. Excellent craftsmanship and simple lines—plus bold colors—distinguish these shirts. The outlet also sells shirts and blouses to women, a clientele that has ranged from Jacqueline Bisset to Candice Bergen. Note that T&A shirts come in only one sleeve length and are then altered to fit, a ritual that takes only a few days, and costs £8 ($12). If you want custom shirts created from scratch, the made-to-measure service takes 10 to 12 weeks, and you must order at least a half dozen. Of course, the monograms are included. 71–72 Jermyn St., SW1. ℂ 020/7808-3000. Tube: Piccadilly Circus or Green Park.

THE CUTTING EDGE

Currently the most cutting-edge shopping street in London is **Conduit Street,** W1 in Mayfair (Tube: Oxford Circus). Once known for its dowdy airline offices, it is now London's smartest fashion street. Trendy shops are opening between Regent Street and the "blue chip" boutiques of New Bond Street. Current stars include **Vivienne Westwood,** 44 Conduit St., W1 (ℂ 020/7439-1109), who has overcome her punk origins. She's now the grande dame of English fashion. See below for her flagship store. **Krizia,** 24 Conduit St., W1 (ℂ 020/7491-4989), the fashion rage of Rome since the 1950s, displays not only Krizia's clothing lines but her luxury home goods as well.

For muted fashion elegance, **Yohji Yamamoto,** 14–15 Conduit St., W1 (ℂ 020/7491-4129), is hard to beat, and **Issey Miyake,** 52 Conduit St., W1 (ℂ 020/7851-4600), is the Japanese master of minimalism.

Finally, one of the most avant-garde, creative British designers in history, **Alexander McQueen,** 47 Conduit St., W1 (ℂ 020/7734-2340), has moved in to give the neighborhood his blessing. No one pays more attention to fashion detail and craftsmanship than the celebrated McQueen.

Accessorize   This aptly named store is often packed with women who have an eye for bargains but want top-notch style. The store stays abreast of the latest fads and trends, especially in evening bags, which range from antique to high fashion. All sorts of treasures are stocked here, everything from hologram-flecked nail polish to silk scarves. 123A Kensington High St., W8. ℂ 020/7937-1433. Tube: Kensington High St.

Anya Hindmarch   Although her fashionable bags are sold at Harvey Nichols, Liberty, Harrods, and throughout the U.S. and Europe, this is the only place to see the complete range of Anya Hindmarch's handbags, wallets, purses, and key holders. Smaller items range in price from £40 ($60), whereas handbag prices start at £200 ($300), with alligator being the most expensive. There's a limited custom-made service; bring in your fabric if you want a bag to match. 15–17 Pont St., SW3. ℂ 020/7838-9177. Tube: Sloane Sq. or Knightsbridge.

Browns   This is the only place in London to find the designs of Alexander McQueen, head of the House of Givenchy in Paris and one of the fashion industry's stars. Producing his own cottons, silks, and plastics, McQueen creates revealing, feminine women's couture and ready-to-wear, and has started a menswear line. McQueen made his reputation creating shock-value apparel that was more photographed than worn. But recently, fashion critics have called his new outfits "consumer friendly." Browns has introduced "Browns Living," an eclectic array of lifestyle products. 23–27 S. Molton St., W1. ℂ 020/7491-7833. Tube: Bond St.

Egg   This shop is hot, hot, hot with fashionistas. It features imaginatively designed, contemporary clothing by Indian textile designer Asha Sarabhai and knitwear by Eskandar. Designs created from handmade textiles, from a workshop in India, range from everyday dresses and coats to hand-embroidered silk coats. Crafts and ceramics are also available. Closed Sunday and Monday. 36 Kinnerton St., SW1. ℂ 020/7235-9315. Tube: Hyde Park Corner or Knightsbridge.

Hennes   Here are copies of hot-off-the-catwalk fashions at affordable prices. While the quality isn't to brag about, the prices are. For disposable cutting-edge fashion, you can't beat it. 261-271 Regent St., W1. ℂ 020/7493-4004. Tube: Oxford Circus.

Joseph   Joseph Ettedgui, a fashion retailer born in Casablanca, is a maverick in the fashion world. He's known for his daring designs and his ability to attract some of the most talented designers in the business to work with him. This is the flagship store of five London branches, and it carries the Ettedgui collection of suits, knitwear, suede, and leather clothing for men and women. The stretch jeans with flair ankles are the label's best-selling items.

 The Comeback of Carnaby Street

What happened to Carnaby Street? A faded echo left over from the Swinging '60s? That was true for a long time. But Carnaby is rising again. A new influx of talented designers and offbeat shops are popping up not only on Carnaby but along its offshoot streets— Newburgh, Foubert's Place, Kingly Street, Marlborough Court, and Lowndes Court. Innovative boutiques seem to open each week behind small Georgian shop fronts.

Among the zillions of shops are such favorites as **Mikey,** 26 Carnaby St., W1 (ℂ 020/7437-1101), London's pioneering jewelry shop, which has chosen Carnaby Street for its flagship store. Join the Spice Girls in their search for street-bred and urban cool ("svelte" is the London word for cool). At **Fletcher,** Newburgh St., W1 (ℂ 020/7437-7871), discover modern wear for men and women. The cutting edge clothes here are priced in the mid-range. **Lambretta Clothing,** 29 Carnaby St., W1 (ℂ 020/7437-7078) retains the mod lifestyle philosophy and has launched a range of casual wear for men and footwear for men and women. The look has a retro feel, but uses the latest fibers and fabric finishes of today. **All Saints,** 8 Fouberts Place, W1 (ℂ 020/7323-3883), is the creation of noted designer Stuart Trevor, one of the most innovative British menswear designers.

To reach the stores above, take the Tube to Oxford Circus.

(Moments   Where Top Designers Go for Inspiration
──

Just for fun, head for **Brick Lane** in E1 in London's East End, taking the
Tube to Liverpool Street, then Bus 8 heading toward the emerging district of Shoreditch. Here, along Brick Lane beginning at 7am (winding
down around noon), vendors from the far corners of the long-gone
British Empire sell "any and everything." The street is lined with inexpensive Indian restaurants, the best of which is **Beigel Bake,** 159 Brick
Lane, E1 (℃ **020/7729-0616**), if you find yourself hungry.

Another tip: If you'd like to see African-Caribbean life in London,
head for the **Brixton Market** along Electric Avenue, SW9. Take the
Tube to Brixton. To the sound of reggae, including lots of Bob Marley,
you can munch on jerk pork and other West Indian eats and search for
bargains, including the cheapest clothing sold in London.

Electric Avenue is the main street of London's African-Caribbean
life; it was immortalized by Eddie Grant, the Jamaican singer. As you
stroll the avenue, which is rife with fruit and vegetable stalls, duck into
Granville Arcade for Britain's widest selection of African fabrics, reggae CDs, and shopping surprises. The market is best visited Monday,
Tuesday, Thursday, and Saturday from 8am to 6pm; Wednesday from
8am to 1pm, and Friday from 8am to 7pm.

The 16 Sloane St. branch carries only the label's womenswear; the 26 Sloane
St. shop displays all Joseph products and stocks the complete menswear line.
The Fulham Road store showcases menswear and womenswear collections by
other designers, including Prada, Gucci, Marni, Misoni, and Anne Deimunister.
23 Old Bond St., W1. ℃ **020/7629-3713**. Tube: Green Park. Also at 26 Sloane St., SW1. ℃ **020/
7235-5470**. Tube: Sloane Sq. and 77 Fulham Rd., SW3. ℃ **020/7823-9500**. Tube: South
Kensington.

Miss Selfridge   This is a hip young women's clothing and accessory store that
sells its own cosmetic brand, Kiss & Make-Up. For pajama parties, there is a
wide selection of sexy cotton pajamas. There is also a large array of products you
can't live without, like two-toned nail polish and shimmery hair mascara. After,
head for the "chill-out" zone where patrons get comfy on sofas and listen to the
latest tunes. 42–44 Kensington High St., W8. ℃ **020/7938-4182**. Tube: Kensington High St.

Paul Smith's Westbourne House   This shop was converted from a stately
three-story Edwardian town house into a showcase for the clothing of Paul
Smith, whose well-made ready-to-wear men's (and to a lesser extent, women's
and children's) clothing defy the preconceptions of Savile Row tailors who
believe that only custom-made garments are made well and will fit well. Preferred colors, with occasional exceptions, include grays, browns, and blacks,
except for a medley of velvet prints inspired by Carnaby Street in the 1960s.
Look for women's clothes and accessories on the building's street level, men's
clothes and accessories on the two floors above street level. 122 Kensington Park Rd.,
W11. ℃ **020/7727-3553**. Tube: Notting Hill Gate.

Vivienne Westwood   No one in British fashion is hotter than the unstop-
pable Vivienne Westwood. While it's possible to purchase some Westwood

pieces around the world, her UK shops are the best places to find her full range of fashion designs. The flagship location concentrates on her couture line, known as the Gold Label. One of the UK's most watched designers Westwood creates jackets, skirts, trousers, blouses, dresses, and evening dresses that manage to be elegant, alluring, and stylish all at the same time. Many of the fabrics and accessories for her garments are made in Britain and at least some of them are crafted and tailored there as well. Westwood came out with her own fragrance in 1997. Westwood's World's End line of clothing focuses on casual designs for youthful bodies, including T-shirts, jeans, and sportswear. 6 Davies St., W1. ✆ 020/ 7629-3757. Tube: Bond St. World's End branch: 430 King's Rd., SW3 ✆ 020/7352-6551; Tube: Sloane Sq.

VINTAGE & SECONDHAND
Note that there's no VAT refund on used clothing.

Annie's Vintage Costume and Textiles *(Finds* This shop concentrates on carefully preserved dresses from the 1920s and 1930s, but has a range of clothing and textiles from the 1880s through the 1960s. A 1920s fully beaded dress will run you about £400 ($600), but there are scarves for £12 ($18), camisoles for £28 ($42), and a range of exceptional pieces priced between £50 and £60 ($75 and $90). Clothing is located on the main floor; textiles, including old lace, bed linens, and tapestries, are upstairs. 12 Camden Passage, N1. ✆ 020/7359-0796. Tube: Northern Line to Angel.

Pandora A London institution since the 1940s, Pandora stands in fashionable Knightsbridge, a stone's throw from Harrods. Several times a week, chauffeurs drive up with bundles packed anonymously by England's gentry. One woman voted best-dressed at the Ascot Horse Races several years ago was wearing a secondhand dress acquired here. Prices are generally one-third to one-half the retail value. Chanel and Anne Klein are among the designers represented. Outfits are usually no more than two seasons old. 16–22 Cheval Place, SW7. ✆ 020/ 7589-5289. Tube: Knightsbridge.

Pop Boutique For the best in original streetwear from the 1950s, 1960s, and 1970s, this clothing store is tops. Right next to the chic Covent Garden Hotel, it has fabulous vintage wear at affordable prices: Leather jackets that would run in the hundreds in the vintage shops of downtown New York go for as little as £45 ($67.50) here. 6 Monmouth St., WC2. ✆ 020/7497-5262. Tube: Covent Garden.

Steinberg & Tolkien London's leading dealer in vintage costume jewelry and clothing also offers some used designer clothing not old enough to be vintage but prime for collectors; other pieces are merely secondhand designer thrills. 193 King's Rd., SW3. ✆ 020/7376-3660. Tube: Sloane Sq.

FILOFAX
All major department stores sell Filofax supplies, but for the full range (and a shopping experience), check out a Filofax store. They also have good sales; calendars for the next year go on sale very early the previous year (about 10 months in advance), so you can stock up and save.

The Filofax Centre Go to the Conduit Street shop if you can; it stocks the entire range of inserts and books at prices that will floor you: half what you pay in the U.S. 21 Conduit St., W1. ✆ 020/7499-0457. Tube: Oxford Circus. Also at 69 Neal St., WC2 (✆ 020/7836-1977; Tube: Covent Garden).

FOOD

English food has come a long way, and it's worth enjoying and bringing home. Don't miss the Food Halls in Harrods. Consider the Fifth Floor at Harvey Nicks if Harrods is too crowded—it isn't the same, but it'll do. Also, check out the internationally famous Fortnum & Mason food emporium. See "The Department Stores," above for other options.

Charbonnel et Walker   Charbonnel et Walker is famous for its hot chocolate in winter (buy it by the tin) and its chocolate-covered strawberries that are available whenever strawberries are available or in season. The company will send messages of thanks or love spelled out on the chocolates themselves. Ready-made presentation boxes are also available. 1 The Royal Arcade, 28 Old Bond St., W1. ✆ 020/7491-0939. Tube: Green Park.

Neal's Yard Dairy   Specializing in British and Irish cheeses, this shop occupies the very photogenic premises of what was originally built as a warehouse for the food stalls at Covent Garden. Today, you'll see a staggering selection of artisan cheeses, including cloth-bound cheddars and a wide selection of mild farmer's cheeses, set in big display windows behind an antique, dark blue Victorian facade. There are also olive oils, breads, fresh produce, and a lot of the fixings of a picnic. 17 Shorts Gardens, WC2. ✆ 020/7240-5700. Tube: Covent Garden.

GIFTS & SOUVENIRS

Asprey & Company   This is as well-known and well-respected a name in luxury gift giving as anything you're likely to find in all of Britain, with a clientele that includes the likes of the Sultan of Brunei and Queen Elizabeth. Scattered over four floors of a dignified Victorian building, you'll find antiques, porcelain, leather goods, crystal, clocks, and enough unusual objects of dignified elegance to stock an entire English country house. 167 New Bond St., W1. ✆ 020/7493-6767. Tube: Green Park.

The Irish Shop   This family business has been selling a wide variety of articles shipped directly from Ireland since 1964. You'll find a selection of colorful knitwear, traditional Irish linens, hand-knitted Aran fisherman's sweaters, and Celtic jewelry. There's a little bit of everything here—even Guinness paraphernalia. 14 King St., WC2. ✆ 020/7379-3625. Tube: Covent Garden.

Muji   An emporium for Japanese wares, this store is known for its bargain offerings. Among its merchandise, the frugal shopper will find everything from "simple and functional chic" clothing to flatware, most of it in avant-garde, minimalist styles that are completely devoid of any traditional or baroque influences of Olde England. The bath soaps are a delight, coming in such unusual scents as grapefruit and mandarin orange. Funky umbrellas and a host of other ever-changing wares tempt shoppers. 157 Kensington High St., W8. ✆ 020/7323-2208. Tube: Kensington High St.

HANDBAGS

Bill Amberg's   Most famous for his logo-free handbags, Amberg has opened his own shop and expanded his line to include luggage, picture frames, and furniture. Supporters of Amberg's designs include Donna Karan, Romeo Gigli, Jerry Hall, and Christy Turlington. Given those celebrity clients, fashion-conscious shoppers may consider the £40 to £400 ($60–$600) price range of most items a steal. 10 Chepstow Rd., W2. ✆ 020/7727-3560. Tube: Chepstow Rd.

HOME DESIGN & HOUSEWARES

The Conran Shop You'll find high style at reasonable prices from the man who invented it all for Britain: Sir Terence Conran. This place is great for gifts, home furnishings, and tabletop ware—or just for gawking. Michelin House, 81 Fulham Rd., SW3. ℂ 020/7589-7401. Tube: South Kensington.

Designers Guild After more than 26 years in business, creative director Tricia Guild and her young designers still lead the pack in all that's bright and whimsical. They are often copied but never outdone. There's an exclusive line of handmade furniture and accessories at the no. 267–271 location, and wallpaper and more than 2,000 fabrics at the neighboring no. 275–277 shop. The colors remain vivid forever, and the designs always irreverent. Also available are children's accessories, toys, crockery, and cutlery. 267–271 and 275–277 King's Rd., SW3. ℂ 020/7351-5775. Tube: Sloane Sq.

Purves & Purves This store has a varied collection of modern furniture from Britain and the Continent. Many designers make individual pieces that are sold here. The light and airy interior holds an eye-catching display of furniture, lighting, fabrics, rugs, and beds. 220–224 Tottenham Court Rd., W1. ℂ 020/7580-8223. Tube: Goodge St.

JEWELRY

Asprey & Garrard Previously known as Garrard & Co., this recently merged jeweler specializes in both antique and modern jewelry, and silverware. The in-house designers also produce pieces to order and do repairs. You can have a pair of pearl earrings or silver cufflinks for a mere £60 ($102)—but the prices go nowhere but up from there. 167 New Bond St., W1. ℂ 020/7493-6767. Tube: Green Park.

Lesley Craze Gallery/Craze 2/C2 Plus This complex has developed a reputation as a showcase of the best contemporary British jewelry and textile design. The gallery shop focuses on precious metals and includes pieces by such renowned designers as Wendy Ramshaw. Prices start at £60 ($90). Craze 2 features costume jewelry in materials ranging from bronze to paper, with prices starting at £20 ($30). C2 Plus features contemporary textile designs, including wall hangings, scarves, and ties by artists such as Jo Barker, Dawn DuPree, and Victoria Richards. C2 Plus has recently added a hanging gallery to display its textiles and wall hangings. 34 Clerkenwell Green, EC1. ℂ 020/7608-0393 (Gallery), ℂ 020/7251-0381 (Craze 2), ℂ 020/7251-9200 (C2 Plus). Tube: Farringdon.

Sanford Brothers Ltd In business since 1923, this family firm sells all styles of jewelry (both modern and Victorian), silver, and a fine selection of clocks and watches. Old Elizabeth Houses, 3 Holborn Bars, EC1. ℂ 020/7405-2352. Tube: Chancery Lane.

LINENS

Irish Linen Company This royal-warrant boutique carries items crafted of Irish linen, including hand-embroidered handkerchiefs and bed and table linens. 35-36 Burlington Arcade, W1. ℂ 020/7493-8949. Tube: Green Park or Piccadilly Circus.

LINGERIE

Bradley's Bradley's is the best-known lingerie store in London; members of the royal family shop here. Established in the 1950s and very fashionable today, Bradley's fits all sizes in silk, cotton, lace, poly-cotton, or whatever else you might desire. 57 Knightsbridge, SW1. ℂ 020/7235-2902. Tube: Knightsbridge or Hyde Park Corner.

LUGGAGE

Mulberry Company   This flagship store offers a complete line of the town's most cutting-edge designer luggage. Their signature grosgrain luggage begins at £195 ($292.50). Mulberry is also earning a name in fashion for its English country–style ready-to-wear clothes for men and women. It also carries fashionable furnishings and accessories for the home, including throws and cushions in chenille and damask. 11–12 Gees Court, W1. ✆ 020/7493-2546. Tube: Bond St.

MUSEUM SHOPS

Victoria and Albert Museum Gift Shop   This is the best museum shop in London—indeed, one of the best in the world. It sells cards, a fabulous selection of art books, and the usual items, along with reproductions from the design museum archives. Cromwell Rd., SW7. ✆ 020/7942-2687. Tube: South Kensington.

MUSIC

Collectors should browse **Notting Hill;** there are a handful of good shops near the Notting Hill Gate Tube stop. Also browse **Soho** in the Wardour Street area, near the Tottenham Court Road Tube stop. Sometimes dealers show up at Covent Garden on the weekends.

In addition to the two below, the ubiquitous **Our Price** chain is worth checking out for current chart-toppers at great prices.

Tower Records   Attracting throngs from a neighborhood whose pedestrian traffic is almost overwhelming, this is one of the largest record and CD stores in Europe. Sprawling over four floors, it's practically a tourist attraction in its own right. In addition to a huge selection of music, you'll find everything that's on the cutting edge of music technology, including hardware and software, CD-ROMs, and laser discs. 1 Piccadilly Circus, W1. ✆ 020/7439-2500. Tube: Piccadilly Circus. Other locations throughout London.

Virgin Megastore   If a record has just been released—and if it's worth hearing in the first place—chances are this store carries it. It's like a giant musical grocery store. You get to hear many of the new releases on headphones at listening stations before making a purchase. Even rock stars come here to pick up new releases. A large selection of classical and jazz recordings is sold, as are computer software and video games. In between selecting your favorites, you can enjoy a coffee at the cafe or purchase an airline ticket from the Virgin Atlantic office. 14–16 Oxford St., W1. ✆ 020/7631-1234. Tube: Tottenham Court Rd. Also at Kings Walk Shopping Centre, Kings Rd., Chelsea SW3. ✆ 020/7591-0957. Tube: Sloane Sq.

SHOES

Also see **Dr. Marten's Department Store** in "Fashion," above.

Natural Shoe Store   A range of shoes for men and women are stocked in this shop, which also does repairs. The selection includes all comfort and quality footwear, from Birkenstock to the British classics. 21 Neal St., WC2. ✆ 020/7836-5254. Tube: Covent Garden.

Tips **Let's Not Go to the Videotape**

Americans should beware of buying videotapes in the United Kingdom; the British standard is PAL, incompatible with the U.S. standard NTSC. Even if a tape says VHS, it won't play in your machine at home.

Finds **One-Stop Shopping in Covent Garden**

The Covent Garden Market is famous, and we predict that the recently opened **Thomas Neal's,** in the heart of the garden on Earlham Street, WC2, between Seven Dials and Neal Street, will also become well known. This offbeat recommendation fills two floors with designer fashion boutiques, cafes, and gift shops. A lot of hard-to-find merchandise is sold here. Tube: Covent Garden.

Office   In spite of its dull name, this is a most unusual store for style-setters on a budget. Its imitations of some of the world's leading shoe designers have earned it the reputation of the "Madame Tussaud's of footwear." All the shoe designers, from Kenneth Cole to Patrick Cox, get ripped off here. 107 Queensway, W2. ✆ 020/7792-4000. Tube: Queensway.

Shelly's   Shelly's flagship on Oxford Circus is the largest shore store in London, selling footwear to fashionable young things and style-conscious individuals at affordable prices. They're famous for their Dr. Marten's, but there's much more. 266–270 Regent St., W1. ✆ 020/7287-0939. Tube: Oxford Circus. Other locations throughout London.

SPORTING GOODS

Harrods (see "The Department Stores," above) has a surprising collection of sporting goods, including everything you'll need for a polo match.

Lillywhites Ltd   Europe's biggest and most famous sports store has floor after floor of sports clothing, equipment, and footwear. It also offers collections of fashionable leisurewear for men and women. 24–36 Lower Regent St., Piccadilly Circus, SW1. ✆ 020/7915-4000. Tube: Piccadilly Circus.

STATIONERY & PAPER GOODS

Paperchase   This flagship store has three floors of paper products, including handmade paper, wrapping paper, ribbons, picture frames, and a huge selection of greeting cards. It's the best of its kind in London. 213 Tottenham Court Rd., W1. ✆ 020/7467-6200. Tube: Goodge St. or Tottenham Court Rd. Other locations throughout London.

TEA

The Tea House   This shop sells everything associated with tea, tea drinking, and teatime. It boasts more than 70 quality teas and tisanes, including wholefruit blends, the best tea of China (Gunpowder and jasmine with flowers), India (Assam leaf and choice Darjeeling), Japan (Genmaicha green), and Sri Lanka (pure Ceylon), plus such longtime favorite English blended teas as Earl Grey. The shop also offers novelty teapots and mugs. 15 Neal St., WC2 ✆ 020/7420-7539. Tube: Covent Garden.

Of course, don't forget to visit **Fortnum & Mason** as well (see "The Department Stores," above).

TOYS

Hamleys   This flagship is the finest toyshop in the world—more than 35,000 toys and games on seven floors of fun and magic. The huge selection includes soft, cuddly stuffed animals as well as dolls, radio-controlled cars, train sets, model kits, board games, outdoor toys, computer games, and more. 188–196 Regent St., W1. ✆ 020/8752-2278. Tube: Oxford Circus. Also at Covent Garden and Heathrow Airport.

TRAVEL SERVICES

British Airways Travel Shop   The retail flagship of British Airways offers worldwide travel and ticketing, as well as a range of services and shops, including a clinic for immunization, a pharmacy, a *bureau de change,* a passport and visa service, and a theater-booking desk. The ground floor sells luggage, guidebooks, maps, and other goods. Passengers who are only carrying hand baggage can check in here for a BA flight. Travel insurance, hotel reservations, and car rentals can also be arranged. 156 Regent St., W1. ✆ **020/7434-4700.** Tube: Piccadilly Circus or Oxford Circus.

5 Street & Flea Markets

If Mayfair stores are not your cup of tea, don't worry; you'll have more fun, and find a better bargain, at any of the city's street and flea markets.

THE WEST END   Covent Garden Market (✆ **020/7836-9136;** Tube: Covent Garden), the most famous market in all of England, offers several markets daily from 9am to 6:30pm (we think it's most fun to come on Sun). It can be a little confusing until you dive in and explore. **Apple Market** is the bustling market in the courtyard, where traders sell—well, everything. Many of the items are what the English call collectible nostalgia; a wide array of glassware and ceramics, leather goods, toys, clothes, hats, and jewelry. Some of the merchandise is truly unusual. Many items are handmade, with some of the craftspeople selling their own wares—except on Mondays, when antiques dealers take over. Some goods are new, some are very old. Out back is **Jubilee Market** (✆ **020/7836-2139**), also an antiques market on Mondays. Every other day, it's sort of a fancy hippie market with cheap clothes and books. Out front there are a few tents of cheap stuff, except on Monday.

The market itself (in a superbly restored hall) is one of the best shopping venues in London. Specialty shops sell fashions and herbs, gifts and toys, books and dollhouses, cigars, and much more. There are bookshops and branches of famous stores (Hamleys, The Body Shop), and prices are kept moderate.

St. Martin-in-the-Fields Market (Tube: Charing Cross) is good for teens and hipsters who don't want to trek all the way to Camden Market (see "North London," below) and can make do with imports from India and South America, crafts, and local football souvenirs. It's located near Trafalgar Square and Covent Garden; hours are Monday through Saturday from 11am to 5pm, and Sunday from noon to 5pm.

Berwick Street Market (Tube: Oxford Circus or Tottenham Court Road) may be the only street market in the world that's flanked by two rows of strip clubs, porno stores, and adult-movie dens. Don't let that put you off. Humming 6 days a week in the scarlet heart of Soho, this array of stalls and booths sells the best and cheapest fruit and vegetables in town. It also hawks ancient records, tapes, books, and old magazines, any of which may turn out to be collectors' items one day. It's open Monday through Saturday from 8am to 5pm.

On Sunday mornings along **Bayswater Road,** artists hang their work on the railings along the edge of Hyde Park and Kensington Gardens for more than 1.5km (1 mile). If the weather's right, start at Marble Arch and walk. You'll see the same thing on the railings of Green Park along Piccadilly on Saturday afternoon.

NOTTING HILL   Portobello Market (Tube: Notting Hill Gate) is a magnet for collectors of virtually anything. It's mainly a Saturday event, from 6am to

---

(*Value* Great Cashmeres at Half the Price

As you stroll along Portobello Market on a Friday and Saturday, duck into the **Portobello Road Cashmere Shop,** 166 Portobello Rd., W11 (℗ **020/ 7792-2571**). It's a hole-in-the-wall, but it sells some of the finest quality cashmeres in London, at half the price you'd pay in Mayfair. The shop lies a few blocks north of Westbourne Grove.

5pm. You needn't be here at the crack of dawn; 9am is fine. Once known mainly for fruit and vegetables (still sold throughout the week), in the past decades Portobello has become synonymous with antiques. But don't take the stallholder's word for it that the fiddle he's holding is a genuine Stradivarius left to him in the will of his Italian great-uncle; it might have been "nicked" from an East End pawnshop.

The market is divided into three major sections. The most crowded is the antiques section, running between Colville Road and Chepstow Villas to the south. (*Warning:* Be careful of pickpockets in this area.) The second section (and the oldest part) is the fruit and veg market, lying between Westway and Colville Road. In the third and final section, there's a flea market where Londoners sell bric-a-brac and lots of secondhand goods they didn't really want in the first place, but poking around this section still makes for interesting fun.

The serious collector can pick up a copy of a helpful official guide, *Saturday Antique Market: Portobello Road & Westbourne Grove,* published by the Portobello Antique Dealers Association. It lists where to find what, be it music boxes, lace, or 19th-century photographs.

Note: Some 90 antiques and art shops along Portobello Road are open during the week when the street market is closed. This is actually a better time for the serious collector to shop because you'll get more attention from dealers and you won't be distracted by the organ grinder.

SOUTH BANK   Open on Fridays only, New Caledonian Market is known as the **Bermondsey Market** because of its location on the corner of Long Lane and Bermondsey Street (Tube: London Bridge, then Bus 78, or walk down Bermondsey St.). The market is at the east end, beginning at Tower Bridge Road. It's one of Europe's outstanding street markets for the number and quality of its antiques and other goods. Many dealers come into London from the country. Prices are generally lower here than at Portobello and other markets. It gets under way at 5am—with the bargains gone by 9am—and closes at noon. Bring a "torch" (flashlight) if you go in the wee hours.

NORTH LONDON   If it's Wednesday, it's time for **Camden Passage** (℗ **020/7359-0190;** Tube: Northern Line to Angel) in Islington, where each Wednesday and Saturday there's a very upscale antiques market. It starts in Camden Passage and sprawls into the streets behind. It's on Wednesday from 7am to 2pm, and Saturday from 8am to 4pm.

Don't confuse Camden Passage with Camden Market (very downtown). **Camden Market** (Tube: Camden Town) is for teens and others into body piercings, blue hair, and vintage clothing. Serious collectors of vintage may want to explore during the week, when the teen scene isn't quite so overwhelming. Market hours are from 9:30am to 5:30pm daily, with some parts opening at 10am.

London After Dark

London's pulsating after dark scene is the most vibrant in Europe. Although pubs still close at 11pm, the city is staying up later, and more and more clubs have extended partying into the wee hours.

London is on a real high right now, especially in terms of music and dance; much of the current techno and electronica originated in London clubs. Youth culture prevails; downtown denizens flock to the clubs where pop-culture superstars are routinely spotted.

London nightlife is always in a state of flux. What's hot today probably just opened and many clubs have the lifespan of fruit flies. At the time of this writing, **Groucho,** at 45 Dean St., W1 (© **020/7439-4685**), is still the *in* club, although it is members only. A few perennials, like Ronnie Scott's, are still around.

London nightlife is not just music and dance clubs. The city abounds with the world's best theater (sorry, New York!), pubs oozing historic charm, and many more options for a night out.

1 The Play's the Thing: London's Theater Scene

Even more than New York, London is the theater capital of the world. Few things in London are as entertaining and rewarding as the theater. The number and variety of productions, and the standards of acting and directing, are unrivaled. The London stage accommodates both the traditional and the avantgarde and is, for the most part, accessible and affordable. The new Globe Theatre is an exciting addition to the theatre scene. Because the Globe is also a sightseeing attraction, it's previewed in chapter 7, "Exploring London."

TICKET AGENCIES   If your heart is set on seeing a specific show, particularly a big hit, reserve way in advance through one of the London ticket agencies. For tickets and information before you go, try **Global Tickets,** 234 West 44th St., Suite 1000, New York, NY 10036 (© **800/223-6108** or 212/398-1468; www.globaltickets.com). Their London office (which operates under the name of both Global Tickets and First Call Tickets) is at the British Visitors Center, 1 Regents St., W1 V1PJ (© **020/7014-8550**), or at the Harrods ticket desk, 87-135 Brompton Rd. (© **020/7589-9109**) opposite the British Airways desk. They'll mail your tickets, fax a confirmation, or leave your tickets at the box office. Instant confirmations are immediately available for most shows. A booking and handling fee of up to 20% is added to the price of all tickets.

Another option is **Theatre Direct International** (TDI) (© **800/334-8457,** U.S. only). TDI specializes in providing London fringe theater tickets, but also has tickets to major productions, including those of the Royal National Theatre

> **Tips** **Finding Out What's Going On**
>
> Weekly publications *Time Out* and *Where* provide the most complete entertainment listings, with information on music and dance as well as London's diverse theater scene, including everything from big-budget West End shows to fringe productions. Daily newspapers, notably *The Times* and the *Daily Telegraph,* also provide listings. The arts section of the weekend *Independent* is also a good source.
>
> If you want to take full advantage of London's arts scene, your best bet is to do a bit of research before you leave. To get a good idea of what's going on, check out *Time Out*'s web page at www.timeout. co.uk. *Time Out* is available at many international newsstands in the United States and Canada. In London, it can be picked up almost anywhere.

and the Barbican. The service allows you to arrive in London with your tickets or have them held for you at the box office.

GALLERY & DISCOUNT TICKETS Sometimes gallery seats (the cheapest) are sold on the day of the performance; head to the box office early in the day to purchase tickets and, since these are not reserved seats, return an hour before the performance to queue up for good seats. Many theaters offer reduced-price tickets to students on a standby basis. When available, these tickets are sold 30 minutes before curtain. Line up early for popular shows, as standby tickets get snapped up. Call the theater directly to find out if gallery or discount tickets are offered for a particular show. Of course, you'll need a valid student ID for student discounts.

The **Society of London Theatre** (© 020/7557-6700) operates the Half-Price Ticket Booth in Leicester Square (see the "Central London Theaters" map on p. 307 for the location), where tickets for many shows are available at half price, plus a £2 ($3) service charge. Tickets (limited to four per person) are sold only on the day of performance. You cannot return tickets, and credit cards are not accepted. Hours are daily from 10am to 6pm. We prefer this ticket agency to the others that populate Leicester Square. Some of the other agencies might offer you a legitimate discount, but over the years readers have lodged dozens of complaints that their so-called discount ticket turned out to be more expensive than tickets sold at the theater box office. Exercise caution when purchasing tickets at other booths.

MAJOR THEATERS & COMPANIES

To find out what's on in all the major theaters, pick out a *Time Out London* or a London newspaper.

Barbican Theatre—Royal Shakespeare Company The Barbican is the London home of the Royal Shakespeare Company, one of the world's finest companies. The core of the company's repertory remains the Bard, but it also presents a wide-ranging program in its two theaters. There are three productions in repertory each week in the Barbican Theatre: a 2,000-seat main auditorium with excellent sightlines throughout, thanks to a raked stage. The Pit, a studio space, is where the company's new writing is presented. The RSC performs here

Central London Theaters

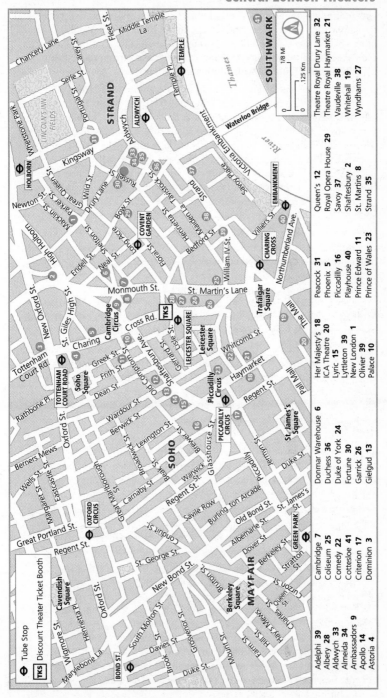

Adelphi **39**
Albery **28**
Aldwych **33**
Almeida **34**
Ambassadors **9**
Apollo **14**
Astoria **4**

Cambridge **7**
Coliseum **25**
Comedy **22**
Cottesloe **41**
Criterion **17**
Dominion **3**

Donmar Warehouse **6**
Duchess **36**
Duke of York **24**
Fortune **30**
Garrick **26**
Gielgud **13**

Her Majesty's **18**
ICA Theatre **20**
Lyric **15**
Lyttleton **39**
New London **1**
Olivier **39**
Palace **10**

Peacock **31**
Phoenix **5**
Piccadilly **16**
Playhouse **40**
Prince Edward **11**
Prince of Wales **23**

Queen's **12**
Royal Opera House **29**
Savoy **37**
Shaftesbury **2**
St. Martins **8**
Strand **35**

Theatre Royal Drury Lane **32**
Theatre Royal Haymarket **21**
Vaudeville **38**
Whitehall **19**
Wyndhams **27**

Φ Tube Stop

TKS Discount Theater Ticket Booth

and at Stratford-upon-Avon. It is in residence in London during the winter; in the summer, it tours England and abroad. In the Barbican Centre, Silk St., Barbican, EC2Y. ℂ 020/7638-8891. Barbican Theatre £5–£35 ($7.50–$52.50); the Pit £15–£22 ($22.50–$33) matinees and evening performances. Box office daily 9am–8pm. Tube: Barbican or Moorgate.

Old Vic This is one of London's most legendary theaters, fabled as the place where Sir John Gielgud made his debut in 1921, and where Lord Laurence Olivier spent much of his career as actor and director of the National Theatre. Kevin Spacey heads a campaign to raise funds to preserve the historic theater, which is still in its original 1818 premises, making it the oldest theater building in London. It is also the most beautiful, though a bit tattered.

Old Vic today is a venue for touring companies that might present everything from the works of The Bard to modern-day prison dramas to Christmas pantomime shows. Each visiting company or troupe sets its own admission prices and box office hours. Waterloo Road, SE1. ℂ 020/7928-7616. Tube: Waterloo.

Open-Air Theatre This outdoor theater is located in Regent's Park. The setting is idyllic, and seating and acoustics are excellent. Presentations are mainly Shakespeare, usually in period costume. Its theater bar, the longest in London, serves both drink and food. In the case of a rained-out performance, tickets are given for another date. The season runs from the end of May to mid-September, Monday through Saturday at 8pm, plus Wednesday, Thursday, and Saturday matinees at 2:30pm. Inner Circle, Regent's Park, NW1. ℂ 020/7486-2431; www. open-air-theatre.org.uk. Tickets £8.50–£23.50 ($12.75–$35.25). Tube: Baker St.

Royal Court Theatre This theater, always a leader in provocative, cutting-edge drama, reopened in February 2000. In the 1950s, it staged the plays of the angry young men, notably John Osborne's then-sensational *Look Back in Anger;* earlier it debuted the plays of George Bernard Shaw. A recent work was *The Beauty Queen of Leenane,* which went on to win a Tony on Broadway. It is home to the English Stage Company. Sloane Sq., SW1. ℂ 020/7565-5000. Tickets £5–£26 ($7.50–$39). Box office 10am–6pm. Tube: Sloane Sq.

Royal National Theatre Home to one of the world's greatest stage companies, the Royal National Theatre is composed of three theaters: the Olivier, reminiscent of a Greek amphitheater with its open stage; the more traditional

---

⸜Tips **Curtain Going Up!**

London theater tickets are not the bargain they used to be. Prices for shows vary from £18 to £60 ($27–$90), depending on the theater and the seat. Matinees, performed Tuesday through Saturday, are cheaper than evening performances. Evening performances begin between 7:30 and 8:30pm, midweek matinees at 2:30 or 3pm, and Saturday matinees at 5:45pm. West End theaters are closed Sundays. Many theaters offer licensed bars on the premises and coffee at intermissions (which Londoners call "intervals").

Many theaters accept telephone bookings at regular prices with a credit card. They'll hold your tickets for you at the box office, where you pick them up at show time with a credit card.

> **Tips** **4 Shows in 2 Days**
>
> That's quite a bit of theater, but true buffs often manage to squeeze that
> much viewing into a fast trip to London. It's possible because so many
> matinees are scheduled throughout the week. For a preview of what's on,
> a pamphlet, "The Official London Theatre Guide," is available at ticket
> brokers and all West End theaters; it's also online at www.officiallondon
> theatre.co.uk.

Lyttelton; and the Cottesloe, with its flexible stage and seating. The National
presents the finest in world theater, from classic drama to award-winning new
plays, including comedies, musicals, and shows for young people. There is a
choice of at least six plays at any one time. As an arts center and gathering place,
it's furnished with an amazing selection of bars, cafes, and restaurants, and
offers free foyer music and exhibitions, short early-evening performances, bookshops, backstage tours, riverside walks, and terraces. You can have a three-course
meal in Mezzanine, the National's restaurant; enjoy a light meal in the brasserie-
style Terrace cafe; or have a snack in one of the coffee bars. South Bank, SE1. ℂ **020/
7452-3400.** Tickets £10–£38 ($15–$57); midweek matinees, Sat matinees, and previews cost less.
Tube: Waterloo, Embankment, or Charing Cross.

Shakespeare's Globe Theatre   In May 1997, the new Globe Theatre—a
replica of the Elizabethan original, thatched roof and all—staged its first slate of
plays (*Henry V* and *A Winter's Tale*) on the site of the 16th-century theater where
the Bard originally staged his work.

Productions vary in style and setting, and not all are performed in Elizabethan
costume. In keeping with the historic setting, the theater is floodlit during
evening performances to replicate daylight because Shakespeare's performances
took place in the afternoon. Theatergoers sit on wooden benches like those of
yore, but now you can rent a cushion. About 500 "groundlings" can stand in the
uncovered yard around the stage, as they did in Shakespeare's day. Mark Rylance,
the artistic director, wants the experience to be as authentic as possible—he told
the press he'd be delighted if the audience threw fruit at the actors, as they did
in Shakespeare's time.

From May to September, the company holds performances Tuesday through
Saturday at 3pm and 7pm, and Sunday at 4pm. The schedule is limited in winter, as this is essentially an outdoor theater. Performances last 2½ to 4 hours.

Also in the works is a second theater, the Inigo Jones Theatre, based on the
architect's designs from the 1600s, where plays will be staged year-round. For
details on the permanent exhibition that tells the story of the painstaking re-
creation of the Globe, as well as guided tours of the theatre, see "More Central
London Attractions," in chapter 7. New Globe Walk, Bankside, SE1. ℂ **020/7902-1400.**
Box office: ℂ 020/7401-9919. Tickets £5 ($7.50) for groundlings, £11–£27 ($16.50–$40.50) for
gallery seats. Exhibition tickets £8 ($12), seniors and students £6 ($9), ages 5–15 £5 ($7.50) Tube:
Mansion House or Blackfriars.

Theatre Royal Drury Lane   Drury Lane is one of London's oldest and most
prestigious theaters. This, the fourth theater on this site, dates from 1812; the
first was built in 1663. Nell Gwynne, the rough-tongued cockney lass who
became Charles II's mistress, used to sell oranges under the colonnade in front.
Nearly every star of London theater has taken the stage here. It has a wide-open

repertoire but leans toward musicals, especially long-running hits. Guided tours of the backstage and the front of the house are given most days at 10:30am and 12:30pm. Call © **020/7494-5091** for information. Evening performances Monday through Saturday 8pm; matinees Wednesday and Saturday 3pm. Catherine St., Covent Garden, WC2. © **020/7494-5060**. Tickets £8–£35 ($12–$52.50). Box office Mon–Sat 10am–7:45pm. Tube: Covent Garden.

FRINGE THEATER

Some of the best theater in London is performed on the "fringe"—at the dozens of theaters devoted to alternative plays, revivals, contemporary dramas, and musicals. These shows are usually more adventurous than established West End productions; they are also consistently lower in price. Expect to pay from £5 to £30 ($7.50–$45). Most offer discounted seats to students and seniors.

Fringe theaters are scattered around London. Check the weekly listings in *Time Out* for schedules and show times. Some of the more popular and centrally located theaters are listed below; call for details on current productions.

Almeida Theatre The Almeida is home to the Festival of Contemporary Music (also called the Almeida Opera) from mid-June to mid-July, featuring everything from atonal jazz to 12-tone chamber orchestra pieces. The Almeida is also known for its adventurous staging of new and classic plays. The theater's legendary status is validated by consistently good productions at lower-than-average prices. Among the recent celebrated productions have been *Hamlet* with Ralph Fiennes and *Medea* with Dame Diana Rigg. Performances are usually held Monday through Saturday. Almeida St., N1. © **020/7359-4404**. Tickets £6–£34 ($9–$51). Box office Mon–Sat 9:30am–6pm. Tube: Northern Line to Angel or Victoria Line to Highbury & Islington.

The Gate This tiny room above a Notting Hill pub is one of the best alternative stages in London. Popular with local cognoscenti, the theater specializes in translated works by foreign playwrights. Performances are held Monday through Saturday at 7 or 7:30pm. Call for shows and times. In the Prince Albert Pub, 11 Pembridge Rd., Notting Hill, W11. © **020/7229-0706**. Tickets £6–£12 ($9–$18). Box office Mon–Fri 10am–6pm. Tube: Notting Hill Gate.

ICA Theatre In addition to a cinema, cafe, bar, bookshop, and galleries, the Institute of Contemporary Arts (ICA) has one of London's top experimental

---

Finds **Something Aesthetic, Something Frenetic: New Theater in London**

Tired of Broadway revivals and English mystery plays that have been running since Queen Victoria occupied the throne? Theater buffs are discovering the **Soho Theatre and Writers' Centre**, a forum for new works in London's Soho district. A former synagogue was converted to make way for a 200-seat theater, plus a restaurant, brasserie, and bar. This is the new home of the Soho Theatre Company, founded in 1969 and credited with launching many successful British playwrights.

The theater is at 21 Dean St., W1 (© **020/7478-0100**). Tube: Tottenham Court Rd. Tickets range from £5 to £15 ($7.50–$22.50).

theaters. The government-subsidized productions usually offer high-quality performances. Bar hours are Tuesday through Saturday from noon to 1am, Sunday and Monday from noon to 11pm. Galleries are open daily from noon to 7:30pm. The Mall, SW1. ✆ 020/7930-3647. Tickets £6.50–£10 ($9.75–$15). Box office daily noon–9:30pm. Tube: Charing Cross or Piccadilly Circus.

The King's Head   London's most famous fringe locale, the King's Head is also the city's oldest pub-theater. Despite its tiny stage, the theater is heavy on musicals; several have gone on to become successful West End productions. Matinees are held on Saturday and Sunday at 3:30pm. Evening performances Tuesday through Saturday are at 8pm. 115 Upper St., N1. ✆ 020/7226-1916. Tickets £9–£14 ($13.50–$21). Box office Mon–Sat 10am–8pm; Sat 11am–8pm; Sun 10am–4pm. Tube: Northern Line to Angel.

Young Vic   Young Vic presents classical and modern plays in the round for theatergoers of all ages and backgrounds, but primarily focuses on young adults. Recent productions have included Shakespeare, Ibsen, Arthur Miller, and specially commissioned plays for children. Call for specific times, as they change. Performances Monday through Saturday 7 or 7:30pm; matinee Saturday 2pm. 66 The Cut, Waterloo, SE1. ✆ 020/7928-6363. Tickets £18 ($27) adults, £12 ($18) seniors, £9 ($13.50) students and children. Box office Mon–Sat 10am–8pm. Tube: Waterloo or Southwark.

2 London's Classical Music & Dance Scene

Currently, London supports five major orchestras—the London Symphony, the Royal Philharmonic, the Philharmonic Orchestra, the BBC Symphony, and the BBC Philharmonic—plus several choirs, and many smaller chamber groups and historic-instrument ensembles. Look for the London Sinfonietta, the English Chamber Orchestra, and of course, the Academy of St. Martin-in-the-Fields. Concerts for many of these groups are presented, with exceptions, in the South Banks Arts Centre or the Barbican. For smaller recitals, venues include Wigmore Hall and St. John's Smith Square.

British Music Information Centre, 10 Stratford Place, W1 (✆ 020/ 7499-8567), is the city's resource center for classical music. It's open Monday through Friday from noon to 5pm and provides free telephone and walk-in information on current and upcoming events. Recitals featuring 20th-century British classical compositions are offered at the information center weekly, usually on Tuesday and Thursday at 7:30pm; call for exact day and time. Since capacity is limited to 40, you may want to check early. The recitals cost up to £5 ($7.50). Take the Tube to Bond Street.

Barbican Centre—London Symphony Orchestra (& more)   The largest art and exhibition center in Western Europe, the roomy and comfortable Barbican complex is the perfect setting for enjoying music and theater. Barbican Hall is the permanent home address of the London Symphony Orchestra, as well as host to visiting orchestras and performers, from classical to jazz, folk, and world music.

In addition to the hall and the two theaters, Barbican Centre includes The Barbican Art Gallery, the Concourse Gallery and foyer exhibition spaces; Cinemas One and Two, which show recently released mainstream films and film series; the Barbican Library, a general lending library that places a strong emphasis on the arts; the Conservatory, one of London's largest greenhouses; and restaurants, cafes, and bars. Silk St., the City, EC2. ✆ 020/7638-8891. www.barbican. org.uk. Tickets £6.50–£40 ($9.75–$60). Box office daily 9am–8pm. Tube: Barbican or Moorgate.

Dance Umbrella   This company's fall season has become *the* contemporary dance event in London. During its 6-week season, new works by up-and-coming choreographers are featured. Performances are held at a variety of theaters. 20 Chancellor's St., W6. ℭ **020/8741-5881**. Tickets £10–£30 ($15–$45) Tube: Hammersmith.

English National Opera   Built in 1904 as a variety theater and converted into an opera house in 1968, the London Coliseum is the city's largest theater. One of two national opera companies, the English National Opera performs a range of works from classics to Gilbert and Sullivan, to new experimental works. All performances are in English. A repertory of 18 to 20 productions is presented 5 or 6 nights a week for 11 months of the year (the theater is dark in July). Although balcony seats are cheaper, many visitors seem to prefer the upper circle or dress circle. London Coliseum, St. Martin's Lane, WC2. ℭ **020/7632-8300**. Tickets £6–£16 ($9–$24) balcony, £17–£61 ($25.50–$91.50) upper or dress circle or stalls; about 100 discount balcony tickets sold on the day of performance from 10am. Tube: Charing Cross or Leicester Sq.

Royal Albert Hall   Opened in 1871 and dedicated to the memory of Victoria's consort, Prince Albert, this circular building holds one of the world's most famous auditoriums. With a seating capacity of 5,200, it's a popular place to hear music by stars. Occasional sporting events (especially boxing) figure strongly here, too.

Since 1941, the hall has hosted the BBC Henry Wood Promenade Concerts, known as "The Proms," an annual series that lasts for 8 weeks between mid-July and mid-September. The Proms, incorporating a medley of rousing, mostly British orchestral music, have been a British tradition since 1895. Although most of the audience occupies reserved seats, true aficionados usually opt for standing room in the orchestra pit, with close-up views of the musicians on stage. Newly commissioned works are often premiered here. The final evening is the most traditional; the rousing favorites "Jerusalem" or "Land of Hope and Glory" echo through the hall. Recently, the hall has seen performances by Liza Minnelli, an avant-garde production of Bizet's *Carmen,* orchestral and symphonic works from orchestras visiting from other cities, lots of British and European pop, and the London production of *Cirque du Soleil.* Kensington Gore, SW7 2AP. ℭ **020/7589-8212**. Tickets £10–£140 ($15–$210), depending on the event. Box office daily 9am–9pm. Tube: South Kensington.

Royal Festival Hall   In the aftermath of World War II, the principal site of London's music scene shifted to the south bank of the Thames. Three of the most acoustically perfect concert halls in the world were erected between 1951 and 1964. They include Royal Festival Hall, the Queen Elizabeth Hall, and the Purcell Room. They hold more than 1,200 performances a year, including classical music, ballet, jazz, popular music, and contemporary dance. Also here is the internationally renowned Hayward Gallery (p. 257).

Royal Festival Hall, which opens daily at 10am, offers an extensive array of things to see and do, including free exhibitions in the foyers and free lunchtime music at 12:30pm. On Friday, Commuter Jazz in the foyer from 5:30 to 6:45pm is free. The Poetry Library is open Tuesday through Sunday from 11am to 8pm, and shops display a selection of books, records, and crafts. The Festival Buffet has food at reasonable prices, and bars dot the foyers. The People's Palace offers lunch and dinner with a panoramic view of the River Thames; reservations by calling ℭ 020/7928-9999 are recommended. On the South Bank, SE1. ℭ **020/ 7960-4242**. www.rfh.org.uk. Tickets £6–£50 ($9–$75). Box office daily 9am–9pm. Tube: Waterloo or Embankment.

The Royal Opera House—The Royal Ballet & the Royal Opera The Royal Ballet and the Royal Opera are at home again in a magnificently restored theater. Opera and ballet aficionados hardly recognize the renovated place, with its spectacular new public spaces, including the Vilar Floral Hall (a chamber music venue), a rooftop restaurant, and bars and shops. The entire northeast corner of one of London's most famous public squares has been transformed, finally realizing Inigo Jones's original vision for this colonnaded plaza. Regular backstage tours are offered daily at 10:30am, 12:30pm, and 2:30pm (not on Sun or matinee days).

Performances of the Royal Opera are usually sung in the original language, but supertitles are projected. The Royal Ballet, which ranks with top companies such as the Kirov and the Paris Opera Ballet, performs a repertory with a tilt toward the classics, including works by its earlier choreographer-directors Sir Frederick Ashton and Sir Kenneth MacMillan. Bow St., Covent Garden, WC2. ✆ 020/ 7304-4000. www.royalopera.org. Tickets £3–£155 ($4.50–$232.50). Box office Mon–Sat 10am– 7:30pm. Tube: Covent Garden.

Sadler's Wells Theatre This is a premier venue for dance and opera. It occupies the site of a theater that was built in 1683. In the early 1990s, the turn-of-the-century theater was demolished, and construction began on an innovative new design completed at the end of 1998. The turn-of-the-century facade has been retained, but the interior has been completely revamped with a stylish cutting-edge theater design. The new theater offers classical ballet, modern dance of all degrees of "avant-garde-ness," and children's theatrical productions, including a Christmas ballet. Performances usually 8pm. Rosebery Ave., EC1. ✆ 020/ 7863-8000. www.sadlers-wells.com. Tickets £9–£60 ($13.50–$90). Box office Mon–Sat 9am–8:30pm. Tube: Northern Line to Angel.

Wigmore Hall An intimate auditorium, Wigmore Hall offers an excellent series of song recitals, piano and chamber music, early and baroque music, and jazz. A cafe-bar and restaurant are on the premises; a cold supper can be pre-ordered if you are attending a concert. Performances nightly, plus Sunday Morning Coffee Concerts and Sunday concerts at 4 or 7pm. 36 Wigmore St., W1. ✆ 020/ 7935-2141. www.wigmore-hall.org.uk. Tickets £8–£55 ($12–$82.50). Box office Mon–Sat 10am– 8:30pm; Sun 10:30am–5pm. Tube: Bond St. or Oxford Circus.

OUTSIDE CENTRAL LONDON

Kenwood Lakeside Concerts These band and orchestral concerts on the north side of Hampstead Heath have been a British tradition for some 50 years. In recent years, laser shows and fireworks have been added to a repertoire that includes everything from rousing versions of the *1812 Overture* to jazz, to operas such as *Carmen*. The final concert of the season always features some of the "Pomp and Circumstance" marches of Sir Edward Elgar. Music drifts across the lake to serenade wine-and-cheese parties on the grass. Kenwood, Hampstead Lane, Hampstead Heath, London NW3 7JR. ✆ 020/7413-1443. Tickets for adults £9 ($13.50) for seats on the grass lawn, £11–£16 ($16.50–$24) for reserved deck chairs. Reductions of 12.5% for students and persons over 60. July to early Sept, Sat 7:30pm. Tube: Northern Line to Golders Green or Archway, then Bus no. 210.

3 The Club & Music Scene

It's the nature of live music and dance clubs to come and go with alarming speed, or shift violently from one trend to another. *Time Out* (available on newsstands in the U.S. and in London) is the best way to keep up.

COMEDY

The Comedy Store This is London's showcase for established and rising comic talent. Inspired by comedy clubs in the U.S., this club has given many comics their start, and today a number of them are established TV personalities. Even if their names are unfamiliar, you'll enjoy the spontaneity of live comedy before a British audience. Visitors must be 18 and older; dress is casual. Reserve through **Ticketmaster** (⊙ 020/7344-4444); the club opens 1½ hours before each show. *Insider's Tip:* Go on Tuesday when the humor is more cutting-edge. Tuesday through Sunday doors open at 6:30pm and the show starts at 8pm, on Friday and Saturday there is an extra show that starts at midnight (doors open at 11:30pm). 1A Oxendon St., off Piccadilly Circus, SW1. ⊙ 020/7344-0234. Cover £12–£15 ($18–$22.50). Tube: Leicester Sq. or Piccadilly Circus.

ROCK AND POP

Bagley's Studios The premises of this place are vast, echoing, a bit grimy, and warehouse-like. Set in the bleak industrial landscape behind King's Cross Station, its interior is transformed 3 nights a week into an animated rave. Its two huge floors are divided into trios of individual rooms, each with their own ambience and sound system. You'll be happiest if you wander the rooms, searching out the site that best corresponds to your energy at the moment. Choices will probably include sites devoted to garage, club classics as promoted by AM/FM radio, "banging" (hard house) music, and "bubbly" dance music. If you happen to be in London on a weeknight, various social groups, including lots of East Indian social clubs, rent the place for gatherings, some of which might be open to the public. Saturday night "Freedom" parties are more fun. A crowd in its 20s and early 30s shows up here, and the joint is jumping at 2am. Guaranteed openings Friday through Saturday from 10pm to 7am. Otherwise, openings depend on whether a promoter has booked the space. King's Cross Freight Depot, off York Way, N1. ⊙ 020/7278-2777. Cover £15–£25 ($22.50–$37.50). Tube: King's Cross.

The Bull & Gate Outside central London, and smaller, cheaper, and often more animated and less touristy than many of its competitors, The Bull & Gate is the unofficial headquarters of London's pub rock scene. Indie and relatively unknown rock bands are served in back-to-back handfuls in this somewhat-battered Victorian pub. The place attracts a young crowd mainly in their 20s. If you like spilled beer, this is off-the-beaten-track London at its most authentic. Bands that played here and later ascended to Europe's clubby scene have included Madness, Blur, and Pulp. There's music nightly from 9pm to midnight. 389 Kentish Town Rd., NW5. ⊙ 020/7485-5358. Cover £5 ($7.50). Tube: Northern Line to Kentish Town.

The Rock Garden A long-established performance site, The Rock Garden maintains a bar and a stage in the cellar, and a restaurant on the street level. The cellar, known as The Venue, has hosted such acts as Dire Straits, Police, and U2 before their rise to stardom. Bands vary widely, from promising up-and-comers to some who'll never be heard from again. These groups appeal to a young crowd from 18 to 35. Simple American-style fare is served in the restaurant. Monday through Thursday from 5pm to 3am; Friday and Saturday from 5pm to 4am; and Sunday from 7pm to midnight. 6–7 The Piazza, Covent Garden, WC2. ⊙ 020/7240-3961. Cover £3–bp]12 ($4.50–$18); diners enter free. Bus: Any of the night buses that depart from Trafalgar Sq. Tube: Covent Garden.

Shepherd's Bush Empire In an old BBC television theater with great acoustics, this is a major venue for big-name pop and rock stars. Announcements appear in the local press. There's a capacity seating of 2,000. The spot mostly attracts fans in their 20s. Shepherd's Bush Green, W12. © 020/7771-2000. Box office hours: Mon–Fri 10am–6pm and Sat noon–6pm. Tube: Hammersmith & City Line to Shepherd's Bush or Goldhawk Rd.

Sound   In the heart of London, this 700-seat venue books the big acts, everybody from Sinead O'Connor to Puff Daddy to the Spice Girls. Sound functions as a restaurant and bar every night, with limited live music and a DJ until 11pm; after 11pm, the mood changes, the menu is simplified to include only bar snacks, and the site focuses much more heavily on live music and dancing. The music program is forever changing; call to see what's on at the time of your visit. Crowds and age levels can vary here depending on what act is featured. Reservations are recommended for dinner, but reservations after 11pm are not accepted. Swiss Centre at 10 Wardour St., Leicester Sq., W1. © 020/7287-1010. Tickets £5–£12 ($7.50–$18). Tube: Leicester Sq.

JAZZ

Bull's Head   This club has showcased live modern jazz every night of the week for more than 30 years. One of the oldest hostelries in the area, it was a 19th-century staging post where travelers on their way to Hampton Court could rest while coach horses were changed. Today, the bar features jazz by musicians from all over the world. Since it's way off the tourist trail, it attracts mainly locals in a wide age group but all appreciative of good music. Live jazz plays on Sunday from 2 to 4:30pm and 8 to 10:30pm; Monday through Saturday, from 8:30 to 11pm. You can order lunch at the Carvery in the Saloon Bar or dinner in the 17th-century Stable Restaurant. Monday through Saturday from 11am to 11pm; Sunday from noon to 10:30pm. 373 Lonsdale Rd., Barnes, SW13. © 020/8876-5241. Cover £5–£10 ($7.50–$15). Tube: Hammersmith, then bus 9A to Barnes Bridge, then retrace the path of the bus for some 100 yards on foot; or take Hounslow Look train from Waterloo Station and get off at Barnes Bridge Station, then walk 5 min. to the club.

Jazz Café   Afro-Latin jazz fans know that this club hosts combos from around the globe. Weekends, described by a patron as "bumpy jazzy-funk nights," are the best time to decide what that means. To fit in here, be young or dress the part. Call ahead for listings, cover, and table reservations (often necessary); opening times can vary. 5 Parkway, NW1. © 020/7916-6060. Reservations recommended. Cover £8–£20 ($12–$30). Tube: Camden Town.

Pizza Express   Don't let the name fool you: This restaurant-bar serves up some of the best jazz in London by mainstream artists, along with thin-crust Italian pizza. You'll find local bands or visiting groups, often from the United States. The place draws an equal mix of Londoners and visitors in the 20s-to-40s age bracket. Although the club has been enlarged, it's still important to reserve ahead of time. Daily from noon to midnight; jazz from 9pm to midnight. 10 Dean St., W1. © 020/7439-8722. Cover £10–£20 ($15–$30). Tube: Tottenham Court Rd.

Ronnie Scott's Club   Inquire about jazz in London and people immediately think of Ronnie Scott's, the European vanguard for modern jazz. Only the best English and American combos, often fronted by a top-notch vocalist, are booked here. The programs make for an entire evening of cool jazz. In the heart of Soho, Ronnie Scott's is a 10-minute walk from Piccadilly Circus along Shaftesbury Avenue. In the Main Room, you can watch the show from the bar or sit at a table, at which you can order dinner. The Downstairs Bar is more intimate; among the regulars at your elbow may be some of the world's most talented musicians. This place is so well known that all visiting musicians along with diehard local music fans show up here—perhaps even Mick Jagger. On weekends, the separate Upstairs Room has a disco called Club Latino. Monday through Saturday from 8:30pm to 3am. 47 Frith St., W1. ⓒ 020/7439-0747. Cover £15–£25 ($22.50–$37.50) for non-members, £5 ($7.50) for members. Tube: Leicester Sq. or Piccadilly Circus.

606 Club   Located in a discreet basement site in Chelsea, the 606 presents live music nightly. Predominantly a venue for modern jazz, styles range from traditional to contemporary. Local musicians and some very big names play here, whether at planned gigs or informal jam sessions after shows elsewhere in town. This is actually a jazz supper club in the boondocks of Fulham; because of license requirements, patrons can order alcohol only with food. Locals show up here along with a trendy crowd from more posh neighborhoods in London. Monday through Wednesday from 7:30 to 1am; Thursday from 8pm to 1:30am; Friday and Saturday from 8pm to 2am; Sunday from 8 to 11:30pm. 90 Lots Rd., SW10. ⓒ 020/7352-5953. Cover Sun–Thurs £5 ($7.50), Fri–Sat £7 ($10.50). Bus: 11, 19, 22, 31, 39, or C3. Tube: Earl's Court.

Vortex Jazz Bar   A bit out of the way, the Vortex is worth the trek, as it books an array of jazz legends as well as new talents. The 20s and 30s crowd that comes here is both cheerful and mellow. Daily from 10am to 11:30pm. Music begins at 9:30pm. 139–141 Stoke Newington Church St., N16. ⓒ 020/7254-6516. Cover £3–£12 ($4.50–$18). British Rail: Stoke Newington.

100 Club   Although less plush and expensive than some jazz clubs, 100 Club is a serious contender, with presentations of some remarkably good jazz. Its cavalcade of bands includes the best British jazz musicians and some of their Yankee brethren. Rock, R&B, and blues are also on tap. Serious devotees of jazz from 20 to 45 show up here. Monday through Thursday from 7:30pm to 11:30pm; Friday from noon to 3pm and 8:30pm to 2am; Saturday from 7:30pm to 1am; Sunday from 7:30 to 11:30pm. 100 Oxford St., W1. ⓒ 020/ 7636-0933. Cover Fri £10 ($15), Sat £12 ($18), Sun £8 ($12). Club members get a £1 discount on Sat nights. Tube: Tottenham Court Rd. or Oxford Circus.

DANCE & ECLECTIC

Nearly all the clubs below cater to a crowd in its 20s and early 30s, with an almost equal mixture of locals and visitors. These clubs hit their groove around 1 to 2am.

Bar Rumba   Despite its location on Shaftesbury Avenue, this Latin bar and club could be featured in a book of "Underground London." A hush-hush address, it leans toward radical jazz-fusion on some nights, phat funk on other occasions. It boasts two full bars and a different musical theme every night. Tuesday and Wednesday are the only nights you probably won't have to queue at the door. Monday's "That's How It Is" showcase features jazz, hip-hop, and drum and bass; Friday's "KAT Klub" grooves with soul, R&B, and swing; and Saturday's "Garage City" buzzes with house and garage. On weeknights you have to be 18 or older; on Saturday and Sunday nobody under 21 is allowed in. Monday through Thursday from 5pm to 3:30am; Friday from 5pm to 4am; Saturday from 9pm to 6am; Sunday from 8pm to 1:30am. 36 Shaftesbury Ave., W1. ⓒ 020/7287-2715. Cover £3–£12 ($4.50–$18). Tube: Piccadilly Circus.

Camden Palace   Housed in a former theater built around 1910, Camden Palace draws an over-18 crowd that flocks here in trendy downtown fashions. Energy levels vary according to the night of the week, as does the music, so call in advance to see if that evening's musical program appeals. A live band performs only on Tuesday. There's a restaurant if you get the munchies. Tuesday from 10pm to 2am; Friday approximately from 10pm to 6am; Saturday approximately from 10pm to 8am. 1A Camden High St., NW1. ✆ **020/7387-0428.** Cover varies, but averages Tues £5 ($7.50), Fri–Sat £12–£20 ($18–$30). Tube: Northern Line to Mornington Crescent or Camden Town.

The Cross In the backwaters of Kings Cross, this club has been hot since 1993. Hipsters come here for private parties thrown by Rough Trade Records or Red Or Dead, or to dance in the space's industrial-looking brick-lined vaults. Music runs the gamut from acid rock to Caribbean/African fusion to Jamaican soca. This place is shadowy, sweaty, raunchy and sometimes down and dirty. Call to find out who's performing. Friday and Saturday from 10pm to 6am. The Arches, Kings Cross Goods Yard, York Way, N1. ✆ **020/7837-0828.** Cover £8–£15 ($12–$22.50). Tube: Kings Cross.

Diva Diva combines a first-class Italian restaurant with a dance club. So get down with your manicotti! Meals, from £8.50 to £14.50 ($12.75–$21.75) per head, are mostly Neapolitan-inspired. Only restaurant patrons are allowed into the disco (where recorded music is played). The atmosphere is sophisticated, yet permissive. Monday through Thursday from 5 to 10:30pm; Friday through Saturday from 5:30pm to 3am; July through September also Sunday from noon to 10pm. 43 Thurloe St., SW7. ✆ **020/7584-2000.** Cover £2 ($3). Tube: South Kensington.

The End This club is better than ever after its recent enlargement. Now there is a trio of large dance floors, along with four bars and a chill-out area. Speaker walls blast you into orbit. The End is the best club in London for house and garage. It draws both straight and gay London. "We can't tell the difference any more," the club owner confessed, "and who cares anyway?" From its drinking fountain to its Ritzy toilets, the club is alluring. Dress for glam and to be seen on the circuit. Some big names in London appear on the weekends to entertain. Wednesday through Thursday from 9pm to 3:30am; Friday through Saturday from 10pm to 6am. 16A West Central St., WC1. ✆ **020/7419-9199.** Cover £5–£15 ($7.50–$22.50). Tube: Tottenham Court Rd.

Equinox Built in 1992 on the site of the London Empire, a dance emporium that has witnessed the changing styles of social dancing since the 1700s, the Equinox has established itself as a perennial favorite. It contains nine bars, the largest dance floor in London, and a restaurant modeled after a 1950s American diner. With the exception of rave, virtually every kind of dance music is featured, including dance hall, pop, rock, and Latin. The setting is illuminated with one of Europe's largest lighting rigs, and the crowd is as varied as London itself. Summer visitors can enjoy the theme nights, which are geared to entertaining a worldwide audience. Monday through Thursday from 9pm to 3am; Friday and Saturday from 9pm to 4am. Leicester Sq., WC2. ✆ **020/7437-1446.** Cover £2–£12 ($3–$18) depending on the night of the week. Tube: Leicester Sq.

Fabric While other competitors have come and gone since opening in 1999, Fabric continues to draw the crowds. Its main allure: it has a license for 24-hour music and dancing from Thursday to Sunday night. This is one of the most famous clubs in the increasingly trendy East London sector. It is said that when the owners power up the underfoot subwoofer, lights dim in London's East End. On some crazed nights, at least 2,500 members of young London, plus a medley of international visitors, crowd into this mammoth place. It has a trio of dance floors, bars wherever you look, unisex toilets, chill-out beds, and even a roof terrace. Live acts are presented every Friday, with DJs reigning on weekends. You'll hear house, garage, soca, reggae and whatever else is cutting edge on London's underground music scene at the time. Thursday through Friday and Sunday from 9:30am to 5am; Saturday from 9:30pm to 7am. 77A Charterhouse St., EC1. © 020/7490-0444. Cover £10–£15 ($15–$22.50). Tube: Farringdon.

Hanover Grand Thursdays are funky, down and dirty. Fridays and Saturdays the crowd dresses up in their disco finery, clingy and formfitting or politicized and punk. Dance floors are always crowded, and masses seem to surge back and forth between the two levels. Age and gender are sometimes hard to make out at this cutting-edge club. Friday and Saturday from 10pm to 3am. 6 Hanover St., W1. © 020/7499-7977. Cover £10–£12 ($15–$18). Tube: Oxford Circus.

Hippodrome Near Leicester Square, the Hippodrome is London's granddaddy of discos, a cavernous place with a great sound system and lights to match. It was Lady Di's favorite in her barhopping days. Tacky and touristy, it's packed on weekends. Monday through Friday from 9pm to 3am; Saturday from 9pm to 3:30am. Corner of Cranbourn St. and Charing Cross Rd., WC2. © 020/7437-4311. Cover £5–£12 ($7.50–$18). Tube: Leicester Sq.

Limelight Although it opened in 1985, this dance club—located in a former Welsh chapel dating from 1754—has only recently come into its own. The dance floors and bars share space with cool Gothic nooks and crannies. DJs spin the latest house music. Monday through Thursday from 10pm to 3am; Friday and Saturday from 9pm to 3:30am. 136 Shaftesbury Ave., W1. © 020/7434-0572. Cover £2–£12 ($3–$18). Tube: Leicester Sq.

Ministry of Sound Removed from the city center, this club-of-the-hour is still going strong. It remains hot, hot, hot. With a large bar and huge sound system, it blasts garage and house music to energetic crowds that pack the two dance floors. If the stimulants in the rest of the club have gone to your head, you can chill in the cinema room. *Note:* The cover charge is stiff, and bouncers decide who is cool enough to enter, so slip into your grooviest and most glamorous club gear. Friday from 10:30pm to 6am; Saturday from midnight to 9am. 103 Gaunt St., SE1. © 020/7378-6528. Cover £10–£15 ($15–$22.50). Tube: Northern Line to Elephant & Castle.

Notting Hill Art Club This is one of the hippest nighttime venues in London, with the action taking place in a no-frills basement in increasingly fashionable Notting Hill Gate. One habitué called it "the coolest night club on earth." Yes, that was Liam Gallagher you spotted dancing with Courtney Love. To justify the name of the club, art exhibitions are sometimes staged here. Most of the clients are under 35; other than that they come from a wide range of backgrounds—from Madonna to Bob Marley wannabes. The music is eclectic, varying from night to night—jazz improv, Latino salsa, hip-hop, indie, jazz, whatever. Wednesday from 6pm to 1am; Saturday from 6pm to 2am; Sunday from 4pm to 1am. 21 Notting Hill Gate, W11. © 020/7460-4459. Cover £3–£6 ($4.50–$9). Tube: Notting Hill Gate.

The Office An eclectic club with a bureaucratic name, one of The Office's most popular nights is Wednesday's "Double Six Club," featuring easy listening and board games from 6pm to 2am. Other nights are more traditional recorded pop, rock, soul, and disco. Ambience wins out over decor. Monday and Tuesday

THE CLUB & MUSIC SCENE **319**

from noon to 11:30pm; Wednesday through Friday from noon to 3am; Saturday from 9:30pm to 3am. 3–5 Rathbone Place, W1. © 020/7636-1598. Cover £3–£9 ($4.50–$13.50). Tube: Tottenham Court Rd.

Smollensky's on the Strand This is an American eatery and drinking bar. At the Strand location, you can dance from Thursday to Saturday nights. Sunday night features a special live jazz session. Meals average £25 ($37.50). Thursday through Saturday from noon to 12:30am; Sunday from noon to 5:30pm and 6:30 to 10:30pm; Monday through Wednesday from noon to midnight. 105 The Strand, WC2. © 020/7497-2101. Cover £5 ($7.50) on Sunday when they have big jazz bands. Tube: Charing Cross or Embankment.

The Velvet Room (formerly The Velvet Underground) The Velvet Underground was a London staple for years, but times changed and the clientele grew older—hence The Velvet Room, a more mature setting that is luxurious but not stuffy. DJs Carl Cox and others spin favorite dance hits—a bit more laid back to better represent the new theme of the club. The Velvet Room hasn't sacrificed a shred of cool, and it still sets a standard for the next generation of Soho bar life. Wednesday through Thursday from 9pm to 3am; Friday and Saturday from 9pm to 4am. 143 Charing Cross Rd., WC2. © 020/7734-4687. Cover £6–£10 ($9–$15). Tube: Tottenham Court Rd.

Zoo Bar The owners spent millions outfitting this club with the slickest, flashiest, and most psychedelic decor in London. If you're looking for a true Euro nightlife experience, replete with gorgeous *au pairs* and trendy Europeans, this is it. Upstairs boasts a menagerie of mosaic animals beneath a glassed-in ceiling dome. Downstairs, the music is intrusive enough to make conversation futile. Clients range from 18 to 35; androgyny is the look of choice. Monday through Saturday from 4pm to 3:30am; Sunday from 4 to 10:30pm. 13-18 Bear St., WC2. © 020/7839-4188. Cover £4 ($6) after 11pm (Fri and Sat after 9pm). Tube: Leicester Sq.

LATIN

Cuba This Spanish/Cuban bar-restaurant, which has a music club downstairs, features live acts from Spain, Cuba, Brazil, and the rest of Latin America. The crowd is equal parts restaurant diners, after-work drinkers, and dancers. Salsa classes are offered Monday and Wednesday from 7:30 to 9:30pm. Classes cost £6 ($9). Happy hour is Monday through Saturday from noon to 8:30pm. Monday through Saturday from noon to 2am; Sunday from 2 to 10:30pm. 11 Kensington High St., W8. © 020/7938-4137. Cover £3–£8 ($4.50–$12). Tube: High St. Kensington.

Salsa This lively bar/restaurant/club for Latin music aficionados mostly features bands from Central and South America. Dance lessons are available nightly starting at 6:30pm; live music starts at 9pm. Some of the best dancers in London strut their stuff here. Monday through Saturday from 5:30pm to 2am. 96 Charing Cross Rd., WC2. © 020/7379-3277. Cover Mon–Thurs £4 ($6) after 9pm; Fri–Sat £2–£8 ($3–$12). Tube: Leicester Sq. or Tottingham Road Ct.

BLUES

Ain't Nothing But Blues Bar The club, which bills itself as the only true blues venue in town, features local acts and occasional touring American bands. On weekends, prepare to queue. From the Oxford Circus Tube stop, walk south on Regent Street, turn left on Great Marlborough Street, and then make a quick

> ### ⌒Fun Fact   Members Only: Gambling in London
>
> Long before Monte Carlo, when Las Vegas was a lifeless desert, London was a gambler's town. However, Queen Victoria's reign squelched games of chance to such an extent that no bartender dared to keep a dice cup on the counter. Only in 1960 did gambling return in gaming clubs.
>
> In the West End there are at least 25 gambling clubs, and many more are sprinkled throughout London. Under British law, casinos may not advertise. Hence, if you wish to gamble away your beer money, your best bet is to ask a knowledgeable concierge. You'll be required to become a member and wait 24 hours before you can play at the tables. Games are cash-only and commonly include roulette, blackjack, *Punto Banco* (a version of baccarat), and baccarat.
>
> Men must wear jackets and ties in all the establishments below; hours for each club are from 2pm to 4am daily.
>
> Some of the popular clubs include **Crockford's,** a 150-year-old club with a large international clientele, located at 30 Curzon St., W1 (② 020/7493-7771; Tube: Green Park), which offers American roulette, *Punto Banco,* and blackjack. Another favorite is the **Golden Nugget,** 22–32 Shaftesbury Ave., W1 (② 020/7439-0099; Tube: Piccadilly Circus), where gamblers play blackjack, *Punto Banco,* and roulette. **Sportsman Casino,** 40 Bryanston St., W1 (② 020/7414-0061; Tube: Marble Arch), features a dice table, American roulette, blackjack, and *Punto Banco.*

right on Kingly Street. Monday through Thursday from 6pm to 1am; Friday and Sat from 6pm to 2am; Sunday from 7:30pm to 1am. 20 Kingly St., W1. ② 020/7287-0514. Cover Fri £3–£5 ($4.50–$7.50); Sat £3–£5 ($4.50–$7.50); free before 8:30pm. Tube: Oxford Circus or Piccadilly Circus.

FOLK

Cecil Sharpe House   CSH was the focal point of the folk revival in the 1960s, and it continues to treasure and nurture the style. Here you'll find a whole range of traditional music and dance, with different evenings devoted to, among others, Irish "set" dances, English barn dances (similar to American square dances), dances from Louisiana's Cajun country, even re-enactments of 18th century quadrilles. Although many of the regular patrons of this bar and dance club know these arcane dances by heart, they're usually charitable towards quick-learning and agile newcomers who can pick up the steps and the beat quickly. Call to see what's happening. 2 Regent's Park Rd., NW1. ② 020/7485-2206. Tickets £5–£8 ($5.50–$12). Box office Tues–Fri 9:30am–5:30pm. Tube: Northern Line to Camden Town.

4 Cocktail Bars

American Bar   The bartender in this sophisticated gathering place is known for his special concoctions "Savoy Affair" and "Prince of Wales," as well as what is reputedly the best martini in town. Monday through Saturday evenings, jazz piano is featured from 7 to 11pm. Near many West End theaters, the location is ideal for a pre- or post-theater drink. In The Savoy, The Strand, WC2. ℂ 020/7836-4343. Smart casual: No jeans, sneakers, T-shirts. Tube: Charing Cross, Covent Garden, or Embankment.

Bad Bobs Bar & Restaurant   Established long ago in Dublin, this lively venue washes Ireland up on the shores of London. Featuring live music (most often Irish), four bars and "Lillie's Bordello" form the ultimate party place and a setting for live music. 66 Chandos Place, W1. ℂ 020/7836-8000 Tube: Leicester Sq.

Beach Blanket Babylon   Go here if you're looking for a hot singles bar that attracts a crowd in their 20s and 30s. This Portobello joint is very cruisy. The decor is a bit wacky, no doubt designed by an aspiring Salvador Dalí, who decided to make it a fairytale grotto (or did he mean a medieval dungeon?). It's close to the Portobello Market. Saturday and Sunday nights are the hot, crowded times for bacchanalian revelry. 45 Ledbury Rd., W11. ℂ 020/7229-2907. Tube: Notting Hill Gate.

The Dorchester Bar   This sophisticated, modern bar is on the lobby level of the hotel, and you'll find an international clientele, confident of its good taste and privilege. The bartender knows his stuff. The bar serves Italian snacks, lunch, and dinner. A pianist performs every evening after 7pm. In the Dorchester, Park Lane, W1. ℂ 020/7629-8888. Tube: Hyde Park Corner, Marble Arch, or Green Park.

The Library   One of London's poshest drinking retreats, this deluxe hotel boasts high ceilings, leather chesterfields, respectable oil paintings, and grand windows. Its collection of ancient cognacs is unparalleled in London. In the Lanesborough Hotel, 1 Lanesborough Place, SW1. ℂ 020/7259-5599. Tube: Hyde Park Corner.

Lillie Langtry Bar   Next door to Langtry's Restaurant, this 1920s-style bar epitomizes the elegance of the Edwardian era. Lillie Langtry, the turn-of-the-century actress and beauty (and mistress of Edward VII), once lived here. Oscar Wilde—arrested in this very bar—is honored on the drinks menu with his favorite libation, the Hock and Seltzer (a combination of sweet white wine and seltzer). Traditional martinis seem to be the most popular drink here. An international menu is served in the adjoining restaurant. In the Cadogan Hotel, 75 Sloane St., SW1. ℂ 020/7235-7141. Tube: Sloane Sq. or Knightsbridge.

The Lobby Bar   This bar and the bar associated with the Axis restaurant are in London's newest five-star hotel. We advise that you check out the dramatic

Finds Drinks a la Americana

Everybody's heard of the Hard Rock Cafe and Planet Hollywood, but the real news coming out of London is the sudden opening of many American-theme bars. We've picked out the two best spots. **Navajo Joe,** 34 King St., WC2 (ℂ 020/7240-4008), offers the largest tequila selection outside of Mexico, and southwestern cuisine that is already starting to win some restaurant awards. For the atmosphere of a different part of the American south, head for **Old Orleans,** corner of Wellington and Tavistock streets, WC2 (ℂ 020/7497-2433), with its colorful cocktail bar and rich decor from the old American south. The restaurant features Creole cuisine. Both are reached by taking the Tube to Covent Garden.

visuals of both before selecting your preferred nesting place. The Lobby Bar occupies what was built in 1907 as the grand, high-ceilinged reception area for one of London's premier newspapers. If that setting doesn't appeal, check out the travertine, hardwood, and leather-sheathed bar in the Axis restaurant. The Lobby Bar is open daily from 9am to 11pm; the Axis bar is Monday through Saturday from 5:45 to 11pm. In the Hotel One Aldwych, 1 Aldwych, WC2. ✆ 020/7300-1000. Tube: Temple.

The Met Bar Very much the place to be seen, this has become the hottest bar in London. Mix with the elite of the fashion, TV, and the music world. A lot of American celebrities have been seen sipping martinis, from Demi Moore to Courtney Cox. Despite the star caliber of the clientele, the bar has managed to maintain a relaxed and unpretentious atmosphere. In the Metropolitan Hotel, 10 Old Park Lane, W1. ✆ 020/7447-1000. Members only and hotel guests. Tube: Hyde Park Corner.

The Phoenix Artist Club What's something so old it's new again? This is where Laurence Oliver made his stage debut in 1930, although he couldn't stop giggling even though the play was drama. Live music is featured, but it's the hearty welcome, the good beer, and friendly patrons that make this redis-covered theater bar worth a detour. 1 Phoenix St., WC2. ✆ 020/7836-1077. Tube: Tottencourt Court Rd.

5 The World's Greatest Pub Crawl

Dropping into the local pub for a pint of real ale or bitter is the best way to soak up the character of the different villages that make up London. You'll hear local accents and slang and see firsthand how far removed upper-crust Kensington is from blue-collar Wapping. Catch the local gossip or football talk—and, of course, enjoy some of the finest ales, stouts, ciders, and malt whiskies in the world.

Anchor You can follow in the footsteps of Shakespeare and Dickens by quenching your thirst at this pub. If literary heroes are not your bag, then per-haps you'll enjoy knowing that Tom Cruise had a pint or two here during the filming of *Mission Impossible*. Rebuilt in the mid–18th century to replace an ear-lier pub, that managed to withstand the Great Fire of 1666, the rooms are worn and comfortable, and you can choose from Scottish and New Castle brews on tap. 34 Park St., Bankside, SE1. ✆ 020/7407-1577. Tube: Jubilee Line to London Bridge.

Antelope On the fringe of Belgravia, at the gateway to Chelsea, the Antelope caters to a hodgepodge of clients from all classes and creeds (including English rugby fans). At lunchtime, the ground floor bar provides hot and cold pub food, but in the evening, only drinks are served. Upstairs, the lunch menu includes principally English dishes: fish and chips, English roasts, and the like. 22 Eaton Terrace, SW1. ✆ 020/7824-8512. Tube: Sloane Sq.

Black Friar The Black Friar will transport you to the Edwardian era. The wedge-shaped pub is swimming in marble and bronze Art Nouveau, featuring bas-reliefs of monks, a low-vaulted mosaic ceiling, and seating recesses carved out of gold marble. It's popular with the City's after-work crowd, and it features Adams, Wadsworth 6X, Tetleys, and Brakspears on tap. 174 Queen Victoria St., EC4. ✆ 020/7236-5474. Tube: Blackfriars.

Bow Wine Vaults Bow Wine Vaults has existed since long before the wine-bar craze began in the 1970s. One of the most famous in London, it attracts cost-conscious diners and drinkers to its vaulted cellars for such traditional fare as deep-fried Camembert, lobster ravioli, and a mixed grill, along with fish. More elegant meals, served in the street-level dining room, include mussels in cider sauce, English wild mushrooms in puff pastry, beef Wellington, and steak with brown-butter sauce. Adjacent to the restaurant is a cocktail bar that's popular with City employees after work (open weekdays 11:30am–11pm). Wines from around the world are available; the last time we were there the wine of the day was a Chilean chardonnay. 10 Bow Chuchyard, EC4. ✆ 020/7248-1121. Tube: Mansion House, Bank, or St. Paul's.

Churchill Arms Stop here for a nod to the empire's end. Loaded with Churchill memorabilia, the pub hosts a week of celebration leading up to the Churchill's birthday on November 30th. Show up and you may be recruited to help decorate the place; visitors are often welcomed like regulars. Decorations and festivities are featured at Halloween, Christmas, and St. Paddy's Day as well, helping to create the homiest village feel you're likely to find in London. 119 Kensington Church St., W8. ✆ 020/7727-4242. Tube: Notting Hill Gate or High St. Kensington.

Cittie of Yorke This pub boasts the longest bar in Britain, rafters ascending to the heavens, and a row of immense wine vats, all of which give it the air of a great medieval hall—appropriate since a pub has existed at this location since 1430. Samuel Smiths is on tap, and the bar offers novelties such as chocolate-orange-flavored vodka. 22 High Holborn, WC1. ✆ 020/7242-7670. Tube: Holborn or Chancery Lane.

Cutty Sark Tavern Retreat here for great antiquarian ambience, inside a 16th-century dwelling with flagstones, barrel tables, open fires, and rough-hewn brick walls. The pub has such an old London feel that you may find yourself seeing Dickensian riffraff after a few pints of Bass or Worthington's Best. Ballast Quay, off Lassell St., SE10. ✆ 020/8858-3146. Tube: Cutty Sark.

Dog & Duck This snug little joint, a Soho landmark, is the most intimate pub in London. A former patron was the author George Orwell who came here to celebrate his sales of *Animal Farm* in the United States. A wide mixture of ages and persuasions flock here, usually chatting amiably. Publicans here stock an interesting assortment of English beers, including Tetleys, Fuller London, and Timothy Taylor Landlord. In autumn customers will ask for Addlestone's Cider. A lot of patrons head to Ronnie Scott's Jazz Club, which is close by, after having a few pints here. The cozy upstairs bar is also open. 18 Bateman St. (corner of Frith St.), W1. ✆ 020/7437-4447. Tube: Tottenham Court Rd. or Leicester Square

Dove You can relax by the Thames at the place where James Thomson composed "Rule Britannia" and part of his lesser-known "The Seasons." To toast Britannia, you can hoist a Fullers London Pride or ESB. 19 Upper Mall, W6. ✆ 020/8748-5405. Tube: District Line to Ravenscourt Park.

George The existing structure was built to replace the original pub, destroyed in the Great Fire. The pub's accolades date to 1598, when it was reviewed as a "faire inn for the receipt of travelers." No longer an inn, it's still a great place to enjoy Flowers Original, Boddingtons, and London Pride Abbot on tap. Off 77 Borough High St., SE1. ✆ 020/7407-2056. Tube: Northern Line to London Bridge or Borough.

Grapes This rustic 16th-century pub served as Dickens's inspiration for "Six Jolly Fellowship Porters" in *Our Mutual Friend*. Whistler came here, too, inspired by the view of the river. Taps include Friary Meux and Tetleys; there are several single-malt whiskies to choose from as well. 76 Narrow St., E14. ✆ 020/7987-4396. Tube: East London Line to Shadwell.

World's Greatest Pub Crawl

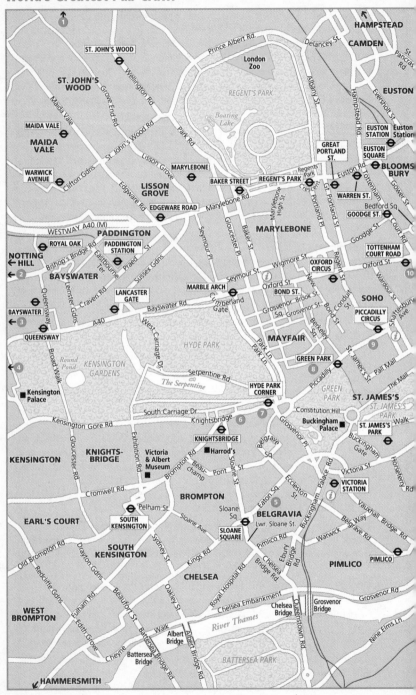

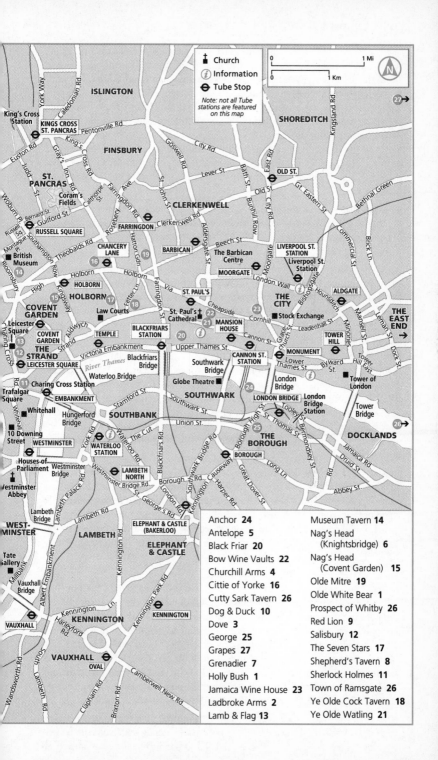

Church
Information
Tube Stop

Note: not all Tube stations are featured on this map

0			1 Mi
0	1 Km		

ISLINGTON
SHOREDITCH
King's Cross Station
KINGS CROSS ST. PANCRAS
Pentonville Rd.
King's Cross Rd.
FINSBURY
City Rd.
Goswell Rd.
Lever St.
OLD ST.
Gt. Eastern St.
Bethnal Green
Euston Rd.
Grays Inn Rd.
ST. PANCRAS
Coram's Fields
Bernard St.
Guilford St.
Calthorpe St.
Farringdon Rd.
CLERKENWELL
Clerkenwell Rd.
Bath St.
Old St.
City Rd.
Bunhill Row
Commercial St.
Brick Ln.
Woburn Pl.
Russell Sq.
RUSSELL SQUARE
Montague Pl.
Southampton Row
Theobalds Rd.
CHANCERY LANE
FARRINGDON
Rosebery Ave.
Hatton Gdn.
Beech St.
The Barbican Centre
LIVERPOOL ST. STATION
Liverpool St. Station
Houndsditch
ALDGATE
British Museum
Bloomsbury
High
Kingsway
HOLBORN
Holborn
Holborn Viaduct
BARBICAN
Aldersgate St.
MOORGATE
Moorgate
London Wall
THE CITY
Bishopsgate
Mansell St.
Leman St.
THE EAST END
COVENT GARDEN
Leicester Square
COVENT GARDEN
Law Courts
Fetter Ln.
ST. PAUL'S
St. Paul's Cathedral
Cheapside
Cornhill
Stock Exchange
MANSION HOUSE
Leadenhall St.
Grace Church St.
TOWER HILL
Minories
Dock St.
Charing Cross
LEICESTER SQUARE
THE STRAND
Strand
Aldwych
TEMPLE
BLACKFRIARS STATION
BOW WINE VAULTS
Cannon St.
Upper Thames St.
MONUMENT
Byward St.
Tower Hill East
Trafalgar Square
EMBANKMENT
Victoria Embankment
River Thames
Blackfriars Bridge
CANNON ST. STATION
Southwark Bridge
Lower Thames St.
Tower of London
Whitehall
Hungerford Bridge
Charing Cross Station
Waterloo Bridge
Globe Theatre
SOUTHWARK
London Bridge
Tower Bridge
10 Downing Street
WESTMINSTER
Stamford St.
Southwark St.
LONDON BRIDGE
London Bridge Station
Tooley St.
Bermondsey St.
DOCKLANDS
Houses of Parliament
Westminster Abbey
SOUTHBANK
WATERLOO STATION
Union St.
THE BOROUGH
St. Thomas St.
Jamaica Rd.
Druid St.
Westminster Bridge
York Rd.
The Cut
Waterloo Rd.
LAMBETH NORTH
Borough Rd.
BOROUGH
Southwark Bridge Rd.
Great Dover St.
Long Ln.
Abbey St.
Lambeth Bridge
Westminster Bridge Rd.
St. George's Rd.
London Rd.
Kennington Causeway
Harper Rd.
WEST-MINSTER
Lambeth Palace Rd.
Lambeth Rd.
ELEPHANT & CASTLE (BAKERLOO)
LAMBETH
ELEPHANT & CASTLE
Tate Gallery
Millbank
Vauxhall Bridge
Albert Embankment
Kennington Rd.
Kennington Park Rd.
KENNINGTON
VAUXHALL
Harleyford Rd.
KENNINGTON
OVAL
Camberwell New Rd.
Wandsworth Rd.
South Lambeth Rd.
Clapham Rd.
Brixton Rd.

Grenadier   Tucked away in a mews, the Grenadier is one of London's reputedly haunted pubs, the ghost here being an 18th-century British soldier. Aside from the poltergeist, the basement houses the original bar and skittles alley used by the Duke of Wellington's officers. The scarlet front door of the one-time officers' mess is guarded by a scarlet sentry box and shaded by a vine. The bar is nearly always crowded. Lunch and dinner are offered daily—even on Sunday, when it's a tradition to drink Bloody Marys here. In the stalls along the side, you can order good-tasting fare based on seasonal ingredients. Well-prepared dishes include pork Grenadier, and a chicken-and-Stilton roulade. Snacks like fish and chips are available at the bar. 18 Wilton Row, SW1. ✆ 020/7235-3074. Tube: Hyde Park Corner.

Holly Bush   The Holly Bush is the real thing: authentic Edwardian gas lamps, open fires, private booths, and a tap selection of Benskins, Eldridge Pope, and Ind Coope Burton. 22 Holly Mount, NW3. ✆ 020/7435-2892. Tube: Northern Line to Hampstead.

Jamaica Wine House   One of the first coffeehouses in England and, reputedly, the Western world. For years, merchants and sea captains came here to transact deals over rum and coffee. Nowadays, the two-level house dispenses coffee, beer, ale, lager, and fine wines, among them a variety of ports. The oak-paneled bar is on the street level, and attracts a crowd of investment bankers. You can order standard but filling dishes such as a ploughman's lunch and toasted sandwiches. St. Michael's Alley off Cornhill, EC3. ✆ 020/7626-9496. Tube: Bank.

Ladbroke Arms   Previously honored as London's "Dining Pub of the Year," Ladbroke Arms is that rare pub known for its food. A changing menu includes chicken breast stuffed with avocado, and garlic steak in pink-peppercorn sauce. With background jazz and rotating art prints, the place strays from a traditional pub environment, but it makes for a pleasant stop and a good meal. The excellent Eldridge Pope Royal is on tap, as well as John Smiths and Courage Directors, and several malt whiskies. 54 Ladbroke Rd., W11. ✆ 020/7727-6648. Tube: Notting Hill Gate.

Lamb & Flag   Dickens once frequented this pub and the room is little changed from the days when he prowled the neighborhood. The pub has an amazing and scandalous history. Poet and author Dryden was almost killed by a band of thugs outside its doors in December 1679, and the pub gained the nickname the "Bucket of Blood" during the Regency era (1811–20) because of the bare-knuckled prizefights here. Tap beers include Courage Best and Directors, Old Speckled Hen, John Smiths, and Wadworths 6X. 33 Rose St., off Garrick St., WC2. ✆ 020/7497-9504. Tube: Leicester Sq.

Museum Tavern   Across the street from the British Museum, this pub (ca. 1703) retains most of its antique trappings: velvet, oak paneling, and cut glass. It lies right in the center of the University of London area and is popular with writers, publishers, and researchers from the museum. (Supposedly, Karl Marx wrote while dining in the pub.) Traditional English food is served: shepherd's pie, sausages cooked in English cider, turkey-and-ham pie, ploughman's lunch, and salads. Several English ales, cold lagers, cider, Guinness, wines, and spirits are available. Food and coffee are served all day; the pub gets crowded at lunchtime. 49 Great Russell St., WC1. ✆ 020/7242-8987. Tube: Holborn or Tottenham Court Rd.

Nag's Head   This Nag's Head (not to be confused with the more renowned one at 10 James St.; see below) is on a back street a short walk from the Berkeley Hotel. Previously a jail dating from 1780, it's said to be the smallest pub in

London. In 1921, it was sold for £12 and 6p. Have a drink up front or wander to the tiny bar in the rear. For food, you might enjoy "real ale sausage" (made with pork and ale), shepherd's pie, or the quiche of the day. This warm, cozy pub, with a welcoming staff, is patronized by a cosmopolitan clientele—newspaper people, musicians, and tourists. This pub touts itself as an "independent," or able to serve any "real ale" they choose because of their lack of affiliation. 53 Kinnerton St., SW1. ⓒ 020/7235-1135. Tube: Hyde Park.

Nag's Head This Nag's Head (as opposed to the one above) is one of London's most famous Edwardian pubs. In days of yore, patrons had to make their way through carts full of fruit and flowers to drink here. But when the fruit and flower market moved, that 300 year-old tradition faded away. Today, the pub is popular with young people. The draft Guinness is very good. Lunch is typical pub grub: sandwiches, salads, pork cooked in cider, and garlic prawns. The sandwich platters mentioned above are served only during the lunch hour (noon–4pm); however, snacks are available in the afternoon. 10 James St., WC2. ⓒ 020/7836-4678. Tube: Covent Garden.

Olde Mitre Olde Mitre is the name of a working-class inn built here in 1547, when the Bishops of Ely controlled the district. It's a small pub with an odd assortment of customers. Friary Meux, Ind Coope Burton, and Tetleys are on tap. 1 Ely Court, EC1. ⓒ 020/7405-4751. Tube: Chancery Lane.

Olde White Bear This is a friendly place for regulars, decorated with Victorian prints, cartoons, and furnishings. Tap offerings include Greene King Abbott and Youngs Bitter. Well Rd., NW31. ⓒ 020/7435-3758. Tube: Hampstead.

Prospect of Whitby One of London's most historic pubs, Prospect was founded in the days of the Tudors, taking its name from a coal barge that made trips between Yorkshire and London. Come here for a tot, a noggin, or whatever it is you drink, and soak up its atmosphere. It's got quite a pedigree. Dickens and diarist Samuel Pepys used to drop in, and Turner came here for weeks at a time studying views of the Thames. In the 17th century, the notorious Hanging Judge Jeffreys used to get drunk here while overseeing hangings at the adjoining Execution Dock. Tables in the courtyard look out over river views. You can order a Morlands Old Speckled Hen from a hand-pump, or a malt whisky. 57 Wapping Wall, El. ⓒ 020/7481-1095. Tube: Wapping.

Red Lion This Victorian pub, with its early-1900s decorations and 150-year-old mirrors, has been compared to Manet's painting *A Bar at the Folies-Bergère* (on display at the Courtauld Gallery). You can order pre-made sandwiches. On Saturday, homemade fish and chips are served. Wash down your meal with Ind Coope's fine ales or the house's special beer, Burton's, a brew made of spring water from the Midlands town of Burton-on-Trent. 2 Duke of York St. (off Jermyn St.), SW1. ⓒ 020/7321-0782. Tube: Piccadilly Circus.

Salisbury Salisbury's cut-glass mirrors reflect the faces of English stage stars (and hopefuls) sitting around the curved buffet-style bar. A less prominent place to dine is the old-fashioned wall banquette with its copper-topped tables and Art Nouveau decor. The pub's specialty, home-cooked pies set out in a buffet cabinet with salads, is really quite good and inexpensive. Both a hot and a cold food buffet are available at all times. 90 St. Martin's Lane, WC2. ⓒ 020/7836-5863. Tube: Leicester Sq.

The Seven Stars In 2001, its 399th year, this tranquil little pub facing the back of the Royal Courts of Justice was taken over by Roxy Beaujolais, author of the pub cookbook *Home From the Inn Contented,* whose former pub was voted the Soho Society's Pub of the Year. Within the ancient charm of two narrow rooms that are listed landmarks, drinking in Queer Street (as Carey Street was called because of the bankruptcy courts) is contrarily pleasant. One can linger over pub food and real ales behind Irish linen lace curtains, with litigants, barristers, reporters, and pit musicians from West End shows. Then, try to navigate to the lavatories up some comically narrow Elizabethan stairs. In mild weather, the law courts' stone balustrade under the trees provides customers with a long bar and beer garden. 53 Carey St., WC2. ℂ 020/7242-8521. Tube: Chancery Lane or Temple.

Shepherd's Tavern One of the focal points of the all-pedestrian shopping zone of Shepherd's Market, this pub is set amid a warren of narrow, cobble-covered streets behind Park Lane, in an 18th-century town house. The street-level bar is cramped but congenial. Many of the regulars recall this tavern's popularity with the pilots of the Battle of Britain. Bar snacks include simple plates of shepherd's pie and fish and chips. More formal dining is available upstairs in the cozy, cedar-lined Georgian-style restaurant; the classic British menu probably hasn't changed much since the 1950s. You can always get Oxford ham or roast beef with Yorkshire pudding. 50 Hertford St., W1. ℂ 020/7499-3017. Tube: Green Park.

Sherlock Holmes The Sherlock Holmes was the gathering spot for the Baker Street Irregulars, a once-mighty clan of mystery lovers who met to honor the genius of Sir Arthur Conan Doyle's famous fictional character. Upstairs, you'll find a recreation of the living room at 221B Baker Street and such "Holmesiana" as the serpent of *The Speckled Band* and the head of *The Hound of the Baskervilles.* In the upstairs dining room, you can order complete meals with wine. Try "Copper Beeches" (grilled butterfly chicken breasts with lemon and herbs). Select dessert from the trolley. Downstairs is mainly for drinking, but there's a good snack bar with cold meats, salads, cheeses, and wine and ales sold by the glass. 10 Northumberland St., WC1. ℂ 020/7930-2644. Tube: Charing Cross or Embankment.

Town of Ramsgate At this old-world pub, overlooking King Edward's Stairs and the Thames, you can enjoy Bass and Fullers London Pride on tap. 62 Wapping High St., E1. ℂ 020/7264-0001. Tube: East London Line to Wapping.

Ye Olde Cock Tavern Dating back to 1549, this tavern boasts a long line of literary patrons: Pepys mentioned it, Dickens frequented it, and Tennyson referred to it in a poem (a copy of which is proudly displayed near the front entrance). It's one of the few buildings in London that survived the Great Fire of 1666. At street level, you can order a pint as well as snacks, steak-and-kidney pie, or a cold chicken-and-beef plate with salad. At the Carvery upstairs, a meal includes a choice of appetizers, followed by lamb, pork, beef, or turkey. 22 Fleet St., EC4. ℂ 020/7353-8570. Tube: Temple or Chancery Lane.

Ye Olde Watling Ye Olde Watling was rebuilt after the Great Fire of 1666. On the ground level is a mellow pub; upstairs is an intimate restaurant where, under oak beams and at trestle tables, you can dine on simple English main dishes for lunch. The menu varies daily, with such choices and reliable standbys as fish and chips, lasagna, fishcakes, and usually a vegetarian dish. All are served with two vegetables or salad, plus rice or potatoes. 29 Watling St., EC4. ℂ 020/7653-9971. Tube: Mansion House.

6 The Gay & Lesbian Scene

The most reliable source of information on gay clubs and activities is the **Lesbian and Gay Switchboard** (© 020/7837-7324). The staff runs a 24-hour service for information on gay-friendly places and activities. *Time Out* also carries listings on such clubs. A good place for finding out what's hot and hip is **Prowler Soho,** 3–7 Brewer St., Soho, W1 (© 020/7734-4031; Tube: Piccadilly Circus), the largest gay lifestyle store in London. (You can buy anything from jewelry to CDs, books, fashion, and sex toys.) It's open until midnight on Friday and Saturday.

Admiral Duncan   Gay men and their friends go here to drink, to have a good time and to make a political statement. British tabloids shocked the world in 1999 when they reported that this pub had been bombed, with three people dying in the attack. Within 6 weeks, the pub reopened its doors. We're happy to report that the bar is back in business and better than ever, now also attracting non-gays who show up to show their support. 54 Old Compton St., W1. © 020/7437-5300. Tube: Piccadilly Circus.

Barcode   This is a very relaxed and friendly bar. With everything from skinheads to "pint-of-lager" types, it has much of a "local pub" atmosphere. The bar is fairly male-dominated, but does not object to women entering. Daily from 1pm to 1am. 3–4 Archer St., W1. © 020/7734-3342. Tube: Piccadilly Circus.

The Box   Adjacent to one of Covent Garden's best-known junctions, Seven Dials, this sophisticated Mediterranean-style bar attracts all kinds of men. In the afternoon, it is primarily a restaurant, serving meal-size salads, club sandwiches, and soups. Food service ends abruptly at 5:30pm, after which the place reveals its core: a cheerful, popular rendezvous for London's gay and counter-culture crowds. The Box considers itself a "summer bar," throwing open doors and windows to a cluster of outdoor tables at the slightest hint of sunshine. Monday through Saturday from 11am to 11pm; Sunday from noon to 10:30pm (cafe Mon–Sat 11am–5:30pm, Sun noon–6:30pm). 32–34 Monmouth St. (at Seven Dials), WC2. © 020/7240-5828. Tube: Leicester Sq.

Candy Bar   This is the most popular lesbian bar in London at the moment. It has an extremely mixed clientele from butch to femme and from young to old. There is a bar and a club downstairs. Design is simple, with bright colors and lots of mirrors upstairs, and darker, more flirtatious decor downstairs. Men are welcome as long as a woman escorts them. Monday through Thursday from 8pm to midnight; Friday and Saturday from 8pm to 2am; Sunday from 7 to 11pm. 23–24 Bateman St., W1. © 020/7494-4041. Cover £2–bp]5 ($3–$7.50). Tube: Tottenham Court Rd.

The Complex   On Fridays, this four-floor club is the site of Pop Starz, one of the most popular nights in London, offering a mix of indie, British pop, 1980s trash, and funk. Started as an alternative to the gay muscle-boy dance parties, the once-weekly night has attracted a mixed and loyal following. Friday from 10pm to 4am. 1–5 Parkfield St., Islington, M1. © 020/7738-2336. Cover £8–($12). Tube: Northern Line to Angel.

The Edge   Few bars in London can rival the tolerance, humor, and sexual sophistication found here. The first two floors are done up with accessories that, like an English garden, change with the seasons. Dance music can be found on the high-energy and crowded lower floors, while the upper floors are best if you're looking for intimate conversation. Three menus are featured: a funky daytime menu, a cafe menu, and a late-night menu. Dancers hit the floors starting around 7:30pm. Clientele ranges from the flamboyantly gay to hetero pub-crawlers. Monday through Saturday from 11am to 1am; Sunday from noon to 10:30pm. 11 Soho Sq., W1. © 020/7439-1313. Tube: Tottenham Court Rd.

First Out First Out prides itself on being London's first (est. 1986) all-gay coffee shop. Set in a 19th-century building whose wood panels have been painted the colors of the gay liberation rainbow, the bar is not particularly cruisy. Cappuccino and whiskey are the preferred libations; and an exclusively vegetarian menu, including curry dishes, potted pies in phyllo pastries, and salads are the foods of choice. Don't expect a raucous atmosphere—some clients come here with their grandmothers. Look for the bulletin board with leaflets and business cards of gay and gay-friendly entrepreneurs. Monday through Saturday from 10am to 11pm; Sunday from 11am to 10:30pm. 52 St. Giles High St., W1. © 020/7240-8042. Tube: Tottenham Court Rd.

Friendly Society This is a Soho hot spot that bustles with young gay life, and there's even a rumor that Mrs. Guy Ritchie (Madonna) made a secret appearance here heavily disguised. "As what?" we asked, but no one knew. The action takes place in the basement of the building which one patron called a "space-age lair." Perhaps the white leather pod seating creates that aura. Come here for the drinks and the company—it's very cruisy. Monday through Friday from 4 to 11pm; Saturday and Sunday from 2 to 11pm. 79 Wardour St., W1. Tube: Piccadilly Circus.

G.A.Y. Name notwithstanding, the clientele here is mixed, and on a Saturday night this could be the most rollicking club in London. You may not find love here, but you could discover a partner for the evening. If you've got the figure for it, you can strip down to your briefs or shorts and give other patrons a treat. A mammoth place, this club draws a young crowd to dance beneath its mirrored disco balls. Monday through Friday from 10:30am to 4am; Saturday from 10:30pm to 5am. London Astoria, 157 Charing Cross Rd., WC2. © 020/7734-6963. Admission £10 ($15). Tube: Tottenham Court Rd.

Heaven This club, in the vaulted cellars of Charing Cross Railway Station, is a London landmark. Owned by the same investors who brought the world Virgin Atlantic Airways, Heaven is one of the biggest and best-established gay venues in Britain. Painted black and reminiscent of an air-raid shelter, the club is divided into at least four areas, connected by a labyrinth of catwalk stairs and hallways. Each has a different activity going on. Heaven also has theme nights, which are frequented at different times by gays, lesbians, or a mostly heterosexual crowd. Thursday in particular seems open to anything, but on Saturday it's gays only. Call before you go. Monday and Wednesday from 10:30pm to 3am; Friday from 10:30pm to 6am; Saturday from 10:30pm to 5am. The Arches, Villiers and Craven sts., WC2. © 020/7930-2020. Cover £5–£12 ($7.50–$18). Tube: Charing Cross or Embankment.

Royal Vauxhall Tavern Originally an 1880s vaudeville pub frequented by London's East End working class, this place has long been a bastion of campy humor and wit. It has been a gay pub since the end of World War II. The tavern received a jolt of fame when, as legend has it, Queen Elizabeth's ceremonial carriage broke down, and the monarch stopped in for a cup of tea. Since then, "Royal" has been gleefully affixed to the name, no doubt suiting the regular queens here. Charington, one of the largest breweries in England, recently acquired this unabashedly gay pub.

Shaped like an amphitheater, the bar has a large stage area and gay themes on weekends. Friday nights are for women only. Saturday is camp night, when the pub overflows with gay men fawning over their favorite cabaret acts. Thursday through Saturday from 9pm to 2am; Sunday from 2pm to midnight. 372 Kennington Lane, SE11. ✆ 020/7737-4043. Cover Thurs–Sun £2–£4 ($3–$6). Tube: Victoria Line to Vauxhall.

Shadow Lounge   This is the current fave hot spot for gay men in Soho. "Our male patrons are fresh and sexy," a seasoned bartender told us. Shadow Lounge is in the vanguard of gay life in London, which, as the millennium deepens, shows a tendency to shift from gargantuan dance palaces like Heaven to more intimate rendezvous points. Young men, who look like the cast of the British version of "Queer as Folk," meet here at 8pm for drinks. Some return after dinner to segue into dancing to raucous house music. Monday through Wednesday from 9pm to 3am; Thursday through Saturday from 8pm to 3am. 5 Brewer St., W1. ✆ 020/7287-7988. Cover Fri–Sat 8–10pm £5 ($7.50); after 10pm £10 ($15). Tube: Piccadilly Circus.

Turnmills on Clerkenwell   For serious gay partygoers, the 2 nights at this otherwise straight venue are a must. Trade, which begins after everyone else has gone home, has a big dance-party atmosphere complete with heavy techno dance music and a literal sea of Adonis-like men with their shirts off. Melt, on Sunday nights, is a slightly more relaxed version of Trade, with a funky house slant. The club is large (capacity: 700) and has two dance floors. Trade: Saturday from 4am to 1pm; Melt: Sunday from 10pm to 6:30am. 63B Clerkenwell Rd., EC1. ✆ 020/7250-3409. Cover: Trade £8–£12 ($12–$18); Melt £7–£10 ($10.50–$15). Tube: Farringdon.

10 Side Trips from London

There's much more to England than London. But you could spend the best part of a year—or a lifetime—exploring *only* London, without risking boredom or repetition. Still, we advise you to tear yourself away from Big Ben for at least a day or two, as the city is surrounded by some easily accessible, wonderfully memorable spots.

1 Windsor & Eton ⊛

34km (21 miles) W of London

Windsor—the site of England's best-known and greatest castle and its most famous boys' school, Eton—would be a captivating Thames town to visit, even if it were not associated with the royal Windsors. In summer it's overrun with tourists, which tends to obscure its charm.

The good news is that, after the disastrous fire of 1992, things are on the mend at Windsor Castle. But not without controversy—some of the new designs unveiled have been called "Gothic shocker" and "ghastly." If you visit, you can decide for yourself.

ESSENTIALS

GETTING THERE   The train from Waterloo or Paddington Station in London takes 30 minutes, involving a transfer at Slough to the Slough-Windsor shuttle train. There are more than a dozen trains per day; fares start at £6.10 ($9.15) one-way or £6.50 ($9.75) for a round-trip ticket. For information, call ☎ 08457/484950.

Green Line coaches (☎ 020/8668-7261), no. 700 and 702 from Hyde Park Corner in London, take about 1½ hours. A same-day round-trip costs £6.70 ($10.05). The bus will drop you near the Town Guildhall in Windsor. It's only a short walk up Castle Hill to the top sights.

If you're traveling by car, take M4 west from London.

VISITOR INFORMATION   A Tourist Information Centre is located across from Windsor Castle on High Street (☎ 01753/743900). There's also an information booth in the tourist center at Windsor Coach Park. Both are open Sunday through Friday from 10am to 4pm and Saturday from 10am to 5pm.

CASTLE HILL SIGHTS

Queen Mary's Doll's House   A palace in perfect miniature, the Doll's House was given to Queen Mary in 1923 as a symbol of national goodwill. The house, designed by Sir Edwin Lutyens, was created on a 1-inch-to-1-foot scale. It took 3 years to complete and involved the work of 1,500 tradesmen and artists. Every item is a miniature masterpiece; each room is exquisitely furnished, and every item is made exactly to scale. Working elevators stop on every floor, all five bathrooms have running water, and electric lighting brightens the house.

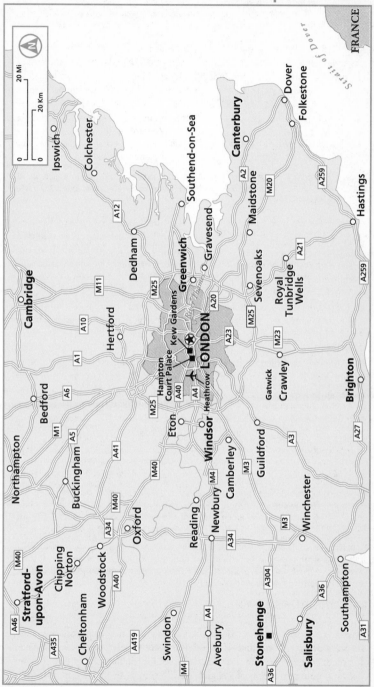

Windsor Castle. ℂ **017/5383-1118.** Castle tickets include admission here. Open same days and hr. as Windsor.

St. George's Chapel ★★★   Along with Westminster Abbey, this Perpendicular-style chapel shares the distinction of being a pantheon of English monarchs. The present St. George's was founded in the late 15th century by Edward IV on the site of the original Chapel of the Order of the Garter. At the chapel's center is a flat tomb containing the vault of the beheaded Charles I, along with Henry VIII and his third wife, Jane Seymour. Other monarchs entombed here include George V, George VI, and Edward IV. History's path forks at Princess Charlotte's memorial; had she survived childbirth in 1817, she—and not her cousin Victoria—would have ruled the British Empire.

The Cloisters, Windsor Castle. ℂ **01753/848883.** Admission included in admission to Windsor Castle. Mon–Sat 9:45am–4:15pm. Sun services open to public, but closed for sightseeing tours. Closed during services, Jan, and a few days in mid-June.

Windsor Castle ★★★ *Kids*   When William the Conqueror ordered Windsor Castle to be built, he established a base for English sovereignty that has known many vicissitudes: King John cooled his heels at Windsor while waiting to put his signature on the Magna Carta at nearby Runnymede; Charles I was imprisoned here before losing his head; Queen Bess (Elizabeth I) renovated; Victoria mourned her beloved Albert, who died at the castle; and the royal family rode out much of World War II behind its sheltering walls.

With 1,000 rooms, Windsor is the world's largest inhabited castle. When Queen Elizabeth II is in residence, the royal standard flies. Many works of art, porcelain, armor, furniture, three Verrio ceilings, and several 17th-century Gibbons carvings are displayed. Works by Rubens adorn the King's Drawing Room. In the relatively small King's Dressing Room are a Dürer, Rembrandt's portrait of his mother, and Van Dyck's triple portrait of Charles I. Of the apartments, the Grand Reception Room, with its Gobelin tapestries, is the most spectacular.

In November 1992, a fire swept through part of the castle, severely damaging it. The castle has since reopened, and its public rooms are available for viewing.

In our opinion, the Windsor changing of the guard is a much more exciting experience than the London exercises. The guard marches through the town whether the court is in residence or not, stopping the traffic as it wheels into the castle to the tunes of a full regimental band; when the queen is not here, a drum-and-pipe band is mustered. From May to August, the ceremony takes place Monday through Saturday at 11am. In winter, the guard is changed every 48 hours Monday through Saturday. It's best to call ℂ **01753/869898** for a schedule.

Castle Hill. ℂ **01753/869898.** www.royalresidences.com. Admission £11.50 ($17.25) adults; £9.50 ($14.25) students and senior citizens; £6 ($9) children 16 and under; £29 ($43.50) family of 4. Mar–Oct daily 9:45am–4pm; Nov–Feb daily 9:45am–3pm. Last admission 1 hr. before closing. Closed for periods in Apr, June, and Dec when the royal family is in residence.

EXPLORING THE TOWN

Windsor is a largely Victorian town of brick buildings, with a few remnants of Georgian architecture. Near the castle, antiques shops, silversmiths, and pubs line cobblestone Church and Market streets. Charles II's mistress Nell Gwynne supposedly occupied a shop on Church Street, which allowed her to be within shouting distance of her beau's chambers. After lunch or tea, you may want to stroll along the aptly named 5 km (3-mile) Long Walk.

On Sundays, in Windsor Great Park and at Ham Common, you may see Prince Charles playing polo and Prince Philip serving as umpire while the queen watches. The park is also the site of Her Majesty's occasional equestrian jaunts. On Sunday she attends a little church near the Royal Lodge. Traditionally, she prefers to drive herself there, later returning to the castle for Sunday lunch. For more information, call the Tourist Information Center (© **01753/743900**).

ETON

From Windsor, Eton is an easy stroll across the Thames Bridge. Follow Eton High Street to the college.

Eton College ★★ (© **01753/671177;** www.etoncollege.com) was founded by the adolescent Henry VI in 1440. Some of England's greatest men, notably the Duke of Wellington, have played on these fields. Twenty prime ministers were educated here, as well as such literary figures as George Orwell, Aldous Huxley, Ian Fleming, and Percy Bysshe Shelley—who, during his years at Eton (1804–10) was called Mad Shelley by his fellow pupils.

The history of Eton College since its inception is depicted in the Museum of Eton Life, located in vaulted wine cellars under College Hall. The displays include a turn-of-the-century boy's room, schoolbooks, sports trophies, canes used by senior boys to apply punishment to their juniors, and birch sticks used by masters for the same purpose. Also on display are letters written home by students describing day-to-day life at the school, as well as samples of the numerous magazines produced by students over the centuries. Many of the items on display were provided by Old Etonians. If it's open, take a look at the Perpendicular Chapel's 15th-century paintings and reconstructed fan vaulting.

Admission to the school and museum costs £2.70 ($4.05) for adults. You can also take guided tours for £4 ($6). Eton College is open from March 29 to April 25 and June 27 to September 5, daily from 10:30am to 4:30pm; from April 26 to July 2 and September 6 to October 1, daily from 2 to 4:30pm. Call in advance; Eton may close for special occasions. These dates vary every year depending on term and holiday dates. It's best to call.

ORGANIZED TOURS OF WINDSOR & ETON

BOAT TOURS Tours depart from The Promenade, Barry Avenue, for a 35-minute ride to Boveney Lock. There's also a 35-minute tour from Runnymede on the *Lucy Fisher,* a replica of a Victorian paddle steamer. The boat passes Magna Carta Island (commemorating the signing of the document), among other places. Both tours cost £4.40 ($6.60) for adults, and £2.20 ($3.30) for children. A 2-hour tour through the Boveney Lock and up past stately private riverside homes, the Bray Film Studios, Queens Eyot (a private beautifully landscaped island), and Monkey Island, is £6.60 ($9.90) for adults, £3.30 ($4.95) for children. Longer tours are offered between Maidenhead and Hampton Court. The boats serve refreshments and have a well-stocked bar, and the decks are covered in case of an unexpected shower. Contact French Brothers, Ltd., Clewer Boathouse, Clewer Court Road, Windsor (© **01753/851900;** fax 01753/832303; www.boat-trips.co.uk).

HORSE-DRAWN CARRIAGE RIDES You can also take a horse-drawn carriage for a half-hour promenade up the sycamore-lined length of Windsor Castle's Long Walk. Horses with carriages and drivers should be lined up beside the castle waiting for fares, which run from £40 ($60) for up to four passengers.

WHERE TO DINE
WINDSOR

The Highlander PUB GRUB   With its Scottish theme, this pub offers a beer garden opening onto a view of Windsor Castle, a choice place for a pub lunch on a fair day. It lies directly south of the fortification of Windsor Castle and is patronized by household staff and security guards who work at the castle. Housed in a 1790s building, it is one of the old town's most popular pubs. Young people come here in the evening, and there is varied live music on Friday. Hot food is served during the day, along with a wide selection of British ales.

Church Lane. ✆ **01753/864257.** Pub meals £4–£8 ($6–$12). AE, MC, V. Mon–Sat 11am–11pm; Sun noon–10:30pm.

Stroks Riverside Restaurant   MODERN BRITISH/FRENCH   A 3-minute walk from the castle, this restaurant is the most elegant and charming in Windsor, with garden terraces and a conservatory. The dining room is designed a bit like a greenhouse, and a pianist entertains at dinner. Enjoy such dishes as roasted squab with goat cheese gnocchi; rosettes of spring lamb with green beans, roasted artichokes, and Yorkshire pudding; and traditional chateaubriand carved at your table with a vegetable medley. The chef, Phillip Wild, studied at two- and three-star Michelin restaurants in Switzerland and cooks with passion and intensity. Each dish is freshly prepared with local ingredients if possible. Lamb and beef are cooked "pink," and vegetables are served al dente.

In Sir Christopher Wren's House Hotel, Thames St. ✆ **01753/861354.** Main courses £19.50–£23.50 ($29.25–$35.25). AE, DC, DISC, MC, V. Daily 12:30–2:30pm and 6:30–10pm.

ETON

Gilbey's Bar and Restaurant   MODERN BRITISH   Just across the bridge from Windsor, this graceful bar is set among the antiques shops on Eton's main street. Inside are pinewood tables, old church pews, and chairs, and there's a glassed-in conservatory out back. A brigade of chefs turns out a fine array of modern British cookery. Appetizers usually include well-prepared soups and a roasted sweet-pepper tart. Main dishes include pine-nut-and-spinach risotto topped with pecorino cheese, and roast lamb filet served with *boulangere* potatoes and vegetables. For dessert, try the tarte tatin, a tasty and creative upside-down apple pie.

82–83 High St. ✆ **01753/854921.** Reservations recommended. Main courses £10–£17 ($15–$25.50). AE, DC, MC, V. Mon–Thurs noon–2:30pm and 6–9:30pm; Fri–Sat noon–10:30pm; Sun 6–9:30pm.

House on the Bridge   ENGLISH/INTERNATIONAL   This charming restaurant is housed in a lovely redbrick and terra-cotta Victorian building, adjacent to the bridge at the edge of Eton. Near the handful of outdoor tables is a steep garden whose plants range down to the Thames. Among the well-prepared main dishes are roasted Aylesburg duckling with poached apple and forcemeat stuffing, and chicken Wellington topped with bacon, Stilton, and creamy sherry sauce. Some specialties, such as roast rack of herb-flavored lamb, are served only for two. Although traditionally based, the preparations have many modern touches, and the chefs always use good fresh ingredients. Desserts include flambés and crêpes suzette.

71 High St. ✆ **01753/860914.** Reservations recommended. Main courses from £14 ($21); fixed-price meal £20 ($30) at lunch, £30 ($45) at dinner; Sun lunch £22 ($33). AE, DC, MC, V. Daily noon–3pm and 6–11pm.

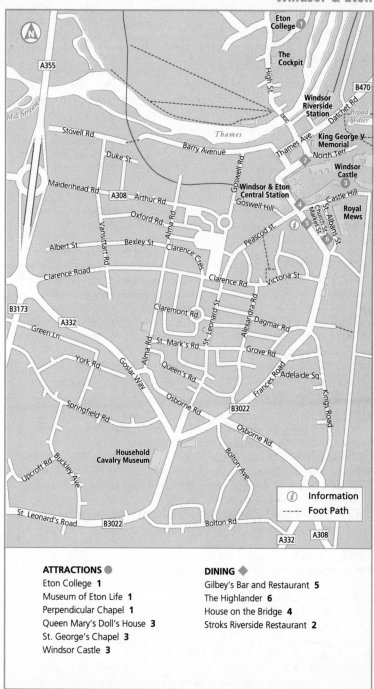

ATTRACTIONS ●

Eton College **1**
Museum of Eton Life **1**
Perpendicular Chapel **1**
Queen Mary's Doll's House **3**
St. George's Chapel **3**
Windsor Castle **3**

DINING ◆

Gilbey's Bar and Restaurant **5**
The Highlander **6**
House on the Bridge **4**
Stroks Riverside Restaurant **2**

2 Oxford, City of Dreaming Spires ✮✮✮

87km (54 miles) NW of London

A walk down the long sweep of The High Street, one of the most striking streets in England; a mug of cider in one of the old student pubs; the sound of May Day dawn when choristers sing in Latin from Magdalen Tower; the Great Tom bell from Tom Tower, whose 101 peals traditionally signal the closing of the college gates; towers and spires piercing the clouds; barges on the upper reaches of the Thames; nude swimming at Parson's Pleasure; the roar of a cannon launching the bumping races (in which each boat tries to bump the boat ahead of it and avoid being bumped by the boat behind it); a dusty bookstall where you can pick up a valuable first edition—all are found in Oxford, home of one of the greatest universities in the world.

Romantic Oxford still exists, but to get to it, you'll have to navigate the bustling and crowded city that has grown about it. A never-ending stream of polluting buses and the fast-flowing pedestrian traffic can make the city core feel more like London than an ancient university town.

At any time of the year, you can enjoy a tour of the colleges, some of the loveliest in all England. The Oxford Tourist Information Centre (see "Visitor Information," below) conducts walking tours throughout the year. Just don't mention the other place (Cambridge), and you shouldn't have any trouble. The city predates the university—it emerged as a Saxon town in the 10th century. By the 12th century, Oxford was growing in reputation as a seat of learning. When the first colleges emerged in the 13th century, Oxford began to churn out powerful and distinguished alumni, among them Roger Bacon, Sir Walter Raleigh, John Donne, Sir Christopher Wren, Samuel Johnson, Edward Gibbon, William Penn, John Wesley, Lewis Carroll, T. E. Lawrence, and W. H. Auden.

ESSENTIALS

GETTING THERE Trains from **Paddington Station** (ⓒ 08457/222-333 or 01603/764776) reach Oxford in 1¼ hours. Service is every 15 minutes. A cheap, same-day round-trip ticket costs £15.50 ($23.25).

The **X90 Oxford Express** departs from Victoria Station (ⓒ 08705/808-080; www.nationalexpress.co.uk) for the Oxford Bus Station daily. Coaches usually leave about every 20 minutes during the day, taking 1¾ hours. A same-day round-trip ticket costs £8 ($12).

Or take the **Oxford Tube,** an express coach that takes you from Oxford to London in 90 minutes off-peak. Coaches leave 3 to 6 times an hour from 6am to 10:30 pm, and hourly overnight. Single fares are £8.50 ($12.75) and £9 ($13.50) for a 24-hour round-trip return. For schedules, call ⓒ 01865/772250 or visit www.stagecoach-oxford.co.uk/tube.

By car, take M40 west from London and follow the signs. Note, however, that parking is a nightmare in Oxford. There are four well-marked "Park and Ride" lots on the north, south, east, and west of the city's ring road. Some car parks are free; others charge 60p or 70p (90¢ or $1.05). From 9:30am on weekdays, all day Saturday and from 8:45am on Sunday, you pay £2 ($3) for a bus ride into the city, which drops you off at St. Aldate's Cornmarket or Queen Street. The buses run every 8 to 10 minutes in each direction from Monday to Saturday, and every 15 to 20 minutes until 9:30 on Sunday. The parking lots are on the Woodstock road near the Peartree traffic circle, on the Botley road toward Farringdon, on the Abingdon road in the southeast, and on the A40 toward London.

Oxford

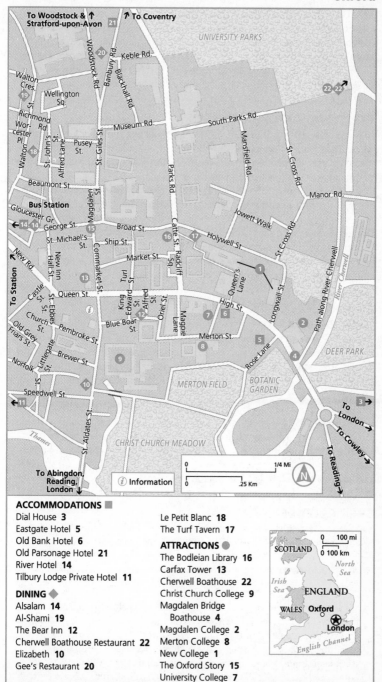

To Woodstock & Stratford-upon-Avon ↑ **21**
↑ To Coventry

UNIVERSITY PARKS

Keble Rd. **20**

Woodstock Rd.

Banbury Rd.

Blackhall Rd.

Walton Cres. **19**

Wellington Sq.

Richmond Rd.

Worcester Pl.

St. John's St.

Alfred Lane

Pusey St.

Walton St. **18**

St. Giles

Museum Rd.

South Parks Rd.

Mansfield Rd.

St. Cross Rd.

Parks Rd.

22-22

Beaumont St.

Magdalen St.

Manor Rd.

Bus Station

Gloucester Gr.

14-14

George St.

Broad St.

Jowett Walk

Cornmarket St.

St. Michael's St.

Ship St.

Catte St.

Radcliff Sq.

Holywell St.

St. Cross Rd.

River Cherwell

New Inn Hall St.

Market St.

16

17

New Rd.

To Station ←

Castle St.

St. Ebbes St.

Church St.

Old Greyfriars St.

13

Turl St.

King Edward St.

Alfred St.

Oriel St.

Queen St.

Blue Boar St.

12

Magpie Lane

Queen's Lane

1

High St.

7 **6**

2

Longwall St.

Path along River Cherwell

Pembroke St.

9

Merton St.

8

5

Rose Lane

4

DEER PARK

Littlegate

Brewer St.

10

Norfolk St.

MERTON FIELD

BOTANIC GARDEN

Speedwell St.

11 ←

St. Aldates St.

Thames

CHRIST CHURCH MEADOW

To London →

To Cowley →

To Reading →

To Abingdon, Reading, London ↓

i Information

0 _____ 1/4 Mi
0 _____ .25 Km

N

ACCOMMODATIONS ■
Dial House **3**
Eastgate Hotel **5**
Old Bank Hotel **6**
Old Parsonage Hotel **21**
River Hotel **14**
Tilbury Lodge Private Hotel **11**

DINING ◆
Alsalam **14**
Al-Shami **19**
The Bear Inn **12**
Cherwell Boathouse Restaurant **22**
Elizabeth **10**
Gee's Restaurant **20**

Le Petit Blanc **18**
The Turf Tavern **17**

ATTRACTIONS ●
The Bodleian Library **16**
Carfax Tower **13**
Cherwell Boathouse **22**
Christ Church College **9**
Magdalen Bridge Boathouse **4**
Magdalen College **2**
Merton College **8**
New College **1**
The Oxford Story **15**
University College **7**

SCOTLAND

North Sea

0 ___ 100 mi
0 ___ 100 km

Irish Sea

ENGLAND

WALES

Oxford ○

London ★

English Channel

VISITOR INFORMATION **Oxford Tourist Information Centre** is at the Old School Gloucester Green, opposite the bus station (© **01865/726871;** fax 01865/240261; www.oxford.gov.uk/tourism/). The center sells a comprehensive range of maps and brochures, as well as the famous Oxford University T-shirt, and provides hotel booking services for a £3 ($4.50) charge. Open Monday through Saturday from 9:30am to 5pm and Sunday from 10am to 1pm and 1:30 to 3:30pm; from Easter Sunday to October and on bank holidays.

EXPLORING OXFORD UNIVERSITY

Many visitors arriving at Oxford ask: "Where's the campus?" If a local chortles when answering, it's because Oxford University is made up of 35 widely dispersed colleges. To tour all of these would be a formidable task. It's best to focus on just a handful of the better-known colleges.

The Oxford Story, 6 Broad St. (© **01865/790055**), has packaged Oxford's complexities into a concise and entertaining audiovisual ride (a la Disneyland). The exhibition reviews some of the architectural and historic features that hurried visitors might miss. The exhibition includes a trip through a three-level former warehouse and takes you through more than 800 years of history. You're also filled in on the backgrounds of the colleges and those who have passed through their portals. The audiovisual presentation runs daily from 10am to 4:30pm. Tickets are £6.10 ($9.15) for adults and £4.90 ($7.35) for children and seniors. A family ticket for two adults and two children is £18.50 ($27.75).

GUIDED TOURS

The best way to get a running commentary on the important sights is to take a 2-hour walking tour of the city and major colleges. Tours leave daily from the Oxford Tourist Information Centre at 11am and 2pm. Tours cost £6 ($9) for adults, and £3 ($4.50) for children; they do not include New College or Christ Church.

For a good orientation, **Guide Friday,** with an office at the railway station (© **01865/790522**), offers hour-long, open-top bus tours around Oxford. Buses leave every half-hour beginning at 9:30am in winter; they run more frequently as summer approaches. Tickets are good for the day and can be purchased from the driver. The cost is £9 ($13.50) adults, £7.50 ($11.25) students and seniors, and £2.50 ($3.75) children age 5 to 12. A family ticket, costing £20.50 ($30.75) for two adults and up to four children, is also available.

THE COLLEGES

CHRIST CHURCH ★★ Begun by Cardinal Wolsey as Cardinal College in 1525, Christ Church (© **01865/276492;** www.chch.ox.ac.uk) was renamed by

---

Moments **A Bird's-Eye View from Carfax Tower**

For a sweeping view of all of the colleges, climb Carfax Tower, located in the center of the city. Carfax Tower is all that remains from St. Martin's Church. The tower used to be higher, but after 1340 it was lowered following complaints that townspeople threw stones and fired arrows at students during town-and-gown disputes. Admission is £1.50 ($2.25) for adults, £1 ($1.50) for children. It's open daily from 10am to 3:30pm (until 5:30pm Apr–Oct). The tower is closed from Christmas Eve until January 2. For information, call © **01865/792653.**

Henry VIII in 1546. Facing St. Aldate's Street, Christ Church—known as the House—has the largest quadrangle of any college in Oxford.

Tom Tower houses Great Tom, the 18,000-pound bell that rings nightly at 9:05pm, signaling the closing of the college gates. Its 101 peals signify the number of students in residence at the time of the founding of Christ Church. Although the student body has grown, Oxford traditions live forever. In the 16th-century great hall, you'll find several notable portraits, including works by Gainsborough and Reynolds. The walls are thick with prime ministers, since Christ Church was the training ground for 13 of them. The college also has a separate portrait gallery.

The chapel was constructed over several hundred years, beginning in the 12th century. (It's also the cathedral of the diocese of Oxford.) The chapel's most impressive features are its 15th-century Norman pillars and the vaulting of the choir.

Outside, in the center of the quadrangle, is a statue of Mercury in the middle of a fishpond. The college and chapel are open from 8am to 6pm. The entrance fee is £3 ($4.50) for adults and £2 ($3) for children. A family ticket costs £6 ($9).

Insider's Tip: Almost overlooked by the average visitor is an unheralded little gem known as Christ Church Picture Gallery, entered through the Canterbury Quad. Here you come across a stunning collection of old masters, mainly from the Dutch, Flemish, and Italian schools, including works by Michelangelo and Leonardo da Vinci. Open April through September Monday through Saturday from 10:30am to 1pm and 2 to 5:30pm (closes at 4:30pm Oct–Mar). Admission is £1 ($1.50) for adults or 50p (75¢) for seniors and students.

MAGDALEN COLLEGE Magdalen (*Maud*-lin) College, High Street (© **01865/276000**; www.magd.ox.ac.uk/), was founded in 1458. Its alumni range from statesman Cardinal Thomas Wolsey to Oscar Wilde. Opposite the botanic garden (the oldest in England), is the bell tower, where the choristers sing in Latin at dawn on May Day (May 1). This 15th-century tower reflects mightily in the waters of the Cherwell below. Visit the equally old chapel, which feels ancient despite many of its latter-day trappings. Ask when the hall and other places of special interest are open. The grounds of Magdalen are the most extensive of any Oxford college; there's even a deer park. You can visit only from Easter to September, daily from 12pm to 6pm. Admission is £2.50 ($3.75) adults, £1.25 ($1.90) children.

Insider's Tip: Often missed by the average visitor, the Botanic Gardens opposite Magdalen were first planted in 1621 on the location of an old Jewish graveyard from the early Middle Ages. Bounded by a curve of the Cherwell, they still stand today and are the best place in Oxford to escape the invading hordes. Open daily from 2 to 4pm; admission is £2 ($3) in summer, free in winter.

MERTON COLLEGE ★★ Founded in 1264, Merton College (© **01865/276310**) is among the three oldest colleges at the university. It stands near Corpus Christi College on Merton Street, the sole survivor of Oxford's medieval cobbled streets. Merton College is noted for its library, built between 1371 and 1379 and said to be the oldest college library in England. One of the treasures is an astrolabe (an astronomical instrument used for measuring the altitude of the sun and stars) thought to have belonged to Chaucer. It costs £1 ($1.50) to visit the ancient library, including admission to the Max Beerbohm Room, honoring the satirical English caricaturist who died in 1956. The library and

---

Moments **Punting on the River Cherwell**

Punting on the River Cherwell remains the favorite outdoor pastime in Oxford. At Punt Station, **Cherwell Boathouse,** Bardwell Road (© **01865/ 515978**), you can rent a punt (flat-bottomed boat steered by a long pole and a small oar) for £8 to £10 ($12–$15) per hour, plus a £40 to £50 ($60–$75) deposit. A punt can take up to six people. **Magdalen Bridge Boathouse** charges similar rates. Punts are available for rent from March to mid-October, daily from 10am to 7pm; a larger inventory of punts is available from mid-June to late August daily from 10am to 10pm. Hours of operation are rather informal; you're not always guaranteed that someone will be here to rent you a boat, even if a punt is tied to the dock.

---

college are open Monday through Friday from 2 to 4pm and Saturday and Sunday from 10am to 4pm. Merton College is closed for 1 week at Easter and at Christmas.

Insider's Tip: A favorite pastime is to take Addison's Walk near here through the water meadows. The stroll is named after former alumnus Joseph Addison, an 18th-century essayist and playwright noted for his contributions to *The Spectator* and *The Tatler.*

NEW COLLEGE New College, New College Lane, off Queen's Lane (© **01865/279555;** www.new.ox.ac.uk/), was founded in 1379. The first quadrangle, dating from before the end of the 14th century, was the first one built in Oxford and formed the architectural boilerplate for many other colleges. In the antechapel are Sir Jacob Epstein's remarkable modern sculpture of Lazarus and a fine El Greco study of St. James. One of the treasures of the college is a crosier (pastoral staff of a bishop) belonging to the founding father, William of Wykeham. In the garden, you can stroll among the remains of the old city wall and the mound (a common decorative feature of Tudor gardens). *Insider's Tip:* New College is known for its notorious gargoyles. Check them out on the bell tower, which is decorated with the seven virtues on one side and the seven deadly sins on the other. The virtues are just as grotesque as the deadly sins. The college (entered at New College Lane) can be visited from Easter to September, daily from 11am to 5pm; off-season, daily from 2 to 4pm. Admission is £2 ($3) adult, £1 ($1.50) children and seniors.

UNIVERSITY COLLEGE University College, High Street (© **01865/ 276602;** www.univ.ox.ac.uk/), is the oldest college at Oxford. It dates back to 1249, when an ecclesiastic, William of Durham, donated money for its foundation (the old claim that the real founder was Alfred the Great is fanciful). All the original structures have disappeared; the architecture of the 17th century predominates today, with additions made in Victoria's day as well as in more recent times. The college's most famous alumnus, Shelley, was expelled for his part in collaborating on a pamphlet on atheism. But with poetical success, all was forgiven, as evidenced by a memorial to Shelley erected in 1894, a mere 72 years after his death.

Insider's Tip: The most famous recent alumnus was William Jefferson Clinton, the Rhodes scholar who did not inhale here. If you'd like to see where America's last president of the 20th century lived, you can walk over to 46 Leckford Road. The hall and chapel of University College are open daily during vacations from

2 to 4pm for a charge of £1.50 ($2.25) for adults, 60p (90¢) for children. Chapel services take place daily at 4 and 6pm.

THE BODLEIAN LIBRARY ☆☆ This famed library on Catte Street (© **01865/277-224;** www.bodley.ox.ac.uk) was launched in 1602, funded by Sir Thomas Bodley. It is home to some 50,000 manuscripts and more than 5 million books. Over the years the library has expanded from the Old Library complex to other buildings, including the Radcliffe Camera next door. The easiest way to visit is by taking a guided tour, leaving from the Divinity School across from the main entrance. In summer there are four tours every day from Monday to Friday, and two on both Saturday and Sunday; in winter, two tours leave per day. Call for specific times.

WHERE TO STAY

The **Oxford Tourist Information Centre,** Gloucester Green, opposite the bus station (© **01865/726871;** fax 01865/240261; www.oxford.gov.uk/), operates a year-round room-booking service for a fee of £3 ($4.50), plus a refundable deposit. If you'd like to seek lodgings on your own, the center has a list of accommodations, maps, and guidebooks.

EXPENSIVE

Eastgate Hotel ☆ Eastgate stands opposite the ancient Examination Halls, next to Magdalen Bridge and within walking distance of the city center. It offers recently refurbished facilities but retains the atmosphere of an English country house. The rooms are well worn but still cozy and comfortable. Mattresses are replaced frequently, and the small shower-tub combination bathrooms are well maintained.

The High Street, Oxford, Oxfordshire OX1 4BE. © **0870/400-8201.** Fax 01865/791681. 64 units. £140–£165 ($210–$247.50) double; £170–£200 ($255–$300) suite. AE, DC, MC, V. Bus: 7. **Amenities:** Restaurant, bar (an undergraduate favorite); room service; laundry. *In room:* TV, coffeemaker, hair dryer.

Old Bank Hotel ☆☆☆ Opened in the last century (1999), this was Oxford's first new hotel in 135 years, and it immediately surpassed traditional favorite Randolph in style and luxuries. The good-size rooms are elegantly appointed, often with views. An understated elegance prevails, and each unit comes with a state-of-the-art marble bathroom with tubs and power showers. Throughout the hotel is an array of 20th-century British art.

92–94 High St., Oxford OX1 4BN. © **0186/579-9599.** Fax 0186/579-9598. www.oxford-hotels-restaurants. co.uk. 42 units. £155–£225 ($232.50–$337.50) double; from £255 ($382.50) suite. AE, DC, DISC, MC, V. Bus: 7. **Amenities:** Restaurant, bar; 24-hr. room service; babysitting; laundry. *In room:* A/C, TV, coffeemaker, hair dryer.

Old Parsonage Hotel ☆☆ This extensively renovated hotel near St. Giles Church and Keble College is so old (1660) that it looks like an extension of one of the colleges. Once a 13th-century hospital, it was restored in the early 17th century. Oscar Wilde lived here for a time; this is where he said, "Either this wallpaper goes, or I do." In the 20th century, a modern wing was added, and in 1991, it was completely renovated and made into a first-rate hotel. The recently redecorated bedrooms are not large, but they're individually designed and have such luxuries as phones in the shower-tub combination bathrooms. All suites and some doubles open onto the private gardens.

1 Banbury Rd., Oxford OX2 6NN. © **01865/310210.** Fax 01865/311262. www.oxford-hotels-restaurants.co. uk. 30 units. £135–£190 ($202.50–$285) double; £200 ($300) suite. Rates include English breakfast. AE, DC, MC, V. Bus: 2 or 6. **Amenities:** Restaurant, bar; room service; laundry. *In room:* TV, hair dryer.

INEXPENSIVE

Dial House   This country house, built in the 1920s, rests beside the highway to London, 3km (2 miles) east of the heart of Oxford. Graced with mock-Tudor half-timbering and a prominent blue-faced sundial, it has roomy and recently renovated bedrooms. Bathrooms are small and most of them have a shower only, but a few offer a combination tub and shower. No smoking is permitted in the house.

25 London Rd., Headington, Oxford, Oxfordshire OX3 7RE. ✆ 01865/769944. Fax 01865/750267. www. oxfordcity.co.uk/accom/dialhouse. 8 units. £60–£75 ($90–$112.50) double. Rates include breakfast. MC, V. Bus: 7, 7A, 2, 2A, or 22. *In room:* TV, coffeemaker, hair dryer.

River Hotel   This hotel lies a quarter-mile west of Oxford's commercial core and charges less than many of its more central competitors. It was built around 1900 by a local craftsman whose casement windows and flower boxes are still in place. About a quarter of the accommodations are across the street in a stone-sided annex. Bedrooms have cozy furnishings and are continually renewed, and you get comfortable beds here. Bathrooms are small and come with showers.

17 Botley Rd., Oxford OX2 0AA. ✆ **01865/243475.** Fax 01865/724306. www.riverhotel.co.uk. 20 units. £70–£90 ($105–$135) double. Rates include English breakfast. MC, V. Bus: 4C or 52. **Amenities:** Restaurant, bar. *In room:* coffeemaker, hair dryer from reception, no phone.

Tilbury Lodge Private Hotel *(Value*   This small hotel lies on a quiet country lane 3km (2 miles) west of the center of Oxford, less than a mile from the railway station. Eddie and Eileen Trafford house guests in well-furnished and comfortable bedrooms. (The most expensive has a four-poster bed.) Rooms vary in size; most have adequate space and each comes with a tiny, well-kept bathroom with a shower. If you don't arrive by car, Eddie can pick you up at the train station; a bus also stops nearby.

5 Tilbury Lane, Eynsham Rd., Botley, Oxford OX2 9NB. ✆ **01865/862138.** Fax 01865/863700. www.oxford city.co.uk/hotels/tilbury/. 9 units. £66–£72 ($99–$108) double; £75 ($112.50) double with four-poster. Rates include English breakfast. MC, V. Bus: 4A, 4B, or 100. **Amenities:** Jacuzzi. *In room:* TV, coffeemaker, hair dryer.

WHERE TO DINE
EXPENSIVE

Elizabeth 🐷 FRENCH/CONTINENTAL   This stone-sided house opposite Christ Church College is named not for Elizabeth II (although her portraits hang near the entrance), but for the matriarch who founded the place in the 1930s. Today, you'll find a well-trained staff from Spain, who serve beautifully presented dishes in the French style. The larger of the two dining rooms exudes a restrained dignity; the smaller is devoted to *Alice in Wonderland* designs inspired by Lewis Carroll. Some of the kitchen's best dishes include a range of Scottish steaks; chicken royale, Dover sole, sea bass in white-wine or lemon-butter sauce, and Basque *piperade,* the famous omelet dish of the Basque country.

82 St. Aldate's St. ✆ 01865/242230. Reservations recommended. Main courses £13.25–£33 ($19.90–$49.50); lunch £16 ($24). AE, DC, MC, V. Tues–Sat 12:30–2:30pm and 6:30–11pm; Sun 7–10:30pm. Closed Easter weekend and Christmas week. Bus: 7.

MODERATE

Al-Shami LEBANESE   Ideal for meals all afternoon and late into the evening, this Lebanese restaurant awakens Oxford's sleepy taste buds. Many diners don't go beyond the appetizers, more than 35 delectable hot-and-cold selections—everything from falafel to lamb's-brain salad. Charcoal-grilled chopped lamb, chicken, or beef constitute most of the main-dish selections. In between, guests nibble on uncut raw vegetables; afterward they choose desserts from the trolley. Al-Shami also serves vegetarian meals.

25 Walton Crescent. © **01865/310066.** Reservations recommended. Main courses £7.50–£12 ($11.25–$18); fixed-price menu £15 ($22.50). MC, V. Daily noon–midnight. Bus: 7.

Cherwell Boathouse Restaurant MODERN ENGLISH/FRENCH This landmark on the River Cherwell is owned by Anthony Verdin, who offers a fixed-price menu that changes every 2 weeks to take advantage of the availability of fresh vegetables, fish, and meat. On any given night, you might try starters such as game terrine with Cumberland sauce or a warm salad of black pudding and bacon with a damson plum dressing. For a main course, you might opt for breast of guinea fowl with tapenade or, for vegetarians, an eggplant gratin with saffron custard and a mixed-bean ragout. For dessert, few have resisted the "fallen" chocolate soufflé with "drunken" prunes and sour cream. The restaurant also has an exciting, reasonable wine list. In summer, dinner is served on the terrace. Before dinner, you can try punting; there's a rental agency on the other side of the boathouse (see "Punting on the River Cherwell," above).

Bardwell Rd. © **01865/552746.** Reservations recommended. Main courses £10–£20 ($15–$30); fixed-price dinner from £22 ($33); fixed-price lunch £19 ($28.50); express lunch £10 ($15). AE, DC, MC, V. Mon–Sat noon–2pm and 6–10pm; Sun noon–2pm. Closed Dec 24–30. Bus: No. 2 Banbury Rd.

Gee's Restaurant ☆ MEDITERRANEAN/INTERNATIONAL This restaurant, in a spacious Victorian glass conservatory, was converted from what for 80 years was the leading florist of Oxford. All the original features were retained by the owners, who also own the Old Parsonage Hotel (see above), who have turned it into one of the most nostalgic and delightful places to dine in the city. It's been around since 1984 but under a new chef has come even more into fashion. Clientele ranges from students to professors, and all enjoy a well-chosen menu that ranges from succulent pastas to chargrilled steaks, from fresh fish to crisp salads. We recently dug into a tagliatelle with smoked haddock, leeks, pancetta, and a thyme butter sauce, and found it a delight; our dining partner was equally satisfied with duck breast with a sherry sauce. Count on a freshly made soup and such Mediterranean-inspired salads as roast pepper, French beans, and olives. The Scottish prime rib-eye steak with mushrooms and shoestring "chips" is always reliable.

61 Banbury Rd. © **01865/553540.** Reservations recommended. Main courses £10–£18.50 ($15–$27.75); fixed-price lunch £9.50 ($14.25). AE, MC, V. Daily noon–2:30pm and 6–11pm. Bus 2 or 6.

Le Petit Blanc ☆ FRENCH/MEDITERRANEAN This buzzing brasserie is located in a former piano shop converted into a stylish restaurant that promises something for every palate. Here you can get a taste of famous chef Raymond Blanc's creations without the high prices charged in his other restaurants. The menu is fairly straightforward, with a special emphasis on fresh ingredients and the restaurant is conveniently located 2 blocks from the bus station.

The aim is simple—to provide the best food, service, and value for the money. The food is wholesome and delicious, based on authentic provincial French cuisine, complemented by Mediterranean and Asian accents. The crab and lobster spring roll with spicy fig compote will get you going if you didn't opt for the goat's cheese-and-thyme soufflé with apple-and-watercress salad. For mains, the braised rabbit with sweet onion tarte tatin and flap mushrooms, or the Oxford sausage and parsleyed mash with Madeira and sweet onion sauce are superb. The desserts are first-rate, especially the raspberry soufflé.

71–72 Walton St. © **01865/510999.** Reservations recommended. Main courses £8.25–£17 ($12.40–$25.50); fixed-price lunch £15 ($22.50). AE, DC, MC, V. Mon–Fri 11am–11pm; Sat noon–3:30pm and 6–11pm; Sun noon–3:30pm and 6:30–10pm.

INEXPENSIVE

Alsalam *Value* LEBANESE   Some Oxford students think this place offers the best food value in the city. The menu depends on what's available in the marketplace and the chef's skill is reflected in such dishes as king prawns sautéed with a garlic and tomato sauce, or spicy lamb with a chili and onion sauce. Long lines can form at the door, especially on Fridays and Saturdays.

6 Park End St. © 01865/245710. Reservations recommended. Main courses £7–£11 ($10.50–$16.50). MC, V. Daily noon–midnight. Bus: 52.

PUBS

The Bear Inn   A short block from The High Street, overlooking the north side of Christ Church College, this village pub is an Oxford tradition. Its swinging sign depicts a bear and a ragged staff, the old insignia of the earls of Warwick, who were among its early patrons. Many famous Oxford students and residents have caroused within the pub's walls since the 13th century, earning it a well-worn place in English literature. Some past owners developed the prankish habit of clipping their guests' neckties. Around the lounge bar you'll see the remains of thousands of ties, all labeled with their owners' names.

Alfred St., at the corner of Alfred and Blue Boar. © 01865/728164. Snacks and bar meals £2.75–£7 ($4.15–$10.50). MC, V. Mon–Sat noon–11pm; Sun noon–10:30pm. Bus: 2A or 2B.

The Turf Tavern   This 13th-century tavern, the oldest in Oxford, stands on a very narrow passageway near the Bodleian Library. Thomas Hardy used it as a setting in *Jude the Obscure,* and it was "the local" of Richard Burton and Liz Taylor when they were in Oxford many years ago making a film. Today's patrons include a healthy sampling of the university's students and faculty. During warm weather you can choose a table in one of the three separate gardens that radiate outward from the pub's core. For wintertime warmth, braziers are lighted in the courtyard and in the gardens. A separate food counter, set behind a glass case, displays the day's fare. The pub is reached via St. Helen's Passage, which stretches between Holywell Street and New College Lane.

4 Bath Place (off Holywell St.). © 01865/243235. Main courses £4.25–£5.45 ($6.40–$8.20). MC, V. Mon–Sat 11am–11pm; Sun noon–10:30pm, last meal served at 7:30pm. Bus: 52.

3 The Pursuit of Science: Cambridge

89km (55 miles) N of London, 129km (80 miles) NE of Oxford

The university town of Cambridge is a collage of images: the Bridge of Sighs; spires and turrets; willows; dusty secondhand bookshops; the lilt of Elizabethan madrigals; lanes where Darwin, Newton, and Cromwell walked; the grassy Backs of the colleges, sweeping down to the banks of the Cam; punters; the tattered robes of hurried upperclassmen flying in the wind.

Along with Oxford, Cambridge is one of Britain's ancient seats of knowledge. In many ways their stories are similar. However, beyond its campus, Cambridge has a thriving, high-tech industry. And while Oxford recalls the arts, Cambridge has embraced the sciences. Both Isaac Newton and Stephen Hawking are graduates, joined by luminaries in every field.

There is much to explore in Cambridge, so give yourself time to wander.

ESSENTIALS

GETTING THERE   Trains depart frequently from London's Liverpool Street and King's Cross stations, arriving an hour later. For inquiries, call © **0345/ 484950** (in the UK only) or 01603/764776. An off-peak same-day round-trip

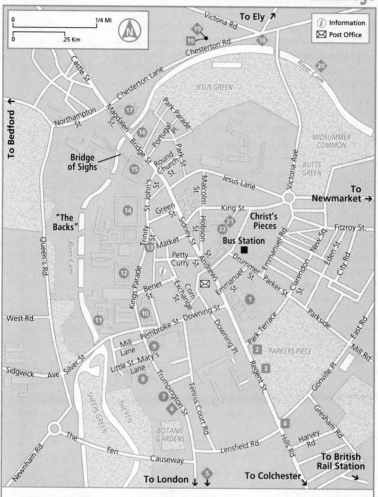

0 1/4 Mi
0 .25 Km

To Ely ↗
Victoria Rd.
Chesterton Rd.

ⓘ Information
✉ Post Office

Castle St.
Chesterton Lane
JESUS GREEN
River Cam

To Bedford ←
Northampton St.
Magdalen St.
Bridge of Sighs
Bridge St.
Portugal Pl.
Park Parade
Round Church St.
Park St.
St. John's
Green St.
Malcolm St.
Jesus Lane
King St.
Christ's Pieces
Bus Station
Victoria Ave.
MIDSUMMER COMMON
BUTTS GREEN
To Newmarket →
Fitzroy St.

"The Backs"
Queen's Rd.
River Cam
Trinity St.
Sidney St.
Market
Hobson St.
St. Andrews St.
Petty Curry
Corn Exchange
Benet St.
Kings Parade
Emmanuel St.
Drummer St.
Parker St.
Emmanuel Rd.
New Sq.
Clarendon St.
Eden St.
City Rd.

West Rd.
Pembroke St.
Downing St.
Downing Pl.
Park Terrace
PARKERS PIECE
Parkside
East Rd.

Sidgwick Ave.
Silver St.
Mill Lane
Little St. Mary's Lane
Trumpington St.
Tennis Court Rd.
Regent St.
Gonville Pl.
Mill Rd.

SHEEPS GREEN
THE FEN
BOTANIC GARDENS
Lensfield Rd.
Hills Rd.
Harvey Rd.
Gresham Rd.

Newnham Rd.
The Fen Causeway
To London ↓↓
To Colchester ↘
To British Rail Station ↘

ATTRACTIONS ●
Christ's College **22**
Corpus Christi College **10**
Emmanuel College **1**
Fitzwilliam Museum **7**
Great St. Mary's **13**
King's College **12**
Magdalene College **17**
Pembroke College **9**
Peterhouse College **8**
Queens' College **11**
Scudamores Boatyards **16**
St. John's College **15**
Trinity College **14**

ACCOMMODATIONS ■
Arundel House **19**
Gonville Hotel **4**
Regent Hotel **3**
University Arms Hotel **2**

DINING ◆
Arundel House Restaurant **19**
Browns **6**
Cambridge Arms **21**
Midsummer House **20**
Out & Out **5**
Twenty Two **18**

0 100 mi
0 100 km
SCOTLAND
North Sea
Irish Sea
ENGLAND
Cambridge
WALES
London
English Channel

is £15.20 ($22.80). A peak-time same-day round-trip is £17.70 ($26.55). An off-peak longer stay round-trip (up to a 5-day period) is £23.40 ($35.10).

National Express (© 08705/808-080; www.nationalexpress.co.uk/) buses run hourly from London's Victoria Coach Station for the 2-hour trip to Drummer Street Station in Cambridge. A one-way trip costs £7.70 ($11.55), a same-day round-trip is £8.50 ($12.75). If you'd like to return in a day or two, the cost is £14 ($21).

To drive from London, head north on the M11.

VISITOR INFORMATION The **Cambridge Tourist Information Centre,** Wheeler Street (© 01223/322640; http://www.cambridge.gov.uk/leisure/index.htm), in back of the Guildhall, offers a wide range of information. From April to October, hours are Monday through Saturday from 10am to 6pm, and Sunday from 11am to 4pm (from Easter to December only); July and August, it's open daily from 10am to 6pm. From November to March, hours are Monday through Saturday from 10am to 5:30pm.

A tourist reception center for Cambridge and Cambridgeshire is operated by **Guide Friday Ltd.** on the concourse of Cambridge Railway Station (© 01223/362444). The center sells brochures and maps, and books rooms. Open daily in summer from 9:30am to 7pm; the center closes at 3:30pm in winter.

GETTING AROUND The center of Cambridge is made for pedestrians, so park your car at one of the car parks (they increase in price as you approach the city center) and stroll the widely dispersed colleges. Follow the courtyards through to the Backs (the college lawns) and walk through to Trinity (where Prince Charles studied) and St. John's colleges, where you'll find the Bridge of Sighs.

Another popular way of getting around is bicycling. **Geoff's Bike Hire,** 65 Devonshire Rd. (© 01223/365629), rents bicycles for £5 ($7.50) for 3 hours, £7 ($10.50) per day, or £12 ($18) per week. A deposit of £25 ($37.50) is required. Open daily in summer from 9am to 6pm; off-season Monday through Saturday from 9am to 5:30pm.

Stagecoach Cambus, 100 Cowley Rd. (© 01223/423578 or 01223/423554), operates a network of buses, with fares ranging in price from 60p to £1.80 (90¢–$2.70). The local tourist office has schedules.

GUIDED TOURS

A good person to know in the Cambridge area is Mrs. Isobel Bryant, who operates **Heritage Tours** from her 200-year-old home, Manor Cottage, Swaffham Prior CB5 0JZ (© 01223/311-602). An expert on the region, she will arrange tours starting from your hotel or Cambridge Railway Station to Lavenham, with its thatched and timbered houses, to the medieval churches of the Suffolk villages, to Ely Cathedral, or to one of the nearby mansions with their many treasures. The cost is £112 ($168) for the day for up to four passengers, with all travel expenses, including the driver/guide, included. Lunch in a pub and admission fees add £4 to £6 ($6 to $9) per person. Mrs. Bryant also offers walking tours around the Cambridge colleges; they cost £36 ($54) for a family-size party and last about 2 hours.

Guide Friday, Ltd., on the concourse of Cambridge Railway Station (© 01223/362444), has daily guided tours of Cambridge via open-top, double-decker buses. In summer, buses depart every 30 minutes from 9:45am to 2:45pm. In the off-season, departures depend on demand. You can hop on or off at any stop; tickets are valid all day. The fare is £9 ($13.50) for adults, £7.50

($11.25) for seniors and students, £3 ($4.50) for children 6 to 12, and free for children 5 and under. A family ticket, costing £20 ($30) for two adults and four children, is also sold. Office hours are from 9:30am to 3:30pm daily in winter and 9:30am to 7pm in summer.

EXPLORING THE UNIVERSITY

Oxford University predates Cambridge, but by the early 13th century scholars began gathering here. Eventually, Cambridge won partial recognition and received funds from Henry III; afterwards approval and funding rose and fell depending on the monarch. Cambridge consists of 31 colleges for both men and women. Colleges are closed to the public during exams from mid-April until the end of June.

The following listing is only a sample of some of the more interesting colleges. If you're planning to be in Cambridge awhile, you might also want to visit **Magdalene College,** on Magdalene Street, founded in 1542; **Pembroke College,** on Trumpington Street, founded in 1347; **Christ's College,** on St. Andrew's Street, founded in 1505; and **Corpus Christi College,** on Trumpington Street, which dates from 1352.

EMMANUEL COLLEGE   On St. Andrew's Street, Emmanuel (© **01223/ 334200;** www.emma.cam.ac.uk/) was founded in 1584 by Sir Walter Mildmay, a chancellor of the exchequer to Elizabeth I. John Harvard, of the university that bears his name in another city called Cambridge, studied here. You can stroll around its attractive gardens and visit the chapel designed by Sir Christopher Wren, consecrated in 1677.

Insider's Tip: Harvard men and women, and those who love them, can look for a memorial window in Wren's chapel dedicated to John Harvard, an alumnus of Emmanuel who lent his name to that other university. Both the chapel and college are open daily during sunlight hours.

KING'S COLLEGE ★★   The adolescent Henry VI founded King's College on King's Parade (© **01223/331212;** www.kings.cam.ac.uk/) in 1441. Most of its buildings today date from the 19th century, but its crowning glory, the **Perpendicular King's College Chapel** ★★★, was built in the Middle Ages and is one of England's irreplaceable monuments. Owing to whims of royalty, the chapel wasn't completed until the early 16th century.

Henry James called King's College Chapel "the most beautiful in England." Its most striking features are the magnificent fan vaulting, all in stone, and the great windows, most of which were fashioned by Flemish artisans between 1517

Which College? Oxford or Cambridge?

Which college should you choose if you can spare only a day out of London? We'd opt for Cambridge over Oxford because Cambridge more closely lives up to the image of what an English university town is like.

In addition to its architecture and university, Cambridge allows you to view the life of East Anglia, still one of the country's most bucolic landscapes (as painted by John Constable). Cambridge is also more compact than Oxford and more easily walked and explored on a day trip.

and 1531 (the west window dates from the late Victorian period). In hues of red, blue, and amber, the long range of windows around the back of the chapel depicts the Birth of the Virgin; the Annunciation; the Birth of Christ; the Life, Ministry, and Death of Christ; the Resurrection; the Ascension; the Acts of the Apostles; and the Assumption. The upper range contains Old Testament parallels to these New Testament stories. The chapel also boasts Rubens's *Adoration of the Magi* and an ornamental screen from the early 16th century. The chapel is famous for its choir and musical concerts. You can call the college for concert dates.

Insider's Tip: For a classic view of chapel, you can admire the architectural complex from the rear, which would be ideal for a picnic along the river. E. M. Forster came here to contemplate scenes for his novel, *Maurice*.

The chapel is open during term time Monday through Friday from 9:30am to 3:30pm; on Saturday from 9:30am to 3:15pm; and on Sundays from 1:15pm to 2:15pm and 5 to 5:30pm. During school vacations, it's open Monday through Saturday from 9:30am to 4:30pm, and Sunday from 10am to 5pm. During term, the public is welcome to attend choral services Monday through Saturday at 5:30pm and Sunday at 10:30am and 3:30pm. It's closed December 23 to January 1. It may be closed at other times for recording sessions, broadcasts, concerts, or other special events.

An exhibition in the seven northern side chapels recounts much of the history of the chapel. Admission to the college and chapel, including the exhibition, is £3.50 ($5.25) for adults, £2.50 ($3.75) for students and children 12 to 17, and free for children under 12.

PETERHOUSE COLLEGE On Trumpington Street, Peterhouse College (*(℃* **01223/338200;** www.pet.cam.ac.uk/) attracts visitors because it's the oldest Cambridge college, founded in 1284 by Hugh de Balsham, the bishop of Ely. Of the original buildings, only the hall remains. It was restored in the 19th century and has stained-glass windows by William Morris. Old Court, constructed in the 15th century, was renovated in 1754; the chapel dates from 1632. Ask to enter at the porter's lodge.

Insider's Tip: Almost sadly neglected, the Little Church of St. Mary's next door was the college chapel until 1632. Pay it the honor of a visit.

QUEENS' COLLEGE ⊛ On Silver Street, Queens' College (*(℃* **01223/ 335511;** www.quns.cam.ac.uk/) is the loveliest of Cambridge's colleges. Dating back to 1448, it was founded by two English queens, Margaret of Anjou, the wife of Henry VI, and Elizabeth Woodville, the wife of Edward IV. Its second cloister is the most interesting, flanked by the early 16th-century half-timbered President's Lodge.

Admission is £1.50 ($2.25) for adults; free for children under 12. A short guide is issued. From November until March 19, hours are daily from 1:45 to 4:30pm; from March 20 to May 15, Monday through Friday from 1:45 to 4:30pm, Saturday and Sunday from 10am to 4:45pm; closed from May 17 to June 19. From June 20 to September 19, it's open Monday through Friday from 10am to 4:30pm, Saturday and Sunday from 10am to 4:45pm; from September 20 to October 31, Monday through Friday from 1:45 to 4:30pm, Saturday and Sunday from 10am to 4:45pm. Entry is by the old porter's lodge in Queens' Lane only. The old hall and chapel are usually open to the public when not in use.

Insider's Tip: Here's your chance to relax from a hectic day of sightseeing. Queens' College's wide lawns lead down to the "Backs," where you may want to go punting. Take in Mathematical Bridge, best viewed from the Silver Street bridge, dating from 1902. By this bridge stop off at the old pub, the Anchor, and contemplate what life would have been like if you'd attended Cambridge.

ST. JOHN'S COLLEGE 🌟🌟🌟   On St. John's Street, this college ((✆ **01223/ 338600;** www.joh.cam.ac.uk/) was founded in 1511 by Lady Margaret Beaufort, mother of Henry VII, who had launched Christ's College a few years earlier. The impressive gateway bears the Tudor coat of arms, and the Second Court is a fine example of late Tudor brickwork. Its best-known feature is the Bridge of Sighs crossing the Cam. Built in the 19th century, it was patterned after the covered bridge in Venice. It connects the older part of the college with New Court, a Gothic revival on the opposite bank, where there is an outstanding view of the famous Backs. The Bridge of Sighs is closed to visitors, but can be seen from neighboring Kitchen Bridge. Wordsworth was an alumnus of this college, which is open March through October, daily from 9:30am to 5pm. Admission is £2 ($3) for adults and £1.50 ($2.25) for children. During the winter months, there is no charge and subject to college activities, the public is welcome to wander the grounds. Visitors are welcome to attend choral services in the chapel.

Insider's Tip: The Bridge of Sighs links the old college with an architectural "folly" of the 19th century, the elaborate New Court, which is a crenellated neo-Gothic fantasy. It's adorned with a riot of pinnacles and a main cupola. Students call it "the wedding cake."

TRINITY COLLEGE 🌟🌟   On Trinity Street, Trinity College (not to be confused with Trinity Hall) ((✆ **01223/338400;** www.trin.cam.ac.uk/) is the largest college in Cambridge. It was founded in 1546 by Henry VIII, who consolidated a number of smaller colleges that had existed on the site. The courtyard is the most spacious in Cambridge, built when Thomas Neville was master. Sir Christopher Wren designed the library.

Insider's Tip: What's fun to do here is to contemplate what has gone on before you arrived. Pause at Neville's Court where Isaac Newton first calculated the speed of sound. Take in the delicate fountain of the Great Court where Lord Byron used to bathe naked with his pet bear. Why a bear? The university forbade students from having dogs but there was no proviso for bears. Years later Vladimir Nabokov walked through that same courtyard dreaming of the young lady he would later immortalize as *Lolita*. For admission to the college, apply at the porter's lodge. There's a charge of £2 ($3) from March to November.

MORE CAMBRIDGE ATTRACTIONS

Fitzwilliam Museum 🌟🌟   This is one of Britain's finest museums, founded by the bequest of the 7th viscount Fitzwilliam of Merrion to the University of Cambridge in 1816. The permanent collections contain remarkable antiquities from ancient Egypt, Greece, and Rome. Galleries display Roman and Romano-Egyptian art along with Western-Asiatic exhibits. The Fitzwilliam's Applied Arts section showcases English and European pottery and glass, as well as furniture, clocks, armor, fans, rugs and samplers, Chinese jades, and ceramics from Japan and Korea. The museum also has married a rare ancient and medieval coin collection with a host of medals created from the Renaissance onward. The Fitzwilliam is best loved for its paintings, which include masterpieces by Simone Martini, Titian, Veronese, Rubens, Van Dyck, Canaletto, Hogarth, Gainsborough, Constable, Monet, Degas, Renoir, Cézanne, and Picasso. There is also a fine collection of other 20th-century art, miniatures, drawings, watercolors, and prints. The Fitzwilliam stages occasional musical events, including

Moments Punting the Cam

Punting along the Cam in flat-bottomed wooden boats is a tradition here. **Scudamores Boatyards,** 8 Bottolph (© **01223/359750**), by the Anchor Pub, has been in business since 1910. Punts, canoes, and rowboats rent for £10 ($15) per hour. A £50 ($75) cash or credit card deposit is required. There's a maximum of six persons per punt or five per rowboat. They're open year-round, although March through October is the high season. Phone to check availability from November to February. They're open daily from 9am until dusk, depending on the weather and number of clients. If you prefer to let a chauffeur do your punting for you, there's a charge of £8 ($12) per adult, and £4 ($6) per child under 14 (babies free).

evening concerts, in Gallery III. Throughout the year, it also plays host to some of the best lectures in England.

Trumpington St., near Peterhouse. © 01223/332900. www.fitzmuseum.cam.ac.uk. Free admission. Tues–Sat 10am–5pm; Sun 2:15–5pm. Guided tours, Sun 2:45pm. Closed Jan 1, Good Friday, May Day, and Dec 24–31.

Great St. Mary's   Closely associated with events of the Reformation because the leaders of the movement (Erasmus, Cranmer, Latimer, and Ridley) preached here, this university church was built mostly in 1478 on the site of an 11th-century church. The cloth that covered the hearse of King Henry VII is on display in the church. There is a fine view of Cambridge from the top of the tower.

King's Parade. © 01223/741716. Admission to tower £2 ($3) adults, £1 ($1.50) children. Tower Mon–Sat 10am–5pm, Sun noon–4:30pm; church daily 9am–6pm.

WHERE TO STAY
EXPENSIVE
University Arms Hotel   Built in 1834, this hotel maintains much of its Edwardian charm and many of its original architectural features, despite modernization over the years. Near the city center and the university, it offers tastefully decorated bedrooms, maintained in tiptop shape, with central heating and radios. Eighty rooms have recently been refurbished with new draperies and firm mattresses. Front rooms are smaller than those in the rear and double-glazed windows cut down on noise. Bathrooms are small and contain a combination tub and shower.

Regent St., Cambridge, Cambridgeshire CB2 1AD. © 01223/351241. Fax 01223/315256. www.devere.com (click on "DeVere Hotels"). 116 units. £160–£180 ($240–$270) double; £250–£275 ($375–$412.50) suite. AE, DC, MC, V. Parking £7 ($10.50). Bus: 1. **Amenities:** Restaurant, bar; room service; babysitting; dry cleaning/laundry. *In room:* TV, coffeemaker, hair dryer, iron/ironing board.

MODERATE
Gonville Hotel   This hotel and its grounds are opposite Parker's Piece Park, only a 5-minute walk from the center of town. The Gonville has been much improved in recent years, and is better than ever, although not yet the equal of the University Arms (above). It's like an ivy-covered country house, with shade trees and a formal car entry. The recently refurbished rooms are comfortable and modern in style. Bedrooms have small but well-kept bathrooms with showers.

Gonville Place, Cambridge, Cambridgeshire CB1 1LY. ✆ **800/528-1234** in the U.S., or 01223/366611 in the UK. Fax 01223/315470. www.gonvillehotel.co.uk. 64 units. £107–£150 ($160.50–$225) double. AE, DC, MC, V. Bus 1. **Amenities:** Restaurant, bar; laundry/dry cleaning. *In room:* TV, coffeemaker, hair dryer, iron/ironing board.

INEXPENSIVE

Arundel House   Occupying one of the most desirable sites in Cambridge, this hotel consists of six identical Victorian row houses—all fronted with dark-yellow local bricks—and all interconnected. In 1994, after two additional houses were purchased, the hotel was enlarged, upgraded, and expanded into the well-maintained hostelry you'll see today. Though not as well appointed as the University Arms, it competes successfully with the Gonville, and has the best cuisine of the three hotels. Rooms overlooking the River Cam and Jesus Green cost more, as do those on lower floors (there's no elevator). Regardless of location, all rooms are clean, simple, and comfortable, with upholstered chairs, carpeting, and small but efficient and tidily kept shower-only bathrooms.

Chesterton Rd., Cambridge, Cambridgeshire CB4 3AN. ✆ **01223/367701.** Fax 01223/367721. www.arundel househotels.co.uk. 105 units. £85–£115 ($127.50–$172.50) double. Rates include continental breakfast. AE, DC, MC, V. Bus: 3 or 5. **Amenities:** Restaurant, bar; laundry. *In room:* TV, coffeemaker, hair dryer.

Regent Hotel   This is one of the most desirable of Cambridge's reasonably priced small hotels. Right in the city center, overlooking Parker's Piece, the house was built in the 1840s as the original site of Newham College. It became a hotel when the college outgrew its quarters. Bedrooms are on the small side, but redecorated frequently. Bathrooms are small, but have adequate shelf space and showers.

41 Regent St., Cambridge, Cambridgeshire CB2 1AB. ✆ **01223/351470.** Fax 01223/566562. www.regent hotel.co.uk. 25 units. £90 ($135) double. Rates include continental breakfast. AE, DC, MC, V. Bus: 1. **Amenities:** Bar. *In room:* TV, coffeemaker, hair dryer.

WHERE TO DINE
EXPENSIVE

Midsummer House ★★ MODERN FRENCH   Located near the River Cam in an Edwardian-era cottage, this is one of our best dining discoveries in Cambridge. The preferred dining area is an elegant conservatory, but you can also find a smartly laid table upstairs. The fixed-price menus are wisely limited, and quality control and high standards are evident despite a frequent change of chefs. The waiters will be glad to assist you as you peruse the menu, which traditionally has offered some of the freshest and best food selections in Cambridge.

Midsummer Common. ✆ **01223/369299.** Reservations required. 3-course lunch £20 ($30); 3-course fixed-price dinner £42 ($63). AE, DISC, MC, V. Tues–Sat noon–2pm and 7–9:30pm. Bus: 6.

MODERATE

Arundel House Restaurant INTERNATIONAL   This acclaimed restaurant in Cambridge is situated in a hotel overlooking the River Cam and Jesus Green, a short walk from the city center. The award-winning cuisine is not only excellent and fresh, but is also a good value. The warm decor features Louis XV–style chairs and spacious tables. The fare changes frequently, and you may dine a la carte or from the set menu. There's also a children's menu with a maximum price of £4 ($6). Appetizers may consist of a homemade golden pea and ham soup, or a white-rum and passion fruit cocktail. Fish choices are likely to include plaice or salmon, which compete against the roasted duckling or ostrich steak.

Chesterton Rd. © **01223/367701**. Reservations recommended. Main courses £10–£16 ($15–$24); fixed-price lunch £17 ($25.50); fixed-price dinner £19 ($28.50). AE, DC, MC, V. Daily 12:30–2pm and 6:30–9:30pm. Bus: 3 or 5.

Browns ★ *Value* ENGLISH/CONTINENTAL   After wowing them at Oxford, Browns now lures Cambridge students in equal numbers. The building lies opposite the Fitzwilliam Museum and was constructed in 1914 as the out-patient department of a hospital dedicated to Edward VII; that era's grandeur is apparent in the building's neoclassical colonnade. Today, it's the most light-hearted place for dining in the city, with wicker chairs, high ceilings, pre–World War I woodwork, and a long bar covered with bottles of wine. The extensive bill of fare includes pastas, scores of fresh salads, several selections of meat and fish (from charcoal-grilled leg of lamb with rosemary to fresh fish in season), hot sandwiches, and the chef's daily specials. If you drop by in the afternoon, you can also order thick milkshakes or natural fruit juices. In fair weather, outdoor seats are prized possessions.

23 Trumpington St. © **01223/461655**. Main courses £7–£14 ($10.50–$21). AE, MC, V. Mon–Sat 11am–11:30pm; Sun noon–11:30pm. Bus: 2.

Twenty Two ★ ENGLISH/CONTINENTAL   Who would expect to find one of the best restaurants in Cambridge in this quiet residential and hotel dis-trict? In the vicinity of Jesus Green, it's a spot jealously guarded by locals. The homey but elegant Victorian dining room offers an ever-changing fixed-price menu based on fresh market produce. Owners David Carter and Louise Crompton meld time-tested recipes with their own inspirations. Typical dishes include grilled loin of tuna with pesto, spring onions, and chili; and supreme of chicken with pearl barley risotto and roasted eggplant.

22 Chesterton Rd. © **01223/351880**. Reservations required. Fixed-price menu £25 ($37.50). AE, MC, V. Tues–Sat 7–9:30pm. Bus 3 or 5.

PUBS

Cambridge Arms   This no-nonsense pub in the center of town, just 1 block from the train station, bustles with atmosphere and dispenses endless platters of food over the bar's countertop. The menu includes the chef's daily specials, grilled steaks, vegetarian meals, and an array of both hot and cold dishes. The pub was recently refurbished and now is a music-oriented theme pub. Guitars and music paraphernalia adorn the walls.

4 King St. © **01223/505015**. Bar snacks £2.50–£6.50 ($3.75–$9.75). MC, V. Restaurant Mon–Thurs noon–3pm; Fri–Sat noon–4:30pm; Sun noon–4:30pm. Pub Mon–Sat 11am–11pm; Sun noon–10:30pm. Bus: 1 or 6.

Out & Out MEXICAN/INDIAN/ENGLISH   Once called The Green Man, this 400-year-old inn is a popular destination for outings from Cambridge. It's located on A604, 3km (2 miles) south of Cambridge in the hamlet of **Grant-chester**. You might enjoy spending a late afternoon wandering through the old church and then heading, as everybody does, to the pub. In winter, a crackling fire welcomes the weary inside, but in summer it's more tempting to retreat to the beer garden, from which you can stroll to the edge of the River Cam. Place your order at the counter; a server will bring your food to your table. The food is an eclectic mix of Indian, Mexican, and English. The fare ranges from Indian curries to burritos and fajitas, and on to traditional English pies and bangers and mash, as well as various vegetarian choices.

59 High St., Grantchester. © **01223/841178**. Reservations recommended. Main courses £5–£12.50 ($7.50–$18.75). MC, V. Restaurant Mon–Fri 11am–2:30pm and 5:30–11pm; Sat 11am–11pm; Sun noon–10:30pm. Pub Mon–Sat 11am–3pm and 5pm–11pm; Sun noon–10:30pm. Bus: 118 from Cambridge.

4 Shakespeare's Stratford-upon-Avon

147km (91 miles) NW of London, 65km (40 miles) NW of Oxford

Crowds of tourists overrun this market town on the Avon River during the summer months. In fact, Stratford so aggressively hustles its Shakespeare connection that it seems at times that everybody here is trying to make a buck off the Bard. If he could return today, Shakespeare would be inundated with T-shirts bearing his likeness and china models of Anne Hathaway's cottage. He might look for a less trampled town to pen his masterpieces in.

One visitor magnet is the Royal Shakespeare Theatre, where Britain's foremost actors perform. Other than the theater, Stratford is nearly devoid of cultural life, and you may want to rush back to London after you've done the literary pilgrimage and seen a show. If you can, visit in winter, when the throngs dwindle.

ESSENTIALS

GETTING THERE   There are no direct trains from London. From London's Paddington Station, you can take a train to Leamington Spa, where you pick up a connection for Stratford-upon-Avon. The journey takes about 3 hours at a cost of £23.20 ($34.80) for a round-trip ticket. Call ✆ **0345/484950** or 01603/764776 for information and schedules. The train station at Stratford is on Alcester Road. It's closed on Sundays from October to May, so you'll have to rely on the bus.

Eight **National Express** buses (✆ **08705/808-080;** www.nationalexpress. co.uk) leave daily from Victoria Station, with a trip time of 3¼ hours. A round-trip ticket costs £12 ($18) if you return on the same day, or £15 ($22.50) if you come back on a different day. To drive from London, take the M40 toward Oxford and continue to Stratford-upon-Avon on A34.

VISITOR INFORMATION   The **Tourist Information Centre,** Bridgefoot, Stratford-upon-Avon, Warwickshire CV37 6GW (✆ **01789/293127;** www. stratford-upon-avon.co.uk), provides all the information you'll need. It's open March through October Monday through Saturday from 9am to 6pm, and Sunday from 11am to 5pm. From November to February, the hours are Monday through Saturday from 9am to 5pm and Sunday from 11am to 4pm.

To contact the **Shakespeare Birthplace Trust,** which administers many of the attractions, send a self-addressed envelope and International Reply Coupon (just ask for one at the post office) to the Director, the Shakespeare Centre, Henley Street, Stratford-upon-Avon, Warwickshire CV37 6QW (✆ **01789/ 204016**).

VISITING THE SHRINES

Besides the attractions around Stratford, there are many Elizabethan and Jacobean buildings in town, some administered by the Shakespeare Birthplace Trust. One ticket—costing £12 ($18) for adults, £6 ($9) for children, or £26 ($39) for a family ticket (two adults, three children)—permits you to visit the five major Shakespeare Birthplace Trust sights: Shakespeare's Birthplace, Anne Hathaway's Cottage, New Place/Nash's House, Mary Arden's House, and Hall's Croft. Seniors and students pay £10 ($15). Get the ticket if you're planning to do a lot of sightseeing (it's obtainable at your first stopover at any one of the Trust properties).

Anne Hathaway's Cottage ✯   Before she married Shakespeare, Anne Hathaway lived in this thatched, wattle-and-daub cottage in the hamlet of Shottery, a mile from Stratford. It's the most interesting and the most photographed of the Trust properties. The Hathaways were yeoman farmers, and their descendants lived in the cottage until 1892. As a result, it was never renovated and provides a rare insight into the life of a family in Shakespearean times. The Bard was only 18 when he married Anne, who was much older. Many original furnishings, including the courting settle and various kitchen utensils, are preserved inside the house. After visiting the house, take time to linger in the garden and orchard.

Cottage Lane, Shottery. ℂ **01789/292100.** www.shakespeare.org.uk. Admission £5 ($7.50) adults, £2 ($3) children, £11 ($16.50) family. Mar 20–Oct 19 Mon–Sat 9am–5pm, Sun 9:30am–5pm; off-season Mon–Sat 9:30am–4pm, Sun 9:30am–4:30pm. Closed Dec 23–26. Take a bus from Bridge St. or walk via a marked pathway from Evesham Place in Stratford across the meadow to Shottery.

Hall's Croft   This house is on Old Town Street, not far from the parish church, Holy Trinity. It was here that Shakespeare's daughter Susanna probably lived with her husband, Dr. John Hall. Hall's Croft is an outstanding Tudor house with a walled garden, furnished in the style of a middle-class home of the time. Dr. Hall was widely respected and built up a large medical practice in the area. Fascinating exhibits illustrate the theory and practice of medicine in Dr. Hall's time.

Old Town. ℂ **01789/292107.** www.shakespeare.org.uk. Admission £3.50 ($5.25) adults, £1.70 ($2.55) children, and £18 ($27) family ticket for the 3 houses in town. Mar 20–Oct 19 Mon–Sat 9:30am–5pm, Sun 10am–5pm; off-season Mon–Sat 10am–4pm, Sun 10:30am–4pm. Open at 1:30pm Jan 1 and closed Dec 24–26. Walk south on High St., which becomes Chapel St. and then later Church St. At the intersection with Old Town, turn left.

Harvard House   The most ornate home in Stratford, Harvard House is a fine example of an Elizabethan town house. Rebuilt in 1596, it was once the home of Katherine Rogers, mother of John Harvard, who founded Harvard College. In 1909, Chicago millionaire Edward Morris purchased the house and presented it as a gift to the famous American university. The rooms are filled with period furniture, and the floors are made of local flagstone. Look for the Bible Chair, used for hiding the Bible during the days of Tudor persecution.

High St. ℂ **01789/204507.** Free admission. Mar–Oct Tues–Sat 10am–4:30pm; Sun 10:30am–4pm. Closed Monday.

Holy Trinity Church (Shakespeare's Tomb)   In an attractive setting near the Avon River is the parish church where Shakespeare is buried (with the famous epitaph "And curst be he who moves my bones"). The church is one of the most beautiful parish churches in England.

On the banks of the Avon, "whit gentle murmur glides," the church dates from the 13th century; its entrance framed by an avenue of lime trees. To see Will's grave, head for the chancel, which was reconstructed from 1465 to 1491 in the Perpendicular style, its tomb lit by stained glass windows. Shakespeare's burial position in the church was not because of his literary prowess. He earned this stellar tomb because he was a lay rector in Stratford-upon-Avon. In 1623, Gerald Janse created a marble bust of Shakespeare on the north wall of the sanctuary over the altar steps. You'll also find the grave of Anne Hathaway, Shakespeare's wife, his daughter, Susanna, and her husband, John Hall. The Parish Register displays the Bard's baptismal entry from 1564 and his burial notice from 1616.

Old Town. ℂ **01789/266316.** www.stratford-upon-avon.org. Church, free admission; Shakespeare's tomb, donation £1 ($1.50) adults, 50p (75¢) students. Mar–Oct Mon–Wed and Fri–Sat 8:30am–6pm, Thurs 8:30am–5:10pm, Sun 2–5pm; Nov–Feb Mon–Sat 9am–4pm (Thurs until 5pm), Sun 2–5pm. Walk 4 min. past the Royal Shakespeare Theatre with the river on your left.

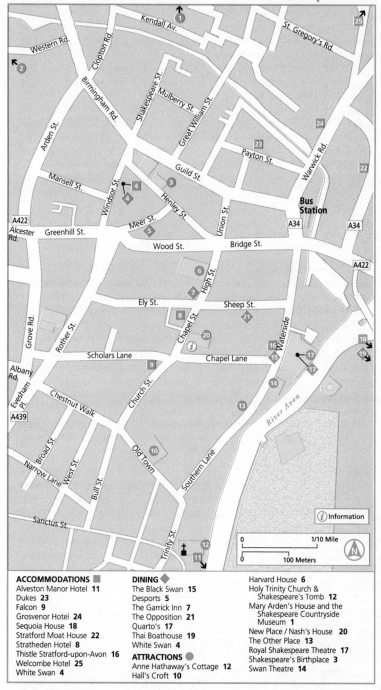

Kendall Av.

St. Gregory's Rd

Western Rd.

Clopton Rd.

Birmingham Rd.

Shakespeare St.

Mulberry St.

Great William St.

Arden St.

Mansell St.

Windsor St.

Warwick Rd.

Payton St.

Guild St.

25

2

24

23

22

Bus Station

A34

A34

A422
Alcester Rd.

Greenhill St.

Meer St.

Henley St.

Union St.

4

3

5

Wood St.

Bridge St.

A422

High St.

6

7

Ely St.

Sheep St.

Chapel St.

8

21

20

Waterside

Grove Rd.

Rother St.

Scholars Lane

Chapel Lane

18

16

17

19

Albany Rd.

9

Church St.

15

17

Evesham Pl.

Chestnut Walk

14

A439

13

River Avon

Old Town

10

Southern Lane

i **Information**

Broad St.

West St.

Bull St.

Narrow Lane

Sanctus St.

Trinity St.

0   1/10 Mile

0   100 Meters

12

11

N

ACCOMMODATIONS ■
Alveston Manor Hotel **11**
Dukes **23**
Falcon **9**
Grosvenor Hotel **24**
Sequoia House **18**
Stratford Moat House **22**
Stratheden Hotel **8**
Thistle Stratford-upon-Avon **16**
Welcombe Hotel **25**
White Swan **4**

DINING ◆
The Black Swan **15**
Desports **5**
The Garrick Inn **7**
The Opposition **21**
Quarto's **17**
Thai Boathouse **19**
White Swan **4**

ATTRACTIONS ●
Anne Hathaway's Cottage **12**
Hall's Croft **10**

Harvard House **6**
Holy Trinity Church &
   Shakespeare's Tomb **12**
Mary Arden's House and the
   Shakespeare Countryside
   Museum **1**
New Place / Nash's House **20**
The Other Place **13**
Royal Shakespeare Theatre **17**
Shakespeare's Birthplace **3**
Swan Theatre **14**

Mary Arden's House & the Shakespeare Countryside Museum ⭐   So what if millions of visitors over the years have been tricked into thinking this timber-framed farmhouse with its old stone dovecote and various outbuildings was the girlhood home of Shakespeare's mother, Mary Arden? It's still one of the most intriguing sights outside Stratford, even if historian Dr. Nat Alcock discovered in 2000 that the actual childhood home of Arden was the brick-built farmhouse, Glebe Farm, next door. It was the trick of tour guide John Jordan in the 18th century, who decided Glebe Farm was too unimpressive to be the home of the Bard's mother, so he told tourists that it was this farmstead instead. Actually the so-called Mary Arden's House wasn't constructed until the late 16th century, a little late to be the home of the Bard's mother. Visit it anyway as it contains country furniture and domestic utensils. In the barns, stable, cowshed, and farmyard you'll find an extensive collection of farming implements that give a window into life and work in the local countryside from Shakespeare's time to the present.

Wilmcote. ✆ **01789/293455.** Admission £5.50 ($8.25) adults, £4.50 ($6.75) students and seniors, £2.50 ($3.75) children. Mar 20–Oct 19 Mon–Sat 9:30am–5pm, Sun 10am–5pm; off-season Mon–Sat 10am–4pm, Sun 10:30am–4pm. Closed Dec 23–26. Take the A-3400 (Birmingham) road for 5.5km (3½ miles).

New Place/Nash's House   Shakespeare retired to New Place in 1610, a prosperous man by the standards of his day, and died here 6 years later. Regrettably, the house was torn down, so only the garden remains. A mulberry tree planted by the Bard was so popular with latter-day visitors to Stratford that the garden's cantankerous owner chopped it down. The mulberry tree that grows here today is said to have been planted from a cutting of the original tree. You enter the gardens through Nash's House (Thomas Nash married Elizabeth Hall, a granddaughter of Shakespeare). Nash's House has 16th-century period rooms and an exhibition illustrating the history of Stratford. The lovely Knott Garden adjoins the site and represents the style of a fashionable Elizabethan garden.

Chapel St. ✆ **01789/204016.** www.shakespeare.org.uk. Admission £3.50 ($5.25) adults; £1.70 ($2.55) children. Mar 20–Oct 19 Mon–Sat 9:30am–5pm, Sun 10am–5pm; off-season Mon–Sat 10am–4pm, Sun 10:30am–4pm. Closed Dec 23–26. Walk west down High St.; Chapel St. is a continuation of High St.

Shakespeare's Birthplace ⭐   The son of a glover and leather worker, the Bard was born on St. George's Day, April 23, 1564, and died on the same date 52 years later. Filled with Shakespeare memorabilia, this half-timbered structure dates from the first part of the 16th century. It was bought by public donors in 1847 and preserved as a national shrine. You can visit the bedroom where Shakespeare was probably born, a fully equipped kitchen of the period (look for the "babyminder"), and the Shakespeare Museum, illustrating his life and times. Walk through the garden, planted with all the flowers mentioned in the plays. You won't be alone: It's estimated that some 660,000 visitors pass through the house annually.

Built next door to commemorate the 400th anniversary of the Bard's birth, the Shakespeare Centre serves both as the administrative headquarters of the Trust and as a library and study center. An extension houses a visitor center, which acts as a reception area for all those coming to the birthplace. It's in the town center near the post office close to Union Street.

Henley St. ✆ **01789/204016.** www.shakespeare.org.uk. Admission £6.50 ($9.75) adults, £2.50 ($3.75) children. Mar 20–Oct 19 Mon–Sat 9am–5pm, Sun 9:30am–5pm; off-season Mon–Sat 9:30am–4pm, Sun 10am–4pm. Closed Dec 23–26.

GUIDED TOURS

Guided tours of Stratford-upon-Avon leave from near the **Guide Friday Tourism Center,** Civic Hall, 14 Rother St. (© **01789/294466**). In summer, open-top double-decker buses depart every 15 minutes daily from 9am to 5:30pm (10am–3pm in winter). You can take a 1-hour ride without stops, or you can get off at any or all of the town's five Shakespeare properties. Although the bus stops are clearly marked along the historic route, the most logical starting point is on the sidewalk in front of the Pen & Parchment Pub at Bridgefoot, at the bottom of Bridge Street. Tour tickets are valid all day, so you can hop on and off the buses wherever you want. The tours are £8.50 ($12.75) for adults, £7 ($10.50) for seniors or students, and £2.50 ($3.75) for children under 14. A family ticket sells for £19.50 ($29.25), and children under 5 go for free.

GOING TO THE PLAYS

On the banks of the Avon, the **Royal Shakespeare Theatre,** Waterside, Stratford-upon-Avon CV37 6BB (© **01789/403-403**), is a major showcase for the Royal Shakespeare Company. The theater seats 1,500 people. The company includes some of the finest actors on the British stage. In an average season, five Shakespearean plays are staged. There are two seasons a year, from November to March and from April to October.

You'll usually need reservations. There are two booking periods, each one opening about 2 months in advance. You can make reservations with a North American or an English travel agent. A small number of tickets are held for sale on the day of a performance, but it may be too late for a good seat if you wait until you arrive in Stratford. Tickets can be booked through New York agents **Global Tickets** (© **800/223-6108** in North America, or 020/7734-4555 in London) or **Keith Prowse/First Call** (© **800/669-8687** in North America, or 020/7878-2081 in London). Keith Prowse will add a hefty (sometimes 20% or more) service charge to your order, so you may prefer to call the Royal Shakespeare Theatre office directly and book tickets with a credit card. The box office is open Monday through Saturday from 9am to 8pm, but closes at 6pm on days when there are no performances. The price of tickets ranges from £8 to £50 ($12–$75). You can make a credit card reservation and pick up your tickets on the performance day, but you must cancel at least 2 full weeks in advance to get a refund.

Opened in 1986, the **Swan Theatre** is architecturally connected to the back of the Royal Shakespeare Theater and shares the same box office, address, and phone number. It seats 430 on three sides of the stage, much as an Elizabethan playhouse would. The Swan presents a repertoire of about five plays per season, from classic to contemporary, with tickets ranging from £10 to £30 ($15–$45).

The most recent addition to the Royal Shakespeare complex is **The Other Place,** a small, starkly minimalist theater located on Southern Lane, near its better-established counterparts. It was redesigned in 1996 as an experimental workshop theater without a permanent stage; seats can be radically repositioned (or removed completely) throughout the theater. Examples of recent presentations include a "promenade production" of *Julius Caesar,* in which the actors spent the whole play moving freely among a stand-up audience. Tickets are sold at the complex's main box office and generally range from £13 to £24 ($19.50–$36), although this is subject to change.

The Swan Theatre has a **painting gallery** (© **01789/412602**) with a collection of portraits of famous actors and scenes from Shakespeare's plays by 18th- and 19th-century artists. The gallery also holds occasional small exhibitions and operates as a base for guided tours of both the Swan and Shakespeare Theatre, with lively running commentary. Guided tours are not conducted daily, but are subject to production schedules. Call beforehand to check times. Tours, which include stopovers at the souvenir shop, cost £4 ($6) for adults, £3 ($4.50) for students or seniors. Call ahead for tour times.

WHERE TO STAY

During the theater season, it's best to reserve in advance. However, the Tourist Information Center (part of the national "Book-a-Bed-Ahead" service, which enables visitors to make reservations in advance) will help find accommodations in all ranges. The fee for room reservations made is 10% of the first night's stay (bed-and-breakfast rate only), deductible from the visitor's final bill.

VERY EXPENSIVE

Welcombe Hotel ★★★ For a formal, historic hotel in Stratford, there's nothing better than the Welcombe. One of England's great Jacobean country houses, this hotel is a 10-minute ride from the heart of Stratford-upon-Avon. Its key feature is an 18-hole golf course. It's surrounded by 63 hectares (157 acres) of grounds and has a formal entrance on Warwick Road, a winding driveway leading to the main hall. Regular bedrooms—some seemingly big enough for tennis matches—are luxuriously furnished; those in the garden wing, although comfortable, are small. Some of the bedrooms are sumptuously furnished with elegant four-posters; all of them have deluxe linens and well-kept bathrooms with shower-tub combinations.

Warwick Rd., Stratford-upon-Avon, Warwickshire CV37 0NR. © **01789/295252.** Fax 01789/414666. www.welcombe.co.uk. 68 units. £180 ($270) double; £265–£300 ($397.50–$450) suite. Rates include English breakfast. AE, DC, MC, V. Take A439 5km (3 miles) northeast of the town center. **Amenities:** Elegant restaurant, bar; golf course, tennis courts; 24-hr. room service; massage; babysitting; laundry/dry cleaning. *In room:* TV, coffeemaker, hair dryer, trouser press.

EXPENSIVE

Alveston Manor Hotel ★★ This Tudor manor is perfect for theatergoers—it's just a 2-minute walk from the Avon off B4066. The hotel has a wealth of chimneys and gables, and everything from an Elizabethan gazebo to Queen Anne windows. Mentioned in the *Domesday Book,* the building predates the arrival of William the Conqueror. The rooms in the manor will appeal to those who appreciate the old-world charm of slanted floors, overhead beams, and antique furnishings. Some triples or quads are available in the modern section, connected by a covered walk through the rear garden. The rooms here have built-in pieces and a color-coordinated decor; 15 are set aside for nonsmokers. All come equipped with well maintained bathrooms with shower-tub combinations. Your opinion of this hotel will depend on your room assignment. You can live in luxury in the original rooms with imported walnut furniture, or be assigned a rather routine standard twin that, though comfortable, will lack romance. Ask for an original.

Clopton Bridge, Stratford-upon-Avon, Warwickshire CV37 7HP. © **800/225-5843** in the U.S., or 01789/204581. Fax 01789/414095. www.heritage-hotels.com. 113 units. £145–£160 ($217.50–$240) double; £230 ($345) suite. AE, DC, MC, V. **Amenities:** Restaurant, bar; use of nearby health club; 24-hr. room service; laundry; nonsmoking rooms. *In room:* TV, coffeemaker, hair dryer.

Stratford Moat House ★ Moat House stands on ample landscaped lawns on the banks of the River Avon near Clopton Bridge. Although it lacks the charm of the Alveston Manor, as far as amenities go, this modern hotel is as highly rated as the Welcombe. It's one of the flagships of Queens Moat Houses, a British hotel chain, built in the early 1970s and renovated in 1995. Every room has a high standard of comfort, especially the bathrooms, which feature generous shelf space and shower-tub combinations.

Bridgefoot, Stratford-upon-Avon, Warwickshire CV37 6YR. **01789/279988**. Fax 01789/298589. 251 units. £120 ($180) double; £200 ($300) suite. Rates include English breakfast. AE, DC, MC, V. **Amenities:** 2 restaurants, 2 pubs; leisure complex with pool; 24-hr. room service; laundry. *In room:* TV, coffeemaker, hair dryer, trouser press.

Thistle Stratford-upon-Avon   Theatergoers flock to this hotel across the street from the entrance to the Royal Shakespeare and Swan theatres. Its redbrick main section dates from the Regency period, although over the years a handful of adjacent buildings were included in the hotel and an uninspired modern extension was added. Today, the interior has a well-upholstered lounge and bar; a covered garden terrace; and comfortable but narrow bedrooms. Though small, rooms have a sitting area with a couple of armchairs and round side tables, plus twin beds (for the most part). Sometimes a room is graced with a four-poster bed. The bathrooms are small but efficient, with a combination shower and tub.

44 Waterside, Stratford-upon-Avon, Warwickshire CV37 6BA. **0870/333-9196**. Fax 0870/333-9296. www.stratford-upon-avon.co.uk/arden.htm. 63 units. £128 ($192) double. AE, DC, MC, V. **Amenities:** Restaurant, pub. *In room:* TV, coffeemaker, hair dryer, trouser press.

MODERATE

Dukes   Located north of Guild Street in the center of Stratford, this little charmer is composed of two Georgian town houses, which were united and restored. The family-operated inn has a large garden and is close to Shakespeare's birthplace. The public areas and bedrooms are attractive, and the furniture tasteful, much of it antique. Bedrooms are a bit small, but they're constantly being renovated. Rooms have small bathrooms that are equipped with shower-tub combinations. No children under 12 are accepted here.

Payton St., Stratford-upon-Avon, Warwickshire CV37 6UA. **01789/269300**. Fax 01789/414700. www.astanet.com/get/dukeshtl. 22 units. £72.50–£100 ($108.75–$150) double. Rates include English breakfast. AE, DC, MC, V. **Amenities:** Room service; laundry/dry cleaning. *In room:* TV, coffeemaker, hair dryer.

Falcon   This inn blends the very old and the very new. The black-and-white timbered inn was licensed a quarter of a century after Shakespeare's death; connected to its rear by a glass passageway is a more sterile bedroom extension added in 1970. In the heart of Stratford, the inn faces the Guild Chapel and the New Place Gardens. The recently upgraded rooms in the older section have oak beams, diamond leaded-glass windows, some antiques and good reproductions. Bathrooms aren't special; some have brown linoleum floors and plastic shower-tub enclosures.

In the intimate Merlin Lounge is an open copper-hooded fireplace where fires are kept burning under beams salvaged from old ships. The Oak Bar is a forest of weathered beams, and on either side of the stone fireplace is paneling removed from the Bard's last home, New Place.

Chapel St., Stratford-upon-Avon, Warwickshire CV37 6HA. **01789/279953**. Fax 01789/414260. www. regalhotels.co.uk. 84 units. £125 ($187.50) double; £140 ($210) suite. AE, MC, V. **Amenities:** Restaurant, pub; room service; laundry/dry cleaning. *In room:* TV, coffeemaker, hair dryer.

Grosvenor Hotel   A pair of Georgian town houses, built in 1832 and 1843, join together to form this hotel, which is one of the second-tier choices of Stratford on equal footing with Dukes or the Arden Thistle. In the center of town, with lawns and gardens to the rear, it is a short stroll from the intersection of Bridge Street and Waterside, allowing easy access to the Avon River, Bancroft

Gardens, and the Royal Shakespeare Theatre. All bedrooms have small bathrooms that are well maintained, and feature showers.

12–14 Warwick Rd., Stratford-upon-Avon, Warwickshire CV37 6YT. © **01789/269213.** Fax 01789/266087. www.groshotelstratford.co.uk. 67 units. £90 ($135) double. AE, MC, V. **Amenities:** Restaurant, bar; room service; dry cleaning. *In room:* TV, coffeemaker, hair dryer, trouser press.

White Swan This cozy, intimate hotel is one of the most atmospheric in Stratford and is, in fact, Stratford's oldest building. In business for more than a century before Shakespeare appeared on the scene, it competes successfully with the Falcon in offering an ancient atmosphere. The gabled medieval front would present the Bard with no surprises, but the modern comforts inside would surely astonish him, even though many of the rooms have been preserved. Paintings dating from 1550 hang on the lounge walls. All bedrooms are well appointed; bathrooms are small but have tub-and-shower combinations.

Rother St., Stratford-upon-Avon, Warwickshire CV37 6NH. © **800/225-5843** in the U.S. and Canada, or 01789/297022. Fax 01789/268773. 41 units. £88 ($132) double; £95 ($142.50) suite. AE, DC, MC, V. **Amenities:** Restaurant, bar; room service. *In room:* TV, coffeemaker, hair dryer.

INEXPENSIVE

Sequoia House ⓥⓐⓛⓤⓔ This privately run hotel stands in its own beautiful garden across the Avon opposite the theater, conveniently located for visiting the major Shakespeare sites. Renovation has vastly improved the house, which was created from two late Victorian buildings. Bedrooms come in various shapes and sizes, and there is a constant program of refurbishment. Bedrooms have fine beds and are warmly decorated and color coordinated. Bathrooms are small, seven with a shower-and-tub combination, the others with a stall shower.

51–53 Shipston Rd., Stratford-upon-Avon, Warwickshire CV37 7LN. © **01789/268852.** Fax 01789/414559. www.stratford-upon-avon.co.uk/sequoia.htm. 24 units. £69–£89 ($103.50–$133.50) double. Rates include English breakfast. AE, MC, V. **Amenities:** Bar. *In room:* TV, coffeemaker, hair dryer.

Stratheden Hotel A short walk north of the Royal Shakespeare Theatre, this hotel is tucked away on a plot of land that was first mentioned in a property deed in 1333. Built in 1673, today it is the oldest remaining brick building in the town center, with a tiny rear garden and top-floor rooms with slanted, beamed ceilings. It has improved again in both decor and comfort with the addition of fresh paint, new curtains, and good beds. Units are small, but each comes with a comfortable bed and small bathroom. Three units have only a tub; the rest have showers.

5 Chapel St., Stratford-upon-Avon, Warwickshire CV37 6EP. © **01789/297119.** Fax 01789/297119. 9 units. £66–£72 ($99–$108) double. Rates include English breakfast. AE, MC, V. *In room:* TV.

WHERE TO DINE
EXPENSIVE

Desports ⭐⭐ ECLECTIC/INTERNATIONAL At last Stratford has a restaurant worth writing home about. In the town center between the Shakespeare Centre and Market Place, Desports was installed in a 16th-century building. Here Paul Desport and his wife, Julie, believe in offering good food in what had been England's gastronomic wasteland (except for our recommendations, of course!). Professional cooking, a vivid use of spices, imaginative menus, and reasonable prices attract a never-ending stream of visitors and locals alike. We like how Paul experiments with Asian flavors and spices and always gets the balance right. Is this the Stratford of yore, you ask, as you taste the aromatic pumpkin and Cerny cheese tagliatelle with almond pesto, tomato, and candied eggplant?

Grilled vegetables in lemon oil with rosemary chickpeas and saffron couscous are followed by cashew nut and herb risotto with wilted rocket and shaved Parmesan. Even such English classics as pan-fried calves' liver, bacon, kidneys, and bubble-and-squeak (cabbage and potatoes) are given new life with an orange Dubonnet sauce.

13–14 Meer St. ✆ **01789/269304.** Fixed-price lunch £16 ($24). Main courses £11–£18 ($16.50–$27). AE, DC, MC, V. Tues–Sat noon–2pm and 5:45–10:30pm.

Quarto's FRENCH/ITALIAN/ENGLISH   This restaurant enjoys the best location in town—in the theater itself—with its glass walls providing an unobstructed view of the swans on the Avon. You can partake of an intermission snack of smoked salmon and champagne or dine by flickering candlelight after the performance. Many dishes, such as apple-and-parsnip soup, are definitely old English; others reflect a continental touch, such as fried polenta with filets of pigeon and bacon. For your main course, you might select Dover sole, salami of wild boar, pheasant, or roast pork loin.

In the Royal Shakespeare Theatre, Waterside. ✆ **01789/403415.** Reservations required. Matinee lunch £16 ($24); dinner £26.50–£30 ($39.75–$45). AE, MC, V. Thurs–Sat noon–2pm; Mon–Sat 5:30pm–midnight.

MODERATE

Thai Boathouse ✦ THAI   The only restaurant set on the Avon, this charming choice is reached by crossing Clopton Bridge toward Oxford and Banbury. The second floor dining room opens onto vistas of the river. This restaurant, originally established 4 decades ago in Bangkok, has brought spice and zest to Stratford's lazy restaurant scene. The decor comes from Thailand itself, with elephants, woodcarvings, and Buddhas. Seasonal specialties such as wild duck and pheasant are a special feature of the menu. Fresh produce, great skill in the kitchen, and exquisite presentations are the hallmarks of this restaurant. Sample a selection of authentic Thai appetizers before going on to such delectable main courses as fresh sea bass in lemon grass; and lime leaves wrapped in banana leaf and grilled on charcoal over salmon stir-fried with curry sauce and coconut cream. One of our favorites is their lamb in a yellow curry with potatoes, onions, and cashew nuts.

Swan's Nest Lane. ✆ **01789/297733.** Reservations recommended. Set menus £19.95–£25 ($29.90–$37.50). Main courses £4.50–£15 ($6.75–$22.50). MC, V. Daily noon–2:30pm and 5:30–10:30pm.

INEXPENSIVE

The Opposition INTERNATIONAL   Located in the heart of Stratford, in a 16th-century building, this is a refreshingly unpretentious restaurant with loyal clients drawn to the good bistro cookery at reasonable prices. Choices include chicken cooked with spinach, stuffed with mango and curry, or prepared Cajun-style; salmon grilled or poached and served with hollandaise; and grilled sirloin or filet of beef. In case you wondered what Banoffi pie is (a specialty here), it's made with toffee, bananas, biscuits, and whipped cream. Most courses are at the lower end of the price scale.

13 Sheep St. ✆ **01789/269980.** Reservations recommended. Main courses £8.50–£14 ($12.75–$21). MC, V. Daily noon–2pm and 5–10:30pm.

PUBS

The Black Swan   Affectionately known as "The Dirty Duck," this has been a popular hangout for Stratford players since the 18th century. The wall is lined with autographed photos of its patrons, such as Lord Olivier. The front lounge and bar crackle with intense conversation; in the spring and fall, an open fire blazes. Typical English grills are featured in the Grill Room, which has never been accused of serving the best food in Stratford. Main dishes include goose pie, roast chicken, or honey-roasted duck. In fair weather, you can have drinks in the front garden and watch the swans glide by on the Avon.

Waterside. ✆ **01789/297312.** Reservations required for dining. Main courses £7–£15 ($10.50–$22.50); bar snacks £4–£7.25 ($6–$10.90). AE, DC, MC, V (restaurant only). Daily 11am–11pm.

The Garrick Inn   Near Harvard House, this black-and-white timbered Elizabethan pub dating from 1595 has an unpretentious charm. The front bar is decorated with tapestry-covered settles, an old oak refectory table, and an open fireplace that attracts the locals. The black bar has a circular fireplace with a copper hood and mementos of the triumphs of the English stage. The specialty is homemade pies such as steak and ale, steak and kidney, or cottage pie.

25 High St. ✆ **01789/292186.** Main courses £6–£12.50 ($9–$18.75). MC, V. Meals daily noon–9pm; pub Mon–Sat 11am–11pm, Sun noon–10:30pm.

White Swan   Housed in the town's oldest building, this is one of the most atmospheric pubs in Stratford. As you step inside, you're drawn into a world of cushioned leather armchairs, old oak paneling, and fireplaces. You're likely to meet a worthy cross-section of amiable drinkers in a setting once enjoyed by Shakespeare himself, when it was known as the Kings Head. At lunch you can partake of the hot dishes of the day, along with fresh salads and sandwiches.

In the White Swan Hotel, Rother St. ✆ **01789/297022.** Reservations recommended for dinner. Bar snacks £3–£6 ($4.50–$9); fixed-price 3-course Sunday lunch £19.95 ($29.90). AE, DC, MC, V. Morning coffee daily 10am–noon; self-service bar snacks daily 12:30–3pm; afternoon tea daily 2–5:30pm; dinner Mon–Thurs 5:30–8:30pm, Fri–Sun 6–9pm.

Index

See also Accommodations, Restaurant, and Afternoon Tea indexes below.

AFTERNOON TEA

BE MOVED

 London's Transport Museum

Covent Garden Piazza

www.ltmuseum.co.uk
24 hr info (020) 7565 7299